Communication Between
CULTURES

NINTH EDITION

Larry A. Samovar

San Diego State University, Emeritus

Richard E. Porter

California State University, Long Beach, Emeritus

Edwin R. McDaniel

San Diego State University

Carolyn S. Roy

San Diego State University

CENGAGE
Learning·

Australia • Brazil • Mexico • Singapore • United Kingdom • United States

Communication Between Cultures, Ninth Edition

Larry A. Samovar; Richard E. Porter; Edwin R. McDaniel; Carolyn S. Roy

Product Director: Monica Eckman

Product Manager: Kelli Strieby

Content Developer: Karolina Kiwak

Product Assistant: Colin Solan

Marketing Manager: Sarah Seymour

IP Analyst: Ann Hoffman

IP Project Manager: Farah Fard

Manufacturing Planner: Doug Bertke

Art and Design Direction, Production Management, and Composition: Lumina Datamatics, Inc.

Cover Image: © Josef F. Stueter

For product information and technology assistance, contact us at **Cengage Learning Customer & Sales Support, 1-800-354-9706**

For permission to use material from this text or product, submit all requests online at **www.cengage.com/permissions**. Further permissions questions can be emailed to **permissionrequest@cengage.com**.

Library of Congress Control Number: 2015948486

ISBN: 978-1-285-44462-8

Cengage Learning
20 Channel Center Street
Boston, MA 02210
USA

Cengage Learning is a leading provider of customized learning solutions with employees residing in nearly 40 different countries and sales in more than 125 countries around the world. Find your local representative at **www.cengage.com**.

Cengage Learning products are represented in Canada by Nelson Education, Ltd.

To learn more about Cengage Learning Solutions, visit **www.cengage.com**.

Purchase any of our products at your local college store or at our preferred online store **www.cengagebrain.com**.

Printed in the United States of America
Print Number: 02   Print Year: 2017

Brief Contents

Contents

| CHAPTER 3 | **The Deep Structure of Culture: Lessons from the Family 68** |

Contents

| CHAPTER 6 | Cultural Values: Road Maps for Behavior   198 |

CHAPTER 8   **Verbal Messages: Exchanging Ideas Through Language   265**

CHAPTER 9   **Nonverbal Communication: The Messages of Action, Space, Time, and Silence   295**

Defining Nonverbal Communication   297

Intentional and Unintentional Messages   297

Verbal and Nonverbal Messages   298

The Functions of Nonverbal Communication   298

   Conveying Internal States   298
   Creating Identity   298
   Regulating Interaction   299
   Substituting for Words   300

Studying Nonverbal Communication   300

   Nonverbal Communication Is a Multichannel Activity   300
   Nonverbal Communication Is Often Ambiguous   301
   Numerous Variables Influence Nonverbal Communication   301

Nonverbal Communication and Culture   301

CHAPTER 10   Intercultural Communication in Contexts: Applications in Business, Education, and Healthcare   339

Preface

Every tale can be told in a different way.

GREEK PROVERB

Our most basic common link is that we all inhabit this planet.

JOHN F. KENNEDY

Real cultural diversity results from the interchange of ideas, products, and influences, not from the insular development of a single national style.

TYLER COWEN

The opportunity to write a ninth edition of *Communication Between Cultures* offered us both rewards and challenges. The realization that earlier texts had been well received by our peers and students to the extent that another edition was warranted imbued us with a sense of gratitude. We interpreted this degree of success to mean that during the past forty-four years our message regarding the importance of intercultural communication appears to have resonated with a sympathetic audience. We welcomed the prospect of being able to refine and improve upon what we had done in eight previous editions. We did, however, realize the requirement to exercise prudence when advancing new perspectives while concurrently retaining the focus that had contributed to the acceptance of earlier editions. Hence, this current volume seeks to respect the past while allowing us to forecast the future prospects of intercultural communication. In short, we have retained the core concepts of the discipline, added contemporary perceptions and research, and also ventured into new territory.

This book still recognizes the synergy between communication and culture and how that interface influences human interactions. More specifically, it is about what happens when people of different cultures engage in communication with the objective of sharing ideas, information, and perspectives. Knowing that the concepts of communication and culture inextricably intertwine, we have endeavored to incorporate the basic principles of both topics throughout the text. Informed by the understanding that intercultural interactions are a daily occurrence for an ever-increasing number of people, we designed this book for those individuals whose professional or private lives bring them into contact with members of other cultures or co-cultures.

RATIONALE

Global interest in the study of intercultural communication has never been more prevalent and necessary. The concern and significance arise from a fundamental premise regarding how the world changed in the past century. The change can be seen in the fact that you live in a dynamic, rapidly evolving era. This global dynamism is characterized by dramatic alterations in technology, increased world travel, many new economic and political institutions, shifts in immigration patterns, growing demographic diversity, and greater population density. These changes have created a world that requires regular interaction with people of different cultural origins—be they next door, across town, or thousands of miles away. Whether or not you embrace these "conversations," they will continue to increase in frequency and intensity. Huston Smith succinctly summarized these circumstances when, in *The World's Religions*, he wrote, "When historians look back on [the twentieth] century they may remember it most, not for space travel or the release of nuclear energy, but as the time when the peoples of the world first came to take one another seriously." His reflections on the past century remain correspondingly valid for our current globalized society.

APPROACH

Our approach is anchored in the belief that all forms of human communication involve some manner of action. Stated in different terms, your communicative behaviors affect you as well as the people with whom you interact. Whether you are generating or receiving words or nonverbal symbols, you are creating and producing messages that influence someone else. Any study of communication must include information about the choices that are made in selecting your messages as well as a discussion of the consequences of those choices. Hence, this book advances the conviction that engaging in intercultural communication is pragmatic (you do something), philosophical (you make choices), and ethical (your chosen actions have consequences).

PHILOSOPHY

A dual philosophy has guided the preparation of this ninth edition. First, we hold that it is advantageous, if not a requirement, for the more than 7 billion of us sharing this planet's limited resources to improve our intercultural communication skills. Globalization and demographic alterations within many countries have created a world so small and interdependent that we must rely on each other—whether we want to or not. As simplistic as it may seem, what occurs in one place can now have a major impact on people in countless other parts of the world. However, many of the obstacles to understanding other people can be mitigated through motivation, knowledge, and an appreciation of cultural differences. Our objective is to provide you with all three.

We realize that writing about culture and communication involves a series of personal decisions and an explicit approach. As scholars and authors, we have made those decisions and developed a point of view regarding intercultural interaction. We contend that the first commandment of any civilized society is the dictum that *allows people to be different as long as their differences do not create hardships for others*. At times, you will find that we have openly stated our personal positions, and for those convictions, we make no apologies. Concurrently, we have made a concerted effort to check our collective and individual ethnocentrism. For those instances where it unintentionally surfaces, we apologize.

NEW FEATURES

The ninth edition contains an abundance of new material. As has been the case with each edition, we have remained mindful of the constructive comments made by users and reviewers of previous editions. We combined those suggestions with our own vision of the discipline. Specifically, we were concerned with where the study of intercultural communication has been and our evaluation of its future direction. Combining these two orientations generated some of the following new features:

- The most apparent new feature of this edition is the additional chapter, Chapter 11, which directly relates to the philosophy we articulated earlier in the Preface. To repeat—communication is an act people engage in that influences other people. To assist you in making those acts more rewarding and successful, the new chapter aims to enable you to become a more effective participant in the countless intercultural encounters in which you will participate. This new chapter has three main goals. First, the chapter examines the challenges of entering another culture by offering a discussion of selected obstacles that can impede effective intercultural communication. Second, suggestions are advanced that can assist you in overcoming those difficulties. Finally, the chapter concludes with an overview of ethical considerations relevant to intercultural behaviors.
- Another visible addition to the text appears at the conclusion of each chapter. Because we consider it essential in this era of intercultural connectedness that you acquire the skills necessary to become a competent communicator and because such competence and skill development is attainable, we now conclude each chapter with a section on developing competency.
- To underscore the importance of intercultural communication in the present, Chapter 1 has been completely revised. We emphasize the need to understand and adjust to the many challenges that require collective management by the international community. Social challenges, ecological concerns, humanitarian demands, political questions, and security issues are just a few of the topics highlighted in the first chapter. To facilitate dealing with these matters, we have added a new section to the opening chapter that discusses the need for compromise in intercultural communication.
- As the role of contemporary information technology has grown throughout the world, so has our treatment of this important topic. In nearly every chapter we indicate the increasing interconnectivity of people worldwide using technology as a communication apparatus. Our analysis looks at issues such as how technology enables the reconstitution of cultures. We also examine how this new technology contributes to the polarization of some segments of society at the same time it fosters social and cultural changes.

- While continuing to address globalization, we have not neglected U.S. domestic intercultural issues. The latest data from the U.S. Census Bureau illustrate the dramatic changes in U.S. demographics, and projections of population changes demonstrate the increasing criticality of intercultural communication.

- Since it is our belief that communication and culture are inseparable, we have increased our presentation of human communication. Part of the expansion includes a detailed explanation of the importance of a communicator being motivated, knowledgeable, and skilled.

- It has long been our conviction that the chief impediments to intercultural understanding are not found in shallow and superficial differences related to food, transportation systems, architecture, and the like. Instead, misunderstandings and conflicts are the product of variances associated with a culture's deep structure institutions. These institutions, such as family, community, and religion, encompass the most significant definitions and meanings regarding life. These messages are transmitted from generation to generation, carry a culture's most important values, endure, and supply a sense of identity to its members. Since family is among the most important of these deep structure elements and because the contemporary world order has altered the face of the family, we have increased the scope of our analysis concerning this key institution. We demonstrate how globalization and social changes are having an impact on traditional family structures. Specifically, we address how globalization is affecting gender roles, individual identity, group orientation, perceptions of aging and the elderly, and personal social skills.

- Worldview and religion remain relevant issues in contemporary society. Continuing media focus and growing misconceptions mandated that we offer a more in-depth examination of religious extremism and conflict. The increasing numbers of people moving away from traditional religion prompted our expanded discussion of atheism and spirituality. We also now include a section related to religious tolerance.

- We continue to believe that history provides a picture of where a culture has been and a blueprint for its future. For this reason, our history chapter has undergone significant changes. The "Country Statistics" tables have been updated, as has "Contemporary Social Issues." We discuss current social conditions and how they may affect both the present and the future. Because of current events, the Islamic history section has been extensively revised. We have also added a new segment to this chapter that explains the connection between historical memory and intercultural competence.

- Two new taxonomies (Minkov's cultural dimensions and Gelfand's "tight" and "loose" cultures) were added to the cultural values chapter. We have also expanded our treatment of the principal values associated with the U.S. dominant culture.

- The language chapter has been completely revised with an emphasis on how language functions and operates in intercultural settings. The discussion of variations within language groups has been updated and amplified. Dissimilarities related to accents, dialects, argot, slang, and texting are presented. The treatment on interpreting has been expanded and now includes material on how new technologies are influencing interpretation and translation. Eight selected cultures are examined as a way of demonstrating how each of them has several unique language characteristics that they employ during interaction. Due to the need to employ an interpreter during many communication events, we have added a detailed section on cultural considerations in these circumstances. A unit on developing competence in using language is also new to this chapter. We explain how understanding in the intercultural setting could be improved by learning a second language, being aware of one's surroundings, knowing about conversational taboos, monitoring speech rates, becoming aware of vocabulary differences, and knowing about variations in conversational styles.

- Chapter 10 concentrates on the setting and context of the intercultural encounter and has been completely restructured. Comprehensive changes in the business, education, and healthcare settings necessitated a revised approach to these three environments.

- Finally, because our reviewers asked for more visual images as a way of teaching some of the strategic concepts of intercultural communication, we significantly increased the number of "cultural photographs" in this new edition.

ACKNOWLEDGMENTS

No book is the sole purview of the authors. Many people contributed to this new edition, and we acknowledge them. We are especially pleased with our publisher for the past forty years. While we have experienced and survived numerous changes in ownership, editors, and management and even corporate name changes, the commitment of Wadsworth Cengage to producing a high-quality textbook has remained intact.

We begin our specific expressions of appreciation with a sincere "thank you" to Karolina Kiwak, our associate content developer. From inception to completion, she offered us direction and support. Whether our problems, questions, or grumblings were major or minor, Karolina constantly responded with efficiency and infinite patience. Also, we wish to recognize the hard work and contributions of Jyotsna Ojha, content project manager, Sarah Seymour, program marketing manager, and Farah Fard, intellectual property project manager. We also extend our sincere thanks to the reviewers of the previous text. Their suggestions contributed significantly to the many improvements found in this edition.

Finally, we express our appreciation to the tens of thousands of students and the many instructors who have used past editions. For forty years they have permitted us to "talk to them" about intercultural communication. By finding something useful in our exchange, they encouraged us to produce yet another edition of *Communication Between Cultures*.

Larry A. Samovar,
Richard E. Porter,
Edwin R. McDaniel,
Carolyn S. Roy

Intercultural Communication: A Requirement for the Interdependent Global Society

Every tale can be told in a different way.

GREEK PROVERB

If there is one lesson from the past 100 years it is that we are doomed to co-operate. Yet we remain tribal.

MARTIN WOLF

In a world where security challenges do not adhere to political boundaries and our economies are linked as never before, no nation can go it alone and hope to prosper.

CHUCK HAGEL

THE INTERDEPENDENT GLOBAL SOCIETY

When Euripides wrote, "All is change; all yields its place and goes" in 422 BCE, he probably did not realize that he would be helping to introduce a book on intercultural communication. Yet, the study of intercultural communication is about change. It is about changes in the world and how the people in that world must adapt to them. More specifically, this book deals with the world changes that have brought us into direct and indirect contact with people who, because of their culture, often behave in ways that we do not understand. With or without our consent, the last three decades [1960–1990] have thrust on us groups of people who often appear alien. These people, who appear "different," may live thousands of miles away or right next door. What is special about them is that, in many ways, they are not like us.[1]

Written nearly thirty years ago to introduce the first edition of *Communication Between Cultures*, the above paragraph is more relevant today. The world is now changing at a much faster pace, requiring rapid adjustment to evolving technology

New technologies allow people almost anywhere in the world to exchange ideas and information.

Courtesy of Edwin McDaniel

and changing social conditions. Our interactions with people of different cultures have become common in the classroom, the workplace, and the healthcare setting, and with growing frequency in our neighborhood. The term "globalization" originally implied an emerging development, a work in progress, but can now be characterized as both an existing condition and a continuing dynamic. With rare exceptions, our lives are increasingly dependent on people and events in other parts of the world. As Cabrera and Unruh point out, "Our economy, environment, resources, education, and health systems all interconnect to, rely on, and affect the economies, environments, resources, and health systems in other countries."[2]

The reliance on food imports serves as an easily understood example of this international interdependency. Population growth and increasing ethnic diversity in the United States have generated a demand for more and diverse food imports.[3] A 2012 government report indicated that "an estimated 15 percent of the U.S. food supply is imported, including 50 percent of fresh fruits, 20 percent of fresh vegetables and 80 percent of seafood."[4] But before any of those items can be imported, international agreements must be reached on innumerable specifications relating to quality, packaging, labels, storage, labor conditions, etc. Food products sent abroad from the United States must also meet import requirements established by the receiving nation, all of which involve cross-cultural negotiations, agreements, monitoring, and inspections. These procedures are carried out and implemented for all U.S. imports and exports, and intercultural communication is the nexus in every step.

Since our first edition, we have offered numerous examples and statistics to convince the reader of the importance of intercultural communication in contemporary

REMEMBER THIS

As the world becomes more interconnected, our lives are increasingly dependent on people and events in other parts of the world.

Overpopulation presents immense challenges to people throughout the world.

© Richard Lord/PhotoEdit

society. However, today, most readers of this text will have grown up in an era when the activities associated with "multicultural," "cross-cultural," "intercultural," "cultural diversity," "ethnic pluralism," and others were common. Therefore, rather than offering a set of examples to illustrate the role of intercultural communication in your social, professional, and even private lives, we now choose to argue that in the globalized world, effective intercultural communication is an increasingly essential requirement in the critical efforts to ensure world peace, improve relationships between co-cultures and the dominant cultures within each country, assure resource sustainability, and promote ecological viability.

THE REQUIREMENT FOR INTERCULTURAL COOPERATION

Discussions of "globalization" most frequently focus on economic benefits and the ramifications of interdependence. However, in addition to economic considerations, globalization has raised awareness of existing and emerging conditions that influence many aspects of our planet and society. The global community is currently faced with a broad spectrum of circumstances that present national governments with pronounced demands on financial and physical resources. Moreover, there are conditions looming on the horizon that portend severe consequences for the future unless properly anticipated and managed. Successful resolution of many of these problems will require global governance—a transnational approach to cooperatively engage and solve multistate problems. Table 1.1 presents a menu of particularly salient issues confronting the globalized society, all of which have to be addressed through competent intercultural communication. We will illustrate some of the issues confronting the global society, many of which will likely influence your lives.

TABLE 1.1	Challenges for the Globalized Society
CONTEMPORARY AND PROJECTED ISSUES REQUIRING INTERCULTURAL COOPERATION	
Social challenges	• World population growth • Mass migration • Urbanization • Intercultural integration • Aging populations/declining birthrates

Ecological concerns	• Competition for natural resources
	  ▪ Raw materials
	  ▪ Water shortages
	  ▪ Food scarcities
	  ▪ Pelagic resources
	• Environmental changes/degradation

Humanitarian and legal cooperation	• Disease control
	• Disaster relief
	• International mishaps
	• Transnational crime
	  ▪ Cyber crime
	  ▪ Intellectual property

Political questions	• International legal system • Scientific advancement ethics • Human rights issue

Security issues	• Weapons of mass destruction
	• Terrorism and piracy
	• Peacekeeping missions
	• Emerging threats
	  ▪ Sectarian and ethnic tensions
	  ▪ Renascent nationalism
	  ▪ Contested territorial claims

SOCIAL CHALLENGES

Scientific and socioeconomic advances in the nineteenth and twentieth centuries resulted in rapid population growth (see Table 1.2). Vastly improved healthcare, increased food production and nutritional knowledge, and greater availability of social support systems contributed to reduced infant mortality and increased life expectancy.[5] Accompanying the many improvements and benefits, this population explosion has exacerbated some older problems and given rise to numerous new ones. Perhaps the most pressing is, "What changes must be made in order to ensure the world's environment can support these levels of human activities?" It is a question that no single organization, government, or nation can answer. It will require shared ideas, interaction, and mutual effort across cultural and state borders.

Social and technological improvements have also facilitated and encouraged large population movement from rural areas to urban environments. We have seen mass migration from regions afflicted by poverty, political oppression, or conflict

TABLE 1.2	World Population Growth[6]	
POPULATION	YEAR REACHED	YEARS TO REACH
1 billion	1804	
2 billion	1922	118
3 billion	1959	37
4 billion	1974	15
5 billion	1987	13
6 billion	1999	12
7 billion	2012	13
8 billion	2025*	13
9.6* billion	2050*	25
10.9* billion	2100*	50

*Estimated.

to areas offering personal safety, economic opportunities, and political stability. Immigration issues are a daily topic in the United States and regularly produce a divided electorate. Movement of people from poverty-ridden and violence-torn African and Middle Eastern nations, along with those from Eastern Europe seeking better employment, has altered the complexion of Western Europe. Immigrants from Latin America and Asia have changed the traditional composition of the United States. Minorities now represent more than 37 percent of the U.S. population, almost 13 percent were born in another country, and more than 20 percent speak a language other than English at home. And changes brought by immigrants are expected to continue—studies indicate that "new immigrants and their children will make up 84%" of the 24 million net increase in the U.S. labor force by 2030.[7] The magnitude of future immigration, the accompanying challenge, and the attendant need for intercultural skills is clearly pointed out by Professor of Evolutionary Biology Mark Pagel:

> the dominant demographic trend of the next century will be the movement of people from poorer to richer regions of the world. Diverse people will be brought together who have little common cultural identity of the sort that historically has prompted our cultural nepotism, and this will happen at rates that exceed those at which they can be culturally integrated.[8]

A majority of new immigrants, both in the United States and in other nations, will seek work and residence in urban areas. According to the United Nations, over half the world's population currently lives in cities, a figure that is expected to reach 66 percent by 2050. In the United States, 80.7 percent of the population already resides in urban areas.[9] Greater population density raises requirements for better waste management, availability of foodstuffs, and reliable freshwater resources. It also places people of different ethnicities, religious practices, worldviews, beliefs, values, etc. in closer proximity to each other. In order to achieve prosperity, they will have to learn to cooperate and respect each other's differences.

CONSIDER THIS

What are some reasons that make intercultural cooperation more important than ever?

Low-cost air travel permits people to experience other cultures with great ease.

Courtesy of Edwin McDaniel

Globalization has additionally resulted in increasing intercultural relationships. Mounting immigration, urbanization, international employment, study abroad, and ease of foreign travel are facilitating contact between people with different racial, ethnic, religious, and cultural backgrounds. In greater numbers, people are living and working abroad. The resultant extended intercultural contact has led to a rise in international marriages in Asia, Europe, and the United States. According to 2010 census data, 9.5 percent of married-couple households in the United States were interracial or interethnic, an increase of more than 2 percent from 2000. Naturally, these cross-cultural marriages, both internationally and domestically, have produced intercultural children, and 32 percent of U.S. citizens self-identified as multiracial in the 2010 census. This growing international phenomenon of cultural mixing gives added emphasis to the important role of intercultural communication and draws attention to identity issues.[10]

In the United States, the white non-Hispanic population is forecast to lose majority status by 2043, after which the nation will be a majority of minorities. By 2060, minority groups will represent an estimated 57 percent of the population. Clearly, this will bring changes to the traditionally "dominant" U.S. culture, a product of the beliefs and values of the historically white majority. This transition will demand greater intercultural insight, acceptance, and communication expertise.[11]

Aging populations represent another emerging problem that will require intercultural communication knowledge and skills. Almost every nation in the world is experiencing an increase in older citizenry (i.e., over 60 years) made more pronounced by declining birthrates. Globally, the older age-group represented 9.2 percent of the total population

Globalization has caused population shifts as people immigrate seeking new opportunities and escaping oppressive conditions.

© Bob Daemmrich/PhotoEdit

in 1990, had expanded to 11.7 percent by 2013, and is expected to reach 21.1 percent by 2050. In the United States, those over 65 years of age represented 13.1 percent of the 2010 population, which was a faster rate of growth than the total population, and is expected to increase to 21.4 percent by 2050. There are numerous social and economic consequences arising from this trend toward expanding aging populations, not the least of which is the ratio of working age to elderly dependency age (i.e., the number of working-age people in relation to those in retirement). This imbalance is a concern because most social support programs for older people are dependent on fiscal support generated by the workforce. Fortunately for the United States, in spite of the declining birthrate, overall population growth is robust due to immigration, which also raises the importance of intercultural understanding.[12]

A prescient summation of concerns about the world's aging population is contained in a U.S. government report on world aging. The report calls for actions that will clearly require intercultural communication exchanges:

Despite the weight of scientific evidence, the significance of population aging and its global implications have yet to be fully appreciated. There is a need to raise awareness about not only global aging issues but also the importance of rigorous cross-national scientific research and policy dialogue that will help us address the challenges and opportunities of an aging world.[13]

ECOLOGICAL CONCERNS

The need and competition for natural resources among nations has a long historical record of creating turmoil and conflict. The globalized economy continues to be characterized by nations seeking to acquire and preserve raw materials needed to fuel their economic engines. In the 1960s and 1970s, Japan scoured the world for needed materials. It was followed by South Korea, and now China is acquiring resources worldwide in order to sustain its industrialization. India's growing economy is also adding to the demand for raw materials. As other nations' populations grow, the requirement for various natural resources will expand. In his 2014 report, the U.S. Director of National Intelligence predicted that "Competition for scarce [natural] resources, such as food, water, or energy, will likely increase tensions within and between states and could lead to more localized or regional conflicts, or exacerbate government instability."[14] Demands for energy resources (e.g., natural gas, oil, and coal), the most vital for economic growth, are expected to increase 37 percent by 2040, and much of this demand will be from China, India, and emerging economies—a situation ripe for political tensions. International agreements will be needed to regulate the extraction of resources from regions of disputed sovereignty and common areas outside national boundaries, such as seabed hydrocarbons and minerals. And cooperative policing mechanisms may be necessary to ensure compliance with treaties and pacts. In some cases, disagreements will have to be mediated through international governance organizations, such as occurred in the World Trade Organization's resolution of a trade dispute between China and the United States over rare earth metals, essential in manufacturing high-tech products, such as smart phones and cameras.[15] In every instance, intercultural communication will be key to the success of these international negotiations and agreements.

Water represents the most indispensable resource for human, animal, and plant life on our planet. Factors such as overconsumption, misuse, pollution, and climate change threaten existing supplies, and serious water shortages are widely predicted for the future. Studies indicate that by 2050, three-quarters of the world's population could experience water scarcity. Potable water is already an issue in parts of the United States, particularly Southern California, and "megadroughts" lasting thirty-five years or more are predicted for the Southwest and Midwest during the latter part of this century. The growing population and increased urbanization are placing enormous demands on existing water sources and creating competition between urban and agricultural populations. In addition to more water for human consumption, increases will be needed for agriculture to grow the necessary food sources. Lack of water has implications for health, economic development, security, and

Expanding populations create pollution that crosses national borders requiring interculturally negotiated solutions.

© GIPhotoStock/PhotoEdit

environmental sustainability. Intercultural communication will play a role in a number of areas related to managing water shortages. International and domestic agreements will have to be negotiated regarding access to water, water distribution rights, and even water trading.[16] An important role for intercultural communication expertise will likely be in developing and implementing educational programs for water management and conservation, especially at the consumer level, where presentations will need to cross multiple cultural lines.

The threat of insufficient food resources is yet another problem arising from population growth, urbanization, and changing dietary habits. In addition to increased numbers of people, socioeconomic improvement has enabled millions to begin consuming more animal protein, in turn requiring expanded land area, water usage, and crops for animal feed. Academic research has revealed that world crop production will have to double by 2050 to meet anticipated demand for human and animal consumption and biofuels. However, crop production is not keeping pace with the projected requirements. A reduction in available food resources will drive prices up, place additional burdens on people living near or below poverty levels, and increase the potential for political instability. As insurance, some nations are already acquiring vast tracts of arable land in Africa, South America, and Southeast Asia for agricultural development.[17]

Adding to the burden of agricultural production is the decline in pelagic resources resulting from fish stock depletion, ocean pollution, and climate change. According to the United Nations, over 10 percent of the world's population relies on fisheries for a living. However, the industry is facing a number of threats, ranging from "illegal, unreported and unregulated fishing to harmful fishing practices to wastage to poor governance."[18] This has resulted in more than 80 percent of ocean fish being harvested at or above their sustainability levels and the wholesale destruction of the world's coral reefs.[19] Amelioration of this situation will require extensive international agreements covering a broad range of topics, such as quotas, permissible practices, type and extent of punishment for violations, and, most challenging, cooperative monitoring and policing of the ocean commons. The extent of the problem and number of involved nations make this an extremely difficult task but a necessary one if we are to ensure that the oceans remain a reliable source of food.

According to the President of the Earth Policy Institute, Lester Brown, "We are entering a time of chronic food scarcity, one that is leading to intense competition for control of land and water resources— in short, a new geopolitics of food."[20] The implications of this evolving situation are multiple. International cooperation will be required on a grand scale to guarantee adequate food availability, avoid detrimental competition, and ensure continued political viability. In addition to cooperative programs and international agreements, some solutions may have to center around changing traditional dietary practices, a daunting cultural challenge.

CONSIDER THIS

How do you believe we can get people throughout the world, and from a variety of cultures, to engage in humanitarian cooperation? Is such engagement possible?

Evolving conditions are worsened by environmental degradation, pollution, and climate change. The destruction of natural habitats, such as wetlands and woodlands, for industrial and residential development (along with other factors, such as pollution) is contributing to the extinction of plant and animal species at an accelerating pace. Pollution is a significant and continually growing problem throughout the world, including our oceans. A 2015 study revealed that as much as 8 million metric tons of plastic trash enters the ocean every year. The Great Pacific Garbage Patch stretches for hundreds of miles across the Pacific Ocean and consists primarily of non-biodegradable plastics that only break down into smaller and smaller particles, ultimately to be ingested by marine life. Domestic water pollution is also a growing problem throughout the world. According to a 2014 government report, almost 60 percent of China's underground water was so polluted that it could not be consumed without treatment. Surveys by the Environmental Protection Agency disclosed that pollution prevented 40 percent of U.S. rivers, lakes, and estuaries from being used for fishing or swimming. The waters are so polluted with runoff sewage and garbage in Rio de Janeiro's Guanabara Bay, site of the 2016 Olympic sailing and windsurfing events, that some officials have registered concern about the health risks to the athletes. Air pollution continues to be an enervating health factor in many parts of the world, especially China and India. Moreover, air pollution does not respect national borders. Recent reports have revealed that industrial emissions produced in

China are carried by wind patterns all the way to the U.S. West Coast, making it a matter of international concern.[21]

The ever-increasing force of climate change is another consideration that necessitates competent intercultural interactions. Extreme weather conditions will bring more frequent tropical storms, droughts, wildfires, flooding, health threats, and a host of other maladies that can be managed only by nations working together. For instance, in low-lying areas, complete towns will have to be relocated, and some islands in the South Pacific are likely to be inundated, requiring relocation of entire populations. Increased ocean temperatures will exert pressure on marine habitats and fishing patterns, impacting traditional industries and altering diets. Insect infestations and plant diseases will become more common with warmer temperatures and result in lower agricultural yields. Adaptation to these many changes will require that nations engage in cooperative efforts and share resources.[22]

We are stressing that ecological changes, both ongoing and in the future, carry the potential to transform many of the beliefs, practices, and habits that have become normal over the past centuries. People, organizations, and states will have to learn new ways of managing and cooperating. Often, this will require reaching across cultural divides.

HUMANITARIAN AND LEGAL COOPERATION

Advances in communication technologies have enabled rapid notification and dissemination of information concerning humanitarian crises, such as contagious disease outbreaks and natural disasters. Modern transport capabilities have offered a means of expeditiously responding to those crises, and nations and relief organizations around the world mobilize and deploy resources to disaster sites. The 2014 outbreak of the Ebola virus in West Africa is a good example of the complexity of responding to such an incident. The disease affected citizens of six West African nations, and infected individuals were also treated in the United States, England, and Spain. In attempting to contain the disease, personnel and materials from around the world were rushed to the area, and coordination required communication across organizational, linguistic, and cultural lines. Additionally, to be successful, the instituted treatment and containment programs had to be culturally sensitive to local customs. For example, caring for the dead traditionally requires touching and even kissing the body in some West African nations. To break the Ebola infection cycle, emergency workers had to identify and implement effective methods of communicating the dangers of this practice to the local inhabitants.

Disaster response is another area of international cooperation requiring intercultural communication competence. The worldwide response to the 2010 Haiti earthquake, the 2011 Japan earthquake and tsunami, and the 2013 Philippine super typhoon offer examples of recent endeavors. International assistance in cases of a major accident has also become common. For instance, the 2014 loss of a Malaysian commercial aircraft thought to have gone down in the Indian Ocean and the AirAsia plane that crashed near Indonesia elicited international deployment of personnel and equipment. These types of calamities increase the need for intercultural communication skills among all parties involved.

Protection of intellectual property is another legal concern in the globalized economy. The negotiation, enactment, and enforcement of regulations arising from international legal agreements are often confronted with issues of cultural divergence. As an example, international copyright law is largely based on the Western concept of creativity being primarily an individual effort, but, as Rajan points out, this conceptualization is not consistent across all cultures:

> A strongly individualistic conception of creativity may not be relevant to cultures which place a higher value on group or communal creation, or locate the work of individual authors within a strong, community tradition of educated understanding and appreciation. They may also be difficult to reconcile with traditions which do not accord primary importance to the identity of the author.[23]

More succinctly, the Euro-American cultural value is on individual ownership and creativity, but many non-European "traditions tend toward a more communal conception."[24] As a result, to reach successful agreements in instances where these varied cultural perspectives collide, the involved individuals will need a strong appreciation for the role of culture in communication.

POLITICAL ISSUES

As globalization has driven the international community into greater economic interdependency, it has presented nations with issues that on occasion conflict with domestic politics. For example, domestic political divisions have kept the United States from becoming a participant in the International Criminal Court, established to prosecute serious crimes against humanity, despite more than one hundred other nations taking part. Due to its opposition to capital punishment, Mexico has been reluctant to extradite criminals to the United States when there is a possibility of the death penalty being imposed. It was only through international pressure that in 2013, the Japanese government ratified an international agreement, first established in 1980, that is used to adjudicate international child custody disputes.[25] Japan's reluctance to sign was due to the strong cultural belief that child custody is the mother's prerogative.

Scientific advances are another area that can become politically divisive. During a period in 2013–2014, the Chinese government halted imports of U.S. genetically modified corn, citing health risks. The national value-related attitude toward genetically modified food also varies between the United States and the European Union, making imports and exports subject to international negotiations and trade agreements. Studies have shown that opinion on research employing human embryo stem cells can also vary internationally based on religion, ideology, and personal values. China and the United States often trade barbs about human rights, and much of their disagreement can be traced to divergent views about human rights. For the United States, human rights are anchored in a legal tradition of political and civil rights. China, on the other hand, grounds its approach to the topic on a perspective that assigns the highest priority to social and economic rights.[26]

These few illustrations should provide ample evidence of the many contentious political issues dividing states in the globalized society. Dissimilar cultural values and attitudes are at the base of many of these controversial issues, and the only prudent course of resolution is through dialogue and agreement—in other words, through employing competent intercultural communication.

SECURITY CONCERNS

Peace and stability in the age of globalization is under constant assault by multiple complex threats, many of which can be countered only through international governmental and military cooperation. To illustrate the continuing need for intercultural communication in the national security arena, we will address a few of the ongoing challenges and operations in the following paragraphs. You should try to keep in mind the many different languages and cultures involved among participants in the programs and operations discussed.

Weapons of mass destruction (WMDs), which include nuclear, chemical, and biological armaments, carry the potential to inflict the greatest number of causalities and are a concern for almost every nation. The desire to prevent the spread of nuclear weapons is exemplified in the multinational efforts to dissuade Iran from further development and to terminate the North Korean program. Negotiations with Iran involve representatives from China, France, Germany, Russia, the United Kingdom, and the United States. In addition to North Korea, the Six Party Talks involve China, Japan, Russia, South Korea, and the United States. The removal and destruction of Syria's chemical arsenal in 2013–2014 involved Syria's acquiescence, an agreement between the United States and Russia, a UN Security Council Resolution, and supervision by the Organization for the Prohibition of Chemical Weapons. Ships from Norway and Denmark provided transport services. Logistic sites were used in Cyprus and Italy. The chemical weapons and associated materials were destroyed aboard a U.S. merchant ship and at sites in Finland, Germany, the United Kingdom, and the United States.[27] The role of intercultural communication in these cases is self-evident.

We are constantly reminded of the danger of global terrorism as it spreads around the world. With the exception of Antarctica, acts of terrorism resulting in loss of life occurred on every continent in 2014. Nor is there any indication that the threat will diminish anytime soon. The ability ultimately to meet the challenge of terrorism will require the cooperation of the entire international community. The Combined Maritime Forces (CMF) offers an example of how the international community can successfully engage and neutralize an asymmetrical threat. Composed of naval units from 30 nations, the CMF maintains a presence in the Arabian Gulf, Northern Arabian Sea, and the Indian Ocean, encompassing "approximately 2.5 million square miles of international waters."[28] This all-voluntary force conducts continuous security operations and has effectively quelled Somali-based maritime piracy. The implementation of these hugely complex operations takes an extraordinary degree of coordination, all anchored in communication that must pass through numerous language and cultural filters.

The UN peacekeeping operations offer another example of international cooperation that must overcome countless cultural and language obstacles. As of January 2015, more than 120,000 uniformed and civilian personnel from 128 nations were deployed to 16 international locations. These men and women were working to maintain peace, protect civilian populations, sustain the environment, and promote human rights at 16 sites in Africa, the Balkans, the Caribbean, the Middle East, and South Asia.[29]

Just as globalization has changed the economic and social landscape, it has given rise to a series of emerging security threats. These include extant and developing sectarian and ethnic tensions. Renascent nationalism has exhibited itself as both a political instrument and an aspirational force. Old and new contested territorial claims are coming between nations. Differences in cultural and ideological perceptions are at the heart of many of these situations, and cooperative mutual interaction to dispel those differences is the key to peaceful resolution.

Religion remains a potent source of divisiveness around the world. A Pew Research Center study revealed that 77 percent of the world's population "was living in countries with a high or very high overall level of restrictions on religion in 2013."[30] These restrictions include government-imposed regulations and acts of social harassment due to religious affiliation. Of the 198 nations in the study, 30 percent had government restrictions against minority religions, and in 61 percent of the countries, religious groups experienced some form of social harassment.[31] After two decades of conflict between Muslims in the north and Christians/Animists in the south, Sudan was divided into two separate states in 2011, but tensions persist. Professed Muslims belonging to the Boko Haram terrorist group seek to impose Islamic law (Sharia) throughout Nigeria. Although it takes many forms, the Sunni–Shia divide is the underlying cause of conflict in the Middle East, with entire nations taking different sides (e.g., Sunni Saudi Arabia vs. Shia Iran). India's enduring Hindu–Christian and Hindu–Muslim animosities give no indication of diminishing, and occasional low-level violent eruptions are not uncommon. Since 2009, Hindus and Buddhist in Sir Lanka have engaged in an uneasy peace following a debilitating civil war lasting more than twenty-five years. The Chinese government has officially banned the Falun Gong religious group. Beginning in 2012, Buddhist mobs have engaged in violent attacks on Muslim-minority Rohingya communities in Myanmar. Nor is the West immune to sectarian conflict, as demonstrated by recent attacks in Denmark, France, and the United Kingdom, part of an alarming rise in anti-Semitism across Europe.[32]

Although not as frequently mentioned in the news as religiously based conflicts, ethnic violence is also an expanding challenge for the international community. The following examples are but a short list of ongoing ethnic struggles. Soon after gaining independence, peace in South Sudan was shattered by conflict between members of the Nuer and Dinka tribes contesting control of land and resources. Since the removal of Muammar Qaddafi as Libya's leader, the country has devolved into a civil war with various tribal, religious, militia, and governmental groups vying for power. Yemen has long been riven by intertribal conflicts, the most recent occurring in early 2015, when rebels from the Houthi tribe overthrew the sitting government. Ethnic strife continues its long history in Myanmar, where Kachin, Shans, Chins, Karens, Mons, and numerous other minority ethnic groups contest the central government for control of their homelands, access to resources, and preservation of their culture. In Russia, ethnic tensions have long been a national concern, and the northern Caucasus region is a site of continuing ethnic violence.

Nationalism, another divisive ideology, has historically been used as a populist call to rally support against such multicultural issues as immigration, foreign products, or involvement in international organizations or pacts. Globalization, with its focus less on individual nations and more on internationalization, has opened the door for emerging, divisive nationalist movements in several areas of the world over the past decade. In Europe, economic recession, unemployment, immigration issues, and sectarianism have promoted nationalist political movements in the United Kingdom,

Denmark, France, and Germany. Since 2012, Russia has invoked emotional nationalistic appeals in its domestic political pronouncements and used nationalism as part of
the rationale for movement into the Crimea and eastern Ukraine. In India, ardent
Hindu nationalists continue to define themselves in contrast to the nation's
Muslim population. As a justification for retaining power and to garner support for
political policies, the Chinese Communist Party instills nationalism through the educational system and popular media. There have also been recent indicators that
nationalism is growing in Japan. Nor is the United States exempt from nationalism,
as demonstrated when some politicos conflate "American exceptionalism" with
nationalism.[33] When faced with any nationalistically based call, one should always
keep in mind that a fundamental function of nationalism is the creation of an "us"
and a "them."

Conflicting territorial claims have been a historical constant due to fluctuating
borders arising from wars, treaties, political intrigues, and mass migration. Many of
the world's established borders are seen as being unilaterally imposed by former colonial powers or viewed through the perspective of divided historical memory. Today,
most historically based disagreements lie dormant, confined to occasional rhetorical
exchanges between the disputants. However, in several areas, these ongoing territorial
differences remain active and carry the potential to disrupt the greater social order.
For example, the absence of a clearly defined demarcation between Israeli and Palestinian territory has been festering almost 100 years and remains an extremely volatile
situation today. An inability to agree on a border in the Kashmir region following the
1947 Partition has left Indian and Pakistani armed forces aligned along the Line of
Control in Kashmir. The situation is made more dangerous due to both nations possessing nuclear weapons. Only a little farther to the north, since their 1962 border
war, Indian and Chinese forces have been separated by an imaginary line extending
over 2,500 miles through an area of disputed territory. In more recent conflicts, China
has used vague historical documents and indistinct claimed boundaries to assert sovereignty over as much as 90 percent of the entire South China Sea, a claim that conflicts with the maritime economic boundaries of six other littoral nations. Incidents
between Chinese and Vietnamese ships in the South China Sea in 2014 led to riots
and the destruction of Chinese properties in Vietnam. Russia's military takeover of
the Crimea, the support of rebels in eastern Ukraine, and President Putin's jingoistic
pronouncements have unsettled the entire European continent.[34]

The foregoing discussion of the numerous challenges confronting the globalized
community was designed to provide you with a broad overview of the current and
evolving circumstances that carry the potential to create friction, instability, and
even conflict between nations. The purpose was to demonstrate the requirement for
international cooperation and, when needed, global governance in managing these
problems. The root cause of conflict often lies in an overemphasis on differences
between the groups involved. This book aims to develop your intercultural skills so
that you may play a role in resolving some of the conflicts in the globalized world.

TECHNOLOGY

Information technology (IT) has globalized and democratized access to information!
No longer are literary, scientific, legal, and educational materials the provenance of
circumstantially advantaged segments of society. With minimal investment in either

CONSIDER THIS

The use of social media networks has expanded far beyond private citizens and now includes government officials, corporations, nongovernmental organizations, and government organizations. For example, in early 2015 the U.S. Naval Academy held an important debate on the future of aircraft carriers. The debate was broadcast simultaneously on Twitter.[35]

money or time, anyone in almost any place in the world can access the Internet for knowledge, entertainment, communication, and other reasons. No longer does one have to travel to a library, locate an expert, purchase a book, send a letter, or even reason out a problem for oneself. A vast body of knowledge is readily available. Even when it is written in another language, a translation can often be obtained online. The ubiquity and accessibility of information has made "I don't know, but I can look it up" the mantra of the digital generations.

The ability to communicate with people around the world is a source of cohesion as well as polarization. Technology has enabled ordinary citizens to form and organize groups quickly around a common interest regardless of veracity or social benefit. The role of social media in the 2011 Arab Spring uprisings that occurred in part of the Middle East is well known. The Internet and social media also played a critical role in the 2013–2014 "Euromaidan" protests, which ultimately drove the Ukrainian president from office and set in motion the chain of events leading to armed conflict between Ukrainian and Russian-backed separatist forces. According to one study, Internet news sites and social media were central in the dissemination of information about the protest and are believed to "have been highly influential—perhaps even at unprecedented levels compared to prior protests internationally—in motivating people and framing their protest claims."[36] Unfortunately, IT is only a medium and is unable to distinguish between use for purposes of positive or negative gain, good or evil intent, or benign or malicious content. ISIS, for example, has employed various modes of IT to distribute videos and messages intended to recruit converts, propagandize its claims, and intimidate opponents. As a result, ISIS has been able to use social media, especially Twitter, to create a virtual image that exceeds actual capabilities. In a more positive vein, while almost 90 percent of the residents of Bell, California, speak a language other than English, the city's website relies on Google Translate to translate city documents into 64 different languages.[37]

The Internet has also launched "international classrooms" by allowing students from different countries to meet for online discussions as part of formal class activities. The "Global Class," conducted by Durham College, is a "live 90-minute class between [sic] four countries, typically three different post-secondary classes and a guest speaker."[38] During these classes, the role of intercultural communication becomes especially salient.

In some instances, media technology is also leading to a more polarized society, particularly in the United States. The availability of varied information sources on the Internet is enormous, making it quite easy to find material that confirms and solidifies almost any conviction. One author ably described this unfortunate trend:

> Out in cyberspace, facts are movable objects, pushed aside when they don't fit
> beliefs, political leanings or preconceived notions. Everybody's an expert. The like-
> minded find each other and form communities online, reinforcing their biases and their
> certitude.[39]

According to Achenbach, current IT venues, which include radio and television, permit people to inhabit a "'filter bubble' that lets in only the information with which [they] agree."[40] Additionally, the Internet provides a degree of anonymity that can be used to strip away social civility and allows individuals to post shrill, demeaning, discriminatory, and even untrue information. Individuals no longer find it necessary to seek compromises with people who hold perceptions and attitudes that differ from their own. Although written in 2009, Nicholas Kristof's comment remains valid today: "Americans increasingly are segregating themselves into communities, clubs and churches where they are surrounded by people who think the way they do…. The result is polarization and intolerance."[41] Evidence of this is seen on a wide range of issues, such as conservative versus liberal, pro-life versus freedom of choice, anti-immigration versus immigration rights, reduced government spending versus social welfare programs, and the schism surrounding gay marriage rights. It is also evident in the vitriolic exchanges often posted on entertainment blogs, even on such mundane issues as what is a good or bad YouTube music video. Amelioration of these divergent perspectives will be achieved only by understanding that people have varying values and worldviews and by acquiring the ability to communicate across those differences.

The continuing growth of digital technologies is also bringing about profound social and cultural changes. For example, users are turning away from hard-copy publications such as newspapers and books in favor of portable electronic devices. Universities offering online degrees are common. Even elite universities, like Harvard, the Massachusetts Institute of Technology, and Stanford, now offer courses online, many of them free. Movies and television programs can be streamed to home television screens or online devices or stored and watched on a portable device during a transatlantic crossing. The Internet also serves as a meeting place for singles. According to a Pew report, 11 percent of U.S. Americans have used "online dating sites or mobile dating apps to meet someone."[42]

Naturally, many more examples could illustrate the ever-expanding role that communication technology plays in your life. And there is little doubt that IT will bring even more change and convenience to your lives in the future. However, we remind you again that IT is a neutral platform. The messages that pass through the many media sources are shaped by the senders. Thus, regardless of the medium used, culture will continue to play an influential role in shaping both the content and the form of the message.

DEVELOPING INTERCULTURAL AWARENESS

In our zeal to convince you to study intercultural communication, we do not want to overemphasize the scale of culture's influence on human behavior. While we strongly hold to the notion that culture is an instrumental variable in human interaction, a number of problems may be encountered as you make culture the centerpiece in your study of intercultural communication. Specifically, we offer five caveats that will clarify the crucial link between culture and communication.

> ### REMEMBER THIS
>
> *Engaging in intercultural communication is a complex activity. You need to be aware of (1) the uniqueness of each individual, (2) the hazards of over generalizing, (3) the need to be objective, (4) the necessity for compromise, and (5) the myth of believing that communication is a cure-all.*

These qualifications deal with (1) the uniqueness of each individual, (2) the perils of generalizing, (3) the need for objectivity, (4) the need for compromise, and (5) the myth that communication is a cure-all.

INDIVIDUAL UNIQUENESS

According to the American philosopher and psychologist William James, "In every concrete individual, there is a uniqueness that defies formulation." In a very real sense, that "formulation" is another way of saying that no two people are (or ever have been) exactly alike. The reason is simple: Our behavior is shaped by a multitude of sources, with culture being but one. Put in different terms, *we are more than our cultures.* Although all cultures offer people a common frame of reference, people are not captives of their culture, nor are they subject to all the lessons of that culture. In fact, it is folly to think of people in terms of being blank slates. As Pinker points out, "The mind cannot be a blank slate, because blank slates don't do anything."[43] Instead, people are thinking, feeling individuals whose biology, environment, history, and personal experiences interact and play crucial roles in their social collective behavior. Consequently, the values and behaviors of a particular culture may not be the values and behaviors of every individual within that culture.

To further clarify the notion of individual uniqueness, reflect for a moment on all the potential responses that could be generated by the simple phrase "I am going to a NASCAR race this Saturday." Depending on the listener's background, one person might think that watching cars go around in a circle is boring, another could consider the event to be environmentally harmful because of the exhaust gases emitted, but another might respond by saying, "I love the sound of the engines and the smell of tires burning rubber." The reason, of course, is that the world does not look the same to everyone. Just for a moment, think about how the following influences can shape your worldview, attitude, behavior, etc.: your genetic makeup (i.e., DNA), social group experiences, language, gender, age, individual and family history, political affiliation, educational level, perceptions of others, the existing circumstances, the region and neighborhood where you grew up, your religious experiences, economic resources, and many other aspects that are at play every moment of your life.

All of these factors (along with culture) coalesce to form your individual personality. Hooker does an excellent job of drawing attention to the interplay of personality and culture and the hazards of relying solely on culture when studying intercultural communication when he writes,

> Personality consists of the traits that are unique to an individual human being. It is partly genetic and partly learned. Because much of personality is acquired, it is strongly influenced by culture. Yet a very wide range of personalities can develop within a given culture, whence the danger of placing too much emphasis on "national character."[44]

We have been stressing that although all learned behavior takes place within a cultural setting, every person has a unique personality. Therefore, you must be cautious and prudent when making cultural generalizations. Throughout this text, you will be constantly reminded of the following precept: Always keep in mind that culture is a powerful force in the shaping of human behavior, but remember that *people are more than their cultures.*

GENERALIZING

When people from other cultures declare that all Americans have tattoos, listen to hip-hop, and eat mostly fast food, they are generalizing. When Americans conclude that Oktoberfest shows that the Germans like beer and sausage, they are generalizing. And when people say that the Irish are usually short tempered, Mexicans are normally late for meetings, and Asians seem to be good at math, they are generalizing. When someone proclaims that California wine is better than that from France or Australia, they are also generalizing. These examples are representative of an endless number of cultural generalizations people use when talking about other groups. When we generalize, we are allowing a few instances to represent an entire class of events, people, or experiences. It is easy to fall into the trap of employing generalizations, as they are easy to arrive at. For example, think how easy it is to make a decision about another culture if, after meeting several international students from India, you concluded that everyone in India spoke English. These sorts of cultural generalizations are popular because they are easy to create, as they rely on limited samples. In addition, when repeated with enough regularity, they become shorthand to represent an entire collection of people, events, or things. As you might expect, the study of intercultural communication, which implies learning about other people and their cultures, is the perfect arena to misuse generalizations, as it is tempting to generalize about an entire collectivity of people when discussing their qualities and "typical" behaviors.

Generalizations are based on limited data and are then applied to a larger population. In intercultural communication, this means ascribing characteristics to a larger group of people based on attributes displayed by a smaller group. Stereotypes differ from generalizations in that they may not be based solely on conjecture and usually appeal to the audience's positive or negative emotions. For example, "All Asian students make good grades" is a stereotype. A generalization would be, "Records indicate that Asian students are likely to make good grades."

Although generalizing can be a problem when studying intercultural communication, certain precautions can be taken (as we have endeavored to do in this book) to minimize the misleading effects of generalizing. First, cultural generalizations must be viewed as approximations, not as absolute representations. Your personal experiences have taught you that people often do not follow the prescribed and accepted modes of cultural behavior. You may read about social conformity as a trait of the Japanese people, but while in Tokyo, you see an elderly woman with green hair and a group of young men wearing hip-hop clothes. In instances such as these, remember the admonition of the English writer Robert Burton: "No rule is so general, which admits not some exception."

Second, when you do make generalizations, they should deal with the primary values and behaviors of a particular culture. It is these core values and learned behaviors that occur with enough regularity and over a long enough period of time that tend to correctly identify the members of a particular culture. If you examine the dominant culture of the United States, you will have little trouble noticing the importance placed on individualism in everything from dress to outward behavior. In the same manner, you could begin to get insight into the different gender roles in Saudi Arabia by noticing how few women drive cars, hold public office, or appear in public in Western attire. What you will notice about these two examples, although there might be exceptions, is that the culturally instilled behaviors in both are easily recognizable. You can see a somewhat consistent pattern in something as simple as greeting behaviors. For example, in Mexico, friends usually embrace; in India, people bow; and in the United States, people typically shake hands. These kinds of behaviors are recognizable because of their consistency over an extended period, usually involving generation after generation.

Third, when employing generalizations, try to use those that can be supported by a variety of sources. Insufficient and/or limited samples often produce unwarranted conclusions. While reading this book, you will notice that we have used hundreds of reliable references to validate many of our conclusions. This sort of "research" is especially useful when seeking to substantiate a generalization concerning a culture where one's fund of knowledge might be limited.

Finally, conclusions and statements about cultures should be qualified so that they appear not as absolutes but only as cautious generalizations. For example, although this is only the first chapter of the book, you might have noticed how frequently we have used words such as "often" or "usually" to avoid speaking in unconditional terms. Coles adds to our list of qualifying terms, suggesting phrases such as "on average," "more likely," and "tend to" as a way to moderate generalization.[45] These qualifiers facilitate thinking and talking about other cultures without implying that every member of the group is exactly alike. We also add that the validity of the generalization often shifts from culture to culture. That is, if the culture is relatively homogeneous, such as that of Japan or Korea, references to group characteristics tend to be more accurate. However, heterogeneous cultures, such as that of the United States, are far more difficult to generalize about because of the variety of backgrounds, religions, and ethnic groups and the importance placed on each person's individuality.

> **CONSIDER THIS**
>
> *Why do you believe that compromise is difficult to achieve in the intercultural setting?*

OBJECTIVITY

Our next consideration involves the issue of objectivity, one of those concepts that is easier to talk about than to acquire. The very definition of objectivity—"Not influenced by personal feelings, interpretations, or prejudice; based on facts; unbiased: an objective opinion"[46]—should highlight the difficulty of trying to communicate with other people while suspending personal judgment. The problem, of course, is complicated when engaging in intercultural communication because you approach and respond to other cultures from the perspective of your own culture—and often, consciously or unconsciously, it is difficult to be objective when observing or experiencing the actions of other cultures. The habit of overemphasizing one's own culture as a template for assessing other cultures is called ethnocentrism. More specifically, as Ferraro and Andreatta note, ethnocentrism is "the belief that one's culture is superior to all other's."[47] Notice in the following brief examples how ethnocentrism and a lack of objectivity operate: An American might consider a Chinese tour group rude and uncivilized because they spit on the sidewalk and talk loudly or believe the Japanese strange because they do not wear shoes inside their homes.

As evidenced by the above, being objective is no simple assignment. For example, it is difficult, if not impossible, to see and to give meaning to words and behaviors unfamiliar to you. How, for example, do you make sense of someone's silence if you come from a culture that does not value silence? You might make the mistake of thinking, "How could someone be so insensitive as to be silent at a time like this?" Someone from an indirect culture might avoid a direct refusal of your proposal by saying, "I'd like to study that," but never get back to you. You might deem the person inconsiderate or even deceitful for not providing an honest answer. In both these scenarios, a lack of objectivity can impede intercultural communication.

Objectivity also requires that you approach each new situation with an open mind and avoid being judgmental. To reject someone simply for having a different skin color, living in a different country, espousing a dissimilar worldview, or speaking English with an accent diminishes the person and keeps you from having new cultural experiences. Objectivity promotes learning to interact and value distinct groups of people regardless of their culture, race, ethnicity, religion, country, or gender.

COMPROMISE IN INTERCULTURAL COMMUNICATION

Intercultural knowledge and skill will not eliminate cultural conflict! If you engage in intercultural communication for any length of time, inevitably you will encounter some type and degree of conflict. The conflict may arise due to differences between you and the other individual(s), or it could be an internal conflict, resulting from having to make decisions when confronted by culturally different beliefs, values, or behavioral protocols. Encountering disagreements is a natural characteristic of interacting with individuals who have differing perceptions of what is right or wrong, good or bad, acceptable or unacceptable, etc. The important aspect is not whether conflicts will occur, because they will, but rather how to successfully manage the situation. Normally, the best resolution of an external conflict is one where both parties are satisfied—mutual agreement. This is often achieved through reciprocal compromise, as in international business and diplomatic negotiations. In these cases, an agreement is usually reached through a compromise over *interests*, such as price, time, or support, e.g., how much an item costs, when it will be delivered, and the type of warranty.

A culturally based conflict involving *values* can be more problematic, especially if it is an internal conflict. For instance, imagine a scenario where you are studying in Madrid and living with a Spanish family. One evening, your host proudly announces that despite great difficulty, she has obtained tickets for Sunday's bullfight featuring Spain's top matador. If you have strong feelings about animal rights and animal cruelty, you may experience an internal conflict. The problem then arises as to how to handle this difficult and delicate situation. You do not want to offend your host, but at the same time, you are rather repelled by the thought of watching a bull being killed. While your culture has taught you that bullfighting is a blood sport, your host family has been brought up to believe that it is an art form. What is to be done? Unfortunately, there is no standardized procedure for handling these types of situations, and you will have to decide on the final resolution yourself.

We do, however, feel it important that in intercultural matters you view compromise as a positive course of action, rather than a negative choice. In the U.S. dominant culture, compromise is frequently associated with losing or giving up. But in other cultures, compromise is a normal approach to conflict. A good example of this was provided by a Japanese friend who told us that the best solution to a disagreement is when "both sides have to cry a little." We are not saying that you always have to "cry a little," but we do suggest that you approach intercultural conflict with an open mind rather than a win–lose perspective. Take the time to consider the other party's perception of the situation, the importance of the issue, and the possible reaction to your response. In other words, try to develop sensitivity to cultural differences and how they may affect interaction. In some cases, finding a middle ground or even accepting the situation may be the best way. However, situations will likely arise where personal feelings, attitudes, beliefs, and values will place you in an uncompromising position. When those situations arise, we suggest that you make your position clear to the other participants in a clear and sincere manner.

REMEMBER THIS

"All government, indeed every human benefit and enjoyment, every virtue, and every prudent act, is founded on compromise and barter." Edmund Burke

COMMUNICATION IS NOT THE UNIVERSAL SOLUTION

Personal experience has no doubt already taught you that there are many situations in life where no amount of talk can assuage bruised emotions, clarify mistakes, or erase hard feelings. Yet there exists an overabundance of self-help videos, celebrity motivational experts, and books on interpersonal relations that expound the virtues of communication as a solution to and panacea for what plagues the individual and society. Although we readily grant that communication is a valuable tool for resolving numerous interpersonal difficulties, we need to make it clear early in our book that communication cannot solve all problems. In fact, there are even occasions when communication may actually worsen the situation. Wood, in the following paragraph, joins us in warning you about the false hope often granted to communication:

> Yet it would be a mistake to think communication is a cure-all. Many problems can't be solved by talk alone. Communication by itself won't end hunger, abuses of human rights around the globe, racism, intimate partner violations, or physical diseases.[48]

You have probably already realized that it is not unusual to encounter situations where the participants have irreconcilable differences. And this occurs not only at the interpersonal level but also through all strata of society, including relations between nations. These unfortunate situations can lead to alienation and even armed conflict.

Our intent in offering these five warnings about the study of intercultural communication is not to dampen your enthusiasm for the topic. Rather, our objective is to alert you to some of the potential problems facing anyone who takes on a topic as large and complex as intercultural communication. However, now that we have offered these admonitions, we are ready to begin the process of helping you improve interactions with people of cultures different from your own.

PREVIEW OF THE BOOK

To help you gain a degree of intercultural communication competence, we have organized this book into eleven interrelated chapters. Chapter 1 was designed to provide you with a compelling reason to engage in studying intercultural communication by highlighting some of the many challenges facing the globalized world. Some of the problems associated with intercultural communication study have also been discussed.

Chapter 2 establishes the connection between human communication and culture. In Chapter 3 we move to the topic of social organizations and examine the role of the family in both communication and culture. Chapter 4 delves into the deep structural organization of culture by investigating how a culture's worldview influences perception of matters relating to gender, suffering, life, death, and similar topics. Chapter 5 examines the role that a culture's historical legacy plays in shaping and informing contemporary beliefs and values and how that culture views itself.

The topic of Chapter 6 is cultural identity—the way it is formed and its impact on perception and communication. Chapter 7 examines values and cultural patterns that shape the perspectives and behaviors of people. Numerous cultural comparisons are used to illustrate the link between cultural patterns and intercultural interaction.

Chapters 8 and 9 move to discussions of the symbols of intercultural interaction. Chapter 8 explores how language is used in intercultural communicative interactions and the ways in which it is often employed differently, depending on the culture. Chapter 9 discusses the effects of cultural diversity on nonverbal communication and how nonverbal messages support verbal communication in a variety of cultures.

Chapter 10 acknowledges the importance of two communication principles. First, communication is rule governed, and, second, those rules are often scenario (or context) dependent. Specifically, our investigation turns to cultural variations in the business, education, and healthcare settings.

Chapter 11, our newest chapter, explores some of the problems associated with intercultural interactions. We discuss culture shock and acculturation and how they can be managed. Obstacles impeding effective intercultural communication, such as stereotyping, prejudice, racism, and ethnocentrism, are discussed. The chapter concludes with an overview of intercultural ethics.

SUMMARY

- Globalization has created an interdependent world community.

- Interdependency has brought many benefits but also raised new challenges.

- The globalized community must work across national and cultural borders to manage growing and potential international problems.

- Social challenges include population growth, migration, urbanization, and aging populations.

- Ecological concerns consist of international competition for natural resources, including water and food stocks, and environmental changes/degradation.

- Nations will have to cooperate over humanitarian and legal issues, such as disease control, natural disaster relief, and transnational crime.

- Political issues relating to international governance include the international legal system, ethics in scientific research, and human rights differences.

- Security issues that require international coordination include weapons of mass destruction, terrorists, and emerging threats such as sectarian and ethnic tensions.

- Problems relating to the study of intercultural communication encompass individual uniqueness, generalizing, lack of objectivity, and compromise.

- Communication is not a panacea for all intercultural difficulties.

ACTIVITIES

1. Working with others, think of some of the ways in which the ethnic and age-group changes in the U.S. demographic composition will impact your lives.

2. In a discussion group, identify problems arising from international water and food shortages.

3. Identify some of the culturally related challenges involved in an international relief response to a communicable disease outbreak.

4. In a class or online group, discuss the role of culture in sectarian and ethnic tensions. Identify ways of ameliorating these tensions in your community.

5. Find a partner and review the internal conflict scenario on bullfighting given in the text. Role-play the situation with each person assuming the position of the student. How do you manage this dilemma?

6. Identify a problem in your own life where communication has only worsened the situation.

7. Go to YouTube and search for videos on "cultural conflict," "intercultural communication," or other related terms. Enjoy the videos, but use your critical thinking skills.

CONCEPTS AND QUESTIONS

1. What are some of the most compelling intercultural communication challenges that will have to be managed over the next 50 years? Why?

2. How do you think the United States becoming a "minority majority" nation will influence dominant culture values?

3. How can culture influence different perceptions of human rights? What is an example?

4. What are some generalizations about life in the United States that an international exchange student might draw from watching *The Big Bang Theory*, *Modern Family*, or your favorite television show?

CHAPTER 2

Communication and Culture: The Voice and the Echo

Precision of communication is important, more important than ever, in our era of hair-trigger balances, when a false or misunderstood word may create as much disaster as a sudden thoughtless act.

JAMES THURBER

Culture is roughly anything we do and the monkeys don't.

LORD RAGLAN

How shall I talk of the sea to the frog, if he has never left the pond? How shall I talk of the frost to the bird of the summer land if he has never left the land of his birth? And how shall I talk of life with the sage if he is a prisoner of his doctrine?

CHUNG TZU

HUMAN COMMUNICATION

If this book were only about culture we would not be compelled to begin our analysis by turning first to the subject of human communication. However, because the study of intercultural communication is the study of culture *and* communication, we begin by examining communication and then move to the area of culture. Although considering communication first and culture second might seem arbitrary, it is not. Our rationale for the order is straightforward: *To understand intercultural interaction, you must first recognize the role of communication in that process.* Communication—our ability to share our ideas and feelings—is the basis of all human contact. As we noted in Chapter 1, today that contact may take a variety of forms. You can interact with another person by meeting in a face-to-face situation, or by employing new media devices you can exchange messages via blogs or social networking sites such as Facebook, Snapchat, Instagram, WhatsApp, and MySpace. You can also "talk" to other people via email, videoconferencing, Skype, and a host of other media methods. What is important is not the tools you use but rather the idea that you are sharing part of yourself with another human being. Keating summarizes this concept of human contact eloquently, saying, "Communication is powerful: It brings companions to our side or scatters our rivals, reassures or alerts children, and forges consensus or battle lines between us."[1] Whether people live in a city in China, in a village in India, on a farm in Kazakhstan, or in the Amazon rain forests of Brazil, they all employ the same activity when they attempt to share their thoughts and feelings with others. The verbal and nonverbal symbols people utilize might sound and look different, but the reasons they have for communicating are universal. To further highlight the uses people make of this important tool, look at some reasons people send and receive messages.

The Uses of Communication
COMMUNICATION HELPS FULFILL INTERPERSONAL NEEDS

Although there may be many times when you feel frustrated with other people and might find comfort in solitude, people are basically social creatures; therefore, communicating with others satisfies a great many needs. So strong is the need to communicate that one of the cruelest punishments found in nearly every society is solitary confinement. Communication is one of the most rewarding experiences people can have. It is one of the major ways you fulfill a social component within yourself. Linking with others allows you to experience a sense of inclusion, affection, and even control. Although cultures might express these feelings and emotions differently, all people, by both nature and nurture, have a need to communicate and interact with others.[2]

Communicating with others is one of the most rewarding experiences we can have since it is the major way we have contact with others, and as such we experience a sense of inclusion, affection, and even control.

Don Smetzer/PhotoEdit

COMMUNICATION ASSISTS WITH PERSON PERCEPTION

Not only does communication allow you to make human connections, but it also assists in collecting data about other people. Personal experience reveals that when you meet someone for the first time, gathering information about that individual is necessary and begins immediately. That information serves two purposes. First, it enables you to learn about the other person so that you may better understand the messages they are producing. Second, it assists in deciding how to present yourself to that person. These judgments affect everything from the topics selected to talk about to whether you decide to continue the conversation or terminate it. This information, collected from both verbal and nonverbal messages, is essential in intercultural communication because in many instances you are dealing with "strangers."

COMMUNICATION ESTABLISHES CULTURAL AND PERSONAL IDENTITIES

Communication does much more than help gather information and meet your interpersonal needs. It is crucial in establishing your personal identity, since you are born into this world without a sense of self. As Wood notes, "Self is not innate, but is acquired in the process of communication with others."[3] Wood is declaring that through contacts with others, information is accumulated that helps define who you are, where you belong, and where your loyalties rest. Identities are not only dynamic but also multidimensional. You have numerous identities, including concepts of self, emotional ties to family, attitudes toward gender, and beliefs about your culture. Regardless of the identity in question, notions regarding all your identities have evolved during the course of interactions with others. So important is identity to the study of intercultural communication that Chapter 7 will examine the link between identity and intercultural communication.

COMMUNICATION HAS PERSUASIVE QUALITIES

This function suggests that communication allows you to send verbal and nonverbal messages that can shape the behavior of other people. In this sense your ability to communicate allows you to exercise a degree of control over your environment. If you take a moment to reflect on the activities of a normal day, you will discover that you engage in innumerable situations intended to influence others. They may include selling products at work, asking someone for directions when lost, soliciting a higher grade from a professor, or rallying a group of friends to work for a charitable cause. In all of these instances you are using communication as a means to regulate the world around you.

Having reviewed the purposes of communication, we are ready to define communication and to discuss some of its basic principles.

DEFINING HUMAN COMMUNICATION

In a class discussion on definitions of communication, a student once offered a very clever response when asked, "What is communication?" She answered, "I know communication when I see it, but there is too much going on to describe it." Perhaps this is the reason the English statesman Benjamin Disraeli once wrote, "I hate definitions." While definitions are necessary (they help establish boundaries), finding a single definition for the word "communication" can be troublesome. For example, nearly forty years ago Dance and Larson perused the literature on communication and found 126 definitions of the word.[4] Since then, because the word "communication" is abstract, countless other definitions have been added to their list. If you type the words "definition of communication" into a search engine on the Internet, you will find thousands of attempts at defining this word. Infante, Rancer, and Womack offer an excellent summary of why a single definition is difficult to pin down:

> Definitions differ on such matters as whether communication has occurred if a source did not intend to send a message, whether communication is a linear process (a source sending a message in a channel to a receiver who then reacts), or whether a transactional perspective is more accurate (emphasizing the relationships between people as they constantly influence one another). Another factor in the lack of agreement on definitions is that the study of communication is not a precise science.[5]

The above critique, however, fails to list the complexities associated with the addition of digital-mediated communication such as television, cell phones, tablets, computers, and the like.

One characteristic that nearly all definitions have in common is that they attempt to stake out the territory that is most germane to the creator of the definition. That specific characteristic applies to our attempt at defining communication. For us, *human communication is a dynamic process in which people attempt to share their thoughts with other people through the use of symbols in particular settings.*

CONSIDER THIS

What is meant by the phrase "People engage in communication for a variety of purposes"?

THE INGREDIENTS OF HUMAN COMMUNICATION

The brevity of our definition has forced us to omit some important specifics regarding how communication operates in real life. By adding some additional detail to our definition, you might be able to get a more realistic view of this complex process. It is a process that is usually composed of eight interrelated activities.

First, there is a *source*—a person who has an idea, feeling, experience, etc. that they wish to share with another person. The source, as well as the other person, is sending and receiving messages. The reason, of course, is that communication is an interactive process. Put slightly differently, while you are sending messages you are also receiving the messages being generated by your communication partner.

Second, because what you are feeling and thinking cannot be shared directly (there is no direct mind-to-mind contact), you must rely on symbolic representations of your internal states. This brings us to our second component—*encoding*.

Encoding is an internal activity. It occurs when the source creates a message through the selection of verbal or nonverbal symbols. Although the process of converting feelings into words and actions is universal, the words and actions selected and how they are strung together have their origins in the culture of the language being used.

Third, encoding leads to the production of the *message*. The message is a set of written, pictorial, verbal, and/or nonverbal symbols that represent a source's particular state of being at a specific moment. While encoding is an internal act (finding a code that represents a personalized reality), the sending of messages is an external undertaking—it is the subject matter to be communicated.

Fourth, messages must have a means of moving from person to person. It is the *channel* that provides that necessary connection. The channel can take a variety of forms. For example, as you read this book, the words on the printed page constitute our message, while the printing on these pages is the channel. Channels, in face-to-face interaction, are sights and sounds. However, channels can include multiple types of media. From television to the Internet to iPhones, a person's messages are moved from place to place.

Fifth, after a message has been generated and moved along through a channel, it must encounter a *receiver*. The receiver is the person who takes the message into account and thereby is directly linked to the source. Receivers may be those with whom the source intends to interact, or they may be other people who, for whatever reason, come in contact with the source's message.

Sixth, in this stage of the communication process, the receiver *decodes* the message. This operation (the converting of external stimuli to meaningful interpretations) is akin to the source's act of encoding, as both are internal activities. The decoding process within the receiver is often referred to as *information processing*. In this stage the receiver attributes meaning to the behaviors generated by the sender.

Seventh, when you send a message to another person you usually perceive the response that person makes to your actions. That response may be words, a nonverbal reaction, or even silence. It matters little; what is important is that your message produced some response that you took into account. The perception of the response to your message is called *feedback*. Feedback typically has two stages. First, it applies to the reactions you obtain from your communication partner. Second, in most instances you use that reaction to decide what to do next. In this way feedback controls the ebb and flow of the conversation. You smile at someone, your smile is greeted with a frown, and you respond by asking, "Are you okay?"

Eighth, the source is not alone in sending messages to the receiver. Every communication event is characterized by a multiplicity of competing stimuli. We intentionally use the word "competing" as a way to call attention to the fact that numerous stimuli are seeking to be noticed. The concept of competing stimuli is referred to as *noise*. Noise is often thought of as interference with the communication process. Noise can be external or internal, and it can influence your capacity to process messages, as it is a kind of competing stimulus. Noise can be produced by people sitting behind you talking on a cell phone or by an air conditioner in need of servicing.

REMEMBER THIS

Because you cannot directly access the internal thoughts of another, you must rely on and interpret their use of verbal and nonverbal symbols to represent those thoughts.

COMPONENTS OF HUMAN COMMUNICATION

Having defined communication and briefly explained its key ingredients, we now expand our analysis to include a discussion of the basic characteristics of communication. As was the case with the examination of definitions and ingredients, a few introductory remarks are in order. First, communication has more characteristics than we can discuss in the next few pages. Just as a description of a forest that mentions only the trees and flowers, but omits the wildlife and lakes, does not do justice to the entire setting, our inventory is not exhaustive. We, too, are forced to leave out some of the landscape. Second, as noted in the introduction to this section on communication, while the linear nature of language forces us to discuss one principle at a time, keep in mind that in reality the elements of communication are in continuous interaction with one another.

COMMUNICATION IS A DYNAMIC PROCESS

You will notice that the words "dynamic process" were contained in our earlier definition of communication. The words "dynamic" and "process" were linked to remind you of a number of factors related to communication. First, the words indicate that communication is an ongoing activity that has no beginning or end. Phrased in slightly different terms, *communication is not static.* Communication is like a motion picture, not a single snapshot. A word or action does not stay frozen when you communicate. It is immediately replaced with yet another word or action. Second, communication is a dynamic process because once a word or action is produced, it cannot be retracted. Once an event takes place, that *exact* event cannot happen again. The judge who counsels the jury to "disregard the testimony just given" knows that such a mental activity is impossible. T. S. Eliot expressed it poetically when he wrote, "In the life of one person, never the same time returns." Third, the phrase "dynamic process" conveys the idea that sending and receiving messages involves a host of variables, *all in operation at the same time.* Each of the parties to the transaction is reacting to the other by seeing, listening, talking, thinking, and perhaps smiling and touching the other, all at once. As Andersen states, "These forces do not work in isolation from one another, nor are they purely additive. Instead, one force may counterbalance or sharply change the nature of the other."[6]

CONSIDER THIS

What is meant by the phrase "Communication is a dynamic process"?

COMMUNICATION IS SYMBOLIC

You will recall that our definition of communication mentioned the importance of symbols to human interaction. Earlier, we alluded to the truism that there is no direct mental connection between people. Of course, this means that you cannot directly access the internal thoughts and feelings of other human beings; you can only infer what they are experiencing by what you see and hear. Those inferences are drawn from the symbols people produce. *In human communication, a symbol is an expression that stands for or represents something else.* Although those symbols may be spontaneous and nonintentional (someone sneezes, and you infer they have a cold) or intentional (someone tells you they have a cold), both involve your attaching meaning to a symbolic event generated by another person. In many ways, this act of attaching meaning to symbols is at the core of human communication. Other animals may engage in some form of communication and even make use of some symbols, but none has the unique communication capabilities found among humans. Through millions of years of physical evolution and thousands of years of cultural development, humans are able to generate, receive, store, and manipulate symbols. This sophisticated system allows people to use symbols—be they sounds, marks on paper, letters on the screen of a cell phone, sculptures, Braille, gestures, or paintings—to represent something else. Reflect for a moment on the wonderful gift you have that allows you to hear the words "The kittens look like cotton balls," and, like magic, you have an image in your head. Because the image you conjure up for "kittens" and "cotton balls" is inside of you, it is essential to remember that each person "defines" those words and phrases from his or her own cultural perspective. Therefore, it is always important to keep in mind that "Language symbols are no more consistent or precise than the experience, values, and belief systems of the people using them."[7]

In terms of intercultural communication, it is important to keep in mind the fact that the symbols you use are discretionary and subjective. There is no innate connection between the symbols and their referents. The relationships are arbitrary and usually shift from culture to culture. In short, although all cultures use symbols, they usually assign their own meanings to them. Not only do Spanish speakers say *perro* for "dog," but the mental image they form when they hear the sound is probably quite different from the one Mandarin Chinese speakers form when they hear *gŏu*, their word for "dog." In addition to having different meanings for symbols, cultures also use these symbols for different purposes. Because symbols are at the core of communication, we examine them throughout this book. For now, remember that symbols, by virtue of their standing for something else, give you an opportunity to share your personal realities. So important is the notion of symbols to the study of intercultural communication that later in this chapter (and again in Chapters 8 and 9), we will return to the topic of symbols.

COMMUNICATION IS CONTEXTUAL

The heading declares that communication is contextual as a way of informing you that communication does not occur in a vacuum. As previously noted, communication, because it is a dynamic process and part of a larger system, is composed of many ingredients. One of those ingredients is *context*. This implies that setting and environment help determine the words and actions you generate and the meanings you give to the symbols you receive. In addition, whether consciously or subconsciously, context plays a role in establishing which behavior is favored and which is deemed inappropriate. Attire, language, nonverbal behavior, topic selection, and vocabulary are all adapted to the context. Reflect for a moment on how differently you would behave in each of the following settings: a classroom, a church, a courtroom, a funeral, a wedding, a sporting event, a hospital, or a nightclub. For example, a male would not attend a university lecture, even in hot weather, without wearing a shirt. However, at a football stadium, you might find a whole row of males without shirts on (possibly with letters painted on their chests), and this would be socially acceptable.

Communication is a dynamic process that involves a host of variables (seeing, listening, talking, smiling, touching) that are all in operation at once.

Courtesy of Carolyn Roy

Even the words we exchange are contextual. The simple phrase "How are you?" shifts meaning as you move from place to place and person to person. To a friend, it can be a straightforward expression used as a greeting. Yet during a doctor's appointment, the same three words ("How are you?") uttered by the physician call for a detailed response regarding your physical condition.

In most instances, the context involves four aspects: (1) the number of people who are interacting, (2) the environmental context, (3) the occasion, and (4) the time.

Number of Participants

The number of people involved in the communication exchange affects the flow of interaction in a variety of ways. You feel and act differently if you are talking to one person, giving a speech, part of a group discussion, or speaking before a large audience. As you can imagine, new technologies have greatly altered the entire notion involving the number of participants who are taking part in any communication event. Instant messaging, email, text messaging, chat rooms, and online social networks such as Facebook have redefined the entire ambiance associated with face-to-face interpersonal communication. From not being able to touch your communication partner to not even knowing who that partner might be, technology has changed how people communicate.

Environmental Context

When we write about the environmental context, we are talking about the "where" of the communication event. Some introspection should tell you that your behavior is not the same in every environment. Whether it is an auditorium, an employment interview, an upscale restaurant, a group meeting, or an office, the location of your interaction provides guidelines for your behavior. Factors such as the noise level, room temperature, or even the way the furniture is arranged influence how people relate to each other. As suggested throughout this section, either consciously or unconsciously, you know the prevailing rules as a member of one culture or another. Most cultures, for example, have classrooms, but the rules for behavior in those class-rooms are rooted in culture. In Mexico, children are encouraged to move around the room and to interact verbally and physically with their classmates. In China, students remain in their seats nearly all of the day, and group interactions are limited.

Occasion

The occasion of a communication encounter also controls the behavior of the partici-pants. The same auditorium or sports arena can be the occasion for a graduation cere-mony, concert, pep rally, convocation, dance, or memorial service. Each of these occasions calls for distinctly different forms of behavior. For example, somberness and silence are usually the rule at a solemn American Protestant funeral, whereas an Irish wake calls for music, dancing, and a great deal of merriment. A pep rally or dance would be an occasion in the same sports arena venue for raucous activity and much movement.

Time

Time is another crucial element that can influence the communication event. Yet the influence of time on communication is so subtle that its impact is often overlooked. To understand this concept, answer these questions: How do you feel when someone keeps you waiting for a prolonged period of time? Do you respond to a phone call at 2:00 a.m. the same way you do to one at 2:00 p.m.? Do you find yourself rushing the conversation when you know you have very little time to spend with someone? Your answers to these questions reveal how often the clock controls your actions. Every communication event takes place along a time–space continuum, and the amount of time allotted, whether it is for social conversation or a formal presentation, affects that event. Cultures, as well as people, use time to communicate. In the United States, schedules and time constraints are ever present. "For Americans, the use of appointment-schedule time reveals how people feel about each other, how significant their business is, and where they rank in the status system."[8]

COMMUNICATION IS SELF-REFLECTIVE

The American philosopher Emerson once wrote, "Wherever we go, whatever we do, self is the sole subject we study and learn." Emerson, whether he employed communi-cation terminology or not, was referring to the idea that human beings have an ability to think about themselves, to watch how they define the world, and to reflect on their past, present, and future. This focus on self can—and usually does—take place while you are communicating. Because of self-reflectiveness, you can think about the encounter you are involved in while being an active member of that encounter. In many ways, it is as if you are talking with yourself while also exchanging messages with other people. In short, this unique endowment lets you be participant and observer simultaneously: You can watch, evaluate, and alter your "performance" as a communicator at the very instant you are engaged in the event. Humans are the only species that can simultaneously be at both ends of the camera.

There is, as you have learned by now, an intercultural dimension to your capacity to be self-reflective, though this capacity may not always be manifest. Some cultures are much more concerned with the self than are others and therefore devote a great deal of energy to watching and even worrying about the self. The "I" is at the heart of Western religion and psychology. For example, from Locke, who said rationality meant you could know the answers to all questions, to modern self-help "experts" who speak of "personal power," Americans grow up believing the individual is at the center of the universe. Cultures that are more group oriented focus on relations with other people, so although they can engage in self-reflective activity during communication, their main concern is with the other, not with the self.

COMMUNICATION IS IRREVERSIBLE

The early Greek philosopher Heraclitus once observed, "You cannot step twice into the same river; for other waters are ever flowing on to you." As applied to human interaction, what Heraclitus was telling us is that once a message is sent, there can be no way to retrieve it. It is as if you had hit the "Send" key on your computer and at the same instant changed your mind about using that key. You could not recover your message. Suppose that, in the heat of an argument with your best friend, you blurt the one insult that you know will hurt the most, directly followed by "I am so sorry." You may indeed be sorry, but that does not expunge the previous message. Both messages have been received and responded to internally if not externally.

The reason, as stated in the heading of this postulate, is because communication is irreversible. A Chinese proverb makes this important point: "A harsh word dropped from the tongue cannot be brought back by a coach and six horses."

CONSIDER THIS

What is meant by the phrase "Communication has a consequence"?

COMMUNICATION HAS A CONSEQUENCE

Our last postulate flows smoothly into this next assumption. Having just discussed how your communication actions once received cannot be reclaimed, this also means that all of your messages affect someone else. To some degree, they also modify your own behavior. This is not a philosophical or a metaphysical theory but a biological fact. It is impossible not to respond to the sounds and actions of others. Obviously, the responses you have to messages vary in degree and kind. It might help you to visualize your potential responses as forming a continuum (see Figure 2.1). At one end of the continuum lie responses to messages that are overt and easy to understand. Someone sends you a message by asking directions to the library. Your response is to say, "It's on your right." You might even point to the library. The message from the other person has thus produced an overt, observable response.

FIGURE 2.1	Communication Responses

1	25	50	75	100
Overt	Covert	Unconscious		Biological

A little farther across the continuum are those messages that produce only a mental response. If someone says to you, "The United States should withdraw from the United Nations" and you only think about this statement but don't respond outwardly, you are still responding. It does not matter that your response does not have an observable action. As you proceed across the continuum, you come to responses that are harder to detect. These are responses to messages you receive by imitating, observing, and interacting with others. Generally, you are not even aware that you are receiving these messages. As your parents act out their gender roles, you receive messages about your gender role. People greet you by shaking hands instead of hugging, and without being aware of it, you are receiving messages about forms of address.

At the far end of the continuum are the responses to messages that are received unconsciously. That is, your body responds even if your cognitive processes are kept to a minimum. Messages that come to you can alter your chemical secretions, your heart rate, or the temperature of your skin; modify pupil size; and trigger a host of other internal responses. These biological responses are covert, and they are the most difficult to classify. They do, however, give credence to our assertion that communication has a consequence. If your internal reactions produce chaos in your system, as is the case with severe stress, you can become ill. Thus, regardless of the content of the message, it should be clear that the act of communication produces change in people.

While everyone receives and responds to messages, the nature of both the message and the response is rooted in your culture. The grief associated with the death of a loved one is as natural as breathing; each culture, however, determines ways of coping with and sharing that grief. These responses to the outside world can range from wailing loudly to maintaining a stoic exterior.

The response you make to someone's message does not have to be immediate. You can respond minutes, days, or even years later. For example, your second-grade teacher may have asked you to stop throwing rocks at a group of birds that were on the playground. Perhaps the teacher added that the birds were part of a family and were gathering food for their babies. She might also have indicated that birds feel pain just like people. Perhaps twenty years later, as you think about eating an animal, you remember those words from your teacher and decide to become a vegetarian. It is important to remember the power of your messages and to consider the ethical consequences of your communication actions, for, whether or not you want to grant those consequences, you are changing people each time you exchange messages with them.

COMMUNICATION IS COMPLEX

One point should be obvious by now: Communication is complex. As you have seen to this point, communication can involve controlling, informing, persuading, and relating to others. And reflect for a moment on all the bodily and mental activity that accompanies even the simple act of saying hello to a friend. From the stimulation of your nerve endings to the secretion of chemicals in your brain to the moving of your lips to produce sound, thousands of components are in operation (most of them at the same time). Not only are there countless biological and physical factors coming into play all at once, but there are also many elements to each person's personality.

For example, during a single interaction there are six "people" involved: (1) the person that you imagine yourself to be, (2) the other person as you perceive him or her, (3) your notion of what you believe the other person thinks of you, (4) the other person as he or she supposes he or she is, (5) how the other person perceives you, and (6) the other person's notion of how he or she believes you perceive him or her. Trying to offer a summary for this idea regarding the complexity of communication, Smith states, "Human communication is a subtle and ingenious set of processes. It is always thick with a thousand ingredients—signals, codes, meanings—no matter how simple the message or transaction."[9]

Communication becomes even more complex when cultural dimensions are added. Although all cultures use symbols to share their realities, the specific realities and the symbols employed are often quite different. In one culture, you smile in a casual manner as a form of greeting; in another, you bow formally in silence; and in yet another, you acknowledge your friend with a full embrace.

MISCONCEPTIONS ABOUT HUMAN COMMUNICATION

Having just spent some time discussing what communication *is*, we now offer a brief explanation of what it is *not*. Below are a few common misconceptions. Avoiding these mistaken beliefs about communication might improve the way you engage in this multifaceted activity.

Communication Can Solve All Problems

First, as you have observed, communication serves a variety of needs in each person's life. From the moment of birth to when we say good-bye to those we love, communication is an essential and important part of what it means to be human. Yet the power and sway of communication are frequently overstated. You often hear people say, "If we could just sit down and talk, we could end war and solve the problem of global poverty." While those declarations are well intended, they contain a not-so-subtle message that communication is a cure-all. This same notion of the magic potion effect of communication is also seen in personal relationships. Many people believe that if they could compose a string of the right words, they could mend a relationship that had been marked with deceit and duplicity. Simply put, there are many occasions, regardless of what self-help gurus might preach, when communication does not work. We should add that from a cultural perspective, a reliance on communication to solve all problems is basically a Western idea. As Wood points out, "Not all societies think it is wise or useful to communicate about relationships or to talk extensively about feelings. Just as interpersonal communication has many strengths and values, it also has limits, and its effectiveness is shaped by cultural contexts."[10]

Some People Are Born Effective Communicators

There is a fallacy about communication that seems to be replicated generation after generation. The myth purports that people are born with or without the ability to be superior communicators. We called that assertion a fallacy and a myth because it is simply not true. Admittedly, some people may have a facility and personality for feeling comfortable around other people, yet every individual can develop the basic skills to be a successful communicator. For example, learning how to compromise, show empathy, and listen intently can be learned. Solomon and Theiss further affirm that effective communication skills can be acquired when they write: "Although people are born with the ability to communicate, creating and interpreting messages requires self-knowledge, attention to a communication partner's perspective, detailed understanding of how the situation shapes meanings, and an ability to select and sequence messages to achieve particular goals. These abilities take effort and practice to develop."[11]

The Message You Send Is the Message Received

We have already mentioned that the communication process is multifaceted and complex. Yet many people believe that the message they send is the one that the other person receives. That notion is bogus, as it is predicated on the false premise that the recipient of the message decodes the message in *exactly* the same way the sender of the message encoded it. Hence, telling is communicating. This myth assumes that people are like computers and that human communication simply involves the direct transfer of information. This view does not allow for variables such as each person's background, memory, values, beliefs, vocabulary, and the like to be in operation when people communicate. This misconception is often at the heart of major conflicts and misunderstandings when people attempt to share their internal states but have very different interpretations for what they believe to be the same messages. Of course, when you add the dimension of culture into that equation, this misconception becomes even more problematic. Later in this chapter, we discuss some ways to minimize some of the problems associated with the misconception that the message sent is the message received.

CULTURE

Moving from communication to culture provides us with a rather seamless transition, for, as Hall points out, "Culture is communication and communication is culture."[12] In fact, when examining communication and culture, it is hard to decide which is the voice and which is the echo. The reason for the duality is that you "learn" your culture via communication and that, at the same time, communication is a reflection of your culture. Worded slightly differently, *culture is both teacher and textbook*.

> **REMEMBER THIS**
>
> *Communication and culture work in tandem.*

This book manifests the authors' strong belief that you cannot improve your intercultural communication skills without having a clear understanding of this phenomenon called culture. The following examples demonstrate the powerful link between communication and culture:

- Some people are delighted and smile when someone pats the head of their young child. Yet in other cultures, such a gesture is deemed an inappropriate act. Why?
- Some people seek the company of others when they are grieving, but other people seek solace. Why?
- Some people scratch their ears and cheeks as a sign of happiness, but people in other places of the world smile when they are happy. Why?

- Some people in many parts of the world put dogs in their ovens, but people in the United States put them on their couches and beds. Why?
- Some people in Kabul and Kandahar pray five times each day while kneeling on the floor, but some people in Jerusalem pray while standing erect and slightly rocking back and forth. Why?
- Some people speak Tagalog, but others speak English. Why?
- Some people paint and decorate their entire bodies, but others spend hundreds of dollars painting and decorating only their faces. Why?
- Some people shake hands when introduced to a stranger, but other people bow at such an encounter. Why?

The general answer to all these questions is the same—*culture*. Each culture presents its members with ways of thinking and ways of behaving. That sentence can serve as one of the basic premises of this entire book. Rodriguez punctuates the influence of culture on human perception and actions when she writes, "Culture consists of how we relate to other people, how we think, how we behave, and how we view the world."[13] Although culture is not the only stimulus behind your behavior, its omnipresent quality makes it one of the most powerful. Hall underscores this point when he concludes, "There is not one aspect of human life that is not touched and altered by culture."[14] Wood further speaks to this notion when she writes, "We are not born knowing how, when, and to whom to speak, just as we are not born with attitudes about cooperating or competing. We acquire attitudes as we interact with others, and we then reflect cultural teachings in the way we communicate."[15] Wood is reminding you that although you enter this world with all the anatomy and physiology needed to live here, you do not arrive knowing how to dress, what toys to play with, what to eat, how to deal with conflict, which gods to worship, what to strive for, how to spend your money or your time, how to define the questions surrounding death, or ways to determine "truth." Those discoveries—and countless others—are part of the domain and function of culture.

Perhaps at this stage in our discussion of culture, it is wise to ask the following question: *What is the basic function of culture?* In its most uncomplicated sense, culture, for over forty thousand years until today, is intended to make life unproblematic for people by "teaching" them how to adapt to their surroundings. The English writer Fuller echoed this idea in rather simple terms when he wrote, "Culture makes all things easy." A more detailed explanation as to the function of culture is offered by Sowell:

> Cultures exist to serve the vital, practical requirements of human life—to structure a society so as to perpetuate the species, to pass on the hard-learned knowledge and experience of generations past and centuries past to the young and inexperienced in order to spare the next generation the costly and dangerous process of learning everything all over again from scratch through trial and error—including fatal errors.[16]

Culture serves a basic need by laying out a somewhat predictable world in which each individual is firmly grounded. It thus enables you to make sense of your surroundings by offering a blueprint for not only how to behave but also what results you can anticipate from that behavior. While people in every culture might deviate from this blueprint, they at least know what their culture expects of them. Try to imagine a single day in your life without the guidelines of your culture. From how to earn a living to how an economic system works to how to greet strangers to explanations of illness and death to how to find a mate, culture provides you with structure and direction.

To further explain the concept of culture and its impact on communication, let us now (1) define culture, (2) discuss the major characteristics of culture, and (3) highlight the essential elements of culture as they apply to intercultural communication.

CULTURE DEFINED

The preceding discussion on the topic of culture should enable you to see that culture is ubiquitous and complex. It is also difficult to define. As Harrison and Huntington note, "The term 'culture,' of course, has had multiple meanings in different disciplines and different contexts."[17] These meanings "range from complex and fancy definitions to simple ones such as 'culture is the programming of the mind' or 'culture is the human-made part of the environment.'"[18] The media also use the word to portray aspects of individual sophistication, such as classical music, fine art, or the appreciation of exceptional food and wine. You also hear the words "popular culture" when people discuss current trends within the culture. But these movements in fashion and style only demonstrate that cultures are always changing. We are concerned with more enduring aspects of culture and with a definition that reveals how culture and communication are linked. One definition that meets our needs is advanced by Triandis:

> Culture is a set of human-made objective and subjective elements that in the past have increased the probability of survival and resulted in satisfaction for the participants in an ecological niche, and thus became shared among those who could communicate with each other because they had a common language and they lived in the same time and place.[19]

We prefer this definition because it highlights the essential features of culture. First, specifying that it is "human-made" clarifies that culture is concerned with non-biological parts of human life. This distinction allows for explanations of behavior that must be learned while at the same time it eliminates (at least from our study) innate acts that are not learned (such as eating, sleeping, crying, speech mechanisms, and fear). Second, the definition includes what can be termed "subjective" elements of culture—such concepts as values, beliefs, attitudes, norms, and foundational behaviors. Think for a moment of all the subjective cultural beliefs and values you hold that influence your interpretation of the world. Your views about the national flag, work, immigration, freedom, aging, ethics, dress, property rights, etiquette, healing and health, death and mourning, play, law, individualism, magic and superstition, modesty, sexual taboos, status differentiation, courtship, formality and informality, and bodily adornment are all part of your cultural membership. Finally, the definition also calls attention to the importance of language as a symbol system that allows culture to be transmitted and shared. This means that a collection of people has established not only a set of symbols but also rules for using those symbols.

CHARACTERISTICS OF CULTURE

Although this book focuses on the cultural differences that influence communication, we will look at a series of characteristics that all cultures have in common. An awareness of these traits is useful for a number of reasons. First, examining these

Early in life children learn about appropriate and inappropriate ways of acting so that they will know how to adapt to their culture's formal and informal "rules."

Courtesy of Edwin McDaniel

characteristics facilitates your appreciation of the importance and influence of culture on human behavior. Second, as we review these commonalities, the strong connection between culture and communication will become apparent. Most experts agree: "The heart of culture involves language, religion, values, traditions, and customs."[20] These are some of the topics treated throughout this book. Finally, this may be the first time you have been asked to seriously look at your own culture. Reflect for a moment on just how often you and your friends sit around and discuss culture. We are not talking about "popular culture" but rather those aspects of culture that often differ from your own. Learning about culture—yours and others—can be an energizing awakening. Shapiro offered such a pep talk when he wrote, "The discovery of culture, the awareness that it shapes and molds our behavior, our values and even our ideas, the recognition that it contains some element of the arbitrary, can be a startling or an illuminating experience."[21]

Culture Is Shared

It should be clear at this point that one of the most distinctive features of culture is that it is *shared*. Whereas your personal experiences and genetic heritage form the unique you, culture unites people with a collective frame of reference. "Culture is to a human collective what personality is to an individual."[22] Nolan reaffirms this idea when he suggests that "culture is a group worldview, the way of organizing the world that a particular society has created over time. This framework or web of meaning allows the members of that society to make sense of themselves, their world, and their experiences in that world."[23] It is this sharing of a common reality that gives people within a particular culture a common fund of knowledge, a sense of identity, shared traditions, and specific behaviors that are often distinct from other collections of people. Haviland and his associates explain this "sharing" process: "As a shared set of ideas, values, perceptions, and standards of behavior, culture is the common denominator that makes the actions of individuals intelligible to other members of their society. It enables them to predict how other members are most likely to behave in a given circumstance, and it tells them how to react accordingly."[24]

We conclude this section regarding the shared component of culture by briefly reminding you of what we wrote in Chapter 1 when we discussed that much of human behavior comes from sources beyond culture. In general terms, three basic factors influence human behavior.[25] The most universal of these is human nature. Our abilities to cry, feel fear, seek food, etc. are inherited traits. Second, culture and various groups (clubs, professions, co-cultures, etc.) present people with thousands of learned behaviors. Finally, there is the unique personality that is the exclusive domain of each individual.

CONSIDER THIS

What is meant by the phrase "Culture is shared"?

Culture Is Transmitted from Generation to Generation

Embedded in our first characteristic is the notion that what is shared by a culture gets transmitted from generation to generation. The American philosopher Thoreau reminded us of that fact when he wrote, "All the past is here." Of course, Thoreau is correct. For a culture to endure, it must make certain that its crucial messages and elements are not only shared but also passed to future generations. In this way, the past becomes the present and helps create and perpetuate the culture. This means that the numerous values, norms, and behaviors that are considered fundamental to a culture need to be handed down from one generation to another. This process of transmitting culture is a kind of cultural inheritance. As such, this "heritage" is made up of the beliefs and actions that may have evolved long before each new generation arrives. The longevity of the beliefs, values, and behavior that are transmitted is clearly delineated by Matsumoto and Hwang when they write, "Our culture determines what it means to be a husband or wife, child, work colleague, acquaintance, or even a stranger."[26]

Like so much of culture, it is communication that makes culture a continuous process, for once cultural habits, principles, values, and attitudes are formed, they are communicated to each member of the culture. While the immediate family begins the "education" process, you need to remember that most of the crucial "lessons" of a culture continue to be emphasized throughout the person's life. Infants, held and touched by parents, do not consciously know they are learning about family and touch, but they are. The essential cultural values continue to be reinforced as children share holidays, both religious and secular, with grandparents, aunts, uncles, and other relatives. So strong is the need for a culture to bind each generation to past and future generations that it is often asserted that a fracture in the transmission process would contribute to a culture's extinction.

Culture Is Based on Symbols

Our discussion of how culture is transmitted from generation to generation allows for an easy transition to our next characteristic—*culture is based on symbols*. Without the capacity of humans to think symbolically and express those symbols, culture could not be passed from generation to generation. The symbols that are important to a culture can take a variety of forms.

Symbols such as flags, wedding rings, gestures, words, dress, objects, statues, and religious icons all have message value. The portability of symbols allows people to package, store, and transmit them. The mind, books, pictures, films, computer memory chips, and videos enable a culture to preserve what it deems important and worthy of transmission. This makes each individual, regardless of his or her generation, heir to a massive repository of information that has been gathered and maintained in anticipation of his or her entry into the culture. Ferraro and Andreatta speak to this "entry into the culture" when they write, "Without symbols we would not be able to store the collective wisdom of past generations, and consequently we would be prone to repeat the mistakes of the past. Symbols tie together people who otherwise might not be part of a unified group."[27]

As we have noted, cultural symbols can take a host of forms, but it is words, both written and spoken, that are most often used to symbolize objects and thoughts. It is language that enables you to share the speculations, observations, facts, experiments, and wisdom accumulated over thousands of years—what the linguist Weinberg called "the grand insights of geniuses which, transmitted through symbols, enable us to span the learning of centuries."[28] Bates and Plog offer an excellent summary of the importance of language to culture:

> Language thus enables people to communicate what they would do if such-and-such happened, to organize their experiences into abstract categories ("a happy occasion," for instance, or an "evil omen"), and to express thoughts never spoken before. Morality, religion, philosophy, literature, science, economics, technology, and numerous other areas of human knowledge and belief—along with the ability to learn about and manipulate them—all depend on this type of higher-level communication.[29]

Culture is shared, transmitted from generation to generation, and needs to be internalized by all the members of each culture.

So important are symbols to the study of intercultural communication that we have set aside Chapter 8 (verbal messages) and Chapter 9 (nonverbal messages) to further develop this connection between symbols and human behavior.

Culture Is Learned

It should be clear by now that culture *is not innate; it is learned.* This means that what is shared, transmitted from generation to generation, and symbolized needs to be internalized by the members of each

culture. This internalization process is not a simple matter. Remember that we are born into a world without meaning. Imagine what a confusing place this is for a newborn. After living in a peaceful environment for nine months, the infant is thrust into this novel place called "the world." It is a world filled with sights, sounds, tastes, and other sensations that, at this stage of life, have no meaning. As the psychologist William James noted, what greets the newborn is a bubbling, babbling mass of confusion. From the moment of birth to the end of life, you seek to overcome that confusion and make sense of the world. It is culture that assists you in that sense-making process. As each person arrives, he or she immediately and automatically becomes a member of a cultural environment that has been coping with thousands of problems and solutions long before the infant is born. The work of culture then becomes one of getting the newborn to adjust to and flourish in a life that includes other people. Nanda and Warms develop this important idea when they write,

> Child-rearing practices in all cultures are designed to produce adults who know the skills, norms, and behavior patterns—the cultural content—of their society. But the transmission of culture involves more than just knowing these things. It also involves patterning children's attitudes, motivations, values, perceptions, and beliefs so that they can function in their society.[30]

This suggestion that culture is learned has direct implications for the study of intercultural communication. If you were reared in a home where your family spoke Spanish, you learned to communicate in that language. If your family spoke in hushed tones, you learned to speak softly. If your family engaged in a great deal of touching, you learned about touch as a form of communication. Even what you learned to talk about was part of your learning experiences. If your family discussed politics and believed people should never gossip, you too, at least early in your life, held these beliefs about appropriate and inappropriate topics for discussion. We are suggesting that all people have learned and carry around an assorted fund of knowledge about communication. However, it is obvious that not all people and cultures have gathered the same information. In one culture, people might have received "training" on how to grow rice and other grains; in another group, people have obtained instructions on how to ride a camel or a horse. Some people have learned to tell others about their personal problems; others believe that a stoic approach is best. Some people talk to God; others sit quietly and wait for God to talk to them.

In many ways, this entire book is about how and what members of particular cultures have learned and how that "learning" might influence intercultural communication. When we speak of "learning," we are using the word in a rather broad sense. *Informal learning* is often very subtle and normally takes place through interaction

> ## REMEMBER THIS
>
> *Like so much of culture, it is communication that makes culture a continuous process, for once cultural habits, principles, values, and attitudes are formed, they are communicated to each member of the culture.*

(your parents kiss you, and you learn about kissing—whom, when, and where to kiss), observation (you observe your parents kneeling at church and learn about correct behavior in a religious setting), and imitation (you laugh at the same jokes your parents laugh at, and you learn about humor).

The *formal* teaching of a culture is far more structured and is often left to the various social institutions of the culture, such as schools and churches. When a school system teaches computer skills, grammar, history, or calculus, it is giving the members of a culture the tools and information the culture deems important. When a child has a Sunday school lesson focusing on the Ten Commandments, he or she is learning about ethical behavior. At times, it is difficult to distinguish between informal and formal learning, as culture influences you from the instant you are born. In addition, much of cultural learning is subconscious, and in most instances, you are rarely aware of many of the messages that it sends. This unconscious or hidden dimension of culture leads many researchers to claim that culture is invisible. There is even a well-respected book about culture by Edward T. Hall titled *The Hidden Dimension*.[31] The title is intended to call attention to the important premise that the "messages" and "lessons" of culture are so subtle that you seldom see them "coming in" or getting "acted out." Most of you would have a difficult time pointing to a specific event or experience that taught you to stand when an important person enters the room or how to employ direct eye contact during a job interview. The roles of silence and the use of space, the importance of attractiveness, your view of aging, your ability to speak one language instead of another, your proclivity for activity over meditation, or your preference for using one mode of behavior over another when dealing with conflict are all rooted in culture. Try to isolate where you learned what is considered "cool" in your culture. You might be able to point to what you think is "cool," but telling someone how you learned to be "cool" would be a near-impossible task.

While you could readily recognize how you learned to solve a specific chemistry problem, you would have a much harder time with your culture's more subtle "teachings." Reflect for a moment on the learning that is taking place in the following examples:

- A child reprimanded for making a hurtful remark about a classmate's weight is learning about compassion and empathy.
- A young boy in the United States whose grandfather reminds him to shake hands when he is introduced to a friend of the family is learning good manners.
- An Arab father who reads the Koran to his daughter and son is teaching the children about God.
- An Indian child who lives in a home where the women eat after the men is learning gender roles.
- A Jewish child who helps conduct the Passover ceremony is learning about traditions.
- A Japanese girl who attends tea ceremony classes is learning about patience, self-discipline, and ritual.
- A fourth-grade student watching a film on George Washington crossing the Delaware River is learning about patriotism and fortitude.

- When a child finds money on the playground and his parents ask him to return the funds, the child is learning about honesty.
- When as part of his school day a young child in North Korea is told to point his wooden gun at a picture of an American, he is learning about hatred.

In these examples, people are learning their culture through various forms of communication. That is why we said that culture is communication and that communication is culture. You have now seen that people learn most of their culture through communication. Through interaction with other members of their culture, they begin to assimilate the rules, norms, values, and language of their culture. We should summarize a few conclusions about culture before we continue with our specific discussion of how it is learned. First, learning about your culture usually takes place without your being aware of it. Second, the essential messages of a culture get reinforced and repeated. Third, you learn your culture from a large variety of sources, with family, school, church, and community being the four most powerful institutions of culture. So significant are those four institutional carriers of culture that we will detail

CONSIDER THIS

Which ten words do you believe best describe your culture?

their specific influences later in the book. But for now, let us look at a few of the "messages" those institutions bring to each generation.

Learning Culture Through Proverbs. Even before a very young child can read, that child is hearing "lessons about life" transmitted through proverbs. "Whether called maxims, truisms, clichés, idioms, expressions, or sayings, proverbs are small packages of truth about a people's values and beliefs."[32] Olajide notes the significance of proverbs to a culture when he writes, "Proverbs are an aspect of culture cherished all over the world and preserved in language which is the medium for expressing them. Also, proverbs have psychological, cosmological and sociocultural roots."[33] These are, in a sense, regarded as storehouses of a culture's wisdom. Proverbs are so important to culture that there are even proverbs about proverbs. A German proverb states, "A country can be judged by the quality of its proverbs," and the Yoruba of Africa teach, "A wise man who knows proverbs, reconciles difficulties." Both of these proverbs emphasize the idea that you can learn about a people through their proverbs. These proverbs—communicated in colorful, vivid language and with very few words—reflect the insights, wisdom, biases, and even superstitions of a culture.

Proverbs are learned early and easily and repeated with great regularity. Because they are brief, their influence as "teachers" is often overlooked. Yet many religious traditions use proverbs to express important messages about life. The Book of Proverbs in the Old Testament represents a collection of moral sayings and "wisdom" intended to assist the reader to behave in a particular and honorable way. Chinese philosophers such as Confucius, Mencius, Chung Tzu, and Lao-tzu also used proverbs and maxims to express their thoughts to their disciples. These proverbs survive so that each generation can learn what their culture deems significant. "Proverbs reunite the listener with his or her ancestors."[34] Seidensticker notes that "[proverbs] say things that people think important in ways that people remember. They express common concerns."[35]

The value of proverbs as a reflection of a culture is further underscored by the fact that "interpreters at the United Nations prepare themselves for their extremely sensitive job by learning proverbs of the foreign language"[36] that they will be interpreting. As Mieder notes, "Studying proverbs can offer insights into a culture's worldview regarding such matters as education, law, business, and marriage."[37] Roy offers a summary as to why understanding cultural proverbs is a valuable tool for students of intercultural communication: "Examination of these orally transmitted traditional values offers an excellent means of learning about another culture because these oft-repeated sayings fuse past, present, and future. These sayings focus our attention on basic principles accepted within the culture."[38]

Because all people, regardless of their culture, share common experiences, many of the same proverbs appear throughout the world. For example, in nearly every culture, some degree of thrift and hard work is stressed. Hence, in Germany, the proverb states, "One who does not honor the penny is not worthy of the dollar." In the United States, people are told, "A penny saved is a penny earned." Because they value silence, the Chinese have a proverb that says, "Loud thunder brings little rain." Taking responsibility for one's actions is also a universal value. Thus, in English, it is "God helps those who help themselves." For Indians, the proverb is "Call on God, but row away from the rocks." However, our concern is not with the commonality of cultural proverbs but rather with the use of these proverbs to teach lessons that are unique to that particular culture. By examining some of these proverbs, you will be able to accomplish two purposes at once. First, *you will discover the power of proverbs as a teaching device.* Second, *from an examination of proverbs, you learn about other cultures' worldviews, beliefs, values, and communication patterns.*

The following are but a few of the hundreds of proverbs and sayings from the United States, each of which attempts to instruct about an important value held by the dominant culture:

- *Time is money, Strike while the iron is hot, Actions speak louder than words, There is no time like the present,* and *He who hesitates is lost.* These proverbs underscore the idea that in the United States, people who do not waste time and make quick decisions are highly valued.
- *God helps those who help themselves, Too many cooks spoil the broth, Pull yourself up by your bootstraps,* and *No pain, no gain.* These sayings highlight the strong belief held in the United States that people should show individual initiative, engage in important activities on their own, never give up, and endure hardship for the desired outcome.
- *A man's home is his castle.* This expression not only tells us about the value of privacy but also demonstrates the male orientation in the United States by implying that the home belongs to the man.
- *The squeaky wheel gets the grease,* and *Fortune favors the bold.* In the United States, people are encouraged to be direct, speak up, and make sure their views are heard.

While we could have selected thousands of proverbs to illustrate our point about the link between these sayings and the teaching of key elements of a culture, we have chosen but a few from non-U.S. cultures[39] that stress important values associated with intercultural communication:

- Many cultures prefer **silence** rather than an abundance of talk. They believe that silence is associated with wisdom. German: *Speaking comes by nature, silence by understanding.* Tanzanian: *The wisest animal is the giraffe; it never speaks.* Thai: *A wise man talks little; an ignorant one talks much.* Peruvian: *From the tree of silence* hangs the fruit of tranquility. Hopi Indian: *Eating little and speaking little can hurt no man.* Hindustan: *From opening the mouth, seven ills may ensue.*

- The belief in and acceptance of **fate and destiny** is a strong view of life and death shared by many cultures. Yiddish: *If you're fated to drown, you may die in a teaspoon of water.* Chinese: *If a man's fate is to have only eight-tenths of a pint of rice, though he traverse the country over, he cannot get a full pint.* Russian: *He who is destined for the gallows will not be drowned.* Japanese: *One does not make the wind, but is blown by it.* Spanish: *Since we cannot get what we like, let us like what we can get.* Mexican: *Man proposes and God disposes.*

- Respect for the wisdom of the **elderly** is found in many collective cultures. Chinese: *To know the road ahead, ask those coming back.* Spanish: *The devil knows more because he's old than because he's the devil.* Portuguese: *The old man is the one who makes good food.* Greek: *A society grows great when old men plant trees whose shade they know they shall never sit in.* Nigerian: *What an old man will see while seated, a small child cannot see even standing.*

- Many cultures teach the value of **collectivism** and **group solidarity** over individualism. Chinese: *A single bamboo pole does not make a raft.* Ethiopian: *When spider webs unite, they can tie up a lion.* Japanese: *A single arrow is easily broken, but not ten in a bundle.* Russian: *You can't tie a knot with one hand.* Brazilian: *One bird alone does not make a flock.* Tanzanian: *Many hands make light work.* Scottish: *He who holds the stirrup is as good as he who mounts the horse.*

- Cultures that place a premium on **education** use proverbs to assist in teaching this important value. Jewish: *A table is not blessed if it has fed no scholars.* Chinese: *If you are planning for a year, sow rice: if you are planning for a decade, plant a tree; if you are planning for a lifetime, educate people.*

- Some cultures stress **social harmony** over direct confrontation. Japanese: *The spit aimed at the sky comes back to one.* Korean: *Kick a stone in anger and harm your own foot.*

- **Privacy** is a key value is some cultures. Here again you can observe the use of proverbs to teach that value. German: *Sweep only in front of your own door.* Swedish: *He who stirs another's porridge often burns his own.*

Learning Culture Through Folktales, Legends, and Myths. While the words "folktales," "legends," and "myths" have slightly different meanings, experts often use the words interchangeably because they present narratives, be they oral or written, that distinguish "significant agents in the transmission of culture."[40] As Imada and Yussen point out, "Narratives are one of the oldest and universal forms of communication in human societies" and also "play an important role in the reproduction of cultural values."[41] In addition to helping to reaffirm cultural identity, these "tales" serve a variety of other purposes. At times, they deal with simple morality lessons focusing on good and evil and right and wrong, or they may address abstract and metaphysical questions regarding creation and "the meaning of life." In addition, the customs, traditions, and beliefs expressed in folktales link people to their history and root them to their past. Rodriguez mentions the many purposes and uses of folk narratives when she writes,

> Folktales are not only regarded as some of the best keepers of our language and cultural memories, they are also great helpers in the process of socialization, they teach our children the sometimes difficult lessons about how to interact with other people and what happens when virtues are tested or pitted against one another.[42]

The communication and social interactive dimensions of these narratives can be seen as a form of "teaching" about culture. They are used in a variety of settings (such as at home, in school, and at church), at all stages of language development (oral, written, etc.), and at each stage of life (infancy, childhood, and adulthood).

As was the case with proverbs, because all people experience many of the same circumstances and events in life, there are some similarities in the messages contained in folktales across cultures. That is, stories of heroes, evil spirits, friendships, animals that talk, good and evil, and even princesses are universal themes. In fact, you can find the story of Cinderella, believed to be the most famous folktale in the world, in many cultures. From China to Saudi Arabia, the little girl waiting for a prince to give her a better life has well over 500 different cultural versions.[43] Walker develops this notion of parallel subjects across cultures:

> Although there is wonderful variety among the tales, there are also striking similarities. As with other folktales, the same basic story is often told by people widely separated by geography and language. For example, the Japanese folktale of Issun Boshi—which I have retold as "One-Inch Boy"—is remarkably similar to the English folktale of Tom Thumb. And both these tales echo stories told in many other lands.[44]

What we have been suggesting in the last few paragraphs is that whether it tells of Pinocchio's nose growing longer because of his lies, Columbus's daring voyage, Captain Ahab's heroics as he seeks to overcome the power of nature, Abraham Lincoln learning to read by drawing letters on a shovel by firelight, Robin Hood helping the poor, or Davy Crockett as the courageous frontiersman fighting to save the Alamo, folklore constantly reinforces important cultural lessons. Some of the "lessons" of folktales are obvious, whereas others are very subtle. Notice, for example, the built-in gender bias in the few examples we presented. In each story, males are the main characters and heroes. When females appear in cultural stories (e.g., "Cinderella," "Snow White," "Little Red Riding Hood," and many others), they are often portrayed as submissive and docile. Since most cultures are male dominated and men create the narratives, it is not surprising that women are seen as passive and meek in the stories told to young people. However, a few contemporary story lines, such as in *The Hunger Games*, incorporate female characters like Katniss. She is not your typical woman in distress but rather is presented as unruffled and brave.

As we have pointed out, the stories that are passed from generation to generation are entertaining and captivating, but in nearly all cases, they are used to stress moral messages and strengthen cultural values. Be it Hopalong Cassidy or John Wayne, Americans revere the tough, independent, fast-shooting cowboy of the Old West; the Japanese learn about the importance of duty, obligation, and loyalty from "The Tale of the Forty-Seven Ronin" and the faithful dog Hachikō, who waited at the same location for nine years for his owner to return; and the Sioux Indians use the legend of "Pushing Up the Sky" to teach that people can accomplish much if they work together. In South Africa, when a child is exposed to the "People of Rock," he is being entertained and learning how the "nunus" (little people with magical powers) "care for all the sad and injured creatures of the world."[45] For the Australian Aborigine, the tale of "The Secret Dreaming" is the story of why the land is sacred and how people are the caretakers of that land. Scandinavian children are confronted with an endless array of strange-looking trolls as they listen to and read stories such as "The Boys Who Met the Trolls in Hedal Woods." In each story, they encounter the trolls and learn lessons for life, ranging from the importance of brushing their teeth to never telling a lie.

Mexican mothers and grandmothers tell the Mayan folktale "The Story of Mariano the Buzzard" to teach children to work hard and not be lazy.[46] And the Chinese folktale "The Taoist Priest of Lao-Shan" teaches young children not to yield to temptation because it causes humiliation.[47]

A common theme in many folktales and myths is the superhero, usually a male protagonist who defends family, country, and even outer space. The United States is not the only country with characters such as Superman, Captain Kirk, Spiderman, X-Men, The Ironman, and Captain America. The Irish still admire the mythical warrior Cu Chulainn. In one of his most famous exploits, he single-handedly fights the armies of Queen Mebh of Connacht and wins the battle that saves Ulster. Greeks learn about Hercules, Jews learn about Samson, and Norwegians learn about Thor. In Zaire, children are told the myth of invincibility. In this tale, young boys learn that if they wrap green vines around their heads, their enemies' weapons cannot hurt them.[48] Shiite Muslims pass on a seventh-century story of how the prophet Muhammed's grandson, knowing he was going to die, fought to his death. In the story of Hanukkah, it is told how, in the second century, a small band of Jews defeated a much larger army. That historic victory, known as the Maccabean Revolt, is commemorated even today with festive religious and family events. Heroic feats are also at the core of the story of Mexico's Cinco de Mayo, celebrated as a national holiday (more by Mexicans living in the United States than in Mexico itself). Here, the historical story tells how on May 5, 1862, a small Mexican armed force defeated a much larger and better-equipped invading French army. In each of these stories, the key participants are successful because of their commendable conduct and strong personal character.

As we have indicated, stories can tell you about what was and still is important to a group of people. Erdoes and Ortiz make this point as they write of stories in American Indian culture:

> They are also magic lenses through which we can glimpse social orders and daily life: how families were organized, how political structures operated, how men caught fish, how religious ceremonies felt to the people who took part, how power was divided between men and women, how food was prepared, how honor in war was celebrated.[49]

We conclude this section on myths, folktales, and legends by reminding you that they are found in every culture and deal with ideas that matter most to that culture— ideas about life, death, relationships, and nature. Because these stories offer clues to culture, Campbell urges you not only to understand your own story but also to read other people's myths.[50] We strongly concur with Campbell: When you study the myths of a culture, you are studying that culture.

Learning Culture Through Art.   A trip to any art museum quickly reveals how the art of a culture is both a method of passing on culture and a reflection of that culture. Nanda and Warms develop this important idea in the following:

> Art forms are not merely a mirror of culture—though they may be that as well—but art also heightens cultural and social integration by displaying and confirming values that members of a culture hold in common. The powerful artistic symbols of a society express universal themes such as death, pride, and gender relationships in ways that are culturally compelling, even when (some might say particularly when) their content is not consciously articulated.[51]

Because art is part of a culture's identity, people throughout the world often feel a historical, emotional, and spiritual attachment to their art forms.

Courtesy of Larry Samovar

Because art is part of each culture's identity, people throughout the world feel a great historical, emotional, and spiritual attachment to their art forms. The systematic pillaging of art during World War II by Nazi forces reverberates even today as efforts to recover "lost" or "missing" items of great cultural value continue, and jubilation occurs when one of these objects reemerges. The organization formed during the war to recover these treasures, as depicted in the film *The Monuments Men*, attests to the widespread interest in recovering these culturally significant paintings, sculptures, and other objects of art. As vessels of cultural heritage, they carry a price far above monetary value. In recent years, Greece and Italy have launched an international campaign to retrieve their cultural treasures taken by the Nazi government during World War II.[52] Many Mediterranean and Middle Eastern countries have long called for the governments of England, France, and Germany to return the antiquities illegally removed by archaeologists in the late nineteenth and early twentieth centuries. In an essay titled "Understanding America Through Art," George Will praises the traveling art exhibition sponsored by the National Endowment for the Humanities called *Picturing America* as a way for Americans to understand "the nation's past and present."[53]

Since the beginning of history, art has provided a reflection of how people lived in and perceived the world. Even the early cave paintings dating back over 40,000 years were communicating to others and also reflecting the daily life of these primitive people. From that period on, we can see art allowing a collection of people to tell the story of how they lived, what they valued, and even their worldview. And in all cases, the art expresses something unique about each time period and culture. For example, because the Romans were not a religious people, most of their art was void of religious symbolism. Yet in the medieval period, much of European art told of the life of Jesus and attempted to depict the content of the Bible. And, of course, insight into the people of the Renaissance can be gleaned by observing the popularity of portraits. In China, the goal was to commemorate the emperor; hence, "paintings of the emperor had to show him with individualized features representing the humanistic Confucian values of compassion and virtue while conveying the imposing demeanor of the absolute ruler, the Son of Heaven."[54] In countless other cases, the stories about any culture and its people can be seen through their art. Strickland highlights the critical effect of these "stories" when she writes, "Art's goal can be communication or expression, a way of interacting with and trying to make sense of the world. All art grows out of a specific climate and culture, giving expression to the ideas and emotions of a particular time and place."[55]

Having established the nexus between culture and art, we offer a few more examples to remind you that art is a vital conduit of the important messages of any culture. We begin with two cultures that for thousands of years have linked religious expression to their artistic displays. India has always had an artistic tradition that has used art for religious purposes. The art, employing countless gods and goddesses, has attempted to fuse spiritual messages with various aspects of culture. As we will discuss in detail in Chapter 4 when we examine the topic of religion, because Hindus believe that God is everywhere and in everything, generally no space is left empty in their paintings. That is, in addition to the main character of the painting, all the space on the painting is filled with images of animals, flowers, and even geographic designs.

A similar link between art and religion can be detected in Islamic art. Through the use of brilliant colors and distinctive geometric patterns and shapes, Islamic art creates a vivid and instantaneous impact. A trip through any Middle Eastern country will reveal stunning and beautiful tile work. Another special quality of Islamic art is its calligraphy. Calligraphy has traditionally been considered by Muslims as the most splendid form of art because of its relation to the Koran. Nydell points out, "Calligraphy usually depicts Qur'anic quotations or favorite proverbs, and patterns are often beautifully balanced and intricate. Calligraphic designs are widely used to decorate mosques, monuments, books, and household items such as brass trays."[56]

This Islamic art form, with its emphasis on shape, form, design, style, and calligraphy—not people, landscapes, or other representations of reality—is unique. Whereas the Roman Catholic tradition has made wide use of depictions of Christ, the Virgin Mary, and the saints, Islam disallows the use of religious images of any kind. That even includes images of the prophet Muhammed.

We turn next to sub-Saharan Africa and mention two major themes in their art—children and nature. According to Ferraro and Andreatta, much of the art of Africa reflects the important social value of having children.[57] Hence, "prominent breasts on female figures are a major theme in much of the wood sculptures from West Africa."[58] You can observe nature's role in the symbolic art of Africa by looking at masks, figures, and jewelry. Here, you will see a great many animals displayed, demonstrating a strong belief that everything in nature is related and alive.

As we alluded to earlier, for centuries, the Chinese have used art to transmit cultural and spiritual values. According to Hunter and Sexton, Chinese art often represents "Buddhist and Taoist concerns with the mind in meditation, with the relative insignificance of human striving in the great cosmos, and with the beauty of nature."[59] This is very different from the art of North America and Europe, where the artistic tradition often emphasizes people. Whether in portraits of a single person or pictures of an entire family, people are the main focus. You will notice when you visit most

Facebook pages that personal pictures of oneself and others is the most common subject matter. This disparity reflects a difference in views: Asians believe that nature is more powerful and important than a single individual, whereas Americans and Europeans consider the individual to be at the center of the universe. In addition, in Western art, the artist tries to create a personal message. You will remember that above we mentioned the popularity of portraits in Western culture. This is not the case with most Asian artists. As Campbell notes, "Such ego-oriented thinking is alien completely to Eastern life, thought, and religiosity...."[60]

As already indicated, art is a relevant symbol, a forceful teacher, and an avenue for transmitting cultural values. We need only look at the art on totem poles to see what matters to American Indians of the northwestern United States. Although totem poles have esthetic value, the carvings on these poles (and even canes) have a more profound purpose. They record and remind American Indians of their identity, ancestors, family, history, wildlife, and nature. This art form, which seeks to tell stories, is very different from the art of Islam discussed earlier. Whereas the Koran forbids the depiction of human figures and animals, Indian art encourages it.

It should be clear from our brief discussion that "through the cross-cultural study of art—myths, songs, dances, paintings, carvings, and so on—we may discover much about different worldviews and religious beliefs, as well as political ideas, social values, kinship structures, economic relations, and historical memory."[61]

CONSIDER THIS

As you watch television for a week, keep a record of the various cultural "lessons" that you believe are being transmitted, either overtly or covertly, through the programs you are watching.

Learning Culture Through Media.   Just as culture is shared through art, the same is true of media. But with media, the types and formats are far more numerous. From television to online discussions to blogs to social networks to the hundreds of other outlets, people share themselves and their culture. The importance of sharing a culture via media is underscored by Newman: "Another powerful institutional agent of socializing is the media. Newspapers, magazines, television, radio, film and the Internet transmit persuasive messages on the nature of reality."[62] As we begin our exploration of this important carrier of culture, we should once again remind you that this is not a book about mass media any more than it is a text about proverbs, folktales, or art. Our purpose is simply to examine those carriers of culture that transmit important lessons. In this section, our goal remains the same. However, we are not talking about those media that are created, designed, and used to reach very large audiences. The impact of these devices on a population is hard to access. That is, it is difficult to draw a definitive cause-and-effect relationship between someone watching a television program, reading a political blog, using Skype, or responding to someone's tweet and concluding that the messages generated by those outlets contributed to the receiver's cultural "instructions." Such an assessment is particularly difficult, as media take such diverse forms and are used for a host of reasons. Nevertheless, the power, reach, and magnitude of this "message carrier" should not preclude us from drawing some conclusions concerning media's role in the socialization process. You know from your own experience that media not only offer information and entertainment but also tell us about our cultural identity and contribute to shaping our beliefs and values. Media offer, as Williams notes, "mass social learning."[63]

The overabundance of media in daily life is perhaps most evident when applied to young people. And it is these young children with whom we are mostly concerned in this chapter, as they are the ones being shaped by the messages they receive at this early age. It is estimated that young children spend about four hours a day watching television. Infants and toddlers alone watch a screen an average of two hours a day. By the time a student graduates from the twelfth grade, he or she will have spent more time watching television than in the classroom. In the average American home, the television in on seven hours a day. This, of course, does not even include the twenty to forty hours children spend each week playing video games.[64]

The issue, of course, is not the amount of time spent watching television or playing with an Xbox but rather the content of the messages young people are receiving from these outlets. A cursory examination of those messages, or a summary of what authorities say about those messages, reveals an overabundance of images that promote undesirable perceptions regarding violence, gender, sexuality, race, the elderly, and drugs and alcohol. Delgado talks about the power of those messages. He asserts that they "help constitute our daily lives by shaping our experiences and providing the content for much of what we talk about (and how we talk) at the interpersonal level."[65] Perhaps the clearest explanation of the role that mass media play in learning about culture is found in Cultivation Theory, which was developed by Gerbner and Gross.[66] At the core, this theory asserts that media, particularly mass media, are an influential "socializing agent" in shaping future perceptions.[67] Specifically, the theory avers that, over time, television shapes the viewers' notion of reality. The words "over time" are important to Cultivation Theory, as "the greater the amount of television you watch, the more your worldview comes to accord with the beliefs, values, and attitudes you see on the screen."[68]

As already indicated, because the messages you receive via most media are so diverse, it is difficult to assign a direct link to media's role in the socialization process. Yet there are thousands of studies that attempt to document the part television plays in the life of young children. The Kaiser Family Foundation and the American Academy of Child and Adolescent Psychiatry offer the following summary of how television viewing among young children gets reflected in their perceptions of the world:

- Extensive viewing of television violence by children causes greater aggressiveness. In addition, children who watch more than four hours of television a day have lower grades in school and are often overweight.
- Television viewing takes the place of activities such as playing with friends, being physically active, reading, and doing homework.[69]

Although the portrayals of sex roles have changed somewhat over the last decade, men, at least on television, "are typically shown as rational, competitive, and violent, while women are sensitive, romantic, peaceful, and submissive"[70] As noted elsewhere, it is not only television that is playing a major role in the socialization process. Young boys in particular are spending as much as 50 hours a week playing video games with names like *Grand Theft Auto*, *Assassin's Creed*, and *Call of Duty*. Each of these (and there are countless others) glorifies aggressive behavior and violence, behavior that many experts believe is having a negative effect on young people. In fact, due to concerns about the adverse effects of too much television, the American Academy of Pediatrics recommends no screen time for children age two and younger. They also

REMEMBER THIS

Most of the behaviors we label "cultural" are automatic, invisible, and usually performed without our being aware of them.

recommend only one or two hours a day of nonviolent, educational programs, with adult supervision, for children.[71]

We conclude our discussion of the characteristic that culture is learned by reviewing a few key points. First, children are born without cultural knowledge. However, because they have the biological "tools" necessary to learn, they quickly discover that the sounds and actions around them have meaning. The same learning process applies to the cultural attributes and characteristics that confront them. In short, the location of your birth sets the tone for what you learn and what you will not learn. Second, most of the behaviors we label as "cultural" are automatic, invisible, and usually performed without our being aware of them. For example, whether you greet people with a handshake or a hug was "learned" without formal instruction. You simply internalized one greeting or another by watching those around you when you were very young. We suggest that this simple behavior—and thousands of others—are learned unconsciously and are performed almost habitually. Third, it is important to repeat that the methods of learning culture we have mentioned are only a few of the many ways culture "is taught." Space constraints have forced us to leave out many subtle yet powerful "teachers." For example, sports are much more than simple games. Football in the United States is popular because it illustrates important themes of the culture. Notice the inconspicuous messages contained in some of the language surrounding the broadcasting of a professional football game. You will hear statements such as "he has the killer instinct," "they are all warriors," "he is a real head hunter," "they are out for blood," and "they all play smashmouth football." You can observe in every culture a variety of activities that have significant meanings that go beyond the actual endeavor. There are "lessons being taught" by Spanish bullfighting, Japanese gardens, French wine, German symphonies, and Italian operas.[72] These cultural metaphors represent and teach, according to Gannon, "the underlying values expressive of the culture itself."[73]

REMEMBER THIS

Cultures are always changing, but the deep structure of a culture is resistant to change.

Culture Is Dynamic

Cultures do not exist in a vacuum; because of multiple influences, they are subject to change. Many of the changes are profound, as in those hundreds of cases involving colonization and/or invasions. In those circumstances, outside forces, be they armies or missionaries, "determine the cultural priorities of those whom they conquered."[74] However, not all change is as intense and devastating as colonization and invasion. Simply reflect for a moment on the cultural changes you have observed in your lifetime. We are speaking not only of surface changes in fashion and music but also of those alterations in culture brought about by new technology and globalization. You have lived through the ongoing impact of these two forces in the world and have also witnessed cultural changes that have altered perceptions of gays, immigrants, and various religions. Although some cultures change more than others (due to isolation or by design), all cultures have been subject to change since the earliest hunter-gatherers moved from place to place. These alterations to a culture, as Nanda and Warms note, may happen in small increments, or ... in revolutionary bursts. Historically, in most places and at most times, culture change has been a relatively slow process. However, the pace of change has been increasing for the past several hundred years and has become extremely rapid in the past century.[75]

Of course, the preceding quotation refers to those changes relating to the spread of American capitalism, worldwide population growth, large movements of immigrants, the proliferation of information technology, wars, and environmental concerns. All of these cultural incursions, whether from within or without, cause both major and minor modifications to culture.

When anthropologists speak of change, they are talking about two interrelated types of change: (1) innovation and (2) diffusion.

Innovation. Innovation refers to the discovery of new practices, inventions, tools, or concepts that may produce changes in practices and behaviors for a particular culture. While you might immediately think of technology as the main force driving innovation, it is just one of many forces confronting cultures. Nanda and Warms expand on this idea when they note, "Although we are likely to think of innovations as technology, they are not limited to the material aspects of culture. New art forms and new ideas can also be considered innovations."[76]

Diffusion. Diffusion is a mechanism of change that is seen by the spread of various ideas, concepts, institutions, and practices from one culture to another. This change is often considered a kind of cultural borrowing. Historically, diffusion has been part of cultural contact for as long as cultures have existed. Whether it be sugar from a plant (i.e., sugarcane) of New Guinean origin ending up in the New World, China introducing paper to the world, missionaries introducing God to everyone, baseball becoming popular in Mexico, or McDonald's hamburgers being sold throughout the world, diffusion is a universal way of life. As we have stressed elsewhere, technology has greatly influenced worldwide diffusion, as it allows for words, sounds, and images to be sent instantly all over the world simultaneously.

Because cultures want to endure, they usually adopt only those elements that are compatible with their values and beliefs or that can be modified without causing major disruption. The assimilation of what is borrowed accelerates when cultures come into direct contact with each other. For example, as we saw Japan and the United States engage in more commercial exchanges, we also observed both countries assimilating the business practices of each other.

We conclude this section on the dynamic nature of culture by linking some ideas we have been discussing to intercultural communication. First, and perhaps most importantly, although many aspects of culture are subject to change, *the deep structure of a culture resists major alterations.* Most of the changes you observe are likely part of what is called "popular culture." This level of culture changes regularly, but that is not the aspect of culture that concerns us here. Beamer and Varner explain the idea of levels of culture and change in the following: "Popular culture, which includes consumer products—for example, music, food, hairstyles, clothing, recreational activities and their equipment, styles of cars, and furnishings—constantly change[s]. But backstage culture—the values, attitudes, and cultural dimensions that have been learned from birth—change[s] very little and very, very slowly."[77]

The changes in dress, music, food, transportation, mass entertainment, and housing are exterior changes and do not go to the root of the culture. In most instances, they are simply blended into the existing culture or eventually discarded as "passing fads." However, values and behaviors associated with such things as ethics and morals, definitions of the role of government, the importance of family and the past, religious practices, the pace of life, folklore, and attitudes toward gender and age are so deeply embedded in a culture that they persist generation after generation. This continual embracing of one's culture is called "cultural boundary maintenance." It is the manner in which a culture maintains its distinctiveness that in the end strengthens its cultural traditions. Barnlund offers a religious example of cultural maintenance when he writes, "The spread of Buddhism, Islam, Christianity, and Confucianism did not homogenize the societies they enveloped. It was usually the other way around: societies insisted on adapting the religions to their own cultural traditions."[78] You can observe the command of these core values in the United States, where studies on American values show that most contemporary foundational values are similar to the values of the last 250 years. Thus, when assessing the degree of change within a culture, you must consider what is changing. Do not be misled into believing that major cultural shifts are taking place in Japan because people in Tokyo dress much like the people in Paris or that Germans are abandoning their love of soccer because people now play basketball in Germany. These are "front-stage behaviors." Most of what we call culture is below the surface, like an iceberg. You can observe the tip, but there are other dimensions and depths that you cannot see. That is the subterranean level of culture.

Second, because much of culture is habitual and deeply rooted in tradition, you can find countless examples where *change is not welcomed* and at times is greeted *with hostility.* France maintains the *Académie française,* which acts as a type of "language police" whose duty it is to monitor outside "infiltration" of their language. The French, it seems, are ever vigilant to keep their language (and their culture) "pure" and free from outside corruption. In the United States, there are still people who rail against women having equal rights with men. In much of the Arab world, some of the aggression aimed at the West can be traced to a fear of having Western values supplant traditional Islamic beliefs. Many Arabs believe that is what happened as part of the "contact" with the West during the Christian Crusades, the Ottoman Empire, and the occupation of much of the Middle East by the West in the early twentieth century.

THE ELEMENTS OF CULTURE

As you have now learned, culture is composed of countless elements (food, shelter, work, defense, social control, psychological security, perceptions of illness, sexual taboos, forms of governing, social harmony, sex roles, purpose in life, etc.). Although each of these plays a role in the life of each culture, a handful of other elements are most germane to the study of intercultural communication. Many of them focus on what people *bring* to a communication encounter and also influence how they *take part* in that encounter. An understanding of these will enable you to appreciate those cultural perceptions and behaviors that usually distinguish one culture from another. Many of them represent the major themes that flow throughout this book.

REMEMBER THIS

Worldview provides some of the taken-for-granted underpinnings for cultural perceptions and the nature of reality. In this sense the worldview of a culture functions to help define reality and in so doing keep the world from being perceived as disordered, accidental, and meaningless.

Worldview

The importance of worldview is clearly affirmed in the following definition advanced by Bailey and Peoples: "World view is the way a people interpret reality and events, including their images of themselves and how they relate to the world around them."[79] This broad description of worldview makes it an "overarching philosophy" of how the world works and how each person fits into that world. Issues such as what truth is and how one discovers "the" truth are part of the domain of a person's worldview. Although every individual has a worldview, a more powerful worldview also pervades each culture and becomes a collective concept of reality. Hoebel and Frost describe this notion of a culture's worldview as an "inside view of the way things are colored, shaped, and arranged according to personal cultural preconceptions."[80] Like culture itself, worldviews are automatic and unconscious. Hall reinforces this key point when he writes, "Often, worldviews operate at an unconscious level, so that we are not even aware that other ways of seeing the world are either possible or legitimate. Like the air we breathe, worldviews are a vital part of who we are but not a part we usually think much about."[81]

As you can see, worldview provides some of the unexamined underpinnings for perception and the nature of reality as experienced by individuals who share a common culture. The worldview of a culture functions to make sense of life, which might otherwise be perceived as disordered, accidental, and meaningless.

As is the case with all the elements discussed in this section, we will return to worldview and reexamine the topic in great detail in Chapter 5.

Religion

Closely related to worldview is the element of religion, which for thousands of years has been found in every culture. Religion, regardless of the form it takes, is used by people to help them understand the universe, natural phenomena, what to die for, and how to dwell among other people. The influence of religion can be seen in the entire fabric of a culture, as it serves so many basic functions. These functions usually include "social control, conflict resolution, reinforcement of group solidarity, explanations of the unexplainable, and emotional support."[82] In many ways, religion is like culture itself, as it provides the followers of the faith with a set of values, beliefs, and even guidelines for specific behaviors. These guidelines consciously and unconsciously impact everything, ranging from business practices (the Puritan work ethic) to politics (the link between Islam and government) to individual behavior (codes of personal ethics). This multidimensional aspect of religion—and its relationship to culture—means that to understand any culture, you must also understand how the members of that culture provide explanations for how the world operates and how they believe they fit into that process. We suggest that now, more than ever, understanding the role of religion in culture is imperative.

History

Over two thousand years ago, the Roman orator Cicero remarked, "History … provides guidance in daily life and brings us tidings of antiquity." Cicero was correct; all cultures believe in the idea that history provides stories about the past that serve as lessons on how to live in the present. These stories also help cement people into what is called "a common culture." This common culture creates a strong sense of unity and identity. As these descriptions of significant historical events get transmitted from generation to generation, people begin to perceive "where they belong" and where their loyalties lie. Stories of the past also provide members of a culture with large portions of their values and rules for behavior. History highlights a culture's origins, "tells" its members what is deemed important, and identifies the accomplishments of the culture of which they can be proud. Although all cultures use history to transmit important messages about that culture, each set of messages is unique to a particular culture. The motivation behind the building of the Great Wall of China, the Spanish conquest of Mexico, the "lessons" of the Holocaust, the Indo-Pakistani War of 1947, the struggles of Nelson Mandela in South Africa, and the events of September 11, 2001, are stories that carry a unique meaning for their respective cultures. These events also help explain contemporary perceptions held by members of those cultures. Succinctly, the study of history links the old with the new while serving as a pointer for the future. However, it is important to remember that authorities often selectively recount and mold historical stories in an effort to construct a desired public perception. The conflict among China, Japan, and Korea over different presentations of history is an example.

Values

Values are another key feature of every culture. Bailey and Peoples emphasize the role values play in culture when they write, "Values are a people's beliefs about the goals or ways of living that are desirable for themselves and their society. Values have profound, though partly unconscious, effects on people's behavior."[83] In this sense, values and the specific behaviors associated with them provide members of a culture standards to live by. The connections among values, culture, and behavior are so strong that it is hard to talk about one without discussing the other, as they "represent the general criteria on which our lives and the lives of others can be judged. They justify the social rules that determine how we ought to behave."[84] The two key words in any discussion of cultural values are "guidelines" and "behavior." In other words, values help determine how people within a particular culture ought to behave. Whether they be values regarding individualism, private property, accomplishment, generosity, change, freedom, etc., each culture defines specific behaviors for nearly every situation.

To the extent that cultural values differ, you can expect that participants in intercultural communication will tend to exhibit and to anticipate different behaviors under similar circumstances. For example, although all cultures value the elderly, the strength of this value is often very different from culture to culture. In Asian, Mexican, and American Indian cultures, the elderly are highly respected and revered. They are even sought out for advice and counsel. This is in stark contrast to the United States, where the emphasis is on youth. So important is the study of values to intercultural communication that we will devote an entire chapter to this topic later in the book.

Social Organizations

Another feature found in all cultures is what are called "social organizations." These organizations (sometimes referred to as social systems or social structures) represent the various social units within the culture. These are institutions such as family, government, schools, tribes, and clans. The basic premise that underlies all these organizations is the need for and reality of *interdependence*. For over 40,000 years, people have formed various interdependent groups as a means of survival. Within these groups, people have developed patterned interactions and "rules" that all members have learned and display. These social systems establish communication networks and regulate norms of personal, familial, and social conduct. "They also establish group cohesion and enable people to consistently satisfy their basic needs."[85] The ways in which these organizations function and the norms they advance are unique to each culture. Nolan underscores the nature of these organizations in the following: "Social structures reflect our culture, for example, whether we have kings and queens, or presidents and prime ministers. Within our social structure, furthermore, culture assigns roles to the various players—expectations about how individuals will behave, what they will stand for, and even how they will dress."[86]

Language

Language is yet another feature common to all people and cultures. We may arrive in this world with all of the biological and anatomical tools necessary to survive, but we must learn language in order to share our ideas, feelings, and thoughts with other people. Language is an element found in all cultures, as the words a young child learns and what those words mean are directly related to culture. By the age of three, children can name and understand a countless number of objects and concepts that they find in their environment, an environment unique to a particular culture. Language and culture are connected in a number of ways. Whether they are English, Swahili, Chinese, or French, most words, how they are used, the meanings assigned, the grammar employed, and the syntax bear the identification marks of a specific culture. Bailey and Peoples further develop the important role language plays in the existence of a culture when they write, "Language underlies every other aspect of a people's way of life—their relationship with the natural environment, family life, political organizations, worldview, and so forth. Most socialization of children depends on language, which means language is the main vehicle of cultural transmission from one generation to the next."[87] As is the case with nearly all of the cultural elements we have examined in this section, we will devote an entire chapter to language later in the book.

Before we conclude this portion of the chapter, we need to underscore two more important ideas about culture. First, throughout this chapter, we have isolated various aspects of culture and talked about them as if they were discrete units. The nature of language makes it impossible to do otherwise, yet, in reality, it is more accurate to perceive culture from a holistic perspective. Hall says it this way: "You touch a culture in one place and everything else is affected."[88] Ferraro and Andreatta expand on Hall's premise when they point out that "cultures should be thought of as integrated wholes, the parts of which, to some degree, are interconnected with one another. When we view cultures as integrated systems, we can begin to see how particular cultural traits fit into the whole system and consequently, how they tend to make sense *within that context*."[89] The crucial point regarding culture being integrated is that you should not "focus on one cultural feature in isolation. Instead, view each in terms of its larger context and carefully examine its connection to related features."[90]

The values regarding materialism in North America exemplify the integrated nature of culture. That is, the thrust behind these values stems from a variety of sources. History, family, and religion can influence family size, work ethic, use of time, and spiritual pursuits. Another complex example of the interconnectedness of cultural elements is the civil rights movement of the United States in the 1960s. This movement brought about change in housing patterns, discrimination practices, educational opportunities, the legal system, and career opportunities. In more recent times, in the last decade of the twentieth century, you can observe how the convergence of "new technologies" mingled with a host of other cultural values, attitudes, and behaviors. Modes of communication brought about by digital technology and the Internet have produced numerous problems associated with privacy, language, and the use of face-to-face communication.

Second, we remind you that the pull of culture begins at birth and continues throughout life—and some cultures say even after life. Using the standard language of her time (sexist by today's standards), the famous anthropologist Ruth Benedict offered an excellent explanation of why culture is such a powerful influence on all aspects of human behavior. Professor Benedict's quote is intriguing in that although she wrote it over sixty years ago, it is as true today as it was then. Actually, it would be accurate if she were describing events forty thousand years ago:

> The life history of the individual is first and foremost an accommodation to the patterns and standards traditionally handed down in his community. From the moment of his birth the customs into which he is born shape his experience and behavior. By the time he can talk, he is the little creature of his culture, and by the time he is grown and able to take part in its activities, its habits are his habits, its beliefs his beliefs, its impossibilities his impossibilities. Every child that is born into his group will share them with him, and no child born into the opposite side of the globe can ever achieve the thousandth part.[91]

The important point to take away from our entire discussion of culture is eloquently expressed in the following sentences: "God gave to every people a cup, a cup of clay, and from this cup they drank life…. They all dipped in the water, but their cups were different."[92] This book is about how those "different cups" influence how people perceive the world and how they behave in that world.

Sports are much more than simple games to a culture in that there are often overt and covert messages in the behavior of the participants.

Clayton Sharrard/PhotoEdit

DEVELOPING INTERCULTURAL COMPETENCE

We continue with the theme of cultural differences here at the end of this chapter by offering some advice on how you can develop the skills necessary to improve your intercultural competency. Before advancing our suggestions, we call your attention to some difficulties you might experience when trying to improve your intercultural skills. First, as we have explained throughout this chapter, much of what we call culture occurs early in life—often prior to age four. Because the "lessons" of culture are learned so early, they become a basic part of the perceptions, thinking, and actions of the child. In this sense, a person's reaction to his or her social environment is often automatic and second nature. Thus, when attempting to develop new communication skills, you bring to the endeavor a lifetime of ingrained habits and unconscious responses. For example, if you are from the culture of the United States, where informality is valued and good manners are not highly esteemed, you might have a difficult time when interacting with Germans. In that culture, "Good manners are part of a child's upbringing" and stressed in everything from family relationships to the business environment.[93]

Second, as Lynch reminds us, "Long-standing behavior patterns are typically used to express one's deepest values."[94] Hence, cultural habits, responses, perceptions, behaviors, and such are hard to change. That they are difficult to change does not mean that they are impossible to change.

We are now ready to answer the significant question: What is intercultural competence? According to Spitzberg, intercultural communication competence is "behavior that is appropriate and effective in a given context."[95] Kim offers a more detailed definition when she notes that intercultural communication competence is "the overall internal capability of an individual to manage key challenging features of intercultural communication: namely, cultural differences and unfamiliarity, inter-group posture, and the accompanying experience of stress."[96] These two definitions, one general and one specific, suggest that being an interculturally competent communicator means analyzing the situation and selecting the correct mode of behavior.

> **CONSIDER THIS**
>
> *What are the advantages of the "culture-general" approach to the study of intercultural communication over the "culture-specific" method?*

THE BASIC COMPONENTS OF INTERCULTURAL COMMUNICATION COMPETENCE

Most of the research in the area of intercultural communication competence includes (1) *being motivated*, (2) *having a fund of knowledge to draw on*, and (3) *possessing certain communication skills*.

Motivation

Motivation, as it relates to intercultural competence, means that as a communicator, you want to be part of a successful intercultural encounter. You know from personal experience that being motivated and having a positive attitude usually bring forth positive results. The problem when talking about motivation is that it is a very subjective proposition. What motivates person A may not motivate person B. In an attempt to motivate you, we suggest that you discover a positive reward that may result from your intercultural meeting. In most instances, such a reward will be achieved when you decide to accomplish certain goals as part of the intercultural encounter. As Morreale, Spitzberg, and Barge point out, "Goals are particularly relevant to communication competence because they are a way of assessing your effectiveness. A communicator who achieves his or her goals is effective, therefore, more competent."[97]

The goals that motivate you might be either *extrinsic* or *intrinsic*. Extrinsically, you might decide that being a competent communicator will provide practical rewards, such as financial gain, respect, or power. Your intrinsic motivations are more personal and harder to access—particularly in the intercultural communication environment. All of us are interested in ourselves and the people who are close to us both physically and emotionally. We are concerned primarily with our families. As our personal circle widens, it includes relatives and friends. Interest in other people then moves to neighbors and other members of the community. As we get farther and farther away from people in our immediate circle, intrinsic motivations in the intercultural event might become more difficult to access. Think for a moment about your reaction to the news that someone you know has been seriously injured in an automobile accident versus your response to reading that 1 million people are suffering from severe famine due to the civil war in Syria. In most instances, you would be more motivated to learn about your friend than about the people thousands of miles away in the Middle East. Although this is a normal reaction, it may keep you from being motivated to deal successfully with people of cultures different from your own. Yet for you to be a competent intercultural communicator, you must learn to go beyond personal boundaries and try to find reasons to be motivated. Make that your goal, and improvement will follow.

Knowledge

Knowledge, as our next intercultural competence element, works in tandem with motivation in that is asks you to be motivated enough to gather a fund of knowledge on other cultures. This element is often referred to as *cognitive flexibility*, as it refers to the ability to augment and expand knowledge about people from cultures different from your own. According to Morreale, Spitzberg, and Barge, you need two kinds of knowledge to be competent—*content knowledge* and *procedural knowledge*. "*Content knowledge* is an understanding of topics, words, meanings, and so forth required for the situation. *Procedural knowledge* tells us how to assemble, plan, and perform content knowledge in a particular situation."[98] Chen speaks more specifically of this cognitive facet of intercultural competence when he writes, "The *cognitive* aspect of intercultural communication competence is represented by intercultural awareness, which refers to the ability to understand cultural conventions that affect how people interact with each other."[99] What makes up those "cultural conventions" is not an easy question to answer. Put in slightly different terms, what are the cultural differences that make a difference? In many ways, this book is about those differences. For example, throughout this book, we plan to offer you "knowledge" regarding cultural values, attitudes, norms, worldviews, language, identity, differing problem-solving methods, levels of self-disclosure, values, and the like.

In gathering information on the components of intercultural communication, scholars and intercultural communication trainers recommend two investigative approaches: (1) *culture specific* and (2) *culture general*. A brief look at these methods of learning will help you appreciate some of the alternatives available to anyone interested in improving intercultural communication. Before beginning, we add that in many instances, some scholars in the area of intercultural competence suggest combining the two methods.

Culture Specific. The culture-specific method assumes that the most effective way to improve intercultural communication is to study one culture at a time and learn all the distinct and specific communication features of that culture. This approach assumes that the person is preparing to visit or work alongside members of another culture; hence, it necessitates an in-depth culture-specific orientation. For example, to interact with an Arab, you should know his or her values regarding gender, hospitality, pride, honor, and rivalry. You should also know that Islam is a regulator of behavior as well as a religion and that Arab males engage in very direct eye contact. You should even make an effort to learn about the Arabic language, as your communication with Arabs will improve if you know that "Arabs are passionately in love with their language."[100] In addition, the Arab language makes abundant use of assertions, metaphors, similes, long arrays of adjectives, and repetition of words. If you were going to Japan, you might benefit from advice about gift giving, the use of first names, greeting behavior, indirect speech, politeness, the use of business cards, the importance of group harmony, social stability, the use of "yes" and "no," and the like. These specific facts regarding some of the communication characteristics of both cultures could offer you cultural guidelines that would help you interact more effectively with both cultures.

Culture General. The rationale of the culture-general method of improving your intercultural competency aims to understand the universal influences of culture on human behaviors through different learning methods.[101] The basic assumption behind this technique is that there are some life experiences and communication traits common to virtually all cultures. These universal experiences and traits are examined in culture-general training classes, videos, textbooks, and face-to-face experiences and are common enough that they can be transferred from culture to culture. As you have learned by now, the approach of this book is culture general. Although we have offered many specific examples, we have looked primarily at cultural traits and behaviors that are shared, to one extent or another, by all cultures. Although there are variations in how each culture manifests its values, worldview, verbal and nonverbal codes, norms, role behaviors, beliefs about healthcare, and the like, these concepts cut across cultures. The content of each might be culture specific, but the need to deal with these topics is universal.

We propose that, regardless of the culture you encounter, it is important to have knowledge that enables you to adapt to any culture. And if you lack that knowledge, know where to find it. The English essayist Samuel Johnson held to this idea when he wrote, "Knowledge is of two kinds: we know a subject ourselves, or we know where we can find information on it." We should add that this entire book is about you finding that information.

Skills

We have mentioned that to be a competent intercultural communicator, you should be *motivated* and have *a fund of knowledge* about other cultures. We now add a third phase of competency—*skills*. Skills are the specific behaviors you engage in to make the communication encounter a successful one. Just a few of these behaviors will be revealed at this juncture, as the remainder of this book will set forth numerous recommendations on how to improve your communication skills.

Develop Intercultural Listening Skills.   Listening is one of those communication activities that is part of all three of the communication competence components we have been discussing. Listening involves being motivated, having knowledge about your communication partner, and possessing the specific skills to listen effectively. You need these three attributes, as there are cultural differences in how people engage in listening. To help you better understand those differences, let us look at a few ways culture and listening work together.

First, as we have noted elsewhere, in many cultures in the Far East, the amount of time spent talking and the value placed on talking are very different from what happens in those cultures that value conversation (Middle East, Latin America, and the United States). Japan is a relatively homogeneous culture; therefore, most people have a pool of common experiences. This commonality has facilitated the development of standardized social behavioral protocols. As a result, the Japanese can often anticipate what the other person will do or say in a particular social context. In fact, at times, they, like many other Asian cultures, believe words can get in the way of understanding. Hence, silence is valued over talk. Think about the connection between speaking, listening, and silence in the Buddhist expression "There is a truth that words cannot reach." Place that against the Arab proverb "Your mouth is your sword." These are two different orientations—one favoring talk and one silence.

Second, when listening to people of different cultures, you must also be aware of cultural variations in how speakers present themselves and their ideas. As you will learn in Chapter 8 when we discuss language, some cultures value a dynamic presentation of ideas, whereas others are passive. For example, in Japan, Thailand, and Cambodia, people tend to speak in soft voices, whereas in the Mediterranean area, the appropriate volume is much more intense. Both of these communication styles put different demands on the listening process.

Third, even the nonverbal responses to what you hear are usually influenced by culture. In the United States, it is often a sign of paying attention when you make the sound "um-humm" or "uh-huh" when someone is talking. Many other cultures find such interruptions by a listener to be impolite. Eye contact is another nonverbal action that influences the listening process. In the United States and other Western cultures, a good listener is seen as paying attention when having direct eye contact with the person talking. But you will recall that direct eye-to-eye contact is not the correct custom in many Asian cultures or in the American Indian co-culture. In short, to be a good listener, you need to know what nonverbal actions are appropriate and which might hamper the communication encounter.

Fourth, be aware of whether the culture of the person you are speaking with uses a direct or an indirect communication style. Although these orientations represent two extremes, they nevertheless provide a useful way of understanding listening. In direct listening cultures, such as those of France, Germany, and the United States, people listen primarily for facts and concrete information. Listeners in these cultures also confront speakers directly and do not hesitate to ask blunt questions. In indirect listening cultures, such as those of Finland, Japan, and Sweden, people listen in a very different manner. Interruptions do not occur while the speaker is talking, and politeness is a crucial part of the listener's behavior.

Fifth, as you listen, you will experience the sway of culture as it affects accents. Accents by people trying to speak English as a second language often make it more difficult for you to listen and comprehend what is being discussed. In these instances, our advice is simple and straightforward—be tolerant, pay attention, and practice being patient. You might also put yourself in the place of someone trying to speak a second language that is new and complex. This attempt at role reversal usually will increase your concentration and your compassion.

Finally, successful listening behavior should include open-mindedness. When you are closed-minded, you end up not listening to new information. However, if you let open-mindedness be part of your listening behavior, you will be accessible to new ideas. You do not have to be in agreement with what is being said, but at least you will be giving the other person a fair hearing. This idea of fairness is extremely important when interacting with people of cultures different from your own, as much of what they are discussing is tied to their culture, and you may lack a direct frame of reference. This, of course, can make listening somewhat problematic. For example, if you are a Christian and believe very strongly in the notion of heaven and hell, you might have trouble listening to someone from India who is telling you about reincarnation.

Develop Communication Flexibility. Our next suggestion asks you to be flexible when deciding how to present yourself to another person—particularly if that person is of a culture different from your own. Flexibility means that you have a large range of behaviors you can call on. This will enable you to regulate, change, and adapt your communication behavior to be appropriate to the setting and the other person. A competent intercultural communicator possesses a repertoire of interpersonal skills that can be applied to specific situations. When speaking to the issue of how communication flexibility applies to international negotiations, Foster used an analogy: "The better [international] negotiators are ultimately pragmatic. They are not oaks; rather, they are more like willows. Unable to predict every situation, every twist and turn, even in a domestic situation, they know that it is nearly impossible to do so in a cross-cultural one."[102]

Regardless of the parts played or the techniques employed, you need to acquire the skills that will allow you to respond to various people, settings, and situations. Having the skills to assume multiple roles means being able to be reflective instead of impulsive when interacting with a culture that moves at a slower pace. It means behaving in a formal manner when encountering a culture that employs a formal style. It means speaking softly instead of loudly when talking with people who use a subdued communication pattern. It means remembering the Spanish proverb "I dance to the tune that is played."

Develop the Skill to Tolerate Ambiguity. A close companion of flexibility is developing tolerance for ambiguity. Because many intercultural encounters are unpredictable and often involve dealing with a new set of values and customs, confusion and ambiguity can often proliferate during the interaction. For example, if your culture values competition and aggressive action and you are around someone from a culture that values cooperation and interpersonal harmony, you might find his or her behavior ambiguous and confusing, yet coping with ambiguity is a key element in intercultural competence. The ability to respond correctly to novel and ambiguous situations with minimal anxiety will enable you to remain calm and will help in familiarizing yourself with the new culture. If you are self-conscious, tense, and anxious when confronted with the unknown, you are apt to use energy to alleviate your frustration instead of trying to decide how best to communicate with the person and adjust to the situation. Perhaps the best advice on how to develop a tolerance for ambiguity is to expect the unexpected, be nonjudgmental, and practice patience.

SUMMARY

- Communication helps fulfill interpersonal needs, assists in gathering information about other people, establishes cultural and personal identities, and allows you to influence other people.

- Communication is a dynamic process in which people attempt to share their internal states with other people through the use of symbols.

- The components of communication include source, encoding, message, channel, receiver, decoding, feedback, and noise.

- Communication is dynamic, symbolic, contextual, self-reflective, irreversible, has a consequence, and is complex.

- Misconceptions about human communication are that it can solve all problems, that people are born good communicators, and that the message sent is the one that is received.

- Culture and communication are so intertwined that it is easy to think that culture is communication and that communication is culture.

- Culture is a set of human-made objective and subjective elements that in the past have increased the probability of survival and resulted in satisfaction for the participants in an ecological niche and thus became shared among those who could communicate with each other because they had a common language and lived in the same time and place.

- Culture informs its members regarding life; therefore, it reduces confusion and helps them predict what to expect from life.

- The central characteristics of culture are that it is shared, transmitted from generation to generation, based on symbols, learned, and dynamic.

- The elements that compose culture are worldview, religion, history, values, social organization, and language.

- Intercultural competence can be developed if you are motivated, have a fund of knowledge about the other person, and possess certain communication skills.

ACTIVITIES

1. Attend a meeting (church service, lecture, social event, etc.) of a culture or co-culture different from you own. Try to notice the various ways cultural characteristics of that culture are being reflected in the interaction.

2. Make a list of the changes in your culture that you have observed during your lifetime. Discuss with a group of your classmates how those changes have affected intercultural communication.

3. Go to YouTube and search for "culture and folk tales." View some folktales from a variety of cultures. Note the "lessons" being taught in each folktale.

4. Type the words "international proverbs" into any search engine and locate proverbs that are trying to "teach" respect, patience, silence, hard work, group solidarity, or trustworthiness.

5. List ten communication characteristics that you would like to develop if you were selected to visit another country as an exchange student.

6. Can you give an example of how each of the three components (motivation, knowledge, and skills) of intercultural communication competence can be improved? Be specific.

CONCEPTS AND QUESTIONS

1. Explain what is meant by the statement "In studying other cultures, we do so very often from the perspective of our own culture."

2. Explain how and why communication and culture are linked.

3. Why is it said that much of culture is invisible?

4. Explain what is meant by the phrase "Communication is contextual." Can you think of examples of how context has influenced your behavior?

5. How does intercultural communication differ from everyday forms of communication?

6. Making inferences about a culture different from your own can often be problematic. Can you think of examples when a lack of information forced you to make the wrong inference?

7. What are some common misconceptions regarding human communication?

8. What are some ways cultures differ in the way they listen?

CHAPTER 3

The Deep Structure of Culture: Lessons from the Family

Children have never been very good at listening to their elders, but they have never failed to imitate them.

JAMES BALDWIN

In every conceivable manner, the family is a link to our past and a bridge to our future.

ALEX HALEY

The family is the nucleus of civilization.

ARIEL AND WILL DURANT

Why do members of some cultures seek solitude, whereas those of other cultures become dejected if they are not continuously in the company of others? Why do people of some cultures frantically cling to youth, whereas others welcome old age and even death? Why do some cultures worship the earth, whereas others mistreat it? Why do individuals in some cultures strive for material possessions, yet in other cultures people believe that wealth hinders a "settled" life? Why do some cultures believe that great insight can be found in silence, but others feel that words contain the world's great wisdom? Why do families in some cultures have children living at home even after marriage, and in others children can hardly wait to flee their homes? These sorts of questions need to be answered in order to understand how people of different cultures see the world, live in that world, and communicate with other people about that world. In the study of intercultural communication it is not enough simply to know that some people bow while others shake hands or that some exchange gifts as an important part of a business transaction while others perceive such an act as bribery. Although these specific behaviors are significant, it is more important to know what motivates people to engage in one action rather than another. The key to how members of a culture view the world can be found in that culture's *deep structure*. It is this deep structure, the conscious and unconscious assumptions about how the world works, that unifies a culture, makes each culture unique, and explains the "how" and "why" of a culture's collective action—action that is often difficult for "outsiders" to understand. Examination of some aspects of a culture's deep structure can provide insight into and improve understanding of that culture's perspectives on ethics, notions of child rearing, ideas about God, nature, aesthetics, and the meaning of life, and even attitudes toward death.

At the core of any culture's deep structure are the *social organizations* we introduced in Chapter 2. These organizations, sometimes referred to as *social institutions*, are the groups and affiliations that members of a culture turn to for lessons about the most important aspects of life. Thousands of years ago, as cultures became more and more advanced and their populations increased, they began to recognize that there was a necessity to organize collectively. These collective institutions, whether family, church, or community, offer their members alliances that they can count on. While these organizations create a social structure that allows members to meet basic needs, they also coalesce the members into a cohesive unit. Bates and Plog repeat this important notion about social organizations, noting, "Our ability to work in cooperation with others in large social groupings and coordinate the activities of many people to achieve particular purposes is a vital part of human adaptation."[1] A number

Families, as a social institution, allow their members to meet basic needs as they learn about cooperation, identity, and the values and behaviors that are important to the culture they were born into.

Courtesy of Robert Fonseca

of groups within every culture help with that adaptation process while also giving members of that particular culture guidance on how to behave. The three most influential social organizations are (1) *family* (clans), (2) *state* (community), and (3) *religion* (worldview). These three social organizations—working in concert—define, create, transmit, maintain, and reinforce the basic and most crucial elements of every culture.

The deep structure institutions are at the core of every culture and provide the fundamental values and attitudes that are most critical to that culture. This chapter looks at the institution of the family and how families shape the social perceptions and communication behaviors of members in a particular culture. In the next chapter, a culture's collective history will be linked to the deep structure of a culture. And, finally, in Chapter 5, worldview and religion are connected to the topic of intercultural communication.

THE DEEP STRUCTURE OF CULTURE

Although many communication problems occur on the interpersonal level, most serious confrontations and misunderstandings can be traced to cultural differences that go to the deep structure of a culture. When Americans were exuberant over the killing of Osama bin Laden on May 1, 2011, they reflected American values of retribution and justice, both part of the historical worldview of the United States. These sorts of examples of deep structure that pit one set of cultural values against another can be found throughout the world. News reports abound with stories of the ongoing persecution of one ethnic group by another. The Kurds in Turkey, Iran, and Iraq have been engaged in a decades-long war to free themselves from ethnic discrimination. In Kosovo, ethnic Albanians declared independence from Serbia—not for economic reasons but for cultural reasons. A kind of "ethnic cleansing" and genocide has been occurring in Rwanda and in the Darfur region of Sudan as the minorities in these areas struggle over divergent cultural norms. In China, discrimination aimed at Tibetans continues on a somewhat regular basis. In Syria and Iraq, the Sunni–Shia fighting that took place in 2014 has a history dating back thousands of years. The same, of course, can be said of the conflict between Israel and much of the Arab world. Here again is a deep structure dispute that began thousands of years ago.

> **REMEMBER THIS**
>
> *It is the deep structure, the conscious and unconscious assumptions about how the world works, that unifies a culture, makes each culture unique, and explains the "how" and "why" of a culture's collective action.*

Hostility and brutality over two contradictory worldviews are as common today as they were thousands of years ago. Christians on a number of fronts are facing oppression and physical abuse around the world. In Pakistan, Malaysia, Iraq, and Nigeria, Christians and their churches have been under attack. In Sudan, the "conflict nurtured by racial and religious hostility"[2] reaches back to the early twentieth century. Even when disagreements do not result in violence, you can still observe how deep structure issues create problems. For example, Japan and China continue exchanging angry words over a series of islands in a dispute that has lasted hundreds of years. We suggest that wherever or whenever there are ethnic, religious, or historical confrontations, be they in Boston, Beirut, Burundi, or Mumbai, it is a culture's deep structure that is being acted out.

Although many of our examples demonstrate clashes that have long historical antecedents, Huntington speaks to future intercultural contact and the potential problems that can arise when deep structure beliefs clash: "The great divisions among humankind and the dominating sources of conflict will be cultural."[3] Although Huntington advanced his proposition nearly twenty years ago, his words are as timely today as when he wrote them. He further explains the rationale behind this in the following:

> The people of different civilizations have different views on the relations between God and man, the individual and the group, the citizen and the state, parents and children, husband and wife, as well as differing views of the relative importance of rights and responsibilities, liberty and authority, equality and hierarchy.[4]

All the issues Huntington cites, as well as the examples noted earlier, penetrate to the very heart of culture. They are what we call in this chapter the deep structure of a culture. Such issues (God, loyalty, duty, family and kinship, community, state, allegiance, etc.) have been components of every culture for thousands of years. In fact, when the world's first cultures started forming—over forty thousand years ago—these same elements were at the core. The earliest expressions of culture reveal that our "ancestors" had interests in spiritual practices, kinship relations, and the formation of communities. These "communities," then as now, assisted cultures in keeping order within the culture and protected the members of the culture from outside threats and influences. Our point is that since the dawn of civilization, the institutions of family, community, and religion have held a prominent sway over the actions of all cultures. Let us look at four reasons their influence is so powerful.

DEEP STRUCTURE INSTITUTIONS TRANSMIT CULTURE'S MOST IMPORTANT MESSAGES

The social institutions of family, state, and religion carry the messages that matter most to people. Whether you seek material possessions to attain happiness or choose instead to seek spiritual fulfillment, the three deep structure institutions help you make major decisions regarding how to live your life. These cultural institutions and the messages they generate tell you whether you should believe in fate or the power of free choice. They form your notions about right and wrong, why there is suffering, what to expect from life, where your loyalties should lie, and even how to prepare for death.

DEEP STRUCTURE INSTITUTIONS AND THEIR MESSAGES ENDURE

Deep structure institutions endure. They work in harmony to preserve the wisdom, traditions, and customs that make a culture unique. From the time when early Cro-Magnon cave drawings appeared in southern France until the present, we can trace the strong pull of family, community, and religion. Generations of children are told about the messages of Abraham, Confucius, Moses, Buddha, Christ, Muhammad, and other spiritual leaders. Whether it is the Eightfold Path, the Ten Commandments, the Analects, the Five Pillars of Islam, or the Vedas, the meanings of these writings survive. Just as every American knows about the values conveyed by the story of the Revolutionary War, every Mexican is aware of the consequences of the Treaty of Guadalupe Hidalgo; likewise, in China, students are being taught about the "one hundred years of humiliation" suffered under Western and Japanese imperialists in the nineteenth and twentieth centuries.

DEEP STRUCTURE INSTITUTIONS AND THEIR MESSAGES ARE DEEPLY FELT

The content generated by these institutions (and the institutions themselves) arouses profound and emotional feelings about loyalty and nationalism. Think for a moment about the fierce reactions that can be produced in the United States when someone takes God's name in vain, burns the American flag, or calls someone's mother an obscene word. Countries and religious causes have sent young men and women to war. And, frequently, politicians have attempted to win elections by urging voters to recognize the importance of God, country, and family. Regardless of the culture, in any hierarchy of cultural values, love of God, country, and family top the list.

DEEP STRUCTURE INSTITUTIONS SUPPLY MUCH OF A PERSON'S IDENTITY

One of the most important responsibilities of any culture is to assist its members in forming their identities. Put in slightly different terms, you are not born with an identity, but through countless interactions, you discover who you are, how you fit in, and where you find security. As mentioned elsewhere, the family is most instrumental in the early stages of the socialization process that establishes a child's personal identity. However, once you encounter other people, you begin to develop a variety of identities. "Everyone has multiple identities which may compete with or reinforce each other: kinship, occupational, cultural, institutional, territorial, educational, partisan, ideological, and others."[5] At some point in your life, you move from identities based only on the "I" ("How attractive am I?" or "Am I a good student?") to identities linked to the "we." That is, you begin to realize that although you still have a personal identity, you also have shared identities. You belong to a "community" and relate to its norms, values, communication behaviors, and the like. We are stressing that you begin to see yourself as part of a larger unit and thus have loyalties to it. Kakar explains this transition in the following: "At some point of time in early life, the child's 'I am!' announces the birth of a sense of community. 'I am' differentiates me from other individuals. 'We are' makes me aware of the other dominant group (or groups) sharing the physical and cognitive space of my community."[6] This "we" identity connects the individual to cultural groups and the main institutions of the culture. This means that when you think about yourself, you most likely conclude that you are a member of a family ("I am Jane Smith"), that you have a religious orientation ("I am a Christian"), and that you live in the United States ("I am from Idaho"). String these three institutions together, and you can observe how people throughout the world employ these cultural organizations for their identity.

These different identities we have discussed are important to the study of intercultural communication because, according to Guirdham, they "can be used to identify similarities and differences in behaviors, interpretations, and norms."[7] Lynch and Hanson agree when they point out, "A person's cultural identity exerts a profound influence on his or her lifeways."[8] For the purposes of this book, those "lifeways" offer insights into how people communicate with one another. The notion of identity is so crucial to the study of intercultural communication that Chapter 7 examines this topic in detail.

FAMILY

The Chinese say that if you know the family, you do not need to know the individual. A Hebrew proverb states, "My father planted for me, and I planted for my children." In Africa, the saying is, "A person who has children does not die." And in the United States, children are told, "The apple does not fall far from the tree." Although these ideas differ slightly, all call attention to the significance and enduring quality of family and the universal form of dependence. Haviland and his associates point out the importance of family in this paragraph: "No matter how each culture defines what constitutes a family, this social unit forms the basic cooperative structure that ensures an individual's primary needs and provides the necessary care for children to develop as healthy and productive members of the group and thereby ensure its future."[9]

Courtesy of Edwin McDaniel

Families are instrumental in "teaching" young people about their identities, how they fit into their culture, and where to find security.

Besides supplying the child's basic physical needs, the family is the first "carrier" of the essential information that the child needs to know as a member of the culture. This means that the family must teach the historical background of the family and the culture, manners and correct behavior, cultural and individual identity, traditions, and language. In short, the family is asked to transform a biological organism into a human being who must spend the rest of his or her life around other human beings. It is the family that greets you once you leave the comfort of the womb. In this sense, the family is the first and chief socializing agent. DeGenova and Rice summarize its importance when they write, "The family is the principal transmitter of knowledge, values, attitudes, roles, and habits from one generation to the next. Through word and example, the family shapes a child's personality and instills modes of thought and ways of acting that become habitual."[10]

As the earliest community to which a person is attached and the first authority under which a person learns to live, the family has a series of responsibilities that directly relate to perception and communication. First, while a culture's core values and worldview derive from its predominant religious and cultural history, the family is the first and primary caretaker of these views and values. As such, the family teaches "communal or collective values; that is, they emphasize the needs, goals, and identity of the group."[11] Second, families are important because they supply all of us with a sense of our identity. Long before we become a separate entity, we are acknowledged and recognized by a family name. The family gives children information about their background, information about their culture, and specific behaviors, mores, traditions, values, and language patterns associated with their culture. Third, families are important from a communication perspective, as they "provide a setting for the development of an individual's self-concept—basic feelings people have about themselves, their abilities, characteristics, and worth."[12]

CONSIDER THIS

Why is it difficult to develop a single definition of the word "family"?

Swerdlow, Bridenthal, Kelly, and Vine eloquently summarize the importance of family to the child:

> Here is where one has the first experience of love, and of hate, of giving, and of denying; and of deep sadness.... Here the first hopes are raised and met—or disappointed. Here is where one learns whom to trust and whom to fear. Above all, family is where people get their start in life.[13]

DEFINITION OF FAMILY

As important as family is to the individual and to the culture, a single definition is difficult to pin down. This difficulty, especially in the United States, has become more challenging during recent decades. It is now nearly impossible to phrase a single definition that would fit all cultures and societies. As Strong and Cohen note, "As contemporary Americans, we live in a society composed of many kinds of families—married couples, stepfamilies, single-parent families, multigenerational families, cohabiting adults, child-free families, families headed by gay men or by lesbians, and so on."[14] Some of the transformations in the United States involve race and ethnicity.

A single definition of family is difficult to construct, since what constitutes a family, especially in the United States, can take a variety of configurations.

© Jim West/PhotoEdit

That is, racial and ethnic diversity among American families and the diversity resulting from immigration have changed the definition of the "typical American family." Hence, there is no simple answer to the question we posed: "How do you define the word 'family'?" We do, however, feel comfortable with a definition advanced by Lamanna and Riedmann:

> A family is any sexually expressive or parent-child or other kin relationship in which people—usually related by ancestry, marriage, or adoption—(1) form an economic unit and care for any young, (2) consider their identity to be significantly attached to the group, and (3) commit to maintaining that group over time.[15]

We accept Lamanna and Riedmann's definition because it is broad enough to include most types of family configurations found all over the world. In addition, their definition is descriptive and nonethnocentric, as it focuses on the social-psychological aspects of family.

FORMS OF FAMILY

Although all cultures deem family one of their most important social institutions, the form and type of the family manifest the cultural and historical beliefs of each culture. Yet even with some cultural variations, most people encounter two families during the course of their lives: (1) the family they are born into (the family of orientation) and (2) the family that is formed when and if they take a mate. Once a person becomes part of either one of these families, he or she also finds him- or herself a member of a *nuclear* or *extended* family. A *nuclear* family is "typically identified as a parent or parents and a child or children as one unit. The *extended* family typically includes grandparents and relatives."[16] Let us further examine the two patterns in greater detail.

Nuclear Families

Nuclear families, usually referred to as "two-generation families," make up the pattern found in most of the United States and in many other Western cultures. Nanda and Warms develop the idea of this important arrangement when they write,

> The nuclear family is adapted in many ways to the requirements of industrial society. Where most jobs do not depend on productive resources owned by family groups such as land and where mobility may be required for obtaining employment and career success, a small flexible unit such as the independent nuclear family has its advantages.[17]

The nuclear family to which Nanda and Warms refer "is made up of two generations: the parents and their unmarried children. Each member of a nuclear family has a series of evolving relationships with every other member: husband and wife, parents and children, and children with each other."[18]

The nuclear family, like all deep structure institutions, manifests many of the values of the culture that stresses this family pattern. For example, we mentioned previously that the nuclear family is characterized by a great deal of geographic mobility. This trait has been part of American culture since the founding of the country. Cultural values of the nuclear family are also reflected in child-rearing practices. According to Triandis, "there is less regimentation and less emphasis on obedience, while exploration and creativity are encouraged."[19] Part of that exploration and creativity can be seen in how early children reared in nuclear families move away from home to "experience life" on their own. American cultural values toward and treatment of the elderly are likewise replicated in nuclear families. In these families older members of the family do not normally spend their "senior" years living with their children.

Extended Families

Anthropologists who study families throughout the world conclude that there are twice as many extended families as there are nuclear families.[20] Tischler offers an excellent description of what constitutes the extended family:

> Extended families include other relations and generations in addition to the nuclear family, so that along with married parents and their offspring, there might be the parents' parents, siblings of the spouses and children, and in-laws. All members of the extended family live in one house or in homes close to one another, forming one cooperative unit.[21]

Even with a larger number of individuals in the household, there is usually one person who can be considered the "head" of the family.

Historically, the cooperative units within the extended family have gathered for economic reasons and to share the workload and rearing of children. In an extended family, a set of behaviors and values may be acted out that differ from those found in nuclear families. For instance, "extended families insist on obedience and are more organized around rules than are nuclear families."[22] Regardless of the culture or the configuration, "The family is regarded as the basic social institution because of its important functions of procreation and socialization, and because it is found in some form in all societies."[23]

CONSIDER THIS

How do extended families differ from nuclear families?

GLOBALIZATION AND FAMILIES

Earlier we noted that for the last twenty years, families in the United States have been in a period of flux. Modifications in what constitutes a family were brought about by a redefining of gender roles, an increase in multicultural and multiracial marriages, changes in dating and mating patterns, new laws regarding homosexuality, and a recognition that many people choose not be married. It is not only families in the United States that have experienced alterations in what constitutes a family. Globalization has redefined families throughout the world. As Karraker points out, "Social scientists recognize that the velocity of social change around the globe in the 21st century is shaping the family as an institution in revolutionary ways."[24] As just mentioned, a major catalyst of this "reshaping" of the family is *globalization*. This dynamic process is one of the major driving forces restructuring many social institutions around the world. It is our contention that families are one of the institutions at the center of this change. Although we discussed globalization earlier in the book, we will revisit the concept as we examine its effect on families. The rationale is simple—globalization is much more than "the process by which *particular* peoples of the world's 170 nations participate in a single system that encompasses all peoples and nations."[25]

Realistically, and from a human perspective, globalization has a series of consequences that go well beyond the exchange of goods and services. Hence, we maintain, along with Trask, that

> Globalization is the critical driving force that is fundamentally restructuring the social order around the world, and families are at the center of this change. In every society traditional notions about family life, work, identity and the relationships of individuals and groups to one another are being transformed due to globalizing forces.[26]

Having recognized that globalization has changed the traditional family structure in many parts of the world, we move to a more detailed explanation of some of these alterations. The most obvious impact of globalization is that it has created a world where millions of workers now leave their families and move from one country to another to seek jobs and higher wages. The World Bank noted in 2014, "More than 250 million people live outside their countries of birth."[27] Many of these people migrate as a way to escape poverty. However, when they "escape," they often transform the makeup and character of their family, as migration places "significant stress on relationships among parents, children, elders, and other family members."[28] The stress of breaking up the family can take a variety of forms. There is an impact on the social lives of both the migrants who move to a new culture and the families they leave behind. There are also countless occasions when parents who are illegal are sent home, and the children often remain in the new country without their parents. As Karraker notes, "The challenges and cultural contradictions of immigration can affect an array of family dynamics, including intergenerational care giving and gender relations."[29] In most instances, migrating individuals are from extended families where for centuries both parents and other family members have taken an active role in child rearing. Our point is that globalization has altered that dynamic. A few specific examples help illustrate our assertion.

The Philippines present a vivid case of how migration, stimulated by globalization, has changed many extended families. In the Philippines, mothers now leave home to take low-paying jobs in Hong Kong, Singapore, Middle East nations, and many other parts of the world in order to support their families. Thousands of nurses have also left the Philippines to seek employment in the United States. While their pay is more substantial than those women who become maids and domestic workers, both groups are often composed of mothers who have left their husbands and children behind. In many instances, personal relationships within the family deteriorate during the long separation. In addition, there is little assurance that those who emigrated will ever be reunited with their families.[30]

This corrosion of traditional families caused by economically motivated migration is not confined to one culture. Countless people from Africa, India, Asia, and Latin America leave their homes because they seek a better life for themselves and their families. When they leave families so that they can survive, the extended family is radically altered. A woman from Zimbabwe offers a poignant example of how family interactions and values can be altered when the family entity is disrupted: "Children no longer sit around the fireplace in the evening to listen to stories that promote the values of respect, integrity, peace, love and unity…."[31]

You can also observe how migrating to a foreign location can produce conflicting family and cultural values as young Muslim women move to European countries. As Newman points out, "young Muslim women are caught between the relative sexual freedoms of European society and the deep, and often very restrictive, traditions of their parents and grandparents."[32]

Perhaps one of the most vivid examples of the lure of jobs away from one's family can be observed in the porous U.S.-Mexican border. Here you see a situation where millions of Mexicans and Central and South Americans have come, both legally and illegally, to the United States in search of employment. When this happens, as we have noted throughout this section, families experience major disruptions and a series of negative consequences. The central question behind all these instances is, *What happens to the core family values as people leave their traditional families in search of employment?* It may take decades to answer this question, but we tend to agree with Giddens when he writes about the worldwide influences of globalization on families: "The traditional family is under threat, is changing, and will change much further."[33]

FUNCTIONS OF THE FAMILY

All families, regardless of type, form, or culture, perform similar functions. We now examine five of those functions.

Reproductive Function

The most important function of the family in any culture is reproduction. While modern technology has added some new dimensions to reproductive methods (artificial insemination, in vitro fertilization, surrogacy), a new infusion of children is necessary for all cultures. The family, therefore, makes continuation of the culture possible by producing (or adopting) children to replace the older members of the culture as they pass on. As simple and obvious as it sounds, this essential function allows a culture to perpetuate itself. Without the infusion of new life, the culture would soon disappear.

Economic Function

The second function of families is to supply children with the necessities of life (food, clothing, shelter). In subtle and manifest ways, the family teaches economic sharing and responsibility. Although the methods for generating goods and services and even the means of distribution vary from culture to culture, the family consumes food and other necessities as a social unit. This means that one of the functions of nearly every family is to supply the basic needs of food, clothing, and shelter. Later in the chapter you will notice how variations in family economic functions often teach important cultural values such as materialism, thrift, sharing, and hard work.

Socialization Function

As mentioned in Chapter 2, the family is one of the "instructors" who transmit the important elements of culture from generation to generation. Strong and Cohen identify part of that instruction when they write, "Children are helpless and dependent for years following birth. They must learn to walk and talk, how to care for themselves, how to act, how to love, and to touch and be touched. Teaching children how to fit into their particular culture is one of the family's most important tasks."[34]

Part of a family's socialization process is teaching the culture's core values, beliefs, ways of behaving, and worldview. This means that "parents teach their children behaviors that are appropriate, expected, moral, or polite."[35] The child's first exposure to emotions such as love, pity, pride, guilt, respect, and fear are experienced in the family setting. Obviously, these kinds of "lessons" and "definitions" also come from other sources, yet it is the family that initially exposes the child to the ideas "that matter most." Not only are norms and values passed along by families to children, but families also "give them their initial exposure to questions of faith."[36] Children are not born into a world that automatically predisposes them to believe in one God, many gods, or no gods. Devotion to a "higher power," be it Allah or Christ, the words of Buddha or Confucius, or the forces of nature, must be learned—and that process begins in the home. Barry and associates offer yet another catalog of the values usually assigned to the family. These include training in obedience, responsibility, nurturing achievement, self-reliance, and general independence.[37] In short, we agree with Al-Kaysi when he writes, "The family provides the environment within which human values and morals develop and grow in the new generation; these values and morals cannot exist apart from the family unit."[38]

Language Acquisition Function

The family is the place where children learn the language of the culture they are born into. All children arrive with the biological and anatomical tools necessary to acquire language. However, in nearly every step of this complex and lengthy process, we find the stamp of family and culture. The process of learning words, what they mean, and how to use them begins at birth and has its origins in the family. As we have said repeatedly, at birth it is the members of the family who are the main caregivers. From how voices sound (learning dialects) to the objects those voices are referring to (the meaning of "mama" and "dada") once again make family the main "teacher." So important is language to intercultural communication that later in the book, we devote an entire chapter to the subject.

Identity Function

As you learned earlier in this chapter, people have multiple identities—individual, national, occupational, cultural, sexual, ethnic, social class, and familial. We maintain that family is perhaps the most important of all identities, as it is a precursor to other identities. Long before we have a notion of ourselves, we are sons or daughters and are identified by family names. In this sense family is not only the basic unit of a society but also provides individuals with their most essential social identity.[39] The family accomplishes this by giving children knowledge about their historical backgrounds, information regarding the permanent nature of their culture, and specific behaviors, customs, traditions, and language associated with their ethnic or cultural group.[40] Because of the importance of identity to intercultural communication, we will have much more to say on the topic later in the book.

REMEMBER THIS

By instruction, observation, imitation, and practice, the child is introduced to the entire spectrum of communication behaviors found within his or her culture.

Having established that there are similarities among most families, regardless of the culture, we now turn to *cultural variations* regarding how family communication patterns get acted out. The connection between families and communication is made clear by Trenholm and Jensen as they write, "The family is a social construction, both a product of communication and a context in which communication takes place. In fact, it is one of the richest sources of communication patterns we have."[41] By instruction, observation, imitation, and practice, the child is introduced to the entire spectrum of communication behaviors. Children first learn about relationships, how to share their feeling, to argue, express affection, make adjustments to other people, and deal with conflict, role relationships, anger, and the like in the context of the family.

CULTURAL VARIANTS IN FAMILY INTERACTION

Before beginning this section on the role of family in cultural interaction patterns, two disclaimers are in order. First, all of the major institutions of a culture are linked. This means the family works in conjunction with other aspects of a culture. As Houseknecht and Pankhurst note, "Family and religion must be viewed in terms of their interactions with other institutions."[42] For example, when a Christian family sits down to dinner and says grace before eating, the children are learning about the importance of God and family rituals at the same time. And when those same children assist their mother in displaying the American flag for a Fourth of July picnic and later sing "God Bless America," they are also learning about three deep structure institutions at once—church, community, and family.

Second, families within a culture may also display a range of differences. It would be naïve to assume that every family in the United States stresses the value of hard work, as there are families where servants pamper even the youngest children. In short, there are variations among and within cultures. As Rodriguez and Olswang observe, "Societies differ, between and within cultures, in their conceptions of the desired traits in children, and therefore, parental beliefs and values might reasonably differ as parents seek to develop culturally defined traits in their children."[43]

Gender Roles

One of the most important family patterns is the teaching of accepted gender roles. As Wood notes, "Families, particularly parents and stepparents, are a primary influence of gender identity."[44] The learning of acceptable gender roles begins as soon as the newborn arrives. As Newman points out, "The gender socialization process begins the moment the child is born. A physician, nurse, or mid-wife immediately starts that infant on a career as male or female by authoritatively declaring whether it is a boy or girl."[45] That initial announcement regarding the sex of the child immediately allows the family to begin the crucial role of socializing the newborn. "The family is a gendered institution with female and male roles highly structured by gender. The names parents assign to their children, the clothes they dress them in, and the toys they buy them all reflect gender."[46] The influence of this early gender identification is made clear by Bailey and Peoples who write, "In any society, gender is a key feature of a person's *social identity*: how other people perceive you, feel about you, and relate to you is influenced by the gender to which they assign you and by how your culture defines gender differences."[47] These differences are reflected in the social roles men and women play, how much authority is given to each gender, who are the major decision makers within the culture, and which gender is most valued.[48]

As you have observed to this point, the task of "teaching" children behaviors associated with each gender falls on the family regardless of the culture. This next section will reveal that in different cultures, boys and girls grow up with very distinct gender identities. These differences are more influenced by culture than biology. Tischler underscores this important idea when he writes,

> Most sociologists believe that the way people are socialized has a greater effect on their gender identities than do biological factors. Cross-cultural and historical research offer

The gender socialization process that begins with the family can be influenced by everything: the toys children are given, family interactions, how children are dressed.

© Steven Lunetta/PhotoEdit

support for this view, revealing that different societies allocate different tasks and duties to men and women and that males and females have culturally defined views of themselves and of one another.[49]

United States.   To this point, we have talked in broad terms about gender differences and the role of families in creating those differences. Let us now turn to some specific cultural differences and how those roles might influence perception and communication. Before we begin our discussion, it is important that we make note of the fact that gender socialization has agents besides the family. For example, media, educational institutions, books, and peer groups, among others, "teach" children "to adhere, often unconsciously, to culturally accepted gender roles."[50]

We commence with the socialization process among families in the dominant culture of the United States. The reason for the attention to gender behavior should be obvious. As Coles points out, "These socially constructed gender expectations for girls and boys frequently translate into different experiences and roles throughout the life course."[51] So powerful are gender roles that children begin to learn how to differentiate between masculine activities and feminine activities when they are just infants. By "age two children can correctly identify themselves and others as boys or girls."[52] Knowing these expectations offers clues as to how interaction is carried out. In the United States, at least within the dominant culture, "appropriateness" is rather specific. Summarizing the research on gender socializing, we offer the following synopsis: males are socialized to be assertive, ambitious, aggressive, sexual, self-reliant, competitive, dominant, distant, logical, and rational, whereas females are socialized to be nurturing, sensitive, interdependent, concerned with appearance, passive, quiet, gentle, emotional, deferential, and cooperative.[53]

The way parents interact with their young child is one of the reasons the various gender differences evolve. Wood, summarizing the research on parent–child interaction, notes that fathers talk more with their daughters than their sons yet "engage in activities more with sons....Mothers tend to talk more about emotions and relationships with daughters than with sons."[54]

Gender roles, like culture, are dynamic and subject to change. We begin our discussion of those changes with the United States. From the start of the twentieth century to the early 1960s, with the exception of World War II when many women replaced men in factories to support the war effort, most females were reared to be wives and assume the roles associated with that position. This, of course, is no longer the case. Events in the United States have brought about conditions that have influenced the notion of gender. From being members of the Supreme Court to being part of a police SWAT team, astronauts, or a military combat pilot, females are now socialized to assume a host of different roles. These new roles mean that "Culturally defined gender expectations in families are certainly changing."[55]

Men have also been affected by a shift in gender roles. As Wade and Tavris point out, "It is no longer news that many men, whose own fathers would no more have diapered a baby than jumped into a vat of boiling oil, now want to be involved fathers."[56]

CONSIDER THIS

In what ways have gender roles changed in the United States?

Having examined some of the research involving changes in the perception of gender in the United States, we are now ready to examine gender roles in other cultures. As part of our transition to an intercultural analysis of gender behavior across cultures, we remind you once again that families in every culture are charged with similar responsibilities, including the need to "teach" appropriate gender roles. However, as you will observe in the following examples, "the way families go about meeting these needs—their structure, customs, patterns of authority, and so on—differ widely across cultures. Thus, ideas about what a family is and how people should behave within it are culturally determined."[57]

Asian. In places such as Japan, Vietnam, China, and Korea, gender roles can be traced to the influence of Confucianism. The basic Confucian assumptions regarding men, women, and child-rearing practices are distinct and prescriptive. The message speaks of male dominance within the family. Expanding on Korea's Confucian legacy toward male dominance, Kim notes, "Confucianism made men alone the structurally relevant members of the society and relegated women to social dependence."[58] These and countless other gender-specific admonitions regarding dissimilar actions were also contained in manuals such as *Lesson for Girls*, written between circa 45 and 120 CE. You can observe this pro-male bias in sayings such as "Woman's greatest duty is to produce a son." You can see the importance of sons over daughters in early Confucian families. In Korea and China, boys studied the classics and played indoors and out, while "girls were confined to the inner quarters of the house where they received instruction in womanly behavior and tasks, such as domestic duties, embroidery, and cooking."[59] Even today, although many young girls work in China (and many may even have important positions), at home, gender roles are still rather rigid. This is the case in many other Asian cultures where homes remain "male-dominated, and women are consigned to subordinate roles."[60] Jankowiak maintains that at the core of these gender attitudes, at least for the Chinese, is the belief that both biological and cultural forces contribute to these differences.[61]

Many of the gender attitudes we have just described for Korea and China can be found in other Asian and East Asian cultures. Among Vietnamese, "Women are raised more strictly and given less freedom than men."[62] Although the practice has changed among Vietnamese Americans, it was the rule in traditional Vietnamese families that only males were educated.[63]

In Japan, a highly industrialized nation where many women attend universities and are in the workforce, there are still major gender differences within the family that go back thousands of years. Within Japanese society, gender roles that men and women engage in at play, in school, at work, and in other settings are learned at home. Even now, "The modern Japanese family, organized to maximize the contribution of men at work, really depends on the devotion of women at home."[64] Within the home, children may even see the father served first at meals, getting the first bath, and receiving nods and deep bows from the rest of the family. All of these activities call attention to the importance of males in Japan. Young boys are indulged, pampered, and even allowed to be a little unregulated. All of this is intended to teach them what it means to become a Japanese man. Young girls receive very different treatment as the family attempts to instruct them in the values associated with being modest and respectable Japanese women. Hall, referring to work by Takie Sugiyama Lebra, offers a clear depiction of that treatment:

> The training young girls receive at home instills cultural values and conditions them to proper comportment. These values include modesty, reticence, elegance in handling such things as chopsticks and dishes, tidiness, courtesy, compliance, discipline for self-reliance, diligence, endurance, and a willingness to work around the house. Japanese girls are groomed to be skilled wives and mothers.[65]

In most Asian cultures, although the structure of the culture perceives men as being superior to women, most of the crucial responsibilities of child rearing fall on the mother. This is exemplified in the Chinese saying "Strict father, kind mother."

Latino. It might be helpful to clarify some of the words we use to define the various types of families that we will place under the umbrella "Latino." While there is an overlap between the words "Hispanic" and "Latino" and many people believe they are interchangeable, they are not. First, "Hispanic" refers to language and constitutes a broad group of Spanish-speaking peoples from places such as South and Central America and the Caribbean. "Latino" is more general than "Hispanic." We should point out that many people consider all Latinos to be Hispanic. For our purposes, Latino is anyone who is from or can trace his or her ancestry to a Latin American country. In many instances, Latinos prefer to call themselves Hispanics. Two clarifications might be helpful. When we speak of "Mexicans," we are referring to someone born in Mexico. "Mexican American" refers to people who live in the United States but have (or have had) some family connections to Mexico.

The sacredness and importance of the family is at the core of Latino cultures. This can be seen in the Mexican proverb "The only rock I know that stays steady, the only institution I know that works, is the family." It is within the context of the family that the individual finds security, emotional support, and a sharp distinction as to how gender roles are defined. Just as Confucian philosophy influenced the shaping of Asian gender roles, the conception of female roles within Christianity derives in part from the masculine representation of God as Father.[66] That is, the male and female roles within Latino families are defined by tradition and religion. For Latina female gender roles, the term *marianismo* is often used when talking about the women being focused primarily on the family while at the same time being subservient to males. As Schvaneveldt and Behnke note, "*Marianismo* is sometimes viewed as women lacking power and being submissive to men."[67] This interpretation is directly linked to the perception of mothers sacrificing their own needs and desires for their children and their husbands. It is the mother who nurtures and educates the children while allowing the father to be the head of the household. This seemingly selfless role does not diminish the fact that "Women ... have great influence in their family, although it may be exercised indirectly."[68] One of their major influences is with young females within the family. For example, because of families' observance of strict female gender roles, young girls "are often less vocal and take less assertive stands than males do."[69]

As you can observe from what we have described thus far, in Mexican culture, the father occupies the dominant role. And, as Hildebrand and his associates note, "The authority of the husband and father is seldom questioned or disputed. The father's role is expected to be one of breadwinner and protector of the family.

He provides for the family's physical needs and monitors and controls all members' participation in the world outside the home."[70] Very early in life, Mexican children learn that "the father makes all of the major decisions, and he sets the disciplinary standards. His word is final and the rest of the family looks to him for guidance and strength."[71] The importance of the male role in the Mexican family can be seen in that when the father is gone from the home, the oldest son takes the position of authority.

Part of the strong role of the father in the family originates in the concept of *machismo*. Although that concept helps explain the notion of male dominance within Latino culture, it is often exaggerated, misused, and misunderstood.[72] In actuality, most of the research regarding *machismo* maintains that *machismo* is characterized by honor, dignity, courage, generosity, and respect for others. When applied to the family, *machismo* encourages the care and protection of all family members. So strong is the protection and concern for family that even "A man's migration to increase economic resources for his family is consistent with traditional male gender roles and brings honor."[73]

We point out once again that changes in migration patterns and globalization have altered the role of women in many countries, including those throughout Latin America. Perhaps the link between gender roles and migration is most vivid as it applies to the United States and Mexico. Writing about this connection, Schneider and Silverman observe, "When men migrate alone, the women left behind assume new responsibilities and freedoms. They must make decisions for their families, and usually they must work."[74] There are now also changes occurring in migration patterns, as women are the ones leaving the family as they find work in *maquila* factories.

> **REMEMBER THIS**
>
> To assure that sons secure "good wives," arranged marriages are still commonplace in India.

Indian.   You have already seen how history, family, and religion are powerful forces in every culture and work together. In each of the cultural families we have talked about, you observed the connection between these social institutions and gender roles. When we look at the position of gender in India, the connections among a culture's history, religion, and its worldview are also apparent. Henderson writes, "Women's status stems from the convergence of historical and cultural factors."[75] These are traditions, as reflected in Hinduism, that go back thousands of years. These traditions, plus the fact that India was cut off from the outside world for much of its early history, helped define the status of women then and, to a degree, even today. In those early days, females wore veils and bulky garments that covered their faces and bodies.[76] During that same period, only men were allowed to interact with the world outside the home. This early orientation promoted an "ideology that separates women and men from one another. Masculinity and femininity become defined as distinct, if not opposing, entities."[77] While strict adherence to this kind of dogma no longer exists, the residual has tended to create a culture where males are considered the superior sex. Male children are thought to be entrusted to parents by the gods. This preference for males, as we noted, has a history as old as Indian society itself. A son guarantees the continuation of the generations and the cycle of life. This, of course, is important for a culture that believes in reincarnation.

The type of family described above has for thousands of years produced a family dynamic where lines to hierarchy and authority are clearly drawn. Male members of the family, acting as authority figures, are heads of the households and make all of the major decisions. Women are seen as caretakers of the children. The roles just mentioned are learned very early in life. Boys are given much more freedom of expression than are girls; boys are encouraged to take part in the religious festivals and activities as a means of introducing them to the spiritual world, and girls are asked to help with the chores that keep the family functioning. It is also hoped that a girl will grow up to be a good wife who devotes herself to her husband's well-being through her performance of religious ritual and household responsibilities. In addition, as a wife, she is expected to "spend much of her time with her husband's family" and reflect "a demeanor of submissiveness and modesty."[78]

To assist their sons in securing "good wives," arranged marriages are still common in India. These types of marriages have been part of Indian culture since the fourth century. For most Indians the rationale behind this practice is as valid today as it was then. In fact, according to UNICEF, arranged marriages make up 90 percent of all marriages in India.[79] There is a belief that arranged marriages benefit not only the parents and the bride and groom but also the entire culture. For many, these arranged marriages continue a long tradition, offer parents control over their children, continue and preserve the ancestral roots, consolidate much of the family property, and enable the elders to preserve the concept of endogamy. The procedure for selecting the correct mate is not a random process but rather "rule governed" and driven by a set of specific objectives. For example, Nanda and Warms note, "Different patterns of choosing a mate are closely related to other social and cultural patterns, such as kinship rules, ideals of family structure, transfer of property at marriage, and core cultural values, all of which are rooted in how people make a living."[80]

The long history of preferring males to females has created what some call "gender disparity" in India. It often means an inequality in employment and a limiting of educational and ownership opportunities. In spite of what we wrote about the roles of males and females in India, the perception and treatment of women are undergoing major changes. As is the case in so many cultures, globalization has had an impact on the Indian workforce, which in turn has brought about some changes in gender stratification throughout India. Today, the number of young women in India receiving higher education is larger than ever. Many of them are becoming scholars, scientists, and medical doctors in greater numbers than their American counterparts.[81]

Arabs. Before we begin our discussion of families and gender roles for our next culture, we need a word or two of clarification. First, as is the case with all cultures, it is important to keep in mind that not all Arabs are the same. Arabs are spread throughout the world and engage in a variety of child-rearing practices. Second, just as we had to make some distinctions between Hispanics, Latinos, and Mexicans, we also have to explain our use of the word "Arab" instead of "Muslims." To begin, not all Arabs are Muslims. And all Muslims are not Arabs. "[O]nly 20 percent of the world's 1.5 billion Muslims originate from Arab countries."[82] There are also Arabs who are Christians and even Jews. However, a majority of experts finds the word "Arab" most appropriate, as it "is a cultural and political term"[83] and relates more directly to the kinds of issues we examine in this section.

You will recall that when we looked at gender issues and child-rearing practices as observed in some Asian cultures, you could see the influence of Confucianism in the socialization process. For Arabs, at least those who are Muslim, one of the clearest delineations of gender roles can be found in the teachings of Islam. "Clear Islamic teachings spell out the roles of women and their rights and duties in the patrilineage. When women marry they retain their father's name and seldom adopt their husband's name. Father and brothers are expected to assume protection over girls and women."[84] When this orientation is applied to the family, you can observe that "An Arab man is recognized as the head of his immediate family, and his role and influence are overt. His wife also has a clearly defined sphere of influence, but it exists largely behind the scenes."[85] These two very distinct roles within the family are predicated on the belief that men are stronger than women, both physically and mentally. Therefore, the argument is that they need protecting. So strong is this decree to protect women that "Young unmarried women need permission from their parents or even their brothers when they seek to venture from their home."[86] The Koran is filled with specific messages for women telling them how they can preserve their honor. These messages range from admonitions against using cosmetics or perfume outside the home to rules about avoiding bathing in public places.[87]

So conspicuous is the preference for male heirs that on the wedding day, friends and relatives of the newlyweds wish them many sons. An Arab proverb states, "Your wealth brings you respect, your sons bring you delight." You can perceive the preferential treatment of males over females in almost any given circumstance. Sait points out just how strong the partiality for males is when he writes, "traditional Palestinian society views women largely through the prism of family, honor, and chastity, and those violating those traditional social norms face reprisals."[88]

In Pakistan, which also has deep religious roots, you can observe a specific example of how gender differences are acted out in the perception and treatment of boys and girls. Irfan and Cowburn explain the Pakistani family and gender: "In Pakistani culture males are more highly valued. They act as the head of the household, the primary wage earner, decision-maker, and disciplinarian. Elder brothers, or on some occasions even younger brothers, take over the role of father and never get challenged by the parents."[89] None of what has been suggested means that girls are not important to Arab families, but their role is to help their mothers and grandmothers in making the home run smoothly.

We would be remiss if we did not point out that in most of the Arab world, the rigid "attitude toward boys and girls is starting to change now that women are being educated and becoming wage earners."[90] This partial shift in gender stratification and family dynamic is taking place throughout the world, not only in the Middle East. Trask reinforces this important idea when she writes, "Westernization and globalization have differentially affected all families with respect to gender roles, child rearing, and maintenance of aging parents."[91] While female gender roles are changing differently from culture to culture, it is nevertheless true that more and more young girls are not limiting themselves to stereotypical roles, jobs, or educational opportunities. That is, in nearly all cultures we are witnessing major transformations regarding gender roles. In numerous countries in the world women are rising to positions of leadership and power. Countries such as Brazil, Germany, Thailand, South Korea, Chile, and Norway now have women as heads of state. There is a strong movement among African young women to question the notion of female circumcision. In Egypt, many parents are sending their daughters to college so that they might secure high-status jobs.[92] In short, women are being integrated into the world economy as they find employment in multinational corporations. This is especially true in developing countries. In other Middle Eastern countries women are asking for, even demanding, the right to vote, along with other privileges. The issue of women driving, according to a report on National Public Radio, is gaining some momentum: Saudi women are employing various social networking sites to air their arguments for easing the driving bans. In Iran thousands of women went to Facebook and posted pictures of themselves bareheaded and not wearing their *hijab* scarves. We are suggesting that you must be careful when thinking about gender roles in a dynamic and changing world.

Individualism and Collectivism

Of great importance to the study of intercultural communication are the notions of individualism and collectivism. Even though these two orientations will occupy a large portion of Chapter 6, we want to introduce the terms now, as they play a significant role in child-rearing practices. Before beginning our discussion of the practices, it is important to realize that although the terms "individualism" and "collectivism" seem to be polar opposites, they are actually the end values of a continuum along which cultures can be situated. As Triandis points out, "Most cultures include a mixture of individualistic and collective elements."[93] For example, this blending can be applied to most Mexican men. While they value the collective nature of the extended family, "The cultural ideal of the Mexican man bravely and aggressively making his way in a hostile world can certainly be described as 'individualistic'."[94] Granting the intermingling of some elements of individualism and collectivism, there are also many very distinct features that mark each orientation. What are these features? In general, "The *individual-collective* dimension is a culture's tendency to encourage people to be unique and independent or conforming and interdependent."[95] More specifically, cultures classified as *individualistic* value the individual over the group. The individual is perceived as a sovereign stand-alone entity. Each person's uniqueness is of paramount value in individualistic cultures. This means that values such as independence, competition, self-determination, pursuing individual goals, independent living, and the "I" being the most important form of identity are the norms.

Collective cultures have a view of the world that is rather different from that of cultures that value individualism. For collective cultures the emphasis is on the needs and goals of the group rather than the self. This means that values such as interdependence, group achievement, cooperation, and the like are stressed. Thomas and Inkson summarize this orientation with the following observation: "In collective cultures, people primarily view themselves as members of groups and collectives rather than as autonomous individuals. They are concerned about [the effect of] their actions on their groups. Their activities are more likely to be taken in groups on a more public basis."[96]

Individualism and the Family

It is not surprising that the two orientations we have described get manifested in the family environment. That is, within each family, children begin to learn (unconsciously at first) values associated with individualism or collectivism. The enactment of these lessons takes a variety of forms. Let us look at some of those forms.

As stressed throughout this chapter, most cultural characteristics have their roots in the deep structure of a culture. For Americans, individualism, as it applies to families, is partially linked to the history of the United States. From earliest colonial times through the present, the nuclear family has been prominent in American culture. It was, however, the Industrial Revolution that saw a major escalation in the concept of individualism. As Lamanna and associates note, "The Industrial Revolution and its opportunities for paid work outside the home, particularly in the growing cities and independent of one's kinship group, gave people opportunities for jobs and lives separate from the family."[97] This meant that most individuals were able— and continue even now—to make decisions that serve their own interests instead of those of the larger group. In most cases, this encourages a shrinking compliance with the authority of the family and stresses self-reliance. Triandis underscores this North American attitude toward individualism within the family when he writes, "In individualistic cultures independence is expected and valued, and self-actualization is encouraged. Mother and child are distinct and the child is encouraged to leave the nest."[98] This independence encourages autonomy. Nomura and his colleagues expand on this idea, writing that "children in America appear to be encouraged to 'decide for themselves,' 'do their own things,' 'develop their own opinion,' or 'solve their own problems.'"[99] Whenever possible, to help their offspring feel autonomous, parents strive to give each child a separate bedroom, computer, television set, and cell phone.

We should remind you in closing that the United States is not the only culture that "teaches" and rewards individualism within the family. Germany, Switzerland, Canada, Australia, France, Finland, and many other cultures can be classified as individualistic.

REMEMBER THIS

Some cultures engage in child-rearing practices that are characterized as dependence training while other cultures emphasize independence training routines.

Collectivism and the Family

An Asian Indian proverb states, "An individual could no more be separated from the family than a finger from the hand." The proverb serves as an excellent introduction to our discussion of collectivism and the family, as it demonstrates the interdependence found in collective cultures. As noted at the outset of this section, in collective cultures, people experience a profound allegiance and attachment to their families. You can see that interdependence in much of India as families often share property, live together, and take part in religious rituals together. You can further observe family loyalty in India in the fact that "feelings of self-esteem and prestige originate more from the reputation and honor of one's family than from any individual attainments."[100]

We now move to the collective cultural orientation found in Latino families. This approach "emphasizes family responsibilities and interdependence to maintain family groups."[101] Ingoldsby offers a synopsis of the Latino experience within the family as a "type of social organization that places the family ahead of the individual's interests and development. It is part of a traditional view of the society that highlights loyalty and cooperation within the family."[102]

As is the case with much of culture, the collective view of family has deep historical roots. Regarding Mexico, for example, Rodriguez unites the three ideas of history,
collectivism, and family:

> From the time of our ancestors, the community has taken care of its children. The Aztecs
> accepted the children from the village into the clan and gave them *cara y corazón*. They
> socialized them, teaching them the traditions, to be self-disciplined and obedient.... It was
> the group that gave the child life and sustained him.[103]

What we have been discussing in regard to families in Mexico also applies to Mexican American families. Sanchez writes, "While it often consists of a household of
husband, wife, and children, people of Mexican origin are more likely to live in an
extended family context, which includes parents, grandparents, brothers and sisters,
cousins, and other blood relatives—commonly referred to as *la familia*, the greater
family."[104] So influential is the power of family ties that when family members
migrate from Mexico to the United States, they usually have someone from their
extended family awaiting their arrival and assisting with the transition period. The
idea of collectivism among Mexican families is further strengthened by a system of
godparenting called *compadrazgo*. Godparents, in most instances, are not blood relations but are part of the extended family. Zinn and Pok explain this broadening of
the Mexican family in the following: "The *compadrazgo* system of godparents established connections between families and in this way enlarged family ties."[105] Godparenting is also an important social institution throughout Central and South America.
   Puerto Rican culture is another example of the socialization process involving a
collective orientation. According to Carrasquillo,

> For the Puerto Rican, the family is an extended social unit that encompasses a wide
> variety of relationships. The extended family functions as a primary agent of socialization,
> as a safety net for its members in times of need, and as a means for obtaining protection,
> companionship, and social and business contact.[106]

This extended collective family is also found in sub-Saharan African culture. In
fact, Wilson and Ngige write, "The nuclear family of husband, wife, and their children (i.e., family of procreation) was considered incomplete without the extended
family."[107] The collective nature of this family structure encourages everyone to contribute to the common good of the family. In these types of families, children are
reared and nurtured by a series of adults. For example, according to Peltzer, child-
rearing practices include "mothering by several adults during infancy and early
childhood."[108] The children engage in "affectionate play with their fathers, held by
the various aunts and uncles, grandparents, and cousins who surround them...."[109]
You can observe the collective nature of these families in the Maasai proverb "The
child has no owner." The meaning, of course, is that all members of the tribe are
responsible for socializing the children.
   Three more cultures (Arab, Japanese, and Chinese) and one co-culture (American
Indian) should be examined before we conclude our section on collectivism and the
family. An excellent preview of the Arab perspective on collectivism is stated by
Esherick:

> Unlike the rugged individualism we see in North America (every person for him or herself,
> individual rights, families living on their own away from relatives, and so on), Arab society

emphasizes the importance of the group. Arab culture teaches that the needs of the group are more important than the needs of one person.[110]

In collective Arab families, people "share work, income, and expenses as a single economic unit."[111] Arab families, as part of their collective orientation, have through the centuries developed a keen sense of family loyalty. Part of that loyalty was reflected in a study that revealed that there is special closeness between Arab youth and their parents even though they were raised with a large series of rules that restricted their conduct.[112]

Not only has the Arab view of collective families been a tradition for thousands of years, but this key value travels with families as they move from place to place. For example, Arab Americans maintain a very traditional view of the collective family, even in the United States. They continue to have "large families in which all aunts, uncles, cousins and grandparents are considered part of the immediate family, even if there is only one breadwinner in the household."[113]

Japan is another culture where collectivism is manifested in the family. Newman offers a summary of the Japanese view of collectivism: "People consider duty, sacrifice, and compromise more desirable traits than personal success and individual achievement. They assume that group connections are the best guarantee for an individual's well-being. Hence, feelings of group loyalty and responsibility for other members tend to be strong."[114] In Japanese families "individuals are encouraged to find fulfillment for their needs within the family and to put the collective interests of the group before their own personal interests."[115] Japanese parents also expect their children to be compliant "and avoid confrontations" that might disturb the harmony within the family.[116] So strong are these family ties that children often live with their parents until they are married. This sort of tight bond creates values such as loyalty and harmony that become part of a person's entire life. The Japanese have a saying that reaffirms the allegiance and duty children have to their parents: "If your parents are living, don't go on a long trip."

The Chinese perception of collectivism is deeply rooted in Confucianism, and "family interests are placed above those of society and other groups within it."[117] The importance of the family has been linked historically not only to Confucianism but also to the geographic nature of China. Because vast areas of the country are widely separated, most Chinese have always felt detached from the central government. There is an important Chinese proverb reminding people that loyalty to family supersedes all other commitments: "Heaven is high and the Emperor is far away." Hence, family devotion goes before any other institution, including the economic forces of globalization. Kissinger examines this essential value and how it might be manifested in the economic arena:

> Nepotism is a special problem, in any event, in a culture as family oriented as the Chinese. In times of turmoil, Chinese turn to their families. In all Chinese societies whether it is China, Taiwan, Singapore, or Hong Kong—ultimate reliance is placed on family members, who in turn benefit in ways determined by family criteria rather than abstract market forces.[118]

So strong is the value of loyalty that ethnographic studies suggest that Chinese children are raised in a manner that teaches them that they should not bring shame to their family, which would be perceived as a lack of devotion. Hence, in China, "Children are socialized to be conscious of what others think of them and are expected to act so as to get the most out of approval of others while trying to avoid disapproval."[119] Chu and Ju make much the same point: "An important Chinese cultural value is filial piety. Traditionally, Chinese children feel a lifelong obligation to their parents, ideally exemplified by an unreserved devotion to please them in every possible way."[120]

American Indians are yet another culture where the extended family transmits ways of living and values. Taylor and Ballard point out that American Indian families are "interdependent and interconnected, in regard to living arrangements, sharing of resources and emotional support."[121] For American Indians the extended family is large. As Cheshire writes, "Individuals identify themselves not only as members of specific families, but as members of a tribe, which creates a larger kinship structure to draw upon, with many families interrelated."[122] An interesting aspect of collectivism among American Indians is that "despite nearly five hundred years of destructive contact with Anglo-European cultures, important differences in family practices persist among Native Americans."[123]

THE ELDERLY

The family is the first institution to introduce the child to the notion of age grouping. Learning about and coping with the life changes associated with aging is also, like gender, a cultural universal. This universal nature of dealing with age and the elderly is explained by Haviland and his colleagues when they write, "All human societies recognize a number of life stages. The demarcation and duration of these stages vary across cultures, but each one provides distinctive social roles and come with certain cultural features such as specific patterns of activity, attitudes, obligations, and prohibitions."[124] The next section deals with some of those roles, features, and perceptions that relate to intercultural interaction. Specifically, we will look at some of the cultural differences found in various families as applied to the elderly.

United States

We begin with the United States. For a number of reasons, most members of the dominant culture have a rather negative perception of the elderly. Because of this perception, members of the dominant culture attempt to avoid growing old. In addition, many of the major values of Western culture celebrate youth and self-reliance. Hence, as one grows old, one's contributions to the culture often become devalued. The English language has even created "derogatory terms" for the elderly. Reflect on the images evoked by the terms "over the hill," "codger," "fuddy-duddy," "geezer," "fossil," or "old coot."

It is, of course, much more than words that foster negative stereotypes. In general, "Ultimately, North Americans retire from their paid jobs at a specified age and, increasingly, spend the final years of their lives in retirement communities, segregated from the rest of society."[125] Since people are living longer, nursing homes and assisted living facilities isolate the elderly even further from the rest of the culture and their children. But the economic recession of 2007–2009 caused a noticeable shift in the composition of American families. By 2012, the number of Americans living in multigenerational households had doubled since 1980. Older family members traditionally made up a higher proportion of individuals living in multigenerational U.S. families than did young adults in their mid-twenties to mid-thirties. But in 2011, of individuals 85 and older, 22.7 percent lived in multigenerational households. Of younger adults, ages 25 to 34, 23.6 percent lived in multigenerational households.[126] This shift in household composition could, in the long term, change attitudes as well.

Perceptions of the elderly common in the dominant culture of the United States are not the rule in many other cultures. In fact, negative perception and treatment of the elderly is not common in most other cultures. Let us now examine some of these countries and cultures.

Latino

We begin with a group of cultures that have a long tradition of positive perceptions of the elderly—Latino cultures. These perceptions are translated into actions where the elderly are highly respected, play a dominant role in the family, and are always cared for. In most Latino families, "older members have authority over younger members."[127] Part of the authority comes from the perception of the elderly as being wise and possessing a great deal of the culture's history. This positive view of old age is seen in many Latino cultures. In Puerto Rican families, grandparents not only live with the extended family but also help with child rearing.[128] So strong is the bond between the elderly and the family in Latino cultures that "placing elderly parents in nursing homes or centers for the aged is virtually unknown. To do so may be looked on as abandonment or rejection of a loved one and as a serious shirking of family responsibility."[129]

Arab

We introduce the Arab culture with a proverb that reflects that culture's perception of the elderly: "A house without an elderly person is like an orchard without a well." Reaffirming that view, Hildebrand and his colleagues point out,

> Prestige and power are attached to age, and especially to Arab grandparents. The grandfather is the undisputed head of the household or clan, and everyone submits to his authority. He passes on the oral traditions of the Arab peoples, using parables for the moral guidance and character development of younger generations.[130]

This deference to the elderly not only is embedded in a culture's deep structure institution of the family but also is part of religious training. For example, Mir states, "Both the Qur'an and the Prophet emphasized the importance of caring for the elderly. In Islamic teaching, it is the responsibility of each individual to care for and honor his or her parents as they age."[131]

You can detect the effects of this attitude toward the elderly when you look at Saudi Arabian culture. There, "the authority, wisdom, and counsel of elder family members are still to a great extent accepted, and younger family members must wait sometimes far into middle age before being accorded that status."[132] They must wait for their turn to experience the respect and admiration associated with age that are part of the process that ensures "the passing on of social values from one generation to another, as the influence of the older relatives is continually present."[133] Because of the attitude toward the elderly we have been explaining, elderly relatives usually remain in the home their entire lives.

Asian

Turning to Asian cultures, we once again observe the interconnectedness of the deep structure institutions we discussed at the onset of this chapter and the elderly. In places such as China, Korea, and Japan, one reason for the respect and reverent attitude toward the elderly is ancestor worship. Perhaps more importantly, in all three of these cultures, there is a strong belief in the "special force" that connects Confucian philosophy to the elderly. Specifically, it is the Confucian notion of filial piety that is concerned with the correct way to treat one's parents and grandparents. That respect and admiration for age even extends after the death of a parent. This belief is illustrated by the proverb "When eating bamboo sprouts, remember who planted them." As Makinen points out, this "2,500-years-old Confucian ideal of filial piety still runs deep."[134] The longevity and strength of this devotion can be seen even today. For example, there is a new "Elderly Rights Law" in China that not only mandates that children visit their parents frequently but also says that they should concentrate on the spiritual needs of their elderly parents.[135] In some urban areas where children are often working and fail to visit their parents or neglect them, their names are posted on a public notice board.[136]

In many cultures the elderly are not only respected and venerated, they are also active members of the family and help "teach" young children about the culture.

© Steve Harrington

Respect for the elderly is manifest not only in deep structure institutions and social laws but also by a culture's use of language. Earlier in this section, we mentioned the negative names applied to the elderly in the United States. This is not the case in most Asian cultures. Here, respect for the elderly is regularly expressed in its language. It reveals a sincere and deep-rooted reverence for the elderly. A family with an old person has a living treasure of gold. And in India the term *ji* allows the speaker to show respect to the older person being addressed.

REMEMBER THIS

Across cultures there are significant cultural differences in both the perception and treatment of the elderly.

Elderly people are not only venerated in Asian cultures; they are also influential both inside and outside the family. In Korean culture, children are taught at a young age that grandparents and other older members of the family are the authority figures.[137] This same attitude is found in China. As Wenzhong and Grove note, "Perhaps the chief determinant of relative power in China is seniority."[138] The hierarchy associated with age in Chinese culture is clear. After the father, the eldest male has the most authority. When Chinese families resettle in the United States, they still follow the customs associated with respecting the elderly and would experience a sense of shame were their elderly parents placed in nursing homes.

East African

While age grouping, and the perceptions and roles associated with each grouping are found in every culture, it is perhaps most detailed in East Africa, particularly when applied to the elderly. Among the Maasai and Tirike in Kenya, males move through four consecutive age grades. Because this section of the chapter is concentrating on age and the family, we will examine only the fourth stage—ritual elders. It is in this stage when elders "preside over the priestly functions of ancestral shrine observances on the household level, at subclan meetings, at semiannual community appeals, and rites initiation into the various age grades."[139] In addition to these special roles granted to the elders, it is also believed that, because of their age, they possess "power as sorcerers and expungers of witchcraft."[140]

American Indian

Before concluding this section, let us mention two co-cultures within the United States. We begin with American Indian families. As is the case with all the families we have examined, any cultural generalizations need a series of disclaimers. For example, American Indians are a very heterogeneous co-culture. Not only are there approximately 500 different tribes, but you also find dissimilarity between those American Indians who live on reservations and those who have relocated to urban areas.[141] However, in spite of these differences, attitudes involving the elderly have remained in place for hundreds of years. At the heart of those views is the same positive perception of the elderly that we have seen in other cultures typified by extended families. There is a deep and clear deference and respect regarding the elderly within American Indian culture—a respect and admiration that can be traced to that culture's deep structure. This respect is seen in everything from their offering advice and care for grandchildren to being served first and also occupying special seats at the table.[142] The elderly are part of the decision-making process and are also responsible for transmitting the collective knowledge and wisdom of each tribe to the younger members of the family. This means the elders are the keepers of oral tradition and tribal stories that are used to pass on important values and beliefs from one generation to the next.

African American

African Americans represent another co-culture in the United States that has a view toward the elderly that differs slightly from the one held by the dominant culture, a view that has been influenced by the history of this co-culture. That is, "The historical past of many African-American families is uniquely different from all the other immigrant groups that have come to the United States. The American experience has resulted in many of the strengths that have helped families to cope with adversities."[143] One of those historical strengths is mentioned by McCoy when she writes, "African American elders became indispensible resources for their wisdom and guidance, and were, in turn, recognized and given strength, empowered, and authenticated."[144] Part of this strength comes from the role of the grandmother, who is one of the most essential figures in the African American family. It is estimated that at one time or another, about seventeen percent of African American children have lived in their grandmother's home.[145] In this role as caregiver for the young, the African American grandmother often becomes both guardian and keeper of the family values.

During the course of this chapter, we have alluded to both obvious and subtle changes to families throughout the world. It is not surprising that many of the changes will influence how the elderly are perceived and treated. There are, of course, numerous reasons for these changes. First, the population is getting older. Across the globe, medical advances have produced a period in history where people are living longer. Second, one of the end products of globalization is that more and more people are moving away from their established communities. For example, Bryant and Lim offer an example as it applies to China: "Chinese culture is undergoing change due to children living away from home for employment."[146] This reduces family size and changes the family structure. This change can be seen today, as "nearly half of the country's seniors live apart from their children, a phenomenon unheard of a generation ago."[147]

Japan represents another clear example of the changes taking place within many Asian countries as it applies to traditional family dynamics. Although the Japanese still embrace the view that senior members of family should be respected and honored, certain events have altered that notion. Izuhara summarizes the causes for those alterations: "There are a number of common pressures and processes confronting family structures and resources. Social change,

---

CONSIDER THIS

Recall as much as you can about your personal family history. Record your answers to the following questions as they apply to the conscious and unconscious learning that took place. It might be interesting to compare your answers to those of someone of a different culture.

a. *In general, would your family be classified as formal or informal?*
b. *What or who were the subjects of jokes?*
c. *What was the attitude toward the elderly?*
d. *Was conflict dealt with in a direct or indirect manner?*
e. *Who made the major decisions in your family? Mother? Father? Both? Other family members?*
f. *If you had siblings of the opposite sex, did you notice different child-rearing practices being followed? What were some of those differences?*
g. *Was competition or cooperation stressed?*
h. *How did you learn about religious matters?*
i. *How were you rewarded?*
j. *How were you punished?*

demographic shifts, and changes in economies and the labor market are some of the key drivers of family change."[148] We need to mention once again that these changes have produced, not a decline in filial devotion, but rather a need to adapt to an ever-changing world. For instance, a continually declining birthrate means that "Japan will have to become a pioneer in figuring out how to run a society top heavy with older people."[149]

SOCIAL SKILLS

Throughout this chapter we have talked about the idea that it is family that is the first institution to socialize the child. Through family interactions, children begin to learn about what are acceptable and unacceptable forms of communicative behavior. When we speak of learning forms of communicative behavior we are talking about much more than language acquisition and the rules of grammar. What we are referring to is how and what families teach their children about effective communication skills. In many ways, parents serve as models for these skills. Burke, Woszidlo, and Segrin develop this indispensable role in the following observation: "Parents serve as models within the family environment, influencing the development of their children's social skills. That is, children learn how to interact with others by observing and imitating the ways in which their parents interact with others."[150] Adler and Proctor underscore the magnitude of those interactions when they write, "Communication in the family of origin can have lifelong effects."[151] The National Association of School Psychologists echoes the importance of these social skills:

> Good social skills are critical to successful functioning in life. These skills enable us to know what to say, how to make good choices, and how to behave in diverse situations. The extent to which children and adolescents possess good social skills can influence their academic performance, behavior, social and family relationships, and involvement in extracurricular activities.[152]

As we have been suggesting, it is a major family responsibly to teach the numerous "cultural skills" a person will need to function effectively. A sampling of some of the basic communication skills each child must learn are listed below:

- When and how to disclose personal information to others.
- How to show respect to other people.
- How to start, maintain, and end a conversation.
- Taking turns when interacting. When to listen and when to speak.
- When not to interrupt.
- The use of silence.
- The correct volume for each setting.
- Knowing appropriate and inappropriate topics of conversation.
- How to use humor.
- Correct use of nonverbal communication. Who can be touched? Where can they be touched?
- Appropriate use of laughter.
- Being responsible for their actions.
- How to respond to criticism.

- How to give and accept compliments.
- Controlling one's ego.
- Developing empathy.
- Respect for others.

Because all cultures prepare their members to live among other people, it should not be surprising that many of the same social skills are taught in every family. For example, instruction in good manners is stressed in every culture, for without some degree of civility, you would have chaos and confusion. Yet the emphasis placed on many common child-rearing "messages" varies as you move from culture to culture. Let us briefly look at two social skills that are often at variance when we compare cultures. These are (1) the importance placed on face-to face communication and (2) aggression behavior.

Communication Skills

You can also observe cultural differences in the teaching of communication skills when you look at family patterns regarding how children are taught the value placed on interaction. Children must learn about words and nonverbal actions so that they can become competent members of their culture. As Park and King note, "Through this language socialization, children learn the behaviors that are culturally appropriate in their community."[153] Of course, what is "appropriate" is rooted in culture. When applied to the dominant culture of the United States, we turn to Cheal, who offers the following commentary on the place of talk in American families: "One of the main things family members do is talk. They talk as they go about their daily routines in the household. They talk when they visit or phone distant members who want to be informed about what is going on within the family."[154] From a very early age, American parents encourage their children to express themselves regardless of the topic or the context. As Kim points out, "Speech and self-expression hold particular importance in individualistic cultures."[155] As you might imagine, such a view regarding oral expression is not universal. For example, "In the East Asian cultural context, expression of one's thoughts may be neither particularly encouraged nor viewed positively,"[156] thus the Confucian saying "The superior man is modest in his speech, but exceeds in his actions." We can see a specific reflection of this view in the Cambodian culture as described by Park and King:

> Among Khmer families in Cambodia, a child's polite behavior is considered a sign of the family's high social status and the child's good moral upbringing. Thus Khmer parents raise their children to display behaviors such as greeting elders in polite ways or addressing others with proper terms that mark relative social status.[157]

Aggressive Behavior

Another example of cultural differences in child-rearing practices can be seen in a culture's acceptance or rejection of aggressive verbal and/or nonverbal behavior. What we know about the link between culture and aggressive action is clearly stated by Rahman when he asserts, "Culture is an important factor that plays a role in aggression."[158] Behind Rahman's observation is a body of research demonstrating that some cultures are low in aggression, whereas others are marked by a high level of aggression.[159] A few cultural examples buttress Rahman's remarks. We begin with families of the dominant North American culture, where studies have shown that parents encourage, approve, and reward aggressive behavior.[160] Rancer underscores the positive image associated with aggression, noting that in the United States, "*Assertiveness* is considered a constructive trait because it involves verbal and nonverbal symbols to exert control, obtain justified rewards, and stand up for one's rights."[161] This tendency is stressed early, and many young males learn to dominate others as a way to increase their status.[162] The tendency toward aggression is not confined to the United States. Studies reveal the propensity toward aggressive behavior in most individualistic cultures.[163]

What we have been describing is not the case with collective cultures. For example, Adler and Proctor reveal that in collective cultures, aggressive messages are perceived somewhat differently: "By contrast, collective cultures (more common in Latin America and Asia) consider the concerns of the group more important than those of any individual. In these cultures, the kind of assertive behavior that might seem perfectly appropriate to a North American would be regarded as rude and insensitive."[164]

Aggressive actions have such a negative connotation in many Asian cultures that even the word "no" is perceived as an indication of being belligerent, impolite, ill-mannered, and aggressive. In these cultures, children are taught the social skills necessary for group harmony, family interdependence, respect for the elderly, and the importance of saving face. Avoidance of the word "no" is just one of many ways this value is made manifest. Another vivid example of how each family teaches various social skills can be seen among the Thai, where the family teaches patterns of interaction that avoid aggressive behavior:

> The child quickly learns that by behaving in a way that openly demonstrates consideration for the feelings of others, obedience, humility, politeness and respect, he can make people like him and be nice to him. This behavior may be summed up in one Thai word, *krengjai*, which is usually translated as "consideration."[165]

The examples provided demonstrate the prominence of the family in the enculturation of communication. It is an institution that helps shape each generation and prepares them to become members of the culture that awaits them.

DEVELOPING COMMUNICATION COMPETENCE THROUGH THE FAMILY

The basic premise of this chapter has been that to communicate effectively with people of cultures different from your own requires an appreciation of the role that family plays within those cultures. The reason for needing such a fund of knowledge about families is uncomplicated. Simply put, a person's family influences how they communicate. An understanding of the role of family in communication exchanges is important on two counts. First, worldwide globalization and demographic changes in the United States have created a situation where settings involving communication have increased in both frequency and variety. As Karraker notes, "Every family in every society—to a greater or lesser degree—is confronted with the issues that globalization portends for culture."[166] Second, many of the professions that you might be pursuing (teaching, healthcare, etc.) will involve working with families from diverse cultures. As applied to the United States, Taylor and Ballard point out, "With the United States having such a diverse population, it is essential that those working with families and individuals in the community be understanding and sensitive to many different cultural beliefs and practices."[167] They suggest that anyone working with families of different cultural heritages should strive to be culturally competent. Although we discussed competency in detail at the conclusion of the last chapter, we now revisit the topic as it applies to the family context.

Ballard and Taylor offer three general traits needed for effective communication with diverse families.[168] Although some of these skills were noted at the conclusion of Chapter 2, they bear repeating:

1. When working with intercultural families, one needs to develop an understanding of self and others.

2. Interpersonal communication proficiency includes listening intently, being empathetic, exercising decision-making and problem-solving skills, and displaying expertise in conflict resolution.

3. A successful communicator interacting with another culture reflects concern, respect, and sincerity.

We add some specific advice to Ballard and Taylor's list:

4. As indicated earlier, cultures and families differ in the degree to which they promote individuality and uniqueness versus conformity and interdependence. When interdependence is the rule, "absolute loyalty is expected to one's immediate and extended family/tribe."[169] This strong emotional attachment that typically lasts the person's entire life might be involved in the decision-making process. Therefore, when asking someone to make a choice, a person of a collective culture will normally ask the advice of family members and place their welfare above all other institutions and individuals.

5. Learn the roles that each family has assigned to gender and the elderly. Those roles will determine how members of each culture will respond to "outsiders." It is not uncommon for females in Asian, Latino, and Arab cultures to allow the male members to make most of the decisions involving healthcare, even if it is a female member of the culture who is visiting the doctor.

6. Learn all you can about age-appropriate behavior for each culture you will be dealing with. What behaviors are expected from members of the family as they move from infancy to childhood to adolescence to adulthood to old age?

7. Be aware of the problems created by the possible changes in family dynamics caused by acculturation into a new culture. As Carteret points out, "It is important to consider the enormous stresses families encounter in the process of acculturation due to sudden and radical shifts in family dynamics."[170] Carteret refers to those situations when a family migrates to a new country and attempts to cling to the values of their original cultural while their children often adapt to the values of the host culture. In many instances, parents and grandparents might well experience feelings of humiliation and betrayal as they see these cultural changes in the children.

SUMMARY

- The deep structures of a culture, which include such elements as family (clans), state (community), and religion (worldview), are important because they perpetuate a culture's most significant beliefs and values. Their messages endure, are deeply felt, and help supply much of a culture's identity.

- Families can take a variety of forms. The two most common are nuclear and extended.

- Traditional definitions of "family" are undergoing major changes in the United States.

- Globalization and shifting migration patterns in recent years have had major impacts on traditional family structures throughout the world.

- Families perform a series of key functions in all cultures. These functions include reproduction, economics, socialization, language acquisition, values and religion, identity, and communication.

- Cultures, by using the family as a transmitter of the key elements of culture, teach gender roles, inculcate views on individualism and collectivism, perpetuate perceptions of aging and the elderly, and develop social skills.

ACTIVITIES

1. Working with others, discuss the following topic: In what ways have globalization and new immigration patterns changed families? Have these changes been beneficial or detrimental to families?

2. Interview someone of a culture different from your own using questions about child-rearing practices. You might inquire about methods of discipline, toys, games, topics discussed at the dinner table, and such. During the discussion, share with them some "dos" and "don'ts" you were taught in your family.

3. Working with others, have each person discuss the "stories" that helped form his or her familial and cultural identity.

4. Go to YouTube and search for "Jewish family Passover." View some of the family videos as they apply to how family rituals are taught to the children who are sharing the religious service associated with the Passover dinner.

5. Working with others, discuss the following questions: Are child-rearing practices throughout the world more alike than they are different? What are the major similarities, and what are the major differences?

6. Go to YouTube and search for "gender stereotypes in the media." After viewing some of the most popular videos, try to answer the following questions: What cultural themes are repeated in many of the videos? How accurate are these themes?

CONCEPTS AND QUESTIONS

1. How are the three deep structure elements interrelated? Are those links the same in every culture?

2. During the chapter, we discussed cultural differences in the perception and treatment of the elderly. Why do you think the differences exist?

3. What are some ways a person's family influences his or her cultural identity?

4. What do you see as the major differences between nuclear and extended families? How do these differences influence communication between members of the family?

5. Why do you believe families in the United States have experienced so many changes in the last two decades? What are these changes? Do you believe the changes are positive or negative?

6. Was the parenting style in your home more authoritarian or laissez-faire?

7. Do you believe mass media and social networking will make major alterations to gender roles in the next ten years? Why or why not?

8. Compare how the following four approaches to child rearing would respond to a child's aggressive behavior: (1) authoritarian, (2) laissez-faire, (3) collective, and (4) individualistic.

9. Will globalization eventually make all families alike? If so, is that good or bad?

10. Is male dominance universal? Is so, why?

CHAPTER 4

Worldview: Cultural Explanations of Life and Death

The creation of a worldview is the work of a generation, rather than of an individual, but each of us, for better or worse, add our brick to the edifice.

JOHN DOS PASSOS

Whatever you are, be a good one.

ABRAHAM LINCOLN

The problem to be faced is: how to combine loyalty to one's tradition with reverence for different traditions.

ABRAHAM JOSHUA HESCHEL

The introduction to Chapter 3 pointed out that family (clans), state (community), and religion (worldview) work interactively to transmit the most important values and beliefs of a culture. Having earlier explained family and state, we now turn to the topic of worldview and religion.

WORLDVIEW AND CULTURE

There are perhaps as many definitions of *worldview* as there are definitions for the words "communication" and "culture." If you examine the word itself, you might assume that worldview means a view of the world. And in a sense, you would be correct. For in its broadest sense, worldview is "the way people interpret reality and events, including how they see themselves in relation to the world around them."[1] What makes interpretation of reality important for our analysis is that this picture of reality is both created and shared by the members of each culture. Schultz and Lavenda develop this idea further when they write, "Members of the same society make use of shared assumptions about how the world works. As they interpret everyday experiences in light of these assumptions, they make sense of their lives and their lives make sense to other members of the society."[2] A culture's worldview focuses on the major assumptions about life that all individuals, at one time or another, must deal with. Klopf and McCroskey note some of those assumptions:

> Worldview is a set of interrelated assumptions and beliefs about the nature of reality, the organization of the Universe, the purposes of human life, God, and other philosophical matters that are concerned with the concept of being. Worldview relates to a culture's orientation toward ontological matters or the nature of being and serves to explain how and why things got to be as they are and why they continue that way.[3]

From Klopf and McCroskey's description you can reason that worldviews deal with some of the following topics:

- What is the purpose of life?
- Does law, chance, or "God" rule the world?
- What is the right way to live?
- What are the origins of the universe, and how did life begin?
- What happens when we die?
- What are the sources of knowledge?
- What is good and bad and right and wrong?
- What is human nature?
- Why do we exist just to die?
- How do we determine "truth"?
- What is our responsibility to other people?

The answers to these kinds of worldview questions can impact a culture's social, economic, and educational systems; destiny; degree of competition; work ethic; risk propensity; gender relationships; level of innovation; perception of authority; and political life.[4] At the same time, worldviews deal with significant questions and provide direction for the more practical features of living. That is, "In selecting its customs for day-to-day living, even the little things, the society chooses those ways that accord with its thinking and predilections—ways that fit its basic postulates as to the nature of things and what is desirable and what is not."[5] As it applies to the basic orientation of this book, we are proposing that knowing about a culture's worldview will assist you in understanding how that culture perceives the world and interacts with other people in that world. Dana underscores the connection between worldview and the study of intercultural communication:

> Worldview provides some of the unexamined underpinnings for perception and the nature of reality as experienced by individuals who share a common culture. The worldview of a culture functions to make sense of life experiences that might otherwise be construed as chaotic, random, and meaningless. Worldview is imposed by collective wisdom as a basis for sanctioned actions that enable survival and adaptation.[6]

REMEMBER THIS

A culture's worldview is directly linked to how members of that culture perceive the world and live in that world.

MANIFESTATIONS OF WORLDVIEW

To this point we have talked about how worldview and culture are linked in general terms. A few specific examples will enable you to see both the perceptual and the communicative components of worldview.

We begin with two differing worldviews regarding nature. In general terms, "The West emphasizes *control* of nature; the East emphasizes *harmony* with nature."[7] For example, the Shinto religion encourages an aesthetic appreciation of nature in which the focus is on reality and not heaven—a reality that makes nature supreme. Shintoism prescribes an aesthetic love of the land. Every hill, lake, mountain, and river is treasured. Cherry trees, shrines, and scenic resorts are indispensable to a full life. People perceive them as lasting icons among which their ancestors lived and died. People thus preserve nature so that nature can preserve the family.[8] When examining the worldview of American Indians, yet another set of preconceptions emerges regarding the universe and how people fit into that universe. In Western logic and science, people move from the specific to the general. American Indians begin with an apprehension of the whole (general) and move to specifics. This worldview reasons that to the extent the universe is a whole, dimensions such as location and time (both specific) become irrelevant. It is the "big picture" that gives meaning to life, not the bits and pieces.[9]

Another link between worldview and behavior can be seen in how a culture perceives the business arena. In two classic texts, Weber's *The Protestant Ethic and the Spirit of Capitalism* and Tawney's *Religion and the Rise of Capitalism*, the bonds among religion, commerce, and production are examined. In both of these historical works, the authors conclude that there are connections among a culture's history, religion, and worldview. Bartels reaffirms these bonds as he writes, "The foundation of a nation's culture and the most important determinant of social and business conduct are the religious and philosophical beliefs of a people. From these beliefs spring role perceptions, behavior patterns, codes of ethics and the institutionalized manner in which economic activities are performed."[10] Even the way a culture engages in business can reflect its worldview. If a culture values "out-of-awareness" processes and intuitive problem solving, it might reach conclusions through processes much different from a culture that values the scientific method. Nisbett summarizes these differences:

> Thus, to the Asian, the world is a complex place, composed of continuous substances, understandable in terms of the whole rather than in terms of the parts, and subject more to collective than to personal control. To the Westerner, the world is a relatively simple place, composed of discrete objects that can be understood without undue attention to context, and highly subject to personal control. Very different worlds indeed.[11]

CONSTRUCTS OF WORLDVIEWS

We have already mentioned that worldview is at the heart of every culture, is transmitted from generation to generation, is composed of many elements, and takes an assortment of forms. Most of these forms can be classified into three categories: (1) atheism, (2) spirituality, and (3) long-established religious traditions. These orientations obviously intersect on a number of important questions. And in many instances, individuals select a portion of all three orientations to construct their view of reality. However, these three constructs have dissimilar answers for inquiries concerning life, death, human nature, and ways of knowing. Let us briefly introduce these three worldviews in general terms before explaining religious traditions in more detail.

REMEMBER THIS

Most of the forms and constructs of worldviews can be classified into three categories: (1) atheism (2) spirituality, and (3) long-established religious traditions.

ATHEISM AS A WORLDVIEW

The idea of atheism, often referred to as a worldview in which "man is the measure," has been a part of the human experience for as long as people have been concerned with questions about the meaning of life and explanations about death. As early as circa 400 BCE, Plato talked about the portion of humankind that did not believe in the existence of any of the gods. Hence, this worldview has a history and "traces its roots from ancient China, classical Greece and Rome, through the Renaissance and the Enlightenment, to the scientific revolution of the modern world."[12] Part of the "modern world" emphasis comes from the theories and personal writings of Charles Darwin.[13] The past two decades have witnessed a new interest in atheism that has been accompanied by an increase in the number of people who subscribe to this worldview. There are numerous surveys that reflect this new popularity. The Pew Forum on Religion and Public Life estimates that approximately 4 percent of the population of the United States holds views associated with atheism.[14] There are now even "Atheist Mega-Churches" that have responded to this recent interest in atheism.[15] Worldwide interest in atheism is even more apparent. Most reports suggest that atheists account for 13 to 16 percent of the world's population.[16] What all these people have in common is a worldview that claims a denial of the existence of God.

There are many definitions and approaches associated with the concept of *atheism*. This should not be surprising given that there are approximately 41,000 different Christian denominations. The major atheist organization actually states on its home page, "atheists come in a variety of shapes, colors, beliefs, convictions, and backgrounds."[17] Many people who hold the atheistic worldview often feel comfortable describing themselves as *agnostics, human secularists,* or *deists*. Although there are some minor shades of differences, there are some core beliefs that explain what these adherents have in common. The most fundamental of these beliefs is that there is a social order and explanation of life that can exist *without* God or organized religion. Not only do atheists deny the existence of God, but they also hold a number of other fundamental beliefs. Let us look at some of these.

Rejection of God

Atheism begins with the premise that religion—and the various deities and Gods associated with it—are a projection of humankind's own aspirations and yearnings. Hitchens, a leading spokesperson for atheism, asserts, "Religion is man-made. Even the men who made it cannot agree on what their prophets, or redeemers, or gurus actually said or did."[18] Because of this attitude, atheists hold that the solution to most problems is not God but rather "extending the scientific method of rational inquiry into all aspects of life."[19] An extension of this position leads to a firm belief in evolution. In fact, most atheists consider that the universe, including the humans within the universe, functions according to the laws of nature. Atheists believe that these are laws that can be observed, tested, and verified.

Role of the Individual

Because atheists begin with a dismissal of God in their worldview, they have a strong belief in the individual. Their teachings and literature stress self-reliance. As Halverson notes, "Each individual determines his or her own purpose in life."[20] While there is also a belief in helping others, that assistance centers on people helping people, not an outside authority.

A Set of Ethical Standards

Like all worldviews, atheism espouses a set of ethical standards. Though many people who rebuff the atheistic worldview charge that atheists are void of ethics, in actuality the ethical standards that atheists propose can be found in nearly all religious traditions. For example, United States Atheists, in an article titled "An Atheist's World View: 15 Principles of Atheism," maintain that atheists cannot avoid responsibility for their actions, should encourage a respect for nature and humanity, and should advance social action that creates a better world.[21]

The Finality of Death

As a secular humanist, the physicist Stephen Hawking's description of death in many ways summarizes the secularist's concept of death when he writes of heaven as a "fairy tale for people who are afraid of the dark." For those who hold this view, death is the end of this life, and there is no other life after this one. Cornish repeats this essential aspect of atheism when he writes, "The simple fact is that all life-forms end in death and the elements of which they are composed return to the air and earth to be taken up and recycled into some new organism."[22] Because of this interpretation of dying, atheists believe that death is not a spiritual matter but rather an undeniable biological truth about our existence. When there are funerals, they are kept very simple. They are intended to offer support to the family by recalling the accomplishments of the deceased.

SPIRITUALITY AS A WORLDVIEW

While the notion of spirituality has been discussed for thousands of years, recently, under the rubric "New Age," this worldview has gained a large following, especially in the United States. As is the case with all worldviews, spirituality has produced different strands. First, because of its popular culture exposure, the concept and the word have become fashionable and chic. In general, spirituality is regarded as a system that stresses that a person does not need formal religion to live a life of faith. This particular approach to spiritualism also draws from a variety of sources. For example, this form of spiritualism "has touches of various Asian and indigenous religions. This is an eclectic group of beliefs and practices: crystal healing, channeling spirits, shamanism, venerations of the Earth, and ritual techniques."[23]

A different and more formalized view of spirituality also exists. It is "concerned with the scared, as distinguished from ordinary reality, but is often individual rather than collective and does not require a distinctive format or traditional organization."[24] It is this idea of having a personalized worldview that appeals to the American value of individualism. The notion of a "religion" wherein people can turn to themselves to discover "inner peace" combines this value of individualism with the value of free choice. Carl Jung, the famous Swiss psychiatrist and popular figure among contemporary spiritualists, expressed this view when he remarked somewhat poetically, "Your vision will become clear only when you look into your heart. Who looks outside, dreams. Who looks inside, awakens." Underscoring the distinction between religion and personal spirituality is the idea of emphasis on the individual versus the institution:

Religion is typically experienced within a social institution with commonly shared traditions, sacred texts, beliefs, and worship practices. Religious institutions usually have a governing structure with designated leaders. Spirituality, on the other hand, is part of each person that searches for purpose, meaning, worth, and wonder, often in quest of an ultimate value or the holy.[25]

From the few lines above, you can observe that spirituality is a personal search for finding the answers to life's essential questions. Followers of this worldview adhere to some of the following guidelines:[26]

- Accept the idea that spirituality is divine and without rules.
- Self-discovery is important. Think not only about what you are but also about what you choose to be.
- Learn to value silence, solitude, and quiet meditation. These will give you inner peace.
- Practice mindfulness. Learn to live in the moment and observe your environment and how you behave when you are in that environment.
- Engage is creative self-expression. Connect yourself to activities such as yoga, dance, music, and other such activities.
- Seek simplicity in your lifestyle.
- Remember that spirituality is individuality.
- Spirituality transcends all and makes you true to yourself.

This brief analysis of spirituality should demonstrate that it contains a number of notions that are general and difficult to pin down, which for some people is part of its appeal. However, you should notice that spirituality has many of the same goals found in organized religions (inner peace, a link with nature, and a search for meaning in life, among others). The major difference is that spirituality uses some atypical methods of achieving those goals and places emphasis on the individual being part of the "discovery process."

> **REMEMBER THIS**
>
> *One of the main functions of religion is to assist people with living their lives and preparing for the end of that life.*

RELIGION AS A WORLDVIEW

Some Africans say, "There is no distinction between religion and the rest of life. All of life is religious." Although that might be an overstatement, it is true that as a worldview religion is an important part of life for billions of people. Roberts makes the connections among worldview, religion, and culture clear: "A distinguishing characteristic of religion is that it provides a worldview."[27]

Perhaps at this point in the chapter, you may have asked yourself, "Why am I studying religions in a course dealing with intercultural communication?" Such a query merits an answer, and our reply comes in three parts. First, religion, as just noted, supplies the worldview for billions of people throughout the world. Second, religion, perception, and behavior are inextricably intertwined. Finally, never in the history of civilization has the behavioral dimension of religion been so widespread, relevant, and volatile. Let us explain those three ideas in more detail before we examine the world's six major religious traditions.

Recall that Chapter 3 discussed the importance of a culture's social institutions. Religion, as pointed out, is one of those institutions that assist people with living life and preparing for death. Kimball expands on this important point when he writes, "For the vast majority of people worldwide, their religious tradition—like family, tribe, or nation—anchors them in the world. Religious traditions provide structure, discipline, and social participation in a community."[28] Friedman uses the image of an olive tree and its deep and stable roots in the title of his book *The Lexus and the Olive Tree* to underscore the powerful and enduring quality of religion to a collection of people.[29] Witness the importance of religion's collective force in the word "religion" itself. "The word *religion* comes from the Latin word *religare*, which means 'to tie.'"[30] The obvious implication is that religion ties people to a set of prescribed beliefs.

An intriguing aspect of religion is that it has attempted to explain the workings of the world—and in some cases the next world—for thousands of years. Whether through institutions such as the Catholic Church, spiritual and social leaders like Buddha and Confucius, or the teachings of the Bible, Vedas, Koran, Torah, and I Ching, people have always had a need to look outside themselves and seek help when addressing questions about mortality, immortality, and the origins of the universe. Religion also takes on the task of trying to explain what are often called the cosmic and complex issues all people must deal with. Fisher and Luyster allude to some of those issues when they write, "All religions help to uncover meaningfulness in the midst of the mundane. They do so by exploring the transpersonal dimensions of life– the eternal and infinite."[31]

What is being stated in all of our examples is that religion offers its followers a worldview that provides a set of principles and beliefs about the nature of life and death, the creation of the universe, the connection of individuals and groups to one another, and the relationship of humankind to the earth. All of these give credence

A major characteristic of religion as a worldview is that it provides people with a belief in the existence of a reality greater than themselves.

to the basic theme of this chapter: *The deep structure of culture deals with issues that matter most to people.* Whether they are wondering about the first cause of all things or the reason for natural occurrences, such as comets, floods, lightning, thunder, drought, famine, or disease, many people rely on religious explanations. Smith eloquently expresses the steadfast importance of religion to the psychological welfare of most people:

> When religion jumps to life it displays a startling quality. It takes over. All else, while not silenced, becomes subdued and thrown into a supporting role.... It calls the soul to the highest adventure it can undertake, a proposed journey across the jungles, peaks, and deserts of the human spirit.[32]

RELIGION AND HUMAN BEHAVIOR

Religion not only deals with the sacred and the spiritual but also helps its adherents manage worldly issues related to human conduct by serving as a mechanism of social control. This role is fulfilled by establishing notions of right and wrong, transferring part of the burden of decision making from individuals to supernatural powers. Tischler explains the social dimension of religion: "Religion responds to the basic human need to understand the purpose of life. This means creating a worldview that can have social, political, and economic consequences."[33] History tells us that religion has been a major source of cultural values, beliefs, and attitudes for as long as humans have used religion as a way of understanding how to function among other people. Haviland and associates point out, "a religion held in common by a group of people reinforces community values and provides moral guidelines for personal contact."[34] From this statement, it should be clear that for the religious individual, theology and everyday experiences cannot be separated.

Each religion offers its adherents structure, a common purpose, and membership in a group made up of people who share beliefs.

M. Freeman/PhotoLink/Getty Images

RELIGION IN THE TWENTY-FIRST CENTURY

We ended the last section by noting the tandem relationship between religious activity and many of the dimensions of culture. This means that religion is part of a larger system. In this way, it is attached to countries' economic, healthcare, political, and educational organizations. As these four organizations and the entire world become more complex, religion is undergoing a modern-day reassessment. From globalization to the rise of religious extremism to domestic changes in demographics to debates between secularists and Evangelical Christians, the world is confronted with an excess of events that are having a profound effect on religion in this century. It seems that "peoples of religion are no longer long distances from each other. Hindus, Buddhists, Muslims, and Christians are highly mobile populations that have crossed geographical and cultural boundaries to meet and live among each other."[35]

Globalization and Religion

As you learned in previous chapters, globalization has both economic and social consequences. The advanced technologies and sophisticated communication systems at the heart of globalization have created unparalleled changes for people throughout the world. "In much the same way that markets have been globalizing over the past decade, the revolution in information and communication has had far-reaching effects on the various ecclesiastical religions of the world."[36] Newman speaks to some of the changes when he points out that "this globalization of religion is creating a crisis for religious communities. Exposure to competing worldviews challenges traditional beliefs."[37]

The idea that globalization should have effects on religion should not be surprising, as globalization, combined with the forces of modern technology, has made human contact inevitable. In the past, religions have usually consisted of the beliefs, values, and practices of a particular religious community. However, now those religious communities are confronted with messages being sent via new technologies as well as the challenges created by major shifts in international migration patterns. Because of these two forces, religious institutions have had to adapt to a series of novel and often disturbing images and ideas. According to Roberts, one of the most troubling new concepts faced by religion today is secularism. He notes, "Globalization impacts religion in a number of ways. The emerging global culture is a highly secularized one stressing a rational-utilitarian outlook on the world and calling for institutional differentiation of religion from other spheres."[38] What is worrisome to many religious leaders is that these "other spheres" pull their adherents away from well-established doctrines and values.

Violence and Religion

For thousands of years violence in the name of religion has been part of the record of nearly every culture. As Schmidt and his colleagues remind us, "Religious experiences are not always positive. Sometimes religiously 'sanctioned' behavior seems more pathological and diseased than ecstatic and liberating."[39] Religious leaders have always had to explain the dichotomy between preaching about peace while engaging in bloody and brutal wars. At the core of this violence is the reality that all religions establish boundaries for their adherents. Each of these boundaries, be they territorial (sacred land) or symbolic (beliefs, values, identity), are important to the religion. When there is a perceived threat to these boundaries, real or imaginary, most religions sense they are under attack. This is one reason people will murder others and even sacrifice their own lives in the name of religion. We have observed this form of violent behavior for centuries. Whether it be the Crusades, the Inquisition, the Reformation, the Holocaust, the events in Rwanda and Bosnia, what happened on 9/11/2001, or China's treatment of Buddhists in Tibet, violent behavior has plagued much of organized religion since its inception. And recent events tell us that not much has changed in this "modern era." In fact, in the first fifteen years of this century we have seen an unprecedented wave of violence among people of various religious groups. The bloodshed in the Philippines, Nigeria, Egypt, Bangladesh, Iraq, and Myanmar continues at an alarming rate. When you add to these the reports of the worldwide increase in anti-Semitism,[40] you can understand why people perceive a connection between globalization, religion, and aggression. You should also be able to appreciate the words of Paden: "The study of religion ... prepares us to encounter not only other centers and calendars, and numerous versions of the sacred and profane, but also to decipher and appreciate different modes of language and behavior. Toward that end, knowledge about others plays its indispensable role."[41] That knowledge about the "other" will help reduce the level of religious violence we have witnessed all over the world. As Van Voorst tells us, "Religious violence committed by groups must be understood in its cultural context—not to excuse it, but to understand it."[42] By introducing the major worldviews of six of the most important religious traditions we hope to contribute to that understanding.

SELECTING RELIGIOUS TRADITIONS FOR STUDY

It is obvious that we must omit numerous worldviews and religions from our analysis. From animism to Zoroastrianism, from Rastafarianism to Scientology, there is no shortage of religions. Many of these religions have within their "tent" thousands of affiliations. For example, as previously noted, there are approximately 41,000 different Christian denominations.[43] There are also people who follow New Age philosophies as a worldview or who practice Wicca (a modern pagan tradition). Turning to Asia, we did not include Sikhism, Taoism, Baha'i, or Shintoism. We also omitted primal religions practiced in parts of Africa, Australia, and the Pacific Islands as well as in the American Indian cultures of North and South America. In short, with thousands of religions, cults, movements, philosophies, and worldviews to choose from, how can we decide which orientations to examine? Drawing on the research of religious scholars, we have decided to examine Christianity, Judaism, Islam, Hinduism, Buddhism, and Confucianism. And though we grant the importance of other religious traditions and worldviews, our decision was based on three widely accepted criteria—*numbers*, *diffusion*, and *relevance*.

First, while statistics of the world's religions are only approximations, most studies reveal that, worldwide, Christianity and Islam have over a billion adherents each, and Hinduism is rapidly approaching that number.[44] Combined, these three religious traditions represent about 66 percent of the world's population. Second, by including diffusion as a criterion, we are referring to the notion of dispersion of a religion throughout the world. For example, while the Jewish population is numerically small

Courtesy of Robert Fonseca

Religion offers security to a collection of people since it helps clarify the baffling questions that everyone must face during their lifetime.

(approximately 14 million—less than 0.22 percent worldwide[45]), Jews can be found in nearly every country in the world. Because of thousands of years of persecution and a long history of migrating, only one-third of all Jews live in Israel. Propelled by missionary zeal, Christianity and Islam are also scattered throughout the world. In fact, while many Africans still follow traditional religions, many of them, because of colonization and missionaries, are either Christians or Muslims.

Finally, the six traditional religions are worthy of serious study because they are as influential and relevant today as they were thousands of years ago. We find guidance in the words of the Buddha and advice for daily living found in Confucianism being utilized by people throughout the world. As Carmody and Carmody note, "When we speak of the great religions we mean the traditions that have lasted for centuries, shaped hundreds of millions of people, and gained respect for their depth and breadth."[46] Because of this respect and longevity, these "are the faiths that every citizen should be acquainted with, simply because hundreds of millions of people live by them."[47] The remainder of this chapter seeks to introduce you to them so that you can understand how members of these religious traditions might perceive and participate in this world.

COMMON ELEMENTS OF RELIGION

It should not be surprising that similar features characterize all of the world's religions, as they all have the same major goal—to make living life more meaningful and death more comprehensible. We will now look at some of these common features before turning to a discussion of some differences that tend to distinguish one tradition from another.

SPECULATION

Most people, from the moment of their birth to the time of their death, face many of the same challenges concerning the uncertainties of life. It is human nature to speculate about some of the mysteries of life that seem difficult to comprehend and often out of our control. To deal with these questions, people have, for centuries, turned to religion. As Ferraro and Andreatta note, "Religion is psychologically comforting because it helps us explain the unexplainable. Every society must deal with imponderable questions that have no definitive logical answers."[48] What religion does is provide a design for those parts of the world that people do not comprehend and thus lessens their feelings of bewilderment. For example, members of each religion find comfort in creation stories that reveal how the world began. In addition, they receive answers to questions about heaven and hell, why they are here, why there is evil, what the nature of the soul is, and why there is suffering. In the course of answering these questions, religions provide their members a sanctuary and a sense of security.

SACRED WRITINGS

At the heart of each of the world's religious traditions lies a body of sacred wisdom— wisdom that must be transmitted from generation to generation. Van Voorst speaks to the importance of these sacred writings, noting,

> The major living religions of the world have all expressed their teachings and practices in writings. Over the course of time some of these writings gained unique standing in their traditions and scriptures. As scriptures, they continue to influence the course of their religions. To read the scriptures of the world, therefore, is to encounter world religions in a direct and meaningful way.[49]

These sacred writings become a repository for a religion's essential principles and teachings. It is important to notice that the word "sacred" is selected when describing these writings. Matthews clearly identifies why that word is used: "Each religion believes its sacred writings have divine or spirit-inspired origin. They were either written or spoken by God, written by divinely guided humans, or spoken by teachers of deep spiritual insight."[50] You will notice that in the last sentence, Matthews is alluding to the variety of forms these scriptures can take. Those who follow Judaism, Christianity, and Islam discover their faith by reading and listening to historical narratives drawn from these scriptures that are usually associated with individuals. These individuals are authority figures who provide guidance and instruction. For Jews, these figures are Abraham and Moses, who speak through the Old Testament. They also find wisdom in the Tanach and Talmud. For Christians, the figure is Jesus, the Son of God. For them, the "book" in the Bible. For the Muslim faith, the figure is a supreme all-knowing God, called Allah, who used Muhammad as a conduit to deliver his message. The sacred book, written in classical Arabic, for Muslims is the Holy Qur'an (in English, usually written as Koran).

Several sacred texts are philosophical in nature and even offer specific directions on how to perform numerous rites and ceremonies. The Hindu Upanishads is an example of this genre of sacred writings. Another text with a philosophical orientation is the Confucian *Analects*. In addition to offering more moral philosophy, the *Analects* offer specific advice as to how people should treat and react to one another.

In the case of Buddhism, there is not a universal scripture written down by Buddha, but the Pali Canon is based on oral tradition and contains the teachings of Buddha.

RELIGIOUS RITUALS

We begin our discussion of religious rituals by turning to one of the "authorities" we have just mentioned—Confucius. In *Analects* 8.2, Confucius notes the value of ritual when he says, "Without ritual, courtesy is tiresome; without ritual, prudence is timid; without ritual, bravery is quarrelsome; without ritual, frankness is hurtful."[51] Rituals are practiced by all religions. Smart offers an excellent restatement of this idea writing:

> Most place a heavy emphasis on ritual. The Catholic is enjoined to attend Mass weekly. The Muslim is told to pray five times daily, according to a set formula. The Hindu attends temple rituals frequently. The Theravada Buddhist will often make a trip to the temple to

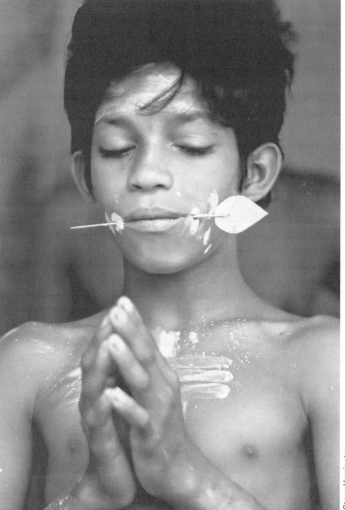

Rituals are repetitive, prescribed, ceremonial actions that allow members of a particular faith to reaffirm important beliefs and, thereby, feel spiritually connected to their religion.

© Steve Harrington

pay his or her respects to Buddha. The Protestant typically has a worship service with a sermon as a vital part of their ritual.[52]

In their strictest form, "Rituals are actions repeated in regular and predictable ways, which create order in the otherwise random process of time."[53] By engaging in rituals, members not only recall and reaffirm important beliefs but also feel spiritually connected to their religion, develop a sense of identity by increasing social bonds with those who share their rituals, and sense that their life has meaning and structure. Rituals, like so many aspects of culture, are not instinctive, so in order to endure, they must be passed from one generation to the next.

The most common of all rituals are rites of passage that mark key stages in the human cycle of life. "Rites of passage are social occasions marking the transition of members of the group from one important life stage to the next. Birth, puberty, marriage, and death are transition points that are important in many different cultures."[54] There are thousands of rituals dealing with the sacred that bring families and the religious community together at the same time they teach important lessons. There are rituals dealing with space (Muslims turning toward Mecca when they pray) and others that call attention to important events (Christian baptisms, Jews marking the importance of Passover, the Hindu young boy engaging in the Upanayanam ceremonial rite of entering manhood).

Rituals can be indirect as well as direct. A good example of an indirect ritual is the Japanese tea ceremony. At first glance, it would appear that the tea ceremony is simply the preparation and drinking of tea, but the importance of the ritual to those who engage in that activity is far greater:

Every detailed act, every move and position, embodies humility, restraint, and awareness. This framing of ordinary action in order to reveal some deeper significance—in this example the values are related to the Zen Buddhist idea of immanence of the absolute in the ordinary—is a common element of ritual behavior.[55]

CONSIDER THIS

All religious traditions examine the topic of ethics and present their members with very specific advice on how to live in an ethical manner. Why do you believe that ethics and religion are linked?

ETHICS

You will recall that the main purpose of this section of the book is to demonstrate that there are many similarities in how the major worldviews approach religious practices and theology. The study of ethics is yet another example of how all these religions include proper behavior as part of their overall "message" to their adherents. Not only do they all examine the topic of ethics, but the guidelines they set forth also have a number of principles in common. In general, they are all admonishing their members to develop the ability to distinguish right from wrong. The admonitions regarding correct behavior are so much alike that Smith notes that they "pretty much tell a cross-cultural story."[56] From warnings to avoid murder, thieving, lying, and adultery to stressing the virtues of "humility, charity, and veracity,"[57] a similar basic core of moral guidelines is found in all cultures. According to Coogan, what they seek to accomplish by the formation of ethical principles is to "enable their adherents to achieve the ultimate objective of the tradition—the attainment of salvation, redemption, enlightenment, and the 'liberation of the soul.'"[58] Because of the importance of ethical behavior to human interaction, we will look at ethics throughout this chapter as applied by the specific denominations.

Before we begin our discussion of the great religions of the world, we urge you to keep a few points in mind. First, remember that religion is but one kind of worldview, and even a secular person who says, "There is no God," has likely sought answers to the large questions about the nature of truth, how the world operates, life, death, suffering, and ethical relationships.

Second, "religion pervades many spheres that others might call secular and it cannot easily be separated from them."[59] It is often difficult to draw a line between secularism and a subtle manifestation of religion. What one person might call "religion" or "worldview" another person might call "philosophy." For example, when a group of people prefers intuitive wisdom to "scientific facts" as a means of discovering reality, they may do so without invoking the principles of Buddhism or Hinduism. For our purposes, labeling is not nearly as important as the notion that a culture's heritage includes ways of dealing with timeless and fundamental questions.

Finally, it is not our intent to offer a course on world religion. Therefore, we have omitted much of the theology and doctrine of the world's great religions and instead concentrated on the ways religion influences perception and communication.

CONSIDER THIS

Why do most religious traditions have so much in common?

CHRISTIANITY

We start with Christianity, a faith that took its name from Jesus Christ, who with a small band of disciples traveled throughout the Holy Land preaching, teaching, and healing the sick. Today, with over two billion adherents (one-third of the world's population), it is the largest of all the traditions and has seen its ideology spread throughout the world. For example, there were 10 million Christians in Africa in 1990—now there are over 365 million. That same explosion in growth can be seen in South America, Asia, and even China. The diversity of people who are Christians produces a multiplicity of denominations. As mentioned earlier, some estimate that there are 41,000 different Christian denominations. However, Christianity has historically been composed of three major branches: the Roman Catholic Church, under the guidance of the papacy in Rome; the Eastern Orthodox churches, with members concentrated in Eastern Europe, Russia, Ukraine, the Balkans, and Central Asia; and Protestantism, which embodies a host of denominations, such as Baptists, Presbyterians, Methodists, Lutherans, and Episcopalians. Although each of these branches and their numerous subsets contain some unique features, they all share many of the same rituals, beliefs, traditions, characteristics, and tenets. In fact, one of the strengths of Christianity throughout the centuries has been its ability to maintain its basic core while being adaptive, varied, and diverse. As Schmidt and his associates point out, "For all their disagreements, however, Christians are united in the belief about the importance of the person and role of Jesus Christ. In every age and in every setting where Christianity is found, there stands at the center a profound and enduring commitment to the person of Jesus Christ."[60]

CORE ASSUMPTIONS

In spite of the assortment and variety of Christian denominations, this tradition has a basic foundation of beliefs that offers its followers a guideline for understanding life and death. Three of the most common guidelines can be found in a few basic tenets and ideologies. Hale expands on these in the following:

> Essentially, Christianity is a monotheistic tradition centered on faith in God (the eternal creator who transcends creation and yet is active in the world) and in Jesus Christ as the savior and redeemer of humankind. Christianity holds that God became incarnate—fully human— as Jesus of Nazareth. Christians believe that Jesus died on a cross and was resurrected, physically rising from the dead. The belief in the Trinity, the sacred mystery of Father, Son, and Holy Spirit as one, triune ("three-in-one") God is central to the Christian tradition.[61]

A number of important precepts emerge from Hale's summary.

- There is a single God who created the universe and also "gave the world" his only son, Jesus Christ. Part of this "giving" involves Jesus giving his life on the Cross (the Crucifixion).
- Christianity is a total worldview that includes both the religious and the secular dimensions of life. Part of this unification of the ways of life is drawn from the belief that Jesus lived among the people and suffered; hence, he understands human pain, problems, and enticements.
- Christians believe that humans are created in God's image and have a responsibility to God.[62]
- The concept of "atonement" is a crucial component of Christian theology. "It is the belief that the things that Jesus did during his lifetime in healing people and restoring them to God, no matter how great their sins may have been, is now done for everyone who has the faith that it can be so."[63]
- The Christian God is personal in that he is not only a God of energy and power but also a personal God.

CULTURAL EXPRESSIONS OF CHRISTIANITY

An important question is how these and other tenets of Christianity are reflected in daily life. Although there are thousands of directives that Jesus and his apostles carried to the world, we have selected a few of those that not only have shaped the Christian tradition but also apply to the study of intercultural communication.

Christianity and Community

In the introduction to this section we pointed out that community was an essential component of Christianity. The link between the community and Christianity has roots that go back to the inception of the religion. For example, from the beginning of his practice, Jesus gathered others to share in his ministry. These relationships were "not a nebulous affiliation, but a concrete group of people that entered into a relationship with Jesus and with other people."[64] The gatherings of these people came to be known as "communion" and "fellowship." These important occasions within the community contributed to feelings of interdependence and group cohesion. This notion of community as part of Christianity goes back to the apostles, who used these communities to take care of the poor (2 Cor. 8:24), provide hospitality to travelers (Rom. 16:2), and generally comfort one another. In each of the instances, the focus was on God's people praying together. Even at the Last Supper, Jesus chose to be with others instead of spending his last night alone. There is not a single reference about that occasion that points to a private prayer session. Schmidt and his colleagues summarize this key component of Christianity with this single sentence: "In essence, all worship is praying with others."[65]

Today, for Christians, the church remains a key element in how community is revealed. Not only is it a "house of worship" and a place of great reverence, but it is also a place where people gather in groups and share a common identity. For our purposes, it is the social dimension of Christianity that offers insight into the communication aspects of this tradition. Visit any Christian church, and you can observe the strong influence of cooperative spirit in how churches have special services for young children, sanctuaries for baptisms, meeting halls, and countless social gatherings.

That sense of community and organized worship has contributed to the social dimension found in Western cultures. Americans are social creatures and belong to numerous clubs, committees, and organizations. The French historian Alexis de Tocqueville pointed out over two hundred years ago that Americans had a large series of networks and associations that went well beyond their family unit.

Christianity and Individualism

At the same time that Christianity encourages community, it also stresses the uniqueness of each individual. The individual is perhaps important because each person is "God's creation." Plus, they can have a one-on-one relationship with God. Most scholars maintain that Christianity and Judaism were the first religions that placed "greater emphasis on the autonomy and responsibility of the self."[66] In short, Christianity and Judaism are the religious traditions that "discovered the individual."[67] Before the arrival of these two religions, people were seen as members of tribes, communities, or families and behaved in ways that reflected the collective nature of their existence. Although family and community remained important, Christianity highlighted the significance of each person. Even the Bible carries examples of individualism. The Gospels are replete with scenes in which Jesus interacts with just one person at a time. It is clear that "Jesus emphasized the personal side of religion."[68] As Matthews points out, Jesus "was content to eat with tax collectors, talk with a prostitute in the home of a host, to defend a woman whom a crowd accused of adultery, to talk with a Samaritan woman at a public well."[69]

You also can see the significance of the individual in that part of Christian theology that begins with the assumption that the world is real and meaningful because God created it. An extension of that idea is that human beings are significant because God created them in his image. In a culture that values the individual, Christianity is an especially appealing religion, as each person can have a one-to-one bond with God.

Christianity and "Doing"

Western culture, as will be discussed in detail in Chapter 6, is one that encourages activity and action. Some of the roots of this philosophy can be traced to Christianity in general and more specifically to the manner in which Jesus lived his life. The story of Jesus is a vivid example of how Christians are told the story of a man who lived in this world. Peter, one of Jesus' disciples, once said of Jesus, "He went about doing good."[70] We call your attention to the word "doing," as that orientation is still part of the Christian tradition. As Schmidt and his coauthors note,

> There are things that Christians "do" that are motivated by their faith, therefore, they are "religious" acts of intention. Christianity has never seen its activity limited to the vertical (God-human) plane. It has always had a vigorous commitment to imitate the example of Christ being in the everyday world and being of service to everyday people, believers or otherwise.[71]

Christianity, as a statement of "doing," has also stressed hard work. The argument was that "material success was taken to be one clue that a person was among the elect and thus favored by God, which drove early Protestants to relentless work as a means of confirming (and demonstrating) their salvation."[72] Even today, hard work is commonly valued in the West. When meeting a person for the first time, you often hear the question "What do you do?" It is the "doing" that can be partially linked to Christianity.

Christianity and the Future

Throughout this book, we discuss cultural attitudes toward time. From those discussions and from your own observations, you can conclude that Americans are future oriented—they are concerned with what will happen next rather than what is happening in the present. We suggest that one of the reasons for this attitude might have some of its roots in Christianity, as one of the lessons of Christianity is that the future is important. For Christians, "no matter what happened in the past, it is the future that holds the greatest promise."[73] God forgives mistakes and offers repentance and incentives to move forward. Many Christians believe the phrase "Forgiveness is the miracle of a new beginning." Acts 3:19 instructs the individual regarding moving forward when it states, "Repent ye therefore, and be converted, that your sins may be blotted out, when the times of refreshing shall come from the presence of the Lord." This sort of theology allows the individual to value the future. Even the notion of a heaven accents the future. You can see that emphasis on the future in Romans 6:23: "For the wages of sin is death, but the gift of God is eternal life in Christ Jesus our Lord." In short, built into Christian ideology is a positive and optimistic outlook toward the future—a belief that *things will be better in the future.*

Christianity and Courage

One of the most enduring legacies of the Jesus story is the message of courage in the face of adversity. As Smith notes, "Through the pages of the Gospels Jesus emerges as a man of strength."[74] It appears that studying the life of Jesus reveals a man who would not be intimidated by his opponents and who repeatedly demonstrated strength, integrity, and daring in the face of overwhelming odds. Without fear, Jesus preached against what was established doctrine during his entire adult life. This made him not only a prophet but also a hero. France, writing about Jesus, points out, "He seemed to delight in reversing accepted standards, with his slogan: 'The first shall be last, and the last first.'"[75] You can conclude that his practice of mixing with ostracized groups (such as the unfortunate and prostitutes) was a brave and courageous act. These same two attributes represent powerful values in American culture.

Christianity and Ethics

Because the basic theme of this section concerns the ways religion is reflected in daily activity, it seems fitting that we turn our attention to the topic of ethics. More specifically, what does Christianity "teach" its adherents about the ethical treatment of other people?

The overriding approach to Christian ethics is clearly stated by Van Voorst:

> As an "ethical monotheism," the Christian religion is based on its view of God. God's self-revelation shows God to be both radically good and radically loving. Christians must worship God but also must live their entire lives according to God's will. Jesus affirmed that the main point of this obedience is to love God and to love one's neighbor. (Matt. 22:37–39)[76]

To carry out this important counsel from Jesus, Christians have always turned to the Ten Commandments and the Sermon on the Mount. Most Christians treat the Ten Commandments as "instructions" written by God, even though they also see them as part of the covenant of the Jews with God. Although everyone might be aware of the Ten Commandments, it might be useful to read them in the following abbreviated form and reflect for a moment on how the advice within each Commandment offers the reader an ethical compass on how to live one's life. The Ten Commandments of God are as follows:

1. Thou shalt have no other gods before me.

2. Thou shalt not make unto thee any graven image.

3. Thou shalt not take the name of the Lord thy God in vain.

4. Remember the Sabbath day to keep it holy.

5. Honor thy father and thy mother.

6. Thou shalt not kill.

7. Thou shalt not commit adultery.

8. Thou shalt not steal.

9. Thou shalt not bear false witness.

10. Thou shalt not covet.

Van Voorst asserts,

> The Sermon on the Mount is, in the three chapters of *Matthew* 5–7, the gospels' longest collection of the moral teaching of Jesus. It is largely a collection by the writer of *Matthew*, probably drawing on an early collection of Jesus' sayings, and it soon became the influential statement of ethics in the Christian faith.[77]

Perhaps the most famous of the teachings fall under the category of the Beatitudes or Blessings. These blessings offer insight into the ethical guidance Jesus offered his adherents:

Blessed are the poor in spirit, for theirs in the kingdom of heaven.

Blessed are those who mourn, for they will be comforted.

Blessed are the meek, for they will inherit the earth.

Blessed are those who hunger and thirst after righteousness, for they will be filled.

Blessed are the merciful, for they shall be shown mercy.

While death is a universal experience, every worldview and religious tradition has developed a way to mark the event with its own interpretation.

© Taylor Ingalls

Blessed are the pure in heart, for they will see God.

Blessed are the peacemakers, for they will be called the sons of God.

Blessed are those who are persecuted because of righteousness, for theirs is the kingdom of heaven.

These two core collections of Christian ethical standards clearly demonstrate that Jesus' message was the universal belief in the Golden Rule ("You shall love your neighbor as yourself") and a deep sense of compassion. As Matthews points out, "Giving money and goods needed by others has long been a part of Christian living."[78]

Christianity and Notions About Death

Even though death is a universal experience, every worldview and religious tradition has discovered a way to mark the event with its own interpretation. That is, regardless of the explanation advanced, religious and secular traditions attempt to enlighten their members about death. Explanations of death, regardless of the tradition, examine the following six questions: "What is the purpose of death? Does existence end at death? If not, what happens after death? Are we embodied in a similar form or in a different form? Is there a final judgment? And how are we to prepare for our own dying?"[79]

The Christian answers to these questions are not simple for two reasons. First, there is a great variety of Christian denominations. Second, interpretations of the Old and New Testaments often differ. However, regardless of the name of the Christian denomination or the teachings it follows, there is a theme about death that links them. All explanations begin with the clear admonition in Ecclesiastes 3:2, namely, that there is "a time to be born, and a time to die." From this scripture grows the foundation for the explanations about death and the afterlife. One of the central explanations is that the manner in which people lived their life is the most significant element in determining their "union with the Lord." As Jackson notes, "One cannot live wrong and die right."[80] Matthews summarizes this core belief as he writes, "Most Christians believe that those who have lived a righteous life will live happily in the presence of God in heaven; those who are wicked will endure hell."[81] Many turn to John 11:25–26 for the following words of guidance and inspiration: "I am the resurrection. If anyone believes in me, even though he dies, he will live, and whoever lives and believes in me will never die. Do you believe this?"[82] A similar passage is found in 1 Peter 1:3–4: "… God has something stored up for you in heaven, where it will never decay or be ruined or disappear." These words tell Christians that death is not something to be feared. In fact, death is often talked of in terms of a "reunion with loved ones." As noted, Christians strongly believe it to be a place where they go to be given the reward of eternal companionship with God. So important is the notion of heaven and eternal life that religious scholars have found the words "heaven" and "eternal life" mentioned over six hundred times in the New Testament.[83]

Because the idea of hell was a late arrival to Christianity (not introduced until the writings of Luke and Matthew), there are a number of versions and descriptions of what hell is and how one becomes a candidate for this "nightmare." In some of the early descriptions, details are scarce and not graphic. But other accounts of hell, especially those suggested by Matthew, are much more explicit and detailed. "Matthew argues, again and again, that Hell exists, is sheer torture, and is reserved for the damned who will be cast 'into the furnace of fire; where there will be wailing and gnashing of teeth.' "[84] Not only do portrayals of hell differ, but who goes to hell instead of heaven is also left to some mild speculation. In most accounts, hell is reserved for people who die without accepting Christ or who have "sinned" and not repented. Hell is most of all "the separation from the love of God."[85] There is yet another, more modern argument suggesting that a loving God would not be party to anything as cruel and sordid as hell, and therefore God needs to be trusted. Regardless of how heaven and hell are defined in various Christian traditions, one conclusion is obvious—Christian doctrine maintains that there is an afterlife, which, as we shall see later in the chapter, is not the case in all religious traditions.

CONSIDER THIS

What can you learn about a culture and its people by studying how their religion explains dying and an afterlife?

JUDAISM

There are fewer than fourteen million Jews worldwide, representing less than 0.22 percent of the world's population.[86] However, their interest in politics, literature, education, medicine, finance, and law have, for thousands of years, made them an influential group no matter where they have lived. As Prothero notes, "This tiny religion has wielded influence far out of proportion to its numbers. It started a monotheistic revolution that remade the Western world."[87]

Van Voorst develops this important point in more detail:

> Our seven-day week with its day of rest is an inheritance from Jewish scripture. The belief that there is only one God is a gift of these writings as well. That all people are equally human, that the human race is one family, and that each individual can fully realize the meaning of life regardless of social or economic class are ideas that have also come to the Western world from the Jewish scriptures.[88]

Not only have Jewish scriptures influenced numerous aspects of Western civilization, but, as Harrison points out, "With the possible exception of a brief period toward the end of the eighteenth century, Jews were the vanguard of intellectual, technological, and economic progress of the West."[89]

REMEMBER THIS

The covenant between God and the Jewish people is predicated on the notion that the Jews are God's chosen people, and this is a basic theme throughout Jewish history.

ORIGINS

Judaism was founded in approximately 1300 BCE, when twelve Israelite tribes came to Canaan from Mesopotamia. Later, many of them settled in Egypt, where they were held as slaves until they fled to Jerusalem in about 1200 BCE. One of the most significant events in the forming of this religion is the role played by the prophet Abraham. According to Jewish history, God chose Abraham to function as the "father" of the Jewish people, a people that God designated as his "chosen people." To be the recipients of this honor, Jews entered into a sacred *covenant* with God. "The covenant was repeatedly renewed. Unlike a contract, the covenant had no date of expiration."[90] Matlins and Magida offer an excellent summary of the covenant:

> Central to this covenant is the concept of being "chosen" as a people. For as Moses tells his people in the Bible: "The Lord has chosen you to be a people for His own possession, out of all the peoples that are on the face of the earth." (Deut. 12:2)[91]

In Jewish theology, this distinctive consideration was never meant to give special advantages to the Jews, only to increase their responsibilities and therefore their hardships.[92]

In the nearly 4,000 years of historical development, the people who practice the Jewish religion have exhibited not only a penchant for continuity but also a remarkable adaptability. Torstrick speaks of this persistent ability to adapt: "The Jewish faith developed over a 4,000-year period. Over that span of time, it has demonstrated a remarkable capacity to adapt and persevere, to absorb elements from the civilizations and cultures which it has come into contact with, but to also retain its own unique identity and heritage."[93]

CORE ASSUMPTIONS

The Jewish worldview is expressed through a number of basic principles:

• We have already mentioned two of the most important assumptions at the heart of Judaism: (1) the covenant between God and the Jewish people that is the basis for the idea behind Jews being God's chosen people and (2) the Ten Commandments, which represent not only the first direct communication between God and the Jewish people but also a set of philosophical and ethical precepts that are as relevant today as they were when they were first written on two stone tablets.

• Jews "believe in one universal and eternal God, the creator and sovereign of all that exists."[94] This creed is clear and brief. It is expressed in Deuteronomy 6:4: "Hear, O Israel: The Lord our God, the Lord is one."

• Humans are inherently pure and good and are given free will. However, they have to accept the consequences of their actions.

• Jews, wherever they are in the world, share a common bond, sense of identity, and responsibility to each other.

These core assumptions compose a belief system stressing the secular notion that places great emphasis on this life rather than an afterlife.

BRANCHES OF JUDAISM

Judaism, like the other major traditions, has experienced a variety of configurations and divisions since its inception. Although the core of the religion has remained the same since its beginning, Judaism has now branched into three main groups: *Orthodox, Reform*, and *Conservative* Judaism. These groups differ in that while most Christian denominations make distinctions based largely on faith and belief, the three Jewish branches "are more like associations, with classifications according to cultural and doctrinal formulas."[95] The American Jewish Committee estimates that 8 percent of the Jewish population in the United States is Orthodox, 28 percent Conservative, and 30 percent Reformed.[96] The Orthodox branch, the most traditional and the oldest of the three branches, seeks to preserve the traditional and historical roots of Judaism. It is the only branch of Judaism officially acknowledged in Israel. Orthodox Judaism retains as much as possible from the long-established religious teachings found in classical and ancient writings. Orthodox Jews maintain that writings should be passed from generation to generation and that each generation should adhere to the principles they teach. This means following dietary laws such as not eating shellfish or pork, not allowing men and women to sit together in synagogue, not working or driving on the Sabbath, and having men wear skullcaps (yarmulkes) and prayer shawls.[97]

Conservative Judaism is often thought of as the middle approach to Judaism, as it attempts to follow basic Jewish teaching and traditions while adapting to contemporary life. Conservative Judaism maintains many of the regulations, canons, rituals, and traditions of Orthodox Judaism as necessary to maintain Jewish distinctiveness and identity. However, some of the traditions reflect the culture in which the temple resides. For example, synagogues "can vary in their practices, following the democratic spirit in America on such matters as whether to use organ music in their worship services."[98] In addition, Conservative synagogues also permit women to fill the role of ordained rabbi.

Reform Judaism is the most pragmatic of the three approaches to Judaism. It began as an attempt in the late eighteenth century to modernize many of the long-established Jewish practices so that Jews worldwide could assimilate into non-Jewish communities without losing their Jewish identity.[99] Conducting prayer services in the local language, not requiring men to wear yarmulkes, the use of choirs and musical instruments, and allowing men and women to sit together are part of the Reform movement. Reformed congregations, like some Conservative temples, even allow ordained women rabbis.

Regardless of which branch of Judaism one follows, it is clear that the Jewish faith is unique in that it is both a culture and a religion. It is common, for example, to find nonreligious Jews who identify fully with the culture but not with the theology. In this sense, Judaism became more of a family and less a religion. In short, Judaism penetrates every aspect of human existence for Jews and provides a means of living in both the secular and the religious worlds.

CONSIDER THIS

Why do you think that people who follow the Jewish religious tradition have experienced such a high degree of repression, genocide, and discrimination during their long history?

CULTURAL EXPRESSIONS OF JUDAISM

As was the case with Christianity, the issue for students of intercultural communication is clear: How is Judaism reflected in the manner in which Jews perceive the world and interact with other people within that world? We now offer a few answers to this question.

Oppression and Persecution

One of the most enduring and horrific aspects of Jewish history—and one that continues to influence Jewish perceptions of non-Jews—has been the oppression, genocide, and persecution Jews have suffered. As Van Doren points out, "The history of Judaism and of the Jews is a long and complicated story, full of blood and tears."[100] As far back as 1500 BCE, the pharaoh of Egypt made an effort to kill all Jewish males. In 70 CE, "The Roman Army destroyed Jerusalem, killed over 1 million Jews, took about 100,000 into slavery and captivity, and scattered many from Palestine to other locations in the Roman Empire."[101] More hatred and massive killings of Jews occurred during the Spanish Inquisition beginning in 1478. In 1523, in an essay titled *Jews and Their Lies*, Martin Luther added to the hostility toward Jews when insisting that they convert to Christianity. Prager and Telushkin offer a summary of this long-standing persecution of Jews: "Only the Jews have had their homeland destroyed (twice), been dispersed wherever they have lived, survived the most systematic attempt in history (aside from that of the Gypsies) to destroy an entire people, and been expelled from nearly every nation among whom they have lived."[102]

While repression, genocide, and discrimination have punctuated Jewish history for thousands of years, it was the Holocaust, the mass killing of six million Jews (1.5 million of them children), and the destruction of 5,000 Jewish communities that emphasized to Jews that anti-Semitism follows them wherever they go. In just a few lines, Matthews captures the horrors Jews experienced during this period. "In camps such as Auschwitz, they were gassed, and their clothes, possessions, and even their body parts were salvaged for the Nazi war effort. Bodies were burned in crematoriums."[103]

Even today, when reflecting on the Holocaust, Jews are still troubled by two aspects of this hideous period in their history. First is the silence of the world leading up to the Holocaust and the lack of response once outsiders knew what was taking place. For example, while the Allies knew about the concentration camps, they did little to help those Jews trying to leave Germany. Moreover, in spite of most of the Western World knowing about the death camps, the international community failed to respond to the German atrocities against the Jews.

Second, Jews perceive the Holocaust as a natural outgrowth of centuries of anti-Semitism that still exists. They observe outbursts of this hostility in this century as they listen to the words of Iran's former president Ahmadinejad calling for Israel to be "wiped off the map." They read a series of reports about property desecration and violence against Jews in fourteen different countries and how in the United States there were 927 anti-Semitic incidents recorded in the last few years.[104] These experiences have created a world where many Jews have a difficult time trusting non-Jews. Yet, in spite of these suspicions and hardships,

> ... Jews are still essentially the same stubborn, dedicated people, now, and forever maybe,
> affirming the same three things. First, they are a people of the law as given in the holy

books of Moses. Second, they are the chosen people of God, having an eternal covenant with him. Third, they are a witness that God is and will be forevermore.[105]

Learning

The Jewish essayist and Nobel laureate Elie Wiesel quotes a Jewish saying: "Adam chose knowledge instead of immortality." There is even a Hebrew proverb: "Wisdom is better than jewels." These two maxims highlight the love of learning that has been a hallmark of the Jewish religion and culture since its beginning. For thousands of years, Jews have made the study of the Talmud (a holy book of over 5,000 pages) an important element of Jewish life.[106] The Jewish prayer book even speaks of "the love of learning" as one of three principles of faith.[107] Even the Jewish synagogue is often referred to as the "*shul.*" This word comes from Greek (and then Latin) *schola.* All of these examples simply underscore the importance of education to Jews. In fact, "As early as the first century, Jews had a system of compulsory education."[108]

Because of this cultural and religious legacy regarding learning, Jews have stressed education throughout their history. When the first Jews arrived in the United States, they immediately realized that education was the path to a good life for them and their children. Today, the Jewish population is one of the most well-educated groups in the United States. One-third of all Jews have advanced graduate degrees, and 58 percent have earned at least a bachelor's degree.[109] Relative to Jews' interest in education, Harrison notes that over the past 105 years, Jews have won 180 Nobel Prizes.[110]

Social Justice

Jews often refer to the words of the prophet Amos (5:24) when discussing their sense of social justice: "Let justice roll down like waters, and righteousness like an ever-flowing stream." This means to them that God wants justice to "flow" over each of them and everyone else in the world. Jews have always believed that they had a historic mandate to fight for social justice. An individual's responsibility and moral commitment to God and other people is even detailed in Jewish religious writings. Markham and Lohr point out, "The God of Israel taught through his prophets that worship of God without social justice is worthless."[111] You can detect this concern for justice in everything from ancient Jewish writings that saw the prophets admonishing kings for indifference to human rights to the active role Jews played during the civil rights movement of the 1960s to the large number of Jewish people involved in the American Civil Liberties Union. So deep-seated is this basic precept that Smith believes that much of Western civilization owes a debt to the early Jewish prophets for establishing the notion of justice as a major principle for the maintenance of "social order."[112]

Family and Community

As pointed out in Chapter 3, all societies value the family, but for Jews, the family is the locus of worship and devotion. As Schmidt and his associates point out, "The strong sense of familial ties transcends any one particular individual's needs."[113] This concern for family has deep biblical roots. Often when Jews summon their God, they speak of a Jewish family. In Jewish social life and tradition, the family constitutes perhaps the most closely-knit unit in any society. All members of the family—husband and wife, parents and children—are bound by mutual ties of responsibility.[114] In this strong pull of Jewish families, there are actually two interrelated families—the larger community of Jews and a person's immediate family. One of the ways Jews have dealt with centuries of hardship was to turn to both of these families for strength and courage. Most Jews have always felt a sense of connectedness with other Jews regardless of where they lived. Being referred to as the "Children of Israel" speaks to the fact that, as Jews, they believe "they are all the physical or spiritual descendants of the same family."[115] In this they share a bond with the entire Jewish community.

Each Jewish family, in addition to the larger Jewish community, plays a key role in the life of all Jews. A famous rabbi once said, "To educate the child without including the entire family is like attempting to heat a home with all the windows open." There is a strong belief among Jews that family is the carrier of religion and culture. On nearly every occasion, be it in the home or the synagogue, the family is an active participant in Jewish life. That life is linked to the larger community by a host of religious traditions and rituals. From circumcisions to Passover seders (ceremonial dinners) to bar or bat mitzvahs to marriage and death to the treatment of the elderly, the family and religion are strongly bound. Rosten summarizes this link: "For 4,000 years, the Jewish family has been the very core, mortar, and citadel of Judaism's faith and the central reason for the survival of the Jews as a distinct ethnic group. The Jewish home is a temple, according to Judaic law, custom, and tradition."[116]

Judaism and Ethics

Although we have already alluded to the history and importance of ethics to Jewish life when we looked at the topics of the Ten Commandments and social justice, the significance of the subject matter warrants further examination. Part of our justification can be found in the works of Markham and Lohr when they write, "There is a sense in which everything in Judaism is ethical. Ethics has to do with behavior, and the entire Torah is preoccupied with behavior."[117] The significance of this all-encompassing view of Jewish ethical behavior is that it applies to everyone. Matthews explains this deep-seated and universal concern regarding ethical behavior in the following:

> Judaism thinks in terms of a community chosen to be responsible to God. Membership in a community of chosen people, however, requires commitment to universal values. Judaism promotes care of humans, animals, and the environment among all people. Ethical behavior is directed not only to Jews but to all peoples. It attends to both its particular origin and its universal vision.[118]

This universal approach to ethics stems from the fact that at the heart of Jewish philosophy is that human beings are created in the image of God. This essential belief in the treatment of others is reinforced by biblical wisdom such as that contained in Exodus 23:9: "You shall not oppress a stranger, for you know the feeling of the stranger, having yourselves been strangers in the land of Egypt."

Jewish Notions About Death

One of the unique aspects of Judaism, at least as perceived by non-Jews, is that there are very few references to death or an afterlife in traditional Jewish writings. As Matthews points out, "Judaism has emphasized a good life on earth more than the joys of heaven."[119] Rabbi Jacobs writes, "The Jewish religion encourages neither a morbid preoccupation with death nor any refusal to acknowledge the fact of human mortality. Judaism teaches that life on earth is a divine gift to be cherished in itself."[120] This attitude is seen in the fact that "The *Torah*, the most important Jewish text, has no clear reference to afterlife at all."[121] Because of this lack of specific material in religious literature, Jews view death as a natural process. According to 2 Samuel 14:14, "We must all die; we are like water spilt on the ground, which cannot be gathered up again."

An important aspect of Jewish notions regarding death is the role of family, friends, and community. While the funeral takes place as soon as possible, the actual mourning practices are elongated, extensive, and marked by a great deal of ritual. The mourning, which usually lasts seven days, and the rituals that follow have two basic purposes: to honor the dead and to bring comfort to the family of the deceased. After the conclusion of the private rituals at the cemetery, most of the comforting takes place when a larger numbers of guests are invited to take part in a social gathering and to have refreshments and share stories about the deceased.

ISLAM

We begin our analysis of Islam with this assertion: For a host of reasons, a large percentage of non-Muslims do not fully understand the Islamic faith. Prothero reaffirms our assertion in the following:

> Most Europeans and North Americans have never met a Muslim, so for them, Islam begins in the imagination, more specifically in that corner of the imagination colonized by fear. They see Islam through a veil hung over their eyes centuries ago by Christian Crusaders intent on denouncing Islam as a religion prone to violence, its founder, Muhammad, as a man of the sword, and its holy book, the Quran, as a text of wrath.[122]

These generalized perceptions took on a new dimension on September 11, 2001. That new element was violence, as we observed how an undeclared war and terrorism could claim thousands of lives. And since 9/11, the vast majority of victims have been civilians.[123] This violence has been accompanied by a wave of hysteria and a blanket condemnation of the entire Islamic faith. We contend that such a sweeping denunciation of all Muslims is misguided on two counts. First, granted that there are some Muslims who perceive the West as evil and engage in violent acts, it is both disingenuous and naïve to assume that all those who follow the Islamic faith are terrorists and seek the complete annihilation of the West. It would be as if the entire world believed that the Christian church in West Virginia that uses rattlesnakes to perform miracles in its worship services represents all Christian churches. Second, the statistical and demographic impact of Islam throughout the world demands that we learn more about what Belt calls the "most misunderstood religion on earth."[124] Islam is the fastest growing of all religions, with approximately 1.6 billion followers scattered throughout the world. Muslims currently represent over 23 percent of the world's population, and their numbers are expected to increase to 26 percent of the world's projected population of 8.3 billion by 2030.[125] We used the word "scattered" as a way of pointing out that the largest share of Muslims live in places other than Arab lands. In fact, Muslims now form the majority in forty-nine countries and a significant minority in many others.[126]

Because of immigration and birthrates, a substantial portion of that percentage lives in the United States. In fact, with a projected growth rate of 67 percent, Islam will soon be the second most commonly practiced religion in the United States.[127] All these numbers imply that whether on the international level, in your neighborhood, or on college campuses, contact with Muslims has become a fact of life.

REMEMBER THIS

The fundamental declaration of Islam is that there is only one God.

ORIGINS

One of the major contentions of this book is that there are connections among culture, history, family, and religion. You can see this point reflected in the Islamic faith. As Sedgwick notes, "Just as the events of Jesus' life matter to a Christian, and just as the history of Israel matters to a Jew, so the events of early Islam matter to a Muslim."[128] So essential is history to the study of Islam that we dedicated an entire section to this topic in the next chapter. However, we need to briefly preview that history, from a religious perspective. Woodward provides a summary of the events that led to the creation of Islam:

> The Arabs were mostly polytheists, worshiping tribal deities. They had no sacred history linking them to one universal god, like other Middle Eastern peoples. They had no sacred text to live by, like the Bible; no sacred language, as Hebrew is to Jews and Sanskrit is to Hindus. Above all, they had no prophet sent to them by God, as Jews and Christians could boast.[129]

The need for a prophet to carry the message from God was resolved in 610 CE when Archangel Gabriel delivered to Muhammad a revelation from God. According to the stories of Muhammad, he was a person with a curious mind who would retreat into a cave near his home and engage in prayer and meditation. It was during one of these meditative periods that "the angel Gabriel appeared to him and told him that God had chosen him to be His messenger to all mankind."[130] This epic event was to cast Muhammad forever as the messenger of God. Muslims believe Allah (Arabic for God) had spoken to human beings many times in the past through other prophets. However, it was Muhammad who delivered the religious messages until his death in 623. These messages were to become recorded in the Koran. Not only did these messages reveal "words from God," but they also established the social order that was to become Islam. Muhammad believed that community and religion were one. Muhammad made the city-state of Medina the capital of Islam. This fusion of church and state was unique in Muhammad's time and remains one of the central characteristics of Islam today.

CORE ASSUMPTIONS

As is the case with all religious traditions, the major premises at the heart of the Islamic worldview are complex and numerous. We have selected six that deserve to be called "core assumptions," for they are the most basic articles of faith and help explain some of the perceptions and actions of people who call themselves Muslims.

One God

The central pronouncement of Islam is that there is only one God. As Matthews points out, "Islam is a firm monotheism. The Shahada recited by every Muslim emphasizes that there is no god but God. God is great; God is merciful."[131] In the Koran, the idea is stated as follows: "He is God, the One God to Whom the creatures turn for their needs. He begets not, nor was He begotten, and there is none like Him."[132] This core belief makes it clear that "there cannot be different or rival gods (for example, a god of the Jews, a god of the Christians, or the many gods of polytheists)."[133] So commanding is this premise that Muslims believe that the worst of all sins occurs when a person gives any share of Allah's special and matchless sovereignty to another body. Regardless of your personal reaction to the specific event, you can recall the protests and even violence that erupted in Pakistan, Afghanistan, Indonesia, and countless Arab countries following publication of cartoons satirizing the Prophet Muhammad. For the protestors, the cartoons diminished the spirituality and uniqueness of Muhammad.

The Koran

We have already referred to the Koran and noted that for Muslims it is the most sacred of all texts. Written in classical Arabic, over an approximately twenty-year period, Muslims believe that the Koran is the word of God. The story of the inception of the Koran is a simple one and one alluded to earlier. "Muslims believe that the angel Gabriel divinely revealed to Muhammad the Qur'an, the perfect copy of an eternal, heavenly book. The name Qur'an means 'recitation,' which reflects the main origin and use of this scripture, oral communication—first from Gabriel to Muhammad, then from Muhammad to his followers."[134] "The *Qur'an* is the basic authority for Islamic religious life, Islam's continuing guide during 1400 years of history and in many cultures."[135]

Unlike the Hebrew Bible and the Christian New Testament, the Koran has very little narrative. Its 114 chapters (often called *surahs*) contain the "wisdom" that Muhammad proclaimed during his life. This makes the Koran a manual on how to live, as it treats topics ranging from how to lead a holy life to proper conduct of social matters. The Koran offers counsel in both spiritual and practical topics because Islam does not distinguish between religious, social, and political life. Prothero expands on this idea: "Islam is a way of life as well as a religion. The Quran tells Muslims not just how to worship Allah, but also how to lend money, divide estates, enter into contracts, and punish criminals."[136] The eclectic nature of the Koran has led some observers to suggest that the Koran is the most memorized book in the world. "To this day there is great prestige in memorizing the text, and one who knows it in its entirety is called *hafiz* (literally 'guardian')."[137] The Koran is so venerated by Muslims that they would never write in the book or damage it in any way.

Submission

As we have mentioned, Islam is a religion based on the idea of one God. A direct corollary of that belief means each Muslim must submit to that God. The Koran (16:52) states, "GOD has proclaimed: 'Do not worship two gods; there is only one god. You shall reverence Me alone.'" Daniel and Mahdia offer a synopsis of this bond between one god and submitting to that God:

> *Islam* itself means "submission" to God and His will. The Koran emphasizes over and over the majesty of God, the beneficence that He has shown to human beings in particular, the acts of obedience and gratitude that creatures owe in return to their Creator, and the rewards that await the faithful at the end of time.[138]

Predestination

A belief in predestination is one of the basic principles of faith for anyone who seeks to practice the Islamic religion. As Van Voorst notes, "Predestination and fate play a large role in affairs both big and small in Muslim life. In Arab countries, perhaps the most frequently heard expression is *enshalla*, if God wills."[139] This simple phrase is not the only example of utterances that represent the Islamic theological concept that destiny unfolds according to God's will. Farah points out that "The sayings of the Prophet are replete with his insistence on God's role as pre-ordainer and determiner of all that takes place."[140] For example, the Koran (3:145) admonishes, "No soul can ever die except by Allah's leave and at a time appointed...." Another prominent lesson from the Koran (22:70): "Did you not know that God knows (all) that is in the heavens and the earth? It is (all) in a record. Surely that is easy for God." To the devoted Muslim, these expressions mean that God's will directs everything.

Judgment

Like Christians, Muslims accept as true the proposition that their present life is only preparation and trial for their next realm of existence. "Muslims believe in a Judgment Day on which each person will be sent by God to either paradise or to hell."[141] Hence, for Muslims, life is a kind of "impending judgment." The Koran states this crucial core concept in many different places and in a variety of ways. Here is but a small sampling:

- "And those who believe and do good deeds, they are the dwellers of Paradise, they dwell therein forever." (Koran 2:82)
- "And whoever seeks a religion other than Islam, it will not be accepted from him and he will be one of the losers in the Hereafter." (Koran 3:85)
- "Those who have disbelieved and died in disbelief, the earth full of gold would not be accepted from any of them if it were offered as a ransom. They have a painful punishment, and they will have no helpers." (Koran 3:91)

The message in all the above is clear: Have one's good deeds outweighed the bad deeds? As we will see later in the chapter, paradise awaits those who have followed God's wishes, while hell is the place where all others must spend eternity. The Koran makes it very clear that merely professing Islam is not enough. In fact, some of the cruelest of all punishments in the afterlife fall on those who were hypocrites during their lives.

Five Pillars of Islam

An important core assumption for Muslims deals with the *Five Pillars of Islam*. These five pillars disclose significant beliefs, values, and perceptions of how Muslims see both this world and the next. The pillars are thought of as a blueprint for worship. They are also a detailed set of instructions for social conduct and a way to include God in every aspect of daily life.

Because the pillars are translated into action, it is important for students of intercultural communication to be aware of the content of these precepts. The Five Pillars of Islam are (1) statement of belief, (2) prayer, (3) alms, (4) fasting, and (5) pilgrimage:

1. **Statement of Belief (Shahadah).** Repetition of the creed (*Shahadah*), often called the *Profession of Faith*, means uttering the following statement: "There is no God but Allah, and Muhammad is the Prophet of Allah." This short sentence is a declaration that affirms the notion that the person accepts the idea of one God and that Muhammad was that God's messenger to humanity. These words, in Arabic, are heard everywhere Muslims practice their faith. They are also the first words a child hears at birth and are repeated throughout life.[142] The next four pillars are conceived of as the "action" dimension of *Shahadah*, as they demand a series of specific behaviors.

2. **Prayer (*Salat*).** Prayer is a central ritual, performed five times a day—at dawn, at noon, in the mid-afternoon, after sunset, and before retiring. The prayer ritual is very structured, as described by Nydell:

> Prayer is regulated by ritual washing beforehand and a predetermined number of prostrations and recitations, depending on the time of day. The prayer ritual includes standing [facing toward Mecca], bowing, touching the forehead to the floor (which is covered with a prayer mat, rug, or other clean surface), sitting back, and holding the hands in cupped position, all while reciting sacred verses. Muslims may pray in a mosque, in their home or office, or in public places.[143]

Even when there is not a mosque available, Muslims will cease what they are doing and engage in *salat*. It is not uncommon to see taxi drivers in New York or people inside office buildings or at airports, putting down prayer rugs and following the directive of this second pillar.

3. **Almsgiving (*Zakat*).** The rationale for almsgiving is deeply rooted in the Islamic tradition and is predicated on the notion that everything is part of God's domain. This means that even wealth and material possessions are held by human beings only because of God's will. "Alms are related to the nature of God, who is merciful and requires mercy in his worshipers toward one another. Compassion toward weak and defenseless persons of the community is a reflection of the compassion of God."[144] Like so much of ritual, there are some deeper meanings embedded in the act of almsgiving. "Consideration for the needy is part of Islam's traditional emphasis on equality. In the mosque, all are equal; there are no preferred pews for the rich or influential—all kneel together."[145]

4. **Fasting (*Sawm*).** Fasting is a tradition observed throughout the holy month of Ramadan. During this period, Muslims do not eat, drink, engage in sexual activity, or smoke between sunrise and sunset. People who are in ill health, women who are pregnant or nursing, and the elderly are excused from fasting. Although Muslims believe that fasting has health benefits, the emphasis is primarily not on abstinence but rather on spiritual self-discipline, introspection, and carrying out good deeds.

Ramadan is also used to encourage families to emphasize family and social relationships during this period. "In the evening after breaking the fast, Muslims socialize, discussing family, community, national and international affairs and reaffirming their values, customs and traditions."[146]

5. **Pilgrimage (*Hajj*).** If physically and financially possible, every Muslim should make a pilgrimage to Mecca (in Saudi Arabia) at least one time as a sign of their devotion to Allah. The trip involves a series of highly symbolic rituals designed to "both celebrate and reinforce the unity of Muslims."[147] This feeling of unity is reinforced by the fact that all the participants, who number in the millions, wear the same-color garments. The pilgrims circle the *Kabha* (a square stone building believed to have been built by Abraham, who struggled against idol worship) seven times.[148] This act, much like the actions associated with all the other pillars of Islam, reaffirms the strong belief Muslims have in their religion.

CULTURAL EXPRESSIONS OF ISLAM

As we have asked of all the religious worldviews, how does theology get translated into the way Muslims live their lives? We admit that the line between religion and worldly events is often a thin one, yet there are clues as to what unites the two. We now search for some of those clues.

The Message and Response to Jihad

There is perhaps no word more incendiary or misunderstood since the events of 9/11 than the word "jihad." A *National Geographic* article echoes the notion: "*Jihad* is a loaded term—and a concept that illustrates a deep gulf of miscommunication between Islam and the West. There are those in each community who see jihad as a clash of civilizations—and act on those beliefs."[149] This dispute and confusion over the term colors both U.S. foreign policy and the perceptions of Islam held by many Americans. Part of the misinterpretation and fear is due in part to the Islamic extremists who employ the word "jihad" as a rhetorical device to inflame the passions of their followers and to threaten their adversaries. As Matthews writes, "In the Middle East, leaders use *jihad* as meaning struggle against Western countries' influence and power in the world, particularly America, which is perceived as bent on destroying the Arab way of life."[150] We have observed specific examples of this confrontational use of the word on numerous occasions. From Osama bin Laden to leaders in Iran to opposition forces fighting in Afghanistan to justification of the violence in Israel, invoking the word "jihad" is a powerful rallying cry.

Part of the problem when using or hearing the word "jihad" is that within Islamic theology the word has multiple meanings. This variety of meanings for the word goes back centuries. A reading of the Koran and interpretations advanced by imams (Muslim prayer leaders) reveal two meanings for the word, both of which are used by followers of the faith. One, *inner jihad*, deals with the individual and designates "the internal struggle each Muslim should engage in to improve himself or herself, to submit to God and restrain from sinful impulses."[151]

It is the second interpretation, the *outer jihad*, that causes problems both inside and outside the Islamic faith. This meaning speaks to those activities that either defend Islam or advance its spread. Hence, early wars that Muslims engaged in to bring new lands or peoples under Islamic control were known as *jihad wars*. Muslims suggest that these wars were similar to the Christian crusades. One of the most famous of these wars is discussed by Armstrong, who points out that Arabs, in the name of Islam, "waged a Jihad against their imperial masters the Ottomans, believing that Arabs, not Turks, should lead the Muslim peoples."[152] Even today, many Arab Muslims believe that their land and their faith are in danger if they do not wage war against the West. It is easy to see how this orientation contributes to a militant vision of the Islamic tradition. Regardless of the merits of this line of reasoning, it behooves you to understand the importance that jihad carries in the Islamic tradition and to try to discover which of the two meanings is being employed when a person speaks about a jihad.

CONSIDER THIS

The Islamic notion of jihad *includes more than one interpretation. What are some of those interpretations?*

A Complete Way of Life

Another cultural manifestation of Islam is that it is a complete way of life. It must be remembered that Muhammad was both a political figure and a religious prophet. In Islam, religion and social membership are inseparable. Islam instructs people on the best way to carry out their lives in private, social, economic, ethical, political, and spiritual arenas. That is, "Islamic law makes no distinction between religion and society, but governs all affairs, public and private."[153] Nydell further develops this idea in the following: "An Arab's [Muslim's] religion affects his or her whole way of life on a daily basis. Religion is taught in schools, the language is full of religious expressions, and people practice their religion openly, almost obtrusively, expressing it in numerous ways."[154] Viewed from this perspective, Islam is a codification of all values and ways to behave in hundreds of circumstances. Instructions are offered in activities such as child rearing, eating practices, treatment of homosexuals, and admonitions about modesty.

We should point out that this notion of Islam being a complete way of life has historical roots that go back to its beginning as a religion. Islamic scholars write, "It is worth recalling that towards the middle of the sixth century AD, mankind lived in pain, oppression, cruelty, and chaos."[155] Because of this anarchy and turmoil, God, speaking through Muhammad, believed that structure, regulation, and guidance was needed. That guidance was supplied by an all-inclusive theological orientation called Islam. It is a religion that provides its members with "an immense body of requirements and prohibitions concerning religion, personal morality, social conduct, and political behavior. Business and marital relations, criminal law, ritual practices, and much more were covered in this vast system."[156]

> **CONSIDER THIS**
>
> *What is meant by the phrase "Islam is a complete way of life"? What are some examples that would validate the truth of this assertion?*

Sharia Law

We now turn to Sharia law (often spelled Shariah) as yet another example of how Islam is a complete way of life. These laws fuse religious theology directly with worldly affairs, such as family, economics, and politics. Like so much of the Islamic approach to the secular aspects of life, Sharia has numerous interpretations—some accurate and others erroneous. Van Voorst speaks to some of the varied interpretations of Sharia when he writes, "If you've already heard of the Sharia, traditional Islamic law enforced in many Muslim lands, it may have been in reports about the stoning of women convicted of adultery or cutting off of the thieves' hands. These sensationalists reports, although generally true, give an incomplete and misleading impression of Muslim law."[157]

What is Sharia law, and why has it been a major topic of discussion in the media? Sharia law (often referred to as Muslim or Islamic law) is a legal code derived basically from three sources: the Koran, the Hadith (sayings from Muhammad), and fatwas (rulings of Islamic scholars).[158] These are very specific laws that deal with nearly all phases of human behavior. They fall into five categories: obligatory, meritorious, permissible, reprehensible, and forbidden. The controversy surrounding these laws centers on two related issues. The first is the degree of influence they have over contemporary Muslims and some of the "punishments" associated with violating any of the laws. Many people in the West (and many in the Muslim community) believe that these laws violate basic human rights, particularly when applied to the treatment of women and those people being punished for what would be considered minor crimes by Western standards. The second half of the controversy is a relatively new one. Simply stated, there is now a belief among some Americans that these laws will find their way into non-Muslim countries. Currently, seven states and numerous communities in the United States have proposed laws actually saying that Sharia law requirements could not be imposed on non-Muslims.[159] Muslims, of course, see Sharia law differently. They turn to the actual meaning of the Arabic word *Sharia* ("a clear path") to help explain its importance in the life of all Muslims. For them, the "path" is a series of mandates that benefits humanity by offering people structure, specific guidelines, and a divine connection to the past.

Gender

Although we discussed gender and Islam as it applied to families in Chapter 3, we now look at the religious aspects of this topic. The subject of gender is difficult to examine because it is emotional, controversial, and subject to a high degree of ethnocentrism. Much of the heated rhetoric is coming from non-Muslims. In addition, the role of Islamic women is also undergoing significant changes. When these factors are combined, it is difficult to study the tie between gender and Islam objectively. It appears that "A priori assumptions, preconceptions, and stereotypes regarding Middle Eastern women abound, and generalizations about women in a region as internally diverse as the Middle East continue to predominate in current discourse."[160] Part of the confusion, both within and outside the Islamic world, stems from the fact that the Koran (as well as other religious teachings) offers a variety of interpretations on the subject of women. Those who support a traditional and strict reading of the Koran point to 4:34, which states, "Men are superior to women on account of qualities with which God has gifted the one above the other, and on account of the outlay they make from their substance for them." Many Muslims take this passage to mean that men are stronger than women physically as well as mentally and morally. Manifestations of this belief can be seen in numerous circumstances. For example, among Muslims, the illiteracy rate is much higher for females than it is for males.[161] In addition, according to Islamic tradition, women cannot teach men, "so Muslim women who have trained in the ways of the Koran teach only girls and other women."[162]

In spite of these different perceptions and interpretations of the role of Islamic women, worldwide attitudes regarding gender roles in many Islamic countries are in a state of flux. All of the changes seem to have one thing in common: Muslim women do not want outside forces to dictate the rate of change or the content of those changes. Esposito and Mogahed quote a series of Gallup polls revealing that "While admiring much about the West, the majority of Muslim women do not yearn to become more like their Western counterparts. While they favor gender parity, they likely want it on their terms and within their own culture"[163] In places such as Egypt, Iraq, Turkey, Morocco, Tunisia, Kuwait, Saudi Arabia, and Indonesia, women are actively protesting and defining those terms.

This section on Islam and gender ends reminding you of two points. First, when observing any cultural difference, it is important that you do not allow ethnocentrism to direct your evaluation. As an "outsider," you are applying Western models to the

Islamic culture's attitude toward women. Although you might find it strange for women to cover their hair with the *hijab*, Muslim women might have a difficult time understanding why so many women in the United States use dye to alter the natural color of their hair. Second, broad generalizations regarding gender often overlook regional differences. For example, the life of a village woman residing in rural Afghanistan is very different from the life of a well-educated Palestinian who is socially and politically active within her community.

ETHICS AND ISLAM

In many ways we introduced the topic of Islamic ethics when we wrote the phrase "Islam is a complete way of life." Since Islam addresses every aspect of life, all that is contained in the Koran is a type of ethical outline. This means that "The ethical dimensions of the Islamic life are spread evenly throughout the *Qur'an*, as one would expect for a religion that calls itself 'submission" to God's way."[164] Besides this overarching principle driving Islamic ethics and morality, there are, sprinkled throughout the teachings, some special behaviors that get called out. Islamic ethics, as reflected in the Koran, forbids gambling, the consumption of alcohol, lying, extramarital sex, and stealing and condemns homosexuality.[165]

ISLAMIC NOTIONS ABOUT DEATH

The idea of death and an afterlife are crucial elements of the Islamic religion. We highlighted some of those elements when we discussed the Islamic view of "judgment." It is important that we return to that topic, particularly due to its current relevance. This issue has been the subject of countless news reports due to the prominence of suicide bombers. Part of the present interest stems from attempts to comprehend the motivation behind bombings that take the lives of women and children as well as that of the bomber. Looking at the concepts of the "final judgment" and afterlife offers some clues to this complex question.

The theology of Muslims, Jews, and Christians, with some variation, all include the Day of Judgment (the Day of Resurrection), when all people will be resurrected for God's judgment according to their beliefs and deeds. The Koran (45:26) makes it clear that Muslims are to view death as a new beginning: "It is God who gives life, then, causes you to die, and then He gathers you all to the Day of Resurrection of which there is no doubt, though most people do not comprehend." This concept of a moral code and living a life that God wants from the individual is the most fundamental and crucial element of Islamic doctrine and helps determine if the person will gain entry into heaven or hell. Muslims believe that

> God will judge people by how they submitted to God's will. Saying that one is a follower of Islam won't save anyone at the judgment; living in an obedient way is the important thing. In fact, the Qur'an states that severe punishments are in store for hypocrites who claim to be Muslims, but haven't lived by Islam.[166]

Unlike most Western traditions, Islam provides graphic details of the punishments and "paradise" that come after death: "Paradise is a pleasant oasis where a man's every desire, according to popular tradition, is satisfied either by his wife or by beautiful houris, or virgins. Hell is a place of burning and heat where excruciating pains are perpetual (Qur'an)."[167] While many Muslim scholars point out that these two descriptions are only metaphors for an afterlife, the two depictions nevertheless underscore the importance of good and evil—and the consequences of each—in Islamic teaching. We should also note that there is debate among Muslim imams and scholars on the issues of suicide bombers, martyrdom, and heaven. Many imams in the leadership of Al Qaeda see the actions of these bombers as an extension of a jihad against the enemies of Islam. They tell suicide bombers that they are dying to save Islam from the West. Other Muslims maintain that the Koran does not approve of the killing of innocent people. Regardless of the authenticity of these positions, one thing seems certain: Those who become suicide bombers and engage in these horrific and gruesome acts do so because they believe their actions will be rewarded in heaven. For this group, death in the name of Allah ensures a place in heaven.

HINDUISM

Hinduism, with approximately a billion followers, is a religion that dates back almost 4000 years. In spite of its many followers and long history, Hinduism, because it is so very different from Western worldviews, remains a mystery to most "outsiders." Part of that mystery is that Hinduism as a "religion has no single founder, creed, teacher, or prophet acknowledged by all Hindus as central to the religion, and no single holy book is universally acclaimed as being of primary importance."[168] Van Voorst explains the uniqueness of this religion writing:

> If this is your first encounter with the Hindu religion you may become bewildered by all its varied beliefs and practices. Calling something a "religion" usually implies a unified system of belief and practice, but Hinduism has little obvious unity. It has no human founder, defined core beliefs, common scripture that guides all Hindus, standardized worship practice, or central authority.[169]

This suggests that it is difficult to pin down Hinduism for a variety of reasons such as those cited by Van Voorst. Yet as distinctive and baffling as this religion can be, there are some concepts and beliefs that will partially explain the worldview of Hindus.

ORIGINS

Hinduism is among the oldest religions in the world, and, as such, providing an accurate history of Hinduism is problematic. In addition, the difficulty of gathering a precise historical account for this tradition is compounded by the fact that Indian culture is not concerned with its past.[170] In addition, Hinduism had its creation long before people were maintaining written records. Even with these limitations, most historians trace the origins of Hinduism to a time four thousand years ago when a group of light-skinned Aryan Indo-European tribes invaded what is now northern India.[171] When this group of people moved into the Indus Valley, a blending of cultures took place. "As these Aryans mixed with the native people, they shared customs, traditions, rites, symbols, and myths. Each contributed and each received."[172] These early stages were marked by a series of orally transmitted texts that expressed the fundamental concepts of what is now call Hinduism. Because of the message contained in these texts and their significance to Hinduism, we now examine some of those "central concepts."

SACRED TEXTS

We have already mentioned that Hinduism is not only one of the oldest of all religions but also the most diverse. You can observe that diversity in the size, use, and influence these scriptures have had on Hindus for thousands of years. Looking at some of the scriptures can help you develop insight into this intriguing religion.

The Vedas

The oldest and most fundamental scriptures are called the Vedas. For thousands of years, the wisdom concerning what is now Hinduism was transmitted orally. In fact, one definition of "Vedas" actually means "hearing." The Vedas are composed of four books that seek to "transmit the ancient revelations in a series of hymns, ritual texts, and speculations composed over a period of a millennium beginning ca. 1400 BC."[173] These four books, with their philosophical maxims and spiritual guidance, are important because they not only deal with the spiritual dimensions of Hinduism but also offer insights into the cultural life in India thousands of years ago. In addition, some authorities believe that the Vedas describe "the origin of the world and human society."[174]

The Upanishads

Sometime between 800 and 400 BCE, another important group of Hindu texts appeared. They are called the Upanishads. These books, written in both prose and verse, are highly metaphysical. They are also instrumental in shaping many of the philosophical beliefs of the Hindu religion. The reason behind their longevity and significance is underscored by Stroud: "These texts contain the core of what would become modern Hinduism—the commitment to reality being undivided at its most basic level and to a renunciation of worldly goods."[175] The texts stress issues of faith dealing with notions of reality, the "oneness" of everything in the universe, the role of one's soul, and the importance of contemplation and meditation. Usha elaborates on the power of the Upanishads when he writes, "The *Upanishads* teach the knowledge of God and record the spiritual experiences of the sages of ancient India."[176]

The Bhagavad Gita

Written around 540 to 300 BCE, the *Bhagavad Gita* contains, in poetic form, a dialogue between a warrior, Prince Arjuna, and the god Lord Krishna. This eighteen-chapter book, revealing the wisdom of Krishna, teaches how to become aware of the "Supreme Reality," a reality that can be known through the pursuit of knowledge, devotion, altruistic behavior, and contemplation. Robinson and Rodrigues speak to the importance of the *Bhagavad Gita* when they write, "In the two millennia since its composition, the *Gita*, as it is often called, has served as a source of inspiration for countless numbers, from Hindu philosophers and politicians such as Shankara and Mahatma Gandhi, to Western authors and poets such as Henry David Thoreau and T. S. Eliot."[177] A major characteristic of the text is that it reinforces the very core of Hinduism: that God is an exalted, stirring, and sublime force within us. Because God is within us, we can rise above our mortal limitations and be liberated.

REMEMBER THIS

Hinduism is a conglomeration of religious thought, values, and beliefs drawn from a variety of sources. As such it does not have a single founder or an organizational hierarchy. Among Hindus one may find magic, nature worship, animal veneration, and an unlimited number of deities.

CORE ASSUMPTIONS

As is the case with all religions, the messages and lessons advanced by the sacred texts, teachers, and prophets of Hinduism are diverse, numerous, and beyond the scope and purpose of this chapter. However, Hinduism does contain some central teachings that you will find useful when interacting with someone who is Hindu.

Divine in Everything

For Hindus, "divine" is the concept that the universe is interconnected in a host of ways. This interrelatedness cuts across time and space and encompasses the belief that plants, animals, and humans are all interrelated. The essence of this worldview is that God is within each being and object in the universe and that the spirit of each soul is divine. Narayanan further develops this concept of the divine when he writes, "The belief that the divine is not only beyond gender and name, but also beyond number, has resulted in its manifestation in many shapes and forms: as human or animal, as trees, or as combinations of these beings."[178] This view of a vast number of deities makes Hindus among the most religious people in the world because they find the divine in everything. As Boorstin notes, "The Hindu is dazzled by a vision of the holy, not merely holy people, but places like the Himalayan peaks where the gods live, or the Ganges which flows from Heaven to Earth, or countless inconspicuous sites where gods or goddesses or unsung heroes showed their divine mettle."[179]

Ultimate Reality

The Hindu interpretation of reality is clearly introduced by Matthews when he writes,

> The distinctive attitude of Hinduism is that there is more to the universe than meets the eye. There is a reality that embraces all we experience; to understand the universe and ourselves, its presence is necessary. Behind all the phenomena of life, a source of energy makes it possible. This unit can be experienced, however, in a great variety of ways. No one way is complete.[180]

This concept suggests the fundamental assumption that the material world, the one we can touch and see, is not the only reality. Instead, Hindus hold that there are other realities that lead to spiritual advancement and reveal the true nature of life, the mind, and the spirit. Hence, Hindus are not satisfied with what they see or hear. This view is reflected in the Hindu saying "Him the eye does not see, nor the tongue express, nor the mind grasp." Counsel for such an orientation even comes from the *Bhagavad Gita* in the following advice: "A man of faith, intent on wisdom, His senses restrained, will wisdom win."[181] An extension of this point of reference leads Hindus to believe that finding satisfaction in the material and physical world (the Western notion of reality) might gratify you temporarily, but eventually the satisfaction of that world will "wear out." To experience true happiness, bliss, or liberation (what Hindus call nirvana), one needs to discover the spiritual existence found outside traditional concepts of reality. Kumar and Sethi summarize this orientation in the following: "The normative implication of this principle is that individuals should strive to unite their inner self with the ultimate reality. The attempt to realize this unity constitutes the heart of spiritualism in the Indian subcontinent."[182]

Brahman

The notion of Brahman is actually an extension of the previous paragraph, as many Hindus believe that "the reality" behind the entire Creation, be it physical, mental, or emotional, is Brahman. Hence, Brahman becomes an all-inclusive, transcendental reality that sustains and supports everything. Van Voorst develops this point when he writes that Brahman is a "single 'world soul' that is the foundation of all physical matter, energy, time and space, and being itself—in short, everything in and beyond the universe."[183] Perceived in this manner, Brahman is the definitive level of reality.

Multiple Paths

In many aspects, Hinduism is a conglomeration of religious thought, values, and beliefs. As discussed earlier, Hinduism does not have a single founder or an organizational hierarchy. Among Hindus, one may find magic, nature worship, animal veneration, and an unlimited number of deities. This all-inclusive orientation has been responsible for Hinduism's popularity even outside of India. Because of this eclectic approach to "God," Hinduism has been able to present various paths to those asking the eternal questions about life and death. There is even a famous Hindu expression: "Truth is one, but sages call it by various names."[184] Granting the "One Goal, Different Paths" orientation of Hinduism, you will also find there are four paths that many teachers of Hinduism believe are the major "stepping stones along one spiritual path, with each building progressively on the previous one."[185] These four are "(1) The Path of Work (Karma-yoga, selfless actions), (2) The Path of Knowledge (Jnana-yoga, philosophy and wisdom, (3) The Path of Physical and Mental Discipline (Astang/Raja-Yoga, exercise and meditation), and (4) The Path of Love (Bhakti-Yoga, path of devotional service)."[186]

> **CONSIDER THIS**
>
> *What do Hindus mean when they say, "Truth does not come to the individual; it already resides within each of us"?*

CULTURAL EXPRESSIONS OF HINDUISM

As we have stressed throughout this chapter, a person's religion is never entirely confined to a church, mosque, synagogue, or temple. Our thesis has been that religion is something people do. This is particularly true of Hinduism. We now turn to some of the ways the religion is reflected in everyday life.

Complete Way of Life

It has been said that religion and culture are interchangeable in terms of Hinduism. It has also been referred to as a holistic way of life because, as the Hindu saying by Swami Vivekananda states, "The Hindu man drinks religiously, sleeps religiously, walks religiously, marries religiously, and robs religiously." For the Hindu, life and religion are the same. "Both are inseparable. Both complement each other. Both exist because of each other and both would lose their meaning and significance without the other. Religion is the center of living and living is the center of religion."[187]

As we have been highlighting, Hinduism is not simply a theology; it is a complete way of life that shows itself in a multiplicity of ways. The sacred writings of this tradition speak of the arts, the birth of children, death, medicine, health, science, governance, education, and a host of other cultural issues. In addition, while temples are a popular place for worship, it is the daily activity in the home that best reflects Hindu practices as an important and integral part of life. Henderson tells of the significance of the home in the following explanation: "Hinduism wears the face of family and home. A home's most sacred spot is its hearth. Most rituals occur amid daily life. The acts of bathing, dressing, and eating are connected to ritual purity."[188]

Dharma

Dharma, because of its influences on how Hindus perceive the world, live that world, and prepare for reincarnation, represents one of the most important concepts of Hinduism. As Van Voorst notes, "Dharma is the foundational concept in Hinduism, a wide-ranging term for righteousness, law, duty, moral teachings, religion itself, or the order of the universe. Dharma is also the god who embodies and promotes right order and living."[189] The multidimensional aspect of the laws of Dharma provides people guidance on how to behave, perform their vocational obligations, and act during various life cycles and even how old people should treat those younger than themselves.[190]

An extension of the belief and command of Dharma is the idea that if you go against Dharma, which is seen as a cosmic norm, you will produce bad Karma. Because Karma affects this life and subsequent lives (through reincarnation), most Hindus seek to live a virtuous life and follow their Dharma.

Karma

Having just alluded to Karma, we now explain the concept in more detail, especially because non-Hindus generally misunderstand the term. The word is now part of popular culture and as such takes on a host of meanings that only serve to distort the concept. "Karma" comes from a Sanskrit word meaning "action." "Karma is the Hindu view of causality, in which good deeds, words, thoughts, and commands lead to beneficial effects for a person, and bad deeds, words, thoughts, and commands lead to harmful effects."[191] Prothero expands on this important concept when he writes, "Just as, according to the law of gravity, what is dropped from a tree will fall to the ground, according to the law of Karma, evil actions produce punishments and good actions produce rewards."[192] The final resolution to a person's Karma has long-range implications. That is, a person "with bad Karma could be reborn many times into lower castes of humans, or even lower animals, and then not released until he or she has been reborn in the Brahmin, or priestly caste."[193] The ethical implications of Karma are obvious. Each new birth is not a matter of chance but rather results from good or bad actions in prior lives.

Four Stages of Life

Another cultural manifestation of Hinduism is referred to as the "Duties of the Four Stages of Life." While writings concerning these stages go back thousands of years, many Hindus attempt to carry out the specific duties even today. These stages represent phases the individual passes through as a means of gathering enough wisdom to become "free" and "spiritual." These stages are of concern to students of intercultural communication in that each stage has specific

For the Hindu, life and religion are the same in that every aspect and ritual of Hinduism has meaning and significance.

© Steve Harrington

interpersonal behaviors and responsibilities associated with it. Before we mention the four stages, we should point out that very few people make it past stages one and two, as the last two stages make enormous demands on the individual. However, the specific guidelines for each stage continue to help shape a Hindu's life. In somewhat abbreviated form, let us look at these four stages: (1) In the *student* stage, a young boy, usually between the ages of eight and twelve, studies the Vedas while serving an apprenticeship with a teacher. (2) The *householder* is that phase in a male's life when he builds his family and attempts to live a highly spiritual and ethical life while meeting his obligations as husband and father. (3) The *forest dweller* is one who has met his obligations to his family and society and is now ready to leave all personal attachments and begin intensive study and meditation. (4) The *ascetic*, an optional state, is when the Hindu renounces the world and is completely independent from all people and possessions and unites with Brahman. In short, he is liberated from ordinary life.[194]

ETHICS AND HINDUISM

Throughout this section on Hinduism we have discussed the idea of ethics on nearly every page. The reason is that Hindus maintain that "everyday life and religious life are not separated because Hindu ethics traditionally play a leading role in everyday life: caste and class, marriage and children, career and retirement."[195] Hindus believe that being true to your moral values is the highest loyalty. It is from the Hindu scriptures, primarily the Upanishads, where most specific "recommendations" concerning ethical behavior, good judgment, and character are drawn. These writings maintain that being ethical "is a means to an end, its purpose being to help the members of society to rid themselves of self-centeredness, cruelty, greed, and other vices, and thus to create an environment helpful to the pursuit of the higher good, which transcends society."[196] In addition to those propositions just cited, the Upanishads "puts the main virtues on Hinduism in their most elemental form as the three *da's: damyata*, restraint and self control; *data*, generosity; and *dayadhvam*, compassion."[197]

NOTIONS ABOUT DEATH

Although we mentioned some perceptions regarding death when we discussed Dharma and Karma, we return to that topic since it is instrumental in how Hindus approach life. The core of a Hindu's conviction regarding death is summarized in one succinct statement: "Hindus believe in the immortality of the soul and in reincarnation."[198] With this basic belief as their anchor, Hindus learn not to fear death or even grieve over the death of loved ones.

As Jayaram V notes,

> Death is therefore not a great calamity, not an end of all, but a natural process in the existence of jiva [being, soul] as a separate entity, a resting period in which it recuperates, reassembles its resources, adjusts its course and returns again to the earth to continue its journey.[199]

The rationale is clear: Even though the physical body dies, a person's soul does not have a beginning or an end but simply passes into another reincarnation at the end of this life. Hindus believe that the state of mind of the person just before death is critical, demonstrating their conviction that the person continues living after death. Were the person's thoughts at the moment of death about family and spiritual matters, or was the person thinking "evil thoughts"? The answer to this question is important to the Hindu.

At the actual time of death, Hindus believe the Atman (the personal enlightened self) moves on. Once the body dies, it is cremated as quickly as possible. The funeral ceremonies surrounding disposition of the remains are extremely ritualistic and involve mourners bathing and stories being shared about the deceased. In India, if at all possible, the ashes of the deceased person are taken by relatives and scattered into a holy river, such as the Ganges.

BUDDHISM

Buddhism is yet another religious tradition that has had profound impact on civilization. Currently, there are approximately 488 million Buddhists worldwide.[200] Even without a missionary component to its philosophy, Buddhism extended itself over cultural areas in South and East Asia and has millions of followers all over the world. It is even one of the fastest-growing religions in the United States.[201] What appeals to many Westerners is that, unlike most Western religions, Buddhism is "grounded in reason not faith and therefore is in harmony with the prevailing spirit of scientific empiricism."[202] Yet in spite of its popularity, many people do not fully understand Buddhism. Thera, quoting the philosopher T. H. Huxley, mentions some of the reasons people are often bewildered by Buddhism: "Buddhism is a system which knows no God in the Western sense, which denies a soul to man, which counts the belief in immortality a blunder, which refuses any efficacy to prayer and sacrifice, which bids men look to nothing but their own efforts for salvation."[203]

ORIGINS

Like Christianity and Islam, Buddhism is also associated with a "founder." However, Buddhism separates itself from those and other traditions because it is nontheistic. Although Buddha "claimed the realization of the ultimate truth, he did not identify himself as the special representative of a transcendent God."[204]

In spite of the fact that oral histories associated with most religious founders have often been altered and embellished, a clear picture of the history of Buddhism is accessible. An Indian prince named Siddhartha Gautama founded Buddhism. The narrative of how the prince became enlightened begins with the fact that at the time of his birth, his father was a king, and the prince was born into great luxury and opulence that he would later reject. As Siddhartha himself said, "I wore garments of silk and my attendants held a white umbrella over me."[205] In spite of all his lavish surroundings, the prince felt a deep discontentment with his life. Garfinkel offers an account of what was to become a major event in the founding of Buddhism:

> At age 29 the married Prince, disillusioned with his opulence, ventured out of his palace and for the first time encountered old age, sickness, and death. So moved was he by this brush with the painful realities of life that he left his comfortable home to search for an end to human suffering.[206]

For the next six years, often called the Period of Enquiry, the prince engaged in deep meditation and lived an austere life as he searched for answers to explain the suffering he saw. After examining his thoughts during this period, he emerged from his self-imposed seclusion and became Buddha. As Clark notes, "Siddhartha became a Buddha (Enlightened One) in a flash of insight one day while meditating. He immediately gathered his disciples and began to teach them what he had learned."[207] *prasada*) the prince experienced when he discovered there was a way to overcome the suffering of life."[208]

From that time until his death at age eighty in 483 BCE, Buddha traveled throughout the Ganges Valley sharing his insights with anyone who would listen. Some communication scholars suggest that part of Buddha's early success was influenced by the fact that he was an excellent communicator. As Dissanayake notes, "The Buddha himself was a supremely persuasive communicator. He preached to the people in an idiom and vocabulary that were readily understandable. He paid close attention to the psychological makeup of his interlocutors and listeners."[209]

CORE ASSUMPTIONS

As is the case with all religious traditions, there are multiple forms of Buddhism (such as Theravada, Mahayana, Zen, Pure Land, Vajrayana, and Tibetan). Over the centuries, each culture and country adapted its existing belief system to what Buddhism had to offer. However, in spite of some minor differences, all the major schools of Buddhism share the same basic principles. Let us look at two of those principles before we examine some of the specific precepts associated with Buddhism.

First, we have already alluded to the idea that Buddha made it clear that *he was not a God but simply a man.* In fact, Buddha went so far as to suggest that "a belief in god is itself a form of human desire and clinging, a product of the ego and another cause of suffering in that it prevents a person from becoming an autonomous and free human being."[210] When Buddha was asked if he were God, the answer he offered his followers demonstrates the importance of this concept to the practice of Buddhism:

"Are you a god?" they asked.

"No."

"An angel?"

"No."

"A saint?"

"No."

"Then what are you?"

Buddha answered, "I am awake."[211]

That simple response, "I am awake," tells all who want to practice Buddhism that the answer to life's questions can be found in the straightforward act of "waking up" and becoming aware of the truths one experiences when being enlightened.

Second, Buddha taught that *all individuals have the potential to seek the truth on their own.* "The Buddha rejected many of the forms of authority that are relied upon by other religious traditions. Instead, he urged his followers to test teachings against their own experiences, and only accept them if they ring true."[212] As just mentioned, it is often difficult for westerners to understand this orientation, as many Western religions stress religious direction from the clergy. One of the most celebrated Buddha sayings reaffirms his strong conviction in "self-discovery": "Be lamps unto yourselves. Be ye a refuge to yourselves. Hold fast to the Truth as a lamp. Hold fast as a refuge to the Truth." This emphasis on self-reliance is explained by the Buddhist teacher Bhikkhu Bodhi: "For the Buddha, the key to liberation is mental purity and correct understanding, and for this reason he rejects the notion that we gain salvation by learning from an external source."[213] The words "external source" represent the

---

CONSIDER THIS

What in Buddhist philosophy led Buddha to instruct his followers that he was "Not a God, but only a man seeking the truth"?

essential message in Buddha's teaching as you can observe in two more celebrated Buddhist maxims that stress the same point: "Betake yourself to no external refuge. Work out your own salvation with diligence" and "You are your own refuge; there is no other refuge." Bodhi explains this core principle in the following:

> The Buddha rests his teaching upon the thesis that with the right method man can change and transform himself. He is not doomed to be forever burdened by the weight of his accumulated tendencies, but through his own effort he can cast off all these tendencies and attain a condition of complete purity and freedom.[214]

The Four Noble Truths

Once enlightened and at the conclusion of his six-year quest, Buddha shared his insights with others. Many of the essentials of that knowledge are found in the Four Noble Truths. "These Noble Truths diagnose the human problem, describe its cause, propose a cure, and prescribe a treatment."[215] It is important to keep in mind that although the Four Noble Truths (and the discussion of the Eightfold Path that follows) are treated as separate categories, they are interrelated, as each flows seamlessly into the other.

The First Noble Truth is that life is suffering (*dukkha*). The basic rationale for Buddha's assertion that life is suffering is further explained by Bodhi: "The reason all worldly conditions are said to be *dukkha*, inadequate and unsatisfactory, is because they are all impermanent and unstable; because they lack any substantial or immutable self; and because they cannot give us lasting happiness; secure against change and loss."[216]

Buddhist teachers point out that if your life is not characterized by some degree of suffering at the moment, you need only look at the world to see the suffering of others. Contrary to Western interpretation, Buddha's philosophy is not a negative one in spite of this first admonition using the word "suffering." The objective of this first truth is not to encourage pessimism but to promote a realistic view of the "human condition."

The Second Noble Truth concerns the roots of suffering. Buddha taught that much of our suffering is caused by craving, self-desire, attachment, anger, envy, greed, ignorance, and self-delusion regarding the nature of reality.[217] Throughout the writings of Buddha, students encounter advice regarding how to learn to see the world as it is. Buddha believed that accepting the world was a major step toward enlightenment. He told his students, "See the false as false. The true as true. Look into your heart. Follow your nature."

The Third Noble Truth is an extension of the first two truths. It asserts that because suffering has a cause, it can be eliminated. Put in slightly different terms, "The means to end our suffering is ending the craving that causes it."[218] Buddha taught that by clearly seeing truth, you can put an end to suffering, ignorance, and craving. As is the case in nearly all of Buddha's counsel, the key component is the person. Notice how these ideas become reinforced in the following famous instruction advanced by Buddha:

> *By your own efforts*
> *Waken yourself, watch yourself.*
> *And live joyfully.*
> *You are the master.*

The Fourth Noble Truth is often called "the remedy," as it is an explanation and prescription for the end of suffering and a path to nirvana (a state of enlightenment).

In many ways, the central core of the teaching of Buddha deals with the Eightfold Path. Because of the importance to the Buddhist worldview and the practical application to how one lives life, we turn to a brief discussion of the tenets of the Eightfold Path.

The Eightfold Path

In many ways, the Four Noble Truths form the central core of Buddhism, as they speak to the symptoms that create unhappiness and suffering. Van Voorst notes, "The Eightfold Path offers practical guidelines to mental and moral development with the goal of freeing individuals from attachments and delusions; it leads to understanding the truth of all things."[219] The various elements that make up the Eightfold Path should not be studied as independent units; rather, they should be learned and practiced simultaneously. The steps are usually reduced to three categories: wisdom, ethical conduct, and mental discipline.

Wisdom[220]

1. *Right view is achieving a correct understanding and accepting the reality and origins of suffering and the ways leading to the cessation of suffering.* This first path sets the tone for all that follow, as it asks the individual to see the universe (reality) as it really is: impermanent, imperfect, and elusive.
2. *Right purpose is being free from ill will, cruelty, and untruthfulness toward the self and others.* To follow in "the path," Buddha encouraged his followers to discover any "unwholesome" ways of thinking they might have and discard them. Instead, they should develop an attitude toward the world filled with loving-kindness and compassion. Buddha told his followers that "Hatred does not cease by hatred, but only by love; this is eternal."

Ethical Conduct

3. *Right speech.* Buddha stressed that people should use discourse that is truthful and considerate. Right speech should be free of falsehoods and slander, be honest, promote harmony, not be divisive, and be void of idle chatter. Buddha advised, "If you propose to speak, always ask yourself, is it true, is it necessary, is it kind."
4. *Right action* is Buddha's version of the Ten Commandments, for this principle seeks to promote moral, honorable, and peaceful behavior. Among other things, this path calls for abstaining from the taking of life, from stealing, from sexual misconduct, from lying, and from drinking intoxicants.
5. *Right livelihood* asks all disciples to avoid occupations that harm living beings and animals. That means refraining for stealing, exploiting people, and selling weapons or intoxicants. Buddha believed that these forms of livelihood were not conducive to spiritual progress.

Mental Discipline

6. *Right efforts* means cultivating and maintaining wholesome thoughts. It was Buddha's belief that allowing the mind to experience anger, agitation, and even dullness would keep a person from cultivating mindfulness and concentration.
7. *Right mindfulness* refers to being able to manage your mind. He continuously urged his students to concentrate on the "here and the now." This, according to Buddha, allows

one to see things as they are. There is a rather famous Buddha saying: "Do not dwell in the past, do not dream of the future, concentrate the mind on the present moment."

8. *Right concentration*, although it comes as the final entry in the Eightfold Path sequence, is one of the most important. It reminds students to aim for a calm, meditative mind. This means complete attentiveness to a single object and the achievement of purity of thought, free from all hindrances and distractions. When the mind is made still through meditation, according to Buddha, the true nature of everything is revealed.

CULTURAL EXPRESSIONS OF BUDDHISM

The Use of Silence

One of the teachings of Buddha that can influence intercultural communication centers on the Buddhist view toward language and silence. First, we have already mentioned the third item on the Eightfold Path, "right speech." This category was included by Buddha because he was keenly aware of the power of language to influence others and oneself. He always encouraged his followers to employ silence when confronted with anger or provocation. Notice the message being given to employ silence in the following Buddhist sayings: "The tongue like a sharp knife …kills without drawing blood," "Remember that silence is sometimes the best answer," and "Whatever words we utter should be chosen with care for people will hear them and be influenced by them for good or ill."

> **REMEMBER THIS**
> Buddha sees reality as impermanent, imperfect, and elusive.

Second, Buddha's view of silence can be seen in the final item of the Eightfold Path that stresses the importance of meditation. This means that "self-reflexivity and critical introspection—the essence of intrapersonal communication—assume a great importance"[221] for Buddhists. Third, meditation is carried out in silence. One of the reasons for the emphasis on silence is that Buddhism requires abandonment of views generated by the use of ordinary words and scriptures. In Buddhism, language can be deceptive and misleading when a person is trying to understand the universe as it really is. Brabant-Smith explains this idea: "Ordinary language tends to deal with physical things and experiences, as understood by ordinary man; whereas Dharma language (Buddha's teaching) deals with the mental world, with the intangible non-physical world."[222] This notion finds expression in three well-known Buddhist admonitions: "Beware of the false illusions created by words," "Do not accept what you hear by report," and "Peace comes from within. Do not seek it from without." These sayings reflect Buddhists' belief that there is a supreme truth that words cannot reach or teach. A Buddhist teacher expressed it this way: "A special transmission outside the scriptures; No dependence upon words or letters; Direct pointing at the mind of man; Seeing into one's nature and the attainment of Buddhahood."[223]

Impermanency

While we have already alluded to the notion of impermanency, we briefly return to it, as it is a fundamental Buddhist concept. For Buddha, "Impermanence means that everything changes and nothing remains the same in any consecutive moment. And although things change every moment, they still cannot be accurately described as the same or as different from what they were a moment ago."[224] Buddha extended this truism about the reality of life rather poetically, stating, "This existence of ours is as transient as autumn clouds. To watch the birth of beings is like looking at the movements of a dance. A lifetime is like a flash of lightning in the sky, rushing by, like a torrent down a steep mountain." Buddha believed that recognizing the truism that nothing is permanent would encourage his followers to appreciate the moment and accept the tentative nature of life. By reminding his followers of the transitory nature of life, Buddha was able to speak to the subject of a code of conduct that could influence human interaction. He told his followers that all things are impermanent and that they should remember the following verse:

Angry in the ultimate dimension

I close my eyes and look deeply.

Three hundred years from now

Where will you be and where shall I be?[225]

Karma

Buddha's teaching regarding Karma is important because it sets the tone for ethical behavior. Buddha repeatedly stressed that a person's actions had consequences. One of his most famous admonitions stated, "Speak or act with a pure mind and happiness will follow you, as your shadow, unshakable." The words "follow you" offer insight into Buddha's notion of Karma, as the result of your action can manifest itself in your current life or in the next life (or, for that matter, several lives). Buddhists have a strong belief in free will; therefore, your actions, over which you have control, determine much of your Karma. In fact, the actual word "Karma" "is used to denote volitional acts which find expression in thought, speech or physical deeds, which are good, evil or a mixture of both and are liable to give rise to consequences, which partly determine the goodness or badness of these acts."[226]

Buddha's way of thinking about Karma is referred to as the *law of action and reaction*. Because he did not believe in a higher being or divine intervention, he taught that people have within themselves the potential to control their own Karma. For Buddha, "All beings are the owners of their deeds (Karma), the heirs of their deeds; their deeds are the womb from which they sprang…. Whatever deeds they do—good or evil—of such they will be the heirs."[227] When Buddha speaks of "heirs," he is referring to the concept that the manifestations of one's Karma remain beyond the physical death of the person. Bogoda underscores this point:

The only thing we own that remains with us beyond death is our Karma, our intentional deeds. Our deeds continue, bringing into being a new form of life until all craving is extinguished. We are born and evolve according to the quality of our Karma. Good deeds will produce a good rebirth, bad deeds a bad rebirth.[228]

BUDDHIST ETHICS

Our discussion of Buddhist ethics is in many ways an extension of our conversation regarding Karma. In addition, even Buddha's Eightfold Path is a statement about ethical behavior. Buddha's approach to ethics was unique in that it was not concerned with what he referred to as "social customs" that could change from location to location. Buddha counseled his students that "ethical values are intrinsically a part of nature, and the unchanging law of cause and effect (kamma)."[229] In this sense, the Buddhist ethical system is both useful and applicable for all time.

As is the case with all the religious traditions, Buddhist ethics are both general and specific. "If you ask any Buddhist what the heart of the Buddhist moral system is, he or she, would probably say, 'Show compassion to all beings.'"[230] Van Voorst adds this simple admonition: "Besides the general command to all Buddhists to be nonviolent, moderate, and compassionate to all beings, Buddhists are urged to live moral, generous lives."[231] In addition to these broad ethical guidelines, Buddha spoke of specific precepts, such as the killing of living beings, stealing, engaging in sexual misconduct, lying, and drinking any intoxicants, mainly because their consumption encourages immoral behavior.[232]

BUDDHIST NOTIONS ABOUT DEATH

A large portion of Buddha's teaching focuses on death. In fact, it was an awareness of the inevitability of death that prompted Buddha to engage in his quest for the "true meaning of life." Buddha believed one could not be happy in this life or create good Karma without understanding the reality of impermanence. He once told his students, "Who, unless he be quite mad, would make plans which do not reckon with death, when he sees the world so unsubstantial and frail, like a water bubble."[233] One of the most often quoted sayings in Buddhism states, "Like a fish which is thrown on dry land, taken from his home in the waters, the mind strives and struggles to get away from the power of Death." The reasoning behind Buddha's teachings regarding death and dying are explained in the following paragraph:

> Contemplation and meditation on death and impermanence are regarded as very important to Buddhism for two reasons: (1) it is only by recognizing how precious and how short life is that we are most likely to make it meaningful and try to live it fully and (2) by understanding the death process and familiarizing ourself [sic] with it, we can remove fear at the time of death and ensure a good rebirth.[234]

Buddha's message was clear and simple—death is certain, the time of death is uncertain, and what can help you at the actual moment of death is your spiritual development.

As noted earlier, according to Buddhism, death is only an end to a temporary phenomenon. Buddhists perceive death as ending one chapter and starting another. When the organic life ends, the forces of Karma take over because they have not been destroyed—*this is rebirth*. As Ottama states, "our past Karma is rebirth itself."[235] As pointed out during our examination of Karma, it is believed that the person's past deeds, both wholesome and unwholesome, play a role in how many times he or she is reborn. As long as the person is greedy, manifests hatred, does not control immoral behavior, and continues to engage in self-delusion, he or she will continue to produce bad Karma. Once there is enough good Karma, the person will experience nirvana. As we also noted earlier, nirvana in its unadorned state is complete bliss that releases a person from all unhappiness.

The state of a person's mind approaching death is also important in the Buddhist tradition. Most religions hold that even a seriously ill person should "keep fighting" and avoid death for as long as possible. The underlying premise for this attitude is that death should be avoided at all costs. Buddhism rejected the idea of trying to cling to life. For Buddha, the state of mind in which one dies is a powerful determinant of the next rebirth. At death, the person should be at peace with oneself and the entire universe. Buddha even offered some specific guidance about one's last few minutes of life. He wanted his followers to think of good deeds. He also recommended that they let go of all anger and "do not think of your enemies or vengeance, because you will reincarnate and take vengeance" with you into your next life.[236]

Buddhism has no specific or dogmatic regulations regarding funerals. In fact, most funerals vary according to the type of Buddhism the deceased practiced, but in most instances, the body is cremated. Buddhist families attempt to have a monk preside over the service. However, as Lamb points out, "The purpose of monks at funerals is not to pray for the deceased but to aid the bereaved and transfer 'merit' to the dead person."[237]

> **CONSIDER THIS**
>
> *Confucius was primarily concerned with maintaining social harmony in all interpersonal relationships.*

CONFUCIANISM

Confucianism, like all the major traditions, has played a principal role in shaping the culture of billions of people for thousands of years. Yin supports this assertion when he writes, "Confucianism is a worldview, a political ideology, a social tradition, and a way of life. As one of the most prominent traditions of thought, Confucianism has lasting and profound bearings on social, political, and value systems in East Asia."[238] Some experts have suggested that much of the economic success of many of the countries in East Asia is, in part, due to Confucianism and its emphasis on values such as concern for the future, hard work, achievement, education, merit, frugality, and cooperation.[239]

At the outset, we should point out that Confucianism, at least in the conventional sense, is not thought of as a formal religion since "Confucianism has no formal religious hierarchy such as the Vatican, no official priesthood, and almost no congregational life."[240] Confucianism began as a series of ethical precepts for the appropriate way of managing a society. If Confucianism is not a religion, what is it? It is, as will be developed in detail later, a worldview that teaches about social, political, and ethical behavior.

CONFUCIUS THE MAN

As was the case with Buddhism, Confucianism centers on the teachings of a single man: Confucius. We have already mentioned the influence of Confucius on Asian history and culture, but he is also remembered and influential for his teachings on the appropriate relationships and manners among people. Confucius was born in China in 551 BCE. He attempted various careers early in his life, including several government positions. However, around the age of thirty he turned to teaching. Confucius believed that because education taught character and created a better society, it should be available to everyone. What Confucius taught grew out of his observations about conditions in China during his lifetime. "He was surrounded all his life by cruel wars, unjust societies, numerous forms of humans' inhumanity to one another, discord in families, and neglect of scholarship, writing, and the fine and performing arts."[241] In response to these observations, "Confucius asserted that government must be founded on virtue, and that all citizens must be attentive to the duties of their position."[242] McGreal points out, "People were impressed by his integrity, honesty, and particularly his pleasant personality and his enthusiasm as a teacher. Three thousand people came to study under him and over seventy became well-established scholars."[243] Those followers are important to Asian history because they carried on the work of Confucius after his death.

> ### REMEMBER THIS
>
> *Why do cultures conceive of death in so many different ways? Which orientation comes closest to your conception of death?*

CORE ASSUMPTIONS

There are a number of principles that help explain Confucianism. First, Confucius was a teacher and philosopher, not a religious figure. Confucianism primarily "focuses on what happens in this world, not the afterlife."[244] Because of this emphasis, Confucius was more interested in issues related to education than theology. Second, it was his hypothesis that people are basically good and only have to learn what constitutes correct behavior. He suggested a means of bringing about this correct behavior, saying that the best "way to actualize this goodness is through education, self-reflection, self-cultivation, and by behavior in accordance with the established norms of the culture."[245] Third, as noted, Confucius had great faith in learning. He stressed that even a common man could greatly benefit from information and formal instruction. Fourth, Confucius stressed a deep commitment to social harmony. That harmony meant fulfilling the familial and secular obligations needed to live and work together. In carrying out these relationships, Confucianism "emphasizes the individual's social relations and social responsibility over self-consciousness: people perceive themselves according to their social relationships and responsibilities as opposed to their individual being."[246] "Proper" relationships involve such things as the protection of "face," dignity, self-respect, reputation, honor, and prestige. Finally, because Confucius strongly believed in a rigid hierarchy for all relations, he put forth five specific relationships where inferior members had the duty to respect, honor, and obey superior members. These relations were "ruler-subject, husband-wife, elder brother-younger brother, elder friend-junior friend, and father-son."[247] This notion of "honoring upper members" often affects how Chinese interact with people of another culture. For example, Chinese students who attend universities in the United States might be reluctant to contradict, question, or even approach an American professor for fear that their action might be taken as displaying a lack of respect.

ANALECTS

While there are many writings attributed to Confucius, it is the wisdom contained in the compilation called *Analects* (sayings) that is most significant. This collection has influenced East Asian thinking and teaching for thousands of years. Because Confucius did not commit his philosophy to writing, it was his students and disciples who recorded his advice. These "sayings" were not written down in a systematic and structured fashion; instead, *Analects* was compiled over a fifty-year period that produced twenty books. Today, this collection continues to exert considerable authority on East Asian values and behavior. *Analects* teaches basic Confucian values and virtues, such as correct governance, goodness, moral development, respect, honor, filial piety, duty, humanity, propriety, and ritual. The ideals are presented in the form of aphorisms, sayings, stories, and proverbs. For example, when expounding on how to treat other people, *Analects* includes the following advice: "In guiding a state of a thousand chariots, approach your duties with reverence and be trustworthy in what you say; avoid excesses in expenditure and love your fellow beings; employ the labor of the common people only in the right season."[248] The importance of this work to Chinese culture was demonstrated when quotes from *Analects* were read by hundreds of performers at the opening ceremonies of the 2008 Olympics in Beijing.

CULTURAL EXPRESSIONS OF CONFUCIANISM

The Chinese philosopher Tu Wei-ming wrote, "The fundamental concern of the Confucian tradition is learning to be human." This one line could be a summary of what Confucius believed about human nature. Because he assumed the best in all people, he taught that a proper and suitable foundation for society is based on respect for human dignity. That dignity means respecting the proper hierarchy in social relationships among family members and within a community. Confucius set forth a series of ideals that describe his thoughts regarding these relationships. An understanding of some of these teachings will help you appreciate East Asian perceptions and interaction patterns.

Jen (Humanism)

Most scholars agree that the idea of *jen* is the cornerstone of what Confucius taught. This core concept is directly related to the notion of reciprocity. In simple terms, *jen* "is the ideal relationship which should pertain between individuals."[249] In Confucian philosophy, *jen* is often referred to as the "humane principle." Essentially, it is based on "Deep empathy or compassion for other humans."[250] This fundamental belief in the integrity of all people is a reflection of the premise that people are by nature good, and *jen* is meant to mirror that goodness. Some attributes associated with *jen* are benevolence, kindness, and compassion. Regardless of one's status or personality, conflict can and should be avoided. In its place, people should strive for harmony in their interactions with other people, be they within the family, government, or daily interactions.

Li (Rituals, Rites, Proprieties, Conventions)

Li is a companion virtue to *jen* in that it also relates to the outward expression of good manners. It is often thought of as the rules to be followed so that "things" are done correctly. Since its original inception, "the term was extended from narrowly defined religious rites to include all formal conduct that structures interpersonal activities."[251] The words associated with *li* are "propriety," "etiquette," "appropriateness," and "conformity." In contemporary times, *li* could be as straightforward as not interrupting the person who is talking or making sure that your bow is performed properly.

Te (Power)

Te literally means "power by which people are ruled." For Confucius, it was power that was properly employed for the betterment of everyone. He strongly believed that to use power correctly, "leaders must be persons of character, sincerely devoted to the common good and possessed of the character that compels respect."[252]

Wen (The Arts)

Confucius had great reverence for the arts. *Wen* deals with an appreciation of the arts, be they calligraphy, poetry, painting, or music. Confucius believed that all people could create beautiful art. He saw the "arts as a means of peace and as an instrument of moral education."[253] You can further observe that veneration in the following quotation attributed to Confucius: "By poetry the mind is aroused; from music the finish is received. The odes quicken the mind. They induce self-contemplation. They teach the art of sensibility. They help to restrain resentment. They bring home the duty of serving one's parents and one's prince."[254]

CONFUCIANISM AND COMMUNICATION

As is the case with all worldviews, Confucianism influences perception and communication in a variety of ways. Let us mention some of those ways that most directly relate to intercultural communication. First, Confucianism teaches *empathy*, as it encourages people to understand the feelings of others. Perhaps you noticed that when we discussed *jen*, the word "empathy" appeared. What you learned is that "Socialization in the Confucian tradition places ultimate emphasis on sensitivity to human relations."[255] Second, when communicating with someone who adheres to the Confucian philosophy, you should be aware of *status and role relationships*. As previously mentioned, one of the goals of Confucianism is to make social relationships work without conflict or discord. To accomplish that goal, it is important that proper status and role relationships be maintained. Chiu and Hong explain this key element, noting that Confucianism "prescribes different obligatory requirements for different role relationships; for example, loyalty of the ruled to their ruler, filial piety of sons and daughters to their parents, respect for brothers, and trust for friends."[256] Even today, these different role behaviors influence such things as using language, displays of respect, status relationships, how leaders are chosen, and seating arrangements in business and educational environments.

Third, closely related to status and role relationships is the Confucian principle of great concern for *ritual and protocol*. In Confucianism, ritual and etiquette help determine one's character. In the business context, ritual and protocol are manifested in the fact that, when negotiating, the Chinese feel uncomfortable if there is not structure, form, and correct manners. They believe that these characteristics will preserve harmony among the participants.

Finally, Confucius was concerned with the *correct use of language*. Schmidt and his associates develop this important idea in the following: "Confucianism is alone among the world's great philosophies in emphasizing the careful and correct use of language."[257] Part of that correct use focused on what is referred to as indirect instead of direct language. In the United States, people often ask direct questions, are sometimes blunt, and frequently use the word "no." Confucian philosophy, on the other hand, encourages indirect communication. For example, "In Chinese culture, requests often are implied rather than stated explicitly for the sake of relational harmony and face maintenance."[258] Yum makes much the same point while demonstrating the link between Confucianism and talk: "The Confucian legacy of consideration for others and concern for proper human relationships has led to the development of communication patterns that preserve one another's face. Indirect communication helps to prevent the embarrassment of rejection by the other person or disagreement among partners."[259]

CONFUCIANISM AND ETHICS

As you have seen throughout this section, Confucius, like Buddha, was concerned more with this life than with the next. Because of that basic outlook, both systems focused their ethical advice on how people treated each other. This approach is reflected in the fact Confucius never used words such as "good" and "evil" when speaking about the human condition. He was interested in what people could do to bring out the best in each other. What he taught his followers was how "one ought to become involved in reforming the larger social and political structures of one's society, and how one ought to conduct oneself when in a position of influence and power."[260] Two of the most important ways of ethical conduct, according to Confucius, were *benevolence* and *reciprocity*. For Confucius, benevolence, as an ethical act, "denotes humaneness, fellow feelings, even love."[261] In *Analects* 4.1–6, Confucius comments on this ethical virtue, noting, "If the will is set on benevolence, there will be no practice of wickedness."

Matthews writes, "The word *reciprocity* is a good description for Confucian ethics."[262] The Confucian attitude toward reciprocity and ethics is one you have been exposed to in nearly all of the religious traditions we have examined. For Confucius, the issue was simple: "People should avoid doing to others what they would not want done to them. They should do those things that they should like done to themselves."[263]

CONFUCIANISM AND NOTIONS ABOUT DEATH

Our discussion of death as applied to Confucianism will be very brief when compared to other traditions, as death and an afterlife were not important to Confucius. He was a practical man and felt there was no need to speculate about things that nobody knew about for sure. When asked questions about death and an afterlife, it was reported that Confucius would always respond, "How can one know about death before he knows clearly about life?" For Confucius, a person should strive to live the best possible life while here on earth. When urged by his disciples to speak on the subject of death, he would proffer a rather simple response. In terms of an afterlife, he would tell his students, "You are not able even to serve man. How can you serve the spirits?"[264]

While Confucius showed little interest in the topic of death, "Rites for the dead are by no means neglected by Confucians."[265] Because of his strong belief in such virtues as filial piety, honor, and formal ritual, Confucius urged his followers to engage in formal practices ranging from funerals to the building of small family shrines to honor the dead. All of these activities were intended to stress ancestor worship for two reasons. First, such worship underscored the importance of family to his followers. Second, for Confucius, this type of worship was "the proper channeling of natural feelings of grief, longing and guilt."[266]

DEVELOPING RELIGIOUS TOLERANCE

It seems that Homer was right when he noted that "all men have need of the Gods." The problem, as we pointed out in the introduction to this chapter, is that many people now believe their god is the only god. Changes in technology and globalization in the twenty-first century have introduced billions of people to a variety of multicultural gods. Some they have understood, and others appear to be threatening and confusing. Disagreements over which god is "the right god" have created a number of problems. It is common knowledge that we are now experiencing a major collision of religious and spiritual beliefs. We have seen discord and conflict between fundamentalism and modernism, the sacred and the secular, and religious pluralism and religious exclusivism and monism. Those who become swayed by these dichotomies do so for a host of reasons. As Prothero notes, some people seek vehemently to advance a theological point, while "others stress religious differences in order to make the political point that religious civilizations are fated to clash."[267] Regardless of their motives, trying to advance rigid, extreme, and dichotomized positions in the name of a single ideology has made this a very dangerous world. As pointed out at the onset of this chapter, perhaps at no other period in world history has it been more imperative to understand various religions. In this chapter, you saw how people turn to their gods to help them deal with the cosmic questions of how to behave during this lifetime and how to cope with death. When comparing what a religion has told followers about how they should behave with what we actually observe, it is crucial to make the distinction between the theological traditions and how people act out that theology. Bowker points out, "Religions offer ways of resisting what is wrong and dispelling ignorance, but they cannot compel people to live in those ways."[268] We agree with Bowker. "To live those ways" is a matter of individual choice. It means taking the best of what one's worldview has to offer and rejecting those who misread the messages of those religions. It also asks us to develop religious tolerance.

We should point out that religious tolerance takes many forms, but primarily it requires that we allow others to embrace religious beliefs that may differ from our own. Laws will not change deep-seated prejudice and hatred. As Albert Einstein, who suffered intolerance for his Jewish heritage, once remarked, "Laws alone cannot secure freedom of expression; in order that every man present his views without penalty there must be a spirit of tolerance in the entire population."

We believe that tolerance takes two different forms: one general and one specific. The general is what the Dalai Lama calls "universal responsibility." This broad and universal appeal asks that each person seek harmony among all the world's religions. This is a kind of moral commitment to tolerate each other's religious beliefs. Adding to these general appeals, we suggest that there are some specific behaviors that you can engage in to help you become more tolerant. Let us examine a few of these.

First, we begin with the advice that has been at the core of this entire chapter. *Learn all you can about religious groups different from your own.* Schmidt and his coauthors develop this point in greater detail when they write, "As you plunge into the study of concrete communities of faith, try to understand their patterns of life, the character of their communities, and the complexity of their worldview. Seek to understand what each tradition regards as sacred and to become familiar with its stories and rituals."[269] Learning those stories means learning about the historical tragedies that helped shape how members of that group might perceive "outsiders." As we noted earlier in the chapter, the Spanish Inquisition and the Holocaust still influence how Jews perceive non-Jews. And, of course, the thirteenth-century Crusades against Muslims is still a major topic of discussion among many Arabs.

Second, part of the learning process involving diverse religious traditions should make you *aware of the significant differences that exist among all of these traditions.* All of the traditions have had dissimilar histories since their inceptions. Accepting these differences, however strange they may appear, is a major key to developing religious tolerance. Hence, "Rather than beginning with the sort of Godthink that lumps all religions together in one trash can or treasure chest, we must start with a clear-eyed understanding of the fundamental differences in both belief and practice between Islam and Christianity, Confucianism and Hinduism."[270]

Third, *religious tolerance can be improved if you attempt to avoid religious stereotypes.* Be aware of the word "all" when either listening to or speaking about another religion. Stereotypes are used to categorize an entire collection of people. What is being implied is that all people in the group are exactly alike. These characteristics are usually oversimplified and misleading. They do not account for diversity within the group. You meet a Christian who says that everyone should celebrate Christmas, and you assume that all Christians are judgmental and dogmatic. The World Trade Center is blown up by Muslim extremists, and you conclude that all Muslims are terrorists. You see that Jewish people are active on Wall Street, and you assume that all Jews are rich. You meet an atheist who tells you he does not understand how people can believe in God, and you assume that all atheists are intolerant. You see many statues and artistic artifacts in the home of a Hindu, and you conclude that all Hindus engage in idol worship. We could, of course, offer hundreds of other examples, but we are sure you understand the point we are making. To repeat, stereotyping is dangerous because your actions, if based on these false notions, can impede religious tolerance.

Fourth, *technology has the potential to contribute to religious intolerance.* The power of technology for both good and evil is well established. It is common knowledge that there are very few gatekeepers filtering out truth from deception. It is also difficult to measure the credentials and credibility of those who produce messages via the Internet. Blair develops this point:

> Technology, so much the harbinger of opportunity, can also be used by those who want to disseminate lessons of hate and division. Today's world is connected as never before. This has seen enormous advances. It means there is a kind of global conversation being conducted. This is exciting and often liberating. But it comes with the inevitable ability for those who want to get across a message that is extreme to do so.[271]

We suggest that you must be on guard to reject those who espouse messages filled with vitriol that are based on untrue information about religions other than their own. In short, to practice religious tolerance means a willingness to refute and even correct the misinformation that seeks to promote religious intolerance.

Finally, although it might seem simplistic, we advocate that practicing the Golden Rule is one of the best ways to manifest religious tolerance. The same "Golden Rule" you learned growing up in the United States is found in variations in all cultures. Although the words are different, the wisdom contained within the words is universal:[272]

Buddhism: "Hurt not others in ways that you yourself would find hurtful." *Udana-Varga* 5:8

Christianity: "All things whatsoever ye would that men should do to you, do ye even so to them." Matthew 7:12

Confucianism: "Do not do unto others what you would not have them do unto you." *Analects* 15.23

Hinduism: "This is the sum of duty: do naught unto others which would cause you pain if done to you." *Mahabharata* 5:1517

Islam: "No one of you is a believer until he desires for his brother that which he desires for himself." Sunnah

Jainism: "In happiness and suffering, in joy and grief, we should regard all creatures as we regard our own self." Lord Mahavira, 24th Tirthankara

Judaism: "What is hateful to you, do not to your fellow man. That is the law: all the rest is commentary." Talmud, Shabbat, 31a

Native American: "Respect for all life is the foundation." The Great Law of Peace

Were it not for space constraints, we could have included an even longer list of cultures that exhort members to practice the "oneness of the human family." However, we believe that from this brief sample, you can begin to appreciate what photographer Edward Steichen wrote about tolerance: "I believe that in all things that are important, in all of these we are alike."

We end this chapter and our section on developing religious tolerance by reminding you, "God speaks multiple languages."[273] Friedman presents the principle slightly differently: "Can Islam, Christianity, and Judaism know that God speaks Arabic on Fridays, Hebrew on Saturdays, and Latin on Sundays, and that he welcomes different human beings approaching him through their own history, out of their own history, out of their language and cultural heritage?"[274] That answer is yet to be determined. It is also an answer that affects each and every person in the world, whether religious or not. Put in rather blunt terms, we must either learn to be tolerant of religious differences or face the obvious consequences.

SUMMARY

- Worldview is a culture's orientation toward God, humanity, nature, the universe, life, death, sickness, and other philosophical issues concerning existence.

- Although worldview is communicated in a variety of ways (such as secularism and spirituality), religion is the predominant element of culture from which one's worldview is derived.

- Atheism is a worldview that does not believe in the existence of God.

- Spiritualism is a personalized worldview that stresses self-discovery.

- While all religions have some unique features, they share many similarities. These include, among other things, speculation about the meaning of life, sacred writings, rituals, and ethics.

- The six most prominent religious traditions are Christianity, Judaism, Islam, Hinduism, Buddhism, and Confucianism. These traditions present their members with definitions of reality, counsel on how to live life, and explanations about death.

- Developing religious tolerance has increased in importance in the twenty-first century.

ACTIVITIES

1. Working with others, answer the following: Why has religion been relevant to humankind for more than ten thousand years? Also, ask those you are working with why religion has been shadowed by so much violence for thousands of years.

2. Go to YouTube and search for videos that show a religious service inside a Catholic church, an Islamic mosque, and a Buddhist temple. Make note of the rituals, messages, art, music, and space that you deem offer insight into each religious tradition. Also, what do these services have in common, and how do they differ?

3. Working with others, discuss the following question: How does my view of death compare with the beliefs found in the six great religious traditions? As part of your discussion, include observations on how a person's perception of death might influence his or her behavior.

4. In a group, identify and discuss the common principles and practices you see among all of the major religions.

5. Working in a group, discuss the following question: Do religious scriptures, in the same manner as the U.S. Constitution, need constant reinterpretation with each generation?

CONCEPTS AND QUESTIONS

1. Do you believe that globalization will have a positive or a negative impact on the world's religious institutions?

2. Explain how its religious views are linked to a culture's lifestyle.

3. Explain the statement: "Religion is only one kind of worldview."

4. What common set of ethics can you identify from the six religious traditions discussed in this chapter?

5. Since religion touches all aspects of human life, should it be separated from government?

6. What role might religion play in an intercultural communication encounter?

CHAPTER 5

Cultural History: Precursor to the Present and Future

A people without the knowledge of past history, origin, and culture is like a tree without roots.

MARCUS GARVEY

Our view of history shapes the way we view the present, and therefore it dictates what answers we offer for existing problems.

DAVID CRABTREE

We use history to understand ourselves, and we ought to use it to understand others.

MARGARET MACMILLAN

HISTORY'S INFLUENCE

So what does history have to do with the study of culture and communication? A short answer to that question is provided by the quotes offered above. However, a reach back into antiquity will provide additional insight as to the role of history in your lives. Herodotus, the ancient Greek famously known as the "Father of History," wrote that the importance of history was "so that the actions of people will not fade with time." The Roman statesman and orator Cicero wrote, "History is the witness that testifies to the passing of time; it illumines reality, vitalizes memory, provides guidance in daily life, and brings us tidings of antiquity." The importance of history to the study of culture and communication is clearly illustrated by Cicero's proclamation and takes on greater significance when you realize that the word *culture* can easily be substituted for the word *history*. Contemporary historians have also offered compelling statements attesting to the role history plays in understanding human society. For instance, Stearns writes, "The past causes the present and so the future."[1]

For any study of culture, an awareness of your historical heritage helps to explain the current values, traditions, and institutions that guide your daily life. As you probably learned as early as primary school, the majority of early immigrants to the

The study of a culture's history can provide insight into its values, traditions, and social institutions.

Courtesy of Edwin McDaniel

United States came from Europe, and they brought with them historically influenced traditions and worldviews. Huber points out that Europe's philosophical and scientific foundations came from Greece, and Medieval Islam subsequently influenced those teachings. The Western legal system is a product of ancient Rome, and Christianity came from Jerusalem.[2] History can also inform us about the communication behaviors we employ today. For instance, throughout this book, we continually aver that Euro-American cultures place great importance on the ability to communicate orally, whereas that skill carries much less significance in Northeast Asian cultures. A look back in time can tell us why:

> In East Asian civilization the written word has always taken precedence over the spoken; Chinese history is full of famous documents—memorials, essays, and poems—but lacks the great speeches of the West. The magic quality of writing is perhaps one of the reasons why the peoples of East Asia have tended to place a higher premium on book learning and on formal education than have the peoples of any other civilization.[3]

Additionally, reverence for the written word is evident in the East Asian art form of calligraphy, for which the West has no real counterpart. The Arab oral tradition is a product of nomadic life, which precluded many of the art forms that sedentary peoples enjoyed.

There is also a direct link between history and identity that helps unify people from diverse backgrounds and cultures. Bender explains that in the nineteenth and twentieth centuries, the national history of the United States became an important force in unifying the nation's varied social strata:

> It [U.S. national history] became the core of civic education in schools and other institutions devoted to making peasants, immigrants, and provincial peoples into national citizens. A common history, which involved both common memory and a tacit agreement to forget differences, was intended to provide a basis for a shared national identity.[4]

Israel offers another example of history being used to construct a national identity and sense of unity. When the nation was established in 1948, the population consisted of peoples from Europe, the Middle East, and other regions. There was no common language, values, or customs. To overcome this, the government drew on the ancient history of the area as the birthplace of the Jewish people to help forge a national unity.[5]

The discussion of history provided in this chapter encompasses much more than a chronology of events and dates. Granted those are important, but taken in isolation, they paint a rather limited and bleak landscape. As part of a culture's

REMEMBER THIS

An awareness of a culture's historical heritage helps to explain the current values, traditions, and institutions guiding that culture.

deep structure, history incorporates the formal and informal governmental procedures, sense of community, political and economic processes, the key historical heroes, and even geography. All of these factors coalesce to give the members of every culture their identity, values, goals, and expectations. For example, a long-held value in the United States is the concept of equal opportunity—anyone can achieve fame and personal wealth if they are willing to persevere and work hard. This value is a constant theme in U.S. historical accounts, such as Bill Clinton's path from rural Arkansas to the White House and Barack Obama's overcoming the divisive issue of racism to become the nation's first African American president. Accounts of how the computer companies Apple and Hewlett Packard had their beginning in garages are used to inspire students of business, as are stories of Microsoft, Google, and Facebook being conceived of by college students. Such stories are examples of how history can influence perception, affect behavior, and shape national character.

The progression of history is important when reflecting on current geopolitical problems. The long-standing conflict between Israel and Palestine becomes more understandable—if mistrust, animosity, and violence can be understood—when you know that Christians, Muslims, and Jews alike have considered the area sacred for almost two thousand years. The current strife in the Middle East between Sunni and Shia can be traced to a seventh-century political decision.[6] Later in this chapter we will illustrate that leaders in both China and Russia today use their nations' early history to build a strong sense of contemporary nationalism.

Interest in learning history is predicated on two assumptions. The first is that historical events help explain the character and actions of a culture. Kerblay enunciates this, noting, "For all people, history is the source of the collective consciousness."[7] From the earliest westward movement of the initial East Coast settlements to the explorations of outer space, Americans have agreed on a history of embracing new challenges, of exploring new frontiers. The second assumption is that what a culture seeks to remember and pass on to following generations is significant in accounting for the values of that culture.[8] U.S. history books are replete with examples of single, determined individuals making a difference, even in the face of intimidating adversity. Everyone has heard of how Rosa Parks, Martin Luther King Jr., and César Chávez brought about social changes that significantly improved the lives of many Americans. U.S. students are often treated to accounts of the historical accomplishments of individuals like Daniel Boone, the intrepid frontiersman; Audie Murphy, the most decorated soldier in World War II; or Helen Keller, the famous author and first deaf and blind person to earn a college degree. The enduring legacy of these and many other similar historical accounts demonstrates the significance of *the individual* in U.S. culture.

In addition to discussing the historical foundations of U.S. culture, this chapter will provide insight on the historical events that shaped several other nations and give you a broad appreciation of Islamic civilization. This will include the following:

- How centuries of authoritarian rule molded the Russian national character
- How China's pride in historical achievements can produce ethnocentric feelings
- How early Japanese agricultural practices contributed to a preference for group activity
- The eleventh-century event that initiated Hindu–Muslim animosity long before the 1947 Partition of India
- How the Spanish conquest contributed to the Mexican sense of fatalism
- How a simple question of leadership resulted in the Sunni–Shia schism

U.S. History

This examination of U.S. history will cover selected events with the objective of demonstrating how cultural traits emerging from those events ultimately formed what is considered contemporary U.S. national character. Those cultural traits are primarily a product of the peoples who created the United States, especially the early immigrants who set the pattern for what was to follow from 1607, when English settlers began arriving on the East Coast, to the present. McElroy maintains that the "primary American cultural beliefs derive from" the initial settlers and that they "began the process of distinguishing American behavior from European behavior, which over the next eight generations led to the formation of a new American culture." McElroy is suggesting that much of what is considered U.S. national character can be traced to the European immigrants who arrived in the early years of the nation's formation—a population that came holding many of the values that continue to characterize the United States, such as hard work, self-improvement, practicality, freedom, responsibility, equality, and individuality.[9]

The initial settlers were predominantly Anglo-Saxons who brought with them selected English values, the English system of law, and the basic organization for commerce used during the sixteenth century. As they were beginning to establish their norms and ideals, these first immigrants were confronted with a wave of non–Anglo-Saxon newcomers, a development that grew and continues even today with the arrival of new immigrants. This continuing influx of immigrants, both legal and illegal, has produced what is sometimes referred to as the first multicultural nation in the world. Remarkably, the later-arriving immigrants adapted to the U.S. culture that had been formed and evolved by earlier immigrants. In his examination of U.S. history Fischer is struck by "the extent to which the American mainstream has overflowed and washed away that [ethnic] diversity, leaving behind little but food variety and self-conscious celebrations of multiculturalism."[10] Fischer is referring to the many immigrant ethnic cultures being subsumed by and incorporated into the dominant U.S. culture.

While cultural integration does not come easily, then or now, the shared desire of the first immigrants to be free from the oppressive dictates of such English institutions as "the Crown," "divine right," and the Church of England motivated them to seek unity. This impetus ultimately led, in part, to the integration of the early English

TABLE 5.1	Country Statistics: United States of America[11]
LOCATION	NORTH AMERICA
Size	Size: $9,826,675$ km^2; third-largest country
Population	>318.89 million (July 2014 est.); fourth-largest population
Ethnic groups	White 79.96%, Black 12.85%, Asian 4.43%, Amerindian and Alaska native 0.97%, native Hawaiian and other Pacific Islander 0.18%, two or more races 1.61% **Note**: About 16.6% of the total population is Hispanic of any race or ethnic group (2013 est.).[12]
Government	Constitution-based federal republic
Language	English 79.2%, Spanish 12.9%, other Indo-European 3.7%, Asian and Pacific Island 3.2%, other 0.9% (2011 census data)[13] **Note**: The United States has no official national language, but English has acquired official status in twenty-eight of the fifty states; Hawaiian is an official language in Hawaii.
Religions	Protestant/other Christian 51.9%, Roman Catholic 23.3%, Mormon 2.1%, Jewish 1.7%, Muslim 0.6%, other non-Christian 2.6%, no religious identity 15.6%, no response 2.2% (2012 survey)[14]

arrivals with Germans, Irish, and other ethnicities that were fleeing the repressive governance of monarchs, religious authorities, or economic privation. The result was a social fabric flexible enough to enfold Catholics, Congregationalists, Methodists, Lutherans, Presbyterians,[15] and a host of others and to unite North, South, East, and West within a national framework.

These early Americans wanted to separate alienable rights (those that could be voluntarily surrendered to the government) from unalienable rights (those that could not be surrendered or taken away, even by a government of the people).[16] The fundamental American proposition became "life, liberty, and the pursuit of happiness" for each individual, and those rights had to be secured against the potentially abusive power of government. A common desire to escape religious authoritarianism and monarchial rule also gave rise to what is referred to as the doctrine of separation of church and state, which prohibits the government from supporting any single form of religion and from preventing anyone from practicing his or her chosen religion.[17] This doctrine is frequently at the forefront of U.S. political activity when questions of abortion rights, school prayer, and religious displays on government property are publicly and passionately debated.

As noted previously, the people who established the initial settlements and populated the subsequent colonies integrated selected English values with a new set of beliefs. Chief among these new ideals were individuality, a lack of formality, and efficient use of time. Centuries later, these values endure. Individualism was perhaps among the initial values to emerge in the new country. As McElroy notes, "The self-selecting emigrants who left Europe for America manifested individualism by their emigration. When they got on the ships, they were already individualists."[18] This sense of individualism also strongly influenced the nation's early political formation. The founders of the United States sought to establish a nation based on "political freedom, personal liberty, rule of law, social mobility, and egalitarianism."[19] A rich, spacious land with abundant natural resources encouraged implementation of these ideals, and personal liberty remains a hallmark of contemporary American society.

The value and importance of individuality in the United States has been heightened through folklore and the popular media. For example, novels often portray the American settler as moving westward into new lands, carving out a homestead in the wilderness remote from others. Rugged individualism is exemplified in the image of the American cowboy—someone unencumbered by restrictive obligations or personal ties, free to roam the spacious American West at will, and able to surmount all challenges single-handedly. Stewart and Bennett, however, have pointed out that the early frontier individualism, so commonly portrayed in popular media, was more myth than reality.[20] Early settlers actually came together in loosely formed, informal groups to help each other accomplish various tasks, such as harvesting crops or building a church or barn, to barter for goods, or simply to socialize. Indeed, the role of groups in early and present-day American life has led Fischer to consider U.S. culture as characterized by voluntarism rather than individualism, where the self-reliant, independent individual recognizes the benefits of communal activity but engages in those activities on a self-selective, voluntary basis,[21] unlike the compelling sense of mutual obligation so prevalent in collectivistic cultures.

Disdain for formality and wasting time was also part of the colonial experience. Settling a new, undeveloped land required that a great deal of hard work be devoted to the daily activities of surviving, a situation that did not lend itself to idleness or pretentious formality. There was no time to be squandered on the nonsense of the rigid European and British rules of formality. Only resourceful, determined people survived. The challenging geographical factors of the Western frontier also had a far-reaching influence on the settlers. The behaviors of survival based on individualism (voluntarism), a lack of formality, and efficiency soon gave rise to corresponding beliefs, values, and attitudes. Accounts of the early immigrants' ability to overcome the many challenges faced in taming the new land have inculcated cultural values of independence and individualism. Anything that might violate free expression and the right to decide for oneself is considered morally wrong.

U.S. history is also replete with instances of violence and war, experiences that shaped both the culture and the geographical borders. Indeed, from some perspectives, it could be said that the United States is a product of conflict. The early history of the United States witnessed the taking of American Indian lands by force; the capture, importation, and enslavement of Africans; and numerous wars, such as the Revolutionary War, the War of 1812, the Civil War, the Mexican-American War, and the Spanish-American War. The latter two profoundly changed U.S. national borders and its overseas domain. The Mexican-American War and its consequences are discussed further in the section on Mexican history. The Spanish-American War placed several of Spain's colonial holdings under U.S. control, where Puerto Rico and Guam remain today. There are, of course, many other examples that reflect the American belief in possessing and using military force. As McElroy points out, "The most remarkable cultural feature of American behavior in the twentieth century is [was] repeatedly deploying huge armies and other military forces on far-distant continents and seas and in transferring colossal quantities of war supplies to distant allies."[22] That pattern has continued into the twenty-first century as witnessed by the conflicts in the Middle East. The United States, with the world's largest standing armed forces, maintains approximately 1,000 overseas military installations.[23] It is also worth pointing out that gratuitous violence is a constant theme in U.S. entertainment media, such as movies, television shows, and video games.

According to Bender, expansion has also been an important part of U.S. history and began when the early English settlers

> took possession of lands they alleged to be empty and unused…. Americans came to associate the meaning of America with an entitlement to unrestricted access to land and markets. Land, freedom, opportunity, abundance, seemed a natural sequence, which nourished something of an American compulsion to use new lands and opportunities to achieve wealth.[24]

This perspective was prominent in the United States' adoption of the concept of Manifest Destiny, a philosophy embraced in the early 1800s to justify an aggressive campaign of westward expansion and territorial acquisition. Although originally used to dispossess American Indians and Mexicans, this philosophy stressed that Americans were the people "who would inevitably spread the benefits of democracy and freedom to the lesser peoples inhabiting the region."[25] The frequent U.S. calls for human rights, free market access, and democratic reforms in other nations can be construed as a continuing application of Manifest Destiny.

Notions of freedom and independence were continually reinforced during the formative period of the United States, as settlers unceasingly pushed westward into new territories. The challenge of developing sparsely populated virgin land also produced a culture with a strong love of change and the notion of progress. Today, change is commonly associated with progress, especially when economically driven.[26] The ability to conceive new ideas and innovative ways of accomplishing tasks is regarded as a highly desirable attribute. The expectation of frequent changes designed to improve products, processes, and individual conditions represents normality among U.S. Americans. The desire for change and innovation pushed early settlers across the vast wilderness of the North American continent and produced a national restlessness that now sends men and women on explorations of space. This can be seen as a continuing manifestation of a cultural heritage that emphasizes egalitarianism, independence, pragmatism, frequent change, and a willingness to engage the unknown.

CONTEMPORARY SOCIAL ISSUES

The United States currently confronts a host of social issues with cultural roots that could ultimately have an impact on established societal norms and also carry considerable potential for intercultural conflict. The first is immigration, which is significantly changing the ethnic composition of the population. Data from the 2010 census show that, collectively, minorities now constitute the majority in many parts of the United States. Members of different ethnicities, particularly those newly arrived, usually bring with them worldviews and practices dissimilar to those of the established majority. This population shift clearly carries the possibility of intercultural discord as new ways and ideals begin to impinge on established cultural norms. A second prominent source of disharmony is the pronounced ideological differences behind a number of social issues that are proving exceptionally divisive. Three of the most contentious are the right to life versus freedom of choice debate, the argument over same-sex marriage, and the question of school prayer. The

Monuments are often used to create a culture's historical memory by highlighting the suffering, hardships, and victories.

Courtesy of Edwin McDaniel

ideological divide behind these differences is primarily between secular and religious beliefs, and those on either side of the arguments show little inclination to seek a middle ground. Varied ideologies have also resulted in a period of U.S. political dysfunction as liberals and conservatives have been unable to find common ground on such issues as capital punishment, climate change, gun control, healthcare, immigration, the role and size of government, social welfare, and a host of others. In the absence of some form of compromise, according to one distinguished U.S. scholar, this gridlock trend is likely to continue unless some extraordinary event can break the deadlock.[27]

RUSSIAN HISTORY

Probably the most striking feature of Russian history is geography. The largest country in the world, Russia is almost twice the size of the United States, encompasses eleven time zones, and stretches across the entire northern tier of the European and Asian continents. The severe climate and vast distances of the Russian steppes and forests, coupled with a lack of any major north–south geographical barriers, have greatly influenced the history and culture of the Russian peoples. The sheer enormity of their country created a people who "would rather settle down by a warm stove, break out a bottle of vodka, and muse about life."[28]

The lack of any significant barriers to east–west movement has historically left the country vulnerable to invasions by armies from both Europe and Asia. The Russian "Motherland" (*Rodina*) has been invaded and occupied by Mongols, Germans, Turks, Poles, Swedes, French, Japanese, and English—subjecting the Russian peoples to war, persecution, and intense suffering. Cities have been brutally occupied and cruelly governed, with the population of entire towns and villages slaughtered. Consequently, Russians have developed a perception of the world that frequently incorporates distrust of outsiders.[29] To illustrate this sense of national paranoia,

Daniels summarizes the differences between U.S. and Russian formative historical perspectives:

> It is of greatest importance for Americans to appreciate how different was Russia's international environment from the circumstances of the young United States. Russia found itself in a world of hostile neighbors, the United States in secure continental isolation. Living under great threats and equally great temptations, Russia had developed a tradition of militarized absolutism that put the highest priority on committing its meager resources to meet those threats and exploit those temptations.[30]

CONSIDER THIS

Can you think of examples to help explain the notion that Russia remains in a transitional phase?

Russia's historical political heritage has helped mold the contemporary Russian worldview. Esler depicts that heritage in the following: "Russia's political tradition has historically been autocratic, from the legacy of the Byzantine emperors and Tartar khans, through the heavy-handed authoritarianism of Peter the Great, to the totalitarian regime of Joseph Stalin."[31] To give you a fuller appreciation of the tradition of Russia being governed by an autocratic, centralized government, a brief overview of the establishment and development of the Russian state is provided.

Early historical records indicate that during the ninth century, a series of city-states was established along the waterways of the western Russian plain, with Novgorod and Kiev the most prominent. Princes ruled these city-states, and Kiev developed into a major center of government until the late twelfth century, when political decay set in. The arrival of the Mongols in 1240 brought about the final collapse of the Kievan state. Although the Mongols maintained a military presence in Russia for well over 200 years, they were generally satisfied to rule from a distance as long as tribute was rendered. Mongol rule was replaced in the fifteenth century by the rise and ultimate establishment of a consolidated Russia governed from Moscow. From the early sixteenth century until the Russian Revolution in 1917, the Russian peoples were

TABLE 5.2	Country Statistics: Russian Federation[32]
LOCATION	**EUROPE AND NORTHERN ASIA**
Size	17,098,242 km^2; world's largest country
Population	142.47 million (July 2014 est.); tenth-largest population
Ethnic groups	Russian 77.7%, Tatar 3.7%, Ukrainian 1.4%, Bashkir 1.1%, Chuvash 1%, Chechen 1%, other 10.2%, unspecified 3.9% (2010 est.) **Note:** Over 190 ethnic groups represented in the 2010 census.
Government	Federation
Language	Russian (official) 96.3%, Dolgang 5.3%, German 1.5%, Chechen 1%, Tatar 3%, other 10.3% **Note:** Total exceeds 100% due some people giving more than one answer on census (2010 est.).
Religions	Russian Orthodox 15% to 20%, Muslim 10% to 15%, other Christian 2% (2006 est.) **Note:** Estimates are of active worshippers; due to seventy years of Soviet rule, there are large numbers of nonpracticing believers and nonbelievers.

subjected to the heavy-handed rule of an authoritarian, centralized government headed by an autocratic, often despotic "tsar."[33] The revolution replaced the tsarist rulers with a Soviet regime but brought little improvement to ordinary Russians' lives. It was not until 1991, when the Communist Party lost power, that the Russian peoples achieved a democratic government. However, the current government under President Putin has become increasingly authoritarian.

These experiences instilled traits that enabled the Russians to accept the diktats of their leaders and endure incredible hardship. One of the most vivid recent examples of the Russians being dominated by harsh, authoritarian rule had its beginning in the 1917 Bolshevik Revolution, which was supposed to overturn the oppressive tsarist regime, eliminate economic inequities, and give the working class a voice. Instead, much of the country was destroyed and the entire sociocultural structure was changed in the name of Communism. Joseph Stalin's program of state agricultural and industrial collectivization brought added turmoil to the Russian populace. Under his rule, "Millions died in the political purges, the vast penal and labor system, or in state-created famines."[34] World War II resulted in more suffering when some 27 million Soviet citizens perished in the struggle against fascist Germany.[35] In 1991, due to economic stagnation and wide popular demand for greater freedom, the repressive Communist system collapsed and was replaced by the Russian Federation, an independent nation. From this sketch of Russian political history, it is easy to understand why Bergelson says that even today, many Russians feel they have "no control over the world."[36] The long legacy of centralized, repressive rule and unwarranted suffering has imparted a sense of fatalism that has become a part of Russian culture.

The Russian historical tradition is also marked by a deep appreciation of and devotion to the arts. During the tenth century, Greek Orthodox Christianity, imported from the Byzantine Empire, became the state religion. Consequently, "Byzantine Christianity has had a profound and permanent effect on Russian civilization," and its legacy can be seen in Russia's architectural, musical, and artistic heritage.[37] Even today, the performing and cultural arts form an integral part of Russian life. Since its inception in the early 1700s, the world-famous Bolshoi Ballet has been a source of great pride and an object of esteem among all Russians. Classical music by Tchaikovsky, Rachmaninoff, Rimsky-Korsakov, and Stravinsky is admired and enjoyed throughout the world. In the field of literature, Russia has produced such literary giants as Chekhov, Dostoevsky, Gogol, Pushkin, and Tolstoy, and five Russian authors have been awarded the Nobel Prize for Literature—Ivan Bunin (1933), Boris Pasternak (1958), Mikhail Sholohov (1965), Alexander Solzhenitsyn (1970), and, most recently, Joseph Brodsky (1987). A contemporary illustration of the important role of the cultural arts in Russian life is the Primorsky Opera and Ballet Theater, which opened in 2013. This seven-story modern, almost futuristic structure is located in Vladivostok, a somewhat isolated city of just over half a million inhabitants located almost four thousand miles east of Moscow on a small peninsula jutting into the Sea of Japan.

Although over two decades have passed since the collapse of communist rule, Russia remains in transition. With very little prior experience of democracy or capitalism to draw on, Russia has encountered many problems in adapting to the international order. Following the establishment of the federation in 1991, Russia was in turmoil until Vladimir Putin became president in 1999. He quickly moved to consolidate and centralize political and economic power over the entire country. In an early speech, Putin acknowledged people's universal values but also asserted three distinctly

Russian values—(1) patriotism, (2) that the state should play a role in world affairs, and (3) "state-centeredness." The latter refers to the belief that the state should be a central influence in Russian society. According to Putin, "It is a fact in Russia the tendency toward collective forms of activity have always dominated over individualism. It is also a fact that in Russian society paternalistic sentiments are deeply embedded."[38] This perception helps explain Putin's movement away from a liberal democratic form of governance in favor of returning to a more authoritarian central government, a structure that has long characterized Russia's history. This has moved Russia toward "state capitalism" and brought about a diminution of political and individual freedoms.[39]

Russia's recent actions in relation to Ukraine and the Crimea can also be explained, at least in part, through the lens of history. As brought out earlier, Russian east–west topography has facilitated numerous invasions, and a large part of Ukraine consists of relatively flat steppes. Over the course of recent history, this has been the route used by Napoleonic French, Imperial German, and Nazi German armies to strike at Russia. Thus, loss of Ukraine as a buffer state against Western European influence and military might be seen as a threat from Moscow's perspective.[40]

CONTEMPORARY SOCIAL ISSUES

The Russian Federation is presently grappling with numerous social issues, some of which are common throughout globalized society and others that are uniquely Russian. The most enervating social problem is endemic corruption, which permeates all segments of contemporary Russian society and has become a normative practice.[41] The pervasiveness of corruption has eroded people's ability to trust government institutions and leaders and inhibited overall social cohesiveness.[42] Rampant drug (heroin) and alcohol abuse also plague Russia. One report indicated that 25 percent of Russian men die before 55 years of age, and alcohol intemperance causes most of those deaths. Intravenous use of heroin has resulted in an epidemic of HIV/AIDS due to addicts sharing dirty needles and the stigma attached to homosexuality.[43] Russia is also beset with a declining population due to high mortality rates and low birthrate. To counter this trend, the government introduced a twelve-year program to provide bonuses, better healthcare, housing, and education for families who have more than two children. Other, more authoritarian measures have been implemented that include taxing divorce and placing limits on abortion.[44] The government has recently become increasingly intolerant of social dissent and now exercises control over key public media outlets. The government's use of historical memory to promote identity-based nationalism by glorifying Imperial Russia's past carries the risk of domestic divisiveness, particularly in relation to Russian ethnic minorities and immigrants from the former Soviet states.[45]

Daniel Triesman's commentary on Russia's socioeconomic plight remains as valid today as when he made it in 2011:

> [Russia is] a country struggling with a combination of challenges, governed under a system that is part democratic, part authoritarian; informed by a press that is only partly free; powered by an economy cued to world commodity cycles; inhabited by citizens who judge their leaders on the basis of economic performance; where alcoholism, encouraged by the extremely low cost of vodka, is taking an extraordinary toll on life expectancy and aggravating crime.[46]

CHINESE HISTORY

Over the past three decades China has achieved extraordinary economic growth and experienced considerable social change. China now occupies a prominent position in the world economy and the ability to influence markets globally. In October 2014, the International Monetary Fund reported that China had surpassed the United States to become the world's largest economy when adjusted for purchasing power.[47] Concurrent with economic growth, Beijing has significantly increased its military capabilities, creating regional tensions and causing concern among many Western nations. Economic and politico-military advances have also given China increased influence in regional and international forums. These developments alone suggest the importance of understanding China and the Chinese. But beyond the economic and political factors, an additional compelling reason is that China is home to almost 20 percent of the world's population—over 1 billion—and globalization has greatly increased the requirement for interaction with Chinese diplomats, government officials, business leaders, and sojourners.

Any understanding of China and the Chinese peoples requires an appreciation of the country's history. China's lengthy legacy of achievements and experiences forms an important part of how the more than 1.35 billion contemporary Chinese perceive and experience the world. One reason for this importance is because historical memory plays an integral role in modern Chinese worldview and "determines most of its approaches to the present."[48]

As befitting a nation with the longest record of civilization, China has an extensive account of its past. Archaeological data suggest that the prehistoric origins

An appreciation and understanding of China's long history is essential to understanding Chinese culture.

Courtesy of Edwin McDaniel

of Chinese society extend back to 7000 BCE.[49] The documented historical record began with the Shang Dynasty (1766?–1122? BCE) and continues unbroken to current times, making China the world's oldest continuous civilization.[50] This record of the past has inculcated in the Chinese an enduring sense of history, a profound pride in past grandeur, and an acute awareness of Western-perpetrated injustices suffered during the modern age.

Geography has played a formative role in China's uninterrupted record of social and cultural development, serving simultaneously to isolate and to unify the nation.[51] Slightly larger than the United States when measured in total land area only, China is surrounded by formidable borders—vast, desolate plateaus and desert to the north, soaring mountain ranges to the west and southwest, mountains and deep valleys to the south, and the ocean to the southeast and east. The formidable barriers to the north, west, and southwest restricted large-scale overland movement. A paucity of good harbors and unfavorable coastal terrain hindered seaborne access to the east and southeast. Collectively, these topographical features, coupled with a strong sense of centrality among Imperial China's governing elite, ensured a degree of geographical and cultural remoteness that continued until the development of modern transportation and communication systems.

This relative geographical seclusion restricted China's awareness of and contact with the world's other early civilizations and facilitated the development of partisan political, economic, and social systems. With only a limited awareness of lands and peoples beyond their borders, Imperial Chinese developed a worldview inscribed with a sense of cultural superiority. Imbued with the belief that they were the foremost social order in the known world, the ancient Chinese elite considered their country to be the center of the world (*tianxia*), and everything beyond its borders was viewed as inferior and unimportant.[52] They referred to China as the "Central Country" (simplified 中国; traditional 中國),[53] and even today those ideograms remain a part of the official name of the People's Republic of China (simplified 中华人民共和国; traditional 中華人民共和國).

Internally, China's irregular topography gave rise to regional separation and differentiation in customs and dialects, discussed in greater detail below. To overcome these impediments to unification and to govern the predominantly agrarian population, the Chinese instituted a system of imperial rule and a bureaucratic, centralized administration. The adoption of Confucianism as a state ideology and development of a written language common throughout the empire facilitated consolidation and control. Thus, although China presented an outward model of uniformity, internally it was marked by social and linguistic diversity, which is a continuing characteristic.

China's premodern history is an enduring cycle of dynastic successions, led by an imperial emperor supported by an extensive bureaucracy. The emperor was referred to as the "Son of Heaven," and his legitimacy and power were derived from the "Mandate of Heaven," the concept that if an emperor were just and virtuous in governing the people, heaven would permit him to rule the land. However, if the people rose up over perceived injustices, natural calamities such as famine or flood occurred, or invading armies breached the borders, the emperor was perceived to have lost his mandate and would be replaced by a new emperor who had received the mandate. The concept of a government formed around a centralized bureaucracy under the rule of a single leader continues today, as exemplified by the Chinese Communist Party (CCP).

TABLE 5.3	Country Statistics: People's Republic of China[54]
LOCATION	EAST ASIA
Size	9,596,960 km²; fourth-largest country
Population	1.35 billion (July 2014 est.); world's largest population
Ethnic groups	Han Chinese 91.6%, Zhuang 1.3%, other (includes Hui, Manchu, Uighur, Miao, Yi, Tujia, Tibetan, Mongol, Dong, Buyei, Yao, Bai, Korean, Hani, Li, Kazakh, Dai, and other nationalities) 7.1%, (2010 est.) **Note**: Has fifty-six officially recognized ethnic groups.
Government	Communist state
Language	Mandarin (official), Yue (Cantonese), Wu (Shanghainese), Minbei (Fuzhou), Minnan (Hokkien-Taiwanese), Xiang, Gan, Hakka dialects, minority languages **Note**: Over eighty languages spoken by various ethnic groups.[55]
Religions	Buddhist 18.2%, Christian 5.1%, Muslim 1.8%, folk religion 21.9%, Hindu <.1%, Jewish <.1%, other 0.7% (includes Daoist [Taoist]), unaffiliated 52.2% (2010 est.) **Note**: Officially atheist.

In addition to the historical legacy of imperial rule, China's contemporary world-view is strongly influenced by events that have transpired over the past two centuries. Western explorers and traders began appearing in Southeast Asia as early as the sixteenth century. By the late 1700s to early 1800s, England, Holland, Germany, Portugal, France, the United States, and other nations had carved out a dominant presence in many Southeast and East Asian countries. China's xenophobic imperial court and ethnocentric disdain for importing foreign products initially led to a one-way flow of trade goods. To redress this imbalance, Western powers, particularly England, began to demand that China open its borders to unrestricted trade. After several humiliating defeats by Western forces, China's weak, corrupt imperial court and ineffective military acquiesced to a series of "unequal treaties" that granted the Western nations "spheres of influence" within China. Conducting commercial activities from these areas, foreign businesses and residents enjoyed special economic privileges and extraterritoriality while ignoring Chinese sovereignty. China's independence was further eroded by Japan's invasion of Manchuria in 1931. Only in the wake of World War II and a subsequent civil war did China regain its full independence. Today, this period of foreign subjugation and occupation is referred to as the "era of national humiliation" and occupies a salient position in contemporary historical memory and political rhetoric.

Since 1949 the People's Republic of China has been governed by the CCP. The early years of CCP rule, particularly those under Mao Zedong, were characterized by widespread internal strife and political turmoil. Left with a backward, underdeveloped, war-ravaged nation, postwar Communist leaders initiated a series of reform programs, such as the Great Leap Forward and the Cultural Revolution. These measures ultimately proved disastrous to the populace and the nation as a whole. While figures vary widely, one estimate is that as many as 45 million, mostly peasants, perished during the Great Leap Forward experiment (1958–1962).[56]

In the early 1970s China began to move away from the debilitating "revolutionary" programs and responded to political overtures from the United States, leading to President Richard Nixon's historic visit to Beijing in 1972. Following Mao's death in 1976, more pragmatic leaders recognized the need for economic and political reforms, and China began to modernize. In the 1990s Chinese leaders opted to move away from a centrally planned economy in favor of one that was more market driven. This has proven enormously successful and improved the lives of millions of China's citizens, especially those living in urban areas. In less than twenty years, the nation has become the world's second-largest economy behind the United States, when measured in gross domestic product (GDP), and is now a key player in the global economy.

COMMUNICATING HISTORY

China is currently in transition and experiencing rapid, increased industrialization and urbanization. Between 1990 and 2013 the urban population more than doubled. However, the country has historically been a predominantly agrarian society, and nearly half the population still resides in the countryside.[57] This rural existence played a formative role in the development of Chinese values. The labor-intensive agrarian lifestyle extending over centuries, blended with Confucian precepts, instilled the Chinese with a strong cultural orientation toward collectivism and hierarchy. Traditionally, Chinese societal organization was composed of four primary groups—family, gentry, bureaucratic officials, and the imperial throne. Unable to rely on the bureaucracy or the emperor during untoward times, the extended patriarchal family, or clan, became the most important social unit. This reliance on a small, select group of people is today exemplified in the concept of *guanxi*, which is based on mutual obligation in a network of close interpersonal relationships. Another key component of the Chinese historically based social structure is respect for hierarchy within and between social groups and individuals. This Confucian-derived value is also seen today in the continuing acceptance of a centralized, authoritative government.

China also offers us an informative illustration of how historical memory can become a source of cultural identity, nationalistic sentiments, and a prominent aspect of political policy. Present-day Chinese are acutely conscious of China's past, and their historical memory is characterized by two distinct themes—traditional and modern. Traditional historical memory recalls the grandeur and legacy of the Chinese empire when it was the "center of the world," and nations from afar sent emissaries bearing tribute gifts to avow their allegiance to the Chinese throne. From this perspective, China is seen as an enlightened, advanced country whose contributions significantly advanced human civilization. Today, it provides the Chinese with a source of national pride and identity. Modern historical memory focuses on the degradations China suffered at the hands of foreign powers during the "era of humiliation." This latter historical perspective has instilled "a sense of entitlement growing out of historical victimization."[58] The nineteenth-century injustices are frequently used by the CCP to validate the Party's legitimacy, justify current policies, and promote nationalism. For instance, the central purpose underlying The Road to Rejuvenation, a permanent display at the National Museum of China in Beijing, is to illustrate how the CCP ultimately defeated and expelled the foreign powers, especially the Japanese, and then successfully rebuilt the nation, returning China to its rightful place on the international stage.

CONTEMPORARY SOCIAL ISSUES

China's rapid economic ascent has prompted significant change in Chinese society, and many of the changes are positive, lifting millions out of poverty into a much better life. However, the rapid economic development has created new societal difficulties and compounded old ones. Economic development and urbanization have resulted in serious environmental degradation. Ecological problems abound in the lack of access to clean water, carbon emissions, desertification, and soil contamination. According to official reports, almost 60 percent of groundwater and 20 percent of farmland is affected by pollution, and Beijing's enervating air quality is a near constant refrain in international media reports. All of these contribute to health problems.[59] Persistent, widespread official corruption continues to threaten economic progress and social stability. China's income inequality ranks among the highest in the world and presents another formidable challenge for China's leaders.[60]

The problem with the greatest potential for transforming traditional Chinese cultural norms is the changing location and structure of the population. Traditional rural Chinese society is rapidly being altered by urbanization and the impact of the one-child policy. In the 2000 census only 36 percent of the population was urban,[61] but by 2014 the figure had risen to almost 54 percent, and the government goal is for 70 percent of the population to live in cities by 2020.[62] As greater numbers of people leave the countryside, the traditional concept of the extended family (and attendant values) will erode, just as has occurred in other industrialized societies.

Due to the culturally motivated desire for sons and availability of selective abortion, China's official one-child policy, instituted over thirty years ago, has both reduced the number of newborns and produced a disproportionate number of males among the younger generations. This has "forcefully altered the family and kin structure of hundreds of millions of Chinese families."[63] The many potential problems resulting from this change are exacerbated by China's falling birthrate and the increased graying of the population. The birth ratio in 2011 was 117 males for every 100 females, and current predictions are that by 2020, there will be an excess of 24 million bachelors. One Chinese official indicated that the imbalance portended a range of social difficulties, including "sex crimes, trafficking in women, and difficulty finding a spouse."[64] The declining birthrate, estimated at 1.5 babies per couple, undermines the Chinese tradition of children supporting their elderly parents. Moreover, a falling youth cohort in an aging society carries major consequences for China's economic growth and social structure—that is, a shrinking labor force insufficient to underpin needed social support systems.[65] The situation is further aggravated by a growing brain drain, with increasing numbers of educated and/or affluent Chinese choosing to move abroad in search of greater opportunity and an enhanced quality of life.[66]

China's economic ascendance has produced social improvement and given rise to new societal challenges. But perhaps the most significant changes and those that portend lasting change have occurred in the traditional social structure:

> Attitudes toward the family have been revolutionized.... The family used to be the state in miniature, with the father-son bond mirroring the ruler-subject relationship. Now though, the vertical relationship in the family is coming second to the horizontal conjugal relationship between man and wife. Youth is triumphing over age in the cities; the individual is becoming more important than the group.... China has become a fount of modern, scientific thinking and go-getting individualism.[67]

JAPANESE HISTORY

The history of Japan is largely a product of geography. Proximity to its two closest Northeast Asian neighbors—China and Korea—produced a lengthy historical record of interaction. Approximately 100 miles of ocean separate Japan from the Korean Peninsula, and China is just 500 miles to the east across the Yellow Sea. This nearness facilitated the early importation of ideas and artifacts from the two nations, particularly China. For example, Confucianism and Buddhism, both brought from China through Korea, exerted a significant and enduring influence on the development of Japanese society. The use of Chinese ideograms is a daily reminder of Japan's historical connection to China. Despite this legacy, however, the Japanese are defined by cultural characteristics quite different from those of its two nearby neighbors.

A relatively small nation composed of four major islands and several thousand smaller ones, Japan was accessible only by sea until the early twentieth century. This insularity made Japan relatively immune to large-scale immigration from the Asian mainland, and the sea often stymied invading foreign armies. This natural isolation was further encouraged by over 250 years of governmentally imposed national seclusion during the Tokugawa, or Edo, era (1603–1867) and resulted in Japan's cultural distinctiveness and self-image.

Historical isolation, low immigration rates, and a feudal-based system of governance produced a society characterized by its relative cultural homogeneity. This sense of ethnic similarity has become a defining characteristic among the Japanese. As Dower writes, "Although all peoples and cultures set themselves apart (and are set apart by others) by stressing differences, this tends to be carried to an extreme where Japan is concerned."[69]

One expression of cultural homogeneity is the Japanese approach to foreigners. As a result of the country being closed to outsiders until the mid-nineteenth century, when it was forcibly opened by Western powers, the Japanese developed an ambivalence toward all foreigners. Demographic separation and geographic isolation "produced in the Japanese a strong sense of self-identity and also an almost painful self-consciousness in the presence of others."[70] This self-consciousness persists today and can sometimes be encountered by foreigners when traveling beyond Japan's major urban areas, where they may find themselves treated as curiosities or even politely overlooked. Such behavior is frequently a result of uncertainty on the part of the Japanese about how to interact with a non-Japanese individual. While their culture specifies the appropriate behavioral and communication protocols for

TABLE 5.4	Country Statistics: Japan[68]
LOCATION	**EAST ASIA**
Size	377,915 km^2; sixty-second-largest country
Population	127.10 million (July 2014 est.); eleventh-largest population
Ethnic groups	Japanese 98.5%, Koreans 0.5%, Chinese 0.4%, other 0.6%
Government	Parliamentary
Language	Japanese
Religions	Shintoism 83.9%, Buddhism 71.4%, Christianity 2%, other 7.8% Note: Total exceeds 100% due to many people practicing both Shintoism and Buddhism.

CONSIDER THIS

How do Japan's demographic separation, geographic isolation, and sense of self-consciousness manifest themselves during inter-action with strangers of other cultures?

working and socializing with other Japanese, no established "correct" way of dealing with foreigners has evolved. The Japanese uncertainty toward foreigners continues today, as evident in contemporary attitudes toward immigration. Foreign residents in Japan in 2014 represented less than 2 percent of the population.[71] Despite a rapidly declining population and the attendant economic and social dilemmas, there is little public support for increased immigration. As one source states, "Simply put, there is a deep cultural aversion to any immigration whatsoever."[72]

Another important link between Japan's long history and its contemporary cultural values is the Tokugawa legacy. In the early 1600s, following a period of debilitating civil wars, Japan was politically unified under the leadership of a military-style governor (*shōgun*). The Japanese population, much of which resided in or around castle towns, was divided into four specific, hierarchical groups—samurai, farmer, artisan, and merchant (*shi-nō-kō-shō*)—each with its own set of subgroups and hierarchy (the Imperial Court was above these, and several lower status groups were below).[73] The central government specified strict codes of behavior to regulate the conduct of every aspect of personal and public life. In other words, the Japanese formed a culture where in almost every context there was a *single correct way* to perform a task, be it sitting, eating, dressing, living, or even thinking, and any other type of behavior was considered deviant.[74] The objective of these protocols was to ensure external peace and internal group stability by subordinating the individual to the central authority and the greater social order. Societal stability was the paramount objective, and this continues to be a central focus of Japanese social activity, demonstrated by an adherence to established norms, a resistance to rapid change, and an aversion to risk,[75] all of which point to a strong inclination to avoid uncertainty.

The Tokugawa-era castle town residents relied on benevolent feudal lords for protection and civil administration. In return for these benefits, the people professed a strong loyalty to the warlords (*daimyō*). This cultural characteristic is evident in modern Japanese social relationships, where workers continue to demonstrate dedication and loyalty to their school, company, and other in-groups. Modern corporations and government institutions became substitutes for the castle town and have traditionally offered lifetime employment, although three decades of economic stagnation have significantly altered this practice. Feudalism also inculcated in the Japanese an acceptance of discipline, sacrifice, and conformity. People were required to conduct every aspect of their lives in a highly prescribed manner, depending on their social class membership. These conditions have been translated into contemporary Japanese dedication to societal and organizational formality and an acceptance of higher authority, status differentials, and conformity to group expectations.[76]

As noted previously, a culture's history is just one of many sources that contribute to the character of its people. This concept is demonstrated in the Japanese attitude toward collectivism, or group orientation. Here again, the link between culture and geography is evident. In total land area, Japan is slightly smaller than Montana, but over 70 percent of the country is mountainous. Ever since people began inhabiting the islands, the rugged topography has forced the majority of the population to live communally in the narrow valleys and along the few coastal plains, where today just over 126 million people are crowded together.

Japanese "premodern village life was a community enterprise"[77] where the people depended on mutual assistance to conduct labor-intensive wetland (rice) cultivation. As Reischauer and Jansen point out, "Probably such cooperative efforts over the centuries contributed to the notable Japanese penchant for group identification and group action."[78] Group affiliation was also inculcated by the feudal government organization and class system, discussed above, which lasted until the 1868 Meiji Restoration. Group orientation continues to guide contemporary Japanese society, where one's status is based more on factors like schools attended, profession, or employer than on individual achievement.

Due to the necessity of group cooperation in early Japanese village life, social ostracism (*murahachibu*), or the threat thereof, became a form of punishment. Unlike early U.S. settlers, whose lives were characterized by frontier semi-isolation, self-reliance, and independence, Japanese farmers were heavily reliant on other villagers. The cooperative demands of wetland cultivation made an isolated existence essentially impossible. As a result, exclusion became "a powerful sanction throughout rural [Japanese] society"[79] to maintain order and punish deviance. To some degree, various forms of social exclusion remain a means of social reprimand in modern Japan.[80]

History has also shaped current Japanese attitudes on contemporary national security issues. Motivated by its inability to resist incursions by Western powers in the mid-1800s, following the Meiji Restoration, Japan began instituting comprehensive national programs to modernize itself in the image of the United States and European nations. Along with economic industrialization, educational restructurings, and social transformation, Japanese leaders sought to build a powerful military capable not only of defending the island nation but also of providing Tokyo a voice in international affairs. This led to imperialistic expansion into Asia in the 1930s and ultimately entry into World War II against the Western Allied Powers. At the end of the war, Japan lay in ruins with industrial and military capacity virtually nonexistent. Almost one hundred years of modernization and industrialization efforts had been comprehensively and completely destroyed. However, drawing on their cultural traits of discipline, the ability to endure hardship (*gaman*), and a strong sense of national identity, the Japanese launched a wide-reaching program of reconstruction, aided by Allied Occupation Forces. By the mid-1980s Japan had become one of the world's leading economies. The historical memory of World War II, especially the impact of the atomic bombs dropped on Hiroshima and Nagasaki, and its aftermath left the Japanese with a strong feeling of pacifism and a reluctance to engage in military operations not directly related to national self-defense.[81]

The primary significance of this summary of Japan's past should be somewhat transparent. The historically based cultural characteristics discussed in this section, such as group orientation, perseverance, hierarchy, social predictability, etc., have endured in Japan for centuries. They have guided the social organization and conduct of the Japanese people through periods of prosperity and of devastation, and they continue to form an integral part of Japanese cultural values.

Japan's history is based on cultural group orientation, perseverance, hierarchy, social predictability, and the love of tradition.

Courtesy of Edwin McDaniel

CONTEMPORARY SOCIAL ISSUES

The era of globalization has given rise to societal problems that are straining the fabric of contemporary Japanese social order and, in some instances, pressuring traditional values. These problems include (1) demographic changes, (2) immigration issues, and (3) risk management.

Japan's once-rural society, characterized by interdependent extended families, now consists largely of urban nuclear families living in high-density population centers. The number of single-person households also had risen to over 32 percent by 2010. Japan's elderly (age sixty-five and above) population represented over 25 percent of the total population in 2013 and is projected to grow to almost 40 percent by 2050. The situation is further exacerbated by increased longevity, a falling marriage rate, a rising marriage age, and a declining birthrate.[82] Stated simply, the Japanese are living longer, fewer are getting married, those marrying are doing so at an older age, and women are having fewer babies. These developments will ultimately exert a significant burden on all social programs, especially pensions, as the native workforce declines. The obvious solution is increased immigration, but this option faces considerable difficulty. As Kingston points out, "The growing presence of foreigners in Japan is generally unwelcome and seen as a risk not only in terms of crime rates, but also to a national identity rooted in a sense of homogeneity."[83] For Japan's consensus-based, conformist, and highly risk-avoiding culture, change comes gradually, even in the face of crisis. This is evident in Japan's continued inability to turn its economy around in the globalized market.[84] However, in the dynamics of the globalized world, change is constant and often rapid, requiring governments and corporations to either adapt or be left behind. Sugimoto indicates "contemporary Japanese society is caught between the contradictory forces of *narrow ethnocentrism and open internationalization*."[85] In short, Japanese society is experiencing considerable social challenges in the process of adapting to the globalized world community and might well be considered a work in process.[86]

INDIAN HISTORY

Many aspects of your everyday life result from events that started in India thousands of years ago. Each time you pull on your cotton jeans, eat chicken, or use the decimal system, you are enjoying the benefits of developments that arose in ancient India.[87] Modern India is no less influential in your life. No doubt you have already had experience talking with a company's representative in India while getting help with an information technology (IT) problem or making an airline or hotel reservation for spring break. And while you sleep, someone in Mumbai, Kolkata, or Noida may be processing your credit card account, developing a new website for use next semester when you register for classes, or reviewing the legal details of the contract for your new job. India's large population of engineers and English speakers provides U.S. companies with IT and business-processing services across a broad range of industries, including animation, computer-assisted design, software development, insurance claim processing, and, of course, customer care call centers.[88] This background should provide convincing illustrations as to why an appreciation of India's history and culture is important today. But in addition to these examples, there are many other reasons for learning about India.

Immigrants from India and their descendants represent a vital, productive segment of the U.S. population. Over 3 million Indian Americans currently live in the United States, constituting the third-largest Asian American ethnic group. Approximately 70 percent of Indian Americans hold at least a bachelor's degree, well above the national average of 28 percent. While these educated professionals love their adopted nation, they also maintain a strong attachment to India and their heritage.[89] Indian Americans are also becoming active in U.S. politics. In 2015 the governors of both Louisiana and South Carolina were first-generation Indian Americans, and California returned an Indian American to the House of Representatives for a second term in 2014. As more Indian Americans become part of the diversity of the United States, it behooves us to have an awareness of the origins of their culture.

The most striking and noticeable characteristic of the Republic of India is the nation's rich diversity of geography, peoples, cultures, languages, and history. The land area of India, the largest nation on the Indian subcontinent, begins in the towering Himalayan Mountains in the north and extends southward for almost two thousand miles, jutting into the Indian Ocean. The diverse terrain and climatic zones include mountain ranges, plateaus, alluvial plains, tropical forests, and deserts. The more than 1.2 billion people who inhabit the world's largest democracy consist of over two thousand ethnic groups and tribes, speak eighteen official languages, and practice a multiplicity of religions, including Hinduism, Islam, Christianity, Sikhism, Buddhism, Jainism, Parsi, and a number of other belief traditions.[90]

The basis of India's contemporary multicultural society is its long and varied historical legacy, which grew out of influences from South and Northeast Asia, Central Asia, the Middle East, and Europe. The archaeological record indicates that hunter-gatherers were active on the subcontinent as early as 2 million years ago. By approximately 2600 BCE, these early groups had evolved into urban dwellers, living in houses along grid-patterned streets with drainage systems. Archaeological data also suggest that they engaged in long-distance trade with Middle Eastern societies.

TABLE 5.5	Country Statistics: Republic of India[91]
LOCATION	**SOUTH ASIA**
Size	$3,287,263$ km^2; seventh-largest country
Population	1.23 billion (July 2014 est.); second-largest population
Ethnic groups	Indo-Aryan 72%, Dravidian 25%, Mongoloid and other 3% (2000)
Government	Federal republic
Language	Hindi 41%, Bengali 8.1%, Telugu 7.2%, Marathi 7%, Tamil 5.9%, Urdu 5%, Gujarati 4.5%, Kannada 3.7%, Malayalam 3.2%, Oriya 3.2%, Punjabi 2.8%, Assamese 1.3%, Maithili 1.2%, other 5.9% (English as lingua franca)
Religions	Hindu 80.5%, Muslim 13.4%, Christian 2.3%, Sikh 1.9%, other 1.8%, unspecified 0.1% (2001 census)

These early inhabitants, who left no written record, are commonly referred to as the Indus River Valley Civilization because they lived along the Indus River in what is now Pakistan. Although the exact cause of its demise remains unclear, the civilization appears to have succumbed to a cataclysmic natural disaster and subsequent climate change.[92]

The next immigration wave into the subcontinent came from the west as nomadic Aryans arrived with cattle and horses. These pastoral tribes conquered and settled northern India, establishing various warring principalities. When Alexander the Great crossed into India in 327 BCE, he found a politically and territorially divided land, highly vulnerable to conquest. Following Alexander's departure, most of the subcontinent was consolidated into the Maurya Empire (321–185 BCE), India's first unified state. The decline of Mauryan culture left the land politically fragmented until the second unification of northern India, the Gupta Dynasty (320–550 BCE). During these two eras, Buddhism and Hinduism took root and flourished in India. The various rulers practiced religious tolerance, which became one of India's principal values. However, it was Hinduism that "provided a unifying framework through which diverse merchant, noble, and artisan groups were integrated into large-scale polities."[93]

> **REMEMBER THIS**
>
> *Perhaps the most striking characteristic of India is its diversity of geography, peoples, cultures, languages, and history.*

Arab Muslim traders carried Islam to the southern part of present-day Pakistan as early as 711 CE, but its influence was initially contained within that region. In the eleventh century Muslim invaders arriving from the west established an enduring presence on the subcontinent. These early Muslim raiders set about conquering the Hindus and destroying their temples, thus planting the seeds of "communal hatred in the hearts and minds of India's populace,"[94] a historical legacy that continues to divide Muslim and Hindu. The presence and influence of Muslims grew to such proportions that the Delhi Sultanate, established in north-central India in the early thirteenth century, lasted for over three hundred years. Concurrently, the south remained an agrarian Hindu state.[95]

The Delhi Sultanate was deposed in 1526 by a new wave of Muslim invaders. Mongols from Central Asia established the Mughal Empire, which eventually ruled most of the subcontinent. The Mughals established "the strongest dynasty in all of Indian history" and nominally held power until the mid-1800s.[96] Indian culture flourished under Mughal rule. A civil service was established to administer the country, religious and ethnic differences were tolerated, meritocracy was practiced, and Persian became the language of the court. The arts were encouraged and thrived.[97] The famous Taj Mahal, a monument to the wife of one of the Mughal rulers, was built during this era.

The decline of Mughal rule opened the door for Western powers to establish a foothold on the subcontinent and ultimately enabled England to turn India into a colony. Western nations had long sought access to the spices of Southeast Asia, historically monopolized by Arab traders following the Silk Road to transport goods overland to Europe. With the development of sea power, Western Europeans were able to circumvent the traditional land route by sailing around Africa to reach Indian Ocean littoral lands. Portuguese ships arrived on the west coast of India in 1510, and Dutch, French, and English vessels soon followed. Capitalizing on the political disorder in the failing Mughal Empire, England's East India Company gained power through a military takeover and established itself as the dominant trader on India's southeast coast.[98]

The East India Company maintained a trade monopoly until 1813, focusing on commercial enterprise with little regard for the native peoples' welfare, economic infrastructure, or culture. According to Grihault, "At the time of the British arrival, India had a strong mercantile capitalist economy. Britain, however, restructured the economy to serve her own imperial interests, disrupting much of the indigenous infrastructure and impeding the development of India's own culture."[99] This development is exemplified in the machinations of British merchants who exported Indian-grown cotton to England, where it was made into cloth and sent back to India, thus displacing millions of "Indian spinners, weavers and other handicraftsmen."[100] Ultimately, British commercial activities proved economically and socially disastrous for the Indian populace, and at the end of the nineteenth century, the nation was "less urbanized than it had been at the beginning [of the century], with over ninety percent of its much larger population dependent upon the land alone for support."[101]

The Indian National Congress was established in 1885 by young, educated Indians with the objective of redressing the excesses of British colonial rule. As a political organization, it was largely ineffective until Mohandas Gandhi was able to build a functional coalition. Gandhi's campaign of passive resistance, which influenced the U.S. civil rights movement of the 1960s, led to India's independence from British rule in 1947. However, due to the long-standing discord between Hindus and Muslims, India was "partitioned" into two separate, sovereign states—India and Pakistan. The partition displaced some 10 million people, the largest migration in history, and unleashed widespread political violence between Hindus and Muslims, resulting in the loss of as many as 1 million lives. The enduring enmity between India and Pakistan and the continuing territorial conflict over the Kashmir region is a legacy of the partition.[102]

Following partition, India instituted a government-controlled, socialist-oriented economy that produced marginal growth, budget deficits, a bloated bureaucracy, and high levels of unemployment. Finally, in the 1990s effective economic reforms were undertaken that began to introduce free market principles, and India's economy began to grow. Based on GDP measurements, India was ranked the world's tenth-largest economy in 2014.[103] Unfortunately, benefits derived from this economic growth have been felt disproportionately among the population, which remains predominantly rural, poor, and not infrequently illiterate, and as many as two-thirds subsist on less than two dollars per day.[104]

Globalization, however, is stimulating some economic and cultural change in traditional Indian society. The large Indian and multinational IT companies have provided employment to many educated, English-speaking young women and men. For women, traditionally accustomed to assuming a submissive role in marriage, economic security has brought empowerment, independence, and ideas of spousal equality.[105] Greater global awareness of the societal position and treatment of Indian women and demands from within the Indian population have resulted in "a new law guaranteeing 33.3-percent female representation on district, municipal, and village councils."[106] Laws have also been enacted mandating women directors on corporation boards.[107]

CONTEMPORARY SOCIAL ISSUES

Despite the many changes brought by globalization, India remains a nation of remarkable contrasts grappling with a lengthy list of social difficulties. The highly educated Indian workers supporting the information technology and service industries account for only a small portion of the nation's inhabitants. According to the 2011 national census (the most recent), over 68 percent of the population continues to live in rural villages, where more than 30 percent remain illiterate.[108] Extensive, persistent poverty plagues India. The World Bank calculated that in 2012, over 23 percent of the total population was living below the national poverty level, a situation further aggravated by high unemployment among young workers.[109] Official corruption, mismanagement, and an incompetent bureaucracy remain problems in almost all levels of Indian society, and a dysfunctional infrastructure hampers needed economic growth.[110] The long-standing schism between Muslim and Hindu remains a source of polarization, occasionally erupting into violent conflict. Such issues as religion, social class, language, educational levels, and Hindu nationalism divide the sides. While Muslims represent approximately 14 percent of the population, they remain underrepresented in government agencies and generally fare worse than do Hindus.[111] Although abolished by law, the age-old caste system of India, which relegated people into predetermined social classes and occupations as a result of birth, "still matters enormously to most Indians," and caste-based discrimination persists.[112] Caste remains especially important in marriages, and most Indians continue to marry within their own caste. Politics is another arena where it can play a part, as many people continue to use caste as a marker when determining for whom to vote.[113] The extent of continuing class-consciousness was revealed when one Indian professor disclosed that in his city, a policeman from a lower caste would never be sent to arrest someone of a higher caste.[114] India is also beset with severe environmental degradation and has some of the world's worst air pollution, along with inadequate freshwater sources and desertification.[115]

MEXICAN HISTORY

The United States and Mexico share a common border extending nearly 2,000 miles from the Pacific Ocean to the Gulf of Mexico. That geographical factor alone is sufficient cause to learn about the history of Mexico. But there are many additional, important reasons to gain insight into Mexico's past. On a daily basis, hundreds of thousands of people and vehicles cross the border. As an example, San Ysidro, near San Diego, California, is the Western Hemisphere's busiest port of entry, with 50,000 vehicles and 25,000 pedestrians crossing into the United States every day.[116] U.S. and Mexican officials at federal, state, and local levels are continually engaged in efforts to coordinate and manage economic cooperation, legal matters, environmental problems, health issues, law enforcement, and many other interests. Some selected statistics below demonstrate the importance of this relationship and the requirement for mutual, effective intercultural communication:

- Approximately 1 million U.S. citizens reside in Mexico.
- Over 20 million U.S. tourists visited Mexico in 2013.
- Over 14 million Mexican tourists visited the United States in 2013.
- Mexico is the second-largest export market for U.S. products.
- Mexico is the third-largest trading partner of the United States.
- Trade and services between the United States and Mexico exceeded $550 billion in 2013.[117]

But perhaps the most compelling reason to learn about the history of Mexico is because "a record 33.7 million Hispanics of Mexican origin resided in the United States in 2012," of which 22.3 million were born in the United States.[118] This means that approximately one-tenth of the total U.S. population—one in every ten people—has a connection with Mexico, suggesting that communication with Mexican Americans is a common occurrence for many individuals. Thus, knowledge of Mexico's history can provide insight into the Mexican worldview, enhance mutual understanding, and improve communicative interactions. For instance, "Mexicans themselves believe that their history holds the key to their character."[119] With this in mind, let us examine the history of Mexico and how that history continues to influence the Mexican people. The discussion is divided into six major periods: (1) the pre-Columbian, (2) the Spanish Conquest, (3) independence from Spain, (4) the Mexican-American War, (5) the Revolution of 1910, and (6) modern Mexico.

Archaeological evidence dates human existence in Mexico and Central America back at least fifty thousand years, but most historians begin the story of the Mexican peoples with the *pre-Columbian era* (300 BCE–1519 CE), during which the agriculturally based Olmec, Maya, Toltec, and Aztec civilizations flourished in different parts of what is now Mexico. With achievements that equaled or exceeded their counterparts

TABLE 5.6	Country Statistics: United Mexican States[120]
LOCATION	**NORTH AMERICA**
Size	$1,964,375$ km^2; fourteenth-largest country
Population	120,286,655 (July 2014 est.); fourteenth-largest population
Ethnic groups	Mestizo (Amerindian-Spanish) 60%, Amerindian or predominantly Amerindian 30%, white 9%, other 1%
Government	Federal republic
Language	Spanish only 92.7%, Spanish and indigenous languages 5.7%, indigenous only 0.8%, unspecified 0.8%
Religions	Roman Catholic 82.7%, Pentecostal 1.6%, Jehovah's Witnesses 1.4%, other Evangelical churches 5%, other 1.9%, none 4.7%, unspecified 2.7% (2010 est.)

in Europe, each of these great societies made unique contributions to modern Mexican culture. Collectively, they constitute an important part of contemporary Mexican worldview and identity. Even today, their legends, artistic heritages, architecture, and foods remain "an integral part of the [Mexican] national identity."[121]

Mexicans are extremely proud of this period of their history not only for its achievements in agriculture, creative arts, and the establishment of large urban settlements but also for scientific advancements. For example, the Maya, who were advanced in astronomy and mathematics, developed the concept of zero independently from its earlier use in Mesopotamia[122] and created one of the world's most accurate calendars. Mexicans are also aware of the many accomplishments of the Aztec, whose social and religious structures, as well as art, have survived for thousands of years.

The pre-Columbian period was brought to an abrupt end by the *Spanish Conquest*, which began in 1519 when Hernando Cortés invaded the Yucatan Peninsula on the southeast coast of Mexico. The arrival of the Spanish conquerors resulted in the wholesale death, destruction, and subjugation of the native inhabitants. Using the advantages of naval power, horses, guns, interpreters, and duplicitous alliances with the different tribes, Cortés eventually defeated the indigenous people. Especially devastating were the diseases brought by the Europeans, such as smallpox, to which the natives had no immunity.[123] It is estimated that slayings, starvation, disease, and overwork decimated about 90 percent of the native population by 1650.[124] The Spanish occupation of Mexico and subsequent colonization profoundly changed the country and the people forever.

To illustrate this transformation, five major changes arising from Spain's military conquest of the land and peoples are examined. The first three changes have proved to be enduring and comprehensive. Beginning with the first arrivals, including Cortés himself, the Spanish were quick to intermix with the native women, a process (*mestizaje*) that created the mestizo (mixed-race) category, which today comprises the majority of Mexico's population. The Spanish conquerors also introduced the Spanish language, which marginalized and ultimately largely displaced the native languages. The third profound change was the introduction of Catholicism.[125] In the beginning, it was left to the Spanish army to destroy Indian idols and replace them with Christian crosses. It was the Spanish friars, following in the wake of the soldiers, who spread throughout the countryside to convert the conquered natives. The conversions proved rather easy because the Indians adapted the new religion to meet their needs, and both cultures "believed in an afterlife and a world created by god(s)."[126] The fourth consequence of the Spanish colonization of Mexico was the development of a rigid social class system that some historians see as imposing great hardship on the indigenous population. As Foster observed, "The Spanish caste system spread illiteracy, racism, and official corruption through the land, setting one group against the others."[127] The fifth effect of Spain's occupation was the granting of vast tracts of land to the Spanish conquerors. This created a large status and socioeconomic gap between the upper and lower classes in much of Mexico and engendered a highly stratified social order—characteristics that remain a part of Mexican society.[128]

For almost three hundred years Mexico suffered under Spanish rule as a feudal and deeply Catholic country where landed aristocrats dominated a population of primarily agrarian peasants under what was called

REMEMBER THIS

Knowledge of Mexico's history can provide insight into the Mexican worldview, enhance mutual understanding, and improve communicative interactions.

the hacienda system.[129] This social organization endured until the summer of 1810, when Miguel Hidalgo y Costilla, a *criollo* (creole/Spaniard born in Mexico) parish priest, rallied a group of followers and started the fight for *Mexican independence.* Although Hidalgo was executed in 1811, he is known as the "Father of Mexican Independence." Actual independence, however, was not achieved until 1821, when Spain and Mexico negotiated a treaty, called the Plan of Iguala,[130] sometimes referred to as the Plan of the Three Guarantees. Final freedom came in 1824, when Mexico became a federal republic under its own constitution. During this period, Mexico abolished titles of nobility and attempted to introduce measures that would produce a more democratic society. However, as Johns points out, "Neither independence from Spain nor the Mexican Revolution changed the basic structure of social relations in which a small, largely Hispanic elite presided over the exploitation of the impoverished populace."[131] The historical legacy of class separation remains evident in contemporary Mexico's hierarchical social structure.

The next twenty years brought great upheaval to Mexico as the people struggled to adapt to a new form of government. It was during this period that the territory of Texas declared its independence from Mexico. Coupled with the U.S. doctrine of Manifest Destiny, this act proved to be a principal cause of the *Mexican-American War,* which began on May 13, 1846. In addition to Texas, President Polk, with the backing of the American people, sought to acquire what amounted to half of Mexico's territory. The two countries fought over the land for two years (1846–1848) in a war that is seldom remembered in the United States but that Mexico considers "its greatest disaster."[132] According to Krauze, "one still sees traces of the war in the defensive and distrustful character of Mexican nationalism."[133]

On February 2, 1848, the war ended with the signing of the Treaty of Guadalupe Hidalgo. Its provisions called for Mexico to cede 55 percent of its territory (present-day Arizona, California, New Mexico, and Texas, and parts of Colorado, Nevada, and Utah) in exchange for 15 million dollars in compensation for war-related damage to Mexican property.[134] For Mexicans, the war was a bitter defeat. But for the United States, it was an example of Manifest Destiny—"to spread the benefits of democracy to the lesser peoples of the continent."[135] The war had an impact that is still felt today. Samora and Simon write, "The Mexican-American War created unparalleled bitterness and hostility toward the United States, not only in Mexico but throughout Latin America.... Even today, Latin American relationships with the United States are often marred by suspicion and distrust."[136] This is reaffirmed by Krauze's assertion that Mexicans continue to harbor a deep suspicion of the United States.[137]

The next period of Mexico's history centers on the *Revolution of 1910.* After over thirty years of a near continuous, repressive dictatorship under President Porfirio Díaz, the Mexican people revolted. During Díaz's rule Mexico's elite saw their wealth grow, while the living standards of the poor continually declined. At the time of the Revolution, "90 percent of Mexico's mestizos and Indians were still desperately poor on the ranches and haciendas of a handful of wealthy land owners."[138] The Revolution ushered in widespread social change because it "rejected Europe as a model, asserted an Indian identity for Mexico, and committed the government to providing security for peasants and workers by redistributing land and income."[139] One of the revolt's leading figures, Emiliano Zapata, remains a national hero among the Mexican general populace.

Contemporary Mexico, our last phase of Mexican history, remains a work in progress. Huge oil and natural gas reserves, manufacturing, agriculture, tourism, and hundreds of maquiladora factories have made Mexico a major economic force. In addition, with the 1994 passage of the North American Free Trade Agreement (NAFTA), Mexico, the United States, and Canada became free trade partners. Although the passage of time and the implementation of economic agreements have improved relations between the governments of Mexico and the United States, there are still critical issues that require effective intercultural interaction. These include border security, drug trafficking, the movement of guns from the United States to Mexico, and, perhaps the most contentious of all, illegal immigrants.

CONTEMPORARY SOCIAL ISSUES

Today, Mexico is struggling with a number of social issues, but two primary causes underlie many of the problems. First, poverty and unemployment, especially in the rural areas, continue to suppress the standard of living for large numbers of Mexicans, with nearly half of the population living below the poverty level.[140] Lacking jobs, many elect to leave their homes in the countryside and relocate to one of the urban centers. Others seek work in the United States as illegal immigrants. Those in the United States often settle for a meager existence in order to send a significant portion of their wages to their families in Mexico. In 2012 Mexican immigrants remitted approximately 22 billion dollars to Mexico, most of it coming from the United States.[141] The lengthy separations between the working immigrants in the United States and their loved ones in Mexico impose considerable strain on families and carry the potential of eroding the traditional Mexican family structure.

Directly tied to poverty and unemployment is the continuing problem of drug-related crime and violence. Since 2006, Mexico's ongoing drug war has taken the lives of some 60,000 people. In 2013 alone, the government spent $172.7 billion on the war, nearly one-tenth of the country's GDP. In addition to the drug violence, kidnappings and extortion have become common. The situation has led to a militarization of civil society, where corruption permeates even social organizations, including political and law enforcement institutions.[142]

The escalating violence, coupled with growing evidence of widespread corruption of government agencies by the cartels, has seriously eroded public confidence. The effectiveness of law enforcement agencies and the legal system to provide law enforcement and public protection has become questionable. This has created a general sense of insecurity and disillusionment at all levels of society, leaving the people to rely on their extended families or local community for support and security. This has produced a growing vigilante movement where local citizens are taking up arms and assuming security responsibilities.[143] Collectively, these events have placed increasing pressure on the traditional Mexican culture once dominated by family and the church.

Of course, Mexico also confronts myriad environmental pollution problems, as is common in almost every developing country. Although major improvements have been made over the past decade, air pollution remains a problem in the industrialized cities, especially Mexico City. Additionally, deforestation, desertification, erosion, polluted rivers, and declining clean water sources threaten Mexico's environment and its people.[144]

HISTORICAL OVERVIEW OF ISLAMIC CIVILIZATION

The preceding sections in this chapter focused on how historical events influenced the cultural characteristics of individual countries. For the final section, however, we will take a broader perspective and examine the sweeping history of Islamic civilization and how it continues to be a major factor in the lives of more than one and a half billion people. Events such as the tragedy of September 11, 2001; U.S. military conflicts in Iraq and Afghanistan; the Arab Spring; Syria's civil war; Boko Haram's atrocities in Nigeria; the rise of the Islamic State of Iraq and the Levant (ISIL); and the continuing global fight against terrorism should serve as motivation for you to learn about Islam. But there are other, equally compelling reasons for acquiring an appreciation of Islamic history and culture. Not the least of these is because Muslims constitute an integral part of the U.S. social fabric. Among the almost 3.5 million U.S. Muslims[145] are congressional representatives, doctors and lawyers, sports stars, your coworkers, and your neighbors, and, most importantly, they form an integral part of our society.

MUSLIM DEMOGRAPHICS

As discussed in Chapter 4, Islam is the world's second-largest religion, exceeded only by Christianity, with Muslims representing the majority of the population in forty-nine nations. Islam is the predominant religion of most North African and Middle Eastern countries and several nations in South and Southeast Asia. Additionally, there are large, growing populations of Muslims in Europe and North America. Muslims numbered approximately 1.6 billion in 2010, constituting over one-fifth of the World's population.[146] These numbers are expected to grow between now and 2030 before leveling off at more than 2.2 billion, exceeding one-quarter of humankind. "If current trends continue, Muslims will make up 26.4 percent of the world's total projected population of 8.3 billion in 2030." In the United States, due to immigration and birthrate, the Muslim presence over the next twenty years is expected to increase to 6.2 million, representing approximately 1.7 percent of the projected population.[147]

As depicted in Table 5.7, the largest number of Muslims is not in the Middle East, as international events tend to suggest. The majority of all Muslims reside in

TABLE 5.7	World Muslim Population by Region[148]			
	TOTAL POPULATION*	MUSLIM POPULATION (MILLION)	MUSLIMS AS PERCENTAGE OF TOTAL POPULATION	MUSLIMS AS PERCENTAGE OF TOTAL MUSLIM POPULATION
Asia-Pacific	4,054.99	985.53	24.3	61.7
Middle East–North Africa	341.02	317.07	93.0	19.8
Sub-Sahara Africa	822.72	248.11	30.2	15.5
Europe	742.55	43.49	5.9	2.7
North America	344.53	3.48	1.0	0.2
Latin America-Caribbean	590.08	0.84	1.0	0.1
World Total	6,895.89	1,598.51	23.2	100

*In millions based on 2010 estimated population.

Indonesia, India, and Pakistan. Conversely, while the Middle East has a much smaller population, over 90 percent of Middle Easterners adhere to the Islamic religion.

THE AGE OF IGNORANCE

In order to better understand the history of Islam and its influence in the globalized world, it is necessary to have an overview of the early Middle East, particularly the Arabian Peninsula, where Islam originated. The geography and climate of the region can be described as generally semiarid and arid, with insufficient rainfall to support agriculture except along river valleys or near oases. This is especially true of the Arabian Peninsula, historically the domain of the nomad. Domestication of the camel around 3000 BCE allowed nomadic groups to move across the peninsula's arid vastness in search of water and fodder for their herds. Constantly on the move, these pastoralists were unable to develop the architectural and cultural artifacts that characterized the early great civilizations of the Middle East, such as the Sumerian and Babylonian to the east and the Egyptian to the west. Instead, they developed cultural expressions more suitable to their mobile lives and what was necessary for survival in the harsh desert environment.[149] During this pre-Islamic era, which Muslims refer to as the "Age of Ignorance" (*jahiliya*),[150] "early Arabs composed poems that embodied their code of values: bravery in battle, patience in misfortune, persistence in revenge, protection of the weak, defiance of the strong, loyalty to the tribe, hospitality to the guest, generosity to the needy, and fidelity in carrying out promises."[151] Loyalty to one's tribe was paramount, and intertribal wars and raids against trade route caravans were common. These early groups practiced a variety of religions, including Judaism, Christianity, animism, and ancestor worship, but a tradition developed among the tribes to annually suspend hostilities and conduct a pilgrimage to an ancient shrine in the city of Mecca.[152] This became an important part of Islamic history and remains the destination of today's Muslim pilgrimages (hajj).

THE RISE AND SPREAD OF ISLAM

Islamic civilization began in the early seventh century and stretches across more than 1,400 years, encompassing far more events than space and time allow for examination here. Thus, our focus will be on the rise of Islam in the Middle East, with only brief mention of its spread to other parts of the world. However, you should keep in mind this is only one part of the story of Islam. Chapter 4 discussed the establishment of Islam as a religion by the prophet Muhammad. Therefore, all you need remember here is that Muhammad, who came from a merchant family in Mecca, received his heavenly revelations about 610 CE and began recruiting followers. It is, however, important to note that Muhammad reportedly received oral revelations from the angel Gabriel and passed them to others orally. It was only after his death that the Koran, which means "the recitation," was transcribed. This is yet another example of the Arab cultural value of orality.

Our historical examination of the rise and spread of Islam will begin with Muhammad's death in 632 CE. When he died, there was no clear line of succession for the Islamic leadership. Muhammad left no male heir and did not designate anyone

TABLE 5.8	Eras of Islamic Civilization
Prophet Muhammad	610–632
Patriarchal Caliphate (Rightly Guided Caliphs)	632–661
Umayyad Caliphate	661–750
Abbasid Caliphate	750–1258
Medieval Islam	1259–1300?
Ottoman Empire	1301–1923
Nation-states	1923–Present

to take his place. This void was filled by a series of caliphs (Arabic for "successor" or "representative"),[153] a role assumed by successive leaders of Islam until the demise of the Ottoman Empire in 1923, in the aftermath of World War I. The first caliphs were drawn from those who had directly served Muhammad and were known as the Patriarchal Caliphate or "Rightly Guided Caliphs" (632–661 CE).[154] Soon after Muhammad's death, many of the Arab groups that had previously submitted to his teachings and leadership sought to disassociate themselves from the new caliphs. Armed groups of "believers" were quickly dispatched to suppress these dissenters, and within a few years, the many nomadic tribes and the urban areas of the Arabian Peninsula had been completely subdued. By the middle of the seventh century, the "believers" held control of most of what is now called the Middle East.[155] As Donner points out, these conquests "established a large new empire in the Near East, with a leadership 'committed to a new religious ideology.'"[156] The new empire provided the political order and organizational structure necessary for the spread of Islam.

The death of the last of the caliphates who had a direct connection to Muhammad ended the era of the Patriarchal Caliphate and ushered in the Umayyad Caliphate (661–750 CE). This period brought many changes to Islam, one of which was the relocation of the capital from Medina in Arabia to Damascus in Syria. Of greater consequence, consolidation of the Middle East enabled Muslims to embark on the conquest of more distant lands. To the west, Muslims spread across all of North Africa, crossing into southern Europe in 710, where they remained a significant presence until 1492, when Christian armies forced them to abandon the city of Granada (in present-day Spain), the last Muslim bastion in Western Europe.[157] To the east, Islam moved across what is now Iran, Afghanistan, and Pakistan and into India and Central Asia, ultimately reaching western China. Southward, Islam extended to present-day Indonesia and the southern Philippines, where it continues to command a dominant position. Despite the geographical advances of Islam during this period, the Umayyad Caliphate was not without internal problems. Questions of leadership succession persisted and ultimately led to civil wars and the division of Islam into its two major branches—Sunni and Shia. Today, Sunnis represent 87 to 90 percent of all Muslims and Shia 10 to 13 percent,[158] with the latter concentrated in Iran, Iraq, Pakistan, and India. The fundamental difference separating them has its roots in the question of leadership of the Muslim community, and the historical basis of those differences justifies a brief review.

Sunnis believe that the leader of Islam should be whoever is best qualified. The Shia, however, contend that leadership is a function of heredity, through lineage traced to Muhammad. Originally, the two groups saw themselves divided not by ideology but by a question of politics, but with the passage of time, varied theological and religious practices have evolved.[159] Moreover, because the Shia have always been a minority, they have developed an interpretation of history quite different from the Sunnis. Esposito provides an insightful summation of the two groups' varied worldviews:

> While Sunni history looked to the glorious and victorious history of the Four Rightly Guided Caliphs and then the development of imperial Islam ... [Shia] history was the theater for the struggle of the oppressed and disinherited. Thus, while Sunnis can claim a golden age when they were a great world power and civilization, which they believe is evidence of God's favor upon them and a historic validation of Muslim beliefs, [Shia] see in these same developments the illegitimate usurpation of power by Sunni rulers at the expense of a just society. [Shia] view history more as a paradigm of the suffering, disinheritance, and oppression of a righteous minority community who must constantly struggle to restore God's rule on earth under His divinely appointed Imam.[160]

These contrasting perspectives should provide you with greater insight to the historical enmity that continues to influence relations between Sunnis and Shia worldwide. Their religious differences play a central role in political tensions and armed conflicts throughout the Middle East, such as the rivalry between Iran and Saudi Arabia and the Syrian civil war. The Sunni–Shia divide is at the heart of Iraqis' seeming inability to form a united polity.

In the mid-eighth century the Umayyad Caliphate was succeeded by the Abbasid Caliphate (749–1258), the seat of government moved to Baghdad, and a cadre of multiethnic Muslims of non-Arab origin supplanted the ruling Arab hierarchy. With Islam as the uniting force, all believers, regardless of ethnicity or place of origin, were considered equal. Under the Abbasids, Baghdad became one of the world's most important cities, and its wealth enabled Muslim emissaries to continue to expand Islamic influence. But this preeminence could not be sustained. As a result of political decline, agricultural failure, and the rise of numerous independent Islamic dynasties in other regions, Baghdad's control of the Islamic empire had become decentralized by the tenth century. These new outlying dynasties continued to expand Islamic culture as they sought to emulate Baghdad, becoming new centers for learning, art, and craftsmanship.[161]

The early years of the eleventh century saw the onset of history's most storied clash between Christianity and Islam—the Crusades, which lasted almost 200 years. Although Muslims had occupied Jerusalem, the seat of both Christianity and Judaism, in 638, they ruled without religious persecution, and the city remained open to Christian and Jewish pilgrims.[162] Arrival of the Seljuk Turks, however, brought change to the Islamic world. Pushing outward from Central Asia, the Seljuks gained a position of power in the Abbasid Caliphate in Baghdad in 1055 and drove the Byzantines from their lands in Asia Minor (now part of Turkey). This gave them control over the Christian pilgrimage routes connecting Europe with Jerusalem. The Byzantine rulers appealed to Rome for assistance, hoping for trained armies. In response, Pope Urban II in 1095 called for the masses to help in "saving fellow Christians" and liberating the Holy Land.[163] Thus were the Crusades launched. Christian forces comprised of nobles, mercenaries, and adventurers were able to gain control of isolated pockets in the Holy Land before ultimately being defeated by the Arab ruler Saladin in the late twelfth century. Smith notes, "Saladin's treatment of the Christian population [in Jerusalem] was humane and reasonable, in notable contrast to the way in which Christians had earlier dealt with Muslims and Jews upon their arrival in Jerusalem."[164]

Mongol invaders moving out of Central Asia through Afghanistan and Persia into the Middle East ushered in the final era of unified Islamic governance. Reaching Baghdad during the mid-thirteenth cen-

tury, Mongol warriors destroyed the city and its inhabitants, bringing an end to the Abbasid Caliphate. The devastation brought by the Mongol armies pushed the Turkish nomads into the eastern regions of modern-day Turkey, where they met and defeated the last of the Byzantine forces. These nomads became known as the Ottomans, and they ruled Islam for more than 600 years. During their reign Ottoman armies advanced into Europe as far as Vienna, Austria, and took control of the Balkans, where large communities of Muslims remain today. In the seventeenth and eighteenth centuries the European powers began to challenge the Ottoman Empire, then beset by internal decay and unable to hold back the Christian nation forces. As the Ottomans retreated, European powers rushed in to fill the void. Noted Middle East expert Bernard Lewis points out the extent of this change:

> By the early twentieth century—although a precarious independence was retained by Turkey and Iran and by some remoter countries like Afghanistan, which at that time did not seem worth the trouble of invading—almost the entire Muslim world had been incorporated into the four European [colonial] empires of Britain, France, Russia, and The Netherlands.[165]

The defeat of the Ottomans at the end of World War I ended more than thirteen centuries of a unified Islam and replaced it with nation-states, many of which remained under the domination of Western colonial masters until after World War II.[166] In the wake of the departing colonial powers, many of the Middle East nations fell under the rule of authoritarian, often autocratic leaders. The ability of these leaders to rely on oil revenues for state capital allowed them to govern without approval of or little concern for the people.

THE LEGACY OF ISLAMIC HISTORY

This brief chronology illustrates the richness of Islamic history, which helps shape the identity and worldview of modern Muslims. History is particularly significant to Muslims. As noted by Lewis, "Islamic history, for Muslims, has an important religious and also legal significance, since it reflects the working out of God's purpose for His Community—those that accept the teachings of Islam and obey its law."[167] From the Muslim perspective, the early era of the caliphates represents a period of one ruler exercising dominion over a single state. The perception of unity persisted even after the caliphate had splintered into a variety of dynastic states, and the people of the Islamic domain identified themselves not by nationality or ethnicity but as Muslims.

For contemporary Muslims, the history of Islam is continually reinforced through (1) language, (2) geography, and (3) tribal affiliation, all of which are derived from the religion's Arabic origins.[168] Classical Arabic was the original language of the Koran, and Arabic became the language of the Middle East and North Africa as a result of the early Islamic conquests. Located in southeast Saudi Arabia, Mecca remains the holiest of all Islamic sites and the annual destination of well over a million Muslims who make the *hajj* each year. Tribal affiliation, the basis of ancient Arabia's societal organization, continues to exert a strong influence among most Muslims. The importance and role of tribal organization was vividly demonstrated in both Iraq and Afghanistan, where U.S. forces belatedly realized the need to work through tribal leaders.

The history of Islamic civilization can easily be oversimplified into a tale of conquest and colonization. One can also use that same lens to view the history of Western civilization. As Lewis indicates, "From the end of the fifteenth century, the peoples of Europe embarked on a vast movement of expansion—commercial, political, cultural, and demographic—which by the twentieth century had brought almost the whole world into the orbit of European civilization."[169]

Space limitations preclude a discussion of the lasting achievements in the sciences, arts, literature, philosophy, and architecture produced by Islam. Those accomplishments originated in the early Islamic centers of civilization, where art, scholarship, craftsmanship, and intercultural borrowing were encouraged. Unification enabled the rapid dispersal of advancements in any branch of knowledge throughout the Islamic realm. Whatever your personal history and culture, it likely bears an Islamic influence. Muslims have been coming to the United States since well before the nineteenth century. They were among the early explorers, traders, and settlers. It is also estimated that Muslims constituted 14 to 20 percent of the slaves brought from Africa to the Americas.[170] Words we use every day, such as *algebra*, *average*, *lemon*, and *magazine*, have Arabic origins. And the next time you are sipping your favorite coffee drink, recall that coffee, along with coffeehouses, was introduced to the West through Islam.

Today, Muslims look back on Islamic history with feelings of both pride and discomfiture. Pride is taken in the fact that while Europe was mired in the Dark Ages, Islam represented "the most advanced civilization in the world."[171] However, as witnessed by the uprisings and continuing unrest across North Africa and the Middle East, many Muslims are greatly dissatisfied with current social conditions in their countries. With few exceptions, Muslim nations in North Africa and the Middle East are plagued by a host of similar conditions arising from inept, authoritarian rulers, conditions that have hampered the ability to improve living standards and participate in democratic institutions. Common problems include repressive authoritarian regimes, official corruption, absence of viable democratic processes, biased social justice systems, stagnant economic development, lack of women's equality, and increased urbanization.[172] Moreover, many young males see little opportunity for economic or social advancement in a region that, according to the United Nations, has the world's highest youth unemployment rate.[173] These conditions have undermined many of the traditional social conventions. For instance, before marriage, a young Arab male is expected to have sufficient economic resources to afford a place to live, a prerequisite made increasingly difficult or even impossible for a large number of young men. This has resulted in disillusion with state leaders and state-sponsored institutions. For some, it has strengthened their connection to Islam.

Much of the turmoil besetting Islam today is a result of its struggle with modernity.[174] Arising in the premodern era, Islamic institutions were designed to combine religious, social, and political functions for the betterment of all Muslims. This objective was achieved, to various degrees, under the consolidated rule of the caliphs. However, the "repudiation of the Caliphate by the Turks"[175] brought to an end the unity that had been a central characteristic of Islam for over a millennium. But unlike Europe, which successfully transitioned from papal governance to independent democratic nation-states during the Enlightenment, the Arab countries have been unable to make the needed changes. For a variety of reasons, many Muslims connect Arabic

TABLE 5.9	Current Divisions of Islamic Thought[177]
FACTIONS	**POSITION**
Modern secularists	Western oriented; advocates separation of state and religion.
Modernists	Islam and modernity are compatible; Islam should inform but not dominate public life.
Conservatives/ traditionalists	Emphasizes past Islamic authority; old Islamic laws and norms should be reinstituted.
Fundamentalists	Calls for a return to Islam's earliest period; Islam must purge itself of corrupting Western influences.

countries' failures with the West and Western values because modern society is usually associated with "Western ideas, institutions, and values."[176] This inability to accommodate to modernity has resulted in a division of Islamic thought. Some of these disparate views are presented in Table 5.9.

It is overly simplistic to consider Islam as the wellspring of current problems in the Middle East and among European Muslim communities. What we see is the historical memory of the "Islamic Golden Age" being employed as a vehicle to recruit impressionable, disaffected young men and women to a radicalized interpretation of their faith. Deeper socioeconomic difficulties and issues of representative political governance lie at the heart of Muslim extremism, and it is essential that we understand that. Moreover, we need to recognize that Islam "will remain a significant political and social force for reform because majorities of Muslims today stress the importance of its role for the progress of their societies."[178] In short, the more we understand Islam and Muslims, the more interculturally competent we become because "religion is embedded in culture."[179]

DEVELOPING HISTORICAL MEMORY COMPETENCY FOR INTERCULTURAL COMMUNICATION INTERACTIONS

The overviews of selected national histories provided in this chapter were intended to illustrate how cultural values can often be a product of past events and to examine the role that collective historical memory plays in the construction of worldview. Those values and worldviews can and generally do come into play during intercultural communication interactions. In some instances, the historical event may be widely known, and all participants will be aware of its potential influence. For instance, the U.S. historical record of slavery, the genocide of indigenous peoples, and the incarceration of Japanese Americans are generally well known, and people usually approach those topics cautiously when interacting with an African American, Native American, or Japanese American, respectively. Less recognized in the United States are Mexicans' enduring feelings about the injustice their country suffered in the Mexican-American War. And people in the United States are also unlikely to realize that the Indian city of Bombay changed its name to Mumbai in 1995 because the former name was considered a reminder of British colonial rule. People in the Middle East view the Crusades quite differently from people in Europe and the United States. A Russian student complained to one of your authors that U.S. students seldom have an awareness of the millions of Russians killed in World War II. There are, of course, many other examples of culturally differing perspectives of historical events.

We are not saying that you need to have an encyclopedic knowledge of world history in order to be a competent intercultural communicator. That is well beyond the realm of reasonability. However, in general, it is recommended that in intercultural exchanges, you need to be mindful that your perception of a historical event may differ from that of the other person(s) and that those differences carry the potential to cause confusion, impede understanding, or even create alienation. There are, therefore, situations where it is advisable to acquire an appreciation of another culture's history. In the event you plan to sojourn or work in a country for any extended period of time, knowledge of the host culture's history will improve both communication and relations with your hosts. Moreover, it will expand your awareness and understanding of the beliefs, values, and behaviors dominant in the host country. What we are trying to convey is this: The more you know about another culture, the greater the likelihood of competent, effective intercultural communication.

SUMMARY

- History and culture are interwoven.

- The study of intercultural communication and the study of history are complementary.

- "The past causes the present, and so the future."

- The influence of history is sometimes difficult to recognize because it contains all the deep structure elements of culture.

- A culture's history affects perception, behavior, and how people relate to other cultures.

- Historical events provide insight into and help explain national character.

- History is a key element in developing a culture's values, goals, expectations, and identity.

- The early U.S. historical experience promoted values of independence and self-reliance.

- Although U.S. Americans are considered individualistic, they often participate in many self-selected groups on a voluntary basis.

- Geography and a lengthy history of authoritarian rule have helped shape the Russian national character.

- China's long history, record of cultural achievements, and Western exploitation in the nineteenth and twentieth centuries strongly influence Chinese contemporary worldview.

- The social divisions instituted during the Tokugawa era continue to be reflected in Japanese modern society.

- The 1947 Partition of India was a result of Hindu–Muslim discord that began hundreds of years earlier and continues today.

- The Spanish conquest and colonization of Mexico instilled in the native population many cultural traits that endure today.

- The historical achievements of Islam are a source of pride and inspiration for contemporary Muslims.

ACTIVITIES

1. Search the Internet for "Why study history?" and make a list of the five best reasons you find. Compare your list with the reasons other class members find.

2. Select a country (or culture) different from your own and examine the history of that country. Try to isolate examples of historical events that have influenced the country's national character.

3. Write down the different groups you belong to now and those you belonged to four to five years ago (include all informal groups, such as a study group). Compare your list with the lists of other classmates to see how frequently membership in a group has changed.

4. Go to YouTube and search for videos on the history of a country or culture you are interested in (use Russia or China to see an example). Try to determine any cultural values that are highlighted in the videos.

5. Interview an older member of your family about the family's history. Try to identify a historical event that resulted in a family tradition carried on today.

CONCEPTS AND QUESTIONS

1. How can the historical legacies of the United States and Russia (China, Islamic nations, etc.) produce discord and conflict? What is a contemporary example?

2. How can a government use a nation's historical legacy to generate popular support among the general population?

3. How does national history play a role in shaping national identity? What is an example for the United States?

4. During a state visit to China in 2010, the United Kingdom's prime minister and his party were asked to remove the poppy flowers they were wearing to honor U.K. war dead, a national tradition observed every November 11. The Chinese indicated that the poppies might remind the Chinese of the Opium Wars of the mid-1800s, in which British forces defeated the Chinese. In your opinion, should the British representatives have worn the poppies? Why?

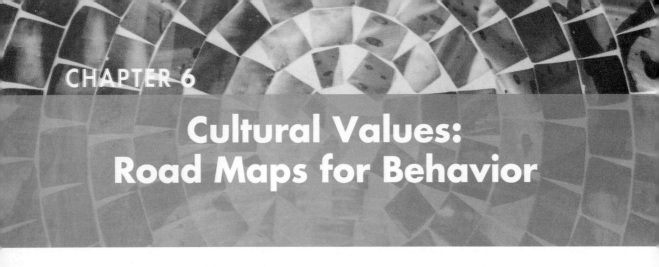

CHAPTER 6

Cultural Values: Road Maps for Behavior

The basic direction of a society is shaped by its values, which define its ultimate goal.

HENRY KISSINGER

Values are not just words; values are what we live by. They're about the causes that we champion and the people we fight for.

JOHN KERRY

The values that we hold inform our principles. The principles that we hold inform our actions.

FRANK MATOBO

From the preceding chapters you should have acquired an understanding of the basic components of communication and culture, learned the various ways that culture is acquired, and examined some of the factors that contribute to culturally based varied worldviews. That information was intended to create an appreciation of just how pervasive culture is in guiding daily social activities and long-term personal objectives. Factors such as family, history, religion, and cultural identity influence your decisions on what to think about, what to disregard, and how to act. It might be something as mundane as what to eat for lunch, whether to sit in the front or back of a large lecture hall, or which movie to see this evening. Alternatively, it can be more consequential, such as influencing your opinion on gun control, abortion, climate change, or capital punishment. How you think and what you do about something is generally based on your perception of the world, which is largely a product of culturally instilled beliefs and values. The things you consider important are often products of beliefs and values learned since childhood, and those values are what motivate your behaviors. A preference for individuality, as is common in the United States, or a more group orientation, such as among Latinos and Asians, is normally a result of culturally based beliefs and values. This can create the perception that personal goals should take precedence over those of the group (or vice versa), depending on your cultural background.

Should race/ethnicity be a consideration for university admissions? Should school prayer be allowed? Should corporations be required to provide insurance that includes contraception to their employees? Should crosses be allowed in public spaces? Your opinion about a moral issue, a question of ethics, a proposed course of action, or what constitutes proper behavior in a particular context is strongly influenced by cultural values, and your values can often conflict with those held by individuals of other cultures. The ability to recognize, prepare for, and manage a conflict of cultural values plays a central role in successful intercultural communication exchanges. To enhance your intercultural skills, this chapter is designed to expand awareness of the role of cultural values in your life and demonstrate how those values can vary across cultures. To accomplish this, we will explore (1) how culture shapes perception, (2) the role of beliefs in forming cultural values, (3) how culture inculcates a set of values, and (4) how values differ across cultures. Considerable time will be devoted to examining different cultural value patterns (or dimensions), how those patterns influence communication, and their impact on intercultural communication. A final section will explain the importance of developing an awareness of cultural values.

REMEMBER THIS

Learning the main values of a culture is essential for successful intercultural communication exchanges.

© S. David Zuckerman

Since much of perception is highly subjective and heavily affected by culture, it is not surprising that many of the meanings we apply to stimuli, even those related to food tastes, are influenced by culture.

PERCEPTION'S INFLUENCE

Take a moment and try to recall having a disagreement with a coworker, friend, or family member that ended with some variation of "I just don't see it that way" or "You just don't understand." Very likely, the inability to resolve your difference was because you each had a different perception of the problem. In other words, each of you had interpreted some or all of the factors relating to the conflict from a different perspective. That people evaluate stimuli differently is a common cause of intercultural disagreements and conflict, and because perception is so important when communicating with someone of another culture, it is essential to have a thorough understanding of the concept.

We live in an information-saturated environment. Daily, our senses are barraged with far more physical and psychological stimuli than we can process and interpret. To survive, we engage in a three-step process—selection, organization, and interpretation—to manage the stimuli considered important. In the first step, we selectively decide which of the stimuli to attend to and which to ignore. Next, the selected information must be organized, or categorized, after which a meaning is assigned. The complete process produces your perception of a situation, emotion, or even another person. In its simplest form, perception is how we make sense of the world, how we construct reality.

The distinguished theoretical physicist Stephen Hawking and his colleague offer a more scholarly description of this process. They contend that just as models are used in science, people construct "mental models … in order to interpret and understand the everyday world," and the resulting perceptions are subjectively influenced because they are "shaped by a kind of lens, the interpretive structure of our human brains."[1] British author and scholar, C.S. Lewis, has provided a more practical view of perception, and one that introduces the role of culture: "What you see and what you hear depends a great deal on where you are standing. It also depends on what sort of person you are." Particularly noteworthy is the last thought, because culture is perhaps the most important social influence in shaping an individual. Thus, the relevant sociocultural factors, such as beliefs, values, and attitudes, provide a template for assigning meaning to the many stimuli, which ultimately coalesce to form our perceptions.

Two examples readily illustrate the interaction between culture and perception. The first contrasts culturally based communication practices. In the United States, a direct, forthright communicative style is expected and valued. Frank exchanges of ideas and animated debates often characterize meetings. In contrast, this type of communication can be threatening to people from Northeast Asian nations (China, Japan, and Korea). Their concern for positive, enduring interpersonal relations leads to a preference for indirect communications between valued associates. Accordingly, negative or adverse information is often couched in ambiguous terms. From this, it is easy to imagine how a culturally uninformed American might perceive a typical Japanese speaker as being evasive or even duplicitous and have reservations about entering into a business arrangement.

The second example concerns how age is perceived across cultures. In the United States, culture emphasizes the value of youth and rejects growing old. As a result, older people are often viewed less positively. This is evident in media commercials that usually appeal to a youth demographic. According to one communication researcher, "Young people view elderly people as less desirable interaction partners than other young people or middle-aged people."[2] This negative view of the elderly is not found in all cultures. For example, as you observed in Chapter 3, in Middle Eastern, Asian, Latin American, and American Indian cultures older people are perceived in a very positive light. Notice what Moran, Harris, and Moran say about the elderly in Africa:

It is believed that the older one gets, the wiser one becomes—life has seasoned the individual with varied experiences. Hence, in Africa age is an asset. The older the person, the more respect the person receives from the community, and especially from the young. Thus if a foreigner is considerably younger than the African, the latter will have little confidence in the outsider.[3]

> **REMEMBER THIS**
>
> *Perception is selective. Perceptual patterns are learned and, therefore, influenced by one's culture.*

These examples illustrate that culture influences one's subjective reality and that there are direct links among culture, perception, and behavior. A more comprehensive appreciation of perception and its functions and deficiencies can be achieved by understanding the following five characteristics listed by Adler and Gunderson:[4]

- *Perception is selective*—Because there are so many stimuli simultaneously competing for the attention of your senses, you focus only on selected information and filter out the rest.
- *Perception is learned*—Life's experiences teach you to see the world in a particular way.
- *Perception is culturally determined*—Culture teaches you the meaning behind most of your experiences.
- *Perception is consistent*—Once you perceive something in a particular manner, that interpretation is usually resistant to change.
- *Perception is inaccurate*—You view the world through a subjective lens influenced by culture, values, and personal experiences. This tends to make you see what you expect or want to see.

The most important aspect of our discussion on perception is that culture "determines both the categories we use and the meanings we attach to them."[5] In many instances, your culturally based perceptions are maintained in the form of beliefs and values. These two concepts, working in combination, form what are called *cultural patterns*, which will be examined at length after a brief definition of beliefs.

BELIEFS, VALUES, AND BEHAVIORS

BELIEFS

What are your beliefs, how did you acquire them, and what do they do? Beliefs are usually reflected in your actions and communication behaviors. For instance, if you believe that a good tan reflects a healthy, active lifestyle, and makes a person more attractive, you will probably find time to lie out in the sun, use a tanning lotion, or perhaps go to a tanning salon. Conversely, if you believe that suntanned skin connotes a lower social status, you will likely make extra efforts to limit exposure to the sun by using sunscreen, wearing a hat and long-sleeved shirt, and perhaps even using an umbrella on sunny days.

But what constitutes a belief? Simplistically stated, a belief is a concept or idea that an individual or group holds to be true. Beliefs represent our subjective conviction in the truth of something—with or without proof. The degree to which we believe that an object, event, phenomenon, person, or group of people possesses certain characteristics reflects the level of our subjective probability and, consequently, the depth or intensity of our belief. Perhaps you believe that life begins at the moment of conception. This belief may be a product of your faith or some aspect of biology you subscribe to. If you hold this belief, you will probably associate with other like-minded individuals, which will serve to reinforce your conviction, as reported by Chiu and Hong: "a shared belief or attitude is usually perceived to be more valid than one that is not shared. When a person holds a certain belief or attitude, knowing that other people share this belief or attitude [will] increase the person's adherence to his belief or attitude."[6]

What makes our belief system important is that it is learned, and subject to cultural interpretation. Therefore, shared beliefs can come to represent cultural norms, or values, characterizing a large collective of people.[7] For example, the belief in individual equality promotes the widely held U.S. value of individuality and reduces the importance of hierarchy and formality. But even within a large collective, people may hold beliefs that run counter to the beliefs of others. For instance, the U.S. population currently has significant differences over social issues such as gun control, government regulations, the use of racial quotas in college admission, capital punishment, and a host of other concerns. Thus, beliefs and the cultural values they may produce can both unite and divide. But in those situations where you find that someone does not share your beliefs and values, you cannot simply throw up your hands and declare the other person's convictions to be wrong. In today's globalized society you have to be able to recognize the importance of other peoples' beliefs and how those beliefs and values shape their worldview and even their manner of communicating.

VALUES

As alluded to earlier, beliefs form the foundation of values. What you consider desirable for yourself and for the society you live in is a product of your values, which can be held both consciously and subconsciously. Although each of us has a unique set of values, there are also values that tend to permeate and characterize a culture. These *cultural values* provide a set of guidelines that assist the culture's members in deciding what is good or bad, desirable or undesirable, right or wrong, and appropriate or inappropriate in almost every context of human activity. Institutionalized cultural values define what is worth dying for, what is worth protecting, what frightens people, which subjects are worthy of study, and which topics deserve ridicule. Varied cultural values can create intercultural conflict at both a personal and an international level. For instance, in the United States people place a high value on individual rights and personal freedom, and they think that those opportunities should be available to everyone in the world. In China, however, the conservative leadership believes that "social harmony and moral rectitude" should take precedence over individual preferences.[8] The Chinese Communist Party also rejects the Western view of human rights as an individualistic concept and considers their responsibility for "lifting millions from poverty and ensuring [societal] stability" to be a more compelling requirement than individual rights.[9]

As discussed in Chapter 2, your cultural values—like all important aspects of culture—are acquired through a variety of sources (family, history, proverbs, media, school, church, state, etc.) and, therefore, tend to be broad-based, enduring, and relatively stable. A culture's value system establishes the expected, normative modes of behavior for members of that culture and institutes the criteria to judge people's conduct. Unfortunately, during intercultural interactions we have a tendency to apply our own criteria to members of other cultures who usually hold different values. This frequently results in misunderstandings, confusion, and even conflict. Clashes arising from variant cultural values can be related to something as seemingly inconsequential as the appropriateness of eating certain foods (e.g., American and Hindu attitudes toward beef or Japan and Australia over whale meat) or more weighty matters, such as human rights or societal ethics. To help mitigate the potential for value-based clashes, we feel that a good rule of thumb for any intercultural encounter is this: *If you consider the other person strange, they probably consider you strange.*

BEHAVIORS

Behaviors are the outward manifestations of our internalized beliefs and values. To illustrate, if you believe that a college degree is the pathway to a better life, you will probably place considerable value on education and diligently apply yourself to your studies. As with almost all things in life, culture also has a regulatory influence on behaviors. Culture tells us the accepted deportment for different social contexts and what is age appropriate, and specifies gender-specific conduct. You know that certain behaviors that are acceptable during a spring-break trip would be considered obnoxious at a family reunion, that senior citizens are not expected to wear hip-hop or Gothic-style clothes, and that assertive actions are more tolerated when done by a man than a woman. To further illustrate, while on a business trip, a Japanese businessman will usually purchase gifts for his office coworkers. This is because the Japanese believe it is important to maintain good interpersonal relations, and they value social harmony, both of which are demonstrated through extensive gift-giving rituals among family, friends, and coworkers. For the study of intercultural communication, it is also important to know that beliefs and values exert an influence on our communicative behaviors. For instance, traditional Arabs believe that God controls everything about a person's life. This has resulted in a strong sense of fatalism, as exhibited in the often-used phrase *Inshallah* (God willing).[10] In the United States, the use of personal titles and honorifics when addressing others is usually restricted to formal settings. This preference for informality is a product of the importance placed on individual equality.

CONSIDER THIS

Your behaviors are a reflection of your values, which are based on your beliefs.

UNDERSTANDING CULTURAL PATTERNS

Culture is a multifaceted social construct. In seeking to reduce this complexity and provide a greater understanding of how culture guides and shapes people's lives, researchers have discerned that the dominant group within a culture often exhibits similar societal characteristics that are derived from their shared set of beliefs and values. *Cultural patterns*, sometimes called value orientations, is an umbrella term used to collectively describe those cultural values that characterize the dominant group within a culture. As used here, the term refers to culturally based beliefs, values, attitudes, and behaviors shared by members of a particular culture. These patterns encompass the conditions that contribute to a social group's perception of the world and how they live in that world. The application of cultural patterns in the study of intercultural communication is beneficial because such patterns offer a systematic structure to help identify and examine recurring values.

When using cultural patterns to help gain added insight relative to various ideas and activities exhibited by other cultures, a few cautionary remarks are in order. We suggest that you keep in mind the following four caveats:

- *You are more than your culture*: As discussed in Chapter 1, all individuals within a cultural group may not share the dominant values of that culture. A variety of factors, such as age, gender, education, income level, personal experiences, and others, influence your view of the world. Because people are more than their culture, assigning national characteristics or typical cultural patterns to a group is a risky endeavor due to the heterogeneity of almost all societies. Think of the many ethnic groups, religious orientations, and political perspectives that make up the U.S. population. Therefore, cultural patterns used to characterize an entire country should generally be limited to the members of the dominant culture in that nation.
- *Cultural patterns are integrated*: Because language is linear in nature, we are forced to talk about cultural patterns individually. It is important, however, to realize that the patterns do not occur or operate in isolation; they are interrelated and integrated. In other words, they act in concert. If a culture values the elderly, that value gets attached to yet other values related to respect and decision making.
- *Cultural patterns are dynamic*: Any review of world history will demonstrate that values can evolve and produce societal change. The U.S. civil rights movement gave rise to actions and legislation that led to equal rights for other minority groups, such as women, gays, and ethnic minorities. The interconnected world created by globalization has enabled people in other nations to learn about different values and social structures. The Arab Spring that swept the Middle East in early 2011 was in part a result of young people who embraced freedom, independence, and democracy—values significantly at odds with those held by the authoritarian elites. However, even after recognizing the dynamic nature of culture, you need to remember that deep cultural structures are often resistant to change and evolve very slowly. Recall that many of the young Egyptian men demonstrating for freedom and democracy later declared that a woman's place was in the home.
- *Cultural patterns can be contradictory*: In many instances you can find contradictory values within a culture. A frequent refrain in the United States is that "all people are created equal," but acts of prejudice toward minorities and violence directed at gays continue. Some of the most divisive issues now confronting U.S. society—abortion, gay marriage, gun rights, capital punishment, immigration, school prayer, wealth distribution, etc.—are a result of contrasting values. Even the divide between conservatives and liberals is at its core a difference of ideologically based values. These types of contradictions are common in all cultures. The Bible advocates helping others, and the Koran teaches brotherhood among all people. Yet in both the United States and

many Muslim nations, some segments of the population are very rich and others are extremely poor.

Even with the caveats just discussed, the study of cultural patterns is a worthwhile endeavor. However, when engaged in any intercultural interaction, you should keep in mind that you are dealing with an individual, and that individual may or may not demonstrate the cultural characteristics generally attributed to the larger cultural group.

> **REMEMBER THIS**
>
> *Cultural patterns are broad generalizations used to characterize a culture's values.*

CHOOSING CULTURAL PATTERNS

Scholars from various disciplines have compiled a variety of cultural pattern typologies. In almost every case the objective has been to discover characteristics that would help to identify and understand dissimilar cultural values. Clearly, there is a degree of overlap among the different classification systems, but each has its own merits. For obvious reasons we have selected cultural pattern typologies that are most commonly seen in works by intercultural communication scholars. Also, we have included Minkov's four cultural dimensions and Gelfand's study of tight and loose cultures, which represent some of the most contemporary research. Thus, the remainder of this chapter presents a comprehensive examination of the following seven value taxonomies:

- Kohls' list of *values Americans live by*
- The Kluckhohn and Strodtbeck classification of *value orientations*
- Hall's categorization of *high-context and low-context orientations*
- Hofstede's set of *value dimensions*
- Minkov's *cultural dimensions*
- Gelfand's research on *tight and loose cultures*
- Ting-Toomey's explanation and application of *face and facework*

As you go through these different typologies, two assumptions should become apparent. First, values presented in cultural patterns are points lying along a continuum rather than polar opposites. The rationale is simple—cultural differences are usually a matter of degree. Second, there is a great deal of commonality and some duplication among the different cultural patterns. In fact, many of the patterns discussed here are also part of other taxonomies.

APPLYING CULTURAL PATTERNS

For each of the seven cultural value typologies discussed in this section we have endeavored to provide a brief theoretical explanation of the individual values along with applied examples.

KOHLS' "THE VALUES AMERICANS LIVE BY"

The diverse, multiethnic population that characterizes, and strengthens, the United States makes the task of constructing an overall set of values quite challenging. This problem is acknowledged in Charon and Vigilant's statement, "Listing American values is a difficult task because there are so many exceptions and contradictions." However, they add, "On a general level, Americans do share a value system."[11] Also, Kim points out, "There are similar characteristics that all Americans share, regardless of their age, race, gender, or ethnicity."[12]

Students beginning their study of intercultural communication are usually interested in learning about other cultures. However, one of our long-standing tenets is that in order to develop competent intercultural skills, a person must understand his or her own culture. So while this book leans toward explaining other cultures, a section exploring American cultural values is also essential. For people who are not members of the dominant culture, this information will provide new insights and understanding. For members of the dominant culture, an analysis of U.S. cultural values is provided for three reasons. First, people carry their culture wherever they go, and that culture influences how they respond to the people they meet. Second, examining one's own values can reveal cultural information that is often overlooked or taken for granted. Finally, personal cultural values can serve as an important reference point for making comparisons between and among cultures.

Professor L. Robert Kohls spent much of his life working to improve cross-cultural understanding. After living in Korea, he returned to the United States and began conducting cultural workshops for the Peace Corps. He also spent time at the United States Information Agency (USIA) as Director of Training. Kohls authored *The Values Americans Live By*, a 1980s monograph intended to help expatriates adjust to living in the United States,[13] and it remains widely available on the Internet. Although written nearly thirty years ago, the thirteen values Kohls ascribed to U.S. Americans (see Table 6.1) continue to provide an accurate characterization of the dominant U.S. culture. Each value is discussed individually.

CONSIDER THIS

Can you think of specific examples that would demonstrate how the following list of U.S. American values gets acted out by members of the culture?

a. *Personal Control over the Environment*
b. *Change*
c. *Time and Its Control*
d. *Equality*
e. *Individualism/Privacy*
f. *Self-Help*
g. *Competition*
h. *Future Orientation*
i. *Action/Work Orientation*
j. *Informality*
k. *Directness/Openness/Honesty*
l. *Practicality/Efficiency*
m. *Materialism/Acquisitiveness*

Personal Control over Nature

The earliest European settlers arrived in America confident they could tame this wild new land and imbue it with political and religious institutions of their own choosing. No doubt, many felt they were simply following God's directive as contained in Genesis 1:28: "And God blessed them, and God said to them, 'Be fruitful, and multiply, and replenish the earth, and subdue it: and have dominion over the fish of the sea, and over the fowl of the air, and over every living thing that moves on the earth.'"

Americans have traditionally approached the environment as something to be conquered, tamed, or harnessed for personal and societal benefit. The idea of exercising dominion over nature and bending the environment to one's own will underwrote the physical and political resolve required continually to push the American frontier

TABLE 6.1	Kohls' American Values Comparison[14]	
U.S. VALUES		**FOREIGN COUNTERPART VALUES**
Personal Control over the Environment	1	Fate
Change	2	Tradition
Time & Its Control	3	Human Interaction
Equality	4	Hierarchy/Rank/Status
Individualism/Privacy	5	Group's Welfare
Self-Help	6	Birthright Inheritance
Competition	7	Cooperation
Future Orientation	8	Past Orientation
Action/Work Orientation	9	"Being" Orientation
Informality	10	Formality
Directness/Openness/Honesty	11	Indirectness/Ritual/"Face"
Practicality/Efficiency	12	Idealism
Materialism/Acquisitiveness	13	Spiritualism/Detachment

Source: © Cengage Learning 2013

westward. In the United States today, the value of mastering nature can be seen in the construction of the Interstate Highway System that crisscrosses the nation, dams that hold back the waters of large rivers, tunnels that go through mountains, bridges that span wide bays, fertile fields that were converted from desert land, and platforms on the sea that remove oil from thousands of feet below. In the United States, the ability to control nature is considered normal and even right. This results in bold approaches to overcome all obstacles and the belief that individuals should have control over their personal environment and the opportunity to achieve any goal.

Change

Closely aligned with control of the environment is the value of change and progress. Since the country's inception, people have subscribed to forward-looking beliefs and attitudes that promote progress through modernization. Various aspects of this orientation are optimism, receptivity to change, emphasis on the future rather than the past or present, faith in an ability to control all phases of life, and confidence in the perceptual ability of the common person. As discussed later in the chapter, many older, more traditional cultures that have witnessed the rise and fall of past civilizations and believe in fatalism, view change and progress as detrimental, and they often have difficulty understanding U.S. Americans' general disregard for history and tradition:

> This fundamental American belief in progress and a better future contrasts sharply with the fatalistic (Americans are likely to use that term with a negative or critical connotation) attitude that characterizes people from many other cultures, notably Latin American, Asian, and Middle Eastern, where there is a pronounced reverence for the past. In those cultures the future is considered to be in the hands of fate, God, or at least the few powerful people or families that dominate the society. The idea that people in general can somehow shape their own futures seems naïve, arrogant, or even sacrilegious.[15]

This dichotomy in perspectives toward change can also be seen in the way that U.S. employment patterns compare with those in some other nations. For U.S.

workers, changing jobs is the accepted norm. Employees see moving to a new company as a way of personal advancement and embracing new challenges. In contrast, in some Asian countries there is often a reciprocal loyalty between employees and their organization.[16]

Time and Its Control

For U.S. Americans, time is a valuable commodity, something to be measured and used wisely. Schedules, which are often divided into hourly, daily, weekly, monthly, and even yearly segments, dictate life in the United States.[17] Deadlines and due dates are a constant reminder of when projects must be completed. U.S. business representatives tend to move quickly past introductory formalities and rapidly "get down to business." This contrasts with other cultures, such as in Mexico and China, where it is considered important to get to know the other person before initiating business discussions. In the United States, schedules are generally inflexible with meetings starting on time, moving through a set agenda, and ending promptly. In other cultures, time may be seen as more flexible, and spending time with someone can take precedence over a schedule.

Even the founding fathers of the United States considered time to be important, as this quotation from Benjamin Franklin demonstrates: "Lose no time; be always employed in something useful." The continuing value U.S. Americans place on time is also illustrated by corporate practices. For instance, "Wal-Mart ... pioneered the daily early-morning meeting at which all stand so as to get down to business quickly, shorten the meeting time, and then go out and execute agreements made."[18]

Equality/Egalitarianism

Equality is a most prized American value and is enshrined in the preamble to the United States Declaration of Independence, which states, "all men are created equal."[19] The concept is further preserved in the Constitution, which specifies, "No Title of Nobility shall be granted by the United States."[20] The founders of our nation had escaped the English social caste system, controlled by the landed, hereditary aristocracy, and sought to ensure that it could not develop in America.

Rather than focus on the literal meaning of "created equal," let us look at the ideals behind those words, which we believe were best explained by Abraham Lincoln in 1860 when he said, "We do wish to allow the humblest man an equal chance to get rich with everybody else." Thus, the value that pervades contemporary U.S. society can best be termed "equal opportunity." All people should have the same opportunity to succeed in life, and the state, through laws and educational opportunities, is expected to guarantee that right.

In the United States the value of equal opportunity translates into equality and informality across social relationships. For instance, most of the primary social relationships within a family tend to promote egalitarianism rather than hierarchy. Formality is generally not important. In secondary relationships, most friends and coworkers are also treated as equals, usually interacting on a first-name basis. People from cultures that adhere to formal social structures often find it disconcerting to work with U.S. citizens, whom they believe diminish the value of social status differences. We are not implying that U.S. Americans completely ignore hierarchy, but it is usually a secondary consideration or applied only in specific contexts, such as seating arrangements, formal introductions, and certain professions.

Courtesy of Edwin McDaniel

In many cultures conformity, rather than individuality, is an important value.

Please remember that contradictions often exist within U.S. values. The history of the United States is replete with examples of discrimination based on skin color, ethnicity, gender, level of education, social class, sexual preference, and even choice of religion. Unfortunately, today, some people continue to employ these criteria to evaluate others. While she acknowledges that many Americans have experienced periods of inequality, Hanson points out, "Not all citizens have had equal rights throughout the course of the country's history, but Americans nevertheless value the notion highly and strive toward this ideal."[21]

Individuality and Privacy

Often referred to as "freedom" by U.S. Americans,[22] individualism is perhaps the most revered U.S. cultural value and is a particularly salient social characteristic. Broadly speaking, individualism, as developed in the works of the seventeenth-century English philosopher John Locke, holds that each person is unique, special, completely different from all other individuals, and "the basic unit of nature."[23] Locke's view is simple—the interests of the individual are or ought to be paramount, and all values, rights, and duties originate in individuals. Individualism commands so much influence among Americans that it gives rise to other U.S. values, such as personal initiative, self-reliance, and equal opportunity.

The emphasis on the individual is also found elsewhere in the world, but it has emerged as the cornerstone of U.S. culture. The origin of this value has a long history. As mentioned in the discussion

REMEMBER THIS
Freedom is the most revered value in the United States.

on U.S. history in Chapter 5, the emphasis on individualism arose from the early settlers' desire to escape the repressive conditions that then characterized European society. Regardless of the context, whether societal, ethical, or sexual, among U.S. Americans, the individual occupies the pivotal position. This notion is so strong that some U.S. Americans see a person who fails to demonstrate individuality as being out of step with society. Irrespective of being conveyed by literature, art, or U.S. history, the message is the same—individual achievement, sovereignty, and freedom are the virtues most glorified and canonized.

Despite today's stress on personal freedom and individual rights, U.S. citizens also have a very distinct group orientation. Chapter 5 reported that one scholar had characterized the United States as a culture of voluntarism, where people participate in groups of their own choosing.[24] Gannon and Pillai bring this point out: "Americans are also group-oriented and being part of a group or network and identifying with it is essential for success in almost all instances. Within the group structure specialization is exalted and everyone is expected to add value to the final product or service because of it."[25] But we add that among the group members, there is no sense of mutual obligation beyond the task at hand.

This concept is readily illustrated by using sports as a metaphor. Baseball has designated hitters, pinch hitters, and relief pitchers. Football has placekickers, specialty teams, punt returners, and other specialists. In each case, a person's specialty is used to benefit the entire team (group) while concurrently providing a degree of individual identity. But the team members may or may not have any contact with each other off the field.

Self-Help

The importance U.S. Americans place on self-help and personal achievement is an outgrowth of the values of independence, equality, and individuality, which are exemplified in commonly heard expressions such as "be self-reliant," "stand on your own two feet," or "don't depend on others." In the United States, your family name or the school attended will normally only help you to get an initial introduction or interview. Any subsequent gain must be earned through personal merit. Theoretically, the concept of equality underlying U.S. societal structure provides everyone the same opportunity for material and social improvement. One just has to work for it. The opportunity to go from rags to riches remains a fundamental American belief and can be seen in the political careers of Presidents Clinton and Obama. Both started from humble beginnings and went on ultimately to sit in the Oval Office. The nineteenth-century English poet William Henley succinctly captured this U.S. value of self-mastery when he wrote, "I am the master of my fate, I am the captain of my soul."

The value of personal self-reliance and individual responsibility in the United States underlies the call for smaller government by some conservative groups. Their attitude is that there should be less governmental intrusion into people's lives, and that includes reducing many of the government-funded social support programs. In other words, these groups think that many of the aid programs erode the individual's self-reliance, a trait that helped found the nation.

Competition and Free Enterprise

A positive attitude toward competition is an integral part of life in the United States and begins during childhood. Whether it is through games or being continually asked to answer questions in the classroom, a competitive nature is encouraged among American children. People are ranked, graded, classified, and evaluated so that everyone will know who is the best. The media continually provide "Top 10" lists of people, schools, hospitals, movies, vacation locations, and endless other topics. The Internet has allowed people publicly to rate almost every commercial and public entity. The U.S. economic system—free market enterprise— is based on competition, and the U.S. government is constantly touting free and open markets. The assumption is that individuals, left to their own means, can more ably and quickly achieve their desired goals. This idea is behind the frequent call to "let the market work." Moreover, the system is considered "fair" because everyone purportedly has the same opportunity.

This competitive spirit can create problems for Americans when they interact with people who do not share the value. For instance, in some cultures, a person's social and economic stature can be a product of family connections, schools attended, length of time with an organization, or even age. In these cultures, competition based on personal merit may become a secondary consideration. Additionally, cultures that promote interdependency and cooperation take a negative view of intragroup competition.

> ## CONSIDER THIS
>
> *Emphasis on the individual leads to a short-term future orientation.*

Future Orientation

An old adage holds that Americans are not especially interested in history because they have so little of it. While that is somewhat an overstatement, it does point out that in the United States, what lies ahead usually takes precedence over the past. What is going to happen holds the greatest attraction because, it seems, whatever we are doing is not quite as good as what we could otherwise be doing or will be doing in the future. Change, taking chances, a stress on youth, and optimism are all hallmarks of U.S. culture and reflect the value placed on the future. As a people, U.S. Americans are constantly thinking about tomorrow. Very young children commonly play with the toys (dolls, cars, guns, and so on) that rush them toward and prepare them for adulthood. What you want, you want now, so you can dispose of this moment and move on to the next. In the classroom, U.S. students impatiently watch the clock as it counts the minutes to the end of class—and cues them to move on to another class or activity. Elementary students are eager to get to high school, then they look forward to college, during which they focus on getting into the workforce, after which they start looking ahead to retirement. Adler and Gunderson aptly capture the U.S. forward-looking focus when they observe, "Future-oriented cultures justify innovation and change mostly in terms of future economic benefits."[26] We will return to this topic when we discuss the Kluckhohn and Strodtbeck's value orientations later in the chapter and again when we examine the use of "time" as employed by each culture.

Action/Work Orientation

Soon after meeting for the first time, people frequently ask each other, "What do you do?" or "Where do you work?" Embedded in this simple query is the belief that working (doing something) is important. For most U.S. Americans, work represents a cluster of moral and affective conditions of great attractiveness, and voluntary idleness is often seen as severely threatening and damaging to society as a whole. Unlike cultures where physical labor is considered the fate of the less privileged, Americans place considerable value on the "dignity of human labor." This value can be seen in the activities of U.S. presidents—Ronald Reagan chopped wood, George W. Bush cleared brush, and President Obama has spent time helping Habitat for Humanity construct homes for the less fortunate.

A major reward for this hard work, and an important aspect of life in the United States, is time away from the job. For U.S. citizens, time for leisure activities is something they have earned as a respite from the demands and stress of work. This emphasis on recreation and relaxation takes a broad array of forms. Each weekend, people rush to get away in their RVs, play golf or tennis, go skiing, ride their mountain bikes, go to the beach, or "unwind" at a gambling casino, a racetrack, or a movie. Vacations are usually spent "doing" something. U.S. Americans often relax by engaging in some form of activity. Yet leisure time is generally seen as an opportunity to "relax" or "refresh" so that one can return to work with rededicated enthusiasm.

Informality

The emphasis on equality and individuality has produced a pervasive sense of informality in the United States, which can be seen in people's dress, deportment, and communication. Casual dress is the norm in most contexts, and blue jeans are a frequent sight among media stars, Silicon Valley entrepreneurs, and occasionally even our presidents. This informality is also evident in the widespread use of first names, even among recent acquaintances. A common practice at U.S. fast-food outlets, such as Starbucks, is to call out the customer's first name when their order is ready. In U.S. restaurants the waitstaff often introduce themselves using only a first name, and even telephone solicitors quickly move to first names. These practices exemplify the informality of U.S. culture and are in contrast with what you might experience in other, more formal cultures. Everyone, regardless of position, rank, wealth, or age, is considered equal, so there is no need for titles of distinction. The exception to this practice is for those in certain professions, such as the military, medicine, the courts, the clergy, high government officials, and a few others. The informality does not connote a lack of respect toward others. Rather, it conveys the feeling of individuality, equality, and outward friendliness inherent in the dominant U.S. culture.

Directness, Openness, and Honesty

The language style used by most U.S. Americans can be characterized as direct, frank, and explicit. Phrases such as "Just tell it like it is," "Don't beat around the bush," and "Give me the bottom line" are frequently heard. In these instances, the speaker is indicating a desire to quickly get to the heart of the matter. This illustrates the value placed on direct, open, and honest communication, which takes precedence over politeness and face-saving measures. Here again, you can see the influence of equality, informality, the importance of time, and the feeling of self-reliance. U.S. Americans see no need to use elaborate courtesy protocols because everyone is equal, and honesty is a positive mark of one's character.

U.S. Americans believe that conflicts are best settled by examining problems in a logical, forthright manner and that personal emotions should be set aside. Indeed, individuals using ambiguous, vague, or indirect communication run the risk of being seen as untrustworthy or duplicitous. A person's ability to openly, directly, and honestly state their position is of such importance that in the United States people attend "assertiveness training" programs. This is in contrast to the normative communication behaviors in many Asian nations, where concern for interpersonal relations takes precedence.[27]

Practicality and Efficiency

Practicality and efficiency are also hallmarks of the dominant U.S. culture. Unlike some Asian cultures, gift giving in the United States is usually kept within the limits appropriate to the giver's budget. Garage sales are common in the United States because U.S. Americans are not embarrassed to buy used items. At a restaurant with a large group, people often "go Dutch," with everyone paying for their own meal. It is easy to see that individuality, independence, and self-reliance are central considerations in the pragmatic attitude evinced by U.S. Americans. Because strong group ties do not play a major role in U.S. societal activities, there is no need to build interpersonal relations based on a system of mutual obligations, as is done in many collectivistic cultures. The role of efficiency in the United States can also be seen in the highly structured use of time, as was discussed earlier. U.S. Americans also tend to be very rational or logical when working on problems. The phrases "Just give me the facts" and "Let's get down to the nitty-gritty" illustrate the importance U.S. Americans place on expediency and impartiality when making a decision or a judgment. Reason, logic, and objectivity take precedence over emotionality, subjectivity, or sentimentality.

Materialism

Acquiring material possessions is an integral part of life for most Americans, so much so that "shopping" is sometimes used as a leisure activity and businesses facilitate purchases by offering easy access to credit cards and installment payment plans, along with frequent sales. From their perspective, U.S. Americans consider their materialistic nature "natural and proper,"[28] which Bender sees as a natural outgrowth of the nation's philosophy of equal opportunity for all.[29] In other words, material well-being and easy access to quality products is not the preserve of an elite class.

However, U.S. Americans have historically been willing to work hard to realize their dreams. Thus, acquisition of material possessions, such as a large home, a variety of clothes for every occasion, convenient personal transportation, and an extensive selection of foods, is considered just reward for hard work. The preference for a wide choice of material items is clearly illustrated in a typical U.S. supermarket, which may carry over 48,000 items.[30] Also, think about the number of sandwich and condiment choices available at Subway, the variety of coffee drinks presented at Starbucks, and the many different brands, styles, and colors of tennis shoes available at Foot Locker.

CONSIDER THIS

Consumerism in the United States is supported by the value placed on materialism.

OTHER CULTURAL PATTERN TYPOLOGIES

With this understanding of the dominant U.S. culture values, you are now ready for a more comprehensive exploration of cultural pattern typologies and to begin making some cross-cultural comparisons. As mentioned earlier in this chapter, scholars have devised a number of taxonomies that can be used to analyze key behavioral patterns found in almost every culture. Among those classification listings, several seem to be at the core of most intercultural communication studies, and we will look at seven of them.

There are, however, other important typologies that you should be aware of, which, due to limited space, cannot be covered in this text. Probably the two most significant are the GLOBE Study and work by Trompenaars and Hampden-Turner. The GLOBE Study is an ongoing research project investigating the relationship between social culture, organizational culture, and leadership within organizations. The extensive project has involved approximately 170 international researchers and more than 17,000 managers from over 900 organizations across sixty-one societies from fifty-eight nations. Trompenaars and Hampden-Turner's work extends over twenty years and focuses on the role of culture in international business and cross-cultural management. They examine five different cultural orientations and cultural differences in attitudes toward time and the environment.[31]

KLUCKHOHN AND STRODTBECK'S VALUE ORIENTATIONS[32]

The first taxonomy of cultural orientations comes from the anthropological work of Kluckhohn and Strodtbeck. They based their research on the idea that every individual, regardless of culture, must deal with five universal questions, referred to as "value orientations." These "orientations," or patterns, inform members of a culture what is important and provide them guidance for living their lives. After extensive study, they concluded that all people turn to their culture for help in answering the same five basic questions:

1. What is the character of human nature?

2. What is the relation of humankind to nature?

3. What is the orientation toward time?

4. What is the value placed on activity?

5. What is the relationship of people to each other?

As with all the cultural value typologies you will study, Kluckhohn and Strodtbeck's orientations (see Table 6.2) are best visualized as points along a continuum. Moving through the five orientations (human nature, person/nature orientation, time, activity, and relational orientation), you will notice that although they have different names, some of the characteristics are similar to the ones discussed in other taxonomies in this chapter. This is understandable because the different classifications are focused on the meaningful values underpinning all cultures. Hence, some of the classifications track the same or similar patterns.

TABLE 6.2	Five Value Orientations from Kluckhohn and Strodtbeck		
ORIENTATION		**VALUE AND BEHAVIOR RANGE**	
Human nature	Basically evil	Mixture of good and evil	Basically good
Humans and nature	Subject to nature	Harmony with nature	Master of nature
Sense of time	Past	Present	Future
Activity	Being	Being-in-becoming	Doing
Social relationships	Authoritarian	Group	Individualism

Source: F. R. Kluckhohn and F. L. Strodtbeck, *Variations in Value Orientations* (New York: Row and Peterson, 1960).

Human Nature Orientation

Nearly all judgments about human behavior, whether moral or legal, begin with this core question: What is the character of human nature? Was Anne Frank right when she wrote in *The Diary of a Young Girl*, "In spite of everything, I still believe that people are really good at heart"? Or was Xunzi, a philosopher in Ancient China, correct when he observed, "Human nature is evil, and goodness is caused by intentional activity." For centuries, religious leaders, philosophers, scholars, and others have pondered and debated questions concerning human nature, answers to which represent a powerful force in how one lives life. Although all people individually answer questions about human nature, there are also cultural explanations for why people act as they do. Since discussions of human nature often deal with divisions of evil, good and evil, and good, each of those issues is examined below to see how they may differ across cultures.

Evil.   Some cultures believe that people are intrinsically evil. Brought from Europe by the early Puritans, this view prevailed in the United States for many years. In the last century, however, Americans have come to consider themselves as a mixture of good and evil. That is, most U.S. Americans now believe that by following certain rules, they can change and improve themselves. According to this idea, an individual can achieve goodness through constant hard work, self-control, education, and self-discipline. A more restrictive view of human nature as good or evil is found in parts of the world where Islam is strong. There, you can find cultures that are imbued with the notion that people have a penchant for evil and therefore cannot be trusted to make a correct decision when left to their own resources. Hence, to help control the actions of their members, numerous social institutions, ranging from the religious to the political, are designed to monitor and manage behavior.

Good and Evil.   People with a Taoist worldview believe the universe is best seen from the perspective of *yin* and *yang*, an infinite system of opposing elements and forces in balanced, dynamic interaction. Two of the forces are good and evil, and since humanity is part of the universe, these forces are naturally present in humankind. This idea is exemplified in the notion of the *yin* and *yang* cycle. Periodic increases in *yin* are accompanied by corresponding decreases in *yang*; this is followed by an opposite cycle in which *yang* increases while *yin* decreases. This view of the good and evil nature of humanity proposes that evil cannot be eliminated because it is an integral part of the universe. For very different reasons, many Europeans also have a dualistic (good/evil) approach to human nature. Specifically, they believe that while we might be born with a propensity for evil, people can become good through learning and education.

Good.   Perhaps the strongest view of the innate goodness of human nature is found in the philosophies of Confucianism and Buddhism. According to the Lu Wang school of Confucianism, "Human nature is originally good." Contemporary Chinese scholar Pei-Jung Fu echoes this belief when he writes, "there is solid foundation for claiming that Confucius regarded human nature as tending toward goodness."[33] Buddhism also maintains that you are born pure and are closest to what is called "loving-kindness" when you first enter this world. Hence, people are good, but their culture often makes them evil.

Cutting across the arguments concerning human nature, whether it is good or evil, is the question of the essential rationality of human nature. Throughout history there has been tension between those who believe in fate or mystic powers and those who feel that thought and reason can solve any problem and discover any truth. Imagine, for a moment, your perceptions of reality if you are French and take the rational approach reflected in Descartes' philosophy or if you are an American Indian and believe that external forces control much of your thinking and behavior. To cite another example, the Hindu relies on mysticism, intuition, and spiritual awareness to understand the nature of reality. A belief in fate, as opposed to one that stresses free will, is bound to yield different conclusions.

Person/Nature Orientation

Different ideas about the relationship between humanity and nature produce distinct frames of reference for human desires, attitudes, and behaviors. In Kluckhohn and Strodtbeck's cultural value taxonomy, three types of relationships characterize how different cultures relate to and interact with nature.

Humans Subject to Nature.   At one end of the scale is the view that humans are subject to nature. Cultures holding this orientation believe the most powerful forces of life are beyond human control. Whether the force is a god, fate, or magic, it cannot be overcome and must, therefore, be accepted. This perspective is found in India and parts of South America. For the Hindu, because everything is part of a unified force, "the world of distinct and separate objects and processes is a manifestation of a more fundamental reality that is undivided and unconditional."[34] This "oneness" with the world helps create a vision of a world operating in harmony. In Mexico and among Mexican Americans, there is a strong tie to Catholicism and the role of fate in controlling life and nature, which leads to a general acceptance of things as they are.

Harmony with Nature.   The middle or cooperative view is widespread and often associated with East Asians. In Japan and Thailand, there is a perception that nature is part of life and not a hostile force waiting to be subdued. This orientation affirms that people should, in every way possible, live in harmony with nature. To cite another

Courtesy of Robert Fonseca

Many cultures instill in their members a desire to live in harmony with nature.

example, the desire to be part of nature and not control it has always been strong among American Indians. Even today, many tribes practice conservation of natural resources and protest the disruption of ancestral lands.

Mastery of Nature.   At the other end of the scale is the view that compels us to conquer and direct the forces of nature to our advantage. This orientation is characteristic of the Western approach, which, as noted earlier in the chapter, has a long tradition of valuing technology, change, and science. Americans have historically believed that nature was something that could and had to be mastered. Even our language reflects this orientation. Early Western European immigrants to North America encountered a vast, unforgiving wilderness that they set about to "tame," and modern astronauts are working to "conquer" space. People with this orientation see a clear separation between humans and nature.

Time Orientation

People's obsession with time and the power they afford it are obvious, and as you would expect by now, cultures vary widely in their perspective toward time. The greatest differences are in the respective values placed on the past, present, and future and on how each influences interaction. This section will highlight some of the major cultural differences in how time is viewed as it applies to Kluckhohn and Strodtbeck's taxonomy.

REMEMBER THIS

Cultures characterized by the practice of rich traditions usually have a strong orientation toward the past.

Past Orientation.   In past-oriented cultures, history, established religions, and tradition are extremely important. There is an intense belief that contemporary perceptions of people and events, decision making, and determinations of truth should be guided by what happened in the past. Respect for the past is especially evident in most Asian nations because of their long and eventful histories. According to Westad, "The past is inscribed in China's mental terrain in a calligraphy so powerful that it determines most of its approaches to the present."[35] There is even a famous Chinese proverb: "The past is as clear as a mirror, the future as dark as lacquer." A similar adage from India advises, "Learn about the future by looking at the past." Great Britain remains devoted to tradition, including the maintenance of a monarchy, and continues to value its historical achievements. France is another culture that can be understood by exploring its view of the past. As Hall and Hall disclose, the French, on many levels, venerate the past:

> The importance of French history to the average French person can hardly be over-stated. The French live surrounded by thousands of monuments to their glorious past. Every quarter in Paris has its historically important statues, buildings, or fountains, daily reminders of past achievements. French villages have statues to local heroes and important political leaders. As a result of this constant immersion in history, the French tend to see things in their historical context and relate contemporary events to their origins.[36]

Present Orientation.   Present-oriented cultures hold that the here and now carries the most significance. The future is seen as ambiguous, capricious, and in a sense, beyond the control of the individual. Because the past is over and the future is unpredictable, present cultures, such as Filipinos and Latin Americans, enjoy living in the moment. These cultures tend to be more impulsive and spontaneous than others and often have a casual, relaxed lifestyle. Mexicans and Mexican Americans believe in living in the present moment, a view that is also characteristic of the African American co-culture.[37]

Future Orientation.   Future-oriented cultures value what is yet to come, and the future is expected to be grander than the present or past. Change, taking chances, a stress on youth, and optimism are all hallmarks of cultures that hold this orientation. As noted when we examined Christianity in Chapter Four, most U.S. Americans, who are constantly thinking about what is ahead, hold this view toward the future. This does not mean that U.S. Americans have no regard for the past or no thought of the present, but it is certainly true that many U.S. Americans, in thought or action, tend to have a short-term, forward-looking perspective. The effect on communication can be seen in business negotiations between a long-term future-oriented country like China and a short-term future-oriented nation such as the United States. While the Chinese side would be looking to establish a relationship that would carry into the future, the U.S. team would be more focused on the immediate project and have much less concern for the future.

Activity Orientation

Activity orientation refers to how people of a culture view activity, and Kluckhohn and Strodtbeck detail three common approaches to activity—being, being-in-becoming, and doing.

While many cultures crave excitement and activity, there are cultures that welcome solitude and members spend long periods of their lives alone in meditation and contemplation.

Being. A being orientation refers to spontaneous expression of the human personality. "People in being-orientated cultures accept people, events, and ideas as flowing spontaneously. They stress release, indulgence of existing desires, and working for the moment."[38] Most Latino cultures consider the activity they are engaged in as the one that matters the most. In Mexico, for example, interpersonal relations are valued more than accomplishments, and people take great delight in the simple act of conversation with family and friends. Mexicans will talk for hours with their companions, for they believe that the act of "being" is one of the main goals and joys of life.

Being-in-Becoming. Being-in-becoming stresses the idea of development and growth. It emphasizes the kind of activity that contributes to the development and improvement of all aspects of the self as an integral whole. This usually correlates with cultures that value a spiritual life over a material one. For example, in both Hinduism and Buddhism, people spend time in meditation and contemplation in an attempt to purify and fully advance themselves. The New Age movement in the United States also stresses the need to develop the being-in-becoming approach to daily life.

Doing. The doing orientation describes activity in which accomplishments are measured by standards external to the individual. The key to this orientation is a value system that stresses action. It is the doing orientation that most characterizes the dominant American culture, as is summed up by Kim:

> Americans are action oriented; they are go-getters. They get going, get things done, and get ahead. In America, people gather for action—to play basketball, to dance, to go to a concert. When groups gather they play games or watch videos. Many Americans don't have the patience to sit down and talk…. Life is in constant motion.[39]

A doing perspective affects many other cultural beliefs and values. Your definition of activity affects your perception of work, efficiency, change, time, and progress. Even the pace at which you live your life—from how fast you walk to how quickly you make decisions—is related to where you fall on the being/doing scale. U.S. Americans admire and reward people who can make quick decisions, "get things done," and exhibit a proactive attitude.

HALL'S HIGH-CONTEXT AND LOW-CONTEXT ORIENTATIONS

E.T. Hall, an anthropologist, was one of the early pioneers in the study of intercultural communication. He categorizes cultures as high-context or low-context, depending on how much meaning is derived from the contextual environment rather than the actual words exchanged during communicative interactions.[40] The assumption underlying Hall's classifications is that "one of the functions of culture is to provide a highly selective screen between man and the outside world. In its many forms, culture therefore designates what we pay attention to and what we ignore."[41]

Hall saw context as "the information that surrounds an event."[42] His work revealed that cultures were often characterized by high- or low-context communication, which he described in the following:

> A high-context (HC) communication or message is one in which most of the information is already in the person, while very little is in the coded, explicitly transmitted part of the message. A low-context (LC) communication is just the opposite; i.e., the mass of the information is vested in the explicit code.[43]

Although all cultures possess some characteristics of both high- and low-context variables, most can be ranked along a scale for this particular dimension. To emphasize this fact, in Table 6.3 various cultures have been placed on a continuum rather than using only two opposing categories.

REMEMBER THIS
High-context cultures rely on the context; low-context cultures rely on words.

High-Context

In high-context cultures, most of the meaning exchanged during an encounter is often not communicated through words. High-context cultures normally possess a significant degree of similarity among the people. This leads to similar perceptions, experiences, and societal expectations, which produce well-defined social protocols. Because high-context cultures are usually quite traditional, they change little over time and produce consistent responses to the social environment. "As a result, for most normal transactions in daily life they do not require, nor do they expect, much in-depth background information."[44] Because the meaning is not necessarily contained in the words in high-context cultures, information is provided through inferences, gestures, and even in what is **not** said.

People of high-context cultures tend to be attuned to their surroundings and can easily express and interpret emotions nonverbally. Meaning in high-context

TABLE 6.3	Cultures Arranged Along the High-Context and Low-Context Dimension

HIGH-CONTEXT CULTURES

Japanese
|
Chinese
|
Korean
|
African American
|
Native American
|
Arab
|
Greek
|
Latin
|
Italian
|
English
|
French
|
North American
|
Scandinavian
|
German
|
German/Swiss
|

LOW-CONTEXT CULTURES

Source: Adapted from E.T. Hall, *Beyond Culture* (Garden City, NY: Doubleday, 1976), 91.

cultures is also conveyed "through status (age, sex, education, family background, title, and affiliations) and through an individual's informal friends and associates."[45] Because of the subtle "messages" used by high-context cultures, members of these groups often "communicate in an indirect fashion."[46] They rely more on how something is said rather than what is said and are acutely aware of nonverbal cues.

As shown in Table 6.3, Northeast Asian cultures tend to be high-context. According to Chang, this is a result of Confucian philosophy, which inclines "Asian culture toward high-context and collectivist communication that emphasizes role hierarchy and relations rather than the expression of self through direct communication."[47]

Low-Context

Low-context cultures typically have a high degree of diversity within the population and tend to compartmentalize interpersonal contacts. Lack of a large pool of common experiences means that "each time they interact with others they need detailed background information."[48] In low-context cultures the verbal message contains most of the information, and very little is conveyed through the context or the participant's nonverbal displays. This characteristic manifests itself in a host of ways. For example, the Asian mode of communication (high-context) is often vague, indirect, and implicit, whereas Western communication (low-context) tends to be direct and unambiguous. "Americans depend more on spoken words than on nonverbal behavior to convey their messages. They think it is important to be able to 'speak up' and 'say what's on their mind.' They admire a person who has a moderately large vocabulary and who can express themselves clearly and cleverly...."[49] As suggested at the end of this quote, differences in perceptions of credibility are another aspect of communication associated with these two orientations. In high-context cultures, people who rely primarily on verbal messages for information are perceived as less credible. They believe that silence often sends a better message than words and that anyone who needs words does not have the requisite communication skills. As the Indonesian proverb states, "Empty cans clatter the loudest."

HOFSTEDE'S VALUE DIMENSIONS[50]

Research conducted by Dutch social psychologist Geert Hofstede was one of the earliest attempts to use statistical data to examine cultural values. He surveyed more than 100,000 IBM employees from fifty countries and three geographical regions. After careful analysis, each country and region was assigned a rank of 1 through 50 in four identified value dimensions (individualism/collectivism, uncertainty avoidance, power distance, masculinity/femininity). A subsequent study involving participants from twenty-three nations revealed a fifth dimension (long-term/short-term orientation), and these countries were ordered 1 through 23. The country rankings discerned through this research offer a clear picture of what is valued in each culture and also help make comparisons across cultures. However, it is important to keep in mind that Hofstede's work measured cultural dimensions at a national rather than an individual level,[51] which means that his value dimensions characterize the dominant culture in that society. As we have said before, within every culture you can find individuals all along each particular value continuum. For example, the United States is classified as a strongly individualistic country, but you may encounter some members of the dominant U.S. culture who exhibit strong collective tendencies. Conversely, in a group-oriented culture such as South Korea or Japan, you can find individuals who subscribe to and assert individuality. Therefore, in any intercultural encounter, you must be mindful that not all individuals adhere to the norms of their culture.

> **CONSIDER THIS**
>
> *In an individualistic culture, people usually have many friends but a weak sense of mutual obligation; in collectivistic cultures, people usually have a few close friends with a strong sense of mutual obligation.*

Individualism/Collectivism

The cultural dimensions of individualism and collectivism were previously mentioned in Chapters 2 and 3. Here, the values receive a more comprehensive examination. The subject of countless studies and research projects, individualism versus collectivism (individual orientation vs. group orientation), might well be considered one of the most fundamental concepts used to help understand and explain social life. The two values produce variations in family structures, how classroom activities are conducted, the way organizations manage work groups, and even how people conduct social relations. The individualism/collectivism continuum can be defined with the following: "Collectivistic cultures emphasize community, collaboration, shared interests, harmony, tradition, the public good, and maintaining face. Individualistic cultures emphasize personal rights and responsibilities, privacy, voicing one's own opinion, freedom, innovation, and self-expression."[52] This synopsis should prepare you for a more focused look at the two dimensions.

Individualism.   Having already touched on individualism in the examination of American cultural values, here some of its components are identified. First, the individual is the single most important unit in any social setting. Second, independence rather than interdependence is stressed. Third, individual achievement is rewarded. Lastly, the uniqueness of each individual is of paramount value.[53] A person's rights and privacy prevail over group considerations in an individualistic culture.[54] Individualists are likely to belong to many groups but retain only weak ties, changing membership when desired. Hofstede's findings (see Table 6.4) indicate that Western democracies have a strong tendency toward individualism.

Collective cultures value the group as the important social unit.

Courtesy of Edwin McDaniel

TABLE 6.4	Individualism/Collectivism Values for Fifty Countries and Three Regions				
RANK	**COUNTRY**	**RANK**	**COUNTRY**	**RANK**	**COUNTRY**
1	United States	19	Israel	37	Hong Kong
2	Australia	20	Spain	38	Chile
3	Great Britain	21	India	39–41	Singapore
4/5	Canada	22/23	Japan	39–41	Thailand
4/5	Netherlands	22/23	Argentina	39–41	West Africa
6	New Zealand	24	Iran	42	El Salvador
7	Italy	25	Jamaica	43	South Korea
8	Belgium	26/27	Brazil	44	Taiwan
9	Denmark	26/27	Arab countries	45	Peru
10/11	Sweden	28	Turkey	46	Costa Rica
10/11	France	29	Uruguay	47/48	Pakistan
12	Ireland	30	Greece	47/48	Indonesia
13	Norway	31	Philippines	49	Colombia
14	Switzerland	32	Mexico	50	Venezuela
15	Germany	33–35	Yugoslavia	51	Panama
16	South Africa	33–35	Portugal	52	Ecuador
17	Finland	33–35	East Africa	53	Guatemala
18	Austria	36	Malaysia		

The lower the number, the more the country promotes individualism; a higher number means the country is more collective. *Source:* Adapted from G. Hofstede, *Culture's Consequences: Comparing Values, Behaviors, Institutions and Organizations Across Nations,* 2nd ed. (Thousand Oaks, CA: Sage Publications, 2001).

Individualism in the United States is seen in the expectation that employees will change jobs in order to advance their careers. The individual is first, and the organization and coworkers are secondary considerations. Conversely, in Japan individuals have traditionally expected to retain affiliation with the same company throughout their working careers. To change jobs would be disloyal to the company and the other employees.

CONSIDER THIS

Individualistic cultures are often low power distance. Collectivistic cultures are often high power distance.

Collectivism. The majority of the world's population lives in collectivistic societies where group interests take precedence over those of the individual.[55] In collective cultures, interpersonal relationships form a rigid social framework that distinguishes between in-groups and out-groups. People rely on their in-groups (e.g., family, tribe, clan, organization) for support, and in exchange, they believe they owe loyalty to that group. The following behaviors are often found in collective cultures:

Collectivism means greater emphasis on (a) the views, needs, and goals of the in-group rather than oneself; (b) social norms and duty defined by the in-group rather than behavior to get pleasure; (c) beliefs shared with the in-group rather than beliefs that distinguish the self from the in-group; and (d) great readiness to cooperate with in-group members.[56]

People in collective societies are often born into extended families, clans, or tribes that support and protect them in exchange for their allegiance. As events in Iraq, Afghanistan, and Libya continue to demonstrate, tribalism is an important social factor in many Middle East nations and African societies. "African thought rejects any view of the individual as an autonomous and responsible being."[57] Collective cultures emphasize group membership, and the individual is emotionally, and in some cases, physically dependent on organizations and institutions. Organizations and the groups to which individuals belong also affect private life, and people generally acquiesce to group decisions, even if they are counter to personal desires. The importance of the group in collective societies is reflected in a Chinese proverb: "No matter how stout, one beam cannot support a house." As is the case with all cultural value patterns, collectivism influences how communication is used. For example, "following traditional Korean values, communicating to become part of an in-group and to strengthen intragroup bonds is more important than communicating for information exchange and persuasion."[58]

Collectivism is also contextual. In a learning environment, a collective classroom will stress harmony and cooperation, often through group activities, rather than individual competition. In the healthcare setting, a hospital patient is likely to receive a continual stream of visitors consisting of family members and friends. The sense of collectivism is so strong among the Japanese that following the March 2011 earthquake, tsunami, and nuclear accident disaster, a national consensus of self-restraint quickly developed. The population as a whole voluntarily became more conservative in their consumption and entertainment activities, wishing to evince a sense of selflessness and a feeling of solidarity with the disaster victims. A similar phenomenon occurred in South Korea in the wake of the tragic ferry sinking that claimed the lives of almost 300 individuals, most of them high school students. A sense of "collective grief and guilt" led the South Korean public voluntarily to cancel or significantly reduce most entertainment events and leisure activities.[59]

Uncertainty Avoidance

Although you may try, you can never predict with 100 percent confidence what someone will do or what might happen in the future, and this is the core of uncertainty avoidance—the future is unknown. As used in Hofstede's research, uncertainty avoidance can be defined as "the extent to which the members of a culture feel threatened by ambiguous or unknown situations."[60] As you will learn below, cultures vary in their ability to tolerate ambiguity and unpredictability.

High Uncertainty Avoidance. High uncertainty avoidance cultures attempt to reduce unpredictability and ambiguity through intolerance of deviant ideas and behaviors, emphasizing consensus, resisting change, and adhering to traditional social protocols. Relatively high levels of anxiety and stress often characterize these cultures. People with this orientation believe that life carries the potential for continual hazards, and to avoid or mitigate these dangers, there is a compelling need for laws, written rules, regulations, planning, rituals, ceremonies, and established societal, behavioral, and communication conventions, all of which add structure to life. Social expectations are clearly established and consistent. Nations with a strong uncertainty avoidance tendency are listed in Table 6.5.

TABLE 6.5	Uncertainty Avoidance Values for Fifty Countries and Three Regions				
RANK	**COUNTRY**	**RANK**	**COUNTRY**	**RANK**	**COUNTRY**
1	Greece	19	Israel	37	Australia
2	Portugal	20	Colombia	38	Norway
3	Guatemala	21/22	Venezuela	39/40	South Africa
4	Uruguay	21/22	Brazil	39/40	New Zealand
5/6	Belgium	23	Italy	41/42	Indonesia
5/6	El Salvador	24/25	Pakistan	41/42	Canada
7	Japan	24/25	Austria	43	United States
8	Yugoslavia	26	Taiwan	44	Philippines
9	Peru	27	Arab Countries	45	India
10~15	Spain	28	Ecuador	46	Malaysia
10~15	Argentina	29	Germany	47/48	Great Britain
10~15	Panama	30	Thailand	47/48	Ireland
10~15	France	31/32	Iran	49/50	Hong Kong
10~15	Chile	31/32	Finland	49/50	Sweden
10~15	Costa Rica	33	Switzerland	51	Denmark
16/17	Turkey	34	West Africa	52	Jamaica
16/17	South Korea	35	Netherlands	53	Singapore
18	Mexico	36	East Africa		

The lower the number, the more the country can be classified as one that dislikes uncertainty; a higher number is associated with a country that feels comfortable with uncertainty.
Source: Adapted from G. Hofstede, *Culture's Consequences: Comparing Values, Behaviors, Institutions and Organizations Across Nations*, 2nd ed. (Thousand Oaks, CA: Sage Publications, 2001).

Japan is a high uncertainty culture with many formal social protocols that help to predict how people will behave in almost every social interaction. Japan's high uncertainty avoidance was illustrated in a 2012 report that disclosed that less than 58 percent of surveyed Japanese students were interested in studying abroad, and the principal reason given was difficulty of living in another country.[61] Evidence of Japanese reluctance to deal with the unknown was further demonstrated in a 2014 report that disclosed that only 12 percent of surveyed students fifteen to eighteen years old were interested in working overseas. Moreover, only 2 percent were interested in employment with a foreign affiliated firm.[62] The Japanese preference for avoiding unfamiliar situations is evident from these surveys.

Low Uncertainty Avoidance. At the other end of the continuum are low uncertainty avoidance cultures. They more easily accept the uncertainty inherent in life, tend to be tolerant of the unusual, and are not as threatened by different ideas and people. They prize initiative, dislike the structure associated with hierarchy, are willing to take risks, are flexible, think that there should be as few rules as possible, and depend not so much on experts as on themselves. As a whole, members of low uncertainty avoidance cultures are much less constrained by social protocol.

As with other value dimensions, there are differences in the degree to which uncertainty avoidance influences communication and activities in varied contexts. In a classroom composed of children from a low uncertainty avoidance culture, such as Britain, you would expect to see students feeling comfortable dealing with unstructured learning situations, being rewarded for innovative approaches to problem solving, and learning without strict timetables. A different behavior is the case in high uncertainty avoidance cultures like Germany, where you find that students expect structured learning situations, firm timetables, and well-defined objectives.[63]

Power Distance

Another cultural value dimension revealed by Hofstede's research is power distance, which classifies cultures along a continuum of high and low power distance (some scholars use the terms "large" and "small" power distance). Power distance is concerned with how societies manage "the fact that people are unequal."[64] The concept is defined as "the extent in which the less powerful members of institutions and organizations within a country expect and accept that power is distributed unequally."[65] In this sense, institution refers to family, school, and community, whereas organizations represent places of employment. The premise of the dimension deals with the extent to which a society accepts that power in relationships, institutions, and organizations is distributed equally or unequally. Although all cultures have tendencies toward both high and low power distance relationships, one orientation seems to dominate.

High Power Distance. "Individuals from high power distance cultures accept power as part of society. As such, superiors consider their subordinates to be different from themselves and vice versa."[66] People in high power distance countries (see Table 6.6) believe that power and authority are facts of life. Both consciously and unconsciously, these cultures teach their members that people are not equal in this

TABLE 6.6	Power Distance Values for Fifty Countries and Three Regions				
RANK	COUNTRY	RANK	COUNTRY	RANK	COUNTRY
1	Malaysia	18/19	Turkey	37	Jamaica
2/3	Guatemala	20	Belgium	38	United States
2/3	Panama	21~23	East Africa	39	Canada
4	Philippines	21~23	Peru	40	Netherlands
5/6	Mexico	21~23	Thailand	41	Australia
5/6	Venezuela	24/25	Chile	42~44	Costa Rica
7	Arab countries	24/25	Portugal	42~44	Germany
8/9	Ecuador	26	Uruguay	42~44	Great Britain
8/9	Indonesia	27/28	Greece	45	Switzerland
10/11	India	27/28	South Korea	46	Finland
10/11	West Africa	29/30	Iran	47/48	Norway
12	Yugoslavia	29/30	Taiwan	47/48	Sweden
13	Singapore	31	Spain	49	Ireland
14	Brazil	32	Pakistan	50	New Zealand
15/16	France	33	Japan	51	Denmark
15/16	Hong Kong	34	Italy	52	Israel
17	Colombia	35/36	Argentina	53	Austria
18/19	El Salvador	35/36	South Africa		

The lower the number, the more the country can be classified as a high power distance culture; a higher number is associated with countries that have low power distance culture. Source: Adapted from G. Hofstede, *Culture's Consequences: Comparing Values, Behaviors, Institutions and Organizations Across Nations*, 2nd ed. (Thousand Oaks, CA: Sage Publications, 2001).

world and that everybody has a rightful place, which is clearly marked by countless societal hierarchies, often based on factors such as family name, education, age, profession, or organizational position. Organizations in high power distance cultures commonly have a strong centralization of power, a recognition and use of rank and status, and adherence to established lines of authority.

Low Power Distance. Low power distance countries hold that inequality in society should be minimized. Cultures considered to be low power distance are characterized by numerous laws, regulations, and rules that tend to minimize power differentials between people. Subordinates and superiors consider and treat each other as equals, and the use of titles is deemphasized. People in power, be they supervisors, managers, or government officials, often interact with their constituents and try to look less powerful than they really are. For example, high-level executives may remove their ties and/or suit coats when interacting with subordinates in an effort to signal equality.

We can observe signs of this dimension in nearly every communication setting, such as the educational context. In high power distance societies, education is teacher centered. The teacher initiates all communication, outlines the path of learning students should follow, and is never publicly criticized or contradicted. In high power distance societies, the emphasis is on the personal "wisdom" of the instructor, whereas in low power distance societies, the focus is on discerning the impersonal "truth," which can be obtained by any competent person.[67] Power distance also plays out in corporate decision making. In a low power distance culture, consensus decision making is usually the norm, with managers consulting subordinates and proposals for new initiatives being thoroughly discussed and debated by everyone concerned, regardless of position. In contrast, decision making in a high power distance organization is usually much more authoritarian, the preserve of only a few top-level individuals.

Cultural values can exert a particularly strong hold on peoples' behaviors, sometimes with tragic consequences. The death of so many high school students in the April 2014 sinking of the South Korean ferry may be partially attributed to the influence of high power distance. Instructed by the crew to remain inside the ship, "many of the children did not leave their cabins, not questioning their elders, as is customary in hierarchical Korean society. They paid for their obedience with their lives."[68]

Masculinity/Femininity

Hofstede uses the words "masculinity" and "femininity" to refer to the degree to which masculine or feminine traits are valued and revealed. His rationale, one that is supported across several academic disciplines, is that many masculine and feminine behaviors are learned and mediated by cultural norms and traditions. Adler and Gunderson feel that the terms "masculinity" and "femininity" do not adequately convey the full meaning behind this dimension and choose to use the terms "career success" and "quality of life."[69] For our discussion here, and throughout the book, we will adhere to Hofstede's terminology.

Masculinity. Masculinity is the extent to which the dominant values in a society are male oriented. In a masculine-oriented culture, "emotional gender roles are clearly distinct: men are supposed to be assertive, tough, and focused on material success, whereas women are supposed to be more modest, tender, and concerned with the quality of life."[70] Gender roles are highly defined and promote achievement in the workplace. "Assertiveness and the acquisition of money and things (materialism)"[71] are emphasized and often take precedence over interpersonal relationships.

The United States offers an example of the influence of strong gender roles in a masculine-based culture (see Table 6.7 for rankings). Despite the high level of economic development and stress on gender equality, in the United States, women continue to occupy a disproportionately low level of political empowerment. This is reflected in the number of women holding public office in 2014. Women were elected to only ninety-nine (18.5 percent) of the 535 combined seats available in the United States Senate and the House of Representatives. Of the 7,383 total number of United States state legislative positions, women held 1,787 (24.5 percent) in 2014.[72]

Femininity.   Cultures that value femininity as a trait stress nurturing behaviors. "A society is called feminine when emotional gender roles overlap: Both men and women are supposed to be modest, tender, and concerned with the quality of life."[73] A feminine worldview maintains that men need not be assertive and that they can assume nurturing roles. It also promotes sexual equality and holds that people and the environment are important. Interdependence and androgynous behavior are the ideals, and people sympathize with the less fortunate. In contrast to the masculine culture reflected by the number of women in the U.S. Congress, Norway and Sweden, the two nations at the top of Hofstede's femininity ratings, have significantly greater representation by women in public office. After Sweden's general election in 2010, women occupied

TABLE 6.7	Masculinity Values for Fifty Countries and Three Regions				
RANK	COUNTRY	RANK	COUNTRY	RANK	COUNTRY
1	Japan	18/19	Hong Kong	37/38	Spain
2/3	Austria	20/21	Argentina	37/38	Peru
2/3	Venezuela	20/21	India	39	East Africa
4/5	Italy	22	Belgium	40	El Salvador
4/5	Switzerland	23	Arab countries	41	South Korea
6	Mexico	24	Canada	42	Uruguay
7/8	Ireland	25/26	Malaysia	43	Guatemala
7/8	Jamaica	25/26	Pakistan	44	Thailand
9/10	Great Britain	27	Brazil	45	Portugal
9/10	Germany	28	Singapore	46	Chile
11/12	Philippines	29	Israel	47	Finland
11/12	Colombia	30/31	Indonesia	48/49	Yugoslavia
13/14	South Africa	30/31	West Africa	48/49	Costa Rica
13/14	Ecuador	32/33	Turkey	50	Denmark
15	United States	32/33	Taiwan	51	Netherlands
16	Australia	34	Panama	52	Norway
17	New Zealand	35/36	Iran	53	Sweden
18/19	Greece	35/36	France		

The lower the number, the more the country can be classified as one that favors masculine traits; a higher score denotes a country that prefers feminine traits. Source: Adapted from G. Hofstede, *Culture's Consequences: Comparing Values, Behaviors, Institutions and Organizations Across Nations*, 2nd ed. (Thousand Oaks, CA: Sage Publications, 2001).

45 percent of the seats in Parliament, and in its 2013 election, Norway saw 40 percent of parliamentary seats won by women.[74]

The impact of masculinity/femininity on a culture can also be observed in the "gender gap" survey. To determine the gender gap in countries, the World Economic Forum conducts a yearly survey to measure these four categories: (1) economic participation and opportunity, (2) educational attainment, (3) health and survival, and (4) political empowerment. In the political empowerment category of the 2013 report (which assessed 136 nations), Iceland, Norway, Finland, and Sweden were ranked as the top four; the United States was twenty-three, Mexico sixty-eight, Italy seventy-one, and Japan 105.[75] These rankings generally parallel Hofstede's findings.

Long- and Short-Term Orientation

Over the years, Hofstede's study has been widely critiqued, and one major complaint concerns the Western bias that influenced data collection. To resolve the problem, Hofstede offered a new dimension called long- versus short-term orientation, also referred to as "Confucian work dynamism."[76] Identification of this dimension came from a study of twenty-three countries using an assessment called the Chinese Value Survey (CVS), developed from values suggested by Chinese scholars.[77] While admitting that westerners might find this fifth orientation perplexing, Hofstede originally linked the dimension to Confucianism, because it appeared "to be based on items reminiscent of the teachings of Confucius, on both poles."[78]

Recognizing the inherent weakness of basing the dimension on data from only twenty-three nations, Minkov and Hofstede drew on World Values Survey (WVS) data to replicate and extend the study to thirty-eight nations.[79] Reporting the results of their analysis in late 2010, the two researchers disclosed, "China and other East Asian countries tended to score high on the dimension, suggesting a long-term orientation. Continental European countries had average scores, whereas Anglo, African, and South Asian countries had low scores, suggestive of a short-term orientation."[80] The research was subsequently extended to encompass ninety-three countries, and the dimension was most recently defined as follows: "Long-term orientation stands for the fostering of virtues oriented toward future rewards—in particular, perseverance and thrift. Its opposite pole, short-term orientation, stands for the fostering of virtues related to the past and present—in particular, respect for tradition, preservation of 'face,' and fulfilling social obligations."[81] After identifying high scores among some East European nations, Hofstede and his colleagues no longer consider the dimension's association with Confucianism to be appropriate. Rather, they now see the long-term/short-term orientation to be "a universal dimension of national culture, underpinned by concepts that are meaningful across the whole world."[82]

For a practical application of the values, you might easily envision how the patterns could influence communication in a business context. Corporate organizations in cultures that rank high on the long-term orientation scale, such as in China and South Korea, would be characterized by a focus on obtaining market share, rewarding employees based on organizational loyalty, strong interpersonal connections, situational ethics, adaptability, and self-discipline. Leisure time would not be a central concern. In contrast, organizations possessing a short-term orientation, like those in Mexico, the United States, and Egypt, would emphasize short-term profits, use merit to reward employees, experience transient organizational loyalty, and consider ethics to be based on a set of universal principles. Personal freedom and leisure time would be significant values.[83]

MINKOV'S CULTURAL DIMENSIONS[84]

Over the past decade, Bulgarian scholar Michael Minkov employed statistical analysis of data taken from large public databases to identify four new bipolar national cultural dimensions. The first two dimensions, industry versus indulgence and monumentalism versus flexumility, are drawn from WVS data. Hypometropia versus prudence and exclusionism versus universalism, the second two dimensions, are produced by data taken from public databases maintained by the United Nations, the World Health Organization (WHO), Transparency International, and WVS. We have elected to omit a discussion of the hypometropia versus prudence dimension, because it focuses on people's physical behavior and conduct and relates very little to communication.

Industry Versus Indulgence

Simply stated, this dimension considers how work and leisure are prioritized differently in national cultures. Not surprisingly, as shown in Table 6.8, most underdeveloped nations place a high priority on industriousness, or hard work, while those countries with a developed economy tilt more toward leisure. This indicates that as a nation's economy improves and people gain more wealth and social security, they begin to value enjoyment of life over work.

Table 6.9 provides a comparison of how some of the values vary across industrious and indulgent cultures. Members of an industrious culture would feel they had less opportunity to enjoy themselves, would consider thrift to be important, and would feel that social order and discipline were more important than individual freedoms.

TABLE 6.8	Industry Versus Indulgence Order Ranking Scores for Forty-Three Countries				
SCORE	COUNTRY	SCORE	COUNTRY	SCORE	COUNTRY
1,000	China	625	Poland	321	Slovenia
968	Vietnam	625	South Africa	316	Argentina
900	South Korea	609	Georgia	251	Colombia
883	India	600	Iran	250	Switzerland
869	Indonesia	563	Jordan	228	Mexico
864	Moldova	548	Turkey	213	Chile
827	Romania	527	Serbia	213	United Kingdom
826	Russia	489	Brazil	196	Australia
744	Bulgaria	463	Italy	167	New Zealand
739	Ukraine	455	France	124	Uruguay
705	Morocco	402	Nigeria	84	Finland
700	Egypt	399	United States	71	Netherlands
653	Iraq	395	Germany	0	Sweden
636	Zimbabwe	372	Spain		
627	Taiwan	343	Japan		

Higher-numbered scores are seen as favoring industry traits; a lower score denotes a preference for indulgent traits. *Source:* Adapted from M. Minkov, *Cultural Differences in a Globalized World* (United Kingdom: Emerald, 2011).

TABLE 6.9	Selected Characteristics of Industrious and Indulgent Cultures
INDUSTRIOUS CULTURE	**INDULGENT CULTURE**
Hard work over leisure	Leisure over hard work
Thrift important	Thrift less important
Economic development most important	Economic development less important
Not fully in control of life	Mostly in control of life
Unhappiness and dissatisfaction with life	Happiness and satisfaction with life
Political liberties less important	Political liberties highly important
Strong governmental control	Loose governmental control
Strong penalties for nonconformity to societal norms	Weak penalties for nonconformity to societal norms

Source: Adapted from M. Minkov, *Cultural Differences in a Globalized World* (United Kingdom: Emerald, 2011).

In contrast, in an indulgent society, people would place a priority on their sense of freedom and personal enjoyment through leisure time and interaction with friends. Consumption and spending would take precedence over fiscal restraint. These differences help explain why the Chinese are more tolerant of strict government control than are people in the United States. Among the Chinese, increased economic growth is currently a greater consideration than individual freedoms, which can come after gaining financial security.

Monumentalism Versus Flexumility

Minkov's analysis of WVS data identified another cultural dimension that he labeled "monumentalism versus flexumility." He likened "monumentalism" to monuments or statues, which are created to reflect pride in a person, event, or thing, and once erected, are relatively unchangeable. Thus, monumentalism describes cultures that exhibit individuals with a high level of self-pride along with "unchangeable identities, strong values, unshakable beliefs, and avoidance of personal duality and inconsistency."[85] "Flexumility," a combination of the words "self-flexibility" and "humility," is the polar opposite of monumentalism and characterizes those cultures that typically exercise humility and situational flexibility, and that easily adapt to changing conditions. Table 6.10 lists selected traits for this dimension.

In the ranking of forty-three nations (Table 6.11), Middle East countries, where religion is a central component of life, scored highest on the monumentalism scale, followed by Latin American nations. At the scale's lower end, indicating a flexumility culture, were Northeast Asian and European countries. The United States ranked in the upper middle of the scale, which reflects how Americans balance self-promotion and humility. In the United States, individuals are often told, "You have to toot your own horn," meaning that some degree of self-promotion is required and expected. The success of Facebook in the United States can be interpreted as an example of the general acceptance of self-promotion. However, if the horn is tooted too loudly or too often, a person risks being labeled a braggart or an egotist. Consider the potential for success or failure when a monumentalism interviewer asks a flexumility interviewee to talk about personal achievements.

TABLE 6.10	Selected Characteristics of Monumentalism and Flexumility Cultures

MONUMENTALISM	FLEXUMILITY
• Self-pride/self-promotion	• Humility
• Self-concept is consistent/fixed	• Self-concept is flexible/fluid
• Truth is absolute	• Truth is relative
• Feelings and expressions equivalent	• Feelings and expressions may differ
• Religion is important; can be dogmatic	• Religion less important
• Interpersonal competition valued	• Interpersonal competition problematic
• Lower educational achievement	• Higher educational achievement
• Strong defense of one's opinions	• Compromise is best
• Difficulty in adapting to another culture	• Easily adapts to another culture
• Direct, forthright negotiating style	• Indirect, conflict avoiding negotiation style
• Suicide unacceptable	• Suicide acceptable
• Low number of women in workforce	• High number of women in workforce

Source: Adapted from M. Minkov, *Cultural Differences in a Globalized World* (United Kingdom: Emerald, 2011), and M. Minkov, "Monumentalism versus Flexumility," SIETAR Europa Congress (2007), http://www.sietareuropa.org/congress2007/files/congress2007_paper_Michael_Minkov .doc.

TABLE 6.11	Monumentalism and Flexumility Scores for Forty-Three Countries				
SCORE	COUNTRY	SCORE	COUNTRY	SCORE	COUNTRY
1,000	Egypt	571	Argentina	276	Moldova
997	Iraq	564	Chile	265	Bulgaria
955	Jordan	527	India	242	Switzerland
908	Nigeria	521	Romania	191	Russia
890	Morocco	505	Poland	184	Sweden
811	Zimbabwe	492	Uruguay	175	Ukraine
747	Iran	436	Australia	165	France
736	South Africa	427	Spain	119	Netherlands
668	Turkey	423	Vietnam	99	Germany
667	Colombia	388	New Zealand	43	South Korea
662	Georgia	359	Serbia	40	Japan
659	Mexico	354	United Kingdom	16	Taiwan
623	Indonesia	352	Italy	0	China
614	Brazil	340	Slovenia		
572	United States	312	Finland		

Higher-numbered scores are seen as favoring monumentalism traits; a lower score denotes a preference for flexumility traits. *Source:* Adapted from M. Minkov, *Cultural Differences in a Globalized World* (United Kingdom: Emerald, 2011).

Exclusionism Versus Universalism

This national cultural dimension bears a strong resemblance to Hofstede's individualism and collectivism. However, Hofstede's dimension was based on work-related values, and, in the case of exclusionism versus universalism, Minkov is concentrating

TABLE 6.12	Selected Characteristics of Exclusionist and Universalist Cultures
EXCLUSIONIST	**UNIVERSALIST**
• Relationships based on group membership	• Individuality
• Close-knit extended family	• Nuclear family common
• In-group members favored over out-group members	• Everyone should be treated equally
• Frequent group discrimination	• Group discrimination minimized
• Agreements are flexible	• Agreements normally adhered to
• Weak safety procedures	• Strict safety procedures
• Low environmental concern	• High environmental concern
• In-group communication clear; out-group communication can be ambiguous	• Clear communication with everyone; ambiguity avoided

Source: Adapted from M. Minkov, *Cultural Differences in a Globalized World* (United Kingdom: Emerald, 2011).

on the role that national wealth, or level of economic development, plays in determining cultural differences in how people treat each other.[86] Exclusionism refers to those national cultures where the type of interaction between people is strongly influenced by group membership, and in universalistic national cultures, as the term implies, relationships are individualistically based. In exclusionist cultures, people develop strong in-group ties and rely on those ties to both receive and grant favors, preferential treatment, and assistance when needed. Conversely, members of universalistic cultures tend to treat everyone the same regardless of group affiliation. Table 6.12 contains a comparison of traits characterizing exclusionist and universalist cultures.

Minkov rank ordered eighty-six national cultures based on their inclination toward exclusionism or universalism, and forty-three of those cultures are presented in Table 6.13. As is evident from the table, economically underdeveloped nations have a strong preference for exclusionism, whereas developed nations scale toward the universalism pole. This separation can be explained by the lack of personal wealth and limited availability of social support systems in developing economies, which results in people having to rely on relations with other people for assistance. Generosity toward strangers, or out-group members, is a seldom-affordable luxury. However, in wealthy nations people generally have greater personal income, and social support programs are more prevalent, which facilitates self-reliance and reduces the need for help from others.

TIGHT AND LOOSE CULTURES

The idea of classifying cultures as *tight* and *loose* arose out of work begun by anthropologists as early as 1950. However, only recently has quantitative evidence been used to substantiate the classifications. This was achieved by Gelfand and associates who analyzed data from thirty-three nations (Table 6.14).[87]

Loose cultures are characterized by relatively weak societal norms and considerable tolerance for deviance from those expectations. Cultures classified as *tight* will exhibit strong established societal norms and a low level of tolerance for deviations from

TABLE 6.13	Exclusionist and Universalist Scores for Forty-Three Selected Countries				
SCORE	COUNTRY	SCORE	COUNTRY	SCORE	COUNTRY
1,000	Ethiopia	681	Mexico	395	Hungary
949	Iraq	664	Philippines	382	Chile
872	Morocco	640	Vietnam	333	Japan
858	Egypt	631	Russia	311	Spain
849	Saudi Arabia	615	Brazil, China	274	Portugal
815	Kyrgyzstan	585	Turkey	262	Ireland
803	India	579	Colombia	237	United
791	Zambia	557	Bosnia	170	France
773	Venezuela	554	Croatia	120	Germany
756	South Africa	542	El Salvador	119	Australia
733	Uganda	529	Poland	107	Canada
727	Jordan	507	Bulgaria	57	United Kingdom
724	Bangladesh	476	South Korea	34	Norway
718	Azerbaijan	425	Italy		
710	Guatemala	397	Singapore		

Higher numbered scores are seen as favoring exclusionism traits; a lower score denotes a preference for universalism traits. *Source*: Adapted from M. Minkov, *Cultural Differences in a Globalized World* (United Kingdom: Emerald, 2011).

TABLE 6.14	Tightness Scores for Thirty-Two Countries				
SCORE	COUNTRY	SCORE	COUNTRY	SCORE	COUNTRY
1.6	Ukraine	5.4	Spain	7.5	Germany (East)
2.6	Estonia	5.6	Belgium	7.8	Portugal
2.9	Hungary	6.0	Poland	7.9	China
3.1	Israel	6.3	France	8.6	Japan
3.3	Netherlands	6.3	Hong Kong	9.2	Turkey
3.4	Brazil	6.4	Iceland	9.5	Norway
3.7	Venezuela	6.5	Germany (West)	10.0	South Korea
3.9	Greece	6.8	Austria	10.4	Singapore
3.9	New Zealand	6.8	Italy	11.0	India
4.4	Australia	6.9	United Kingdom	11.8	Malaysia
5.1	United States	7.2	Mexico	12.3	Pakistan

Lower-numbered scores are seen favoring looseness; a higher score denotes a preference for tightness. *Source*: Adapted from M. J. Gelfand et al., "Differences Between Tight and Loose Cultures: A 33-Nation Study," *Science*, (May 27, 2011), 332, 1100–4.

accepted behaviors. Tight cultures, such as Japan, have a well-defined set of societal protocols that govern social interaction between individuals. For example, greetings during formal first meetings are governed by a rigid set of procedures determining who bows first, how low, and for how long, depending on the interactants' status levels. Contrast this with the United States, a loose culture, where a handshake is the norm and difference in status has little bearing on who initiates it or how long

Individualist cultures, because they are concerned primarily with self-face, tend to favor confrontational approaches to resolve problems and misunderstandings.

© Richard Hutchings/PhotoEdit

it lasts. The use of titles can also be a reflection of a culture's *tightness* and *looseness*. In the United States, as we have repeatedly pointed out, titles enjoy limited use, often depending on the social context. However, in Germany, a tight culture, titles play an extremely important role in social interaction.

FACE AND FACEWORK

Our final cultural value concerns the concept of face, which, according to Hu, was identified and categorized in China as early as the fourth century BCE.[88] The term "face" is commonly used as a metaphor to designate the self-image a person projects to other people. In other words, your "face" is your public identity, how you are perceived by others. And because face is how others see you, it is acquired, maintained, and lost through social interactions, primarily communication. This process is referred to as facework, which Domenici and Littlejohn define as "a set of coordinated practices in which communicators build, maintain, protect, or threaten personal dignity, honor, and respect."[89] Facework consists of those actions you engage in to acquire or maintain face for yourself or give face to someone else.

In an effort to make a favorable impression on your prospective employer during a job interview, you will try to "put on your best face." You will probably wear your best suit and arrive a few minutes before the scheduled time. During the interview you will remember to sit erect, maintain eye contact, respond to questions with thoughtful answers, use formal terms of address, and avoid slang. These efforts amount to self-directed facework because you want to make a positive impression. Complimenting a friend on new clothes, on landing a new position, or when accepted to graduate school are examples of other-directed facework.

Research conducted by Ting-Toomey highlights the role of face and facework in intercultural communication, especially in conflict situations. Her work assumes that people from all cultures strive to "maintain and negotiate face in all communication situations."[90] Face and facework, however, are influenced by cultural

> **REMEMBER THIS**
>
> *Asian cultures commonly place greater emphasis on "face" than do Western cultures.*

values and vary across cultures. In individualistic cultures, for example, a person's face is usually derived from his or her own self-effort and is normally independent of others. Accordingly, people from individualistic societies are usually more concerned with maintaining their own face. Because U.S. Americans do not normally rely on group affiliation for their identity or social support, they have less concern with how they influence someone else's face. This results in a direct, forthright communication style. Common expressions in the United States, such as "tell me what you really think" and "don't hold anything back," demonstrate the value placed on open, candid communication. In some contexts, harmonious interpersonal relations become secondary to frankness.

In collectivistic cultures, however, there is much greater concern for others' face. This is because group membership is normally the primary source of identity and status. Considerable value is placed on establishing and sustaining stable, harmonious relationships with in-group members. This is evident in what constitutes face in collectivistic societies. Among the Japanese, face involves "honor, appearance of propriety, presence, and the impact on others."[91] For the Chinese, according to Gao and Ting-Toomey, "gaining and losing face is connected closely with issues of social pride, honor, dignity, insult, shame, disgrace, humility, trust, mistrust, respect, and prestige."[92] As you might expect, extreme politeness and positive interpersonal relations are important means of face-saving in collective social groups. "The preference for harmony in collectivistic groups is focused around anticipating and forestalling any loss of face within one's dyad or group. The focus upon context and upon indirect styles of communication can therefore be seen as forms of preventive facework."[93]

Varying attitudes as to what represents face, how facework is conducted, and the objective of facework have a very noticeable impact on how cultures view and approach conflict. According to Ting-Toomey's Face Negotiation theory, during a conflict situation, three different face concerns can come into play. These are (1) "self-face," where the individual is concerned about his/her own face; (2) "other-face," which focuses on the other person's face; and (3) "mutual-face," which encompasses both parties in the conflict.[94] These three face concerns vary in importance depending on one's cultural orientation. For example, Kim tells us that in collective cultures, in-group conflict "is viewed as damaging to social face and relational harmony, so it should be avoided as much as possible."[95] As a result, in collectivistic cultures maintenance of mutual and other-face receives greater emphasis than self-face.

The different values placed on face, what constitutes face, and how it is managed have a very noticeable influence on facework. Drawing on the individualism/collectivism cultural dimension, Ting-Toomey posits that when confronted with the potential for conflict, collectivists will be more inclined toward avoidance and obligating measures. This is a result of concern for both mutual face and others' face and how one's actions may affect others. Individualists, however, are concerned primarily with self-face and tend to favor confrontational and solution-oriented approaches to resolve conflicts.[96] This attitude toward problem solving by individualistic cultures is evident in the number of U.S. lawyers, the frequency of lawsuits, and the requirement to sign a lengthy contract for such basic services as a mobile phone or a cable service account. Collectivistic nations, such as Japan and China, have far fewer lawyers and prefer to resolve disputes through intermediaries.

These contrasting attitudes toward conflict give rise to quite different culturally based communication styles. During intercultural communication events, the divergent styles can result in confusion, misinterpretation, or even animosity between the participants. Adherence to an indirect communication style to sustain amicable relations, as used in high-context cultures, can actually produce the opposite effect among individualistic participants, who may well view the indirectness as duplicity. Conversely, the use of open, direct, forthright communication, common in low-context cultures, can be perceived as rude and inconsiderate by collectivistic participants, who will likely consider the interaction as face threatening.

The differences between face and facework across cultures are a function of dissimilar cultural values. Just as we have discussed throughout this chapter, the differences in cultural values have a direct and continuing influence on how you perceive the world, behave, and communicate. The hope is that you will be motivated to learn more about variations in cultural patterns so that you will be able to understand, predict, and even adapt to the behavior of people of different cultures.

> ## CONSIDER THIS
>
> *Gaining an awareness of cultural values is essential to understanding another culture.*

CULTURAL PATTERNS AND COMMUNICATION

By now, you have probably realized that cultural patterns occupy a very prominent position in the study of intercultural communication. This chapter has provided only a preliminary overview of how cultural patterns can help you understand and anticipate varied communicative behaviors that may arise during an intercultural exchange. A succinct overview of the most common patterns and their influence on behavior and communication is provided in Table 6.15.

DEVELOPING CULTURAL VALUE AWARENESS

When someone wants to learn about another culture, it is easy to go to a website or pick up a book that offers a general background on a country and commonly either lists or provides concise paragraphs on how that culture differs from others. Usually, these "differences" focus on such basics as greetings, introductions, business protocols, dress, food, punctuality, gender issues, important holidays, and similar topical subjects. This information is essential to gaining an appreciation of how a culture can differ from your own but offers little or no actual understanding of the causes that underlie those differences. In other words, they seldom provide insight into what we consider to be a fundamental part of learning about other cultures—understanding *why* cultural differences exist. Without an appreciation of why members of another culture have beliefs and behaviors that differ from your culture's, you can inadvertently fall into the trap of simplistically viewing those differences as exotic, strange, oppressive, or even misguided.

TABLE 6.15	The Influence of Cultural Patterns

CULTURAL PATTERNS

Individualism Versus Collectivism

Individualism (e.g., U.S., Australia, Canada)	*Collectivism* (e.g., ROK, China, Mexico)
• Focuses on the individual and self-promotion	• Focuses on the group/affiliations and self-criticism
• Independency	• Interdependency
• Task dominates relationship	• Relationship dominates task
• Social obedience through sense of guilt	• Social obedience through sense of shame

Egalitarian Versus Hierarchal (Power Distance)

Egalitarian (e.g., Australia, Canada, U.S.)	*Hierarchal* (e.g., Mexico, India, ROK)
• Horizontal relationships	• Vertical relationships
• Equality expected	• Inequality accepted

Low Versus High Uncertainty Avoidance

Low Uncertainty Avoidance (e.g., Ireland, U.S.)	*High Uncertainty Avoidance* (e.g., Japan, Spain)
• Change is normal and good	• Change is disruptive and disliked
• Few behavioral protocols	• Many behavioral protocols
• Greater cultural diversity	• Less cultural diversity

Monochronic Versus Polychronic (Use of Time)

Monochronic (e.g., Germany, U.S.)	*Polychronic* (e.g., Arabs, Africans, France)
• Time is linear and segmented	• Time is flexible
• Focus on a single task	• Focus on multiple tasks
• Adherence to schedules	• Weak ties to schedules

Low Versus High Context Communication

Low Context (Direct) (e.g., Germany, U.S.)	*High Context (Indirect)* (e.g., ROK, Japan)
• Meaning inherent in verbal message	• Meaning dependent on context
• Nonverbal communication low importance	• Nonverbal communication high importance
• Silence is avoided	• Silence is normal

Low Versus High Face Concerns

Low Face Concerns (e.g., Canada, U.S.)	*High Face Concerns* (e.g., China, Korea, Taiwan)
• Conflict/disagreement is constructive	• Conflict/disagreement is threatening
• Concern for self-face	• Concern for mutual and other-face

Universalism Versus Particularism

Universalism (e.g., U.S., UK, Australia)	*Particularism* (e.g., China, Russia, Japan)
• Rules and regulations apply equally to all in every situation	• Adherence to rules and regulations is situational
• Relationship is subordinate to principle	• Relationship obligations may take precedence over principle
• There is only one truth; reality is objective	• Truth is perception based; reality is subjective

Source: Adapted from Edwin R. McDaniel, "Bridging Cultural Differences in International Trade in Services: Communication in the Globalized Market," *Taiwanese Journal of WTO Studies* XXXIV (2013): 1–39.

To explain this more fully, let us examine a very basic difference in beliefs and values between China and the United States concerning the role of interpersonal relations. In China, the practice of *guanxi* (reliance on interpersonal relations) plays a central role in business and private interactions. It is not uncommon for a Chinese company to hire employees from a small circle of family members or well-known, longtime acquaintances, with personal qualifications playing a secondary role. Without the requisite cultural understanding, someone from the United States might quickly consider the practice of *guanxi* as nepotism or corruption. This view would arise from the U.S. value of equality, individuality, and being judged on merit, all of which are supported by clearly defined rules and laws and a well-established system of social services. To gain a more balanced perspective of the differences, you would need to know that China is a collectivistic-oriented culture, with a developing economy, and only a nascent social services system. Succinctly, in China, personal contacts are considerably more important than in the United States because the Chinese have historically had to rely on each other rather than depending on an existing societal infrastructure.

Once you gain an awareness of *why* there is such a contrast between the value placed on interpersonal relations in China and the United States, it becomes easier to understand the other person's motivation. You may not agree with that person's values, but knowing why they think or act a certain way can reduce or even eliminate potential intercultural communication discord. Therefore, when confronted with confounding cultural differences, we urge you to examine the cause behind those differences, the motivating cultural value, rather than simply assuming it is a wrong way of thinking or acting.

SUMMARY

- Perception may be defined as the process whereby people convert external events and experiences into meaningful internal understanding.

- Perception is the primary mechanism by which you develop your worldview.

- Perception is selective, learned, culturally determined, consistent, and often inaccurate.

- Values are enduring attitudes about the preference for one belief over another. Behaviors are the observable demonstration of internally held beliefs and values.

- Cultural pattern taxonomies are used to illustrate the dominant beliefs and values of a culture.

- When applying cultural patterns, you should keep in mind that we are more than our culture; cultural patterns are integrated, dynamic, and can be contradictory.

- According to Kohls, the dominant American cultural patterns include personal control over the environment, change, time and its control, equality, individualism/privacy, self-help, competition, future orientation, action/work orientation, informality, directness/openness/honesty, practicality/efficiency, and materialism/acquisitiveness.

- The Kluckhohn and Strodtbeck value orientation taxonomy includes (1) human nature, (2) the perception of nature, (3) time, (4) activity, and (5) relationships.

- In Hall's context orientation, high-context and low-context describe the degree to which individuals rely on internalized information.

- A prominent taxonomy of diverse culture patterns that explains both perceptual and communication differences is Hofstede's Values Dimension, which includes (1) individualism/collectivism, (2) uncertainty avoidance, (3) power distance, (4) masculinity/ femininity, and (5) long-term/short-term orientation.

- Work by Minkov has recently revealed the value dimensions of industry/indulgence, monumentalism/flexumility, and exclusionism/universalism.

- Gelfand and her colleagues have used empirical data to demonstrate the classifications of tight and loose cultures.

- For Ting-Toomey, face and facework take different forms and are valued differently across cultures.

- Face is a function of group affiliation in collectivistic cultures and is self-derived in individualistic cultures.

- In conflict situations, collectivistic cultures focus on other-face and mutual face, while individualistic cultures focus on self-face.

ACTIVITIES

1. Working with others, list the American cultural values mentioned in this chapter. Try to think of other values that are not included in the text. Then find examples from American advertising campaigns that illustrate those values. For instance, the advertising slogan "Just do it," from an athletic shoe manufacturer, has endured for twenty-five years because it reflects the American values of perseverance and accomplishment.

2. Working with others and using Hofstede's value dimensions, prepare a list of behaviors found in American culture that reflect individualism, uncertainty avoidance, and masculinity.

3. Working with others, make a list of typical American behaviors that relate to evil, good and evil, and good. How widespread are these behaviors within the culture?

4. Reflect on your behavior and determine how well you fit into the various degrees of time orientation.

5. Compile a list of cultural characteristics that you think characterize the United States as a tight or loose culture. A video on tight and loose cultures is available by searching the Internet for "Michele Gelfand discusses what makes cultures restrictive versus permissive."

6. Think about a recent conflict situation in which you participated (e.g., an argument with your significant other, your parents, or a stranger). What communication strategies did you use to give, maintain, or take face?

CONCEPTS AND QUESTIONS

1. How does a study of cultural values help you understand other cultures?

2. What differences in behavior might be exhibited by people of cultures that have different activity orientations?

3. Examine the concept of high- and low-context cultures. What problems can you anticipate when you are communicating with someone who holds a different context orientation?

4. How can cultural differences in perception affect the intercultural communication process?

5. The United States ranked in the upper third as a monumentalism culture. What cultural traits from Khols' American values list do you think contribute to this ranking?

6. What cultural values help explain why face is more important in Asian societies than in the United States?

CHAPTER 7

Culture and Identity: Situating the Individual

Who you are is determined by your past; who you will become is a product of your future.

ANONYMOUS

We define our identity always in dialogue with, sometimes in struggle against, the things our significant others want to see in us. Even after we outgrow some of these others—our parents, for instance—and they disappear from our lives, the conversation with them continues within us as long as we live.

CHARLES TAYLOR

I move back and forth between the racial divides.

BARACK OBAMA

*I*dentity is a term frequently used in media reports, popular culture discussions, academic studies, and numerous other contexts, but all too often it is inadequately defined or explained. Even here, you are probably wondering why identity has its own chapter in an intercultural communication textbook. A very good question, and by the end of this chapter you should have an answer as well as greater insight as to what identity is and an appreciation for the complexity of the concept.

Identity is a multifaceted, dynamic, abstract concept that plays an integral role in daily communicative interactions and particularly in intercultural communication. The accelerated mixing of cultures arising from globalization has added to the complexity of identity through increased immigration, cross-cultural marriage, international adoption, and an overall broadening of opportunities for people of different cultures to meet and interact across a variety of professional and social settings.

Because identity is so pervasive in social interactions and can be such a critical factor in intercultural communication, it is necessary to have a thorough understanding of what it entails. To help you attain that understanding, we begin by providing a theoretical definition of identity. This is followed by a discussion of how identity influences social roles and guides social behaviors. We then examine a few of your many social identities and the different ways they are acquired and developed. A discussion of the different ways that you establish and enact your various identities and the role they play in communication is then provided. Next, the growing phenomenon of binational and multiethnic identities emerging from the globalized social order is examined. Finally, the chapter concludes with a brief discussion on ways of developing competency when dealing with people possessing dissimilar identities in intercultural communication interactions.

IDENTITY: DEFINING THE CONCEPT

As we have just indicated, identity is an abstract, complex, dynamic, and socially constructed concept. As a result, identity is not easily defined, and scholars have provided a rich variety of descriptions. For instance, Tracy finds identity to be both inclusive and contradictory: "Identities, then, are best thought of as stable features of persons that exist prior to any particular situation *and* as dynamic and situated accomplishments, enacted through talk, changing from one occasion to the next. Similarly, identities are social categories *and* are personal and unique."[1] Ting-Toomey echoes this inclusive nature when she considers identity to be the "reflective self-conception or self-image that we derive from our family, gender, cultural, ethnic and individual socialization processes. Identity basically refers to the reflective views of ourselves and other perceptions of our self-images."[2]

> **CONSIDER THIS**
>
> Who am I? Who and what help to define me? Pause for a moment and reflect on those two questions. Write down a few of your thoughts. The answers you produce will provide insights into some of your many identities and the sources of those identities.

These two definitions treat identity in a broad sense, but some communication scholars address "cultural identity" more specifically. For instance, Fong contends, "culture and cultural identity in the study of intercultural relations have become umbrella terms that subsume racial and ethnic identity."[3] Fong goes on to define cultural identity as "the identification of communications of a shared system of symbolic verbal and nonverbal behavior that are meaningful to group members who have a sense of belonging and who share traditions, heritage, language, and similar norms of appropriate behavior. Cultural identity is a social construction."[4]

Cultural identity for Ting-Toomey and Chung is "the emotional significance that we attach to our sense of belonging or affiliation with the larger culture."[5] Klyukanov sees cultural identity as "membership in a group in which all people share the same symbolic meanings."[6] Dervin defines cultural identity as "what we construct whenever we are in contact with other human beings—regardless of the fact that they are from the same 'environment' or not."[7] This series of definitions is not an attempt to confuse you. Instead, we are trying to demonstrate that due to its complexity and abstractness, it is difficult to construct a single, concise definition of identity that will be agreed on by everyone across the various academic disciplines. Some of the definitions use "identity," while others rely on "cultural identity." However, as we will illustrate throughout this chapter, we believe that culture plays a role in each of your many identities, no matter how they are acquired.

Regardless of the definition or term used, it is important to recognize that identities are dynamic and multiple. Throughout life you are continually acquiring new

People have a number of different identities as they move through life.

© Taylor Ingalls

identities and discarding old ones. To illustrate these two points—dynamic and multiple identities—reflect on how you identified yourself in grade school, in high school, and after entering college. As you grew older, you gained new identities and left behind some old ones. For instance, after graduation from high school, you set aside many of the identities you had and on entering the university, acquired new ones. However, you also retained some of your previous identities, such as the regional identity of your hometown and state. Perhaps you gave up your identity as a member of a high school sports team or being in the band. In college you may have taken the identity of a sorority or fraternity member, and in that case you also assumed the identity of the specific organization.

It should be clear that identity is not a single entity but a composite of multiple, integrated identities; they do not work in isolation, but rather operate in combination based on the social context or situation. For example, when you are in the classroom, your identity as a student takes priority, but you are still a male or a female, a friend to some of your classmates, perhaps an employee, a son or daughter, and for some, even a wife or a husband. Identities can also be associated with the sports teams you root for, your favorite genre of music, and many other aspects of your social life.

To better comprehend people's seemingly countless identities, researchers have con-

> ## REMEMBER THIS
>
> *Identity is not a single entity. But rather it is a combination of multiple integrated identities that operate in combination based on the social context or situation.*

structed taxonomies categorizing the different types. Turner provides three identity categories—human, social, and personal.[8] *Human identities* are those perceptions of self that link you to the whole of humanity and separate you from other life forms. *Social identities* are represented by the many groups you belong to, such as racial, ethnic, occupational, age, hometown, and numerous others. Social identities are a result of being a member of some social groups and nonmember of others (i.e., the in-group/out-group dichotomy). *Personal identity* is what sets you apart from other in-group members and marks you as special or unique. This form of identity can come from an innate talent, such as the ability to play a musical instrument without formal training or from some special achievement, like winning an Olympic gold medal. Personal identity can also come from something as intangible as a gregarious personality.

> ### Turner's Identity Categories
>
> Human ←→ Social ←→ Personal

Hall's three identity categories are similar—personal, relational, and communal. *Personal identities* are those that set you apart from other people and make you distinct. *Relational identities* are a product of your relationships with other people, such as husband/wife, teacher/student, and supervisor/employee. *Communal identities* are "typically associated with large-scale [social] communities, such as nationality, ethnicity, gender, or religious or political affiliation."[9]

> ### Hall's Identity Categories
>
> Personal ←→ Relational ←→ Communal

Hall's communal identities are essentially the same as Taylor's social identities, and these identities carry importance during intercultural communication interaction, which is made clear in Gudykunst's explication of social identity:

> Our social identities can be based on our memberships in demographic categories (e.g., nationality, ethnicity, gender, age, social class), the roles we play (e.g., student, professor, parent), our memberships in formal or informal organizations (e.g., political parties, social clubs), our associations or vocations (e.g., scientists, artists, gardeners) or our memberships in stigmatized groups (e.g., homeless, people with AIDS).[10]

The objective of this discussion has been to provide a theoretical understanding of identity and illustrate that you have a variety of identities, which can change as a result of the social context. Because of its great relevance to intercultural communication interaction and study, we will now look at the influence of identity.

THE INFLUENCE OF IDENTITY

Identity represents an extremely important psychological component for the individual. Phinney writes that adolescents who fail to develop a "secure identity are faced with identity confusion, a lack of clarity about who they are and what their role is in life."[11] From this perspective, the need to understand your sense of identity is obvious.

The 2010 census survey was only the second time that respondents could indicate belonging to more than a single race. Over 9 million U.S. Americans, 2.7 percent of the respondents, identified themselves as belonging to two or more races, a 32 percent increase from the 2000 census.[12] Although not included in the 2010 census survey, a question on the 2000 census form allowed individuals to write in their "ancestry or ethnic origin," which resulted in "about 500 different ancestries" being reported, with ninety of those categories having U.S. populations exceeding 100,000.[13] These figures illustrate the ethnic diversity in the United States and the level of awareness that people have about their identities. The dynamics of globalization have also made identity an important factor in contemporary social life. In other words, as people struggle to adapt to the new technology-driven social order, the push of globalization and pull of traditional norms are becoming considerations in how they live their lives and with whom they interact.

The study of identity in intercultural communication tends to focus on how identity influences and guides expectations about one's own and others' social roles and provides guidelines for communicating with others.[14] For example, the cultural model for university classroom interaction in the United States is defined as student-centered because students are free to interrupt lectures to ask questions, offer personal opinions, and respectfully question the professor's claims. Also, students are aware that they may be called on to answer questions about the lesson, which instills a motivation to come to class prepared. One's identity as a professor or a student provides the blueprint for assuming the appropriate U.S. classroom behavioral role. But is that blueprint applicable to other cultures? The short answer is, "No." China and Japan, both of which are collective, hierarchical cultures, usually adhere to an instructor-centered blueprint. While the identity roles are the same as in the United States, the culturally instilled expectations are quite different. Normally, Japanese university students do not expect to be asked questions in class, and they seldom interrupt the professor's lecture. Culturally established norms can also be seen in the way occupational identity can influence intercultural communication. In many cultures, teachers are afforded considerable social respect and shown deference by both students and the population as a whole. In the United States, however, status is more a function of material gain, and educators do not usually occupy an especially elevated societal position.

While somewhat oversimplified, these examples demonstrate the importance of understanding the role of identity in an intercultural environment. There are, of course, many more reasons to gain an appreciation of identity and its influence on intercultural communication, but the above discussion should convince you of the benefits of a greater awareness of your own identity and that of others. To help you with that task, we will discuss some of your many social identities and examine how they are influenced by culture.

Examining Social Identities

As noted earlier, it is important to recognize that your identity is actually a product of multiple identities, sometimes acting in concert and at other times acting singularly. The community you are born into and those that you elect to belong to constitute a large part of your identity. And while identity serves to bind us to a larger group and makes us feel part of something bigger and more enduring, it can also isolate and even alienate us from other groups.[15] The schism between Shia and Sunni Muslims exemplifies how identity can contribute to alienation.

The salience of any identity generally varies according to the social context. As situations vary, you usually choose to emphasize one or more of your identities. In the classroom, identity as a student is paramount, but at work, occupational and organizational identities take precedence. When visiting your parents, you are first a daughter or son. In any context, however, other identities, such as race and biological sex, are also present, albeit usually in a secondary role.

Regardless of the identity or identities on display, all are influenced to various degrees by culture. In this section we will examine a few of your many identities and illustrate how each is influenced by culture.

RACIAL IDENTITY

Perhaps the most important single aspect to remember about race is that it is a social construct arising from historical attempts to categorize people into different groups. The concept grew out of efforts by eighteenth-century European anthropologists to place people into hierarchically ranked categories based largely on their outward appearance. In retrospect, it is easy to see how those early endeavors were influenced by feelings of prejudice and ethnocentrism grounded in a strong sense of Western superiority. This concept of classifying groups of peoples as superior or inferior has, unfortunately, "been used as justification for brutalities ranging from repression to slavery to mass murder and genocide."[16] Today, racial classifications and identity are usually associated with a person's external physical traits—principally skin color but also physiognomy and hair texture. Modern science, however, has discovered very little genetic variation among human beings, which erodes the belief that race can be used to categorize people. The concept is further discredited by centuries of genetic intermixing.[17]

However, as in many other countries, social categorization employing racial identity persists in the United States, no doubt abetted by the historical legacy of slavery, early persecution of American Indians, and issues of civil rights. The vestiges of early racial differentiation can be seen in question 9 of the 2010 census form, which offered respondents a choice of fifteen different racial categories, and clearly confused race (e.g., White, Black) with nationality and ethnicity (e.g., Chinese, Guamanian).[18] More recently, issues of racial differentiation have become prominent in discussions on immigration and the relationship between police forces and minority community members.

Although "race" remains a commonly used term in the United States, it is usually ill defined and often used interchangeably with the term "ethnic group." This lack of a clear definition and resulting confusion leads us to agree with Kottak and Kozaitis's recommendation that "it is better to use the term *ethnic group* instead of *race* to describe *any* such social group, for example, African Americans, Asian Americans, Irish Americans, Anglo Americans, or Hispanics."[19]

GENDER IDENTITY

Gender identity is quite different from biological sex or sexual identity, which is derived from an individual's anatomy at birth. Gender is a socially constructed concept that refers to how a particular culture differentiates masculine and feminine social roles. Ting-Toomey considers gender identity as "the meanings and interpretations we hold concerning our self-images and expected other-images of 'femaleness' and 'maleness.'"[20]

Dennis MacDonald/PhotoEdit

Gender identity refers to ways particular cultures and co-cultures differentiate masculine and feminine roles.

What constitutes displays of gender identity varies across cultures and is constantly changing. For instance, the normative U.S. male appearance in the 1960s was characterized by long hair, often accompanied by beards and mustaches, as typified in the counterculture rock musical *Hair: The American Tribal Love-Rock Musical*. Today, however, style dictates short or no hair, which is evident in the many advertisements for men's fashions. The growing number of men opting for colored nails, including toenails, is another indication of changing male gender appearance.[21] In Japanese certain words are traditionally reserved for use by women exclusively, while men use entirely different words to express the same meaning. In English there is little or no distinction between male and female vocabulary.

A culture's gender norms can also influence career decisions. For instance, male flight attendants are common on U.S. airlines, but in Northeast Asia the occupation is almost exclusively the domain of women. Traditionally, most people in the United States viewed nursing as a woman's occupation.[22] This was evidenced by the 1970 statistic reporting that only 2.7 percent of all U.S. registered nurses were male. However, in another indication of changing attitudes about gender roles and identity, by 2011 the figure had risen to 9.6 percent.[23]

In contrast to the rigid, binary classifications of either male or female traditionally used in the United States, many European nations, and the Middle East, there are a few cultures that offer a socially acceptable middle ground for transgender individuals. Some Native American Indian tribes historically held transgender individuals in high esteem, considering them to be blessed with the spirit of both man and woman.[24] Thailand's *kathoeys*, or "lady boys," do experience some discrimination but enjoy more social acceptance than their U.S. counterparts.[25] In South Asia, the *Hijras*, generally men who assume feminine identities, are viewed as neither male nor female but rather as a third gender.[26] In the United States, public media shows, such as the comedy-drama *Orange is the New Black*, have raised awareness of the country's approximately 1.5 million transgendered individuals and eroded the conventional societal idea of gender as being only male or female.[27]

Ethnic identity, like all identities, can be communicated through art forms that are unique to a particular ethnicity.

© Taylor Ingalls

ETHNIC IDENTITY

As stated earlier, racial identity is traditionally tied to one's biological ancestry, which results in similar physical characteristics in skin tone, facial characteristics, eye shape, etc. Ethnic identity, or ethnicity, on the other hand, is derived from a sense of shared heritage, history, traditions, values, similar behaviors, geographical area of origin, and in some instances, language.[28]

Most people consider their ethnic identity to come from the nation-state where they or their forefathers were born—German or German American, for example. However, some people's ethnic identity is derived from a cultural grouping that transcends national borders and is grounded in common cultural beliefs, practices, and in many cases, a shared language. The three groups listed below are illustrative:

• The Basques, located along the Spanish–French border, who speak Euskara
• The Kurds, a large ethnic group in northeast Iraq, with communities in Iran, Syria, and Turkey, who speak Kurdish
• The Roma (more commonly called Gypsies), scattered across Eastern and Western Europe, who speak Romani

As mentioned above, many U.S. Americans view their ethnicity as a product of their ancestors' home of origin prior to immigrating to the United States, such as Italy, Mexico, Vietnam, Liberia, or any one of a host of other geographic locations. Members of generations following the original immigrants frequently refer to themselves using such terms as "Italian-American," "Mexican-American," or "Vietnamese-American." For Chen, the hyphen both separates and connects the two social groupings.[29]

The United States is commonly characterized as a nation of immigrants, and during the nation's formative years, new arrivals often grouped together in a specific location or region to form ethnic communities, such as Germantown, Pennsylvania, founded by German settlers. Some of these communities continue today, as seen in San Francisco's Chinatown and Little Italy in New York. Newer ethnic enclaves, like Little Saigon in the Los Angeles area and Hong communities in Saint Paul, Minnesota, have developed in the wake of more recent immigrant arrivals. In these areas, the people's sense of ethnic identity tends to remain strong because traditional cultural practices, beliefs, values, religion, and often language are followed and perpetuated. However, as time passes, members of the younger generations often may move to areas of greater ethnic diversity and many marry into other ethnic groups. For some, this may dilute their feelings of ethnic identity and today it is not uncommon to hear U.S. Americans explain their ethnicity by offering a lengthy historical account of their family's many ethnic mergings. Others, especially those with a Euro-American heritage, will often simply refer to themselves as "just an American" or even "a white American." Frequently, they are members of the U.S. dominant culture that grew out of Judeo-Christian religious traditions imported from Western Europe and whose lineage is characterized by an extensive history of interethnic Euro-American marriages.

> **CONSIDER THIS**
>
> *How have you observed the dominant cultural values of the United States coming into contact with people of different nationalities or ethnicities? What have been some of the effects, both positive and negative, of these contacts as they apply to the beliefs and values of the dominant culture?*

NATIONAL IDENTITY

The majority of people associate their national identity with the nation where they were born. However, national identity can also be acquired through immigration and naturalization. People who take citizenship in a country other than their birthplace may eventually adopt some or all aspects of a new national identity, depending on the strength of their attachment to their new homeland. This attachment can be influenced by where the individual resides. For example, someone originally from Mexico may retain strong ties to their native land if they settle in the southwestern United States, where there is a large Mexican immigrant community. Strong nationalistic ties can be sustained in an immigrant enclave, like Little Saigon, in Orange County, California, where displaying the flag of the former South Vietnam government remains common practice. Alternatively, those ties may be eroded if the new arrival settles in an area of the United States that has a limited demography. Normally, national identity becomes more pronounced when people are away from their home country. When asked where they are from, international travelers will usually respond with their national identity, for example, "I'm from

South Korea." In some cases, however, a regional or local affiliation can outweigh nationality. Texans, for instance, are noted for identifying themselves as being from Texas rather than from "the United States." Strong and sometimes emotional displays of national identity are common at international sporting events, such as the World Cup or the Olympics.

As indicated earlier, identity is dynamic and can change contextually over time. A particularly interesting example of this dynamism is ongoing in the European Union (EU) where younger generations are moving away from the national identity of their parents and adopting what might be termed a "transnational" identity. According to Reid, many young adults from the EU tend to "think of 'Europe' as their native land."[30] A particularly prominent display of this emerging attitude came from Anne (Ana) Hidalgo, the first woman to be elected mayor of Paris, France. Ms. Hidalgo was born in Spain, immigrated to France with her parents, and subsequently took French citizenship. When asked during an interview in 2014 if she felt Spanish or French, Ms. Hidalgo responded, "I feel European."[31]

Most nations are home to a number of different cultural groups, but one group usually exercises the most power and is often referred to as the dominant culture because its members maintain control of economic, governmental, and institutional organizations. This control leads to the establishment of a "national character," as defined by Allport: "'National character' implies that members of a nation, despite ethnic, racial, religious, or individual differences among them, do resemble one another in certain fundamental matters of belief and conduct, more than they resemble members of other nations."[32]

In the United States the dominant culture is considered to be people with Western European ethnicity, and the cultural traits arising from that heritage are ascribed to the nation as a whole and referred to as the "national character." The advent of globalization, however, has brought challenges to the primacy of U.S. dominant cultural values as people of different nationalities, ethnicities, and varied beliefs and values increasingly come into contact with each other. The "transnationalism" promoted by globalization has also given rise to growing numbers of individuals with dual citizenship who carry two passports.[33]

National identity often plays a central role in contemporary geopolitics. In some instances national identity is seen as a panacea for overcoming divisions created by tribal ethnicities. For example, in an effort to heal the wounds of the 1994 conflict between the Hutu and Tutsi tribes, a struggle that claimed over 800,000 lives, the Rwandan government has outlawed references to tribal ethnicity and is seeking to have new generations see themselves only as Rwandans.[34] A similar effort was undertaken in Afghanistan, where U.S. military trainers worked to create a sense of nationality among Afghan soldiers that would transcend culturally instilled tribal loyalties.[35] The crisis in Ukraine, which resulted in a commercial airliner being shot down in 2014, has its basis in a question of national identity—the Ukrainians see themselves being more oriented toward Europe, but the nation's Russian-speaking minority maintain allegiance to Moscow.[36] And political divisions resulting from war have imposed different national identities on residents of North and South Korea.

REGIONAL IDENTITY

With the exception of very small nations like Lichtenstein, Monaco, or San Marino, every country can be divided into a number of different geographical regions, that are often characterized by varying cultural traits. These cultural contrasts may be manifested through ethnicity, language, accent, dialect, customs, food, dress, or different historical and political legacies. Residents in these areas often use one or more of those characteristics to exhibit their regional identity. For example, although the population of Belgium is just over 10 million, the country has three official languages—Dutch, French, and German, spoken by the Flemish, Walloon, and German ethnic groups, respectively, living in the Flanders, Wallonia, and Brussels areas. Thus, individuals from the northern part of Belgium are likely to identify themselves as Dutch-speaking (linguistic and ethnic identity) Belgians (national identity) from Flanders (regional identity).

In the United States, state boundary lines define many regional identities, and almost everyone is proud of his or her home state. Louisiana is marked by a variety of distinct cultural traditions and in the Bayou Country, a regional language (Cajun French) derived from its Acadian French historical heritage. Residents of Alaska, California, and Texas offer prime examples of pride in regional identity. U.S. regional identity can also be based on a larger or smaller geographical area, such as New England, "back East" (i.e., East Coast), "down South" (i.e., southeastern United States), "West Texas," or "Southern California."

Regional identity in Japan is manifested through a variety of different dialects (e.g., Kanto, Kansai, Tohoku, etc.), and some of the dialects (e.g., Kagoshima and Tohoku) are difficult for Japanese from other regions to understand. Japanese living abroad often form clubs based on their home prefecture and hold periodic gatherings to celebrate their common traditions. In China, the majority Han ethnic group is also characterized by regional differences such as linguistic variation (e.g., Mandarin, Hakka, and Min), cuisine (e.g., Cantonese and Szechuan), and housing styles (e.g., wood in the south and brick in the north). Although reunited in 1990, East and West German identities remain a reality among the older generation. Mexicans demonstrate their regional identity when they tell you they are from Sinaloa, Michoacán, Oaxaca, or Mexico City.

ORGANIZATIONAL IDENTITY

A person's organizational affiliation(s) can be an important source of identity in some cultures. This is especially true in collectivistic cultures but much less so in individualistic cultures. This dichotomy is clearly illustrated by contrasting organizational identity practices in Japan, a strongly group-oriented culture, with those in the United States, a very individualistic culture. Although becoming less prevalent, especially among younger workers, Japanese businessmen employed by large corporations have traditionally worn a small lapel pin to signal their company affiliation. There is no similar practice among managers and executives in the United States, although in some instances a polo shirt or a tie with a company logo may be worn.

Organizational identity is so important in Japan that in business introductions, the company's name is given before the individual's name. For example, Ms. Suzuki, an employee at Tokyo Bank, would be introduced as *Tōkyō Ginkō no Suzuki san* ("Ms. Suzuki of Tokyo Bank"). But in the United States, an individual is introduced first by his or her name, followed by their organizational affiliation (e.g., "This is Mr. Smith from ABC Construction Corporation"). On Japanese business cards the company and the individual's position are placed above his or her name. On U.S. business cards, the company name is normally at the top, followed by the individual's

There are many identities that play significant roles in the daily lives of people—identities they share in a very personal way.

Courtesy of Edwin McDaniel

name in large, bold letters, with organizational position under the name in smaller type. These illustrations offer insight into how collective cultures stress identity through group membership, and individualistic cultures emphasize individual identity. The examples also demonstrate how hierarchy is emphasized in Japan and egalitarianism is stressed in the United States. In other words, among the Japanese the school you attended and the company you work for are indicators of your personal status. Although there are, of course, some status differentials among U.S. schools and corporations, they exert far less influence than in Japan.

PERSONAL IDENTITY

As noted earlier, your personal identity arises from those characteristics that set you apart from others in your in-group—those things that make you unique and influence how you see yourself. Scholars typically use the term "self-construal" to denote how individuals view themselves in relation to others.[37] Research by social and cultural psychologists has disclosed that an individual possesses an independent, an interdependent, and a relational self-construal and that "cultural differences in self-definition arise through differences in the relative strength or elaboration of these self-construals."[38] People from individualistic cultures, such as in the United States and Western Europe, with a high level of independent self-construal are likely to be self-promoting and favor direct communication. Conversely, someone of a collectivistic-oriented culture, such as those in Northeast Asia, may tend to emphasize their group membership and prefer indirect communication. Relational self-construal, according to Cross and her colleagues, can be considered a global dimension that expresses the degree to which people define themselves by their close, dyadic relationships (e.g., relationship with spouse, child, sibling, close friend, etc.).[39] Someone motivated by relational self-construal can be expected to engage in efforts to enhance that relationship.

CYBERIDENTITY AND FANTASY IDENTITY

Our lives increasingly focus around the Internet. On a near daily basis, we spend time online engaged in a variety of activities—communicating, searching for information, shopping, seeking leisure, conducting work-related tasks, social exchanges, and a variety of other endeavors. It is common to see people in a coffee shop working on a laptop or walking along absorbed in some type of activity on their mobile device. The Internet allows you quickly and easily to access and exchange information on a worldwide basis. As Suler informs us, the Internet also provides an opportunity to escape the constraints of our everyday identities:

> One of the interesting things about the Internet is the opportunity it offers people to present themselves in a variety of different ways. You can alter your style of being just slightly or indulge in wild experiments with your identity by changing your age, history, personality, and physical appearance, even your gender. The username you choose, the details you do or don't indicate about yourself, the information presented on your personal web page, the persona or avatar you assume in an online community—all are important aspects of how people manage their identity in cyberspace.[40]

The Internet allows individuals to select and promote what they consider the positive features of their identity and omit any perceived negative elements or even construct an "imaginary persona." The Internet is replete with a variety of websites, such as Internet forums, online chat rooms, massively multiplayer online role-playing games (MMORPG), and massively multiplayer online worlds (MMOW) that construct a computer-driven virtual environment allowing users to construct a cyberidentity, that may or may not correspond to their actual identity. Infatuation with these invented identities can become so strong they can "take on a life of their own."[41]

CONSIDER THIS
How does the Internet allow for individuals to select and promote what they consider the positive features of their identity and omit any perceived negative elements, or even construct an "imaginary persona"? What are some dangers of this feature of the Internet?

Fantasy identity, which also extends across cultures, centers on characters from science fiction movies, comic books (*manga*), and *anime*. Every year, people attend domestic and international conventions devoted to these subjects. For example, the 2014 Hong Kong Ani-Com and Games convention drew a record attendance of 752,000 and attracted 550 commercial exhibitors.[42] Comic-Con International has been held annually in San Diego, California, since 1970, and in 2014 attendance exceeded 130,000.[43] At these gatherings many attendees come dressed, individually or in groups, as their favorite fantasy character(s). For a few hours or days, they assume, enact, and communicate the identity of their favorite media character. But conventions are not the only opportunity for people to indulge their fantasy identities. "Cosplay" (short for "costume play") is another venue that lets people attend events or parties dressed as media characters.

OTHER IDENTITIES

Space limitations preclude our addressing the many other forms of culturally influenced identity that play a significant role in the daily lives of people. For example, we have not examined the role of religion, which occupies a significant place in the lives of many people. To illustrate, New York City is home to the largest Jewish population outside of Israel,[44] and a visit to Brooklyn will demonstrate the important role that religion plays in the identity of the Jewish community, especially the large number of Hasidic Jews, who adhere to a strict dress code and diet. Christian women often include a cross in their accessory wardrobe, and the *hijab* head covering and the *abaya* cloak represent a part of many Muslim women's identity.[45] Age, political affiliation, socioeconomic class, physical ability, and minority status, all of which are part of most individuals' culturally influenced identity, have not been addressed. Nor have we examined the very important role that tribal identity plays in such places as Afghanistan, Iraq, Libya, and Pakistan. Indeed, much of the ongoing Middle East conflict can be attributed to renascent tribal affiliation, which became prominent after several of the authoritarian leaders were removed from power.[46] However, the various identities discussed here should provide you with insight into the complexity of the topic and the important influence of culture on identity. Let us look now at how we acquire our identities.

IDENTITY ACQUISITION AND DEVELOPMENT

As previously discussed, identities are a product of contact with others. Ting-Toomey sees identities as being acquired and developed "through interaction with others in their cultural group."[47] Thus, your individual identity(ies) are derived from your larger group identities (e.g., you can only identify as a male, daughter, college student, etc. due to the existence of the larger collectivity of similar individuals).[48] Identity development, then, can be described as a dynamic process of familial influences, cultural socialization, and personal experiences. We have already looked at the family in Chapter 3, but familial influence on identity is so great that we need to touch on a few points here.

The initial exposure to your identity came from your family, where you began to learn culturally appropriate beliefs, values, and social role behaviors.[49] Development of gender identity commences at a very early age when family members start teaching children culturally based behaviors specific to boys and girls. Interacting with extended family members also instills age-appropriate behaviors. Moreover, it is the family that first begins to inculcate the concept of an individual- or group-based identity. At the start of your school years, you were required to learn and enact the culturally mandated behaviors of a student. Media also play a major role in your identity development. The near-constant exposure to media stereotypes creates a sense of how you should look, dress, and act in order to exhibit age- and gender-appropriate identities. Media also serve to recruit people to join different groups, for example those for or against a specific activity, such as gay marriage, abortion, or the use of enhanced interrogation techniques.

From a theoretical perspective, Phinney provides a three-stage model to help explain identity development. Although the model focuses on adolescent ethnic identity, it is equally applicable to the acquisition and growth of cultural identity. The initial stage, *unexamined ethnic identity*, is "characterized by the lack of exploration of ethnicity."[50] During this phase individuals are not particularly interested in examining or demonstrating their personal ethnicity. For members of minority cultures, diminished interest may result from a desire to suppress their own ethnicity in an effort to identify with the majority culture. Majority members in the United States, on the other hand, seem to take for granted that their identity is the societal norm and give little thought to their own ethnicity.[51]

> **Phinney's Three-Stage Identity Development**
>
> Unexamined ethnic → Ethnic identity → Ethnic identity
>   identity   search   achievement

Ethnic identity search, the second stage, begins when individuals become interested in learning about and understanding their own ethnicity. Movement from stage 1 to stage 2 can be stimulated by a variety of events. An incident of discrimination might move minority members to reflect on their own ethnicity. This could lead to a realization that some beliefs and values of the majority culture can be detrimental to minority members[52] and provoke movement toward one's own ethnicity. As an example, Dolores Tanno grew up in northern New Mexico and had always considered herself Spanish. After leaving New Mexico, she discovered that some people saw her as Mexican rather than Spanish, and this motivated her ethnic identity search.[53] Increased interest in ethnic identity could also come from attending a cultural event, taking a culture class, or some other event that expands greater awareness of and interest in one's cultural heritage. *Ethnic Identity achievement*, Phinney's final stage of identity development, is reached when individuals have a clear and confident understanding of their own cultural identity. For minority members, this usually comes with an ability to effectively deal with discrimination and negative stereotypes.[54] Identity achievement can also provide greater self-confidence and enhance feelings of personal worth.

Drawing on social science research, Martin and Nakayama offer multistage identity development models for minority, majority, and biracial individuals respectively. In the *minority development model*, the initial stage, *unexamined identity*, is similar to Phinney's model, in which individuals are unconcerned about identity issues. During stage 2, *conformity*, minority members endeavor to fit in with the dominant culture and may even develop negative self-images. *Resistance and separatism*, stage 3, is usually the result of some cultural awakening that motivates increased interest in and adherence to one's own culture. Concurrently, rejection of all or selected aspects of the dominant culture may occur. In the final stage, *integration*, individuals gain a sense of pride in and identify with their own cultural group and demonstrate an acceptance of other groups.[55]

Multistage Identity Development Models

> ***Minority Identity Development:***
> Unexamined identity → Conformity → Resistance and separation → Integration
> ***Majority Identity Development:***
> Unexamined identity → Acceptance → Resistance → Redefinition → Reintegration
> ***Biracial Identity Development:***
> General difference awareness → Personal difference awareness → Awareness/acceptance of duality

Multistage Identity Development Models

Majority identity development follows a five-step model with identity in the initial stage, *unexamined* identity, being of little concern. *Acceptance*, the second stage, is characterized by acquiescence to existing social inequities, even though such acceptance may occur at a subconscious level. At the next stage, *resistance*, members of the dominant culture become more aware of existing social inequities, begin to question their own culture, and increase their association with minority culture members. Achievement of the fourth and fifth stages, *redefinition* and *reintegration*, brings an increased understanding of one's dominant culture identity and an appreciation of minority cultures.[56]

In the first stage of Martin and Nakayama's *biracial identity* development model, biracial individuals may rotate through three phases where they (1) become conscious of differences in general and the potential for discord, (2) gain an awareness of their personal differences from other children, and (3) begin to sense they are not part of the norm. The second stage entails a struggle to be accepted and the development of feelings that they should choose one race or another. In the third and final stage, biracial individuals accept their duality, becoming more self-confident.[57] This development model is demonstrated in the historical experience of Japanese biracial children, often called *hafu* (half) in Japanese. The occupation of Japan by Allied forces after World War II saw the birth of increasing numbers of biracial children who generally encountered derision and overt discrimination. However, as their numbers have gown, especially with the increase of international marriages arising from globalization, they have become common figures in the contemporary social order, establishing a formal, worldwide organizational structure promoting organized events and public

As you go about daily activities, entering and exiting various contexts, different identities come into play.

Rudi Von Briel/photoEdit

lectures about the biracial experience.[58] As another example, the Hapa Project strives to "promote awareness and recognition of the millions of multiracial/multiethnic individuals of Asian/Pacific Islander descent [and] to give voice to multiracial people and previously ignored ethnic groups...."[59]

Identities can also be classified as *ascribed* or *avowed*, based on how they are acquired,[60] a distinction referring to whether an identity was obtained involuntarily or voluntarily. Racial, ethnic, and sexual identities are assigned at birth and are considered ascribed, or involuntary. In hierarchical cultures where social status is often inherited, such as in Mexico, a person's family name can be a strong source of ascribed identity. By contrast, your identity as a particular university student is avowed because you voluntarily elected to attend the school. Even though being a university student is a voluntary identity, your culture has established expectations that delineate appropriate and inappropriate social behavior for college students. When enacting your student identity, you will normally try to conform to those socially appropriate protocols, sometimes consciously and at other times subconsciously.

ESTABLISHING AND ENACTING CULTURAL IDENTITY

By now you should have an appreciation of identity as a social construct, what constitutes identity, an awareness of some of your own identities, and insight into how identities are acquired. This background will help you understand how cultural identities are established and expressed.

As you go about your daily activity, entering and exiting various contexts, different identities come into play. By interacting with others you continually create and re-create your cultural identity through communication,[61] which can take a variety of forms, including "conversation, commemorations of history, music, dance, ritual, ceremonial, and social drama of all sorts."[62] Family stories told by family members connect us to the past and provide a "sense of identity and connection to the world."[63] These stories are also infused with cultural beliefs and values that become part of one's identity.

Culture's influence in establishing identity can be demonstrated by returning to the classroom and contrasting student interaction styles in the United States and Japan. In the United States individualism is stressed, and even young children are taught to be independent and develop their personal identity. Schools in the United States encourage competition in the classroom and on the playing field. Students quickly learn to voice their ideas and feel free to challenge the opinions of others, including teachers, as a means of asserting their own identity. Being different is a common and valued trait. This is in contrast to the collective societies of South America, West Africa, and Northeast Asia, where children learn the importance of interdependence and identity is "defined by relationships and group memberships."[64] This results in activities that promote group-affiliated identity. In Japanese preschool and elementary classrooms, students are frequently divided into small groups (*han*) where they are encouraged to solve problems collectively rather than individually.[65] This practice teaches young Japanese students the importance of identifying with a group.

> **CONSIDER THIS**
>
> *Once established, identities are enacted in multiple ways, beginning in childhood and progressing through adolescence into the adult years.*

Identities are also established and displayed through cultural rites of passage that help adolescents gain an increased awareness of who they are as they enter adulthood.[66] In some underdeveloped societies the rite can involve a painful physical experience, such as male or female circumcision, but in developed nations, the ceremony is usually less harsh and is often a festive event. The bar mitzvah, for instance, is used to introduce Jewish boys into adulthood when they become more responsible for religious duties. In Mexican culture, girls look forward to celebrating their fifteenth birthday with a *quinceañera*. This occasion is a means of acknowledging that a young woman has reached sexual maturity and is now an adult, ready to assume additional family and social responsibilities. In addition, the celebration is intended to reaffirm religious faith, good morals, and traditional family values.[67] In the dominant U.S. culture, rites of passage into adulthood are generally not as distinctive but are often associated with the individual attaining a greater degree of independence or "freedom."[68] Graduation from high school or college, for example, brings increased expectations of self-sufficiency and a new identity.

Once established, identities are enacted in multiple ways, beginning in childhood and progressing through adolescence into the adult years. For instance, individuals in almost every culture have ways of displaying their religious or spiritual identity. As we noted earlier, many Jews wear yarmulkes or other distinctive clothes, and Christians frequently display a cross as an item of personal jewelry. As a display of humility, Muslim men often go unshaven, which can also convey their religious identity. Some men and women wear a red dot (*pottu*) on their forehead as a sign of their devotion to the Hindu religion. Male adherents of Shikism commonly wear a turban and refrain from cutting their hair as part of their devotion. Each of these outward symbols identifies the wearer as belonging to a specific religious group and thus is a sign of both inclusion and exclusion.

Identity can also be evinced through involvement in commemorative events. The Fourth of July in the United States, Bastille Day in France, and Independence Day in Mexico are celebrations of national identity. The annual Saint Patrick's Day parade in New York City is an opportunity for people of Irish heritage to take pride in their ethnic identity. Oktoberfest celebrations allow people to rekindle their German identity, and the Lunar New Year is a time for the Chinese and many other Asian cultures to observe traditions that reaffirm their identities.

While many customs of identity enactment are tradition-bound, evolving circumstances can bring about new ways. This type of change was discovered by David and Ayouby's study of Arab minorities in the Detroit, Michigan, area. They found that a division existed between how early immigrants and later arrivals understood Arab identity. Immigrants who arrived in the United States years earlier were satisfied "with meeting and enacting their ethnicity in a ritualistic fashion by eating Arabic food, perhaps listening to Arabic music, and even speaking Arabic to their limited ability."[69] The more recent Arab immigrant arrivals, however, had a "more politicized identity,"[70] resulting from their experiences in the conflicts and political turmoil of the Middle East. They felt that being an Arab involved taking a more involved role in events in their native land, such as sending money back or becoming politically active.[71]

There are certainly many more ways of establishing and evincing your identity than we have discussed here. For instance, we did not address the obvious cultural identity markers of language, accents, or family names. But this overview should convince you of the complexity of your identities and how they are shaped by culture.

REMEMBER THIS

Increasing numbers of people are acknowledging multiple cultural identities.

GLOBALIZATION AND CULTURAL IDENTITY

There is no denying that the contemporary world social order is increasingly characterized by multiculturalism. In Chapter 10, we will talk about how business is now routinely conducted in a transnational environment, the growing field of cross-cultural healthcare, and how multicultural education is a contemporary challenge. Contrary to the belief and dire predictions made by some, globalization does not appear to be producing a culturally homogenized global society. Giddens claims that rather than increased similarity, globalization is actually abetting cultural diversity and giving rise to "a revival of local cultural identities in different parts of the world."[72] Advances in technology have enabled people of similar backgrounds, ideologies, philosophies, etc. to quickly and easily interact with each other, both virtually and in person, regardless of their location. This capability promotes activities that tend to strengthen, and in some cases revive, feelings of cultural identity. However, openness to cross-border information flow and international travel can represent a threat in conservative states, where the introduction "of foreign content can erode the traditional values and indigenous cultural identity."[73] In Western European countries there is concern about how traditional national identities might be affected by the increasingly vocal immigrant communities and the rising numbers of new arrivals.[74] So great is this concern that France established a government agency charged with "promoting national identity" and subsequently launched a national debate on the topic.[75]

From another perspective, people acknowledging multiple cultural identities are becoming more common. The globalized economy, immigration, ease of foreign travel, communication technologies, and intercultural marriage are bringing about an increased mixing of cultures, and this mixing is producing people who possess multiple cultural identities. Chuang notes, "cultural identity becomes blurry in the midst of cultural integration, bicultural interactions, interracial marriages, and the mutual adaptation processes."[76] Martin, Nakayama, and Flores further support this idea by reporting, "increasing numbers of people are living 'in between' cultural identities. That is, they identify with more than one nationality, ethnicity, race, or religion."[77] As mentioned earlier, dual citizenship has become common. For instance, citizens of any EU nation are also legal citizens of the EU, with the right to live and work in any other EU nation.

In the United States, immigration, intercultural marriage, and multiracial births are creating a social environment where the younger generations consider cultural diversity a normal aspect of social life.[78] Kotkin and Tseng contend that among U.S. Americans there is "not only a growing willingness—and ability—to cross cultures, but also the evolution of a nation in which personal identity is shaped more by cultural preferences than by skin color or ethnic heritage."[79] Hitt points out that "more and more Americans have come to feel comfortable changing out of the identities they were born into and donning new ethnicities in which they feel more at home."[80]

Globalization has also given rise to "intercultural transients," those people who frequently move back and forth across cultural borders and must manage both cultural changes and identity renegotiations.[81] Over the past decade a growing number of nations have made dual citizenship available, thereby increasing the community of intercultural transients.

Issues of identity can be expected to remain complex—and perhaps become more so—as globalism and multiculturalism increasingly characterize contemporary society. It is clear, however, that the old understanding of a fixed cultural identity or ethnicity is outdated, and identity is rapidly becoming more of an "articulated negotiation between what you call yourself and what other people are willing to call you."[82] Regardless of how they are achieved, the form they take, or how they are acquired, your identities will remain a product of culture.

COMPETENCY AND IDENTITY IN INTERCULTURAL INTERACTIONS

We have already discussed that identity is established through communicative interaction with others. Hecht and his colleagues also point out that identity is "maintained and modified through social interaction. Identity then begins to influence interaction through shaping expectations and motivating behavior."[83] As was previously mentioned, you are constantly assuming different identities as you interact with other people, and with each identity you employ a set of communicative behaviors appropriate for that identity and context. Culture has shaped your understanding and expectations of appropriate communicative behaviors for various social settings—for example, a classroom, hospital, sales meeting, wedding, or funeral. But what is appropriate in one culture may be inappropriate in another. We have also illustrated how students and teachers in Japan and the United States have quite different culturally established standards for classroom communicative behavior. However, what if a Japanese student is placed in a U.S. classroom or vice versa?

In an intercultural meeting, the varying expectations for identity display and communication style carry considerable potential for creating anxiety, misunderstandings, and even conflict. This is why Imahori and Cupach consider "cultural identity as a focal element in intercultural communication."[84] Continuing with our student/teacher example, try to imagine how students from a culture that does not value individuality and communicative assertiveness would feel in a typical U.S. classroom. Being unaccustomed to having an instructor query students, they would probably be reluctant to raise their hands and would likely consider U.S. students who challenged the teacher to be rude or even arrogant. These factors would probably produce a degree of confusion and stress. To avoid potential problems during intercultural interaction, you need to develop what Collier calls intercultural competence, which is achieved when an avowed identity matches the ascribed identity.

> For example, if you avow the identity of an assertive, outspoken U.S. American and your conversational partner avows himself or herself to be a respectful, nonassertive Vietnamese, then each must ascribe the corresponding identity to the conversational partner. You must jointly negotiate what kind of relationship will be mutually satisfying. Some degree of adjustment and accommodation is usually necessary.[85]

Collier is saying that in order to communicate effectively in an intercultural situation, to lessen the potential of tension and misunderstanding, an individual's avowed cultural identity and communication style should match the identity and style ascribed to him or her by the other party. But since the communication styles are likely to be different, the participants will have to search for a middle ground, and this search will require flexibility and adaptation. As a simple illustration, the Japanese traditionally greet and say good-bye to each other by bowing. However, in Japanese-U.S. business meetings, the Japanese have learned to bow only slightly while shaking hands. In doing this, they are adjusting their normal greeting practice to accommodate U.S. visitors. Longtime U.S. business representatives to Japan have learned to emulate this behavior. Thus, a mutually satisfying social protocol has evolved. In achieving this, the participants have demonstrated the principal components of intercultural communication competence: motivation, knowledge, and skills.

SUMMARY

- Identity is a highly abstract, dynamic, multifaceted concept that defines who you are.

- Identities can be categorized as human, social, and personal; another classification scheme uses personal, relational, and communal.

- Every individual has multiple identities—racial, gender, ethnic, national, regional, organizational, personal, and perhaps cyber/fantasy, and others—that act in concert. The importance of any single identity is a result of the context.

- Identity is acquired through interaction with other members of one's cultural group. The family exerts a primary influence on early identity formation.

- Identities are established through group membership and are enacted in various ways, including rites of passage, personal appearance, and participation in commemorative events. Concepts of identity within the same group can change over time.

- Competent intercultural communication is achieved when the participants find commonality in ascribed and avowed identities.

- As society becomes increasingly multicultural, new concepts of cultural identity are evolving.

ACTIVITIES

1. Construct a list of as many of your identities as you can. Using the list, draw a pie chart with each identity receiving space proportional to that identity's importance to you. Compare your chart with other classmates' charts. Do members of the dominant and minority cultures differ in the amount of space allotted to their racial/ethnic identity? If so why?

2. In a group of at least three individuals, have each person go to YouTube and view at least two videos on one of the following topics—Christian, Jewish, or Muslim/Islamic identity. Afterward, compare notes for similarities and differences on how the respective identities are established, displayed, etc.

CONCEPTS AND QUESTIONS

1. Why is an awareness of identity important in your personal life? What are some of the situations in which this awareness would be beneficial?

2. How would you define identity? How would you explain your identities to another person?

3. What are some of your different identities and how did you acquire them? What are some differences between your identities and those same identities in another culture?

4. How did you establish some of your identities? How do you enact those identities?

CHAPTER 8

Verbal Messages: Exchanging Ideas Through Language

A language is a part of a culture, and a culture is a part of a language; the two are intricately interwoven so that one cannot separate the two without losing the significance of either language or culture.

DOUGLAS BROWN

We look around us, and are awed by the variety of several thousand languages and dialects, expressing a multiplicity of world views, literatures, and ways of life.

DAVID CRYSTAL

Whether clear or garbled, tumultuous or silent, deliberate or fatally inadvertent, communication is the ground of meeting and the foundation of community. It is, in short, the essential human connection.

ASHLEY MONTAGU AND FLOYD MATSON

As is the case with many everyday activities, we seldom pause to appreciate the significance and power of language for human existence and survival. Schultz and Lavenda call attention to the importance of language in our lives when they write, "All people use language to encode their experiences, to structure their understanding of the world and of themselves, and engage one another interactively."[1] Language gives meaning to humans by allowing them to symbolize their feelings and the world around them. That ability permits you to transmit to others your beliefs, values, attitudes, worldviews, emotions, aspects of identity, and myriad other personal features. In addition, as Newman writes, "Language can also pack an enormous emotional wallop. Words can make us happy, sad, disgusted, or angry, or even incite us to violence. Racial, ethnic, sexual, or religious slurs can be particularly volatile."[2] A very specific example of the power of words occurred when the French foreign minister urged the international community to no longer refer to the terrorist group ISIS as an Islamic state. His argument was simple: Those two words grant credibility to ISIS as both Islamic and a state. The foreign minister's point was that ISIS is neither.

Because this book examines communication and culture, it should not be surprising when we assert that language and culture are indispensable components of intercultural communication.

Together, they illustrate synergism, each working to sustain and perpetuate the other while creating a greater phenomenon—language allows the dissemination and adoption of culture. The link between language and culture should be obvious, for as the American philosopher John Dewey remarked, "language is…fundamentally and primarily a social instrument." Because it is a social instrument, language provides the means for a group to create a collective societal structure encompassing political, economic, social, and educational institutions.

Since language and culture are linked, it behooves students of intercultural communication to become aware of what can be learned by studying some of the language characteristics of cultures other than their own. In addition, contemporary society, both domestic and international, is increasingly characterized by interactions among people of different cultures speaking different languages. For example, a 2011 U.S. Census ascertained that over 21 percent of the U.S. population, five years of age or older, speak a language other than English at home.[3] This statistic offers a compelling reason to understand how culture and language complement each other. Not only is there a domestic need to understand language differences, but international interactions also demand an awareness of the connection between language and culture. As globalization increases, multiple business transactions each day between people who do not speak the same language also increase. Ferraro highlights the importance of those international exchanges, writing, "If international business people are to succeed, there is no substitute for an intimate acquaintance with both the language and the culture of those with whom one is conducting business."[4] Hence, the objective of this chapter is to provide you with an appreciation and understanding of some of those languages and cultures. The statement by the American writer Rita May Brown reflects our motivation: "Language is the roadmap of a culture. It tells you where its people came from and where they are going."

REMEMBER THIS

Language and culture are interconnected in a multiplicity of ways.

FUNCTIONS OF LANGUAGE

We have suggested to this point that language is a means of preserving culture, a medium for transmitting culture to new generations, and the chief means utilized by humans to communicate their ideas, thoughts, and feelings to others. Language is significant because it is capable of performing a variety of functions. A look at some of these functions will serve as a vehicle for revealing the importance of language to the study of intercultural communication.

SOCIAL INTERACTION

Stop for a moment and consider some of your normal activities that necessitate the use of language. These activities might include chatting with your roommate, talking with your professor before class, asking a college librarian for help finding a journal, using your cell phone, surfing the Internet, writing a report, or using your iPad. All of these activities—and many more—form a part of your daily routine. Without language, however, none of

Language can take a variety of forms and enables a group to share common systems and use symbols to preserve past events.

© Kathleen K. Parker

these events would be possible. Language allows you to speak, read, write, listen to others, and even talk to yourself—or to think. Language allows you verbally to convey your internal emotions and relieve stress by simply uttering a phrase (darn it) or a swear word (damn). You use language to express pain (ouch!), elation (great!), disappointment (oh no!), and amazement or surprise (OMG!).[5] Often, these or similar expressions are used subconsciously, even when no one is around. Language is also employed to invoke assistance from the supernatural. A Jewish rabbi, a Buddhist priest, a Mongolian shaman, the Pope, a Muslim, or a young child reciting a prayer are all using language to appeal to a greater power. For all of them, words allow for a special type of social interaction.

SOCIAL COHESION

A common language allows individuals to form social groups and engage in cooperative efforts. A shared vocabulary enables a group to preserve a record of past events, albeit often with a selective interpretation. Because the past is an important means for teaching children their culture's normative behaviors, these records provide the people with a communal history that becomes a unifying force for future generations. As you may recall from Chapter 2, language allows a group of people to maintain a record of the cultural values and expectations that bind them. The maintenance of social relations also relies on language for more than communicating messages. For example, the type of language used to express intimacy, respect, affiliation, formality, distance, and other emotions can help you sustain a relationship or disengage from one.[6]

EXPRESSIONS OF IDENTITY

In Chapter 7 we dealt extensively with how culture contributes to the construction of individual and cultural identity. Language, of course, is the major mechanism through which much of individual and group or cultural identity is constructed. Identities do not exist until they are enacted through language. As Hua asserts, "Identity is constituted in discourse."[7] Not only does language present information about identity, but the linguistic expression of identity unites people by reinforcing group identification. Cheering at a football game, reciting the Pledge of Allegiance, or shouting names or slogans at public meetings can reinforce group identification.

The deep-seated loyalties attached to linguistic activities go well beyond cheering and slogans. In the United States, for example, there is an ongoing controversy over making English the official language of the United States, which is often seen as a reaction to the rising tide of illegal immigrants. The French believe so strongly in the value of their language and the need to keep it pure that in 1635 they established the Académie Française to regulate and standardize their language. Yet another example showing how language plays a part in establishing and expressing ethnic identity can be seen within the co-culture of African Americans. Black English Vernacular (BEV), or Ebonics, helps create and reinforce a sense of mutual identity among African Americans. Dialects or accents can also be a part of one's identity. Think for a moment about the stereotypical southern drawl, the variety of accents encountered in the metropolitan areas of Boston and New York City, or the surfer's lingo heard in Southern California. Each of these different linguistic conventions contributes to the user's regional identity.

Language usage, and its relationship to identity, can also categorize people into groups according to factors such as age and gender. The terminology used can easily mark one as young or old. Recall how you have sometimes thought the words used by your parents or grandparents sounded old fashioned. Additionally, language is part of your gender identity. Women and men use language differently, both in word choice and in behaviors. Among U.S. English speakers, women tend to ask more questions, listen more, and use a supportive speech style. Men, on the other hand, are more prone to interrupting and asserting their opinions and are poor listeners.[8] In Japan, women employ more honorific terms and the genders often use a different word to say the same thing. Language has also been used to categorize people into varying social and economic levels. Because the way that people speak

CONSIDER THIS

Why do members of a culture or co-culture have such ingrained loyalties and intense attachments to their language?

carries an unimaginable weight in each society, it also influences how they are perceived by that society. They can be viewed as "civilized" or "uncivilized," sophisticated or unsophisticated, and educated or uneducated by the way they use language. Hence, although language can be a form of identity, a shared language can also become a divisive force when people identify too strongly with their native tongue, become ethnocentric, and feel threatened by someone speaking a different language.

WHAT IS LANGUAGE?

Let us start with a definition of language. *Language may be thought of as an organized system of symbols, both verbal and nonverbal, used in a common and uniform way by persons who are able to manipulate these symbols to express their thoughts and feelings.* While countless other animals use a form of language, it is the human brain and body that are best adapted for this complex symbol system. In the next chapter we look at how nonverbal symbols operate as part of this multifaceted and elaborate system, but for now we turn our attention to verbal language.

> **REMEMBER THIS**
>
> *Language may be thought of as an organized system of symbols, both verbal and nonverbal, used in a common and uniform way by persons who are able to manipulate these symbols to express their thoughts and feelings.*

CHARACTERISTICS OF LANGUAGE

Words Are Only Symbols

While we spent some time in Chapter 2 explaining how communication is symbolic, we now return to that notion as we examine how it applies to language. English philosopher John Locke offered an excellent introduction to words as symbols observing that, "Words, in their primary or immediate signification, stand for nothing but the ideas in the mind of him that uses them." Simply put, *words are substitutes for "the real thing."* You can't eat the word "apple" or drive the word "car." You face the same dilemma, in a much more serious situation, when you attempt to string words together in your effort to tell someone how sorry you feel over the death of a loved one. In this sense, we live in two different worlds: the one made up of words (symbols) and the one composed of what the words are attempting to represent.

Words Are Arbitrary

The frustration created by words only being symbols is compounded by the fact that the relationship between the selected symbol and the agreed meaning is arbitrary. As Solomon and Theiss state, "Language is arbitrary because there is no inherent reason for using a particular word to represent a particular object or idea."[9] This concept is easily illustrated by looking at some of the varied symbols used by different cultures to identify a familiar household pet. In Finland, they have settled on *kissa*, but in Germany, *katze* has been chosen, and Swahili speakers use *paka*. Tagalog speakers in the Philippines prefer *pusa*, and in Spanish-speaking countries, *gato* has been selected. In the English language "*cat*" is the term used. As you can see, none of the words has any relation to the actual characteristics of a cat. These are simply arbitrary symbols that each language group uses to call to mind the common domestic pet, or sometimes a larger wild animal, such as a tiger, lion, or leopard. It is also common to find significant differences within a major language group. Although English can vary within national boundaries, more prominent differences, such as pronunciation, spelling, and terminology, can be found when comparing English-speaking countries such as Australia, England, and the United States. For example, in England, the trunk of a car is a "boot," and the hood is the "bonnet." Australians pronounce the "ay" sound as "ai." Imagine the confusion and consternation when an Australian asks his U.S. friend how she will celebrate "Mother's Dai."

Words Evoke Denotative or Connotative Meanings

We have already explored the idea that when someone selects a particular word or phrase, he or she may not be using it in precisely the same manner as someone else. Hence, different meanings for that word are built into the communication experience. In addition, meanings are also affected by the denotative or connotative meanings. The "denotative meaning refers to the literal, conventional meaning that most people in a culture have agreed is the meaning for the symbol."[10] The category of words associated with denotative meanings is somewhat impartial and neutral and seldom contains expressive overtones. There can be general agreement as to what is a tree, a table, a car, and the like.

Connotative meaning is the private, emotional meaning that the word evokes. It is the meaning that reflects your personal and cultural experiences with the word or words being used. Because connotation in language involves the deep structure of words and expressions that are strongly related to culture, they can be problematic during intercultural exchanges. You may observe this point with words such as "freedom," "devotion," "disgust," "democracy," and "love." For example, you may love good food, love your mate, love your parents, and love your country. Yet while you used the word "love" in all of these instances, the connotations are very different. Understanding the subtlety of these differences when communicating with someone of another culture often takes time to develop.

LANGUAGE AND CULTURE

One of the most difficult and persistent problems encountered in intercultural communication is that of language differences. We now turn to some of those differences and see how they might influence intercultural interactions. Our examination will include some examples (1) of how language and thought are linked; (2) cultural variations in accents, dialects, argot, slang, and texting; and (3) differences in the special ways cultures employ language. All of these examples illustrate the values of those cultures. Several features of interpretation, a critical link in intercultural communication, are then examined. We next explore some aspects of language in communication technology. The chapter concludes with a look at language considerations that can increase intercultural communication competence.

LANGUAGE AND THOUGHT

You may assume that everyone speaks and thinks in much the same way—that they just use different words. This is not the case. While words and meanings differ from one culture to another, thought processes and perceptions of reality also differ. And

Language allows people to establish relationships and to express and exchange ideas and information.

© David Frazier/PhotoEdit

these differences in perception, many of them subconscious, have an influence on how people think and use language. This cultural dynamic is known as *linguistic relativity* and was set forth in the Sapir–Whorf hypothesis. The hypothesis asserted "that language profoundly shapes the perceptions and world view of its speakers."[11] Sapir and Whorf suggested, "differences between languages must have consequences that go far beyond mere grammatical organization and must be related to profound divergence in modes of thought."[12] Hence, the Sapir–Whorf hypothesis argued that language is not simply a means of reporting experience but, more importantly, a way of defining experience. To explain this concept, Sapir and Whorf wrote,

> Human beings do not live in the objective world alone, nor alone in the world of social activity as ordinarily understood, but are very much at the mercy of the particular language which has become the medium of expression for their society…. The real world is to a large extent unconsciously built up on the language habits of the group. No two languages are

ever sufficiently similar to be considered as representing the same social reality. The worlds in which different societies live are distinct worlds, not merely the same world with different labels attached.[13]

Sapir and Whorf proposed that "even ideas such as time, space, and matter are conditioned by the structure of our languages."[14] If this be the case, those who support linguistic relativity conclude that people who speak different languages also perceive certain portions of the world in dissimilar ways. Perhaps a few examples will help to demonstrate this notion. In the Hindi language of India, there are no single words equivalent to the English words for "uncle" and "aunt." Instead, as Rogers and Steinfatt relate, Hindi has different words for your father's older brother, your father's younger brother, your mother's older brother, your mother's older brother-in-law, and so forth.[15]

CONSIDER THIS

How would you explain the following phrase: "Language profoundly shapes the perceptions and worldview of its speakers"?

Another cultural example deals with the Hopi language (spoken by the Hopi, an American Indian people). Hua offers the following examples to explain how language and experiences are linked in that culture:

> According to Whorf, in the Hopi language, there is no plural form for nouns referring to time, such as days and years. Instead of saying "they stayed ten days," the equivalent in Hopi is "they stayed until the eleventh day" or "they left after the tenth day." In addition, all phrase terms, such as summer, morning, etc., are not nouns, but function as adverbs.[16]

Bonvillain demonstrates yet another cultural trait and how it is reflected in their language. In this case, it is the Navajo's concern for individual autonomy:

English Speaker: "I must go there."

Navajo Speaker: "It is only good that I shall go there."

English Speaker: "I make the horse run."

Navajo Speaker: "The horse is running for me."[17]

Although complete acceptance of linguistic relativity is controversial, even critics agree that a culture's linguistic vocabulary emphasizes what is considered important in that culture. Salzmann contends that "those aspects of culture that are important for the members of a society are correspondingly highlighted in the vocabulary."[18] For example, Ronnie Lupe, chairman of the White Mountain Apache tribe, noted, "To the white man, he thinks, land is just 'real estate.' But in Apache the word for land is also the one for mind: 'So I point to my mind, I also point to my land.'"[19]

This kind of culture–language synergy is also illustrated by comparing a food staple from the United States with one from Japan. As Table 8.1 reveals, each nation has a large vocabulary for the product that is important but few words for the less used product. In the United States "rice" refers to the grain regardless of context—whether it is cooked, found in the store, or still in the field. Similarly, when discussing "beef," the Japanese use only the traditional word *gyuniku* or the adopted English word *bifu* or *bifuteki*.

TABLE 8.1	English and Japanese Words Reflecting Culturally Important Items

U.S. CUTS OF BEEF	JAPANESE RICE
• chuck	• *ine* – rice growing in the field
• rib	• *momi* – rice with the husk still on
• short loin	• *genmai* – unpolished (brown) rice
• sirloin	• *kome* – uncooked white rice (e.g., at the store)
• round	• *shinmai* – rice harvested this year
• brisket	• *komai* – rice harvested last year
• fore shank	• *gohan* – steamed glutinous rice
• short plank	• *okayu* – rice gruel

LANGUAGE VARIATIONS

In addition to the differences discussed to this point, cultures are also characterized by a number of internal linguistic variations. These differences are culturally influenced and frequently offer hints as to the nation or region where a person lives or grew up and his or her age, level of education, and socioeconomic status.[20] It is particularly important to have both an awareness of these distinctions and an appreciation of their role in intercultural communication.

Accents

While later we look at those occasions when the participants are speaking different languages, we begin with those countless occasions when English is the language being used by all parties to the transaction. However, we should not be fooled into believing that language problems cannot occur. As Cargile reminds us, "it must be realized that even when interacting people speak the same language, such as English, they don't always speak the same 'language.'"[21] A good example of Cargile's assertion can be found in accented language. Novinger explains an accent and its relationship to intercultural communication in the following, "An accent can range from perfectly native pronunciation (no discernible foreign accent) to pronunciation of the foreign language using the same sounds that the non-native learned in order to speak his or her own mother tongue (a very heavy foreign accent)."[22] As you can tell from Novinger's description, accents can take a variety of forms. These often result from geographical or historical differences, such as those among English speakers in Australia, Canada, England, South Africa, and the United States. In the United States you also often hear regional accents characterized as "Southern," "New England," or "New York."

Accents have the potential to create two problems in intercultural exchanges. First, if the speaker's accent is prominent, comprehension might be impeded. For example, people from the United States might be able to understand an accent used by someone from New England but might encounter a problem with a speaker from India who is speaking English with a Hindi accent. Second, as Schmidt and his coauthors point out, "Speakers may be negatively stereotyped by their accent. Speaking with an accent may create negative impressions with the listener when the speaker's accent differs significantly from that of the dominant group."[23]

Dialect

Closely related to the pronunciation variations that characterize accents is the topic of dialects. Crystal explains the difference between accents and dialects noting, "Accents refers just to distinctive pronunciation, whereas dialect refers to spoken grammar and vocabulary as well."[24] What they have in common is that they are differences in a given language as spoken in a particular location or by a collection of people. English spoken in the United States is characterized by a number of dialects. Most social scientists suggest there are three basic dialects (New England, Southern, Western). However, some estimates range as high as twenty-four when adding dialects of such specific regions as Mid-Atlantic, Northern, Midland, and the like.[25] Add to these Chicano English, Black English Vernacular (BEV), and Hawaiian "pidgin." Considering this large variety of dialects, take a moment and place yourself in the position of an international visitor, using English as a second language, confronted with a group of U.S. Americans speaking several of these dialects.

Dialects not only identify someone as being from a certain region, but also are distinctive of a person's country. And within these countries are even further distinctions. For example, the Japanese, often considered a homogeneous culture, have a number of dialects, and some, like Kagoshima-*ben* and Okinawa-*ben* in the extreme south, are very difficult for other Japanese to understand. Chinese is usually considered to have eight distinct, major dialects (Cantonese, Mandarin, Hakka, etc.) that are bound by a common writing system but are mutually unintelligible when spoken. Indeed, some scholars consider the dialects as separate languages.[26] The most common dialect categories of German are High, Middle, and Low, but there are numerous subdialects of these classifications that are often unintelligible to someone speaking Standard German. There are different dialects of the Spanish language spoken in Spain, such as Andalusian in the south, Castilian in the center, and Galician in the northwest. Significant dialectical differences exist between the Spanish spoken in Europe and that used in North and South America, and most regions have their own unique variations.

In intercultural communication, dialects, like accents, present challenges. One reason is that dialects are often looked down on as people use the dialect to stereotype the speaker. For example, French Canadians believe that European-style French is more sophisticated and intellectual, and Spanish speakers in Barcelona tend to observe their distinctive dialect as superior.

> **REMEMBER THIS**
>
> *In intercultural communication, dialects and accents present challenges. It seems that these two language characteristics can carry negative connotations since some people wrongly use them to stereotype the speaker.*

Argot

People who are members of a co-culture not only share membership, participation, and values as part of their social and cultural communities but also share a common language. In most instances, that language takes the form of argot. Argot is specialized informal language used by people who are affiliated with a particular co-culture. This dedicated vocabulary serves two main purposes. First, it is an in-group and secret language. While "outsiders" may understand the language and even try to use it, it is, nevertheless, part of the domain of the co-culture. Second, the language establishes a strong sense of identity, as it is associated only with members of the co-culture.

In the United States many individuals employ a specialized vocabulary that identifies them as members of a particular co-culture or group, such as surfers, prisoners, street gangs, and such. Members of these groups may employ a specialized vocabulary to obscure the intended meaning or to create a sense of identity. These co-cultures (and others) will often change words and their meanings or invent new words so that "in-group" members can communicate with fellow members while excluding outsiders who might be listening. In this sense, most words of argot are short lived.

Slang

Carl Sandburg once wrote, "Slang is a language which takes off its coat, spits on its hand—and goes to work." The problem in intercultural communication is that slang usually fails to work when the participants are from different cultures. That is, while it is found in nearly every culture and co-culture, slang typically does not cross cultures. Slang designates those nonstandard terms, usually used in instances of informality, which serve as a "means of marking social or linguistic identity."[27] The notion of "marking identity" is at the core of slang in that, as Crystal notes with a clever rhyme, "The chief use of slang is to show you're one of the gang."[28] That "gang" means that slang can be regionally based, associated with a co-culture, or used by groups engaged in a specific endeavor. At one time, slang was considered to be a low form of communication. However, many now agree that slang offers people a kind of alternative second language that allows them to identify and interact with members of an in-group. In addition, using slang can make the user sound novel, witty, and "one of the gang." In any event, slang has been around for centuries and is widely used today.

As we offer you a few examples of slang, it is important to keep in mind that slang, like argot, is always in a state of flux. As Ferraro notes, "Since many slang words are used only for several years before disappearing or becoming incorporated into the standard form of the language, keeping up with current slang trends is difficult."[29] We suggest, therefore, that the few examples shown below might well have vanished by the time you are reading (or at least turning the pages) of this book. Hence, the examples are not nearly as important as the idea that if someone has English as a second language and/or is not a member of the group using the slang, problems can occur. As you read the twenty random examples, imagine someone who knows very little English trying to determine the meaning of each word:

United States

Jerk – Stupid or un-cool person.

Ballistic–Furious.

Fazed–Worried.

Postal – Uncontrollably angry.

Dope–Excellent.

Hassle–Bother.

Zip–Nothing.

Flaky–Unreliable.

Twit–Stupid person.

Wicked–Fantastic.

Britain

Knackered–To be exhausted.

Chuffed–Pleased, very happy.

Peanuts–Something cheap.

Cracking–Stunning.

Shirty–Annoyed.

Get Stuffed–Go away.

Narky–Ill-tempered.

Barmy – Foolish, silly.

Tosh–Nonsense.

Dodgy–Something risky.

Texting

In the past decade a new form of slang has emerged—texting. Texting involves employing a cell phone or some other electronic device to send a message as text. Because it is a kind of instant messaging and saves the users both time and energy, texting has grown in popularity. By some estimates, the average cell phone user sends eighty to one hundred text messages a day. By using acronyms and abbreviations, messages can be sent much faster than by typing out long passages on the keyboard. Those abbreviations now represent a form of slang. The problem is that this new shorthand uses the English alphabet. If someone does not know that alphabet, he or she may not understand the slang. Plus, many of the text abbreviations may contain concepts that are culture specific. Below are a few examples that might be confusing to someone who is not familiar with some of the subtleties of the English language:

ROF–Rolling on the floor.

TMI–Too much information.

BM – Bite me.

SC – Stay cool.

SUX – It sucks.

WTG–Way to go.

ZUP – What's up?

WTF – What the freak?

CUL – See you later.

KIT – Keep in touch.

AMOF – As a matter of fact.

PIR–Parent in room.

Idioms

As we have stressed throughout the last few pages, in much of the world, English is taught as a second language; therefore, you may face countless situations when you are in a country where you are speaking English to someone who might not be as fluent in the language as you. And in the United States, the Census Bureau, as we noted at the beginning of the chapter, points out that English is the second language for over 60.6 million of the people who now live in the country.[30] A major problem non-English-speaking people face, whether in the United States or somewhere else in the world, is that thousands of words and phrases are unique to particular cultures. Idioms fall into that category. In fact, it is estimated that the English language has over 15,000 idioms that native English speakers use on a regular basis. By definition, idioms are a group of words that when used together have a particular meaning different from the sum of the meanings of the individual words in isolation. Hence, idioms are not capable of literal translation. Try to imagine having English as a second language and defining each word of the following on its own because you do not know the cultural meaning of the idiom:

"There are people all over the world who are born with two strikes against them."

"Now just hold your horses."

"Of course it is true, I got it from the grapevine."

"Let's look at the nuts and bolts of the deal."

"We must stop beating our heads against the wall."

"We need to be careful that the tail doesn't wag the dog."

"Do not listen to John—he's got an ax to grind."

"John dropped the ball on this one."

"Just play it by ear."

"You need to get off the dime."

"By continuing with this course of action she is opening a can of worms."

USING LANGUAGE

Language, as we have stressed throughout this chapter, frequently differentiates one culture from another. The British author Freya Stark expressed this thought when she wrote, "Every country has its way of saying things. The important thing is that which lies behind people's words." And what lies behind those words is a reflection of the country's values, beliefs, and countless linguistic "rules." Linguistic "rules" can apply to who talks first, what is a proper topic of conversation, how are interruptions perceived, what is the correct sequencing of subjects for discussion, and how is humor treated. To help you understand the different ways people use their language, we will examine a few select cultures and attempt to demonstrate the links among language, perception, and communication.

English

As mentioned previously, language usage reflects many of the deep structure values of a culture. The directness of a language represents an excellent example of this point. Most members of the dominant U.S. American culture tend to be direct in their communication style. Your own experiences tell you that Americans are rarely reserved. Instead, the language used by most U.S. Americans can be characterized as direct, blunt, frank, and unequivocal. These traits are developed very early in life. Kim elaborates on this idea when she notes,

> From an early age, Americans are encouraged to talk whenever they wish. American parents tend to respect children's opinions and encourage them to express themselves verbally. Schools encourage debates and reward verbal skills. This environment has created people who love to talk and are not afraid to say what they think.[31]

An outgrowth of people seeking to have their opinions heard can be seen in the passion many U.S. Americans have for "talk shows," from Jerry Springer, to Maury Povich, to the hundreds of other programs that allow people to tell others how they feel regarding a wide array of very personal topics. In short, people are willing to talk about anything—just so they can talk. Internet blogs and Twitter are also instances of the desire people have to "be heard."

Another cultural value that is part of U.S. American interaction patterns is how frequently people use "I" in conversation and writing. When constructing your résumé, personal accomplishments and rewards take precedence over group efforts. During communicative interactions, you will probably be more concerned with protecting your own ego than that of others. This encourages U.S. Americans to use a very direct, forthright style of communication that promotes the individuality so valued in the United States. This means that U.S. Americans try to avoid vagueness and ambiguity and get directly to the point. If that means saying "no," they will say "no" without hesitation.

> ## REMEMBER THIS
>
> Linguistic "rules" can determine who talks first, what is a proper topic of conversation, how interruptions are perceived, what is the correct sequencing of subjects for discussion, and how is humor treated.

As briefly noted earlier in this chapter, the English language in other national cultures can vary in usage, vocabulary, and even speaking style. For instance, the British place more emphasis on social status, or class, which can be reflected through one's accent. Additionally, they tend to be more formal, and first names are normally not used until a relationship has been established.

Spanish

An exploration of how the Spanish language is used in Mexico can provide insight into Mexican society and further demonstrate the codependency of language and culture. First, communicative interaction, especially conversation, is an important part of Mexican life, and Mexicans readily engage in casual talk and even delight in wordplay. Condon points out that during interactions, even in business settings, puns, double entendres, and colloquialisms are frequently interjected,[32] which give conversations a feeling of liveliness and warmth. If there are opportunities to engage in talk, the Mexican is ready, even among casual acquaintances. And, as Riding reports, once an emotional bond is established, Mexicans are open and generous, willing to confide and be very hospitable.[33]

The male orientation that characterizes Mexican society, which we discussed in Chapter 3, is evident in the Spanish language use of gendered nouns and pronouns. For instance, men in an all-male group are referred to as *ellos*, and women in an all-female group are *ellas*, the *o* ending denoting masculine and the *a* ending being feminine. However, *ellos* is used for a group of several men and one woman, as well as a gathering of women and one male. Small girls in a group are called *niñas*, but if a boy joins the girls, *niños* is used.

The Spanish use of separate verb conjugations for formal and informal speech also helps Mexicans express the formality that is important in their culture. To understand this distinction, we can look at the pronoun "you." In formal speech, *usted* is used, but when talking to family or friends, or in informal situations, *tú* is more appropriate. Mexicans also employ language as a means of demonstrating reverence, status, and hierarchy. As Crouch notes, "Giving respect for achievement is part of the Mexican linguistic blueprint. Titles such as *ingeniero* (engineer), *profesor* (professor or teacher), *licenciado* (attorney or other professional designation), and others are generously accorded."[34]

Finally, it should be mentioned that "One of the key language use differences between Americans and Mexicans involves direct versus indirect speech."[35]

Therefore, you can observe the Mexican preference for indirectness in their use of language. Interpersonal relationships are very important among Mexicans, and they try to avoid situations that carry the potential for confrontation or loss of face. Their values of indirectness and face-saving are evident in their use of the Spanish language. Direct arguments are considered rude. The Mexican usually attempts to make every interaction harmonious and in so doing may appear to agree with the other person's opinion. In actuality, the Mexican will retain his or her own opinion unless he or she knows the person well or has enough time to explain his or her opinion without causing the other person to lose face. This indirect politeness is often viewed by North Americans as dishonesty and aloof detachment when in actuality it is a sign of individual respect and an opportunity for the other person to save face.

Brazilian Portuguese

Many people assume that Brazilians, because they live in South America, have Spanish as their native language. They do not. The Brazilian national language is Portuguese, which is spoken by 99 percent of the population. It is also one of the strongest components of Brazilian identity and unity. As Novinger points out, "Brazilians are proud of their language and protective of its use, and people who do not know that Brazilians speak Portuguese rather than Spanish label themselves as ignorant."[36] This pride often creates exchanges where a pleasant sound to the word is just as important as what the word is conveying.

The hierarchy found in interpersonal relationships is also a major characteristic of the Brazilian Portuguese language. This hierarchy "governs forms of address such as the use of formal and informal pronouns, names, and titles."[37] This use of language to mark status and rank also applies to the forms of address used to speak to the elderly. Younger people will show respect by "using 'o Senhor' and 'a Senhora' in deference to the person's age, regardless of social rank."[38] Here again, you can detect the link between a culture's values and the use of language.

Northeast Asian

While the languages of China, Korea, and Japan are quite different, there are commonalities in how those respective languages are used. All three nations are considered high-context cultures and commonly employ language in an indirect manner to promote harmony and face-saving measures. At the heart of this approach to communication is the teaching of Confucianism.

Yin develops this point in the following: "The care for harmonious relationships in Confucian teaching steers East Asians away from overreliance on direct communication. Indirect modes of communication are valued precisely because of the concern for the other person's face."[39]

With this style of language use, you can appreciate how politeness takes precedence over truth, which is consistent with the cultural emphasis on maintaining social stability. Members of these three cultures expect their communication partners to be able to recognize the intended meaning more from the context than the actual words used. The languages of the Northeast Asian cultures also reflect the need for formality and hierarchy. This

CONSIDER THIS

What are some important ways that a culture's values might influence a culture's use of language?

orientation varies sharply from the more direct, informal, low-context speech common among U.S. Americans. This contrast is, in part, a result of varying perceptions of the reason for communication. In Northeast Asia, communication is used to reduce one's selfishness and egocentrism. This is diametrically opposite to the Western perspective that views communication as a way to increase one's esteem and guard personal interests.[40] To provide more insight, we will examine some specific examples of the similarities between how Chinese, Korean, and Japanese are used.

Chinese. Wenzhong and Grove suggest that the three most fundamental values of Chinese culture are (1) collectivism or a group orientation, (2) intergroup harmony, and (3) societal hierarchy.[41] The latter two values are easily discernible in Chinese language use. For instance, the focus on social status and position among the Chinese is of such importance that it also shapes how individuals communicatively interact. Accordingly, a deferential manner is commonly used when addressing an authority figure.[42] Widespread use of titles is another way of demonstrating respect and formality in Chinese culture. Among family members given names are usually replaced with a title, such as "younger" or "older" brother, which reflects that individual's position within the family.[43]

The Chinese exhibit the importance of in-group social stability, or harmony, through a number of different communication protocols. Rather than employing precise language, as is done in the United States, the Chinese will be vague and indirect, which leaves the listener to discern the meaning.[44] Conflict situations among in-groups will be avoided when possible, and intermediaries are used to resolve disputes. Any criticism will be issued in an indirect manner.[45] The concern for others' face can be pervasive, and to demonstrate humility, Chinese will frequently engage in self-deprecation and attentively listen to others, especially seniors or elders.[46]

Korean. The cultural values of (1) collectivism, (2) status, and (3) harmony are also prevalent in the way Koreans use language. For instance, the family represents the strongest in-group among Koreans, and a common way of introducing one's parent is to say "this is our mother/father" rather than using the pronoun "my." This demonstrates the Korean collective orientation by signaling that one's family is a comprehensive unit, encompassing parents and siblings, extending beyond self-considerations.[47] Status is another important cultural value, and one's position as a senior or a junior will dictate the appropriate communication style. As a result, Koreans will use small talk in an effort to ascertain each other's hierarchical position.[48]

In addition, it is considered improper behavior to address high status people by name when in the presence of lower-status people. This contact ignores the position of the person being addressed. Another manifestation of status and formality among Koreans can be seen in the fact that they "distinguish five distinct styles of formality, each with a different set of inflectional endings, address terms, pronouns, lexical items, honorific prefixes and suffixes, particles, among others."[49]

Because Korea is a high-context culture, communicative interactions are often characterized by indirectness, with the meaning embedded in the context of how something is expressed rather than what is actually said. For example, instead of asking a subordinate to work on a project over the weekend, a Korean manager may say, "The success of this project is important to the company, and we cannot miss the deadline."

Japanese. As with China and Korea, Japan is a (1) high-context, (2) hierarchical culture with a distinct group orientation and (3) stresses social harmony. These cultural characteristics are manifest in the Japanese language, which is highly contextual and often ambiguous. There are many words that have identical pronunciations and written form but quite different meanings. For instance, *sumimasen* can mean "excuse me," "sorry," or "thank you" or can be used simply to attract someone's attention. The listener is left to determine the meaning from the context. *Osoi* is another word that has dual meanings ("slow" or "late") but is written and pronounced identically. Japanese verbs come at the end of sentences, which impedes a full understanding until the sentence has been completed and allows the speaker to gauge listeners' reactions before deciding on which verb form to use.

Social position, or status, is an important consideration among the Japanese and is evident in their use of language. One's social position will determine the type of language and choice of words to use during every interaction. Even within "the family, older children are addressed by younger ones with a term meaning 'older sister' or 'older brother,' sometimes as a suffix to their names."[50] Also within the family, women will use more honorific words than men. Within the business context, juniors will employ polite speech when addressing their seniors, who may reply with informal speech. Terms of address are also determined by one's hierarchical positioning. Given names are rarely used between Japanese, who prefer to use last names followed by a suffix term that is determined by the type or level of the relationship. Professor Mari Suzuki's students, for example, would call her Suzuki *sensei* (teacher), and she would refer to the students by their last name and the *-san* (Mr. or Ms.) suffix. There are many other hierarchically determined suffix terms used with an individual's name. In addition to the Japanese concern for social position, this practice also indicates that Japan is a formal culture.

As is the case with the previous two cultures we examined, social harmony is a hallmark of Japanese interactions. Both Buddhism and Confucianism teach that in human relationships, it is crucial that harmony be maintained and that one's use of language not be acrimonious.

One expression of this value is that there is less personal information being exchanged about people. As Barnlund points out, "This tendency toward limited disclosure, combined with a desire to avoid or absorb differences, promotes the harmony so valued in the Japanese culture."[51]

Arabic

Linguistic identity within Arab culture transcends ethnic origins, national borders, and with certain exceptions (e.g., Coptic, Jewish), religious affiliation.[52] Among Arabs, "anyone whose mother tongue is Arabic" is considered an Arab. Thus, language is what defines and unites the greater Arab community. The importance placed on language is, in part, a function of their history. Recall from Chapter 5 that the early Arabs developed cultural expressions, such as poetry and storytelling, which were suited to their nomadic life. This long love affair with their language has created a strong belief that Arabic is "God's language," and as such, Arabs treat their language with great respect and admiration. Nydell provides an insightful summation of the prominence of language among Arabs: "The Arabic language is their greatest cultural treasure and achievement, an art form that unfortunately cannot be accessed or appreciated by outsiders."[53] Arabs see their language as possessing a powerful emotional content. There is even an ancient Arab proverb that highlights that power: "A man's tongue is his sword."

Arabs employ language in a dynamic, direct fashion that is often elaborate and forceful.

© Jim West/PhotoEdit

Arabs approach their language as a "social conduit in which emotional resonance is stressed," which contrasts with the Western view that language is a means of transferring information.[54] Because of this orientation the Arab language contains a rich vocabulary and well-rounded, complex phrases that permit educated and illiterate alike to have a strong mastery of their language. Words are often used for their own sake rather than for what they are understood to mean. This creates a situation where assertion, repetition, and exaggeration are used with regularity. It also means that whereas a U.S. American can express an idea in ten words, the Arabic speaker may use one hundred.

In Chapter 3 we indicated that Arab societies are characterized by the cultural values of collectivism, hierarchy, and a present orientation, which are mirrored in how Arabic is used. As with nearly every collective society, social harmony among in-group members is valued among Arabs, who rely on indirect, ambiguous statements to lessen the potential for loss of face during interactions.[55] While employing indirectness to ensure smooth relations, Arabs will often appeal to the listener's emotions. The noisy, animated speech often associated with the Arab communication style is normally limited to interactions with social peers. When engaging elders or superiors, "polite deference is required,"[56] which demonstrates the value placed on hierarchy. Arabs also tend to focus more on the present and consider future events with some degree of incertitude. This attitude is evident in the frequent use of *inshallah* (if God wills) when discussing future events. Additionally, when connected to some action, the phrase can be used to indicate "yes" but at an unspecified future time, "no" in order to avoid personal responsibility, or an indirect "never."[57]

German

The German people represent yet another culture that takes great pride in its language. Historically, you will find that many of the world's great achievements were first conceived and delivered in the German language. Be it music, opera, literature, science, or other fields of endeavor, the German language was the vehicle that revealed these creations and discoveries to the world. As is the case with all cultures, the Germans also have their unique way of using language. This uniqueness shows itself in their approach to (1) formality, (2) concern for detail, and (3) directness.

In German culture, special forms of address are employed when conducting business. One feature deals with formality. As Hall and Hall point out, "Germans are very conscious of their status and insist on proper forms of address."[58] This desire for formality not only is used in the business context but also can be found when communicating among close relationships. Germans almost always address people by their last name. They even make a distinction between the formal you (*Sie*) and the familiar (*du*). You can also observe the link between language and formality in the fact that if someone inquires about an individual's name, the person being asked usually offers his or her last name. This desire to remain formal when using language can also be seen in how Germans perceive and cope with conflict. If and when conflicts do arise, Germans generally avoid them "not by emphasizing harmony in personal relationships or by smoothing over differences of opinion, but rather by maintaining formality and social distance."[59]

Another major characteristic of German language use can be found in the degree to which they detail when they speak. That is, "Germans provide much more information than most people from other cultures require."[60] According to Ness, "This leads to an explicit style of speech in which precision of expression, exactness of definition, and literalness play important parts."[61] Not only do Germans employ great detail, but they also tend to ask the people they are interacting with to supply detail. As Morrison and Conaway note, "Germans will ask every question you can imagine and some you can't."[62]

German fondness for directness is actually an extension of our last two explanations of the German language. Because Germans are rather straightforward, they often appear to be very blunt and direct—and they are. They will get to the point quickly during conversations and assume others will do the same. They will ask you directly "for the facts." In many ways, according to Ness, their directness is related to their desire for clarity. We urge you not to be misled by their directness. Germans are a very polite and caring people.

INTERPRETING

In a world in which 80 percent of the world's translated books are in English[63] and half of the world's population speaks that language,[64] it seems that learning a foreign language is no longer a major necessity—but it is. As noted previously, the impact of globalization on the world community presents all of us with countless situations that demand the use of an interpreter. The importance of interpreting in our globalized, multicultural society is exemplified by the requirements of the European Union. Today, the European Union, with its twenty-eight country members, must manage meetings and correspondence in its twenty-four official languages[65] as well as several others, such as Arabic, Chinese, and Russian. While the United Nations has only six official languages (Arabic, Chinese, English, French, Russian, and Spanish), it utilizes over 190 interpreters. International agencies are not the only government groups where you might deal with interpreters. For example, the Judicial Council of California reports that its court system maintains a pool of interpreters representing

The need to use and to understand how to work with interpreters is central in the business, healthcare, and educational settings.

© Kayte Deioma/PhotoEdit

over 147 languages.[66] Yet the U.S. Department of Justice ruled in 2013 that the County of Los Angeles and California's Judicial Council were violating the Civil Rights Act by not providing free interpreters in all court proceedings.[67] There is clearly a pressing need for interpreters in the civil court system.

The same need for interpreters occurs in both the healthcare and business setting. For example, a recent article in the *Los Angeles Times* reported that the California legislature was proposing a bill intended to deal with language barriers in the health-care context by adding more interpreters. The rationale behind the bill was that "People with limited English proficiency face a higher risk of being misdiagnosed or receiving unnecessary treatments that could hasten their deaths."[68] The need to use and to understand how to work with interpreters is central to any multinational cor-poration. As Rudd and Lawson note, "Even though more and more businesspeople around the world speak English, most people are more comfortable speaking in their native language. Thus, including an interpreter as part of your negotiation team is a wise decision."[69] We are suggesting that in today's multicultural society, the presence of interpreters is common. As noted, interpreters are frequently used in healthcare centers, courtrooms, business conferences, and even classrooms.

We should mention early in our analysis that the terms "translating" and "inter-preting" are often confused. Translators work with written material and have the advantage of being able to consult references if needed and are not subject to the same time constraints as interpreters, as interpreters deal with spoken and signed lan-guage. Because interpreting is usually in "real time," not delayed, it is often not as accurate as translating. In addition, interpreters are usually required to be familiar with the cultures of both the original language and the target language. This means they need an extensive vocabulary and must be ready to make quick decisions.

The two most common forms of interpreting are consecutive or simultaneous. *Con-secutive* interpreting is most often used in high-level private activities, business meet-ings, and small, informal gatherings. In this method, the speaker will talk for a short time and then stop to allow the interpreter to convey the message to the other party. *Simultaneous* interpretation uses audio equipment, with the interpreter located in a soundproof booth away from the participants. This is a much more demanding method because the speaker does not pause, which requires the interpreter to listen and speak simultaneously. In each method, a high degree of fluency in the target languages is obviously necessary.

Because this book is basically about face-to-face communication, we will deal with interpretation rather than translating because, as noted, it implies changing oral or signed messages from one language into another. Awareness of this difference is especially important when interacting with organizations that must continually manage information in two or more languages.

> **REMEMBER THIS**
>
> *An interpreter works with spoken or signed language. A translator works with written text.*

CULTURAL CONSIDERATIONS IN INTERPRETING

The process of interpretation is much more complicated than merely taking a word from one language and replacing it with one from another language. There are numerous cultural considerations that come into play. Often, there is no single word equivalent, or the word may have a different meaning in another language. *Football*, for instance, means something quite different in Europe and South America than in the United States or Canada. In the United States, the suggestion to "discuss" something connotes a desire to talk over a topic in a mutually agreeable, friendly manner, but in Spanish, "*discusión*" implies a more intense, discordant attitude. A humorous example of the effect of the lack of an equivalent for an entire sentence took place in China when the KFC slogan "Finger Lickin' Good" was translated as "Eat Your Fingers Off."

Although the last example might be a bit humorous, there are countless other instances when words, ideas, and concepts cannot be translated directly. Strong affection is expressed in English with the verb "to love." In Spanish, there are two verbs that may be translated into English as "to love": *amar* and *querer*. *Amar* refers to nurturing love, as between a parent and child or between two adults. *Te quiero* translates literally as "I want you" or "I desire you," a concept not present in the English expression "I love you." Commonly used to express love between two adults, *te quiero* falls somewhere between the English statements "I love you" and "I like you." Another example of direct translation difficulties occurs with the Spanish language as spoken in Mexico. Mexican Spanish has at least five terms indicating agreement in varying degrees. These include *me comprometo* (I promise or commit myself), *te aseguro* (I assure you), *sí, como no, lo hago* (yes, sure, I will do it), *tal vez lo haría* (maybe I will do it), and *tal vez lo haga* (perhaps I might do it). The problem, of course, is to understand the differences between *me comprometo* and *tal vez lo haga*. Misunderstandings and confusions may arise if we simply translate each of these phrases of agreement as "okay." Earlier in the chapter, we pointed out that some cultures (e.g., Chinese, Japanese, and Korean) rely on an indirect communication style, and others (e.g., the United States) use a straightforward, direct style. These style differences influence the translation of many words and phrases. For example, in cross-cultural negotiations with a U.S. group, representatives from one of the Northeast Asian countries might respond to a request with "maybe," "I will try my best," or "we will have to consider this" to signal a negative reply. In this case, a literal translation devoid of any cultural nuances can be potentially misleading. Members of the U.S. team are conditioned to hearing a more direct reply, such as a simple "no" or even "that is out of the question." Thus, they could easily misconstrue a literal interpretation to be a positive reply.

Many other examples may be offered when the translation process can alter the meaning of what is being said. The Spanish word *ahora* offers a specific instance of what we are referring to. Among Spanish speakers, the common meaning is that something will be done within a few minutes to several hours. However, the word is usually translated into English as "now," which implies immediately or right away. To add greater urgency, the Spanish speaker in Mexico would use *ahorita* or *ahoritita*. But in Venezuela or Costa Rica, to indicate that the action will be immediate, the word used might be "*ahoritico.*" So, even *within* the Spanish language, there are major linguistic differences among what is used in Spain, South America, Central America, Mexico, and other Spanish-speaking nations. These variations are so great that it is impossible to translate any given passage in a way that would suit all of the parties.

It is obvious that translation tasks require an extensive awareness of cultural factors. As an illustration, if translating a Japanese novel into English, the translator would need to be aware of contemporary colloquialisms and slang. For example, if the novel mentions a large truck (*oki torakku*), it could become "eighteen-wheeler" or "semi" in American English, but in the United Kingdom, "articulated lorry" would be a more appropriate term. Similarly, if the Japanese novel mentioned an "American dog" (*Amerikan doggu*), the Australian version would use "Dagwood Dog," and the U.S. adaptation would be "corn dog."

Equivalency problems across cultures are not only common with single or multiple words but also on countless occasions when the issue or concept that is being translated is without an equivalent. One case involves the Dalai Lama. When two American psychologists asked the Dalai Lama, who speaks perfect English, to discuss the topic of low self-esteem at a conference, the Dalai Lama told them that he would be delighted but that he did not know what low self-esteem meant. Although the two Americans tried in a variety of ways to explain the concept to the Dalai Lama, he continued to be confused. After countless examples and detailed explanations, the Dalai Lama said he now understood what they were trying to say. He added, however, that the reason he was having trouble with what the Americans were trying to say was that in his culture, people did not think poorly of themselves and, therefore, had no concept of low self-esteem. In this example, you see yet another difficulty in translation—difficulties that deal with a lack of matching concepts.

WORKING WITH INTERPRETERS

As stressed throughout this chapter, interactions with people from other cultures speaking different languages continue to increase. Hence, the ability to work through an interpreter becomes essential if your message is to be conveyed correctly. Use of an interpreter involves establishing a three-way rapport among you, the interpreter, and the audience. Thus, it is important to select an interpreter or translator who best suits your particular situation. The following are some of the more important considerations.

Preparing for the Session

Being prepared for an encounter that uses the services of an interpreter entails a series of important steps: (1) Locate someone with whom you are comfortable. This usually means a person who is neither domineering nor timid. (2) The individual you select needs to be completely bilingual. Moreover, this knowledge should encompass contemporary usage that includes metaphors, slang, and idioms. The person should also be aware of the problems inherent in the use of humor, as jokes usually do not translate well. (3) Be sure that the interpreter is aware of any specialized terminology to be employed. The specialized terminology used in different fields can be very confusing to an outsider. Therefore, it is essential that an interpreter or translator be well versed in the terms, jargon, and acronyms of the topic being addressed. For instance, an interpreter unfamiliar with medical terminology would be an impediment to effective intercultural communication in a healthcare setting. How might they translate "copayment," or "HMO"? (4) In addition, the individual should also have a facility in any dialect that might come into play. While this may seem minor, during the 2010 Gulf of Mexico oil spill, to work with the Vietnamese-speaking residents of the Gulf area, BP hired interpreters who spoke a North Vietnamese dialect and used what was considered "Communist terminology." This created a situation that caused the Gulf Coast Vietnamese, who were originally from South Vietnam, to mistrust the interpreters. (5) There is a growing recognition that interpreters and translators must be culturally competent, and this requires knowledge of their own culture as well as that of the target language culture. (6) Decide long before the actual event if the interpreter is to use *simultaneous* or *consecutive* interpreting. Simultaneous interpretation is usually employed in large settings. The interpreter typically sits in a soundproof booth or room wearing a set of earphones and offers the interpretation of the target language into a microphone.

One of the central elements of this form of interpreting is the interpreter's ability to be decisive, as the response to what is said is almost instantaneous. In consecutive interpretation the interpreter, who often takes notes, waits for the speaker to conclude a sentence or an idea and then delivers the speaker's words into the target language. The wait between the speaker's original words and the interpreter's response can vary from thirty seconds to five minutes. Consecutive interpretation is normally found in situations involving a small number of people. It is well suited to business meetings, interviews, teleconferences, or any form of one-on-one exchanges.

During the Session

(1) One of the first and most important rules in using an interpreter deals with the speed at which you will talk. Interpreting is a demanding and mentally exhausting assignment. Hence, your interpreter will be pleased and can do a better job if you do not rush, use short sentences, and pause often. (2) While speaking through an interpreter, remember that he or she is not the "audience" you should be directing your remarks to. Although you may not know what he or she is saying, you must show an interest in the people you are addressing. This means using eye contact and even appropriate facial expressions. (3) Remember the importance of feedback. What we mean is that you must be aware of the "audience's" (be it one person or one hundred) response to the interpreter. If they appear to be confused, slow down or even pause for

REMEMBER THIS

Why has it become important to learn how to speak using an interpreter?

questions. (4) Allow for some rest periods for the interpreter. As you might well imagine, interpreting takes a great deal of intense concentration.

INTERPRETING AND TECHNOLOGY

There is little doubt that technology has increased and changed the way people throughout the world "talk" to each other. From cell phones (6.8 billion users) to the Internet (3 billion users), technology has brought cultures closer together. In fact, one of the themes we have carried in and out of nearly every chapter is that new technology has greatly enhanced the ability of people around to world to easily and quickly "connect" with others. One technological innovation is software for computer-aided human interpreting. This new "tool," developed by Microsoft, allows people who are speaking different languages to communicate over video with real-time translation. More specifically, this "new feature, called Skype Translator, will let you talk in your native language to a user who speaks a different language and instantly translates the conversation."[70] This innovative device can be employed in business and government settings. It could also aid students in learning a new language. For example, it can provide some sample foreign words and phrases in a person's own voice instead of a mechanical reproduction. This would make it much easier to imitate.

Microsoft admits that the device is not fully developed and has some problems that they continue to work on. Part of the difficulty lies in a machine's inability to detect the subtle aspects of language, such as emotions and sarcasm, which can be conveyed by the way words are *used* rather than the actual words. Moreover, machines cannot interpret nonverbal communication. Yet even with these drawbacks, the potential for accurate real-time translation holds great promise for the future.[71]

DEVELOPING LANGUAGE COMPETENCE IN THE INTERCULTURAL SETTING

We begin this section on competency by reminding you of two important points stressed earlier in the chapter. First, we again call your attention to the truism that words are only symbols and can never be precise, as they mean different things to different people. This, of course, demands that you be especially vigilant in how you use words. Second, almost every intercultural communication interaction involves one or more individuals relying on a second language. Thus, it is impossible for us to discuss all of the many scenarios where language is used to create understanding. Later in the book, we devote an entire chapter to intercultural communication interactions in business, healthcare, and education contexts and discuss a broad spectrum of factors that influence understanding. But here we want to acquaint you with some general measures relating to language use that can enhance your intercultural communication competence.

LEARN A SECOND LANGUAGE

Charlemagne, the emperor who around 771 CE sought to unite all the German people, once noted, "To have another language is to possess a second soul." We are not sure how a second language would influence your soul, but we do know that learning a second language will give you insight into another culture. It could also assist you in coping with culture shock since it may reduce undue irritations and misunderstandings. Admittedly, learning another language can be extremely demanding, requiring considerable time and effort. However, the advantages are so numerous as to make the effort worthwhile. Not only does knowledge of a second language help you communicate with other people and even see the world differently, it also tells the native speakers that you are interested in them and their culture. As Crystal reminds us, "Languages should be thought of as national treasures, and treated accordingly."[72] Learning and using another language can also help you better express yourself or explain certain concepts or items. Lal, a native Hindi speaker, explains that English, his second language, has no "words for certain kinds of [Hindi] relationships and the cultural assumptions and understandings which go with them."[73] Wong, who speaks Chinese (both Mandarin and Cantonese) and English, echoes this: "Relying only on English, I often cannot find words to convey important meanings found in Chinese."[74] Thus, learning a second language can provide greater insight into the emotions and values of another culture, which will increase your intercultural understanding and competence, and also provide a greater awareness of cultural influences in general.

A Belgian businessman explained that one of the first questions asked during employment interviews is, "Do you speak languages?"[75] This priority is a product of Belgium's small geographical size, which creates a need for international commerce, and as a member of the European Union. In many ways the language ability that the people of Belgium need to effectively interact within the greater sphere of the European Union is a microcosm of globalization. As world society becomes more interconnected and more integrated, there is a corresponding need to speak more than one language. While bilingualism is official in only a small number of nations—such as Switzerland, Belgium, India, and Canada—it is practiced in almost every country.[76] The criticality of language to successful interactions in a globalized world is seen in the European Commission's intent of "encouraging all citizens to be multilingual, with the long-term objective that every citizen has practical skills in at least two languages in addition to his or her mother tongue."[77] A similar objective was voiced on the other side of the world by the Japanese Minister of Education, Culture, Sports, Science and Technology (MEXT), "Since we are living in a globalized society, I am keenly aware of the necessity of children acquiring the ability to communicate in foreign languages."[78]

BE MINDFUL

While we have used the phrase "being mindful" elsewhere in the book, it is worth examining again as it applies to language. As we noted in Chapter 4, "The cultivation of mindfulness has roots in Buddhism, but most religions include some type of prayer or meditation technique that helps shift your thoughts away from your usual preoccupations toward an appreciation of the moment."[79] It is that concentration on the moment that, as Gudykunst notes, allows the person to create new categories, become receptive to new information, and realize that other people may not share your perspective.[80] Creating new categories means moving beyond the broad, general classifications you may have been using for many years. As an example, instead of categorizing someone as an Asian, you should try to form a more specific classification that considers gender, age, national and regional identity, occupation, and such (e.g., "a young Chinese male college student from Beijing"). Being receptive to new information may mean something as simple as learning that some people consider horsemeat a delicacy or do not wear shoes inside their homes. Yet learning about different perspectives can also be as complicated as trying to understand why another culture sees nothing wrong in bribing government officials or aborting a fetus because it is not male.

Being mindful can also entail being aware that using a second language is more physically and cognitively demanding than speaking one's native language. During a conversation, someone speaking a second language must be more alert to what the other person is saying and how it is being said. They must simultaneously think about how to respond. Depending on the degree of fluency, this may require the second language speaker to mentally convert the received message into his or her native language, prepare a response in the native language, and then cognitively translate that response into the second language. If their second language vocabulary is limited, the cognitive demands are even greater. This difficulty is increased if the second language speaker is unfamiliar with the native speaker's accent. Plus, as is the case in all communication encounters, distractions occur. This means that the second language speaker is confronted with a much greater mental task than the native speaker. This cognitive process can produce both mental and physical fatigue. Thus, the native speaker must be alert for signs that the second language speaker is tiring.[81] Should this be the case, you should make an effort to be specific, be patient, and even ask if your "partner" needs clarification regarding something you said.

> ## REMEMBER THIS
>
> *Cultural differences regarding conversation can be seen in how conversations are opened and terminated, how participants take turns talking, how silence is used, reactions to being interrupted, and what subjects are taboo when interacting with "strangers."*

BE AWARE OF CONVERSATIONAL TABOOS

We have just finished talking about being mindful as a special kind of awareness. Part of that awareness involves being sensitive in the words you select. We make this recommendation because all cultures have taboos related to the use of language. As Ferraro points out, "All linguistic communities have certain topics of conversation, *conversational taboos*, that are considered inappropriate in either polite conversation or in a business setting."[82] Crystal tells us that a culture's verbal taboos generally relate "to sex, the supernatural, excretion, and death, but quite often they extend to other aspects of domestic and social life."[83]

From personal experience you know that at first meetings, whether for business or pleasure, people usually engage in "small talk" as a way of getting to know each another. However, the choice of topics discussed during these meetings must follow established cultural norms. In intercultural interactions this requires that you learn which topics are acceptable and which are taboo. In the United States early conversations often center on the weather or some aspect of the physical setting, such as the scenery or furnishings in a room. As the interaction becomes more comfortable, topics relating to sports, food, or travel may be discussed.[84] If both parties continue the conversation, which is a positive sign, they begin gathering information about each other through personal questions related to likes and dislikes and family matters. For U.S. American businesspersons personal questions are not actually considered taboo in the business context. Hence, you might hear the most well-intentioned U.S. citizen ask questions such as "What do you do?" "How long have you been with your company?" or "Do you have a family?" But those personal topics are considered taboo in many cultures. For example, in Saudi Arabia, asking about a person's family can cause considerable offense.[85] Discussions of politics with "strangers" in Germany and Iran can also be taboo.[86] People in Chile, Argentina, and Venezuela also are uncomfortable talking about political issues.[87]

BE ATTENTIVE TO YOUR SPEECH RATE

One problem encountered by second language speakers, and as we noted earlier when discussing using an interpreter, is that native speakers often talk quite rapidly. For example, if you are interacting with someone who is using English as a second language, you cannot automatically assume that he or she is completely fluent. Therefore, until the other person's level of language competence is determined, you should speak a bit more slowly and distinctly than you normally do. By closely monitoring feedback from the second language speaker, you can adjust your speech rate accordingly. It is also important to look in the direction of the other person, as this can aid in understanding a second language.

BE CONSCIOUS OF DIFFERENCES IN VOCABULARY

Determining the second language speaker's vocabulary level is also important. Until you are sure that the other person has the requisite second language ability, avoid professional vocabulary, technical words, acronyms, and words with multiple meanings. In a healthcare setting, instead of using "inflammation," it might be more effective to say, "The area will get red and a little sore." Metaphors, slang, and colloquialisms can also impede understanding and should not be used. In the United States, for instance, the phrase "we are on a parallel course" is used to indicate that you agree with the other party's proposal. However, in Japan it means that the proposal will never be accepted because parallel lines never meet. In addition, please recall our earlier warning that humor does not travel well across cultures.

ATTEND TO NONVERBAL BEHAVIOR

When interacting with a second language user, you need to be alert to the individual's nonverbal responses. This can provide cues about your speech rate, type of vocabulary, and whether the individual understands what you are saying. Moreover, in an intercultural situation you need to be aware of cultural differences in nonverbal cues, which will be discussed more in depth in Chapter 9. For instance, if your Japanese counterpart is giggling at something you said that you know is not humorous, it might be a signal that your message is not fully understood. At the same time you should expect a second language speaker to exhibit unfamiliar nonverbal behaviors. Standing farther apart than you are used to, being less demonstrative, refraining from smiling, or avoiding direct eye contact may be normal nonverbal behaviors in their culture.

USE "CHECKING" DEVICES

By "checking" (often referred to as seeking feedback), we mean that you should employ measures to help ensure that your intercultural partner understands your messages. If you feel the second language speaker is having difficulty comprehending something said, simply say, "Let me say that another way," and rephrase your statement. Also, while checking for understanding, try to do so from a subordinate position. That is, instead of asking, "Do you understand?" which places the burden on the other person, ask, "Am I being clear?" In this manner you take responsibility for the conversation and lessen the potential for embarrassing the other person. This can be of considerable importance when interacting with someone from a culture where face is highly valued. Another means of checking is to write out a few words of the message you are trying to convey. Some people's second language reading skills may be greater than their listening ability.

BE AWARE OF CULTURAL VARIATIONS IN THE USE OF LANGUAGE

Throughout this chapter the idea was reiterated that while the ability to use language is a universal trait, that attribute as acted out is rooted in culture. Hence, you should be aware of some of the following cultural differences: (1) how conversations are opened and terminated, (2) how the participants take turns talking, (3) the importance of silence in interaction, (4) reaction to being interrupted, (5) knowing what are appropriate and inappropriate topics of conversation with "strangers," and (6) the sequencing of topics from specific to general or general to specific.

SUMMARY

- Language allows people to exchange information and abstract ideas, and it is an integral part of identity.

- Language is a set of shared symbols used to create meaning. The words that people use are not only symbolic, but the relationship between the symbol and the meaning is often arbitrary. Symbols can evoke both denotative and connotative meanings.

- A culture's use of language influences how that culture perceives the world and communicates within that world.

- There are usually variations within language groups, such as accents, dialects, argot, and slang.

- Cultures differ in how people use language as can be seen in an examination of English, Spanish, Brazilian Portuguese, Chinese, Korean, Japanese, Arabic, and German.

- Interpreters work with spoken or signed language and translators work with written messages. Consecutive interpretation is when you stop every minute or so to allow the interpreter to relay your message in the other language. Simultaneous interpretation is done while the speakers are talking in their native language. A good interpreter should have knowledge of the target language, dialect, special terminology, and culture.

- New technologies have changed the ways people can now interpret different languages.

- Every culture has conversational taboos—restrictions against some topics in certain contexts.

- Competence in using language in an intercultural context can be improved if you learn a second language, are mindful of the surroundings, are aware of conversation taboos, monitor your speech rate, are aware of vocabulary differences and nonverbal feedback, and are responsive to variations in conversation styles.

ACTIVITIES

1. Take four different English proper nouns (other than someone's name) and use online translation dictionaries to translate each noun into five different European languages. Do some of the translated nouns have a resemblance to the English nouns? If so, what are some possible reasons?

2. Find someone who is of a culture that uses the type of indirect communication we discussed in the chapter. Ask that person to note some of the difficulties he or she often experiences when speaking with people who employ a direct communication style.

3. Talk with two or three people over sixty years of age and ask them for some examples of the slang they used in their younger days (e.g., "groovy man"). Try to compare it with slang that is popular now. You can also do this by watching a movie made before 1960.

4. Meet with one or two speakers of English as a second language to identify the kinship terms they use in their native language (e.g., mother, brother, aunt). Do they have kinship terms that vary with age differences? Do their kinship terms differ between their own kin and others' kin? What cultural values do you think their terms reflect?

5. An Internet search for "Where is the Speaker From?" should take you to the PBS website regional dialect quiz. Take the quiz. Explore the "Do You Speak American" site for additional information on U.S dialects. The quiz is at http://www.pbs.org/speak/seatosea/americanvarieties/map/map.html (accessed June 18, 2015).

6. To become aware of the multiple meanings found in most words, meet in a group with a number of people who have English as their second language. Ask them to give as many meanings as they can for the following words: comb, dart, bank, bark, bright, lap, jam, spring, rock, toast, point, place, board, block, swallow, ruler, wave, and miss.

CONCEPTS AND QUESTIONS

1. What is meant by the phrase "Language influences our view of reality"?

2. What images come to mind when you hear someone speaking English with an accent? Do different accents create different images? Try to decide why you form those images? Talk with others to see if they have the same experience.

3. Some countries have an official language (or languages), but others do not. What are the advantages and disadvantages of a country having an official language? Should the United States have an official language? Why?

4. Some scholars think the world is moving toward an "oligarchy" of major economic power languages. Do you think this would be a good or a bad occurrence? Why? What will happen to minority languages, and what will be the result?

5. Do you believe technology helps or hinders intercultural communication?

6. What techniques can you employ that will assist you when you are in a situation that is employing an interpreter?

CHAPTER 9

Nonverbal Communication: The Messages of Action, Space, Time, and Silence

Do not the most moving moments of our lives find us all without words?

MARCEL MARCEAU

The power of communication to draw others near or to drive them away derives as much from how we appear as from the language we deploy.

CAROLINE KEATING

Sometimes one creates a dynamic impression by saying something, and sometimes one creates as significant an impression by remaining silent.

THE DALAI LAMA

The alarm clock on your iPhone tells you that this day you thought would never come has finally arrived. After more than four years of life as a university student, graduation day is only weeks away. It's the end of late-night cram sessions, mass lecture classes, endless meals of instant ramen, and part-time employment. Life begins today! (You hope.) Your first interview at the company went well, and today's follow-up is the final hurdle before being offered your dream job. Knowing the importance of making a good first impression and recalling what you learned about nonverbal messages in a communication class, you pay particular attention to every detail of your appearance. After showering and a quick glance in the mirror, you begin to wonder about your short beard. After a moment of reflection, including a fleeting thought about selling your soul to corporate America, off goes the beard, followed by a dash of aftershave for that clean scent. Next come the freshly ironed shirt, new tie, and the shined business shoes. As you pick up your new leather briefcase and head for the door, your roommate offers a "thumbs-up" for good luck.

At precisely 9:20 A.M., right after placing a small breath mint into your mouth, you enter the building, approach the receptionist and inform her that you are there for a 9:30 appointment. Ten minutes later, you are ushered into a large, carpeted corner office. An engraved nameplate on the elegant oak desk lets you know this is the office of the executive vice president for human resources. The smartly dressed woman seated behind the desk smiles, rises, and walks around to meet you. Returning the smile, you step forward and firmly grasp her outstretched hand to signal your self-confidence. With a nod of her head, she invites you to sit in a comfortable chair while she takes a seat in another chair across the coffee table from you. The interview is about to begin.

This hypothetical (and perhaps exaggerated) episode was intended to demonstrate a few of the many and subtle ways nonverbal communication affects your life. In our little drama, it was assumed that the interviewer would have positive responses to your nonverbal "messages" of punctuality, grooming, apparel, expression, handshake, odor, and the like. But would these same behaviors be as successful if you were applying for a position in another country? The answer is *no*. Our negative response can perhaps be better explained with a few examples to demonstrate that misinterpreting the nonverbal actions of people of different cultures is common.

Arab men often greet by kissing on both cheeks. In Japan, men and women greet by exchanging bows. Remember that the interviewer greeted you with a simple handshake. In Thailand, to signal another person to come near, one wags one's fingers back and forth with the palm down. You will recall that the interviewer sent you a beckoning message with her palm facing up. In Vietnam, that same motion is reserved for someone attempting to summon a dog. In Italy and various Arab countries, it is not uncommon for people to be thirty minutes tardy for an appointment. And there you were, making sure you were on time for your interview! Tongans sit down in the presence of superiors; in the West, you stand up, as you did with the interviewer. Crossing one's legs in the United States is often a sign of being relaxed; in Korea, it is a social taboo. In Japan, gifts are usually exchanged with both hands. Muslims consider the left hand unclean and do not eat or pass objects with it. The simple thumbs-up used in the United States to say "okay" is an offensive gesture in Nigeria. The Buddha maintained that great insights arrived during moments of silence. In the United States, people talk to arrive at the truth.

All of the examples to this point were presented for three reasons. First, we wanted to pique your interest in the subject of nonverbal communication. Second, we used our examples to underscore the importance of nonverbal communication in human interaction. Or, as Descartes noted, "To know what people think, pay regard to what they do, rather than what they say." Finally, we sought to demonstrate that although much of nonverbal communication is universal, many nonverbal actions are shaped by culture.

REMEMBER THIS

Remember that although much of nonverbal communication is universal, many nonverbal actions are shaped by culture.

To further appreciate the significance of nonverbal communication, reflect for a moment on the countless times, besides employment interviews, when nonverbal messages play a significant role in the transaction. For example, Silverman and Kinnersley point out that in the medical setting, nonverbal communication "is the channel most responsible for communicating attitudes, emotions and affect."[1]

Barnlund highlights some additional occasions when nonverbal messages come into play:

Many, and sometimes most, of the critical meanings generated in human encounters are elicited by touch, glance, vocal nuance, gestures, or facial expressions with or without the aid of words. From the moment of recognition until the moment of separation, people observe each other with all their senses, hearing pause and intonation, attending to dress and carriage, observing glance and facial tension, as well as noting word choice and syntax. Every harmony or disharmony of signals guides the interpretation of passing mood or enduring attribute. Out of the evaluation of kinetic, vocal, and verbal cues, decisions are made to argue or agree, to laugh or blush, to relax or resist, or to continue or cut off conversation.[2]

DEFINING NONVERBAL COMMUNICATION

Because the objective of this chapter is to examine how and why people communicate nonverbally, we begin with a definition of nonverbal communication. A single definition, like our definitions of "culture" and "communication" in Chapter 2, is difficult to compose. Having reviewed numerous definitions, we propose that *nonverbal communication involves all those nonverbal stimuli in a communication setting that are generated by both the source and his or her use of the environment and that have potential message value for the source and/or receiver.*

It is not by chance that our definition is somewhat lengthy. We wanted to offer a definition that would not only establish the boundaries of nonverbal communication but also reflect how the process actually functions. Part of that functioning involves (1) intentional and unintentional messages and (2) the reciprocal relationship between verbal and nonverbal messages.

INTENTIONAL AND UNINTENTIONAL MESSAGES

Our definition permits us to include *intentional* as well as *unintentional* behavior. One of the features that separate humans from most other animals is that humans can usually plan certain actions before they execute them. Observing a friend approaching, you offer a broad smile as part of your greeting. This is an intentional act. Yet nonverbal messages are most often produced without a conscious awareness that they may have meaning for other people. These are unintentional messages. For example, frowning because the sun is in your eyes may make someone mistakenly believe that you are angry; looking upset after receiving a phone call could make a person approaching you think that you're unhappy to see him or her; and touching someone's hand for an extended time could cause that person to think you are flirting when that was not your intent. These are all examples of how your actions, unintentionally, can send messages to others. The sociologist Goffman describes this fusing of intentional and unintentional behavior:

> The expressiveness of the individual (and therefore his capacity to give impressions) appears to involve two radically different kinds of sign activity: the expression that he gives and the impression that he gives off. The first involves verbal symbols or their substitutes, which he uses admittedly and solely to convey the information that he and the other are known to attach to these symbols. This is communication in the traditional and narrow sense. The second involves a wide range of action that others can treat as symptomatic of the actor (communicator), the expectation being that the action was performed for reasons other than the information conveyed in this way.[3]

CONSIDER THIS

What are some examples of intentional and unintentional behavior that you have observed? Have any of these instances involved people of cultures different from your own?

VERBAL AND NONVERBAL MESSAGES

We have already indicated that nonverbal communication is a multidimensional and complex activity. You can observe the truth of that assertion by realizing that nonverbal messages can serve as substitutes for verbal messages. In addition, verbal and nonverbal messages often work in unison. Knapp, Hall, and Horgan emphasize this idea: "We need to understand that separating verbal and nonverbal behavior into two separate and distinct categories is virtually impossible."[4] The interfacing of the verbal with the nonverbal is reflected in a number of ways. For example, you often use nonverbal messages to repeat a point you are trying to make verbally. You could place your index finger over your lips while whispering, "Please don't yell," to someone who was shouting. You can also observe the reciprocal relationship between words and actions if you tell someone you are pleased with his or her performance while patting him or her on the shoulder.

THE FUNCTIONS OF NONVERBAL COMMUNICATION

As you can tell from the previous few pages, nonverbal communication is both omnipresent and an indispensable constituent of human interaction. This point is demonstrated by the fact that nonverbal messages serve a number of specific functions. Examining a few of those functions will illustrate why any study of intercultural communication must include information about nonverbal behavior.

CONVEYING INTERNAL STATES

As illustrated in our initial story about the college student and the employment interview, consciously and unconsciously, intentionally and unintentionally, people make important judgments about each other through nonverbal symbols. These symbols express attitudes, feelings, values, and emotions. If you see someone with a clenched fist and an inhospitable expression, you do not need words to tell you that the person may not be happy. If you hear someone's voice quaver and witness their hands tremble, you may infer that the person is fearful or anxious, despite what might be said. If someone smiles as you approach, you feel far more at ease than if they were scowling.

Be it fear, joy, anger, or sadness, your posture, face, and eyes can convey your feelings without you ever uttering a word. For this reason, the interpretations assigned to nonverbal messages influence how one assesses the quality of a relationship. From the amount of touching that takes place, to the tone of voice being used, to the distance between you and your partner, you can gather clues to the closeness of your relationship. The first time you move from holding hands to touching your partner's face, you are sending a message, and that message takes on added significance if your touch is returned. In short, "people use nonverbal cues to define the social and emotional nature of their relationships and interactions."[5]

CREATING IDENTITY

Not only do you use nonverbal communication to tell others about what you are thinking and feeling, but you also utilize nonverbal symbols to "tell" yourself and

Be it fear, joy, anger, sadness, or a host of other emotions, your posture, face, and eyes can convey feelings without your uttering a single word.

© Kathleen K. Parker

others who you are. In this sense, nonverbal messages are partially responsible for establishing your identity. From personal experience you know how judgments are often made about another person based on such things as skin color, use of makeup, facial expression, manner of dress, accent, jewelry, and even the nature of the handshake offered. This use of nonverbal symbols to express a person's identity is universal, as observed in the following discussion of tattoos. In New Guinea, a swirl of tattoos on a Tofi woman's face indicates her family lineage. The dark scrawls on a Cambodian monk's chest reflect his religious beliefs. A Los Angeles gang member's sprawling tattoos depict his street affiliation and may even reveal if he has committed murder. Whether the bearer is a Maori chief in New Zealand or a Japanese mafia lord, tattoos express an indelible identity.[6]

REGULATING INTERACTION

Nonverbal actions offer clues regarding how people navigate conversation. In a classroom you might raise your hand to signal that you want to talk. As you approach someone you do not want to visit with, you may look down to indicate your lack of willingness to interact. Conversely, direct eye contact and a smile could send a message that you want to talk with the person who is approaching you. In other situations you could lean forward, point a

CONSIDER THIS

How would you explain the phrase "Nonverbal actions offer clues regarding how people navigate conversation"?

finger, or even pause as a way of altering the conversation. These and other actions can regulate everything from when the conversation can begin, when it is your time to speak, and even when it is time for the interaction to conclude.

SUBSTITUTING FOR WORDS

Another function of nonverbal messages is that they can be used as substitutes for words. For example, there are many occasions when someone who is carrying terrible news will end up signaling sorrow without uttering a sound. A teacher may place an index finger to the lips as an alternative to saying, "Please be quiet." People often use the hands to beckon someone to come closer or use the same hands to say "good-bye." In each of these examples, an action is replacing a verbal utterance, and that action becomes the language.

We should point out that while we treated the functions of nonverbal communication as if they were separate or independent elements, they are not. These elements usually work in tandem. Although on some occasions they operate in isolation, "more commonly there is interaction between nonverbal behavior and verbal behavior to produce meaning in the minds of others."[7]

To help you understand the language of nonverbal communication and its role in intercultural communication, we will (1) suggest some guidelines for studying nonverbal communication, (2) link nonverbal communication to culture, (3) discuss the major classifications of nonverbal messages, and (4) offer some advice on how to better employ nonverbal communication within the intercultural context.

STUDYING NONVERBAL COMMUNICATION

Because the study of nonverbal communication has become part of "popular culture," this complex and multifaceted subject is often trivialized. Many "news" programs and talk-shows, for example, frequently employ an "expert" in nonverbal communication to inform viewers of what politicians are "really saying." This marginalizing often means that nonverbal communication is presented in a disingenuous and frivolous manner. Therefore, we need to pause before pursuing the topic any further and mention some potential problems and misconceptions associated with this area of study.

NONVERBAL COMMUNICATION IS A MULTICHANNEL ACTIVITY

The above heading alludes to the notion that nonverbal communication usually involves more than one message being sent at a time. For example, you might be talking with a friend while you are holding his or her hand and looking at your friend. Here, three communication activities (talking, touching, eye contact) are going on simultaneously. The problems associated with the multichannel nature of nonverbal communication often show themselves when people focus on one channel and forget the others. For example, your friend might not have direct eye contact with you while you are talking. What is this behavior signifying—if anything? In short, a great amount of information is exchanged during an interaction, and not being aware of that fact can cause confusion.

NONVERBAL COMMUNICATION IS OFTEN AMBIGUOUS

We noted the problem of ambiguity earlier when we discussed the intentional and unintentional nature of nonverbal communication. Ambiguity, however, and the problems it creates are worthy of further discussion. Simply stated, nonverbal communication can be ambiguous. The potential for ambiguity increases when the variable of culture is introduced. For example, a lack of eye contact in the dominant U.S. American culture often carries a negative connotation. In China, a reluctance to make eye contact may be seen as a sign of respect. For many Muslim females, eye contact is avoided as a sign of modesty. Ambiguity can also be linked to the context. The ambiguity of setting is seen if someone brushes your leg on an elevator—was it merely an accident or an aggressive sexual act? Our point should be obvious: When you use nonverbal communication, you need to be aware of the ambiguous nature of this form of interaction.

NUMEROUS VARIABLES INFLUENCE NONVERBAL COMMUNICATION

The next obstacle in studying nonverbal communication relates to the idea of individual differences and the complex nature of human communication. As noted elsewhere, people are the products not only of their culture, but also of their gender, region, occupation, political affiliation, educational background, and countless other factors that have shaped their perceptions, values, attitudes, beliefs, and nonverbal communication. We are suggesting that nonverbal communication, like much behavior, is produced by a host of variables, and culture is but one of them. Nonverbal interactions are influenced by factors such as "cultural background, socioeconomic background, education, gender, age, personal preferences and idiosyncrasies."[8]

NONVERBAL COMMUNICATION AND CULTURE

We have already mentioned that culture is but one of the dynamics that influence the manner in which people send and receive nonverbal messages. However, while granting the assorted causes behind human behavior, we nevertheless advocate that nonverbal communication mirrors the learned behaviors embedded in a culture. As we pointed out in Chapter 2, nonverbal behavior is part of the socialization process and presents the members of each culture with "cultural rules." These rules "are manifested in norms, values, attitudes, traditions, customs, and heritage and are communicated across generations."[9] Rosenblatt links these cultural rules to nonverbal communication, as he writes, "What emotions are felt, how they are expressed, and how they are understood are matters of culture."[10] Key in Rosenblatt's sentence is that culture has taught you which nonverbal actions to display (crying or laughing), the meaning of those actions (sadness or happiness), and the contextual backdrop (funeral or wedding). Our thesis should now be clear: *Nonverbal communication is a vital component whenever people of different cultures come together to share ideas, information, and feelings.*

As a student of intercultural communication, learning about the connection between culture and nonverbal behavior will help to improve the manner in which you engage in intercultural interactions. Hall underscores the need to learn about nonverbal behaviors in the following:

> I remain convinced that much of our difficulty with people in other countries stems from the fact that so little is known about cross-cultural communication.... Formal training in the language, history, government, and customs is only a first step. Of equal importance is an introduction to the nonverbal language of the country. Most Americans are only dimly aware of this silent language, even though they use it every day.[11]

By understanding cultural differences in nonverbal behavior you will also be able to gather clues about underlying attitudes and values being expressed by your communication partner. How far people stand from each other during normal conversation can offer clues to their views on privacy. Bowing tells you that a culture values formality, rank, and status. It is not by chance that Hindus greet each other by placing their palms together in front of their chests while tilting their heads slightly downward. This salutation reflects their belief that the deity exists in everyone.

CLASSIFICATIONS OF NONVERBAL COMMUNICATION

MESSAGES OF THE BODY

As we begin our discussion of the classifications of nonverbal communication, you will notice that our analysis of each category starts with the behaviors found in the dominant culture of the United States. We remind you of the integrated nature of these categories. The messages you produce do not take place as individual units. Rather, there are usually many messages being sent. Keeping this notion in mind, most classifications divide nonverbal messages into two comprehensive categories: (1) those that are primarily produced by the body (appearance, movement, facial expressions, eye contact, touch, and paralanguage) and (2) those that the individual combines with the setting (space, time, and silence).

APPEARANCE

In the West, concern for how one looks takes a variety of forms. From hair sprays to hairpieces, from fat-reducing diets to twenty-four-hour fitness centers, from false eyelashes to blue contact lenses, and from cosmetic surgery to tanning salons, people show their concern for how they appear to others. The popularity of tattooing is another good example of how large numbers of people strive to make themselves more attractive. In the United States, 23 percent of women and 19 percent of men now have tattoos.[12]

The importance of appearance can be seen daily in each of your personal interactions. Whom you approach and whom you avoid, particularly in regard to first impressions, might well determine future interaction or, indeed, if there will be any interaction. Concern with personal appearance is not confined to the West. It can be found in every culture. People from around the globe have been altering the way they appear for thousands of years. As far back as the Upper Paleolithic period (about 40,000 years ago), your ancestors were using bones for necklaces and other body ornaments. From that period to the present, historical and archaeological evidence has shown that people are fixated on their bodies. The alterations to their bodies have helped them "tell" others about who they are and where they belong. They have painted them, fastened objects to them, dressed them, undressed them, and even deformed and mutilated them in attempts to have some control over how they appear.

Judgment of Beauty

An important component of appearance is the perception of beauty. In the West, this fascination with beauty begins early. For example, many department stores and online businesses now offer a complete line of beauty aids to preteens. There are numerous studies that clearly document the advantages and disadvantages of being attractive. And many of these pros and cons surface at an early age. Knapp, Hall, and Horgan cite several studies that conclude that young students who are attractive are more popular and are perceived to be "more intelligent, more socially adept."[13] These positive perceptions toward being attractive become more magnified during adulthood. Whom you select to avoid and/or approach is often determined by a person's attractiveness. Studies reveal, at least in the United States, that attractive individuals are

Tattoos are often used to express identity.

Courtesy of Ed McDaniel

perceived as more persuasive and are hired for sales positions over less attractive individuals.[14]

In the United States, people tend to value the appearance of males who are tall and muscular. As for women, they are considered more attractive if they are tall and slender.[15] This view of attractiveness is not the rule in all cultures. For example, in large parts of Africa, plumpness is considered a sign of beauty, health, and wealth, and slimness is evidence of unhappiness, disease, or mistreatment at the hands of one's husband.[16] Buxom and stout women are also valued in much of Russia. There is even a Russian proverb that states, "One need not worry about fat, only about being hungry." It is not only the perception of the body that is part of a culture's attitude toward beauty. In Myanmar, an extended neck is considered a sign of beauty. Face painting is still common in parts of Africa and South America and among some American Indian tribes. In China, social change has brought about a transformation in how female beauty is viewed. "The tendency to conform to a modest standard of dress is strong only in small cities or rural areas.... In large cities, young people crave individual styles and world-famous brands."[17]

Ethnocentrism often heavily influences perceptions of attractiveness. A person usually internalizes the definitions of attractiveness related to the particular culture in which they live. Hence, what is called beauty in one culture may appear repugnant to people of another culture. A case in point is the face painting we just mentioned. Some people might be repulsed by other people painting their faces and bodies, but at the same time, many women in the United States use lipstick, makeup, and other means to change their appearance. For them, the use of makeup is often important but not the use of paint. We also see signs of ethnocentrism appear among males. In Iran, for instance, men are banned from having "decadent Western haircuts."[18]

Remland offers an excellent summary of cultural perceptions of beauty and ethnocentrism:

> The many exotic rituals we often see in PBS documentaries or in the pages of *National Geographic*, such as neck stretching, lip enlargements, earlobe plugs, teeth filing, and so on, represent the beautifying practices common in many parts of the world. Of course, liposuction, hair implants, facelifts, laser surgery, and the like, while not the least bit extraordinary to many Westerners, may seem abhorrent to people from other parts of the world.[19]

Because cultures are always in flux, perceptions of attractiveness are beginning to change as cultures have greater contact with one another. Even today, doctors are reporting an increase in plastic surgeries in places like China, Russia, Korea, and Brazil. In addition, within the United States, plastic surgeons have noticed an increase in the requests for cosmetic surgeries coming from people with a variety of ethnic and international backgrounds.[20]

Skin Color

Perhaps we should have begun our discussion of appearance with skin color, as it is the first characteristic people notice when they approach a stranger and the one that has the greatest impact on perception and interaction. For centuries and in nearly every culture, the lightest-skinned individuals were perceived to have the greatest social status and power. Even today, within the United States, "skin color is the first racial marker children recognize and can be considered the most salient of phenotypic attributes."[21] Often, that marker is perceived negatively. Folb stresses how these harmful perceptions of what she calls "caste markers" are manifested through issues of dominance and social control.[22] Skin color "may also be the basis of the allocation of economic and psychological privileges to individuals relative to the degree those privileges are awarded to valued members of the dominant culture."[23] The "awards" are so large that many advertisers are accused of using "digital manipulation to lighten ethnic models' skin tone" in their ads.[24]

The United States is not the only location where members of a culture are judged by their skin tone and seek various means to alter that tone. Because of this skin tone preference, skin bleaching in employed in many parts of the world. Avoiding sunlight to keep their skin light is a common practice among Asian women. U.S. Americans who visit Thailand are often surprised to see women sitting at the beach fully dressed. It is not uncommon to see women in China at the beach sporting face masks and sun-protective gloves.[25] They, along with women from Brazil, Jamaica, and India, are even using an assortment of creams and lotions to achieve a lighter tone to their skin. We should point out that women are not the only ones concerned with pale skin tones. In Japan, male-oriented parasols have become popular among younger men who seek to maintain a whiter, paler look.

Attire

As highlighted in this chapter's opening vignette, clothing goes well beyond protection from the elements. Clothing can be used to tell others about economic status, educational level, social position, current status, occupation, interests, public and private affiliations, and the like. Perhaps most importantly, as Ross points out, "The things that people say, or are forced to say, through their clothing are thus above all statements about an individual's identity."[26] In the United States you can also observe the link between clothing and individual identity in a variety of ways. Whether it is a military uniform, the sweatshirt that carries a logo of a favorite football team, the black clothing of Goth "adherents," the specific tilt of a baseball cap, or the attire of the hip-hop co-culture, clothing attempts to tell other people something about your identity. Among gang members, even the color of a bandana or T-shirt is a proclamation of group affiliation. So strong is this nonverbal proclamation that in 2013, a gang member from Los Angeles was sentenced to ninety years in prison for mistakenly killing a fourteen-month-old child. The shooter indicated that he was aiming at the child's father, as he "believed the father was a member of a rival gang because of the color of his T-shirt."[27] Women also know the language and power of clothing, as they, unlike men, have had to adapt and adjust their attire to the workplace for more than forty years.[28]

Nowhere is the controversial nature of clothing more apparent than in the various types of scarves, veils, and robes associated with Muslim women. For these women, clothing is much more than apparel to cover the body. As Torrawa points out, garments often reflect important values of Arabs.[29] As is the case with so many aspects of culture, there is often a "below the surface" reason for cultural behaviors. This deep structure and its significance in the Arab world are explained by Torrawa: "In all its guises, clothing inscribes ideologies of truth and deception, echoing the words of scripture, and revealing—and unraveling—that honor can only be attained when every robe donned is a robe of honor and every garment a garment of piety."[30]

The clothing Torrawa is referring to takes an assortment of forms. The first is called the *hijab*, which basically covers only the head, while the second scarf, known

Clothing can convey a variety of aspects, such as identity, group affiliation, religious preference, and individuality.

© Susan Van Etten/PhotoEdit

as the *alamira*, is a two-piece veil that also includes a scarf. There is also the *niqab*, a more extensive veil that leaves an area open only around the eyes. However, most controversy has been generated by the *burqa*, which consists of a robe covering the entire body and veils over the entire face of the woman. Even the eyes are covered with the exception of a mesh screen that allows the woman to see what is in front of her. These coverings, particularly the ones over the entire face, have been a point of contention in some non-Muslim countries. For the last decade in many European nations, there have been government attempts to ban the veils from being worn in public places.[31] France took the first step in this debate with the bold action of banning Muslim head scarves and other so-called religious symbols from classrooms.[32] Attempts at outlawing the veils have even come to North America, where "Lawmakers in Quebec are pushing a bill that would deny public services—including health care and education—to Muslim women who wear the *niqab*."[33] And in the United States, the issue of dress for Muslim women has even found its way to a location that in many ways is an icon of the United States—Disneyland. A young woman received an internship to work at Disneyland without having to be interviewed for the position. When she appeared for her first day of employment, she was wearing a *hijab*. She was told to remove the *hijab*. She refused and was relegated to a room at Disneyland where she had no contact with park visitors. The woman took legal action against Disneyland.

Muslim men, like the women, have attire that differs from that seen in the West. And like the attire of women, there is often a link between religion and dress. The traditional apparel for men in Arabic nations would "include a long loose robe called a *dishdasha* or *thobe* and a headpiece, a white cloth *kaffiya* banded by a black *egal* to secure it."[34] The subtlety of color in garments "tells others" about an individual's status and affiliation. An all-white *kaffiya* means that the person wearing the headpiece has not yet made the pilgrimage to Mecca.

REMEMBER THIS

Attire is often used to establish one's cultural identity.

The link between cultural values and clothing can be seen in nearly every culture. For example, as a symbolic gesture of their faith, the Amish dress in clothing that demonstrates humility and severance from the dominant culture. Both males and females wear clothing that is simple, unadorned, and predominantly dark in color. You can also observe the relationship of values and attire in German culture, where status and authority are significant. Hall and Hall write,

> Correct behavior is symbolized by appropriate and very conservative dress. The male business uniform is a freshly pressed dark suit and tie with a plain shirt and dark shoes and socks. It is important to emulate this conservative approach to both manners and dress. Personal appearance, like the exterior appearance of their homes, is very important to Germans.[35]

You can witness that same tie between cultural values and clothing among Filipinos. Gochenour tells us, "Values relating to status and authority are the root of the Filipino's need to dress correctly."[36] Japan is another culture that merges attire and the culture's value system: "The general proclivity for conservative dress styles and colors emphasizes the nation's collectivism and, concomitantly, lessens the potential for social disharmony arising from nonconformist attire."[37] This desire for social harmony can even be seen in the white coats that are part of a physician's attire in Japan. A recent study revealed not only that patients preferred the white garments, but also that "wearing a white coat could favorably influence patients' confidence in the relationship with their physician in all types of practices."[38]

Throughout this segment on attire, we have attempted to demonstrate how clothing represents a series of messages used by individuals and their cultures. Adamo summarizes this important set of messages in the following: "Dress is a symbolic language. It is one of the many ways in which people create and exchange meanings in communication. It helps to separate group members from non-members and to place the individual in a social organization."[39]

We offer a final admonition to conclude this particular section. Whether it be the women of Guatemala wearing their colorful tunics (*huípiles*) or African men in white *dashikis*, traditional garments are still common in many cultures. Whether they are Sikhs in white turbans, women in Iran wearing their *hijabs*, Japanese in kimonos, Hasidic Jews in black yarmulkes, or the dark attire of the Amish in the United States, you need to learn to be tolerant of others' external differences and not let them impede communication.

BODY MOVEMENT

We remind you that a major thesis of this chapter is that communication involves much more than words. As Benjamin Franklin noted, "None preaches better than the ant, and she says nothing." Imai underscores this point in a little more detail: "The world is a giddy montage of vivid gestures—traffic police, street vendors, expressway drivers, teachers, children on playgrounds, athletes with their exuberant hugging, clenched fists and 'high fives.' People all over the world use their hands, heads, and bodies to communicate expressively."[40]

The study of how movement communicates is called *kinesics*, which are those visible body shifts and movements that can send both intentional and unintentional messages. For example, your attitude toward the other person can be shown by leaning forward to "communicate" that you are comfortable with him or her. Something as simple as walking can also send messages. Americans, particularly males, tend to walk in a manner that is distinct from most other cultures. Stevenson highlights this distinguishing gait thusly: "We walk big—swinging arms, letting our legs amble wide—in a manner that's fitting for folks from a country with plenty of empty space. Citizens of densely populated Europe exhibit a far more compact posture, with elbows and knees tucked tight and arm swings restrained."[41]

In attempting to understand the influence of body movement, a few points need clarification. First, in most instances, the messages the body generates operate in combination with other messages in somewhat instantaneous fashion. People may greet a friend by smiling, saying "hello," and even hugging all at the same time.

Richmond, McCroskey, and Hickson summarize this "multidimensional" notion of kinesics in the following:

> Researchers have studied these motions from many perspectives, but most nonverbal scholars today agree that it is virtually meaningless, and probably inappropriate, to study kinesic behaviors apart from their contexts. It is rare that a particular body movement symbolizes a specific message outside the restrictive environs of the context or culture where it occurs.[42]

Second, it is often difficult to control kinesic behavior. In most instances, you have at least a fraction of a second to think about what you are going to say, but a great deal of body action is spontaneous and linked to the moment. If you are hiking with friends and without any warning, see a rattlesnake at your feet, your movements are certainly not calculated but instead are controlled by adrenalin. Finally, there are thousands of distinct physical signs that a person can make. Therefore, any attempt at cataloging them would be both frustrating and fruitless. Our basic purpose is to point out that although all people use movements to communicate, culture teaches them how to use and interpret the movements. In the upcoming sections, we look at a few cultural differences in a person's (1) posture and (2) movements (gestures) that convey ideas and feelings.

Body movements can transmit both intentional and unintentional messages.

© Kathleen K. Parker

Posture

A person's posture can send a multiplicity of messages. Posture can be a sign of whether people are paying attention, the level of status in the encounter, if people are friends or strangers, if they like or dislike each other, and it can provide a variety of other information about the relationship. One study revealed "that body posture may be as important as the face in communicating emotions such as fear."[43] Think for a moment of all the meanings associated with slouching, being stiff, slumping over, crouching, kneeling, pulling back one's shoulders, twitching one's legs, putting one's hands in pockets, bowing, and the like.

On an intercultural level, posture can offer insight into a culture's value system, as President Obama discovered a few years ago when he visited Japan and engaged in a polite bow in front of Japan's Emperor Akihito. The arguments surrounding this seemingly innocuous nonverbal action created a firestorm of media attention. *Newsweek* magazine summarized the positions on both sides of the argument in the following two sentences: "The President was pilloried last week for his deep bow to Japan's Emperor Akihito during a visit to Tokyo. Was he groveling before a foreign leader—or just being polite?"[44] For many, Obama was engaging in an act of subservience. To the Japanese, the bow (*ojigi*) is not a sign of capitulation but rather mirrors their value of status and respect.[45] Actually, the Japanese have a wide range of uses for the bow. It can be a nonverbal way of expressing "thank you," a greeting, an apology, a congratulatory gesture, or a simple means of acknowledging another person.

To outsiders, the act of bowing appears simple. The actual Japanese ritual is rather complicated. For example, the person who occupies the lower station begins the bow, and his or her bow must be deeper than the other person's. The superior, on the other hand, determines when the bowing is to end. When the participants are of equal rank, they begin the bow in the same manner and end at the same time. In fact, there are so many nuances to the act of bowing in Japan that young children begin to learn about this nonverbal behavior at a very early age. Many large companies even hold classes in correct bowing protocol for their employees.

Thai people use a bow that is similar to the one employed by the Japanese. This movement (called the *wai*) is made by pressing both palms together in front of one's body, with the fingertips reaching to about neck level. Although the basic value behind the bow is to demonstrate respect, it is also used to communicate "thank you." Many Buddhists will also keep the hands in the *wai* position while listening to a Dharma talk (Buddhist teaching).

Another nonverbal greeting pattern linked to religion is used in the Indian culture, where *namaste* is spoken while making a slight bow and bringing both hands together in front of the heart. This practice of greeting someone reflects the Hindu belief that God is in everything—including other people. Hence, all human beings, along with all the gods of Hinduism, are to be honored and respected. Hindus will even bow before eating as a way of bestowing thanks for yet another one of God's gifts.

As eccentric as it sounds, the way people sit is often a reflection of important cultural characteristics. In the United States, being casual and friendly is valued, and people often demonstrate this through their manner of sitting. For males, it is usually a casual sitting position that might include slouching and leaning back. American males often, consciously or unconsciously, sit with their feet up on their desk as a sign of being relaxed. In many countries, such as Germany, Sweden, and Taiwan, where lifestyles tend to be more formal, slouching is considered a sign of rudeness and poor manners. In fact, "German children are still taught to sit and stand up straight, which is a sign of good character. Slouching is seen as a sign of a poor upbringing."[46] Even the manner in which you position your legs while sitting has cultural overtones. For example, in Turkey, it is a sign of rudeness to sit with your legs crossed. Remland offers further instances of the crossing of legs when he notes, "An innocent act of ankle-to-knee leg crossing, typical of most American males, could be mistaken for an insult (a showing of the sole of the foot gesture) in Saudi Arabia, Egypt, Singapore, or Thailand."[47] People in Thailand also attribute distinct significance to the soles of the feet. For them, the feet are the lowest part of the body, and they should never be pointed in the direction of another person.[48]

In the United States, co-cultural differences exist in how people perceive and utilize posture and movement during interaction. The walk assumed by many young African American males illustrates this characteristic. "The general form of the walk is slow and casual with the head elevated and tipped to one side, one arm swinging and the other held limply."[49] The walk is often used to "show the dominant culture that you are strong and proud, despite your status in American society."[50]

Gestures

Consider all of the messages that can be sent by waving, placing hands on hips, folding the arms, scratching the head, biting fingernails, pointing, making a fist, shaking a finger, etc. Gestures are a nonverbal "vocabulary" that people use, both intentionally and unintentionally, to share their internal states. Reflect for a moment on "signing" as a major form of communication utilized by the deaf co-culture in the United States. Here, you can observe a rich and extensive vocabulary composed almost exclusively of gestures. Crew members on the deck of an aircraft carrier do most of their talking via hand gestures. Another example of the power of gestures can be found in the hand signals used by motorcycle and ethnic gangs. The slightest variation in performing a certain gesture can be the catalyst for a violent confrontation. An inability to "read" the meaning of a gesture, particularly in an intercultural communication setting, has the potential for confusion and awkwardness. You can witness some of the uncertainty of intercultural gestures in the following examples:

- The "thumbs-up" gesture in the United States has positive connotations because it indicates that "everything is okay" or "you are doing very well." However, in Australia, Bangladesh, Iran, and Nigeria, it is seen as a rude gesture. And in Turkey, it actually represents a political party.
- In the United States, pointing at someone usually does not carry negative connotations. In fact, directions are often given by pointing in one direction or another with the index finger. Germans point with the little finger, while in Japan pointing is done with the entire hand with the palm held upward. In China, pointing can be taken as a sign of rudeness. In much of the Arab world, pointing is thought to be an offensive gesture. And in much of Asia, pointing the index finger at a person is considered rude.
- In the United States, "making a circle with one's thumb and index finger while extending the others is emblematic of the word 'okay'; in Japan (and Korea) it traditionally signified 'money'[51] (okane); and among Arabs this gesture is usually accompanied by a baring of teeth, signifying extreme hostility."[52] To a Tunisian,

the gesture means, "I'll kill you." In some Latino cultures, the circle with the thumb and index finger is often perceived as an obscene gesture.

- In Mexico, when asking someone to wait for "just a minute, please" (*un momento, por favor*), the speaker also makes a fist and then extends the thumb and index finger so that they form a sideways "U," as though measuring a short span of time.
- Greeks express "yes" with a nod similar to the one used in the United States, but when communicating "no," they jerk their heads back and raise their faces. Lifting one or both hands up to the shoulders strongly emphasizes the "no."
- In Chile, to "say" that someone is unintelligent or dense, one holds the palm upward with the fingers spread.

We could present more examples, as there are thousands of gestures prevalent in every culture. But instead of offering a protracted catalog of gestures from all over the world, we will include just a few examples to demonstrate how gestures and culture are linked. We remind you of the mutually dependent nature of all nonverbal actions. As applied to gestures, the thin line between gestures and all the messages a person generates cannot be clearly drawn. Hence, we agree with Ekman and Friesen's view of nonverbal communication when they speak of a "comprehensive approach."[53] For them, studying nonverbal gestures in isolation provides "an incomplete picture of what is occurring." With this qualification behind us, we propose to examine (1) idiosyncratic gestures, (2) beckoning, and (3) the frequency and intensity associated with gestures.

> **CONSIDER THIS**
>
> *Consider that you have met someone who has recently arrived in the United States and they ask your help in deciding what certain gestures mean. What would you tell them about the meaning for the following gestures used in the United States?*
>
> - Fingers crossed
> - Thumbs up
> - Thumbs down
> - Making a round ring (O) with the thumb and index finder
> - Pointing directly at someone

Idiosyncratic Gestures. As already indicated, there are limitless idiosyncratic gestures found in each culture. These are the distinctive gestures whose meanings are usually the feature and property of a particular culture. Even gesturing with the same specific part of the body can differ from culture to culture. For example, in Nepal, pulling both earlobes is a form of apology for offending someone. Yet pulling one earlobe in China means a person is "saying" that he or she touched something that was very hot.[54] The Japanese also have a gesture whose actual movement is not unique to that culture, yet the meaning is exclusive to that culture. The gesture is made by pointing both index fingers above the head, at the top of the ears, as if they were the horns of an ogre. The gesture means the man's wife is angry.[55] In China, if you place your right hand over your heart, it means you are making a sincere promise. In Iraq, the same gesture can mean "thank you." For the French, pulling the skin down below the right eye can mean, "I don't believe you." In Argentina, one twists an imaginary mustache to signify that everything is "okay."

Meanings for gestures with sexual connotations may also be exclusive to a specific culture. In the United States, someone might use the middle finger to send an insulting, obscene gesture. This sexual insult gesture is not universal. For the Japanese, the thumb protruding out between the index finger and the middle finger is a sexual sign with a variety of interpretations. This same gesture is the letter "T" in American Sign Language (ASL).[56]

Beckoning Gestures.   The sign used for beckoning is also attached to culture. In the United States, when a person wants to signal a friend to come, he or she usually makes the gesture with one hand, palm up, fingers more or less together, and moving toward the body. In much of Latin America, this gesture takes on romantic connotations. And in the Philippines, that same gesture is often used to call one's dog. Chinese and Koreans signal someone to come by cupping "the hand with the palm down and drawing the fingers toward the palm."[57] Vietnamese use this same beckoning sign. When Americans see this gesture, many often think the other person is waving good-bye. In Germany and much of Scandinavia, tossing the head back constitutes a beckoning motion. For many Arabs, holding the right hand out, palm upward, and opening and closing the hand is nonverbally asking someone to "come here."[58] And to beckon someone in Spain, you stretch your arm out, palm downward, and make a scratching motion toward your body with your fingers.

Frequency and Intensity of Gestures.   There are also cultural differences that regulate the frequency and intensity of gestures. Italians, Africans, and people from the Middle East are more outwardly expressive and utilize gestures with greater frequency and intensity than do Japanese, Chinese, and Scandinavians. Writing about Brazilian culture, Novinger notes, "Brazilians say that if you tie their hands they cannot speak. They use hand gestures and broad arm gestures as they talk."[59] The use of gestures to promote meaning is also common among Arab men. Here you can see large gestures that seem to go along with almost every word.[60] Members of many Asian cultures perceive such outward activity quite differently, often equating vigorous action with a lack of manners and personal restraint.[61] Germans are also made uncomfortable by bold hand gestures. Ruch offers the following advice to American executives who work with German corporations: "Hands should be used with calculated dignity. They should never serve as lively instruments to emphasize points in conversation. The entire game plan is to appear calm under pressure."[62] Germans are not alone in their aversion to large and ostentatious gestures. Canadians and other people with British lineage usually do not employ extensive gesturing.

Facial Expressions

The early Greek playwrights, Beijing Opera performers, and the Noh actors of Japan were keenly aware of the shifts in mood and meaning that facial expressions convey. Each form of drama uses masks or an abundance of makeup to demonstrate differences in each actor's character and expression. Whether it is the Mexican adage that "One's face is the mirror of one's soul" or the Yiddish proverb that "The face tells the secret," people everywhere have always been captivated by the face. What is intriguing is that we are talking about three faces. First, there is your assigned face, the one you are born with. Although it is altered by age, health, and even cosmetics and surgery, this is your "basic" face. Second is the face that can be manipulated at will, often called the voluntary face. Here is where you can deliberately hide or reveal your true feeling regarding the person and/or situation you are confronting. You can signal your happiness and put on a broad smile when your best friend is approaching. Alternatively, you can hide your true feelings and smile when you dislike having to talk with yet another person. In short, this second face is the one you control. Finally, you have the face that is changed by your surroundings and the messages you receive, such as when you involuntarily blush after receiving a compliment.

Among scholars, the importance of facial expressions is well established. Richmond, McCroskey, and Hickson summarize this importance when they write, "Experience and research have helped us to understand that the human face is a primary tool used for transmitting emotional expressions."[63] The role of culture in those expressions has been a matter of debate for a great many years. The dispute is rooted in a nature–nurture controversy that goes back to the work of Charles Darwin. Although much of the debate deals with facial expressions, the arguments reach into all dimensions of nonverbal communication. Here lies the question: Is there a universal language of facial expressions? Darwin posited, and researchers such as Eibl-Eibesfeldt uphold, that "some primary facial expressions are inherently linked with moods and feelings" and have their origin in our evolutionary past and are universal.[64] Ekman, a principal proponent of this view, asserts that, "The subtle creases of a grimace tell the same story around the world, to preliterate New Guinea tribesmen, to Japanese and American college students alike."[65] Further, Ekman and others affirm that there is "a basic set of least six facial expressions that are innate, universal, and carry the same basic meaning throughout the world."[66] The six pan-cultural and universal emotions conveyed by facial expressions are happiness, sadness, fear, anger, disgust, and surprise. However, despite the biologically based nature of facial expressions, there seem to be clear cultural expectations and norms that often dictate when, where, how, and to whom facial expressions are displayed.[67]

Different cultures create their own rules for what are appropriate facial expressions and how those expressions are to be interpreted. While granting the assorted causes behind human behavior, we advocate that nonverbal communication mirrors the learned behaviors embedded in a culture. Richmond, McCroskey, and Hickson offer a summary of how these acquired behaviors grow out of the cultural factors:

1. Cultures differ concerning circumstances that elicit emotions.

2. Cultures differ about the consequences that follow certain emotional expressions.

3. Different cultures have different display rules that govern the use of facial behavior, which their members must learn.[68]

Each culture "teaches" its members what nonverbal actions to exhibit (crying or laughing), the meaning of those actions (sadness or happiness), and the contextual setting of those actions (funeral or wedding).

Because the face is often the first part of the body observed when you meet someone, usually it is given greater weight than are vocal messages.[69] Think for a moment about what is being implied about the power of the face with phrases such as "face-to-face" meeting or "losing face." People usually send messages, consciously or unconsciously, that predict a course of action, help define power relationships, or reflect a level of interest and the degree of involvement regarding the specific encounter.

A few years ago, the world was treated to a vivid example of how facial expressions impact intercultural communication. A group of executives from the Toyota automobile company appeared before a congressional panel in the United States to explain the problems associated with the recall of over 6 million Toyota vehicles. The executives' presentation before the panel was criticized by members of the congressional committee and the news media. They believed that the Toyota spokespersons failed "to show adequate remorse for those who had been killed in accidents involving acceleration problems."[70] At the core of these negative reactions was the perception that the Toyota representatives failed to outwardly display any signs of emotion. What the critics failed to realize is that many Asian cultures control and suppress facial expressions. For example, it is not uncommon for Japanese, Chinese, and Koreans to show restraint even when experiencing intense feelings (anger, irritation, sadness, and love or happiness). Although the "rule" in many Asian cultures calls for a degree of control and restraint with regard to outwardly displaying emotions, in some cultures, such as those of the Mediterranean, facial expressions are animated and exaggerated.[71] It is not uncommon in this region of the world to see men crying in public.

We now move to yet another facial expression: the smile. While the smile is a universal act and everyone is born knowing how to smile, it is also influenced by culture. The stimulus that produces the smile—and even what the smile is communicating—often shifts from culture to culture. In North America, a smile usually sends a positive message and is often used as a greeting. The individual who is smiling is typically perceived as happy or amused. However, as just noted, culture can "influence smiling both by determining the interpretation of events, which affects the cause of happiness, and by shaping display rules, which determine when it is socially appropriate to smile."[72]

A few examples will illustrate the role culture plays in the use and interpretation of a smile. Like North Americans, Thais are another people noted for their use of the smile. In fact, Thailand has been called the "Land of Smiles," and so common is the smile that to an outsider, it seems to be the response to just about any situation. Therefore, people from other cultures find it difficult to "read" the Thai smile, as it can be used to display sadness, joy, embarrassment, fright, anxiety, and numerous other emotions. Vietnamese also make use of the smile to represent phrases such as "Hello," "Thank you," and "I am sorry." In Japan you can observe another culture where there are many meanings associated with smiling. According to Nishiyama, "the Japanese may smile when they feel embarrassed and laugh when they want to hide their anger."[73] Smiling is also used to denote acceptance of a command from a person of higher status.

There are many cultures where smiling is not a common or widely accepted nonverbal action. In Korean culture too much smiling is often perceived as a sign of shallowness. Dresser notes that the "lack of smiling by Koreans has often been misinterpreted as a sign of hostility."[74] Russians also suffer from the same misunderstanding regarding their limited use of smiling. Russians are not exhibiting rudeness or impoliteness by not smiling, but rather they are reflecting that culture's "rules" regarding when and to whom to smile. They are also distrustful of people who smile at what they believe are inappropriate occasions. The same restrained attitude toward smiling exists in Germany, where a smile "is used with far more discretion, generally only with those persons one knows and really likes."[75]

Eye Contact and Gaze

Making eye contact is one of the earliest and most powerful modes of communication used by human beings and other primates. After touch, a newborn infant's first "contact" with the world is through the eyes. Eyes have always been a topic of fascination. You can witness the potential communication component of eye contact when professional poker players seek to hide behind their dark glasses or a hooded sweat-shirt during a tournament. The impact of eye contact on communication is also man-ifest in the countless literary and musical allusions to eyes made over hundreds of years. Emerson wrote, "An eye can threaten like a loaded and leveled gun or can insult like hissing and kicking." Shakespeare also knew the communicative potency of the eyes when he wrote, "Thou tell'st me there is murder in mine eye." Bob Dylan underscored the same power in his lyrics: "Your eyes said more to me that night than your lips would ever say." Even the concept of "the evil eye" has been present in nearly every culture for centuries. The notion of an evil eye means being able to send another person a thought (transmitted through the eyes) that can cause damage in a host of ways. By some estimates there are approximately seventy cultures covering nearly every part of the world that believe in the influence of the evil eye.[76] For example, Nydell points out that "Belief in the evil eye (often just called 'the eye') is common, and it is feared or acknowledged to some extent by most Arabs."[77] Con-victions regarding the power of the evil eye (*mal de ojo*) are also seen in Mexico and Puerto Rico, where "Mothers may isolate their children for fear of having one become a victim of *mal de ojo*."[78]

Eye contact and gaze are essential to the study of human communication for a number of reasons. First, eyes can give clues to the nature of the relationship, indicate if the channels of communication are open or closed, assist in monitoring feedback, indicate degrees of attentiveness and interest in the interaction, regulate the flow of the conversation, reflect positive or negative emotions, and help define power and status relationships between the participants.[79]

Second, eyes are significant to the communication process because of the abun-dance of messages they can send. We have all heard some of the following words used to describe a person's eyes: "direct," "sensual," "sardonic," "cruel," "expressive," "intelligent," "penetrating," "sad," "cheerful," "worldly," "hard," "trusting," and "suspicious." Finally, and most importantly for our purposes, much of eye contact is directly related to culture. On both a conscious and an unconscious level, you have "learned" the significance of eye contact and the "rules" for employing (or not employing) eye contact. These rules become quite evident when people are in an ele-vator with strangers. Also, reflect on the discomfort felt when someone stares at you for a long period of time.

Before offering some comparisons that demonstrate culture's influence, we shall briefly discuss how eye contact is used by the dominant culture in the United States. As Triandis notes, looking another person directly in the eye is very com-mon in the United States.[80] Not only is it common, but this interpersonal act is highly valued by members of the domi-nant culture. It is expected in most inter-personal exchanges and perceived as an indication of good manners. The implica-tion is that if you fail to use direct eye contact, you risk being perceived as showing a lack of interest, trying to hide something, or being deceitful.

REMEMBER THIS

Avoidance of eye contact and/or prolonged eye gazing varies from culture to culture.

What is normal in the United States may be unacceptable in other cultures. In Japan, prolonged eye contact is often considered discourteous and disrespectful. It is not uncommon for Japanese to look down or away or even close their eyes while engaging in conversation. You can appreciate the problems that might arise if

Americans are not aware of the Japanese use of eye contact. U.S. Americans who are culturally uninformed often assume that Japanese eye contact (or lack of it) is an indication that their Japanese partner disagrees with what is being said or is disinterested.

Koreans also have a view of eye contact that differs from that held by most Americans. Richmond, McCroskey, and Hickson offer an excellent summary of how this culture employs eye contact:

> some cultures, such as the Korean, place much more emphasis on the observance of the eyes than do others. That is, Koreans are highly aware of eye behavior because it is believed that real answers to questions they ask may be found there, even though the other's words say something else.[81]

Dresser offers further information about culture when she notes that "People from many Asian, Latino, and Caribbean cultures also avoid eye contact as a sign of respect."[82] This same orientation toward eye contact is found in many parts of Africa, where "Making eye contact when communicating with a person who is older or of higher status is considered a sign of disrespect or even aggression."[83] There is even a Zulu saying: "The eye is an organ of aggression." India and Egypt provide two additional examples of eye contact mirroring a cultural value. In India, the amount of eye contact that is employed is often related to a person's social position. This, of course, means that people of different socioeconomic classes often avoid eye contact with each other. In Egypt, where the issue is not social status but gender, "Women and men who are strangers may avoid eye contact out of modesty and respect for religious rules."[84] We should point out, at least as it applies to gender and globalization, that the use of eye contact involving women is changing as women all over the world join the workforce.

The avoidance of eye contact is not the case among Arabs, who use very direct eye contact between same-sex communicators. This contact not only is direct, but also extends over a long period of time. For "outsiders," this directness often appears as a form of staring. Yet for Arab males, this visual intensity is employed so that they can infer the "truthfulness" of the other person's words.[85] Notice how the words "same-sex" were used in our reference to Arab eye contact. The reason is that where gender segregation is the custom, direct eye contact between men and women is often avoided. Germans also engage in very direct eye contact. The direct gaze is also part of Russian culture. As Morrison and Conaway note, "Do not be surprised if Russians stare at you."[86]

In the United States the prolonged stare is frequently part of the nonverbal code used in the gay male co-culture. When directed toward a member of the same sex, an extended stare, like certain other nonverbal messages, is often perceived as a signal of interest and sexual suggestion.[87] A few other differences in the use of eye contact in the United States are worth noting. Eye contact (or a lack of it) can create misunderstandings between African Americans and members of the dominant culture. The reason is simple: African Americans often do not find it necessary to engage in direct eye contact at all times during a conversation. This same uncomfortable feeling toward direct and prolonged eye contact can be found among Mexican Americans,

CONSIDER THIS

Can you recall how you learned the nonverbal communication "rules" for greeting a stranger, a mate, a professor, a best friend, or your grandparents?

who "consider sustained eye contact when speaking directly to someone as rude. Direct eye contact with superiors may be interpreted as insolence. Avoiding direct eye contact with superiors is a sign of respect."[88]

Eye contact is an important consideration when communicating with members of the deaf community who are employing ASL. Among members of the deaf co-culture who are "signing," there is a belief that eye contact is an especially important part of their communication process.[89] Turning your back to people who are "signing" is essentially the same as ignoring them. So delicate is the use of eye contact that you seldom realize the modifications you make when communicating. For example, the next time you are speaking with a disabled person, perhaps someone in a wheelchair, notice how little eye contact you have in comparison with someone who is not disabled. This practice is all too common and, unfortunately, may be interpreted as a lack of interest and concern.

Touch

Touch as a form of communication can be as effortless and rewarding as holding your partner's hand or as powerful and frightening as being touched in a sexual manner by a stranger. The meanings you assign to being touched and your reasons for touching others offer insights into the communication encounter. This is vividly illustrated by the character Holden Caulfield in the American classic *The Catcher in the Rye*:

> I held hands with her all the time. This doesn't sound like much, but she was terrific to hold hands with. Most girls, if you hold hands with them, their goddam hand *dies* on you, or else they think they have to keep *moving* their hand all the time, as if they were afraid they'd bore you or something.[90]

Touch is often considered the most fundamental and primitive of all the senses. It is our first form of "language" and point of contact with others. It is not until after birth that infants utilize all their senses as a means of defining the reality that confronts them. During this early period, they are highly involved in tactile experiences with other people. They are being held, nuzzled, cuddled, getting cleaned, patted, kissed, and in many cases breast-fed. As you move from infancy into childhood, you learn the rules of touching. You are taught whom to touch and where they may be touched. By the time you reach adolescence, your culture has taught you the "rules" of touch behavior. You have learned about shaking hands by employing various types of handshakes—firm, gentle, etc. You have even become skilled at knowing whom to hug and the intensity and location of contact associated with the person you are hugging (parent, friend, lover). Culture has also "taught you" what occasions (greeting, expression of affection, etc.) call for a hug. Because of all the contextual and relational variables involved with touching, you have also been "informed" about sexual harassment and what constitutes inappropriate touching. In spite of the complexities that are often associated with touching, it is generally believed that in the dominant U.S. culture, there are six basic types of touching:

1. Accidental touching is when someone inadvertently bumps into you.

2. Professional touching is carried out by individuals such as doctors, nurses, hairdressers, or even a swimming coach moving the arms of a pupil.

3. Social politeness touching is associated with greeting and showing appreciation. These contacts can range from a handshake to a respectful pat on the back.

4. Friendship touches demonstrate concern and caring between family members and close friends. In this type of touching, you might see actions ranging from an extended embrace to an arm placed on a shoulder.

5. Love-intimacy touches are those touches that usually occur in romantic relationships (caressing, hugging, embracing, kissing, and the like).

6. Sexual touch, the most intimate type, is used for sexual arousal.[91]

As is the case with all the topics in this book, each culture has "directives" aimed at its members concerning how to use touch as a means of communication. That is, each culture "instructs" its members as to who can touch whom, on what parts of the body, and under what situations. So prescriptive are these "cultural definitions" regarding touch that in the United Arab Emirates, a British couple was sentenced to one month in prison for kissing in public. You may recall the disturbance created in Great Britain when First Lady Michelle Obama was introduced to Queen Elizabeth and touched the queen as part of her greeting. Shaking hands and even hugging dignitaries is common in the United States; it is taboo in Great Britain.

One of the best settings to observe cultural variations in touch behavior is in international departure situations. Drawing from a study involving these at an international airport, Andersen offers the following observations:

> A family leaving for Tonga formed a circle, wove their arms around each other's back, and prayed and chanted together. A tearful man returning to Bosnia repeatedly tried to leave his sobbing wife; each time he turned back to her, they would grip each other by the fingertips and exchange a passionate, tearful kiss and a powerful embrace. Two Korean couples departed without any touch, despite the prolonged separation that lay ahead of them.[92]

Let us supplement Andersen's list and examine a few other cultural examples. We begin with Arabs, a group of people who frequently employ touching behavior as part of their communication style. In fact, it is not uncommon to see men in such places as Saudi Arabia holding hands while walking. Men will often kiss each other on the cheek in many Arab countries. This type of contact as a greeting has led Feghali to note that "Touching in Arab societies 'replaces' the bowing and handshaking rituals of other societies."[93] Because of religious and social traditions, Arab Muslims eat and engage in other activities with the right hand but do not greet (touch) with the left hand because this is a social insult. The left hand is used to perform basic biological functions. Muslim women seldom touch or are touched by individuals outside of their family. Men also have "rules" about being touched by women. An athlete from Iran refused to shake hands with Duchess Kate Middleton after winning a medal in the 2012 Paralympic Games. It seems that Iranian culture bans men from shaking hands with unrelated women.

In South America and Mexico, touch is routine. Brazilians may even continue to "touch you intermittently on the arm, hand, or shoulder during much of the conversation."[94] In Mexico a physical embrace, called an *abrazo*, is common among both males and females. "Hugs, pats on backs, and other physical contact are an important part of communication in Mexico."[95] A high frequency of touching is also prevalent among the people of Eastern Europe, Spain, Greece, Italy, Portugal, and Israel.[96]

Touch is less frequent among Germans and Finns.[97] Intentional touching is also not a prevalent form of communication in Asia.[98] For example, in Japanese business practices, "Touching fellow workers and associates is not common."[99] Even the simple act of kissing has cultural overtones. Although mouth-to-mouth kissing is sexual in Western cultures, it is not widespread in many parts of Asia. In fact, the Japanese have for centuries rhapsodized about the appeal of the nape of the neck as an erotic zone. Having no word for "kiss" in their language, the Japanese borrowed the English word, and *kissu* is now used. In some cultures, touch can have a religious meaning. For instance, "Many Southeast Asians believe that touching their heads places them in jeopardy because that is where their spirits reside."[100]

Gender differences also occur in the use of touch as a form of communication. Women, for example, tend to welcome touch more than do men, especially when it is from the same sex. They initiate touch behavior more than men.[101] As noted earlier, gender differences as they apply to touch, particularly in the workplace, have become the source of many sexual harassment cases. A male colleague who strokes a female coworker on the arm or even pats her on the back might be perceived as engaging in sexual or condescending behavior. Hence, you need to remember that touching is contextual and often carries multiple meanings. While being greeted with a hug at a party with friends might seem appropriate, that same contact may be highly inappropriate in the workplace, especially between supervisors and subordinates.

Co-cultures within the United States often employ touch in ways unique to their members. African Americans "give skin" and "get skin" when greeting each other, but they do not normally use "skinning" (touching) when greeting white people unless they are close friends.

As we have noted throughout this book, cultural norms and "rules" are subject to change. One of those changes applies to touch behavior among young people throughout the world. This is especially true in the United States. Growing weary of the handshake, the high-five, and fist bump, some are greeting each other with hugs. Kershaw writes, "Girls embracing girls, girls embracing boys, boys embracing each other—the hug has become the favorite social greeting when teenagers meet or part these days."[102]

Scents

The Russian writer/historian Solzhenitsyn was reminding us of the role of scent in human interaction when he wrote, "We are all human, and our senses are quicker to prompt us than our reason. Every man gives off a scent and the scent tells you how to act before your head does." Although you receive most of your messages from the outside world through vision and hearing, the sense of smell can also be a conduit for meaning. From the burning of incense in India, to the aroma of flowers and herbs used in China for medicinal purposes, to people using aromatherapy to cure certain illnesses, cultures have been using odor in a variety of ways. In fact, the following paragraph by Low underlines some of the ways:

> Whether we like it or not, we remain as odouriferous beings despite all of our cleaning regimes, and these odours play important roles in virtually every realm of our everyday life social experiences, running the gamut from gustatory consumption, personal hygiene, the home, the city, to class, gender and racial dimension of social life.[103]

Speaking more directly about the role of smell in human communication, Richmond, McCroskey, and Hickson tell us, "The air around us is filled with scents that express a variety of messages to us. Scents can communicate memories, fear, love, dominance, and excitement—and may even arouse powerful feelings about another person."[104] The importance of scent, at least in the United States, can be seen in the fact that "Each year American men and women spend millions of dollars on deodorants, soaps, mouthwashes, breath mints, perfumes, aftershave lotions, and other products to add to or cover up natural body scents."[105] What makes scent part of the communication experience is that people attach meaning to how we smell. According to Howes, we even "Establish group identity through some odor, whether natural, manufactured, symbolic, or some combination of these."[106] A number of elements affect the meaning we give to a smell: (1) *the strength of the smell in relation to competing fragrances and odors* (French perfume vs. an inexpensive aftershave lotion), (2) *smell's distance from the other person*, (3) *the perceived relationship between the parties involved*, and (4) *the context of the encounter*.

Although everyone experiences the world of smell through the same sense organ, culture also plays a part in how that scent is perceived and responded to.[107] A few examples will help illustrate the point. The traditional Eskimo kiss, what is commonly depicted as rubbing noses, also includes "mutual sniffing."[108] In Bali, when lovers greet one another, they often breathe deeply in a kind of friendly sniffing. The Maori of New Zealand use much the same greeting when they meet close friends. Smell also plays a large role among Filipinos. It is not unusual for young Filipino lovers to trade small pieces of clothing on parting so that the smell of the other person will evoke their affection for each other.[109] In Japan, where smell is an important part of the culture, young girls often play a game involving the placing of five fragrances in tiny boxes. The girl who identifies the most aromas wins the game. And it is not uncommon in Japan to have various fragrances emitted in the workplace. Aromatherapy is an accepted healthcare practice in many cultures.

As mentioned, Americans represent an example of a culture that tends to be uncomfortable with natural body smells and, therefore, attempts to cover up innate smells with perfumes and lotions. Many other cultures regard natural odors as normal. For example, most Italians do not mask their scents with other aromas.[110]

There is a belief among Muslim women that "wearing perfume on clothes either outdoors or when meeting strangers indoors should be avoided."[111] The reason is that Arabs perceive a person's smell as an extension of the person. Hall describes this cultural value:

> Olfaction occupies a prominent place in Arab life. Not only is it one of the distance setting mechanisms, but it is a vital part of the complex system of behavior. Arabs consistently breathe on people when they talk. However, this habit is more than a matter of different manners. To the Arab good smells are pleasing and a way of being involved with each other. To smell one's friends is not only desirable, for to deny him your breath is to act ashamed. Americans, on the other hand, trained as they are not to breathe in people's faces, automatically communicate shame in trying to be polite.[112]

REMEMBER THIS

Paralanguage is concerned with the communicative characteristic of the voice and with how people use their voices. Paralanguage includes such things as giggles, laughter, accents, groans, sighs, pitch, tempo, volume, and resonance.

Paralanguage

This next form of nonverbal communication is predicated on the belief that the sounds we generate, apart from the meaning contained in the words, often communicate more than the words themselves. Most of you have seen a foreign film with English subtitles moving across the screen. During those intervals when the subtitles were not on the screen, you heard the actors uttering an unfamiliar language but could essentially understand what was happening on the screen just from the sound of the voices. Perhaps you inferred that the performers were expressing anger, sorrow, joy, or any number of other emotions. From the sound of the voices, you could even tell who the hero was and who was cast in the role of the villain. The rise and fall of voices also may have told you when one person was asking a question and another was making a statement or issuing a command. Whatever the case, certain vocal cues provided you with information with which to make judgments about the characters' personalities, emotional states, ethnic background, and rhetorical activity. To be sure, you could only guess at the exact meaning of the words being spoken, but sound variations still told you a great deal about what was happening. Shakespeare suggested this with great style when he wrote, "I understand the fury in your words, but not the words." What we have just been considering is often referred to as *paralanguage*, which "includes all oral cues in the stream of spoken utterances except the words themselves."[113] Research reveals that those utterances can influence perceptions related to the individual's emotional state, social class and status, personality traits, ethnicity, educational level, credibility, comprehension, and personality.[114] Most classifications divide paralanguage into three categories: (1) *vocal qualities*, (2) *vocal characterizers*, and (3) *vocal segregates*.

Vocal Qualities.   As just indicated, a great many inferences about content and character can be made from the paralinguistic sounds that people produce. Let us now look at some paralanguage behaviors that have message value in particular cultures. Although vocal qualities have numerous components, cultural differences are most apparent in the use of volume. Arabs speak with high levels of volume. It might even appear to be theatrical to "outsiders." For Arabs, loudness connotes strength and sincerity. A softer voice suggests weakness and even deceitfulness. Nydell explains the Arab use of volume in more detail: "Loudness of speech is mainly for dramatic effect and in most cases should not be taken as an indication of aggression or insistence on the part of the speaker."[115] Germans conduct their business with a "commanding tone that projects authority and self-confidence."[116] At the other end of the continuum, there are cultures that have a very different view toward loud voices. For example, people from the Philippines speak softly, as they maintain that this is a sign of good upbringing and education. Speaking in soft tones is also valued in Thailand. A visitor from Thailand once asked one of the authors if the loud voices she was hearing in the United States meant that U.S. Americans were upset or mad at a specific person or event. Her question made a great deal of cultural sense. In Thailand, people speak in quiet voices and believe it is an indication of anger when a person elevates his or her volume. These strident tones contradict what Buddhist teaching calls "disciplined in quietness." In Japan, raising one's voice often implies a lack of self-control. For the Japanese, a gentle and soft voice reflects good manners and helps maintain social harmony—two important values in Japanese culture.

Co-cultures also use vocal qualifiers in subtle and unique ways. For example, many African Americans use more inflection and employ a greater vocal range than most white Americans.[117] Differences in paralanguage also mark the communication patterns of males and females. Research indicates that men's voices tend to have louder volume, lower pitch, and less inflection. Notice that these features are likely to conform to cultural perceptions of men as assertive and emotionally controlled. Women's voices typically have higher pitch, softer volume, and more inflection. Again, these are characteristics associated with cultural views of women as emotional and polite.[118]

Vocal Characteristics.   Vocal characteristics are vocalizations that convey a meaning for members of a specific culture. In both France and Argentina, it is considered rude to yawn in public. And in much of Europe, whistling during a public performance is a message of disapproval and ridicule. For many Muslims, the simple act of sneezing is interpreted as "a blessing from God."[119] In fact, after a sneeze, a Muslim would say, *Al-hamduillah* ("praise and thanks to God"). Laughing also sends different messages, depending on the culture. Lynch and Hanson note this difference:

> Laughing and giggling are interpreted as expressions of enjoyment among most Americans—signals that people are relaxed and having a good time…. Among other cultural groups, such as Southeast Asians, the same behavior may be a sign of extreme embarrassment, discomfort, or what Americans might call "nervous laughter" taken to the extreme.[120]

Vocal Segregates.   Vocal segregates are sounds that are audible but are not actual words. These sounds are used as substitutes for words. A case in point is the "shh" sound produced by Americans when they are asking someone to be silent. In many cultures certain sounds also take on special meanings. For instance, the Maasai in Africa use a number of sounds that have significance. The most common one is the "eh" sound, which the Maasai draw out and which can mean "yes," "I understand," or "continue."[121] In Kenya, the "iya" sound tells the other person that everything is okay. In Jamaica, the "kissing" or "sucking" sound expresses anger, exasperation, or frustration. The Japanese make use of vocal segregates in their conversations. To demonstrate reluctance or concern, a Japanese worker might "suck in his breath, look doubtful and say 'Saa…. '"[122] Japanese will also make small utterances to demonstrate their attentiveness, such as *hai* ("yes," "certainly," "all right," or "very well"), *so* which has the same sound as the English "so" ("I hear that" or an indication of agreement), or *eto* ("well…" or "let me see…").[123] Many members of the African-American co-culture are familiar with the "whoop" used by many preachers, a sound to arouse members of the church. This sound has been employed in African American churches since the time of slavery.

Having previously examined how body movement communicates, we now move to a review of how space, time, and silence communicate. Although these variables are external to the communicator, they are used and manipulated in ways that send messages. For example, imagine your reaction to someone who stands too close to you, arrives late for an important

CONSIDER THIS

Have you ever felt uncomfortable when someone you had just met stood very close to you? How did it make you feel?

appointment, or remains silent after you reveal some personal information. In each of these instances you would find yourself reading meaning into your communication partner's use of (1) *space and distance*, (2) *time*, and (3) *silence*.

SPACE AND DISTANCE

The variation in distance between you and other people is as much a part of the communication experience as the words being exchanged. The study of this message system is called *proxemics*. Hall defines proxemics as "the interrelated observations and theories of man's use of space as a specialized elaboration of culture."[124] While Hall's definition was advanced over forty years ago, it remains the anchor for most discussions of space and distance in a cultural context. Expanding on Hall's analysis, today proxemics is concerned with such things as (1) *personal space*, (2) *seating*, and (3) *furniture arrangement*.

Personal Space

Personal space is often thought of as a kind of "bubble" that encircles each individual. This "bubble" increases and decreases depending on the person's reaction to the setting and the person "invading" his or her space. Employing the example of the "bubble," Hall and Hall discuss the significance of personal space to communication:

> Each person has around him an invisible bubble of space which expands and contracts depending on his relationship to those around him, his emotional state, his cultural background, and the activity he is performing. Few people are allowed to penetrate this bit of mobile territory, and then only for short periods of time.[125]

As indicated, your personal space is that area you occupy and call your own. As the owner of this area, you usually decide who may enter and who may not. When your space is invaded, you react in a variety of ways. You may retreat, stand your ground, or sometimes react violently. Use of personal space is learned on both the conscious and unconscious levels. Personal space used in the United States is divided into four categories.

1. Intimate distance (actual contact to 18 inches) is normally reserved for very personal relationships. You can reach out and touch the person at this distance. Because of the closeness of the participants, voices are usually at the level of a whisper.

2. In personal distance (18 inches to 4 feet) there is little chance of physical contact, and you can speak in a normal voice. This is distance reserved for family and close friends.

3. Social distance (4 to 12 feet) is the distance at which most members of the dominant U.S. culture conduct business and take part in social gatherings.

4. Public distance is usually used in public presentations and can vary from relatively close to very far.[126]

As with most forms of communication, space is associated with cultural values. A good example of the link between the use of space and culture can be seen in the values of individualism and collectivism. Cultures that stress individualism and

People's use of space, like most aspects of nonverbal communication, can be influenced by the setting and context.

Courtesy of Larry Samovar

privacy (England, the United States, Sweden, Germany, and Australia) generally demand more space than do collective cultures. According to Triandis, Arabs, Latin Americans, and U.S. Hispanics fall into this collective category.[127] These are cultures in which people are interdependent and often work, play, live, and even sleep in close proximity to one another. "Brazil is a wonderful example of a culture that communicates in close proximity."[128] With regard to Arabs, Ruch writes, "Typical Arab conversations are at close range. Closeness cannot be avoided."[129]

Differences in personal space can even be seen in how cultures perceive and respond to standing in lines. For most U.S. Americans "regulations" for standing in line are simple. The line should be straight and people are expected to wait their turn. As Dresser noted, "Many new immigrants don't understand the American rules for standing in lines."[130] When waiting for a bus or an elevator most Arabs will not stand in neat straight lines. There is often a degree of pushing as they work their way toward the front of the crowd. For them, this is not considered rude, but simply a reflection of their perception of personal space.

Some co-cultures have their own special use of space. In prisons, where space is limited and controlled, space and territory are crucial forms of communication.

New inmates quickly learn the culture of prison by finding the correct ways to use space. They soon discover how and when to enter another cell, what part of the exercise yard they can visit, how reduction of a person's space is a form of punishment, and that they must form lines for nearly all activities.

Women and men also use space differently. For example, women normally "establish closer proximity to others" than do men.[131] Years of research have also revealed other gender differences in the use of space: (1) men claim more personal space than women, (2) women manifest less discomfort than men when confronted with a small amount of space, (3) men seem to approach females more closely than females who move toward men, (4) women, when given the opportunity, seek to interact at a closer distance than do men, and (5) men more frequently walk in front of their female partner than vice versa.[132] Spatial distance is also a variable when interacting with members of the deaf culture. When using ASL, it is necessary for the person signing to sit far enough away from the other person so that they can be seen. It would not be uncommon for two signers to sit across from one another at a distance that hearing people might perceive as impersonal.[133]

Seating

As is the case with many features of nonverbal communication, seating arrangements send both inconspicuous and obvious messages. The producing of a very subtle message could be witnessed at an important diplomatic meeting between the Turkish ambassador and his counterpart from Israel. The Turkish representative was extremely distressed that he was asked to sit on a sofa that was lower than the one occupied by the Israeli officials. His anger was so intense that he refused to allow the media to take a picture of the meeting since he felt it humiliated him and his country. This real-life example vividly demonstrates that seating arrangements can be a powerful

The way people use space, including how they arrange themselves in a group, is often rooted in their culture.

form of nonverbal communication. Not only do seating arrangements signal power relations, as was the case with the Israeli and Turkish examples, but research points out that perceptions related to leadership, dominance, sex roles, and introversion and extraversion are influenced by seating arrangements.[134]

Notice that when you are a member of a group in the United States, people tend to talk with those opposite them rather than those seated beside them. And in most instances, the person sitting at the head of the table is the leader. These seating "rules" are not the same arrangements used in other cultures. For example, in some Asian cultures students do not sit close to their teachers or stand near their superiors; the extended distance demonstrates deference and esteem. This regard for admiration and ritual can also be seen in China. Because of their Confucian background, the Chinese respect proper etiquette and ceremony. Therefore, seating arrangements are frequently dictated by cultural and historical norms, particularly at formal events such as banquets, and diplomatic and business meetings. At banquets, which are very common in China, seating arrangements place the honored person (often decided by seniority and age) facing east or facing the entrance to the hall. The higher a person's status, the closer they sit to the person of honor.[135] At business meetings the Chinese experience alienation and uneasiness when they face someone directly or sit opposite them at a desk or table.[136] If you view a news story about American diplomats meeting with government officials from China, you might observe that the meeting is taking place with people sitting side by side—frequently on couches. In Korea seating arrangements reflect status and role distinctions. In a car, office, or home, the seat on the right is considered to be the place of honor.

For the Japanese, much like the Chinese, seating at any formal event is determined based on hierarchy. When conducting business or diplomatic negotiations, the Japanese will arrange themselves with the most senior person sitting in the middle and those next highest in rank sitting to the left and right of this senior position. Low-ranking members will sit away from the table, behind the other representatives.[137] Ways of reflecting "lower-ranking" members take a somewhat different seating arrangement among Samoans and Fijians. For them, respect and status "means being physically lower than a superior."[138]

Furniture Arrangement

The way people arrange furniture (cubicles, chairs, tables, desks, sofas, etc.) can, as Shah and Kesan note, "play a communicative role by expressing cultural or symbolic meaning."[139] The importance of seating arrangement as a form of communication, and the role it occupies within a specific culture can be observed in the Chinese traditional philosophy of *feng shui* that dates back over 3,000 years. This approach to the arrangement of furniture and space is based on the Taoist tradition that stresses the need for people and nature to live in harmony. The heart of this perspective is that people must live with, rather than against, their environment. Further, it is believed that striking the balance between self and one's physical environment brings good health, happiness, and wealth. You can observe the signs of this philosophy in Chinese homes and the way some members of the family organize themselves at a table. For example, when at a business meeting, Chinese executives will often seek out a seat that they believe is synchronous with the environment.

Just as *feng shui* reflects some of the history and values of China, furniture arrangement can also mirror some of the values found in the United States, where furniture is often arranged to achieve privacy and interpersonal isolation. It is a way of circumventing interaction. People who value conversation, such as the French, Italians, and Mexicans, are often surprised when they visit the United States and see that the furniture in the living room is pointed toward the television set so people can focus on the television program rather than the other people in the room. They believe that such an arrangement is rude and stifles conversation.

In Japan, offices are usually open and shared with many colleagues, and the furnishings are, like the workers, placed in close proximity. The contrast between office arrangements in the United States and Japan can create problems. As Nishiyama notes, "Because of its lack of privacy, Westerners, especially individualistic Americans, might find the Japanese office arrangement very uncomfortable and annoying."[140]

The arrangement of furniture in offices can also give you a clue to the character of a people. "French space is a reflection of French culture and French institutions. Everything is centralized, and spatially the entire country is laid out around centers."[141] Hence, offices are organized around the manager, who is at the center. In Germany, where privacy is stressed, seating is dispersed throughout the office. By comparison, in Japan, where group effort and hierarchy are important, office seating is arranged according to seniority, with desks abutting each other.

TIME

When the Dutch mathematician Christian Huygens built the first pendulum clock over three centuries ago, he probably had little idea that his invention would have such an impact on the world. This intrusion on how people live is now more profound than ever. As Flaskerud illustrates,

> In these days of speed up communication, there are messages to us about time from many sources: smartphones, desktop and laptop, and iPads, not to mention clocks, watches, and their bells that ring and chime. These sources of communication demand that we speed up our responses to one another.[142]

Gonzalez and Zimbardo echo Flaskerud's observation when they add, "There is no more powerful, pervasive influence on how individuals think and cultures interact than our different perspectives on time—the way we mentally partition time into past, present and future."[143] After some reflection you will see how time communicates. In the United States, if you arrive thirty minutes late for an important appointment and offer no apology, you send a certain message about yourself. Telling someone how guilty you feel about your belated arrival also sends a message. Studies point out that one of the markers of a successful and intimate relationship is the amount of time people spend together and how patient they are with each other.[144]

The connection of time to culture is profound, and like most aspects of culture, it is part of the enculturation process early in life:

> Culture begins to educate each of us at an early age as to the value of and the means by which we distinguish time. Each culture has its own particular time norms, which are unconsciously followed until violated. When such violations occur, however, they are perceived as intentional messages associated with that particular culture. In this regard, each culture teaches its people what is appropriate or inappropriate with regard to time.[145]

Let us look now not only at *how* cultures teach, but also *what* they teach about the use of time. To accomplish this, we will examine two cultural perspectives: (1) *informal time* and (2) *monochronic and polychronic classifications*.

Informal Time

Informal time is usually composed of two interrelated components—punctuality and pace.

Punctuality. Rules that apply to punctuality are taught implicitly and explicitly. On a conscious level, young children are taught the importance of being prompt. They are told that a lack of punctuality equals being inconsiderate, lazy, and discourteous. In addition to these conscious messages, there are numerous messages sent and learned on an unconscious level. You would probably have some difficulty remembering where you learned some of the following informal rules:

- The boss can arrive late for a meeting without anyone raising an eyebrow.
- A secretary arriving late might receive a reprimand in the form of a stern glance.
- A rock star or a physician can keep people waiting for a long time, but the warm-up band and the food caterer had better be at the event on time.

You know these "rules" about time but cannot point to the moment you learned them, as they operate below the level of consciousness. The imperatives about time are also often linked to a culture's worldview. For example, in the Western perception, response to time can be traced to the Judeo-Christian worldview. We see time beginning with the Creation and ending with the Second Coming or the arrival of the Messiah.[146]

Experience tells you that in the United States, most members of the dominant culture adhere to Benjamin Franklin's pronouncement that "Time is money." Think of what is being said about the use of time in these common expressions: "Don't put off until tomorrow what you can do today," "He who hesitates is lost," and "Just give me the bottom line." For U.S. residents, time is fixed and measurable, and where we feel seconds ticking away, we attach much significance to schedules. We measure our efficiency according to our ability to meet deadlines and cross off items on our checklist by the end of the day. Getting things done on schedule has a value in itself.[147]

> ## REMEMBER THIS
>
> *Cultures vary in how they perceive punctuality, the amount of time they set aside for socializing, whether they value a fast or slow pace of life, and the importance of work versus leisure time.*

As mentioned, cultures vary in their punctuality standards. Argyle highlights a few of those variations:

> How late is "late"? This varies greatly. In Britain and America, one may be 5 minutes late for a business appointment, but not 15 and certainly not 30 minutes late, which is perfectly normal in Arab countries. On the other hand, in Britain it is correct to be 5 to 15 minutes late for an invitation to dinner. An Italian might arrive 2 hours late, an Ethiopian after, and a Javanese not at all—he had accepted only to prevent his host from losing face.[148]

Status relationships can influence punctuality in Japan. As Nishiyama points out, "The time usage in Japan is usually determined by the status relationships between the people involved."[149] A lower-status person in Japan would wait much longer for someone of higher status than they would for a lower-status individual. For the Japanese, a person's use of time is yet another way of showing respect.

A few additional examples will help illustrate how reactions to punctuality are rooted in culture. In Spain, Italy, and Argentina it is typical for people to be thirty or more minutes late for a meeting or dinner appointment. Punctuality is also not highly regarded in much of the Arab world. Comparing Arabs to westerners, Nydell notes, "Arabs are thus much more relaxed about the timing of events than they are about other aspects of their lives."[150]

In Africa, people also might "show up late for appointments, meetings, and social engagements."[151] There is even a Nigerian expression that says, "A watch did not invent man." These views of tardiness might be perceived as rudeness in places such as the United States, Canada, Germany, and the United Kingdom.

Pace. The Irish have a saying: "Life is a dance not a race." This somewhat cavalier approach to life is often confusing to westerners, who are raised to adhere to the biblical statement that "Idle hands are the devil's workshop." These two examples demonstrate cultural attitudes toward pace. Because of the tempo of life in the United States, to "outsiders" U.S. citizens always appear to be in a hurry. As Kim observes, "Life is in constant motion. People consider time to be wasted or lost unless they are doing something."[152] From fast-food restaurants to gas stations where you can do your shopping while putting gas in your car, to microwave cooking, to computers that use the fastest available processors, U.S. Americans live life at a frenzied pace. Even the expression "rush hour" describes how commuters in major cities are dashing to get from point A to point B. Children in the United States grow up hearing others tell them not "to waste so much time" and to "hurry up and finish their homework." Think how those expressions differ from the Latin proverb "Haste manages all things badly" or the Mexican saying "You don't have to get there first, you just have to know how to get there."[153]

People in much of the world use time differently than the pace found in the United States. For instance, "the French do not share the American sense of urgency to accomplish tasks."[154] Japanese culture considers time in ways that often appear at cross-purposes with U.S. American goals. Brislin illustrates how the Japanese pace is reflected in the negotiation process:

> When negotiating with the Japanese, Americans like to get right down to business. They were socialized to believe that "time is money." They can accept about fifteen minutes of "small talk" about the weather, their trip, and baseball, but more than that becomes unreasonable. The Japanese, on the other hand, want to get to know their business counterparts. They feel that the best way to do this is to have long conversations with Americans about a wide variety of topics.[155]

The Chinese also value a slow pace. For them, the completion of the mission is what matters, regardless of the amount of time it takes. The Chinese proverb "With time and patience the mulberry leaf becomes a silk gown" captures the notion of time being unhurried. In Africa, where a slow pace is the rule, "People who rush are suspected of trying to cheat."[156]

The idea that nonverbal behavior is directly linked to a culture's religious and value orientation is manifest among Arabs. Earlier, we pointed out that Muslims believe that their destiny is predetermined. The connection between this religious view and the pace of life is pointed out by Abu-Gharbieh: "Throughout the Arab world, there is nonchalance about time and deadlines: the pace of life is more leisurely than in the West. Social events and appointments tend not to have a fixed beginning or end."[157]

Monochronic (M-Time) and Polychronic (P-Time)

Hall established a classic taxonomy for examining the link between culture and time. He proposed that cultures organize time in one of two ways—either *monochronic* (M-time) or *polychronic* (P-time),[158] which represents two approaches to perceiving and utilizing time. While Hall's system of analysis has been part of intercultural literature for over thirty years, it has taken on added significance in this era of globalization and electronic methods of communicating. Not only are international messages often received and responded to in different time zones, but the ways people create and respond to electronic "tools" like email are influenced by how each culture perceives the various notions of time. For example, issues such as punctuality, time set aside for socializing, fast or slow paces of life, and the importance of work versus leisure time are just some of the concerns facing people who use electronic devices to send and receive messages to people from cultures different from their own.

In reference to Hall's classifications, we should add that although M-time and P-time are presented as two distinct categories, it is much more realistic to perceive the two classifications as points along a continuum. There are many cultures that do not fall precisely into one of the two categories but instead contain degrees of both M-time and P-time.

M-Time. As the word "monochromic" implies, this concept views time as linear, sequential, and segmented. More specifically, "A monochronic view of time believes time is a scarce resource which must be rationed and controlled through the use of schedules and appointments, and through aiming to do only one thing at any one time."[159] Cultures with this orientation perceive time as being *tangible*. When speaking of the M-time orientation Hall states, "People talk about time as though it were money, as something that can be 'spent,' 'saved,' 'wasted,' and 'lost.'"[160] Acting out this view of time a person would value punctuality, product over process, and the judicious use of time. The English naturalist Charles Darwin glorified this approach when he wrote, "A man who dares to waste one hour of time has not discovered the value of life."

Cultures that can be classified as M-time include Germany, Austria, Sweden, Norway, England, Finland, Canada, Switzerland, and the dominant U.S. culture.[161] As Hall explains, "People of the Western world, particularly Americans, tend to think of time as something fixed in nature, something around us and from which we cannot escape; an ever-present part of the environment, just like the air we breathe."[162] In the business or educational setting, M-time culture people would schedule appointments in advance, try to be on time to meetings, be concise in making presentations, and have a strong penchant for following initial plans. When those plans are not adhered to, they are apt to become frustrated.

P-Time. People from cultures on polychronic time live their lives quite differently from those who move to the monochronic clock. The pace for P-time cultures (Arab, African, Indian, Latin American, South Asian, and Southeast Asian) is more leisurely than the one found in M-time cultures. In P-time cultures, human relationships, not tasks, are important. "A polychronic view of time sees the mainte-nance of harmonious relationships as the important agenda, so that use of time needs to be flexible in order that we do right by the various people to whom we have obligations."[163] These cultures are normally collective and deal with life holistically. For P-time cultures, time is less tangible, and people are usually not in a hurry to finish an assignment or chore. In addition, P-time participants can interact with more than one person or do more than one thing at a time. Because P-time has this characteristic of engaging in several activities at once, people of these cultures often find it easier to employ "multitasking." As Dresser notes, this trait "explains why there is more interrupting in conversations carried on by people from Arabic, Asian, and Latin American cultures."[164] African cultures also place great stock in the activity that is occurring at the moment and emphasize people more than schedules. The person they are interacting with is more important than an event or individual that is someplace else. In short, "Time for Africans is defined by events rather than the clock or calendar."[165]

As we conclude this section on how time communicates, it is important to remem-ber that specific settings and occasions can influence how a person "acts out" M-time or P-time. In one context, you might be extremely prompt (M-time); in another situ-ation, you might be multitasking or making a decision that what you are doing at a particular moment is essential and hence postpone your next appointment (P-time). Two cultural examples will further underscore the contextual nature of the use of time. While Arab culture manifests all the characteristics of P-time cultures, "Mod-ernization has influenced approach to time in the Arab regions, particularly in regional business centers and other urban environments."[166] Hall offers another instance of how the setting can determine which orientation a person utilizes: "The Japanese time system combines both M-time and P-time. In their dealings with foreigners and their use of technology, they are monochronic; in every other way, especially in interpersonal relations, they are polychronic."[167]

Table 9.1 summarizes the basic aspects of M-time and P-time. The table takes many of the ideas we have mentioned and translates them into specific behaviors.

SILENCE

We conclude our analysis of the types of nonverbal messages by looking at how silence can be an important component in intercultural communication. Within the interpersonal setting, silence can provide an interval in an ongoing interaction during which the participants have time to think, check or suppress an emotion, encode a lengthy response, inaugurate another line of thought, call attention to certain words, express various emotions, or indicate thoughtfulness.[168] Silence also provides feed-back, informing both sender and receiver about the clarity of an idea or its signifi-cance in the overall interpersonal exchange. In most Western cultures, talk is highly valued, and as such, it is often difficult to determine the meaning behind someone's silence. It can be interpreted as an indication of agreement, anger, lack of interest, injured feelings, shyness, a means of showing respect, contempt, or even a way con-cealing the truth.[169] And reflect for a moment on the meaning of silence when young children in the United States are given a "time-out"—a period when they are expected to be silent and not have any sort of human interaction. Hence, many

TABLE 9.1	A Comparison of Monochronic and Polychronic Cultures
MONOCHRONIC TIME PEOPLE	**POLYCHRONIC TIME PEOPLE**
• Do one thing at a time	• Do many things at once
• Concentrate on the job	• Easily distracted and subject to interruption
• Take time commitments (deadlines, schedules) seriously	• Consider time commitments an objective to be achieved, if possible
• Are low context and need information	• Are high context and already have information
• Are committed to the job	• Are committed to people and human relationships
• Adhere to plans	• Change plans often and easily
• Are concerned about not disturbing others; follow rules of privacy	• Are more concerned with people close to them (family, friends, close business associates) than with privacy
• Show great respect for private property; seldom borrow or lend	• Borrow and lend things often and easily
• Emphasize promptness	• Base promptness on the relationship
• Are accustomed to short-term relationships	• Have tendency to build lifetime relationships

Source: Adapted from E.T. Hall and M.R. Hall, *Understanding Cultural Differences: Germans, French, and Americans* (Yarmouth, ME: Intercultural Press, 1990), 15.

U.S. Americans grow up perceiving silence as a frightening experience. This is one reason they try to fill up the silence with "small talk."

The intercultural implications of silence as a means of interpreting ongoing verbal interactions are as diverse as those of other nonverbal cues:

> Cross-cultural differences are common over when to talk and when to remain silent, or what a particular instance of silence means. In response to the question, "Will you marry me?" silence in English would be interpreted as uncertainty.... In Igbo, it would be considered a denial if the woman were to continue to stand there and an acceptance if she ran away.[170]

Knowing how cultures use silence can offer essential information for anyone who interacts with a different culture. As Braithwaite points out,

> One of the basic building blocks of competence, both linguistic and cultural, is knowing when not to speak in a particular community. Therefore, to understand where and when to be silent, and the meaning attached to silence, is to gain a keen insight into the fundamental structure of communication in that world.[171]

As noted, silence is not a meaningful part of the life of most members of the dominant U.S. culture. Conversing at coffee houses, talking or texting on cell phones (even when driving an automobile), watching television, or listening to music on an iPod keeps U.S. Americans from living in a silent world. In fact, silence often takes on a negative connotation. Think of the U.S. American saying that "the squeaky wheel gets the grease" or the words of Ralph Waldo Emerson when he wrote, "Speech is power: Speech is to persuade, to convert, to compel." We can observe a fascination with "talk" over silence in the popularity of radio and television programs called "talk shows." Members of the dominant culture not only enjoy talking and avoiding silence, but also "often experience problems when they go international and place themselves in face-to-face contacts with more silent people of the world."[172]

U.S. Americans are not the only group who prefer talking rather than silence. In the commercial world, "a silent reaction to a business proposal would seem negative to American, German, French, Southern European and Arab executives."[173] You will notice that the German culture appeared on the list we just presented. The German proverb that states that "Silence is a fence around wisdom" illustrates how some Germans might diminish the importance of silence. There is a link between cultures that emphasize social interaction (Jewish, Italian, French, Arab, and others) and their perception of and use of silence. Talking in these cultures is highly valued. In Greek culture, there is also a belief that being in the company of other people and engaging in conversation are signs of a good life. The concepts of solitude and silence are overshadowed in Greek history and literature, which contain numerous allusions to rhetorical techniques and dialogues. The culture that produced Aristotle, Plato, and Socrates is not one that will find silent meditation appealing. For people who follow this Greek tradition, talking is often used as a means of discovering and communicating the truth.

Let us now look at a few cultural variations in the use of silence so that you might better understand how a lack of words can influence the outcome of a communication event. In the Eastern tradition, the view of silence is much different from the Western view. As you learned in Chapter 5, Buddhists feel comfortable with the absence of noise or talk and actually believe that words can contaminate an experience. They maintain that inner peace and wisdom come only through silence. This idea is brought out by the Buddhist scholar A. J. V. Chandrakanthan:

CONSIDER THIS

How would you explain the African proverb, "Silence is also speech"?

> In the stories and discourses attributed to Buddha, one can clearly see a close link between Truth and Silence. Wherever Truth is mentioned in references to Buddha it is always said in relation to silence. In fact, popular Buddhist religious tradition attests that whenever someone asked Buddha to explain truth, he invariably answered in silence.[174]

Barnlund associates this Buddhist view of silence with communication: "One of its tenets is that words are deceptive and silent intuition is a truer way to confront the world; mind-to-mind communication through words is less reliable than heart-to-heart communication through an intuitive grasp of things."[175] Silence is also used by many Asian people as a means of avoiding conflict. "A typical practice among many Asian peoples is to refuse to speak any further in conversation if they cannot personally accept the speaker's attitude, opinion, or way of thinking about particular issues or subjects."[176] The Chinese represent an excellent example of how silence is a part of many Asian cultures. Going back 2,500 years, Confucius stressed the importance of social harmony. Embedded in that philosophy is a belief that direct face-to-face conflict should be avoided. Silence is one way to circumvent that conflict. To help accentuate that point Confucius wrote, "Silence is the true friend that never betrays."

Silence is also important to the Japanese. In many instances, people are expected to sense what another person is thinking and feeling without anything being said. Some scholars even refer to this mode of communication as "implying rather than saying."[177] The Japanese emphasis on silence serves a variety of purposes. First, among family members, silence is actually seen as a way of "talking." The following example offers an explanation of how silence takes the place of words for the Japanese: "When people say, 'There's no communication between parents and children,' this is an American way of thinking. In Japan we didn't need spoken communication between parents and children. A glance at the face, a glance back, and we understand enough."[178]

Second, silence in Japan is linked to credibility. Someone who is silent is often perceived as having higher credibility than someone who talks most of the time. Think of the message contained in the Japanese proverb that states, "The silent man is the best to listen to." In Japanese culture, the restrained individual is one who is perceived as honest, genuine, and straightforward. Finally, the Japanese also use silence to avoid conflict and as such lessen the chance that they may lose "face." This Japanese view of silence is reflected in the following proverb: "It is the duck that squawks that gets shot." You can imagine how this use of silence might create communication problems when U.S. Americans and Japanese come together. For example, during business negotiations, each will give a different interpretation to the same silent period. The Japanese might use silence to evaluate the Americans' recommendation before responding so that their response will not embarrass or humiliate them. The U.S. Americans could read the silence of the Japanese as a rejection of the proposal. The same use of silence to save "face" can be seen in the classroom settings. And, of course, it has the same potential to be misunderstood if the person observing the silence fails to understand how the Japanese employ silence. In one study using Japanese studying in Australia, it was found that when the Japanese used face-saving silence, they were evaluated negatively.[179]

Silence plays a central role in Indian culture. Hindus believe that "self realization, salvation, truth, wisdom, peace, and bliss are all achieved in a state of meditation and introspection when the individual is communicating with himself or herself in silence."[180] Many Scandinavians also have a view of silence that differs from that of the dominant U.S. culture. In Finland, Sweden, Denmark, and Norway, silence conveys interest and consideration. In fact, your silence tells the other person that you want them to continue talking.[181]

Some co-cultures in the United States also use silence differently than does the dominant culture. A good example is American Indians. Silence for them is a major value. It can be a sign of acceptance or a manifestation of group harmony or used as a marker for a person of great wisdom or as a means of showing respect to persons of authority and age. In fact, for American Indians the tendency to respond too quickly when asked a question is considered immature, as it indicates that the person did not have the insight to use a period of silence to think about their response. The lack of speaking can create intercultural communication difficulties. Plank points out that these difficulties are often seen during employment interviews, in doctor–patient relationships, and in the classroom.[182]

DEVELOPING NONVERBAL COMMUNICATION COMPETENCY

In the Preface and during many of the discussions that followed, we have accentuated the idea that *communication is an activity*. This was a way of declaring that communication is a behavior that you engage in and that others respond to. Therefore, we conclude this chapter by offering a brief section on how you can exercise some control over that behavior and become a more competent communicator.

YOUR INTERPRETATIONS SHOULD BE TENTATIVE

At the beginning of this chapter, we noted that nonverbal messages can be intentional (waving good-bye to a friend) or unintentional (frowning because you are looking into the sun and your friend believes you are upset). In our second example, it was as if you were nonverbally "saying" two different things at the same time. The same stage for confusion can also be seen if you tell someone, "I am so happy to see you again," while at the same time you are pulling away as they try to embrace you. What we are suggesting is that nonverbal messages are subject to a great deal of ambiguity. *This potential for ambiguity can be partially minimized by making your conclusions tentative.*

BE CONSCIOUS OF THE CONTEXT

As you have already learned, *communication is rule governed.* Some self-reflection tells you that your behavior is different as you move from place to place. Think of all the "rules" that are in operation in school rooms, courtrooms, churches, business meetings, parties, restaurants, sporting events, funerals, and the like. Each of these settings requires behaviors that you have learned as part of the acculturation process. When trying to improve nonverbal communication skills, you need to understand how each situation might influence the meaning given to a specific action. During a job interview, a person's actions might reflect a degree of nervousness brought about by the formal setting (fidgeting, talking fast, etc.), while at home, that same person might be relaxed and speak at a slower pace.

Culturally, you can also observe vast differences in how people respond nonverbally when thrust into an unfamiliar environment. In North American classrooms, students move around, interact with the teacher, and are often animated. In Japan and China, nonverbal behavior is much more subdued and restrained as students follow the classroom "rules" in these cultures, where silence and constrained gestures are the norm. When trying to improve your ability to read nonverbal behaviors, ask yourself if the observed actions are appropriate for the setting.

UTILIZE FEEDBACK

Utilizing feedback means being aware of the interactive nature of communication; that is, the recipients of your messages are not passive observers. They receive your verbal and nonverbal symbols and respond in a variety of ways. As explained in Chapter 2, these responses are known as *feedback.* Hence, our next suggestion is that you *encourage feedback as a way of improving the accuracy of your perceptions of the communication encounter.* Utilizing both verbal and nonverbal feedback devices allows you to make qualitative judgments about the communication encounter. Feedback also affords you the opportunity to immediately correct and adjust your next message. When appropriate, it even means that you can ask questions of your communication partners so that you can better understand the nonverbal messages they are sending.

Because feedback is critical, you need to create an atmosphere that encourages it. Communication skills that promote feedback include smiling, head nodding, leaning forward, and even laughing. Although the nonverbal actions just mentioned are found in Western cultures, they often produce positive reactions in other cultures as well. Each of these nonverbal activities contributes to a relaxed atmosphere that fosters an accurate "reading" of your receiver's nonverbal response to your messages.

KNOW YOUR CULTURE

That you need to know your own culture should be obvious, as at this stage, you have learned that perceptions of how you and other people use nonverbal communication is colored by culture. Aspects of communication, such as what is considered attractive or how close to stand to someone, are influenced by culture. Therefore, a certain degree of introspection about your own culture is an important step in improving nonverbal behavior. A cultural accounting can provide you with important insights regarding how you might be presenting yourself and judging other people.

MONITOR YOUR NONVERBAL ACTIONS

We turn to that overused yet significant expression "know thyself" as we conclude this chapter. Our reason for this admonition is simple: What you bring to the encounter influences all aspects of that encounter. The novelist James Baldwin highlighted the idea of self-knowledge when he wrote, "The questions which one asks oneself, begin, at last, to illuminate the world, and become one's key to the experiences of others." Hence, to understand these "others," you need to monitor your actions in order to better understand the experiences of others. By knowing how you "present" yourself, you can gain insight into how people are reacting to the messages you are sending. We urge you to consider some of the following questions that will help you understand the responses displayed by your intercultural communication partner:[183]

1. Is my behavior making people feel comfortable or uncomfortable? Am I smiling or glaring at the other person? Am I standing so close that I am making him or her feel uncomfortable? Does my body appear relaxed, or do I appear stiff and nervous?

2. Am I adjusting my nonverbal messages to the feedback I am receiving from my communication "partner"? Does it appear that I am talking at such a rapid pace that I am confusing him or her? Am I pausing often enough to allow the other person to talk?

3. If my messages are being misinterpreted, is it because my unintentional messages, rather than my intentional messages, are confusing my communication "partner"?

4. Am I positioning my body as if I want to end the conversation and move on to someone or something else? Am I standing such that I appear to be seeking a power position? Am I observing and respecting cultural "rules" as they apply to the use of space?

5. Am I engaging in touching behavior that is inappropriate because of gender or cultural reasons?

6. Am I yielding to physical distractions in the setting instead of focusing on the other person?

SUMMARY

- Nonverbal communication is important to the study of intercultural communication because people use nonverbal communication to express internal states, create identity, regulate interaction, repeat messages, and substitute actions for words.

- Nonverbal communication is culture bound.

- Nonverbal communication involves all nonverbal stimuli in a communication setting that (1) are generated by both the source and his or her use of the environment and (2) have potential message value for the source and/or the receiver.

- Nonverbal messages may be intentional or unintentional.

- Nonverbal messages can work alone or in tandem with verbal messages.

- When studying nonverbal communication, it should be remembered that nonverbal messages involve multichannel activity, can be ambiguous, and are composed of numerous interacting variables.

- Nonverbal behaviors and culture are similar in that both are learned, both are passed from generation to generation, and both involve shared understandings.

- The body is a major source of nonverbal messages. These messages are communicated by means of general appearance, judgments of beauty, skin color, attire, body movements (kinesics), posture, gestures, facial expressions, eye contact, touch, and paralanguage.

- Cultures differ in their perception and use of personal space, seating, and furniture arrangement.

- A culture's sense of time can be understood by learning how members of that culture view informal time and whether their orientation toward time is monochronic or polychronic.

- The use of silence varies from culture to culture.

- You can improve your nonverbal communication skills by keeping your interpretations tentative, being conscious of the context, employing feedback, knowing your culture, and monitoring your nonverbal actions.

ACTIVITIES

1. Go to YouTube and view videos of services of three different religions: Catholic, Buddhist, and Jewish. Observe the nonverbal elements, noting particularly the differences in how members of each group use paralanguage, space, and touch.

2. Locate pictures from magazines, newspapers, and the Internet that you believe are showing the following emotions through facial expressions: (a) anger, (b) joy, (c) sadness, (d) fear, and (e) revulsion. Show these pictures to people from various cultures and see what interpretations they give to the facial expressions.

3. Go to YouTube and type in "culture and body language." View some of the videos for examples of how cultures differ in their use of body language.

4. Watch a foreign film and look for examples of proxemics, touch, and facial expressions. Compare these to those of the dominant culture of the United States.

CONCEPTS AND QUESTIONS

1. Why is it useful to understand the nonverbal language of a culture?

2. What are some potential obstacles to accurately reading the nonverbal messages of other people?

3. What is meant by the following: "Most nonverbal communication is learned on the subconscious level"?

4. Give your culture's interpretation of the following nonverbal actions:

- Two people are speaking loudly, waving their arms, and using many gestures.
- A customer in a restaurant waves his hand over his head and snaps his fingers loudly.
- An elderly woman dresses entirely in black.
- A young man dresses entirely in black.
- An adult pats a child's head.

- Two men kiss in public.

5. How can studying the intercultural aspects of nonverbal behavior assist you in discovering your own ethnocentrism? Give personal examples.

6. How late can you be for the following: (a) a class, (b) work, (c) a job interview, (d) a dinner party, or (e) a date with a friend? Ask this same question of members of two or three cultures other than your own.

7. What is meant by "Nonverbal communication is rule governed"?

8. Do you believe that in the United States a person who knows how to effectively employ nonverbal communication has an advantage over other people? How would the use of these same skills be received in Japan, China, Mexico, and India?

Intercultural Communication in Contexts: Applications in Business, Education, and Healthcare

Live together like brothers and do business like strangers.

ARABIAN PROVERB

Education must, then, be not only a transmission of culture but also a provider of alternative views of the world and a strengthener of the will to explore them.

JEROME S. BRUNER

If you are not in tune with the universe, there is sickness in the heart and mind.

NAVAJO SAYING

CULTURE AND CONTEXT

We have stressed throughout this book that communication is context dependent. Social interaction is not arbitrary, nor disorderly, nor randomized. It occurs in culturally determined, patterned rituals that dictate normative ways of speaking and behaving in each specific situation, such as in the classroom, interviews, casual conversation, sports events, etc. Our point is that communication does not occur in a void; to some degree, the social and physical setting, more commonly referred to as the communication context, influences communication.

Culture plays a primary role in establishing specific, shared rules that stipulate the communicative behaviors appropriate for different social and physical contexts. When communicating with members of your own culture, you rely on deeply internalized cultural protocols that define acceptable behavior for each particular communication situation. These rules, which facilitate your ability to communicate effectively, are so ingrained that you do not have to think consciously about which rule to use when moving from one context to another.

During intercultural communication interactions, difficulties can arise because you and your communication partners rely on different standards. Communication rules exhibit a great deal of cultural diversity, making the possibility of miscommunication an ever-present consideration. To avoid these pitfalls, you need to be aware of the potential problems that differences in culturally based protocols can bring to an intercultural exchange. This chapter aims to demonstrate how cultural norms can vary

Human interaction does not occur in a void. To some degree the social and physical setting, commonly referred to as the communication context, can influence everything, including seating arrangement, topic selection, attire, posture, and eye contact.

© Linda Winski/PhotoEdit

across three social contexts common to intercultural communication—the business, education, and healthcare settings.

ASSUMPTIONS GROUNDING COMMUNICATION CONTEXTS

Before beginning our examination of context influence and in order to further emphasize just how important the social context is in any intercultural communication contact, we will examine three basic assumptions about human communication that are directly applicable to any discussion of context: (1) communication is rule governed, (2) context prescribes the appropriate communication rules, and (3) communication rules vary across cultures.

COMMUNICATION IS RULE GOVERNED

Both consciously and unconsciously, people expect that their interactions will follow appropriate and culturally determined rules—rules that inform both parties about the proper communicative behavior for specific circumstances. Communication rules act as guidelines for both one's own actions and others' actions. As Wood points out, these rules "are shared understandings of what communication means and what kinds of communication are appropriate in particular situations."[1]

Communication rules govern both verbal and nonverbal behaviors and specify not only *what* should be said but also *how* it should be said. Nonverbal rules, as we saw in Chapter 9, apply to paralanguage, touch, facial expressions, eye contact, and other nonverbal behaviors. Verbal rules govern such things as topic selection, turn taking, voice volume, and the formality of language used as well as directness and indirectness.

Rules are also used to manage interpersonal relationships. Morreale, Spitzberg, and Barge explain that an extensive set of rules governs friendships (emotionally trusting the other person vs. keeping secrets) and conflict (raising your voice vs. not showing any emotion).[2] These cultural rules, like most aspects of culture, are learned, integrated into the self, and adhered to when communicating.

CONTEXT DICTATES COMMUNICATION RULES

Our second assumption is that the context specifies the appropriateness of the rules to be employed. Your personal experiences should validate that position. Consider how such diverse contexts as a classroom, bank, church, hospital, courtroom, wedding, funeral, or sporting event determine which communication rules you follow. In an employment interview, you might use formal or respectful words, such as "sir" or "ma'am," when responding to the interviewer. Yet, at a football or basketball game, your language would be far less formal, incorporating slang phrases and quite possibly good-natured derogatory remarks about the opposing team. For that job interview, men might wear a dark suit with white or blue shirt and conservative tie, and women would probably dress in a dark suit with a white or pastel blouse. At the sports event, jeans or shorts and a T-shirt could be appropriate. Your nonverbal behavior would also be different. At the interview, you would probably shake hands and maintain eye contact with your prospective employer, but at the football game with friends, you might embrace them when you meet, slap them on the back, or hit a "high-five."

COMMUNICATION RULES VARY ACROSS CULTURES

Our third assumption is that communication rules are, to a large extent, determined by culture. While social contexts are similar across cultures (e.g., negotiations, classrooms, hospitals), the rules governing communication in those contexts are often dissimilar. Consequently, concepts of dress, time, language, manners, and nonverbal behavior differ significantly among cultures. A few examples will illustrate the point.

When conducting business in the United States, it is not uncommon for men and women to welcome each other to a meeting by shaking hands. In the Middle East, however, some Muslim businessmen may choose to avoid shaking hands with a woman. This should not be perceived as rude or insulting but rather as a reflection of the man's religious proscriptions. This was seen during President and Mrs. Obama's 2015 visit to Saudi Arabia to express condolences after the passing of the late King Abdullah. As Saudi officials filed past to greet the Obamas, some men shook Mrs. Obama's hand, but others did not, instead acknowledging her with a nod.[3]

In an Asian college classroom, students may appear reserved, hesitant to participate in discussions, and reluctant to ask questions. This is due to the cultural standards regarding the hierarchy that governs interaction between Asian students and their professors. Cultural differences can also be found in the business context when you compare business hospitality in Turkey and the United States. In Turkey, for

Because many contextual rules are influenced by culture, it is important to learn those rules if you find yourself in a cultural setting different from your own.

Courtesy of Ed McDaniel

example, your Turkish colleagues will be adamant about paying for everything associated with your entertainment. Turkish hospitality is legendary, and you will not be permitted to pay for any part of an official meal.[4]

INTERNATIONAL COMMUNICATION IN CONTEXTS

To provide a perspective on how intercultural communication varies across cultures and contexts, we have selected the business, education, and healthcare settings for analysis. The level of cultural diversity within the United States will necessitate that many of you interact with a wide variety of cultures if you seek a career as a teacher, a healthcare provider, or business executive. Some of you may find yourself working abroad for a globalized organization. In that position you will certainly have to interact with members of the host culture in both a professional and a social capacity. Additionally, you may require medical care during your sojourn. To be successful in those settings, it is essential that you be aware of your own culture's rules and how they might differ from the rules of the person with whom you are interacting. It is also important for you to keep in mind that intercultural communication plays a vital role in many other contexts, a few of which are illustrated in Table 10.1.

INTERCULTURAL COMMUNICATION IN GLOBALIZED BUSINESS

The extensive changes that globalization has brought to nearly every aspect of life on this planet have been noted throughout this book. There is probably no segment

TABLE 10.1	Contexts for Contemporary Intercultural Communication

Business

- Negotiations
- Management
- Advertising
- Finance

Healthcare

- Clinical
- Psychological
- Traditional

Diplomatic

- Coalition building
- Maintaining alliances
- Treaties
- Trade pacts
- Goodwill programs

Legal

- Courts
- Law enforcement
- Contracts
- Oversight/regulatory compliance

Social Services

- Immigration assistance
- Welfare/unemployment benefits
- Domestic services

Politico-Military

- Peacekeeping forces
- Military exchanges/Joint exercises
- Weapons sales
- Arms reduction verification
- Armed conflict (interrogations)

Source: E. R. McDaniel.

more impacted by these many changes than the business community. Over the past several decades, "outsourcing," "offshoring," "multinational enterprise," "globalized markets," "workforce diversity," "cultural intelligence," and similar terms have become common business terms. U.S. corporations' customer-service call centers are just as likely to be located in India, the Philippines, or Mexico as in Utah, Texas, or Florida. Online shopping has accelerated commercial exchanges across national borders. PayPal, for instance, manages approximately 2,000 international transactions every minute. This type of activity requires companies to open storage warehouses in various countries in order to expedite merchandise delivery.[5]

U.S. corporations focusing on the domestic economy must also be prepared to manage the contemporary cultural diversity that characterizes both their clientele and their workforce. For multinational corporations (MNCs), the requirement for competent intercultural skills extends across all phases of their enterprise—management, production, marketing, and sales. To gain market location-specific advantages, MNCs commonly establish manufacturing sites, distribution centers, and sales and marketing forces in separate countries. This type of organization requires executives, managers, and often members of the workforce to be familiar with cultural differences among clients, employees, and local government regulation enforcement agencies. These same people need to possess the ability necessary to communicate across these multicultural boundaries. Hence, cultural knowledge and intercultural communication skills have become fundamental to almost every type of commercial endeavor—international or domestic.[6]

REMEMBER THIS

"Globalization can be conceptualized as a situation where political borders become increasingly more irrelevant, economic interdependencies are heightened, and national differences due to dissimilarities in societal cultures are central issues of business."[7]

The requirement to engage in intercultural communication always increases the potential for misunderstanding and conflict, but in business relations, it can also mean the difference between success and failure. To illustrate the very vital role that culture plays in globalized commercial activities, we will examine five culturally sensitive areas: (1) business protocol, (2) leadership and management, (3) decision making, (4) conflict management, and (5) negotiations.

Business Protocol

Business protocol involves forms of behavior such as establishing initial contact, greeting conventions, personal appearance, gift giving, and communication improprieties, with cultural differences in these protocols varying widely. For instance, while informality is the norm in most U.S. business settings, that protocol is not shared by all cultures. When conducting business in another culture it is highly important to understand and follow the prevailing customs. Knowing how to dress and introduce yourself, for instance, is especially important during initial interactions, when making a positive impression is critical to continued good relations.

Making *initial contact* is an important aspect of globalized business. The methods used to establish these contacts vary among cultures and can range from sending an email, to placing an unsolicited telephone call, to writing a formal request for a meeting, to using a "go-between" or emissary to help obtain an appointment. The appropriate procedure to use relates directly to the culture of the person you wish to contact. In the United States, initial contacts are often facilitated by a third-party introduction, but this is not a necessary requirement. "Cold calls" can also be used to gain access, and every U.S. embassy has an office dedicated to helping businesses make preliminary contact. In many cultures, however, business is based on established, trusted relationships. For instance, in Northeast Asia (China, Japan, and Korea), India, and Latin America, having a trusted third-party provide the initial introduction is often the only way to gain access to an organization's executives.

After gaining entry, it becomes important to acknowledge and attempt to practice the established cultural *greeting behaviors* of that nation. By knowing the appropriate greeting behavior and a few expressions in the language of the host culture, you will have a general idea of what to expect. This will enable you to reduce uncertainty and anxiety. You will also have an advantage in making a positive first impression. A significant consideration when meeting someone of another culture for the first time is knowing the proper form of address. What is the order of names? Should you use the first name, last name, or title? What gestures are appropriate?

Your experience has taught you that in the United States, first names precede family names, a firm handshake is expected, and after exchanging initial greetings, individuals often begin using first names. Titles such as "doctor" or "professor" are appropriate only in certain settings and are often dropped after establishing relations. However, in Japan, Korea, Vietnam, and several other cultures, the family name precedes the given name. Thus, in Seoul, Kim Eun-Ju would be Ms. Kim, whose given name is Eun-Ju (there are no middle names in Korea). If Ms. Kim has a professional title, that should be made part of any address to her. It is also important to know that in Korea, married women retain their own family name. Thus, Ms. Kim's husband may be Mr. Lee or Dr. Park. On meeting, a bow is usually rendered to Korean women and men, accompanied by a handshake between men. Although it may be normal in the United States for men to grasp the shoulder or upper arm of another man when meeting, this behavior should be avoided in Asian cultures. However, among close associates in Mexico, a brief embrace (*abrazo*) on meeting and departing is entirely appropriate. In the more formal German culture, where all titles are used, *Herr Professor Doktor* Schmidt would expect a firm handshake.

Personal appearance is yet another critical aspect of business protocol, as it creates a first impression and plays a significant role in establishing credibility.[8] The relaxed dress code common in many U.S. organizations is a reflection of the informal U.S. culture. Casual dress has become even more popular among the dot-com generation in the United States, and the late Steve Jobs, founder of Apple, made informal dress his hallmark. But while this informality is often seen as a mark of status among the younger U.S. generations, it can be perceived quite differently in cultures where formality is the norm. In China, Germany, France, much of Latin America (including Mexico), and many other nations, conservative dress, such as dark suits and white or pastel shirts, is the norm for the business environment.

The *exchange of gifts* in the international business context can be somewhat challenging, as expectations differ among cultures. In individualistic Western cultures, gift giving can be associated with attempts to curry favor. The attitude against corruption is so strong that the United States has a federal statute prohibiting bribery, and the Internal Revenue Service limits gift deductions to \$25.[9] Such restrictions make it necessary for the international business representative to be able to distinguish between what may be considered a gift and what might be seen as a bribe. From the perspective of the United States, suitable gifts for exchange with representatives of another organization are small, relatively inexpensive mementos intended to commemorate an event or organization or to serve as an expression of appreciation and solidarity. These include such things as cups, key rings, glasses, books, etc., which are inscribed with the company's logo.

When engaged in business with a foreign organization, it is useful to know not only the local views concerning gift giving but also what is considered an appropriate gift. In some cultures the color white is associated with death, so white flowers and white gift wrap should be avoided. Of course, giving alcohol to a Muslim host would be most inappropriate. In China, Korea, and Japan, you should use both hands when offering or receiving a gift. In the United States the number thirteen is considered bad luck, but in China, Korea, Japan, and Vietnam, a gift set containing four items should be avoided because their words for "four" and "death" have similar sounds. There are, of course, numerous other cultural nuances related to gift giving, so before setting out to visit a business counterpart in another country, learn as much as possible about what is considered suitable in the host country, when to present the gift, and how it should be presented. Although these details may seem trivial, without an appreciation of what is appropriate and inappropriate, you run the risk of destroying any goodwill before discussion of the business proposal even begins.

You undoubtedly know the value of using "small talk" to get to know another person. You will also have learned that there are some topics that should not be addressed during these early meetings or perhaps ever discussed at all. The choices of *initial conversational topics* during social interactions are dictated by standards that often differ across cultures. In order to avoid embarrassing social blunders, it is necessary to understand which topics are acceptable in the host country and which subjects are considered off limits.

In the United States, an initial meeting may begin with comments about the weather and quickly proceed to more personal questions, such as "Do you have a family?" or "Where did you go to school?" While these may be perfectly acceptable between Americans, they could be considered too personal in many other countries. In Saudi Arabia, for example, one should avoid asking about a man's wife.[10] Because status plays such an important role in Japan, asking what school someone attended could be a source of embarrassment. In the United States, the topics of personal salary and income are seldom part of social conversation, and the question of one's age can be a sensitive topic for many people. But in China, employees at state-owned enterprises (SOE) usually know the salary structure and may inquire about yours. And the Japanese may ask you very early on about your age, if you have a hobby, and even your blood type, which they believe can forecast personality. The Taiwan situation can be a controversial subject in China. Again, before traveling to another country, we encourage you to conduct research to determine which topics should be avoided.

As we discussed in the chapter on language, humor generally does not travel well across cultural lines, particularly in professional settings—a joke in one culture can be an insult in another. Irony is common in the United States but is seldom understood in Japan. A standard attention-getting technique for Americans is to begin a presentation with a joke. But in Germany and France, this would be inappropriate because business meetings are serious events. Our advice is to wait until you have established a good relationship with your international counterpart before attempting to inject humor into your conversations.

REMEMBER THIS

In the global market, both employees and clients come from an international pool.

Leadership and Management

According to the U.S. Department of Labor, there were 25.3 million foreign-born workers in the U.S. labor force in 2013. Another report indicated that there were as many as 600,000 people working in the United States under the H-1B visa program, which allows foreign specialists to stay in the country for as long as six years.[11] These workers are integrated into U.S. organizations alongside native-born employees, requiring the management of cultural and linguistic differences within work teams. Nor is this situation unique to the United States, as globalization has internationalized workforces around the world. Concern about the changes arising from globalization prompted one organization to commission a major study on the changing nature of work and growing workplace diversity. Two key findings related to intercultural communication are provided here:

[A 2009] survey found that it is cultural and linguistic differences that present by far the most pressing challenge for virtual-team managers. Differences in culture appear in a broad range of attitudes and values, greatly increasing the potential for a breakdown in team cohesiveness. Such differences span a wide range of areas, including attitudes toward authority, teamwork and working hours. Cultural and linguistic misunderstandings, both internally and with prospective clients, can be very costly.

[A 2012 survey] found that one-half of companies admit that communication misunderstandings have stood in the way of a major cross-border transaction, incurring significant losses for their company.[12]

Eric Miller/World Bank Group

Globalization has created circumstances where business executives from all over the world are meeting face-to-face to establish joint ventures and negotiate contracts.

In these increasingly culturally diverse work groups, every employee possesses culturally specific expectations toward management issues such as organizational structure, employee-supervisor relationships, motivational factors, and reward allocation, all of which can vary. To be successful, a global manager must be aware of the potential that cultural differences carry. Table 10.2 contains some culturally influenced management considerations and provides a generalized comparison of normative practices and employee expectations in Northeast Asian and Euro-American organizations.

Most Euro-American organizations subscribe to a "flat" structure, where work team members and managers consider each other more or less equal. Communication is informal and forthright. This organizational structure is thought to encourage a collegial atmosphere that promotes individual creativity and initiative. Pervasive individuality among Euro-Americans results in worker responsibilities and entitlements being contractually specified and little sense of organizational loyalty, which creates a highly mobile workforce as employees move from job to job in pursuit of greater personal benefits. In contrast, companies in Northeast Asia are usually characterized by a

TABLE 10.2	Cultural Variances in Organizations	
MANAGEMENT CONCERN	**NORTHEAST ASIAN**	**EURO-AMERICAN**
Organizational structure	• Vertical	• Horizontal
Organizational relationships	• Hierarchal	• Egalitarian
Basis of trust	• Interpersonal relations	• Legal system
Basis for promotion	• Time/age	• Merit
Reward allocation	• Equal for all	• Equitable to individual
Involvement in personal life	• High/expected	• Low/undesired

Source: E. R. McDaniel.

"vertical," or hierarchical, organizational structure, and employees subscribe to a well-defined hierarchy, showing deference to seniors. Work groups are expected to follow the directives of their supervisors. In China, Korea, and Japan, traditional norms dictate that employees of large, multinational organizations demonstrate loyalty to the company,[13] although there are signs that this is changing. The role that relations play among Northeast Asians was revealed in a report that showed that 60 percent of the Chinese surveyed considered interpersonal relationships as being important in their lives but that only 29 percent of the U.S. Americans in the study felt that way.[14]

Employee morale and motivation are also influenced by a worker's cultural preference for individuality or group membership. In Western organizations, especially in the United States, individuals are normally singled out for recognition and reward. This trend is evident in many workplaces where photos are prominently displayed of "Employee of the Month, Quarter, and/or Year." These individuals may receive a certificate or a plaque at a formal ceremony, along with additional rewards, such as a small bonus or perhaps a dedicated parking space for a specific period of time. In contrast, employees in Northeast Asian organizations consider all work group members to be part of an integrated team and equally responsible for the success or failure of a project. Accordingly, rewards are expected to be distributed equally. Personal recognition can lead to friction within the group and potential embarrassment for the individual.

CONSIDER THIS

A globalized Silicon Valley firm sought to motivate its multicultural workforce using posters saying, "Slay the Dragon." However, the Chinese workers objected because in China, dragons are considered good luck. The posters were removed.[15]

Different cultures also have varied perspectives on how mentoring should be conducted. In Euro-American organizations, mentoring often assumes a structured, programmed format designed to assist a specific group, such as the highly talented, socially disadvantaged, or physically challenged, for a specific time period. Quite in contrast, in Japanese corporations, the mentor–mentee relationship is personal, often emotionally based, and intended to be long term.[16]

Dissimilar culturally instilled attitudes toward work and leisure can also impact globalized organizations. Recalling our discussion of values in Chapter 6, the United States is considered to be a "doing culture," where work is an important, valued activity that usually takes precedence over almost everything else. However, employees from some other cultures may have very different attitudes and priorities. Table 10.3 illustrates the different views of work and leisure that must be managed in a multicultural workforce.

Religion is yet another consideration for global managers. In some cultures, religion is personal and separate from professional life, but in other cultures, religion permeates every aspect of work and social activity. Religion presents a host of considerations for the global manager—workweek schedule, holidays, diet, alcohol consumption, dress, accessibility to place of worship, worldview, etc. Some nations have laws governing how religion can be treated, as a New Zealand manager of a bar and restaurant in Myanmar discovered. After an advertising poster of a blue Buddha, wearing headphones, on a psychedelic-colored background was posted on Facebook, he and two other individuals were arrested and sentenced to two and a half years in

TABLE 10.3	Attitudes Toward Work[17]

STATUTORY MINIMUM ANNUAL DAYS LEAVE

NATION	DAYS
• United States	0
• China	≤ 10
• South Korea	≥ 15
• Russia	≥ 20
• Brazil	≥ 20
• France	≥ 24

prison. Myanmar has a national law prohibiting the insulting, damaging, or destruction of any religion, and the Facebook posting was considered an insult.[18]

Decision Making

A central part of any business venture is decision making. Every executive and manager, regardless of culture, must continually weigh a range of variables and decide on the best course of action. In a globalized organization, culture takes on added importance in decision making. In diverse contexts, such as personnel management, new product development, market expansion, and sales campaigns, cultural norms have significant impact. Global managers must weigh cultural variables for both domestic and international markets while managing cultural differences among employees, clients, and any other stakeholders. Globalization has also increased awareness of the role of culture in the decision-making process. Effective multinational corporation managers must understand *who* makes decisions and *how* those decisions are made. Table 10.4 compares decision-making styles in Northeast Asian and selected Western cultures.

Broadly speaking, decision making for Northeast Asians is a collectivistic process that attempts to reach an orchestrated consensus that sustains group harmony and preserves the participants' face. There are, however, distinct differences among the three cultures. "Leader-mediated compromise" is how Wenzhong, Grove, and Enping

TABLE 10.4	Cultural Variations in Decision Making

NORTHEAST ASIAN NATIONS (China, Japan, Korea)	WESTERN NATIONS (Australia, Canada, United Kingdom, United States)
• Deliberative	• Delegated authority
• Consensus oriented	• Individual oriented
• Shared responsibility	• Individual responsibility
• Group cohesion and harmony	• Positive results

Source: E. R. McDaniel.

have described decision making in Chinese organizations. This process incorporates data collection and analysis, canvassing subordinates for their opinions, distribution of background data, and meetings to discuss the issues. Senior members retain and exercise personal power by ultimately making a top-down decision crafted to reflect the group's assessments and efforts. The final result is a "harmony-within-hierarchy arrangement" designed to convey a sense of shared responsibility, create cohesion, and lessen loss-of-face opportunities among the work group participants.[19] In Japanese organizations, the stronger sense of institutional collectivism produces a much more inclusive consensus-based decision-making style, one structured to avoid relational disharmony. Japanese managers employ what could be called a middle-level up-and-down process. All affected personnel subject disseminated ideas and proposals to comprehensive discussion. If an agreement is reached, the proposal will be sent to upper-management and executive levels. When a consensus emerges, the proposal becomes policy. This method provides the opportunity for everyone to engage in the process of decision making. But shared decision making often requires considerable time to reach a final decision.

In Western nations, specifically those listed in Table 10.4, decision making is more individualistically oriented, with delegated authority usually vested in one person or a small group of personnel who are expected to take full responsibility for the final decision. This results in an expedient, top-down decision style based on the careful analysis of various options and potential outcomes. The opinion of experts and others may be solicited during the process, but there is no requirement or guarantee that their advice will be followed. This type of decision making is a reflection of the strong sense of individualism, egalitarianism, independence, and low levels of uncertainty that characterize Western culture. A Western manager working in a globalized organization will have to recognize and accommodate to the importance placed on face, group orientation, and positive social relations when engaged in decision making with employees from Northeast Asian nations.

Conflict Management

At almost every level of commercial activity, the potential exists for interpersonal and organizational conflict. Given that cultural beliefs and values contrast, the methods, opinions, and attitudes regarding the completion of tasks and achievement of goals also differ. Quite naturally, these variations provide fertile ground for disagreements that can adversely impact organizational relationships, both internally and externally. Yuan points out that in globalized organizations, the array of cultural differences within employee work groups and between clients presents an environment that heightens the potential for conflict and the ability to intensify discord.[20] Indeed, conflicts can even be caused by cultural variances that are beyond participants' awareness.

It is imperative that global managers be able to recognize when a conflict is driven more by cultural differences than by substantive disagreement. They must also be cognizant of how different cultures perceive and manage conflict. Some of these differences are listed in Table 10.5, which provides a comparison of how conflict is perceived in Northeast Asian and several Western nations, respectively. To illustrate, among in-group members in Northeast Asian cultures, conflict is considered undesireable because it carries the possibility of harming interpersonal relations and can be face threatening. As a result, open, direct conflict between in-group members is

TABLE 10.5	Conflict Management/Resolution
NORTHEAST ASIA (China, Japan, Korea)	WESTERN NATIONS (Australia, Canada, United Kingdom, United States)
• Detrimental	• Beneficial
• Conflict and parties connected	• Conflict and parties separate
• Holistic; logical analysis	• Linear; logical analysis
• Indirect approach	• Direct approach
• Confrontation avoided	• Confrontation is okay
• High face concerns	• Low face concerns
• Respected mediator	• Legal action; expert mediator
• More information	• Less information

Source: E. R. McDaniel.

normally avoided if possible or managed indirectly. For someone from Japan, the strong interpersonal connections within an in-group can create a sense of interrelatedness between a conflict and the members' personal relationships. Moreover, an open conflict can result in loss of face for one or more of the group. As a result, disagreements are usually approached indirectly and resolved through lengthy discussion of the problem. And discussions can continue outside the workplace during the evening in bars and restaurants where alcohol serves as a social lubricant. If the conflict cannot be reconciled informally, Northeast Asians, driven by particularistic inclinations, prefer to use trusted intermediaries to help reach an amicable solution.[21]

This contrasts with individualistic Western nations, where debating conflicting opinions and ideas is seen as a useful tool for airing differences and finding compromise. Face concerns in the West are individual based, and there is generally less concern for that of others. This is, of course, amplified by the lack of close, interdependent relationships in the work setting. Professional conflict situations are considered separate and apart from one's relationship with the other party. This detachment from the professional conflict allows Westerners, particularly those from the United States, to engage in heated, sometimes boisterous debate over an issue but concurrently retain affable relations with each other. The universalistic perspective of Westerners pushes them to quickly move to employ legal counsel or professional, third-party mediators for conflict resolution.

Negotiations

In the business world, negotiations are fundamentally a formal process designed to assist disparate parties in the management of differences and to assist in making decisions that lead to mutually agreeable, cooperative interactions. In the global market, corporate agents are continually negotiating mergers, joint ventures, imports/exports, patent licensing agreements, intellectual property rights, foreign direct investment, and a host of other cross-cultural commercial endeavors. The central element in these or any type of negotiation is communication. When representatives of different cultures engage in bargaining, the critical role of communication brings added challenges. Thus, intercultural communication can be the key to success or failure in cross-cultural negotiations.

Every negotiator will develop a strategy that reflects his or her personal style, but each individual is also influenced by a national negotiating style as has been substantiated by numerous academic studies and research reports. The varying national styles are products of dissimilar historical legacies, definitions of trust, cultural values, decision-making processes, approaches to risk taking, attitudes toward formality, perceptions of time, cognitive patterns, and of course, communication styles.[22] Research has also disclosed that national negotiating styles are strongly influenced by culture, and the behaviors displayed during bargaining sessions often reflect the more prominent cultural characteristics of that nation. For example, although China, Japan, and Korea have different national negotiation styles, all adhere to bargaining procedures that reflect a collectivistic theme. On the other hand, Western nations normally display individualistic-based negotiation behaviors. To demonstrate further, Table 10.6 presents an overview of the primary Chinese and U.S. culturally based negotiation characteristics, which will be more fully developed in the following discussion. But before beginning that discussion, we need to explain our decision to use China and the United States as examples. Our rationale is quite simple—in the global market, China and the United States represent the two largest economies, which means that both commercial and diplomatic negotiations between representatives of the two nations will continue to occupy a prominent position well into the future.

The national negotiation styles generalized to Chinese and U.S. business representatives are rather disparate. The most conspicuous difference is the ultimate objective. Although each side strives to obtain the most advantageous agreement possible, there are signal differences in the underlying attitude. The Chinese approach negotiations with a vision toward establishing a continuing, lasting collaborative relationship. They usually seek agreements that have a long-term, relational basis. This will be evident in the Chinese initial efforts to socialize and become better acquainted with their U.S. counterparts. This objective of building a trusting relationship is another reflection of the importance of *guanxi* (i.e., social network/relationship) in Chinese society. The goal is to develop an affiliation founded on mutual respect and trust, an association that not only will smooth the way for the current project but also holds

TABLE 10.6 Negotiation Styles	
CHINA	**UNITED STATES**
Objective	
• Cooperative relationship	• Written legal contract
Characteristics	
• Relationship based	• Task based
• Between individuals	• Between organizations
• Long-term focus	• Short-term focus
• Process oriented	• Goal oriented
• Holistic	• Objective, logical, linear
• More information needed	• Less information needed
• Low initial trust	• High initial trust
• Nonconfrontational	• Assertive, confrontational
• Particularistic ethics	• Universal ethics

Source: E. R. McDaniel.

the possibility of future collaborations. To achieve their goal of a cooperative relationship, the Chinese spend considerable time discussing issues, examining data, and engaging in social entertainment.

In contrast, U.S. negotiators, driven by the value of individualism and self-reliance, normally prefer a logical, linear procedure, where points are examined and bargained over individually and sequentially. Due to the cultural value placed on time, U.S. negotiations move through the bargaining sessions as quickly as possible. They are focused on the immediate end result of a contractually based agreement and are much less concerned about relationships and future collaborative projects than are their Chinese counterparts. The shorter time horizon among U.S. business representatives is also due to the importance given to quarterly earnings statements, stockholder expectations, and bonus agreements. In contrast to the Chinese, negotiations for the U.S. team are between organizations, and personal relationships are a separate, unrelated entity.

The Chinese prefer negotiations that develop through a holistic process rather than a linear advance. Intraorganizational and governmental oversight considerations, coupled with cultural concerns for face, hierarchy, and group consensus, tend to lessen the ability to make quick decisions. Considerable time must be spent in discussions with colleagues and gathering data to respond to actual and anticipated questions. As a result, negotiation topics may be discussed in random order, and previously concluded topics may be reopened due to Chinese deliberations with the greater work group. This slower pace may be perceived as a delaying tactic by U.S. negotiators, who regularly exercise considerable autonomy in decision making. U.S. delegates usually have little concern for the thoughts and opinions of their general employees and would seldom see a need to consult them. Employee turnover is normal in the United States, and the greater concern is for the well-being of the organization.

Chinese and U.S. representatives approach the establishment of trust, instrumental to almost any negotiation, differently. Despite its long history, China has never had a comprehensive legal system that protected the rights of all its citizens. This helps explain the importance of interpersonal relations and social networks (*guanxi*). Unable to rely on an established legal framework, the Chinese turned to a network of family, clan, and close friends. Today, trust is extended only after a period of social interaction that, if successful, leads to a positive, dependable interpersonal relationship. The U.S. view is to immediately extend a degree of initial trust to others, a "hail fellow, well met" attitude arising from the cultural preference of egalitarianism and universalism. For U.S. negotiators, long-term trust will be guaranteed by a highly detailed, legally binding contract that clearly specifies requirements for each side. Moreover, contracts in the United States are considered static, and any proposed change requires renegotiation. The Chinese view contracts as a dynamic agreement among friends that is subject to adjustment as conditions change. These different views of contracts once again illustrate the inclination by the United States toward universalism and the Chinese preference for particularism.

Their varied approaches to conflict management can also conflate relations between Chinese and U.S. negotiators when problems or differences occur during the bargaining sessions. Chinese negotiators may endeavor to promote and maintain positive relations with the U.S. side and employ an indirect communication style to avoid confrontation when discussing differences. U.S. representatives, accustomed to dealing with negative information in a direct manner, may be confused by the indirect approach and even consider the Chinese to be disingenuous, possibly leading to a breakdown in the negotiations. Conversely, the U.S. direct style, a product of a historical legacy of rhetorical argumentation, could also create problems. If a U.S. negotiator resorted to abrupt, confrontational dialogue as a means of persuasion, the Chinese side could well consider this behavior as offensive and immature, resulting in a loss of face for the U.S. bargaining team and their company.[23] This aptly demonstrates the necessity of intercultural competence among cross-cultural negotiators.

THE ROLE OF LANGUAGE IN GLOBALIZED ORGANIZATIONS

Throughout this text we have stressed the need to gain second-language competency, and nowhere is that skill more critical than in a globalized organization. Whether working abroad or with a multicultural workforce, knowing another language provides numerous benefits. One of the most important aspects of second-language skills when combined with cultural knowledge is the awareness that literal translations do not always carry the same meaning into the other language. As an example, in the United States, the phrase "we are on a parallel course" is commonly used to indicate agreement with the other party. However, for the Japanese, the phrase would connote irreconcilable differences because "parallel lines" never meet. From the U.S. individualistic cultural perspective, being on a parallel course suggests agreement but retention of everyone's individuality. But the group-oriented Japanese would be more comfortable with terms conveying feelings of inclusiveness.

When working abroad, knowledge of the host country's language will greatly ease the stress of cultural adaptation and integration. A common problem that plagues newly arrived expatriates is an inability to function in the new culture as efficiently as in their own. Learning about the host nation's cultural norms before departure will reduce a great deal of uncertainty about your new environment, but knowing some of the language provides exponential benefits in adapting. Moreover, the ability to speak even a little of the new language will facilitate your development of interpersonal relationships with members of the host population.

BENEFITS OF GLOBALIZED ORGANIZATIONS

The preceding discussions have clearly illustrated that global business managers are faced with a variety of culturally based challenges when working in a multinational environment. Being successful in meeting these challenges requires a comprehensive appreciation for cultural differences and the ability to employ competent intercultural communication skills. In an effort to convince you to exert the time and energy to prepare for these challenges, it is worthwhile to examine the benefits of the multicultural workplace.

Given the globalized market and the growing diversity of U.S. demographics, contemporary organizations face little option but to incorporate cultural diversity and adapt to the new requirements. Today, companies must market their product to appeal to a variety of cultures and concomitantly draw on employees of that same variety. Although these requirements have presented new challenges and problems, they have also brought numerous benefits to the workplace, and we will explain three of them: (1) increased perspectives, (2) greater flexibility and adaptability, and (3) expanded market share.

As you have learned, it is common for people of different cultures to have dissimilar worldviews and approaches to life. This lack of commonality in a multicultural workforce offers the benefit of expanded perspectives, which in turn can increase creativity within the organization. Having people with different perspectives focus on a problem will produce more innovative, viable solutions, and collaborative solutions are normally adopted and implemented much faster than when directed from above. A multicultural work environment also brings about greater flexibility and adaptability for the organization as a whole. Employees of a globalized organization, possessing attributes of various cultures, have already learned to adapt to changing environments and how to best deal with uncertainty. That experience provides them with insight into helping the organization as a whole adapt to changing market conditions and manage new customer requirements. This diversity of talent and experience also offers the organization a venue for expanding their customer base.

On the off chance that you remain unconvinced of the merits of diversity and the need for corporations to meet the demands of the globalized marketplace, we offer you the following example of what can happen when organizations fail to accommodate. In 1995, the *Fortune* Global 500 list included 147 Japanese companies, but only sixty-two were listed in 2013, a 42 percent drop. According to academic reports, this decline was a result of Japan's inability to adapt to the forces of globalization. Diversity is a major driver of innovation in organizations today, but Japanese companies and many of their technologies have remained surprisingly insular and unable to integrate into the larger global market, a condition commonly called the "Galapagos syndrome." Japan's resistance to change, a product of high uncertainty avoidance, has also inhibited the growth of start-ups, a prominent driver of the global economy. The misfortunes of Japanese MNCs attest to the requirement for contemporary organizations to embrace cultural diversity and acquire intercultural competence.[24]

EDUCATION IN THE GLOBALIZED SOCIETY

Globalization and accompanying migration patterns have significantly changed the demographic composition of nearly all U.S. and most European Union (EU) nations' classrooms. Many EU countries have long had diverse populations due to immigrants from their former colonies. Now, new arrivals from the Middle East and Africa are making their way to Italy, Greece, and Spain and moving northward into other European nations. The United States is not immune to these kinds of demographic shifts in its school populations, as immigrants from Latin America, Asia, and the Middle East are coming, both legally and illegally, to classrooms in the United States. Many of these new arrivals bring their children—or in some cases, are children

TABLE 10.7	U.S. Public School (Pre-K–12) Enrollments[26]		
RACE/ETHNICITY % BY YEAR	2001	2011	2023*
White	60	52	45
Black	17	16	15
Hispanic	17	24	30
Asian/Pacific Islander	4	5	5
American Indian/Alaskan Native	1	1	1
Two or more races	—	3	4

*Projected.

themselves—who add to the diversity of U.S. primary and secondary school classrooms. The impact of these changes can be seen in Table 10.7, which shows the continued growth of the cross-cultural student population in the United States. Moreover, in the 2011–2012 school year, more than 9 percent of U.S. public school students were English language learners, and over 20 percent of U.S. students spoke a foreign language at home, according to census data. In California, 45 percent of households speak a foreign language. At one high school in San Diego, California, 80 to 90 percent of the 1,100 students were first-generation immigrants in 2013. The students, teachers, and staff had to manage communication that crossed thirty-four languages and thirty-seven dialects.[25]

Increased cultural diversity in the U.S. educational system has not been limited to primary and secondary schools. Higher education has also experienced larger numbers of co-culture enrollees. Perhaps you have noted this diversity on your own campus and in some of your classes. Globalization has also raised the number of international students and foreign-born faculty in U.S. universities. In 2011 there were 115,000 foreign-born educators and researchers working at U.S. higher education institutions, an increase of approximately 29,000 over a ten-year period. The number of international students enrolling in U.S. universities and colleges has grown over 70 percent since 2000.[27] The numbers of educators and students would probably have been

TABLE 10.8	International Students Attending U.S. Universities, 2013–2014 (Top 10 Countries)[28]	
COUNTRY	NUMBER OF STUDENTS	% OF TOTAL
All nations	886,052	100.0
China	274,439	31.0
India	102,673	11.6
South Korea	68,047	7.7
Saudi Arabia	53,919	6.1
Canada	28,304	3.2
Taiwan	21,266	2.4
Japan	19,334	2.2
Vietnam	16,579	1.9
Mexico	14,779	1.7
Brazil	13,286	1.5

higher except for the restrictions placed on visas in the aftermath of 9/11 and other worldwide terrorist attacks.

Increased cultural diversity in today's classrooms presents challenges for students, teachers, counselors, and administrative staff. In addition to the language issue, learning styles, attitude toward education, classroom deportment, and student–teacher relationships are some of the factors that vary across cultures. Educational systems that for decades have served their communities well must now adapt to the needs of a growing, dynamic multicultural student body. It is the responsibility of schools and educators at all levels to prepare students to participate fully in the ever-evolving global community. This requires an expanded knowledge of the role of culture in the classroom.

Our discussion on culture and communication in the educational context is designed to inform you on how the approach to education varies across cultures, the different ways that students learn, and the demands of the multicultural classroom. Before beginning that discussion, however, we will take a moment to illustrate what and how culture teaches.

Courtesy of Robert Fonseca

What a culture teaches, and how it teaches it, can provide insight into that culture.

CULTURE AS A TEACHER

By now, you know that culture is a tireless teacher that starts your learning process at birth and never pauses. You will also have discerned that every culture adheres to a very selective curriculum. This selectivity is embodied in the ancient Chinese proverb "By nature all men are alike, but by education widely different." The Chinese sage was pointing out that cultural variations are the result of people being taught different beliefs, values, customs, and perspectives. What is taught in a culture is critical to the maintenance and perpetuation of that culture, and much of the responsibility for that instruction comes from the formal educational systems within the culture.

Formal education, regardless of the culture, includes a variety of common subjects—mathematics, science, history, language, literature, and in some nations, religion. Although the subjects are similar, the content often varies. For instance, history is taught in almost every culture, but the focus is usually different because each culture emphasizes its own past. As we discussed in Chapter 5, history teaches you the values of your culture, assists you in making sense of the present, and helps you identify with a larger group. With only infrequent variation, each culture highlights those events that serve to promote positive ideals and tends to deemphasize actions that carry a negative connotation. As the late Israeli scholar and diplomat Abba Eban pointed out, "A nation writes its history in the image of its ideal." To illustrate, U.S. history classes devote considerable time to the Founding Fathers, the Declaration of Independence, the American Revolution, and the westward growth of the young nation. Until the latter half of the twentieth century, much less attention was devoted to the topic of slavery and the plight of American Indians. History classes in China are accustomed to examining the achievements of 5,000 years of continuous civilization and the Chinese Communist Party's rescue of the nation from the tyranny of Western and Japanese colonial powers. Often left unsaid is the devastation brought about by the Great Leap Forward and the Cultural Revolution. Mexico's history would likely focus on the cultural heritage of the pre-Columbian era and the Mexican Revolution, while little attention would be paid to the long record of political corruption and drug cartels.

Formal education can easily become an outlet for cultural ethnocentrism because every culture tends to glorify its own achievements and focuses less on the accomplishments and contributions of other cultures. This is particularly true of history but also occurs in other subjects. In the United States, the Pulitzer Prize–winning poet Carl Sandburg receives more attention than the Chilean Pablo Neruda, who was awarded the Nobel Prize in Literature. Studying only one religious text—Bible, Koran, Torah, Vedas, etc.—while disregarding others is a quiet form of ethnocentrism. The pitfalls of ethnocentrism and the constraints of prejudicial nationalism that can creep into educational curricula can be avoided. Through exposure to a range of different perspectives, philosophies, and histories, complemented by critical thinking skills, you can develop a greater awareness and understanding of cultural diversity and enhance your intercultural competency.

LEARNING FROM CULTURE

After reading that what is taught in schools varies among cultures, it should be no surprise to discover that there are also differences in how students and teachers participate in the educational process. Knowledge of *what* a culture teaches can provide an understanding of what that culture considers important; knowing *how* a culture teaches is equally significant because (1) it provides insight into the characteristics of the culture, (2) student–teacher relations offer a perspective on the structure of interpersonal relations throughout the culture, and (3) it illustrates the importance that a culture places on education.

The *process* of formal education in a culture is tied directly to its beliefs, values, and characteristics. In some cultures, the normative way of teaching is for the teacher to lecture while students sit quietly and dutifully take notes. Tests involve iterating the previously received facts. In other cultures, students actively engage their instructors in give-and-take verbal sparring. Exams may involve creative and critical thinking skills. The relationship between teacher and student also varies among cultures. In some countries where teachers enjoy considerable social status and power, the student–teacher relationship is very formal, but in other nations, the relationship is more relaxed and egalitarian. Even nonverbal aspects, such as space, distance, time, and dress codes, are cultural variables reflected in classroom behavior. For example, in some cultures, informal attire is acceptable in the classroom, but other cultures demand that students attend class in identical uniforms. To further illustrate this aspect of education, we will look at some of the behaviors that characterize culturally based educational differences in Japan, the United States, and China.

Students walking to school are a familiar sight on any weekday morning in Japan, as well as the United States, although less common in the latter due to parental concerns and fewer public transportation options. But there are some other marked differences. Japanese elementary students usually assemble at a neighborhood location and proceed together to their classes. They will form one or two lines, with one older student at the front and one at the back. All will be wearing hats identical in color and shape. The younger students are learning the cultural values of group membership, hierarchy, and social conformity. The older students are learning about leadership, social responsibility toward others, and mentorship. In the classroom, interdependence is stressed as students work on projects in assigned groups and are seldom called on to answer questions individually. Upon entering middle school and throughout high school, the students will wear uniforms reflective of their school and will generally remain with the same group of classmates from class to class, a continual reinforcement of the importance of group solidarity.

CONSIDER THIS

What is taught in the formal education system of a culture is determined by its values and also promulgates those values.

For U.S. high school students, however, choice and freedom of expression are constants. Their day begins by deciding what to wear and perhaps even how to get to school—walk, ride, or drive. Their choice of classes can vary yearly and even by semester. Each high school class is likely to have a diverse group of students as they move from room to room for each lesson. Additionally, there will be a wide selection of extracurricular sports and clubs for after-school activities. For any group project, U.S. students may even be allowed to choose their own teammates. In student-centered classes, learners will be encouraged to voice their own opinions (hopefully with supporting evidence), even if different from the instructor's. Students rarely experience open, public critical feedback in their classes. These practices serve to inculcate the cultural values of individual self-worth, independence, self-reliance, and freedom of choice.

Traditional Chinese classrooms are characterized by the teacher lecturing and students furiously copying everything so that it can be memorized and replicated on exams. The instructor's questions, when asked, will frequently be responded to en masse. This form of classroom teacher-centered behavior is a reflection of China's Confucian heritage, which elevated the values of hierarchy and social cooperation and placed memorization of established precepts above creative thinking. The student–teacher relationship is formal at all times, and like their Japanese counterparts, Chinese secondary school students usually wear uniforms, have a larger class size than in the United States, and remain together as a class for all subjects. In their study of preschools, Tobin and Hayashi observed that Chinese students received open, honest critical comment from their teachers and peers, another Confucian attribute. As an example, a student experiencing difficulty with a math problem may be requested to come to the front of the classroom and try to work through the problem. This allows the teacher and the class as a whole to offer assistance. The thought is that this experience will cause the student to reflect on his or her efforts and work harder, quite in contrast to the individualistically oriented positive feedback procedures used in U.S. classes. From this brief overview, you should be able to appreciate that in addition to subject material, the Chinese classroom also instills the cultural values of a hierarchical social structure, group identity, social harmony, and the importance of determination and perseverance.[29]

CULTURAL ATTITUDES TOWARD EDUCATION

How you perceive education is strongly influenced by culture, or, as stated by McHugh, "the cultural attitudes of the society toward education greatly affect the education of its citizens."[30] The contrasting attitudes across cultures can readily be seen by comparing the United States with two Asian nations—China and Korea.

Clearly, education is seen as important in the United States, but it is not considered an absolutely essential prerequisite for success. The strong sense of independent meritocracy among U.S. Americans, partly fed by media stories and programs, conveys a belief that if someone has an idea and the determination, one can fulfill one's dreams. Stories abound of young dot-com entrepreneurs dropping out of college to start their own businesses—Bill Gates, Steve Jobs, and Mark Zuckerberg being but three among many.[31] Declining U.S. test scores in comparison to other nations have also contributed to a growing ambivalence toward the contemporary U.S. education system. Today's parents demand choices for the education of their children, as seen in the growth of charter schools, homeschooling, and private schools. There is also vocal concern that the federal government has too much influence on local schools and the curricula. And although U.S. American parents take an active role in school activities, Ripley found that they tended to focus on the "nonacademic side of their children's school" and felt that the best setting for learning was an unstructured environment. Additionally, building self-esteem was considered an important part of the classroom experience.[32]

In China and Korea, along with most Asian cultures, including Asian Americans, educational achievement is among the highest of values, and parents are involved in all phases of their children's schooling. Unlike in the United States, where students expect to do "fun things" in class, Chinese and Korean students see education as a serious undertaking centered on "hard work." This is, in part, a result of the Confucian influence that persists in both nations and results from the status and material benefits acquired through education. Each year, graduating high school students in both nations take a single exam that largely determines the course of their adult life. In China, the *gaokao* (high exam), lasting two days, is administered at the conclusion of the school year. In June 2015, over 9.4 million Chinese students participated in the exam. Korean high school seniors take the College Scholastic Ability Test (*suneung*), an eight-hour exam administered in the fall. The importance of these nationally administered tests cannot be overstated. The exam scores determine which university a student will attend, and the institution attended is the single most influential factor in a student's future success—the more prestigious the school, the more success in life. This procedure is highly reminiscent of the ancient Chinese imperial exam system that was based on knowledge pertaining to the Confucian classics.[33]

During the years of schooling leading up to the modern-day exams, Chinese and Korean parents become actively involved in the education of their children, often functioning as at-home coaches and teachers. After scheduled classes Chinese and Korean students regularly attend private cram schools for a few hours before returning home, where they continue to study. As the exam date draws near, family life centers on creating an environment conducive to study. Many students are escorted to the exam center by a parent or grandparent, who then goes to a nearby temple or shrine to pray for success. In status-conscious China and Korea, parental involvement is also motivated by the fact that a child's accomplishments (or failures) also reflect on the family as a whole. Pressure on the students is enormous; they shoulder the future fortunes and social standing of their families. This high value placed on education carries over to Asian Americans, who spend more on education than any other ethnic group in the United States. Their dedication to scholastic achievement has resulted in Asian Americans having a larger representation among students at elite universities than they do in the U.S. population as a whole. This is easily seen in the University of California system, where Asian Americans represented 30 percent of the 2013 enrollment but only 14 percent of the state's total population.[34]

This comparison of educational attitudes and class deportment should convince you that culture is a very influential factor in your value of and approach to education. Moreover, it also offers a preview of the level of competition for jobs in the globalized workplace.

LANGUAGE AND EDUCATION

Language is an important and requisite dynamic in multicultural education. As was brought out in Chapter 8, language, an integral part of all social interaction, allows you to share your experiences, feelings, and acquired knowledge with others. In an ideal setting, the use of a common language helps foster mutual understanding by enabling the construction of shared meanings with others. However, in the United States and many other nations, the increase in population diversity has eroded the use of a common language in the community collective. This same diversity also exists in the growing multicultural classrooms. At the beginning of this section, we mentioned the many different languages and dialects used in a San Diego school.

That diversity is a common characteristic of schools in the United States and other nations as well. Consider the primary school in England, where 414 students spoke thirty-one languages, or the high school in Nashville, Tennessee, with students coming from sixty-three different nationalities and 70 percent not speaking English at home.[35]

The lack of a common first language in a classroom is problematic, and the implications are obvious—the learning process can be impeded for the individual and the class as a whole. The language-deficient student can experience psychological dissonance and diminished self-esteem. A lack of fluency can also result in nonnative speakers being pejoratively categorized into groups. Accents and nonfluency can lead to negative perceptions and stereotyping by classmates and instructors. Students seeking to speak their native language may inadvertently produce in- and out-groups, with the resulting intergroup tensions.

Language assists individuals to construct an identity that connects them to their ethnic in-group and concurrently sets them apart from other reference groups.[36] Your first language not only helps in identity construction, but also ties you to the historical legacy of the group. When non- or limited-English-speaking students enter the U.S. school system, they are faced with the challenge of assimilating into the dominant, English-speaking culture. This need to assimilate can act as a wedge between the student's native-language identity and the English language social system they are encountering. Classroom instructors can help to mediate this difficult process by demonstrating respect for their students' native languages and recognizing that they may be experiencing difficulties in adapting to an English language educational environment.

REMEMBER THIS

Culture plays a role in every learning situation.

THE MULTICULTURAL CLASSROOM

The multicultural classroom is a distinguishing characteristic of globalized society. Recall the statistics presented in Table 10.7 that illustrate the ever-increasing diversity in U.S. public schools. It is quite probable that you will find yourself in other multicultural classrooms after completing your university career. Some of you may become teachers or professors, and others may work as corporate trainers. Almost everyone can expect to participate in professional workshops. Today, schools, universities, and corporate training all require that culture be considered in the design and implementation of educational programs. Even when engaged in on-the-job training, different cultural learning styles are a factor. In every multicultural classroom, success depends on the instructor being knowledgeable about, and responsive to, cultural diversity. Teachers need intercultural communication skills in order to effectively prepare presentations, construct teaching aids, and interact with students. The importance of this ability is highlighted in the following statement: "Communication in the learning environment is influenced by cultural, psychological, and contextual factors and it involves the application of interpersonal and intrapersonal values."[37]

Cultural Considerations in the Multicultural Classroom

While the list will not be exhaustive, we will discuss a few of the considerations that must be taken into account when teaching a multicultural class. Perhaps one of the first issues that should be addressed is recognition that a culturally diverse class will likely have students who have been conditioned to learn differently. Students from the United States will have been taught that debate, argumentation, public speaking skills, and critical thinking are important classroom attributes. However, Asian students, especially if they are coming from abroad, will have learned that the proper classroom deportment is to sit silently, to not challenge the teacher, to take copious notes, and to memorize all the materials. Left unaddressed, this situation could result in a class divided along cultural lines—some sitting quietly and others dominating any discussion.

Second, in learning situations, regardless of the level, it is vital to understand that different cultures have varied thinking patterns that influence reasoning, problem solving, and social interaction. Cross-cultural psychology research has demonstrated that Westerners generally use a linear, cause-and-effect thinking process that emphasizes logic and rationality. Problems are approached through a systematic, in-depth analysis of each component, progressing individually from the simple to the more difficult. In contrast, the research showed that people from Northeast Asia (Chinese, Japanese, and Koreans) rely on a holistic thinking pattern. Problems are seen as complex and interrelated, requiring a greater understanding of and emphasis on the collective, rather than on separate, individual parts. This produces an emphasis on intuitive and contextual thinking. These varied patterns of cognitive processing will influence the way students and employees communicate, interact with others, and perform problem-solving tasks.[38]

Third, cultures also have distinctive ways of presenting educational information. Some prefer to present information orally, and others emphasize texts. Elsewhere in this book we mentioned that Arabs have an oral tradition. This is also true for many West African cultures, North American Native tribes, the peoples of Central Asia, and Australian Aboriginals. Societies with a tradition of oral learning will engage in more conversation, use storytelling to transmit knowledge, and rely more on what they hear. We also pointed out in our discussion of history that East Asian cultures have historically emphasized written text over verbal eloquence. This is why the use of books and other print formats tend to take precedence in Asian schools. From this background, it would not be unusual to see Vietnamese students sitting quietly and being somewhat reticent to join in classroom discussions while African American students eagerly voiced their thoughts. Western cultures generally tend to give greater precedence to while African cultures emphasize orality.[39]

Fourth, Limited English Proficiency (LEP) in the U.S. classroom is an obvious impediment to learning and will only worsen if left unattended. LEP students are faced with both cognitive and linguistic issues. The requirement to move between languages involves managing different grammatical structures, inexact word meanings, vocabulary shortfalls, unfamiliarity with colloquialisms, and other issues. This not only deters comprehension but also demands greater cognitive effort, which produces mental fatigue. In other words, in addition to grasping subject content, LEP students also have to make the new language express what they are learning. Therefore, they must perform at a much higher cognitive and linguistic level than their native English-speaking peers who need only manage the cognitive aspects of learning. When teaching a multicultural audience, instructors need to be attentive to signs of incomprehension by the students and must also self-monitor for speaking rate and appropriate vocabulary usage.

Finally, a consideration in the multicultural classroom is student–teacher interaction protocols. Students from different cultures will have varied attitudes toward their teachers. Those coming from hierarchical cultures will probably see teachers as high-status authority figures and interact formally. In contrast, students of egalitarian cultures, such as the United States, may frequently be on a first-name basis with their instructor, who will likely dress informally. In Israeli schools, students may openly criticize the instructor[40] and will often use first names. Eye and physical contact can also vary, with Asian students avoiding both, while Mexicans are likely to be more open to touching the shoulder or arm. Student expectations of their teacher's appearance and conduct are also culturally driven. Professors in formal, hierarchical cultures will be expected to dress formally and maintain a proper relationship of distance with students.

The considerations discussed in this section were intended to demonstrate the complexities of cultural influences in a multicultural classroom. We now provide some recommendations on how to become a culturally responsive teacher in any setting.

Multicultural Classroom Communication Strategies

As previously mentioned, there is a very good possibility that you will find yourself in an instructional position during your professional career, and your students or clients will almost certainly come from a variety of cultural backgrounds. Communicating effectively in a culturally diverse educational setting will present you with a variety of challenges and calls for the development and implementation of appropriate communication strategies. With this in mind, we offer the following guidelines that can assist in creating a beneficial learning environment for a multicultural audience:

- **Develop an appropriate attitude**

    o Recognize that your own perspectives and behaviors are culturally based and may be different from some of your students'

    o Increase self-awareness and knowledge of cultural differences

    o To improve understanding and tolerance, continually expose students to other cultures

- **Promote conversations about culture**

    o Create student awareness of their own and other cultures

    o Engage students in discussions of cultural similarities and differences

    o Employ classroom activities that require student collaboration

    o Ensure that all groups have cross-cultural representation

- **Be alert for cultural conflict**

    o Recognize the potential for culturally based misunderstanding and conflict

    o Make it clear that cultural differences are to be viewed from a tolerant perspective

    o Establish ground rules for classroom discussions (e.g., ethnic-based humor is off limits)

    o Stress the need for an unbiased attitude toward other peoples' beliefs, values, and behaviors

- ○ Explain potential cultural differences in intellectual property rights (i.e., what is plagiarism)
- ○ Make clear the policy and consequence of academic dishonesty

- **Be aware of family and community backgrounds**

  - ○ Be aware of the student's home and community environment
  - ○ Recognize that cultural intolerance and stereotypes learned in the home may present classroom challenges
  - ○ Explore the resources in your students' community that can help you reach all of your students
  - ○ Invite outside speakers to address culturally related topics

- **Be culturally responsive**

  - ○ Be cognizant of the different ways of learning and vary your instructional format
  - ○ Design classroom activities to illustrate cultural differences
  - ○ Recognize the cultural variations in communication styles[41]

We expect that you now understand and appreciate the impact that cultural diversity has in the educational context. Gollnick and Chinn provide a succinct reminder of this influence when they say, "Not all students can be taught in the same way because they are not the same. Their cultures and experiences influence the way they learn and interact with their teachers and peers."[42] Effectiveness in the multicultural classroom requires an understanding of the students' culturally based learning behaviors and communication styles. In order to extend and enhance the learning experience, the competent educator will have the ability to use the richness of values, worldviews, and lifestyles represented in the students' diversity.

HEALTHCARE IN A MULTICULTURAL CONTEXT

By now you should be convinced that you live, study, work, and play in a truly globalized society, a society characterized by the continued commingling of people of different cultures. This mixing is not likely to abate, given the many humanitarian crises, political oppression, and desire for economic betterment facing much of the world's population. In the previous sections we sought to demonstrate the influence of culture and the role of intercultural communication in the business and education contexts. For our final example of applied intercultural communication, we have selected a context that all of you will experience throughout your life—healthcare. If you have not already done so, at some point in your life, you will encounter people of different cultures in the healthcare setting. This can occur during treatment involving yourself, a family member, or a friend. Some of you may find employment in the burgeoning healthcare industry where knowledge of culture and competent intercultural communication skills are increasingly required, as indicated by Purnell:

> Health ideology and health-care providers have learned that it is just as important to understand the patient's culture as it is to understand the physiological responses in illness, disease, and injury.... A lack of knowledge of patients' language abilities and cultural beliefs and values can result in serious threats to life and quality of care for all individuals.[43]

GLOBALIZATION AND HEALTHCARE

Any examination of the role that intercultural communication plays in the healthcare context cannot be limited to doctor–patient interactions. The topic is much more comprehensive and calls for an appreciation of just how prevalent cultural diversity is in both international and domestic healthcare. From the global perspective, recall the many natural disaster relief efforts that have taken place over the past several years, such as the Haiti earthquake (2010), the Japanese earthquake and tsunami (2011), the Philippines typhoon (2013), and the Nepal earthquake (2015). In each instance, medical relief teams were quickly dispatched by a host of different nations.

Humanitarian relief operations to relieve suffering resulting from armed conflicts, disease outbreaks, refugee displacement, and other crises are also areas where multicultural medical aid teams are on duty. Both government and nongovernment agencies staff these operations. Doctors Without Borders alone maintains operations in seventy nations,[44] and at every location, the healthcare providers must manage cultural differences in language and healthcare treatment beliefs along with varied value systems. The 2014 Ebola outbreak in West Africa saw personnel from around the world working to coordinate logistics, administer care, institute prevention programs, and help with recovery operations, including body disposal and bereavement counseling.

The diversity of the population of the United States is also mirrored in the healthcare system. Today, it is not uncommon to encounter a doctor, nurse, office staff, hospice worker, pharmacist, physical therapist, dentist, hospital attendant, dental technician, psychologist, lab technician, etc. with a cultural background different from your own. According to a Migration Policy Institute report,

> In 2010, the foreign born accounted for 16 percent of all civilians employed in health care occupations in the United States. In some health care professions, this share was larger. More than one-quarter of physicians and surgeons (27 percent) were foreign born, as were more than one out of every five (22 percent) persons working in health care support jobs as nursing, psychiatric, and home health aides.[45]

In 2012, doctors who had graduated from international medical schools represented over 35 percent of the total physician workforce in both New York and New Jersey. This situation is not unique to the United States. England's National Health Service relies on workers from over 200 countries, with foreign nationals accounting for 14 percent of the clinical staff and 25 percent of the physicians.[46]

INTERCULTURAL COMMUNICATION IN HEALTHCARE

The preceding discussion makes it clear that whether you have a career in healthcare, or interact with a member of that profession, cultural differences will influence that experience. Of course, culturally sensitive, competent healthcare delivery is directly dependent on clear, unambiguous communication among all involved individuals. If communication between healthcare providers and patients is not mutually understandable, the entire medical treatment process is hindered. The challenge of effective communication is even greater when the participants are of diverse cultural backgrounds. Lack of knowledge about a patient's language, values, and cultural beliefs can endanger their life and impair the overall healthcare experience.[47]

People of diverse cultures often hold quite different perspectives about illness, healthcare, and death. Some cultural belief systems related to health and well-being vary considerably from Western views, producing challenges for both patients and providers. To overcome these differences, healthcare providers must develop and practice competent intercultural communication skills. This requires that those in the healthcare professions have a fundamental understanding of the relationships among healthcare, culture, and communication.

HEALTHCARE BELIEF SYSTEMS ACROSS CULTURES

All cultures possess basic beliefs about illness and health that are derived from their worldviews. These beliefs often vary among cultures and can lead to different, sometimes idiosyncratic concepts of illness. Culture and ethnicity create unique patterns of beliefs and perceptions relating to well-being and the cause, prevention, and cure of illness. Cultural notions about health and illness differ not only internationally but also domestically among U.S. co-cultures. For instance, spiritual beliefs, the church, and family play a very strong role in the African American concept of healthcare. People living in the Appalachian region of the United States, or with heritage links to the area, commonly have a strong tradition of self-reliance and independence, which leads to a tradition of folk cures and self-medication taking precedence over consulting a doctor. A very large and growing number of people of rural Latin American heritage now living in the United States have of necessity relied on herbal medicines, whose efficacy even modern pharmaceutical companies recognize. These examples illustrate the need for healthcare providers to understand that contemporary healthcare cannot be approached from a single cultural perspective.[48]

Andrews offers a comprehensive paradigm that divides health belief systems into three major categories— (1) supernatural/magico/religious, (2) holistic, and (3) scientific/biomedical—each with its own corresponding set of related beliefs.[49] We will utilize these categories to organize our discussion of the wide variety of culturally derived beliefs about the causes, treatment, and prevention of illness.

Supernatural/Magico/Religious Perspective

The *supernatural/magico/religious* healthcare tradition is based on a belief system that perceives the world as being dominated by supernatural forces. Followers of this tradition hold strong beliefs about the existence of sorcery, magic, and evil spirits. Disease is thought to result from the active intervention of supernatural beings (deities or gods), paranormal beings (ghosts or evil spirits), or evil humans (witches or sorcerers). An illness is seen as punishment rendered by the supernatural agent. As an example, there is a belief among Haitians that some diseases are brought about by evil spirits displeased with some action that the person has done. As was previously mentioned, one of the oldest and most widespread beliefs as to the cause of illness is the evil eye—someone can project harm on another by gazing or staring at them—a common belief in Mediterranean countries, the Middle East, Central America, and other areas.[50]

Treatment of illnesses by followers of the supernatural/magico/religious perspective may take a variety of forms to include folk healers and prayer. Depending on the

Cultures differ in their understanding of the causes, treatments, and prevention of illness.

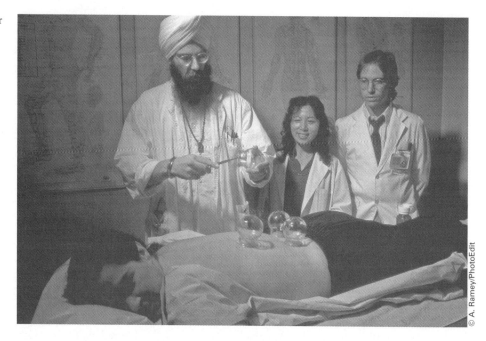

culture, traditional folk healers may be called medicine men, shamans, *kahunas*, *curanderos*, *santeros*, *hatali*, *houngan*, or a variety of other terms that can be grouped under the rubric of spirit healers. For their followers, traditional healers are believed to possess the power to call on supernatural forces. Many Cubans, Puerto Ricans, and Brazilians follow Santería, a religion with West African origins. When someone is ill, a folk healer called a *santero* will call on an *Orisha* (a saint-like spirit) for help in finding a cure. African Americans may resort to prayer for assistance in overcoming an illness and surround themselves with fellow church members. Adherents of Christian Science beliefs will also place emphasis on prayer and may eschew medications. Galanti relates an instance when a young Hmong woman was brought to the hospital emergency room with severe abdominal pains and diagnosed with acute appendicitis. However, her parents refused to permit an operation, and the woman died. The parents believed that an incision would provide an opening for the woman's soul to depart and possibly for an evil spirit to enter.[51]

While these beliefs and practices may seem strange and at odds with Western concepts of healthcare, for the believers, they represent a very normal response to illness. Thus, it becomes incumbent on healthcare providers to find ways to accommodate these differences.

Holistic Perspective

The *holistic* perspective considers an entity not as discrete parts but as an integrated whole. That is, an entity consists of interdependent, interacting parts. When applied to the medical profession, an individual is seen as a whole composed of interdependent parts, including physical, mental, emotional, and spiritual. *Mosby's Medical Dictionary* describes holistic healthcare as follows: "A system of comprehensive or total patient care that considers the physical, emotional, social, economic, and spiritual needs of the person; his or her response to illness; and the effect of the illness on the ability to meet self-care needs."[52] To achieve and sustain an individual's well-being, the various parts cannot be considered separately because what happens to one part of the body also influences all the others. In other words, if one component is not functioning properly, it degrades the performance of the other parts and can impede the entire system as a whole. For example, someone with financial difficulties may experience stress that can in turn produce different physical maladies, such as a stomachache, headache, or even depression.

Holistic health is concerned with a person's entire well-being, not just the symptoms of an illness. It can be seen as a lifestyle that seeks to integrate the physical, psychological, and spiritual aspects of life. In holistic healthcare, the individual is encouraged to engage in beneficial behaviors, such as a good diet, regular exercise, and maintenance of a positive mental outlook, all of which make positive contributions to health. This requires that they remain in balance with their environment, that they maintain a state of "harmony" with the world around them. For instance, "maintaining harmony is the driving force in Navajo life."[53] Another form of the holistic approach is Chinese Traditional Medicine (CTM), which can take a variety of forms. Followers of Taoism believe that good health requires maintaining a balance between the opposing forces of *yin* and *yang*:

> According to TCM, the two opposing principles in the universe are yin and yang. Yin is the female principle; it represents cold, darkness, and other qualities. Yang is the male principle; it represents heat, light, and so forth. When yin and yang (or cold and hot) are in balance, the individual is healthy. When they become out of balance, illness results.[54]

The importance assigned to TCM practices is illustrated by the modern Chinese hospital ship *Peace Ark*. In addition to being fully prepared to treat almost any emergency with the latest medical equipment, *Peace Ark* also has a TCM treatment and consultation room where such therapies as massage, acupuncture, and cupping are practiced.[55]

Other treatments employed by holistic medicine practitioners may include yoga, meditation, chiropractic care, moxibustion, and the use of herbal medicines or other naturopathic remedies. In the Native American tradition, to help maintain "harmony," a Navajo may enlist the help of a medicine man to conduct an elaborate ceremony that can involve chants, singing, sweat lodges, dance, prayer, sand paintings, and other rites, some lasting several days. The traditional treatment of illness among Mexican Americans may involve prayer, poultices, herbal teas, and adhering to a diet that balances "hot" and "cold" foods.[56]

Again, we should remind you that although some of these beliefs and treatments may seem unusual when compared to the Western science–based model, healthcare practitioners in other cultures have successfully employed many of these methods for centuries.

Scientific/Biomedical Perspective

Just as the name implies, the *scientific/biomedical* tradition is based on the scientific method and rests on the premise of cause and effect. The human body is seen in a biological and chemical context. Through careful observation and study the cause and effect related to illnesses, diseases, and physical disorders can be determined. Once the cause of a malady has been identified, medicines and therapy are then developed and used to manipulate the body's physical and biochemical processes in order to achieve a palliative solution. This is the dominant healthcare paradigm in the United States and much of the developed world. Recently, however, the U.S. medical profession has become more cognizant of the influence of the psychological aspects of patient healthcare, and many Americans are also exploring alternative medicines, such as acupuncture, massage therapy, folk remedies, and other measures.[57]

Practitioners subscribing to the biomedical model consider a primary cause of illness to be pathogens—foreign agents (e.g., bacteria, viruses) that invade and disrupt the body's normal biophysical functions. Other causes of illness include such factors as deterioration of skeletal structures or organs that can result from aging or malnutrition; abnormal cell growth, such as occurs with cancer; deposits in the heart, such as those formed from elevated levels of cholesterol; or genetically inherited disorders. Scientific/biomedical treatment protocols, normally based on scientific studies and research, are designed to destroy or remove the illness-causing agent, repair the impaired body part, or control the affected body system. These approaches, dominant in the United States and most Western nations, are based on the scientific principle of cause and effect. A negative aspect of this approach is that "social, spiritual, and psychological factors" often receive little attention.[58]

The three medical paradigms discussed here offer an overview of contrasting perspectives on the cause and treatment of illness. A practitioner of one model can expect challenges when faced with healthcare issues for patients who subscribe to a different model, and culture can further exacerbate the difficulties. For instance, a U.S. biomedical specialist confronted with a Chinese patient who refuses to take medication for lower back pain may need to communicatively establish rapport to determine if the individual prefers to pursue more holistic treatments, such as acupuncture or "cupping" (a traditional form of heat treatment).

Hopefully, the preceding has convinced you that culture plays a determining role in how the causes and treatment of illnesses are viewed. We now move to an examination of how different cultures approach the prevention of illnesses.

ILLNESS PREVENTION ACROSS CULTURES

Just as culture has led to a variety of beliefs and practices related to the cause and treatment of illness, methods to prevent illness also vary across cultures and in some cases combine ideas from the different belief systems. In the United States, as well as other highly technologically developed nations, the maintenance of good health is based on the ideals of annual physical examinations, immunizations, exercise, good nutrition, and other lifestyle regimens. Yet many people also adhere to healthcare practices that include stress-reducing massage and meditation as well as the use of herbal and probiotic supplements. In addition, they may employ preventive measures with healthcare practices, such as chiropractic treatment, acupuncture, or even colonic irrigation.

Some cultural groups believe that illness may be prevented by maintaining a "hot–cold" balance. In this belief, diseases are thought to be the result of an imbalance between hot and cold. Hot conditions are sustained by cold therapies, such as eating foods classified as hot; cold conditions are maintained through the use of hot therapies, such as consuming hot foods. As an example, someone of Mexican heritage could classify a kidney problem as a hot condition and elect to eat large amounts of fruits and vegetables, considered cold foods, to regain the hot–cold balance. People from Pakistan will avoid hot foods in the summer and cold foods in the winter. Both Chinese and traditional Islamic medicine subscribe to the hot–cold food theory as a means of maintaining health and warding off illness.[59]

According to Giger, some Mexican Americans "believe that health may be the result of good luck or a reward from God for good behavior,"[60] which could provide motivation for piety. Many cultural groups believe that disease can be the result of supernatural causes and subscribe to the use of amulets or charms to ward off illness and ensure good health. Amulets made of blue beads or blue stones may be worn by Afghans to guard against the evil eye.[61] In Japan, amulets (*omamori*) for good health, childbirth, prosperity, and a variety of other goals can be purchased at almost every Shinto shrine or Buddhist temple.

Our examination of explanations, treatments, and prevention of illnesses should convince you that a patient's cultural beliefs can affect healthcare and well-being. However, before moving to the next facet of cultural influences in healthcare, we need to apprise you of an important consideration. Even though some of the beliefs and practices may seem unusual, keep in mind that many cultures have not yet experienced the technological and economic benefits so common in developed societies. As a result, these less developed societies have little choice but to rely on traditional healthcare customs, even though they might be harmful. However, Western medicine, like the Western media, is rapidly reaching more people worldwide. As a consequence, while still adhering to some of their traditional healthcare practices, many cultures are becoming aware of and adopting Western scientific/biomedical approaches, either alone or in conjunction with traditional cultural practices, to treat illnesses.

LANGUAGE DIVERSITY IN HEALTHCARE

The criticality of language in the healthcare setting is obvious, and it pervades all levels of patient–caregiver interactions. To ensure a correct diagnosis and treatment prescription, the doctor–patient exchange requires a full and accurate understanding of the patient's symptoms. The nursing staff must be able to comprehend the patient's questions and responses in order to provide needed care. Pharmacists and therapists have to be able to give understandable instructions about prescribed medications and treatment regimens. As illustrated by the exchange between Hanako and the laboratory technician in the box below, the lack of a common language, coupled with usage of medical specific terminology, can complicate even simple exchanges.

The issue of language in U.S. healthcare is especially acute due to the great population diversity and varied levels of language skills. According to U.S. census data, in 2011 approximately 38 percent of the people five years or older spoke English "less than very well," and the figure rose to 50 percent for the 46 million individuals reporting having no health insurance coverage.[62] (While the Affordable Care Act has reduced the number of people without health coverage, it has no impact on English-speaking skills.) These

CONSIDER THIS

Hanako, a first-year graduate student from Japan, had visited the campus infirmary and was told she needed a blood test. At the medical laboratory, the lab tech asked, "Are you fasting?"

Hanako replied, "No, I am Hanako Suzuki."

Health care
professionals need
special communication
skills when dealing
with diverse cultures.

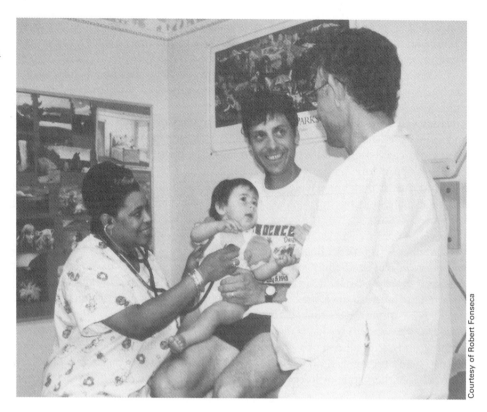

Courtesy of Robert Fonseca

figures highlight the need for interpreters and translators to assist healthcare providers
in order to deliver effective care. A study by Kaiser Permanente in Los Angeles indicated that Spanish-speaking patients were better able to manage their maladies when
they could see a Spanish-speaking doctor.[63]

Unfortunately, in many instances, healthcare workers are forced to rely on a member of the patient's family or a bilingual staff employee to serve as an interpreter, as
was mentioned in Chapter 8. This raises a host of problems relating to privacy and
linguistic issues. In almost any culture, a son would likely find it troubling to have
to translate his mother's gynecological problems for an attending physician. Likewise,
a daughter would probably be very uncomfortable relaying her father's request for
Viagra, due to erectile dysfunction difficulties. Also, bilingual staff members may not
be sufficiently skilled in the language or the patient's dialect. Even a linguistically
proficient translator can encounter difficulties if he or she has not been trained in
medical terminology. To guarantee proficiency, healthcare providers should always
try to use a certified medical interpreter.

The use of professional medical jargon can also complicate healthcare interactions.
For example, telling patients that they have *rhinitis* rather than hay fever, *ageusia*
rather than a loss of taste, or *hypesthesia* rather than a diminished sense of touch
would confuse even native English speakers. Those individuals with only a limited
English capability would almost certainly not understand. Similar words can also
have vastly different meanings in other languages. Imagine an American expatriate
hospitalized in Germany being told it was time for his *dusche* (shower) or a Filipino

nurse telling a Mexican patient she would bring her a *puto* the next day. *Puto* in Spanish is a male prostitute, but in Tagalog it is the name for a rice cake.[64]

As a final thought on language, a review of how English is used in discussing disease and healthcare issues can reveal cultural differences. Stop for a moment and think about the terms commonly used when talking about some malady in the United States—"fight off a cold," "heart attack," "cancer survivor," "[disease] warning signs," and so on.[65] These terms, along with many others, illustrate how disease is seen as an enemy attacking the body, an entity that must be conquered in order to ensure good health. But recall our earlier comments that some cultures see health as being achieved by keeping different elements in a state of harmony. For them, disease and sickness are the result not of an attack but of various elements being out of balance. Thus, telling a Chinese immigrant that taking an antibiotic will help "fight off the infection" may not be as effective as telling him the medicine will restore the body's balance.

DEATH AND DYING ACROSS CULTURES

If this were a book focused only on comparing cultural practices, it would be easy to fill this section with examples of how people in different cultures manage death and dying. For example, as we related in Chapter 1, the people of West Africa, where Ebola ravaged the population in 2014, wash the body of the deceased before burial and eschew cremation. In contrast, people in Nepal were unable to carry out cremations quickly enough due to overwhelming numbers of deceased following the devastating 2015 earthquake. Islamic law dictates that Muslims be interred as quickly as possible after death, and cremation is forbidden. In the United States, burial may be days or even weeks after death, and cremation is becoming more widely accepted. A traditional practice in Tibet and some areas of western China, referred to as "sky burial," involves dismembering the corpse in an open area exposed to the natural elements to be consumed by vultures. In some areas of China and on Taiwan, a funeral may include female strippers as a means of drawing larger crowds to convey the impression that the deceased was held in high esteem. But this is a text about intercultural communication, not about cultural burial protocols. Accordingly, we will now address the role of communication as it relates to death and dying in different cultures.

As noted in Chapter 4 when we discussed religion, cultures have evolved different perceptions and procedures to deal with the topic of death and dying. They range from active participation to completely ignoring the issue. However, in the healthcare professions, death cannot be ignored. Effective and timely communication assists patients and their families in gathering relevant data about health threats and in developing appropriate strategies for responding to those threats. The requirement for healthcare professionals to deliver unpleasant news to patients and their family members is a daunting task demanding compassion and sensitivity, further intensified by the need to understand how cultures differ in the delivery and reception of such information.

Healthcare practice in the United States reflects the belief in the importance, uniqueness, dignity, and sovereignty of every person; the sanctity of individual life; and everyone's legal entitlement to patient autonomy and self-determination. From this perspective, it is assumed that the patient is always the best person to make health decisions. In many other cultures, however, the interdependence between patient and family can override individual self-determination. In other cultures, the family is vested with the decision-making authority and the task of informing the patient. In Japan, for instance, it is common for physicians to consult with family members rather than the patient about treatment regimens. In the Filipino community, family members will decide among themselves if a patient should be informed of a terminal condition.[67] Euro-American healthcare practitioners have to recognize that the Western practice of disclosing diagnostic information directly to the patient may not be applicable in all cultures.

The discussion of death is also marked by cultural differences. Although end-of-life decisions and procedures are often only reluctantly discussed in the United States, patients are continually urged to execute advanced healthcare directives to specify desired treatment and procedures should they become incapacitated and unable to communicate. Among many other benefits, an advanced directive relieves family members and loved ones of having to make difficult decisions, thereby preserving everyone's autonomy. However, the hesitancy to address end-of-life issues is evident in that only around 30 percent of the people in the United States have an advanced healthcare directive. But imagine how difficult it would be to discuss an advanced healthcare directive with someone from the Navajo culture, where even the mention of death is thought to invite it. Mexicans, on the other hand, take a more stoic view of death as just another part of life and God's will.[68]

To conclude our examination of multicultural healthcare, we remind you again that an understanding of varied medical perspectives, communication styles, and individual beliefs will assist healthcare providers in becoming more sensitive to the culturally based health expectations held by people from different cultures.

DEVELOPING INTERCULTURAL COMMUNICATION COMPETENCE IN CONTEXTS

From reading this chapter, along with others, you have probably already discerned the importance of becoming interculturally competent, which can be broadly defined as "the knowledge, motivation, and skills to interact effectively and appropriately with members of different cultures."[69] This general definition provides a template that can be used in identifying more specific requirements for attaining intercultural competence in various contexts. Therefore, as a conclusion to this chapter, we offer a brief discussion on means of acquiring those skills as they relate to business, education, and healthcare contexts.

While they differ significantly in appearance and objectives, each of the contexts discussed in this chapter share some common traits, the most salient being they each require an organizational structure and involved personnel. These shared characteristics allow us to make the claim that the responsibility for the acquisition and employment of intercultural communication competence rests with the service provider and its employees. That is, regardless of whether it is a multinational corporation, an elementary school, a rural healthcare clinic, or any other service or product provider, the organization and its personnel are accountable for engaging in competent intercultural practices. The challenge, then, is for providers to ensure that all employees are sensitive to the cultural variations existing within the workforce, among customers, and in the relevant cultural groups in the local community and that workers possess the necessary skills for effective interaction. And the first requirement is for personnel at all levels—executive, managerial, and workforce—to understand that acquiring those skills requires effort and time.[70]

The first step in achieving the goal of intercultural competence in any occupational context is to create and nurture an organizational policy (i.e., organizational culture) that recognizes the need and benefits of multiculturalism. Such a policy will create a sense of organizational inclusiveness and promote successful intercultural engagement with clients and stakeholders. The most widely employed means of creating greater intercultural awareness and skill development is through formal or informal training programs that create cross-cultural understanding and raise own-culture awareness. However, self-study offers another viable means of gaining cultural knowledge.

Training programs are normally structured to meet specific organizational requirements, and the content can be "cultural general," "cultural specific," or a combination. Programs focusing on cultural general training are designed to provide employees with an appreciation of what culture is and how it varies and its influence on individual behaviors and communication to include one's own culture. Organizations staffed by employees from a variety of cultures will find this type of training beneficial, especially supervisory personnel charged with overseeing a multicultural workforce. Teachers who manage classrooms with students from a variety of cultures and health workers serving culturally diverse patients would benefit from cultural-general training.

Culture-specific training focuses on specific culture with the objective of providing in-depth knowledge and understanding. These programs benefit organizational personnel who must interact with individuals from a single culture, such as a Filipino nurse working in a predominantly Vietnamese American neighborhood or a Euro-American teacher in a Hispanic-majority school district. Likewise, a U.S. business team negotiating a contract with a large Korean firm would be better prepared by having an appreciation of Korean culture and communication styles.

Regardless of the context, organizations operating in culturally diverse environments require cultural competence and effective intercultural communication skills in order to manage employees and serve clients successfully. As an illustration, we will conclude with a short description of how one large multinational corporation has made multiculturalism a core competency.

ABB is a large corporation headquartered in Geneva, Switzerland, with some 150,000 employees working in approximately 100 countries and whose website is available in over thirty languages. In 2014, ABB was ranked 259 on *Fortune's* Global 500 list:[71]

> Formed in 1988 from the merger of two international engineering companies—the Swiss BBC company and the Swedish ASEA—ABB acquired more than 230 companies in 50 countries within a decade. It didn't build its corporate culture on that of its parent companies, but on its diversity. The core of its management philosophy was to respect

local culture and acculturation. English is the language of management at ABB, even at its headquarters in Switzerland, where there are employees from 19 countries. The company is led by managers who know the local culture and the company's global strategy. *ABB spends almost US$1 billion annually on management training and research into trans-cultural communication.* [emphasis added][72]

This description offers tangible evidence that cultural awareness contributes to success as well as being a necessary part of global business.

SUMMARY

- Basic assumptions about human communication in contexts:
    1. Communication is rule governed.
    2. Context determines what communication rules should be used.
    3. Communication rules vary across cultures.

Business

- The greatest influence of globalization has been in the business context.
- Knowledge of cultural differences and competent intercultural communication skills are fundamental to success in the multinational business community.
- Business protocols, such as greetings, personal appearance, communicative behaviors, etc., vary across cultures.
- Leadership and management styles are marked by cultural differences.
- Culturally instilled individualism or collectivism can influence how employees are motivated and rewarded.
- Culture is an important factor in decision making.
- The attitude toward conflict and how it is managed is a function of culture.
- Broadly speaking, every nation has a preferred negotiation style, which usually reflects the communication style of the dominant culture.
- Language skills are absolutely critical when working in multinational organizations.

Education

- Multicultural classrooms are common in the United States and many European Union nations.
- Diversity in U.S. schools is forecast to continue increasing.
- Culture never stops teaching, but it tends to be self-perpetuating and self-focused.
- Some educational content varies across cultures.
- To avoid ethnocentrism, students should be exposed to different perspectives, philosophies, and histories.

- *What* and *how* a culture teaches is a reflection of its beliefs, values, and characteristics.

- Culture influences attitudes toward education.

- Lack of a common language is a challenge in the multicultural classroom.

- To be proficient in the contemporary learning environment, instructors must have intercultural communication skills.

- Competency in the multicultural classroom requires the following:

  o Awareness that culture teaches different ways of learning

  o Knowledge that cognitive patterns are culturally conditioned and vary

  o Awareness that culture can create a preference for oral or literate learning

  o Recognition that Limited English Proficiency places extra demands on nonnative speakers

  o Knowledge of culturally different teacher–student relationship behaviors.

- Success in the multicultural classroom requires development of culturally sensitive instructional strategies.

Healthcare

- The healthcare industry is characterized by cultural variation among both care providers and patients.

- Perspectives about illness, healthcare, and death vary among cultures.

- Every culture has a set of basic beliefs concerning illness and health:

  o The supernatural/magico/religious healthcare tradition perceives the world being controlled by supernatural forces.

  o The holistic perspective considers the individual as a "whole," consisting of interdependent parts, such as physical, mental, emotional, spiritual, etc.

  o The scientific/biomedical tradition is based on the Western scientific method, relying on cause and effect.

- Illness prevention methods vary across cultures and can combine concepts from different belief systems.

- Language is the critical nexus at all levels of patient–caregiver interactions.

- Whenever possible, healthcare providers should use a certified medical interpreter.

- Cultures have developed different procedures for managing death and dying.

- In the United States, the patient is considered the best person to make health decisions, a reflection of strong individualistic beliefs.

- In some collectivistic cultures, healthcare decisions are the responsibility of the family.

- Broadly defined, intercultural competence is having the knowledge, motivation, and ability to interact effectively with people from other cultures.

- Organizations and their personnel bear the responsibility for employing competent intercultural practices.

- Formal and informal training programs, along with self-study, are used to instill intercultural awareness and develop skills.

ACTIVITIES

1. This chapter discussed three different contexts—business, education, and healthcare. Think of another context (e.g., environmental nongovernmental organizations (NGOs), social work organization, legal assistance volunteers) and identify as many potential cultural challenges as you can.

2. Find two or three online articles that discuss globalization of the economy/marketplace. Working with others, identify three positive and three negative cultural aspects related to globalization.

3. Make a list of the culturally related problems that you think might arise in a multicultural workforce, either domestically or internationally. Compare your list with several other classmates' lists and then work together to identify how those problems could be avoided or overcome.

4. Table 10.6 lists the characteristics of Chinese and U.S. negotiation styles. Select several of the characteristics and discuss how they might influence communication between the two negotiating teams. Provide applied examples.

5. Identify several examples of how cultural ethnocentrism could occur in the classroom. Meet with other classmates to compare examples and then devise some recommended actions that would eliminate the ethnocentric practices.

6. Form a small group (three or four people) and select one of the recent natural disasters where aid responders from different countries came to offer assistance. Identify some of the cultural difficulties they may have encountered and ways the difficulties could be solved.

7. Using online searches, compile a list of hot–cold foods and the health benefit that is attributed to each. Can you identify any cultural relation to the listed foods?

8. You have been asked to conduct a culture general training course for marketing department employees, a class of elementary school teachers, or a group of multicultural nurses. Draw up a list of topics for one of the courses.

CONCEPTS AND QUESTIONS

1. What is meant by the phrase "communication is rule governed"? Compare some of the different "rules" that govern your communication in the following contexts:
   (a) A meeting with your professor to discuss grades and a meeting at a social event.
   (b) Giving your professional opinion to the company president and to a co-worker.
   (c) Discussing a medical concern with a doctor and with a close friend.

2. In almost any context, first-time meetings will involve initial conversational talk. The rules governing what are appropriate or inappropriate topics for these interactions vary across cultures. Work with other classmates to compile a list of what would be correct and

incorrect topics among Euro-Americans (or another culture you are interested in).

3. In the globalized marketplace, contemporary business leaders must manage a variety of cultural expectations and adapt them to the workplace. What cultural differences of values and behaviors are most important for a manager to be aware of? How could a business manager best handle cultural conflicts?

4. What are some of the ways that a culture's attitude toward education can become manifest in the classroom? In the workplace? Identify some of the outcomes of a culture's overemphasis and underemphasis on education.

5. Examine you own beliefs about the causes and prevention of disease. Which healthcare perspective do you most identify with? Why? Do you engage in health practices that would be considered a part of one of the other traditions? If so, why?

6. Recall the *Consider This* example of Hanako's visit to the medical laboratory. How could the lab tech have better phrased his question to promote understanding?

7. Imagine you are a doctor and have just diagnosed one of your patients with a terminal illness. How would you present the news to a German American, a Mexican immigrant, and someone from China?

CHAPTER 11

The Challenges of Intercultural Communication: Managing Differences

Honest differences are often a healthy sign of progress.

MAHATMA GANDHI

Differences were what made up the human race; similarities were what made up drones and clones.

VICKTOR ALEXANDER

The highest result of education is tolerance.

HELEN KELLER

INTERCULTURAL COMMUNICATION IN A DYNAMIC WORLD

The Renaissance philosopher Niccolo Machiavelli advised, "Whosoever desires constant success must change his conduct with the times." Although written 500 years ago, this advice clearly remains relevant today. To succeed in our rapidly evolving globalized world, you must learn to recognize and manage the differences brought about by near continuous sociocultural change, much of which is the result of intercultural dynamics. Growing domestic diversity, increasing migration, enhanced transportation systems, the advance of information systems, interdependent economies, political developments, and global conflicts are bringing people from different cultures and religions into contact with each other with a regularity and urgency never seen. Indeed, by both chance and design, encountering people of different cultures is now common. This increased contact with people who often speak another language and hold values different from yours has created a critical need to develop and employ competent intercultural communication skills.

To help you become an effective intercultural communicator, this final chapter is designed to assist you in overcoming some of the common problems encountered when interacting with people of other cultures. We begin by discussing the challenges of entering another culture, followed by an examination of selected obstacles that can impede effective intercultural communication. The chapter concludes with an over-view of ethical considerations relevant to intercultural behaviors.

ENTERING ANOTHER CULTURE

The novelist Louis L'Amour wrote that "each of us is convinced that our way is the best way," underscoring the generally accepted hypothesis that people are normally more comfortable with the familiar than the unfamiliar. Social psychology scholars contend that

> individuals are more likely to seek out, enjoy, understand, want to work and play with, trust, believe, vote for, and generally prefer people with whom they share salient character-istics. These include interests, values, religion, group affiliation, skills, physical attributes, age, language, and all the other aspects on which human beings differ.[1]

To illustrate this concept, among family and close friends you usually know what to expect, how to behave, and the established communication norms. The situation is the same when interacting with people of your own culture. In other words, culture provides you with a general frame of reference on how to act, speak, feel, think, etc., which closely approximates the other members of your culture. The shared set of nor-mative cultural values, social behavioral conventions, language, and communication protocols reduces uncertainty and creates a common bond among the culture's mem-bers. However, when entering a different culture, some of the predictable societal norms may be different, producing both uncertainty and an inability to function com-petently. For instance, on a short vacation trip to London, England, you would prob-ably encounter some cultural differences and a small degree of uncertainty due to varying norms, social procedures, and unfamiliar terminology but still be able to func-tion with a relatively high degree of competence. This is due to the numerous cultural similarities between the United States and England, although there are some very dis-tinct differences. However, when undertaking a semester abroad in Shanghai, China, your ability to function would be significantly impeded, even if you have had a year or two of Mandarin language study. The new cultural environment would render almost all of your normative, established patterns of behavior ineffective and make nearly every social situation challenging and in some cases unsolvable. This inabil-ity to operate as usual would produce both cognitive anxiety and physical stress, and in some cases, a syndrome referred to as *culture shock*. Because almost every

REMEMBER THIS

People are usually more effective and comfortable with familiar situations than unfamiliar conditions.

sojourner entering a new cultural environment for a sustained period initially experi-ences some degree of culture shock, we will examine the phenomenon in greater detail.

CULTURE SHOCK AND ITS IMPACT

For a summer vacation adventure you decide to spend a few weeks with your older brother, an IT engineer who has been working in Beijing, China, for a year. After several weeks of preparation you are ready to board a flight to Beijing, but the night before leaving, you receive an email from your brother saying he will be unable to meet you at the airport. Instead, he asks that you meet at a hotel and provides the following directions:

> *After arriving, take the Airport Express to Dongzhimen Station. Walk east on Dongzhimen Outer Street. Turn right on Chiuxiu Road. The hotel will be on the right side a few blocks after turning. You can't miss it. I'll be in the lobby.*

Sounds easy enough, and the Google map you print out looks quite simple. On arrival at the airport English language signs guide you through immigration and customs stations, to the baggage claim area, and then to the Airport Express station. It is only then that you discover that your U.S. currency is not accepted, requiring a trip back into the terminal to find an ATM, where it takes a minute to locate the button that changes the Chinese language screen to English. After purchasing a ticket and taking a twenty-minute ride, you arrive at the underground Dongzhimen Station and make your way up to the street. The first task is to find Dongzhimen Outer Street and walk in an easterly direction. This is when you discover that reality is quite different from what the map depicts. You are confronted with tall buildings, speeding cars, bicycles, pedicabs, large bustling crowds, few street markers, and only limited English signs. After considerable effort you make your way to the hotel, only to find that your brother has left a note saying, *Called away to Shanghai for a meeting, be back in two days. Enjoy exploring Beijing.*

Exhausted from the thirteen-plus-hour flight, you check into the room reserved by your brother and set out to find something to eat. The hotel's restaurant is closed, but the desk clerk directs you toward a local place close by. But on arrival, you discover people sitting around small, low tables on the sidewalk, talking loudly, and ordering from a menu in Chinese hanging on a wall. Unable to communicate with the waiter, you give up and stop at a convenience store, pick up some type of crackers and a soda, and retreat to your hotel room. The next morning you set out to explore the city of over 11 million people. Very quickly you discover that finding your way can be a challenge, requiring much longer than expected, and that trying to make yourself understood to non-English speakers is very difficult. After spending the morning exploring a shopping center where you must deal with large, loud, jostling crowds, you feel mentally and physically exhausted and return to your room to rest. That is when you decide to just stay in the hotel watching the international channel on television until your brother returns.

You have just experienced culture shock!

Reactions associated with culture shock can vary widely among individuals and take the form of any or all of three components—affective, behavioral, and cognitive.[2] An individual confronting the impacts associated with culture shock can experience a sense of disorientation, feelings of rejection, homesickness, withdrawal, irritation, physical and mental fatigue, and even depression in severe cases. However, culture shock will not affect everyone to the same degree. People who have considerable experience living in diverse social settings will usually adapt much more quickly than someone who has little experience encountering other cultures. Our discussion on the impact of culture shock is not intended to make you apprehensive about venturing into another culture. Rather, the intent is to help you be prepared should you experience some of these reactions.

THE PROCESS OF ACCULTURATION

We consider culture shock as the *initial* mental and physical stress experienced, to varying degrees, when an individual enters a culture different from his or her own. If the amount of stress exceeds a person's tolerance level, he or she can essentially become nonfunctional, withdrawing emotionally and physically from the new culture, either returning home or limiting one's interactions exclusively to the local expatriate community. On the other hand, if the culture shock is not severe, as is usually the case, people commence a process of acculturation—learning to become functional and comfortable in their new cultural setting.

Although there are variations in how people respond and in the amount of time they need to adjust to a different culture, most of the early literature on culture shock relied on a U-curve-shaped model to illustrate four phases, or stages, of adjustment (see Table 11.1). The U-curve model was subsequently extended and called the W-curve,[4] which included the adjustment period that expatriates go through when they return home after extended periods living in another culture. The greatest appeal of these two models is their intuitiveness. They are easily understood, appear quite commonsensical, and are simple to illustrate. Unfortunately, there is insufficient empirical data to verify the models, leading some to consider them overgeneralizations of the adaptation process.[5]

In more contemporary work, Kim has developed a theoretical model that proposes the cultural adjustment experience to be more complex than the U- and W-curve models.[6] She sees acculturation as a continuing process of "stress-adaptation-growth." Initial entry into a new culture produces *stress* because the sojourner's ability to function is normally diminished. In other words, the traveler experiences some degree of stress when dealing with new and different procedures, behaviors, and communication standards. To mitigate stress, sojourners begin to develop and incorporate the cultural norms needed to function competently in the new environment. They start *adapting* to the other culture. Through continual interaction with people and managing the daily requirements of working and living in a different social environment, the stress-adaptation process broadens sojourners' perspectives and produces personal *growth*. The three components of stress-adaptation-growth constitute a dynamic process that continues to advance throughout the expatriate's stay.

TABLE 11.1	U-curve Model of Cultural Adjustment[3]
STAGE	**CHARACTERISTICS**
Honeymoon	Anticipate living/working in the new culture, which is considered exciting/exotic.
Disillusionment/Culture Shock	Encounter the difficulties of daily living and communicating in the new culture. Experience various levels of stress.
Recovery	Begin to learn how to function in the new culture. Levels of stress decline.
Adjustment/Effective Functioning	Gain a higher degree of functionality and start feeling comfortable in the new culture.

FIGURE 11.1   The Stress-Adaptation-Growth Dynamic

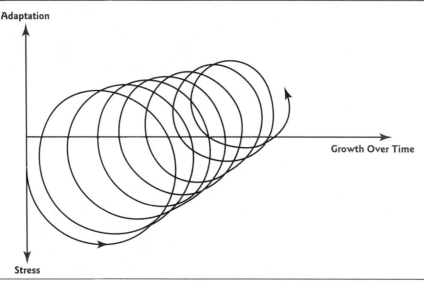

Source: Y. Y. Kim, *Becoming Intercultural: An Integrative Theory of Communication and Cross Cultural Adaptation* (Thousand Oaks, CA: Sage, 2001), 59.

According to Kim,

> The *stress-adaptation-growth dynamic* does not play out in a smooth, steady, and linear progression, but in a dialectic, cyclic, and continual "draw-back-to-leap" pattern. Each stressful experience is responded to with a "draw back," which, in turn, activates adaptive energy to help individuals reorganize themselves and "leap forward." … [This] process continues as long as there are new environmental challenges, with the overall forward and upward movement in the direction of greater adaptation and growth.[7]

In less theoretical terms, Kim's theory contends that when someone enters a new cultural environment, his or her initial reaction will be some level of stress as he or she learns how to become functional. If the sojourner remains in the new culture, the process of stress and adaptation will continue but produce lessening levels of stress as he or she becomes more culturally competent. The progression is graphically illustrated in Figure 11.1.

MANAGING CULTURE SHOCK AND ENHANCING ACCULTURATION

As has been noted throughout previous chapters, people are moving from place to place around the world in greater numbers and with increased regularity. Regardless of whether they are relocating for a defined period of time, such as a vacation, a study program, or a business opportunity, or permanently, as in the case of immigrants, these individuals are faced with the demanding task of learning to live in a new cultural environment, and they often encounter difficulties adapting to their host culture. The process of cultural adjustment can be a lengthy, formidable task that requires attaining a large body of knowledge about the new culture. New arrivals must acquire additional linguistic and social skills in order to fit in and become functional in their host culture. Fortunately, as discussed by Ward, Bouchner, and Furnham,[8] there are a number of measures that can be taken to facilitate cross-cultural adjustment. These recommendations are set forth below.

Learn About the Host Culture

A major theme of this book is the principle that developing a bank of knowledge about other cultures is a necessary first step toward improving intercultural communication skills. Culture shock can be lessened and adaptation accelerated if one becomes aware of the host culture's fundamental characteristics. In this context we consider cultural awareness to include understanding the new culture's religious orientation, historical background, political system, primary cultural values and beliefs, verbal styles, nonverbal behaviors, family organization, social etiquette, and other similar aspects.

Learn About the Language of the Host Culture

Of the many challenges facing someone living in a new culture, language is the most obvious and perhaps the most demanding. However, the importance of learning about the host culture's language cannot be overestimated, as is explained by Masgoret and Ward:

> Knowledge of the language spoken in the receiving community plays a central role within the cultural learning process, since language is viewed as the primary medium through which cultural information is communicated. Because language and cultural learning are intimately linked, miscommunications will likely result if migrants and sojourners do not acquire at least some fundamental verbal skills.[9]

The difficulties associated with exposure to a new language are twofold: language acquisition and the speaking style unique to the new culture, both of which can contribute to culture shock and impede the adaptation process. As brought out in our discussion of language in Chapter 8, cultural variations in language usage encompass a variety of topics, from the use of idioms and conversational taboos to linguistic ways of showing respect. We are not saying that you must be fluent in the host culture's language. Obviously, it would not be practical for someone going to another culture for a short time to try to attain fluency. However, learning a few phrases to help express greetings, render courtesies, and perhaps ask directions will serve you well. Moreover, learning *about* the language will provide insight into turn taking, directness and indirectness, logical or relational orientation, and other culturally specific language traits.

Guard Against Ethnocentrism

As we have discussed throughout this book, *ethnocentrism* is the conviction that one's own culture is superior to other cultures. Everyone is vulnerable to ethnocentrism—sojourners, immigrants, and even members of the host culture. A sojourner with feelings of ethnocentrism can expect to encounter difficulties adjusting to a new set of cultural norms. Taken to an extreme, ethnocentrism can lead to prejudice, which in

It is difficult to recognize and control ethnocentrism because it is learned early, it is hard to isolate, and it is usually unconscious.

Courtesy of Edwin McDaniel

turn can produce mistrust, hostility, and even hate.[10] Host culture members may exhibit feelings of ethnocentrism by developing negative judgments about outsiders who have different cultural traits. This situation can easily create a downward spiral in relations between members of the host culture and sojourners. The best way to facilitate effective adaptation is for all parties to recognize and work to resist the strong pull of ethnocentrism. One way of reducing the potential of ethnocentrism is for individuals to learn how their own culture influences and shapes their beliefs, perceptions, values, and behaviors.[11]

Stay Connected to Your Own Culture

By now, you should know that entering a new culture has the potential to be physically and mentally overwhelming. You will probably experience some degree of culture shock, and the adaptation process will demand increased levels of emotional and physical energy. One way of mitigating these demands is to maintain contact with your own culture. Simply spending time with people from your culture can reduce the stress of managing life in another culture. It is quite common for people moving abroad to find a specific neighborhood that has culturally familiar conveniences, which can range from religious institutions to food stores. In large urban areas, expatriates often join a club or professional organization where members are from the same culture, such as the American Club of Paris or the American Chamber of Commerce in Shanghai. When confronted with dietary challenges in a new culture, an American sojourner can now easily retreat to one of many U.S. fast-food franchises located in almost every major overseas metropolitan center. Today, unlike only a few years past, modern technology has made staying in touch with family members and friends in one's home country both affordable and easy. "A 19th-century Russian immigrant might never see or speak to his family again. A 21st-century migrant can Skype them in the taxi from the airport."[12]

OBSTACLES TO EFFECTIVE INTERCULTURAL COMMUNICATION

Our discussion of the potential difficulties that can arise when entering a different culture was framed primarily around the cognitive and physical aspects. In this section, we turn to some of the impediments to effective communication when communicating with someone of a different culture. An awareness of these potential pitfalls will enable you to avoid some of the common problems that can diminish intercultural communication competency.

TENDENCIES TO SEEK SIMILARITIES

Found in multiple variations, "Birds of a feather flock together" is an adage common to many cultures. Regardless of the variation, however, the meaning is clear—we are more comfortable being around people who have similar outlooks, habits, and traits. Think for a moment about the people with whom you most frequently associate. Very likely, you have a number of things in common with those people, and these shared interests can include matters as mundane as liking the same type of food, music, or sports and extend to complex issues, such as similar political or religious views. These similarities allow you better to gauge the other person's likely feelings, attitudes, reactions, and communication styles. Thus, when meeting someone for the first time, it is a natural inclination to seek topics that both parties find interesting, and if enough commonality can be found, it is equally likely for friendships to form and evolve. The more you have in common with another person, the more comfortable you feel being together. In contrast, we can often feel ill at ease or unsure when encountering strangers, and this sometimes makes conversation difficult, especially when a second language is involved.

The connection between intercultural communication and the inclination to associate with people who reflect your own beliefs and values should be obvious. As previously illustrated, a culture provides its members specialized patterns of communication—patterns that are often dissimilar to those of another culture. We are not suggesting there is anything wrong with favoring ethnic or cultural congruity. In fact, we have already pointed out how common it is to seek the familiar and avoid what is different or strange. It is when the pull of similarities leads to the exclusion or even elimination of those who are different that problems arise. Persecution of people with differences can be seen in the recent tragic events in Myanmar, where Buddhist majorities attacked Muslim minorities, and in Iraq, where Islamic extremists waged war on Yazidi Christians. Here in the United States, the movement of Euro-Americans from ethnically mixed neighborhoods to racially divided areas has been termed "white flight."

The message we are attempting to convey is that culture often separates you from people with a history different from your own. Well over one hundred years ago, the famous poet Emily Dickinson lyrically alluded to the tendency to separate from those who are different:

> The Soul selects her own Society —
>
> Then — shuts the Door —
>
> To her divine Majority —
>
> Present no more —

The message is clear. Most people prefer the familiar and too often "shut the door" on the unfamiliar. This bias for similarity poses a potential problem when engaging in communication with someone of a different culture who may look, act, speak, and think differently from you. Overcoming that bias requires making an extra effort to appreciate and understand those differences.

MANAGING UNCERTAINTY

Uncertainty is another potential intercultural communication problem and one that is directly related to the natural inclination to seek similarities. As suggested above, during initial meetings, conversation generally involves efforts to learn about the other person, which helps you reduce the cognitive feelings of uncertainty and increase predictability. In other words, it helps you reduce uncertainty about your communicative interaction and lessen your feelings of apprehension. First-time meetings with anyone carry some level of uncertainty, but if the person is from a different ethnic group, that sense of uncertainty and anxiety will be increased. This is especially true when you are unable to anticipate the other person's behaviors or understand the reasons for their actions. Simply stated, uncertainty is magnified when you meet people of cultures different from your own.[13]

When engaging with someone of another culture, it is important to realize that the other person will also experience feelings of uncertainty. To help alleviate this mutual sense of uncertainty, Gudykunst advocates being "mindful." By this, he means assuming an increased awareness of your own behaviors and being more accepting of different practices and perspectives.[14] In other words, Gudykunst is telling us that when we communicate interculturally, we need to be more attentive to the behaviors and what is said both by ourselves and the other party.

WITHDRAWAL

The potential for withdrawing from an intercultural communication event is increased when you cannot find similarities and/or fail to adequately reduce uncertainty to a satisfactory level. In this case, withdrawal can occur at the interpersonal or group level. In short, your withdrawal from a face-to-face interaction or an international negotiation can increase the potential for difficulties. Characterized by a rapid-paced lifestyle, increased urbanization, and ideological alienation, contemporary society can represent an overwhelming challenge for some individuals, causing them to withdraw from some or all social activities. For instance, Japan may have as many as 1 million individuals, called *hikikomori*, who have withdrawn from society and spend their time socially isolated from others.[15] On the international level, the reluctance of Israel and Hamas to negotiate with each other has led to a series of devastating conflicts in Gaza.

See if you can recall ever having a seemingly irreconcilable difference with a family member or very close friend and ended the argument by withdrawing. Did the withdrawal resolve the difference? Probably not. When this occurs, the consequences are obvious—communication becomes impossible, and in the absence of communication, the problem usually remains unresolved. In many cases, withdrawal of one intercultural participant is motivated by differences such as skin color, sexual orientation, religious affiliation, or cultural heritage. But in this age, when what happens in one place reverberates throughout the world, retreat and withdrawal can have devastating effects. As the philosopher Flewelling wrote, "Neither province, parish, nor nation, neighborhood, family, nor individual, can live profitably in exclusion from the rest of the world." When confronted with a challenging intercultural communication situation, we urge you to be mindful, seek some type of commonality with the other person, and do not let uncertainty push you into withdrawing from the contact.

STEREOTYPING

Stereotyping is a natural, often subconscious way of dealing with unknown situations. When confronted with unfamiliar circumstances, you normally draw on previously acquired knowledge to analyze, evaluate, and classify the new situation. While stereotyping may be a normal cognitive process when meeting strangers, problems can arise when negative stereotypes are assigned.

Stereotyping Defined

Stereotyping is a complex form of categorization that mentally organizes your experiences with and guides your behavior toward a particular group of people. It is a means of cognitively organizing your perceptions into simplified categories that can be used to represent an entire collection of things, processes, or people. A more formal definition can be found in the psychology literature: "A stereotype is a cognitive structure containing the perceiver's knowledge, beliefs, and expectancies about some human social groups."[16] Stereotyping is a pervasive human activity due to the need for cognitive structure. The world is too big, too complex, and too dynamic to comprehend everything in detail. To help make sense of your physical and social environment, you tend to filter, classify, and categorize in order to reduce uncertainty. Although this is a natural and necessary process, problems arise when you tend to overgeneralize.

Stereotypes can assume either a positive or a negative form. The generalization that people with PhD degrees in astrophysics from MIT are good at mathematics is a positive generalization and probably pretty accurate. However, this characterization is referring to a quite small number of individuals who represent a specialized context. The assumption that all Asian students are hardworking, well mannered, and intelligent is an example of a positive stereotype that represents an overgeneralization of a large group of people. Classifying all people who dress in Goth fashion as drug addicts is a negative stereotype. In both examples, a group of people is ascribed common characteristics that not everyone in the group possesses. You know that not all Asian students are hardworking and intelligent and that not everyone who wears Goth clothes does drugs. Each group, Asians and Goth dressers, is composed of individuals who may or may not exhibit the ascribed stereotypical characteristics. Because stereotypes tend to narrow your perceptions and can easily take a negative tone, they often result in erroneous, overgeneralized categorizations of a group of people. This overgeneralization, especially when negative, can adversely impact intercultural communication.

Acquiring Stereotypes

We are surrounded by stereotypes, and they seem to endure. Why? One way to understand the power and lasting impact of stereotypes is to examine how they are acquired. Like culture, stereotypes are learned, and they are learned in a variety of ways. The most obvious and probably the most important source is the socialization process, which begins in the home during childhood. Although many parents actively work to avoid teaching their children to think about things in a stereotypical manner, often they may directly or indirectly promote a stereotype classification.[17] A child who overhears a family member say, "All those illegal immigrants are taking our jobs," is learning a stereotype. The socialization process continues when a child enters school and begins to hear stereotype categorizations from their peers. Religious and social organizations are also sources of stereotype learning. These groups, although teaching the virtues of a particular point of view, might intentionally or unintentionally impart stereotypes about an opposite view. For example, by learning one specific view of religion and at the same time hearing of the "evils of Islamic-based religious terrorists," children might acquire stereotypes about all Muslims.

Many stereotypes are generated by mass media and widely disseminated through a variety of formats, such as advertisements, talk shows, movies, television sitcoms, soap operas, and reality shows. Television has been guilty of providing distorted images of many ethnic groups, the elderly, and the gay community, as well as others. Media have also played a role in creating and perpetuating certain stereotypical perceptions of women and men. Wood offers an excellent summary of television's portrayal of men and women: "Media most often represents boys and men as active, adventurous, powerful, sexually aggressive, and largely uninvolved in human relationships, and represents girls and women as young, thin, beautiful, passive, dependent, and often incompetent."[18] When the media highlight incidents of crime committed by illegal immigrants or a specific ethnic group, an image is created that all immigrants or members of that ethnic group are engaged in criminal activities. In other words, a series of isolated behaviors by a few members of a group unfairly creates a generalized perception that is applied to all members of that group. Stereotypes can also evolve out of fear of the unknown. People from groups that differ from one's own and who dress differently, speak another language, practice an unfamiliar religion, and celebrate holidays different from the mainstream population can easily become targets of suspicion and derision.

Stereotypes and Intercultural Communication

Generally speaking, most stereotypes are the product of limited, lazy, misguided, and erroneous perceptions. These misperceptions can become the source of numerous and quite serious problems when brought into intercultural interaction. Adler points out the detrimental effect that stereotypes can have on intercultural communication:

> Stereotypes become counterproductive when we place people in the wrong groups, when we incorrectly describe the group norm, when we evaluate the group rather than simply describing it, when we confuse the stereotype with the description of a particular individual, and when we fail to modify the stereotype based on our actual observations and experience.[19]

In addition to Adler's listing, let us examine four other ways in which stereotypes obstruct intercultural communication. First, stereotypes act as a type of filter; they let in only information that is consistent with what the individual already knows. Thus, the correct, or truthful, descriptions may be filtered out. For instance, for many years, women were stereotyped as a rather one-dimensional group—the weaker sex—confined to the role of mother and homemaker. Those labels kept women from advancing in the workplace, even when more skilled than their male counterparts. Second, it is not the act of categorizing or classifying that creates the intercultural problems. Rather, it is the assumption that culture-specific information applies to all members of that cultural group. For example, national and ethnic stereotypes project the same traits on all members of the culture. To say that every U.S. American is an individualist overlooks the fact that some people in the United States prefer group activity. Additionally, it disregards the many collectivistic ethnic groups that are a part of the U.S. multicultural population. Third, stereotypes also hamper successful intercultural communication because they present an oversimplified, exaggerated, and overgeneralized portrait of the individual. Often based on half-truths, untrue premises, or unfounded assumptions, stereotypes offer a distorted representation of the concept, thing, or person. Stereotypes alter intergroup communication because they lead people to base their preparation, transmission, and reception of messages on false assumptions.[20] Fourth, stereotypes are resistant to change. Stereotypes are usually learned early in life, tend to be repeated and reinforced through in-group interaction, and become more solidified with the passage of time. Contact between in-groups and out-groups may only strengthen the inaccurate perceptions. Meshel and McGlynn bring out this potential: "Once formed, stereotypes are resistant to change, and direct contact often strengthens the preexisting associations between the target group and the stereotypical properties."[21]

Avoiding Stereotypes

Because learning stereotypes, along with culture, begins early in life, it should be obvious that the best time to initiate measures to circumvent them is during childhood. Research has revealed that children who experience positive contact with other groups hold fewer negative stereotypes than children who have not had the opportunity for such contact. Studies also show that positive contact among different groups of children will diminish many of the effects of stereotyping by dispelling fictitious and negative perceptions.[22]

To help control stereotyping, Ting-Toomey and Chung advocate learning to "distinguish between inflexible stereotyping and flexible stereotyping."[23] As the words suggest, inflexible stereotyping is rigid and intransigent and occurs almost automatically. Because the stereotypes are so deeply embedded, you usually reject information that runs counter to these inflexible categorizations. However, the employment of flexible stereotyping starts when you become aware that categorizing is a natural tendency—you become more "mindful." This involves being open-minded, receptive to new information, avoiding assigning judgmental opinions, and recognizing that intercultural interactions can produce stress and discomfort.[24]

PREJUDICE

In the context of intercultural communication, prejudices are deeply held positive or negative feelings associated with a particular group. Your identity and self-image favorably incline you toward your in-group's characteristics and norms. This creates a positive in-group prejudice. Conversely, this prejudice promotes a tendency to use your in-group's standards to evaluate members of out-groups, both individually and collectively.[25] As a result, prejudice toward another group or a member of that group can arise when their attributes are evaluated unfavorably. Due to a lack of information, misconceptions, suspicion, misinformation, or other irrational feelings, unfavorable attitudes can easily develop toward other ethnic groups or their members. Allport provides one of the most widely used definitions of ethnic prejudice: "Ethnic prejudice is an antipathy based on a faulty and inflexible generalization. It may be felt or expressed. It may be directed toward a group as a whole or toward an individual because he is a member of that group."[26]

A more concise explanation is offered by Rogers and Steinfatt: "Prejudice is an unfounded attitude toward an outgroup based on a comparison with one's ingroup."[27] During communicative interactions, prejudicial perspectives are often displayed through the use of group labels, hostile humor, or vocabulary that stresses the superiority of one group over another.[28] It should now be evident that negative feelings and attitudes are an integral part of prejudice.

As with stereotypes, beliefs linked to prejudices possess certain characteristics. First, they are directed at a social group and its members. While this text focuses on prejudices between different cultural groups, negative prejudices can also be directed toward groups distinguished by gender, age, religious affiliation, sexual preference, and the like. Second, prejudices involve an emotional evaluation concerning "what is good and bad, right and wrong, moral and immoral, and so forth."[29] Prejudices can lead one to adopt an inflexible position about someone or something, and this intransigence can result in a heated, loud, and unproductive exchange rather than a reasoned discussion. Finally, the strength of a prejudice influences its longevity. A strongly held attitude toward a group is difficult to change, even when presented with facts that disprove a prejudicial opinion. The less intense a belief, the greater the opportunity for success in changing the prejudice.

> ## REMEMBER THIS
>
> *Prejudice occurs when a person holds a generalization about a group of people or things, often based on little or no factual experience.*

Functions of Prejudice

Like stereotypes, prejudices are learned and fulfill a variety of functions for the people holding them. For instance, prejudices can provide an individual a sense of superiority and power. Four of the more common functions of prejudice are discussed below:[30]

1. The *ego-defensive function* allows individuals to hold a prejudice while denying to themselves that they possess negative beliefs about a group. An example is the statement "I didn't get the promotion because they wanted to increase the number of minorities in upper management." This type of remark allows the speaker to articulate a prejudicial statement while avoiding self-examination to determine why he or she was not promoted.

2. The *utilitarian function* enables people to believe that their prejudicial beliefs result in a positive outcome. This is frequently found in situations where economic gain is involved. For instance, someone hiring immigrants might think, "Those

immigrants have so little education and training, they are lucky to have the jobs we offer them." This sort of statement reflects a prejudice because the holder can use the belief as justification for providing minimal wages to the workers.

3. A *value-expressive* function occurs when people maintain a prejudice in the belief that their attitude(s) represents the highest moral values of the culture. This usually revolves around the values associated with religion, government, and politics. Someone who believes that his or her religion is the only true faith and denigrates other beliefs is being prejudicial against people who hold different religious convictions. Political commentators on television often display a prejudice toward one political party or another.

4. Using the *knowledge function*, people can categorize, organize, and construct their perceptions of other people in a matter they consider rational—even if that perception is woefully incorrect. This makes dealing with the world much simpler because people can be viewed as a homogeneous group rather than individually. This results in an abundance of labels. People are considered not as individuals with a diversity of characteristics but rather as "Arabs," "Jews," "gays," "feminists," or some other label, which denies the person's unique characteristics.

Causes of Prejudice

There are no simple explanations for the origins of prejudice, and in most instances, the causes are multiple. Experts have isolated a few of the basic motivations behind prejudice, and we will look at three in order to better understand how they can be a major deterrent to successful intercultural interaction:

1. *Societal sources*: A considerable degree of prejudice is built into the major organizations and institutions of a society. These organizations produce norms, regulations, and rules that enable the dominant group to maintain power over subordinate groups. In so doing, they give rise to societal prejudice. The period of racial segregation in the United States and the era of apartheid rule in South Africa are classic examples of how the social structure can be used to establish, enforce, and sustain prejudice.

2. *Maintaining social identity*: The important role that identity plays in connecting people to their culture was discussed in Chapter 7. Identity is a very personal and emotional link because it creates the bond that binds people and culture. Anything that poses a potential threat to that connection, such as out-group members, can become a target of prejudice. For example, some members of the dominant U.S. culture view increased immigration as a threat to contemporary social values and the traditional way of life. This attitude produces a prejudice against immigrants, especially those who are illegal.

3. *Scapegoating*: Scapegoating is a process where a particular group of people, usually a minority, is singled out to bear the blame for certain events or circumstances, such as economic or social ills, that adversely affect the dominant group. Scapegoating uses arguments and justifications based on fear and imagined threats posed by an out-group. These assumed, unsubstantiated threats can be political, economic, or social concerns considered threatening to the in-group's well-being.[31] Throughout history, black people, Jews, immigrants, gays, and other minority groups have been used as scapegoats in order for the dominant group to escape responsibility.

Being motivated to communicate with people different from yourself is perhaps the first step in overcoming stereotyping, prejudice, racism, and the misuse of power.

© A. Ramey/PhotoEdit

Expressions of Prejudice

Prejudice expresses itself in a variety of ways, some subtle and indirect, and others overt, direct, and blatant. Over sixty years ago Harvard University Professor Gordon Allport's work revealed five escalating levels of prejudice.[32] That scale maintains its relevancy today and continues to be cited by contemporary scholars. We discuss the five levels below:

1. *Antilocution*: Allport uses the term "antilocution" to refer to negative verbal comments about a person or group. These discriminatory remarks can take a variety of forms, such as an ethnic joke or a stereotypical characterization like "Asians are bad drivers." Another example is the statement "Don't give the homeless people money because they just spend it on dope or alcohol," which attributes negative behaviors to an entire group. Antilocution can also be seen in the use of racial or ethnic slurs, such as "Mick" (Irish), "Gook" (Asian), "Kraut" (German), "Dago" (Italian), and others.

2. *Avoidance*: The next level of prejudice occurs when a person(s) physically avoids or withdraws from contact with a disliked group. Not attending a Cinco de Mayo festival because there will be Mexicans present is an example of avoidance.

3. *Discrimination*: Prejudice at this level is represented by efforts to exclude all members of a group from access to opportunity, institutions, services, and other forms of social life. When a company promotes a less qualified man instead of a more competent woman, you have discrimination. Denying a group access to a country club based on their ethnicity, gender, or religion is another form. Discrimination often combines ethnocentrism, stereotyping, and prejudice in a form of extremism that obstructs any type of successful intercultural communication.

4. *Physical Attacks*: At this stage, prejudice becomes so intense that it is acted out by physical aggression against another group or their property. Painting the swastika

(卐) symbol of Nazi Germany on a Jewish synagogue represents a prejudicial physical attack, as is any form of physical action against gays. Historical examples include the violence committed against blacks during the segregation era, pogroms against Jews in Russia, and recent attacks on Muslims and mosques in the United States in the wake of the events of 9/11.

5. *Extermination*: The most heinous form of prejudice is extermination, where a target group is subjected to physical violence with the intent of total elimination. The U.S. government's program against Native Americans in the 1800s, Hitler's "master plan," the "killing fields" of Cambodia, Serbian "ethnic cleansing," and "tribal warfare" in Rwanda are examples of this form of prejudice. A more recent illustration is the radical Islamic State militants' actions against members of the Yazidi minority group in northern Iraq.

As Allport brings out, most individuals are content to express their prejudices verbally to friends and seldom move to the more intense levels.[33] However, a close monitoring of daily news events will disclose that prejudicial instances of discrimination and physical aggression remain an all-too-common event both domestically and internationally.

> **CONSIDER THIS**
>
> In what ways have you personally observed prejudice being expressed?

Avoiding Prejudice

Avoiding prejudice is neither easy nor simple. As with most aspects of culturally instilled perception, prejudices are learned early and reinforced through repeated exposure. However, research has disclosed two techniques that are often successful in dispelling prejudicial views—personal contact and education.[34] Research on the merits of personal contact as a means of reducing prejudice dates from the early 1950s. The rationale is actually quite simple—the greater the frequency of positive interaction between in-group and out-group individuals, the lower the level of perceived prejudice. This contact does, however, need to meet certain criteria in order to be successful, with the most important being groups of equal status and cooperation for common goals.[35]

From an educational perspective, two types of programs have been found to reduce prejudice. The first centers around what is called multicultural education curricula, which focus on presenting the "history and cultural practices of a wide array of racial and ethnic groups."[36] The material is related from the point of view of the minority group(s) rather than that of the dominant culture. Cultural diversity training, the second type of program, is widely used in business and organizational settings. These programs are designed for all corporate employees, from worker to executive. Objectives are to increase employee cultural awareness, heighten intercultural understanding, create self-awareness of one's own cultural behaviors, and demonstrate the value of cultural diversity.[37] Regardless of the program selected, the explicit goals remain the same—to reduce prejudice through intergroup contact and cross-cultural dialogue.

The most fundamental method of decreasing prejudice is being personally mindful. You can examine your own prejudices and work to avoid remarks that could be interpreted as prejudicial against another group or person from that group. Too often, ethnic jokes or slurs are spoken in jest or in order to feel like part of the in-group. In addition to being self-mindful, it is important to make others mindful that you do not use or tolerate prejudicial statements.

RACISM

Racism represents a shameful stain on the course of history and unfortunately continues even today. In modern U.S. history, Congress passed a law in 1924 severely restricting immigration quotas for immigrants from eastern and southern European nations while eliminating all quotas for Asian countries.[38] During World War II, Japanese Americans living in the western states were relocated to concentration camps. Segregation in the southern states denied African Americans equal access to public facilities until the Civil Rights Act of 1964. Nazi Germany forced Jews to wear a yellow Star of David and ultimately instituted a program of mass extermination. Apartheid was official government policy in South Africa until 1994.

Despite the appalling record of the past, racism remains evident in contemporary society. According to Vora and Vora, "Both blatant and very subtle forms of racism permeate organizational and personal levels of our society, from governmental, business and educational institutions to our everyday interactions."[39] Events during the summer of 2014 attest to the continuance of racial tensions in the United States. Expressions of racism toward President Obama have a constant presence on the Internet, in emails, and in online cartoons.[40] Nor is racism confined to the United States. Minority groups around the world are subjected to racism simply because of their perceived biological differences—usually their physical appearance—from the majority group. There is growing resentment in Western Europe against immigrants from Africa and South Asia; in western China, the Uyghur minority is harshly subordinated to the Han majority; and Japan's immigration policies are extremely restrictive. While the underlying causes are many, at its core, racism is driven by "culture, economics, psychology, and history."[41]

It is impossible to make a complete assessment of the consequences of racism because the effects are both conscious and subconscious. However, we do know that racism damages both those who are subjected to it and the racists themselves. Racism denies the target individual(s) his or her identity and destroys the culture by eroding social cohesion and creating divisions in the population. This occurs when a selected group of people is excluded from access to society's social, economic, and educational institutions.

Racism Defined

In many ways, racism is but an extension of stereotyping and prejudice, as brought out in Leone's classic definition: "Racism is the belief in the inherent superiority of a particular race. It denies the basic quality of humankind and correlates ability with physical composition. Thus, it assumes that success or failure in any societal endeavor will depend upon genetic endowment rather than environment and access to opportunity."[42] The key phrase in this explanation is "inherent superiority." This false belief of superiority allows one group to mistreat another group on the basis of race, color, ancestry, national origin, or other perceived difference. Racist thinking is irrational because it is not only unethical and cruel but also founded on false premises.

There are no biological abilities or skills that differentiate groups of people. For those who are willing to accept it, "the big differences among human groups are the result of culture, not biological inheritance or race. All

CONSIDER THIS

Do you think racism has decreased or increased in your lifetime?

human beings belong to the same species and the biological features essential to human life are common to us all."[43] Yet despite this obvious truth and wisdom, racism remains a major hindrance to successful intercultural communication.

Categories of Racism

Racism comes in a variety of forms, some of which are almost impossible to detect, such as a company's hiring practices. But others, like the Ku Klux Klan's activities, are blatant and transparent. In broad terms, however, the different forms can be categorized as either personal or institutional. In the former category, racism is the manifestation of the individual's beliefs and behaviors. On the other hand, "Institutional racism refers to racial inferiorizing or antipathy perpetrated by specific social institutions such as schools, corporations, hospitals, or the criminal justice system as a totality."[44] The history of voting rights for Jews in the United States offers an example of institutional racism. The U.S. Constitution initially left voting rights to the individual states, and in several cases, Jews, as well as Catholics, were disenfranchised until ratification of the Fifteenth Amendment in 1870.[45] Whether intentional or inadvertent, the consequences of racism have a detrimental effect on the targeted group specifically and society as a whole.

Countering Racism

Views about race are often deeply entrenched, especially those learned during childhood, but there are some measures that can help reduce racism:

1. *Try to be honest*: When deciding if you hold any racist views, be truthful with yourself. Although an easy proposition to write but somewhat difficult to accomplish, confronting personal racist views is an important and necessary first step.

2. *Object to racist jokes and insults*: Although a simple act, this will often take considerable courage, especially when confronting family and close friends. However, it will send a clear message to other people that you condemn racism in any form.

3. *Respect freedom*: This seemingly simple proposal is actually a fundamental part of the American legacy. The Fourteenth Amendment to the U.S. Constitution specifies, "nor shall any State deprive any person of life, liberty, or property, without due process of law; nor deny to any person within its jurisdiction the equal protection of the laws."[46] This makes clear that liberty can be preserved only when all individuals are free from politically and socially imposed limitations.

4. *Examine racism's historical roots*: In order fully to comprehend and challenge the adverse impact of racism, you need to be able to understand and explain the origins of racist ideas and why they appeal to some people.

We conclude this discussion by reminding you that racism, stereotyping, and prejudice are pervasive because they are often acquired early in life and, like much of culture, become part of your way of seeing the world. The late African American author Maya Angelou employed an eloquent metaphor to reinforce this point: "The plague of racism is insidious, entering into our minds as smoothly and quietly and invisibly as floating airborne microbes enter into our bodies to find lifelong purchase in our bloodstreams."[47] We add that only individuals can purge those microbes from their bodies.

POWER

Much of our previous discussion reveals that prejudice and racism have roots in issues related to power. Power has played a significant role in relations among people, cultures, nations, and civilizations throughout history. Spears, guns, bombs, language, territory, money, and even historical memory have been—and continue to be—used to acquire and maintain power over others. The reason is apparent even though not wholly justifiable—power enables people to achieve their will regardless of the relationship. The integral position of power in all human relations was made clear when British philosopher Bertrand Russell observed, "the fundamental concept in social science is Power, in the same sense in which Energy is the fundamental concept in Physics."[48] Granted that there are many kinds of power (e.g., physical, psychological, spiritual, political, economic) that occur in a wide variety of contexts (e.g., interpersonal, organizational, governmental), we will focus on power in the intercultural context.

> ## REMEMBER THIS
>
> The concept of power is absolutely central to any understanding of society.[49]

Power Defined

In general, humans tend to seek power whenever they can, but why? Perhaps the answer lies in its definition. German philosopher Max Weber considered power as the ability to exert your will even in the face of opposition.[50] More broadly viewed, power is the ability to cause things to happen, to control what happens, and to prevent things you do not want to happen.[51] It is this idea of enabling you to control not only your own life but also the lives of others that makes power an important dimension in intercultural communication. In many cultures, the use of power enables people to pursue their own self-interests and to disregard the well-being and aspirations of others.

The methods of power are as diverse as they are widespread. Power is present in nearly every human experience, from global politics to contact between the dominant culture and co-culture members, and even in interpersonal interactions with friends and family members. As a result, the dynamics of power greatly influence all phases of intercultural communication. The historical memory that each party brings to any intercultural communication exchange carries an element of power. For instance, the tensions between African Americans and the police in Ferguson, Missouri, during the summer of 2014 were filled with different power issues—the history of racial segregation in the United States, local political authority, level of community unemployment, police appearance and perception of being abusive, and many others. On a global scale, official exchanges between China and the United States are colored by existing economic considerations, availability of military force, the memory of

China's exploitation by Western powers, etc. The point we are trying to make is that when you engage in intercultural communication, there will probably be a power imbalance that could influence the exchange. Something as seemingly minor as limited second-language ability can create a power differential.

Power in Intercultural Communication

Power in intercultural communication conversations can manifest itself in a variety of ways. In interpersonal exchanges, the amount of power you have or do not have influences with whom you talk, what you talk about, and how much control you have when talking. Power gives people the ability to impact what is appropriate and what is not, including topics of discussion, which level of formality to use, how to dress and behave, and even what to think or believe. The phrase from George Orwell's *Animal Farm* that "All animals are equal, but some animals are more equal than others" is often used metaphorically to illustrate that even in a society based on individual equality, those with power usually exert greater influence.

The level of power you have during any conversation is contingent on the person(s) you are interacting with and the resources you control. In intercultural communication exchanges these two factors take on added significance because the sources of power are culturally based. What may be seen as a source of power in one culture may have no bearing on power in another culture. For example, in England, the level of English used can often be seen as a sign of potential power because it signals one's class and social station. In some cultures, power and status are associated with one's family name. Level of education can also be a source of power. In the United States, older white males have historically enjoyed more power in social interactions than women or minority groups.

In the United States, there is a strong cultural message that one needs to have and exercise power. Children grow up being told they "need to stand on their own two feet," to be the "masters of their own fate" or "captain of their ships." Not only do they want power and think they deserve it, but they do not want other people to have power over them. In the United States, people often leave home as soon as possible to elude their parents' influence, and teachers, police, and bosses are made the brunt of jokes because they have power over us. Power is incorporated into the slogans of minority groups, such as gray power, black power, and gay power. In short, people in the United States are taught that they need to have power. In contrast to the United States, many cultures do not seek individual power and believe that power exists outside of them, that power resides in fate, nature, or God. Power is not something they have. Muslims use the phrase *inshallah*, "God willing" or "If God wills it." Among Hindus, power exists in one's karma, and in Mexico, a strong belief in fatalism often replaces power.

In the context of intercultural communication, it is important that you become aware of the different cultural approaches to power and try to mitigate its influence as much as possible. Measures to reduce the impact of power differentials can be as mundane as your posture and as complex as your vocabulary. We have previously posited that in any intercultural communication encounter, one person is probably using his or her second language. In these cases, as mentioned above, the individual using his or her first language enjoys a degree of power over the other person. This can be even more pronounced on those occasions when someone from a culture that has high face concerns is using their second language.

ETHICAL CONSIDERATIONS

The previous discussions in this chapter have focused on problems that can arise in an intercultural situation and issues that can impede communication between people of different cultures. At this point, we feel the need to examine some of the ethical issues that can arise in intercultural scenarios. As an introduction to ethics, we offer a series of contentions:

- Only God should decide when it is time to die.
- Assisted suicide should be made legal.
- Racial profiling is necessary and justified.
- Racial profiling violates the individual's personal freedom.
- Women have the right to control their reproductive behaviors.
- Artificial birth control is wrong.
- School prayer is just exercising freedom of religion.
- School prayer violates the concept of separation of church and state.

Deciding how you feel about these propositions involves making judgments that contain ethical implications and considering what is right or wrong, proper or improper, good or bad. The propositions may also require that you think about them in a global sense and decide if what is appropriate for your society is suitable for the global society as a whole. Ethics can be seen as a reflection of convictions that are rooted in culture. As a set of principles, ethics also provide guidelines that influence your manner of communicating with other people. Ethics, therefore, helps you determine what you ought to do, how you ought to act, and how you should interact with people.

ETHICS IN COMMUNICATION

A basic concept of this text is that communication is an instrument that can be used for an infinite number of purposes—sell a car, run for public office, teach children, obtain directions, make friends, persuade others to believe your views, express feelings, etc. Communication always has an impact, good or bad, desirable or undesirable, significant or insignificant, intended or unintended. Something happens when you send someone a message. Your words can change behavior, attitudes, beliefs, perceptions, moods, and even a person's sense of self. While the change may be immediate or delayed, public or private, short term or long term, when you communicate, you produce changes. This very fact speaks of the ethical component associated with intercultural communication.

REMEMBER THIS

Ethics is a tool that you may use when making difficult moral choices. These choices often involve the balancing of competing rights when there does not appear to be one "correct" answer.

Most cultures recognize the ethical dimension of communication on both a legal and an interpersonal level. In the United States, for instance, the legal aspects of communication are manifested in laws governing libel, slander, truth in advertising, and political campaign practices. Although most of your communication contexts are beyond the realm of legal control, you still need to consider the effects of your actions in the interpersonal setting. Whether the consequences of our messages are simple or profound, we cannot hide from the fact that our communicative actions affect other people.

You have probably realized by now that ethics is an elusive, multifaceted topic. And while the motivations for your ethical decisions come from a host of sources (parents, church, school, mass media, etc.), in the final analysis, the decision to act in one way or another is your responsibility. The choice of which course of action to take is complicated by the fact that many ethical decisions are automatic, made subconsciously due to prior conditioning. Additionally, a person's set of ethics serves to provide him or her with instructions on how to make difficult moral decisions in both professional and personal settings. Ethical choices are even more challenging when ethical practices collide—as they often do in intercultural exchanges. We are positing that ethical systems are subject to cultural diversity.

This observation of varying moral systems raises the question of whether there is an absolute morality and set of universal ethical principles. We conclude that the answer is "no." Although people hold many of the same ethical precepts, they advance diverse arguments about what is the "true" morality, whether morality is absolute, or whether it is relative to specific cultures. It is not our intent to settle this dispute. Rather, we offer you a brief overview of two of the most common perspectives—*relativism* and *universalism*—employed by people and cultures to deal with ethical issues.

Relativism

Cultural relativism is predicated on the belief that ethical systems can vary among cultures, all systems are equally valid, and there is no single system that is better than the others. In other words, what is believed and valued in one culture may be different in another culture. From the relativist perspective, what is correct or incorrect, right or wrong, true or untrue, is determined within that culture. More specifically, this orientation holds that ethical principles are culturally bound, context dependent, and applicable only to their respective cultures.[52] Relativism underscores the fact that different cultures not only often fail to agree on specific practices and beliefs but also contrast on moral codes concerning right and wrong, virtue and vice. The basic philosophical premise behind relativism is that "there is no single true morality."[53] As indicated, this ethical philosophy advocates the view that there is no one correct moral code for all times and all people, that each group has its own morality relative to its wants and values, and that moral ideals are necessarily relative to a particular group of people.

Stop for a moment and recall the examples given in Chapter 6 about the United States and China viewing the application of human rights from different perspectives and China's practice of hiring in-group members, even when less

> ## REMEMBER THIS
>
> *The relative perspective of ethics holds that values and morality are culturally bound and primarily depend on the perspective of the respective culture.*

qualified, before employing out-group members. From the ethical relativistic view, China's approach to human rights and giving in-group members precedence would be no more or less ethical than the opposite principles followed in the United States.

A secondary dynamic that follows from cultural relativism is that ethical standards are subject to change. Robertson and Crittenden suggest that the dynamics of convergence will cause standards and norms everywhere to shift as globalization leads to common values regarding economic and work-related behavior.[54] This convergence can be seen in labor-related issues as Western corporations, in response to client demands, pressure offshore manufacturing sites in Asia to improve employee working conditions. However, as a cautionary note, we point out that the two authors restrict this merging of ethics to economic and labor practices. There is little prospect for a single global culture at this time; indeed, there is some evidence that "globalization of culture creates heterogeneity, but within the context of one world culture, namely as local adaptations of world cultural forms."[55]

Universalism

Cultural universalism takes a position diametrically opposed to that of relativism. Universalism maintains that regardless of the people, context, time, or place, there are immutable universal ethical precepts that apply to all cultures. This stance maintains that there is in fact a single set of values, standards, morals, and the like that weave their way in and out of every culture. In simpler terms, cultural universalism believes that what is right or wrong, true or false, is applicable to all people everywhere in every circumstance.[56]

The problems with the universalism approach seem rather obvious and, like relativism, underscore the difficulty of deciding on a standard of ethics applicable to all cultures in every situation. Think for a moment how problematic it would be even to suggest that there is only one correct way for people to act. Moreover, should the attempt be made, what criteria would be used to select one culture's ethical system and deem it superior to those of all other cultures?

Cultural relativism is often defended because it purportedly results in tolerance, and cultural universalism is frequently seen as the only way to avoid nihilism.[57] However, it is not our objective to persuade you to accept the correctness of either ethical relativism or universalism. Rather, we will defer to the Taoist philosophy, which proposes that humans exist simultaneously in both a real and an ideal world. That is, the world of reality is the world that is the one you function in daily. The idealized world is the world that should be. In the world of reality, ethics and morality are culturally relative. Perhaps ethics and morality would be absolute in the world that should be. But because we live in the world that is, we will proceed on the assumption, rightly or wrongly, that ethics and morality are culturally relative. We will also take the position that regardless of one's basic philosophical worldview, ethical decisions are a part of everyone's daily life. A decision may be as simple as deciding to confront your best friend over a disparaging racial remark. Alternatively, it may be as complex as having to decide to report your foreign employer for using bribes to obtain a contract. With this in mind, we now offer some guidelines that can help you practice ethical behavior when interacting with people of diverse cultures.

CONSIDER THIS

How does universalism differ from relativism? Which do you believe holds the greater promise for intercultural interaction?

GUIDELINES FOR INTERCULTURAL ETHICS

Be Aware That Communication Produces a Response

A basic premise expressed throughout this text has been that the intercultural messages you send produce a response from the recipient(s). When communicating with someone from your own culture, you can often anticipate the response although not always. In an intercultural exchange, where diversity is a factor, it is much more difficult to foretell the type of reaction your message may produce. For example, in the culture of the United States, when asked a direct question, the response is usually a clear "yes" or "no." Also, a smile normally accompanies a positive reply. Quite in contrast, among Northeast Asian cultures, a direct question may elicit an ambiguous response along with a seemingly sincere smile. Without an appreciation for the nuances of communication in Northeast Asia—where "yes" can mean "no"—it can be easy to misinterpret what is said and what is actually meant.

The point is that it is difficult to know always how people will react to messages, and in intercultural communication, the intended meaning behind the outward reaction may be difficult to discern. Therefore, we recommend that you try to focus on both the other person and the social environment. In other words, as we discussed earlier in this chapter, you need to be "mindful." Obviously, concentrating on personal actions is far more difficult in actual practice than can be explained here. But the primary message is clear—being mindful during intercultural communication encounters requires giving your full attention to the moment. This will enable you to adjust your messages to the person and the context as well as being self-aware of how you may be affecting the other person, which is an ethical concern.

Respect Others

How do you feel when someone belittles you, ignores you, embarrasses you in front of others, or otherwise tends to diminish your sense of self-worth? The answer is obvious. Your emotions would range from anger to hurt. No one likes to feel belittled. Everyone wants some level of respect and dignity along with a positive self-image. Our contention is that ethical standards demand that respect be given to every human being regardless of their culture or station in life. And we are not alone. The *United Nations Declaration of Human Rights*, written in 1948, avers the following in the first of thirty articles: "Article 1: All human beings are born free and equal in dignity and rights. They are endowed with reason and conscience and should act towards one another in a spirit of brotherhood."[58] From the ethical perspective, this means that during communicative actions, you must display respect for the dignity and feelings of the other person(s). Confucius also advocated this sense of ethical concern: "Without feelings of respect, what is there to distinguish men from beasts?" In the globalized society, you must reach beyond your own cultural norms and respect the norms of other cultures.

Seek Commonalities

This book spends a great deal of time discussing how cultural differences can influence intercultural communication. But cultural similarities must also be considered because those similarities can act as an ethical guide. The search for commonality is

At the core of meaningful ethics are the twin beliefs that while we are different, in most of the things that matter—children, family, faith in something, and commitment—we are very much alike.

Courtesy of Robert Fonseca

an important ethical consideration because it helps you decide how to treat other **people** regardless of race, ethnicity, gender, age, etc. Looking beyond surface differences, you find multiple similarities. DeGenova points out that "Stripping away surface differences will uncover a multiplicity of similarities: people's homes, aspirations, desire to survive, search for love and need for family—to name just a few."[59]

CONSIDER THIS

How do cultures find similarities when cultures, in many instances, are dissimilar?

The similarities that unite people and that make everyone a part of the globalized society range from the obvious to the subtle. For example, all people share the basic desire to live their lives without external constraint—to be free. There is also a universal link between children and family. All people share the excitement of a new birth. Mating and wanting friendship is a common need. Everyone must eventually face old age, and people are joined in knowing that death is inevitable, a part of life's process. The enjoyment of music and art, in all their many forms, is universal. There are also countless religious and philosophical values that bind people.

From this brief discussion, you can recognize that people are very much alike in many significant ways. In a multicultural world, it is important to recognize these commonalities. As the late Professor Samuel Huntington said, "People in all civilizations should search for and attempt to expand the values, institutions, and practices they have in common with people of other civilizations."[60]

Recognize and Respect Cultural Differences

In addition to finding commonalities among people and cultures, it is equally important to recognize, understand, and respect cultural differences. Former President of Israel Shimon Peres provides an eloquent summation of this ethical precept: "All people have the right to be equal and the equal right to be different." A foundational objective of this text has been to instill an appreciation that culture produces varying beliefs, values, and behaviors. Understanding and respecting those cultural variances enables you to develop an intercultural awareness with an ethical perspective. In short, you must keep in mind that people are both *alike* and *different*!

World travelers today can order a latte at a Starbucks in Mumbai, eat a McDonald's Big Mac in Berlin, drink a Coca-Cola in Nairobi, visit an Apple store in Beijing, purchase a Toyota Corolla in Cairo, try on a pair of Zara jeans in Moscow, find a Louis Vuitton store in Rio de Janeiro, and connect to Google.com almost anywhere in the world. And there is a very good chance that in each city, you will be able to speak English with the salesperson. The internationalization of commercial activities can give the impression that everyone everywhere has a similar lifestyle and enjoys the same things. However, this is an illusion. Over twenty-five years ago, Barnlund vividly illustrated this double-sided nature of cultures:

> If outwardly there is little to distinguish what one sees on the streets of Osaka [Japan] and Chicago—hurrying people, trolleys and busses, huge department stores, blatant billboards, skyscraper hotels, public monuments—beneath the surface there remains great distinctiveness. There is a different organization of industry, a different approach to education, a different role for labor unions, and a contrasting pattern of family life, unique law enforcement and penal practices, contrasting forms of political activity, different sex and age roles. Indeed, most of what is thought of as culture shows as many differences as similarities.[61]

The observable similarities that Barnlund wrote about not only remain today but also, in many cases, have increased. Yet the cultural differences endure and continue to influence interactions.

The need to recognize, appreciate, and accept cultural similarities and differences is essential to developing a complete and honest intercultural ethical perspective. This perspective will help you better access the potential consequences of your communicative acts and become more tolerant of others. It is appropriate here to recall Thomas Jefferson's advice about accepting differences: "It does me no injury for my neighbor to say there are twenty gods, or no God."

Be Self-Responsible

Earlier, we referred to our ability to exercise free choice and the need to be "mindful" because our choice of communicative behaviors can cause both intended and unintended consequences for other people. Our final ethical consideration places those two ideas into an intercultural context. We advocate a three-point perspective that acknowledges individual uniqueness, the ability to exercise free choice, and the increasing interdependence of contemporary society. Support for this idea is found in Evanoff's communicative approach to intercultural communication ethics:

> The communicative approach recognizes that while we are situated in a particular culture and socialized in certain norms, we are nonetheless able to reflect back on those norms and change them if necessary. We are also able to critically reflect on the norms of other cultures and to selectively adopt (or reject) those norms that seem plausible (or implausible) to us.[62]

The central message we are trying to convey is that if we are going to live in this crowded, interconnected world, we need to recognize our individual roles within that world and hold ourselves accountable for our own actions. Recall, as we have endeavored to demonstrate throughout this book, that people and cultures are inextricably linked. As the English anthropologist Gregory Bateson rhetorically queries, "What pattern connects the crab to the lobster and the orchid to the primrose and all the four of them to me? And me to you?"[63]

A FINAL APPEAL

We have come to the end of our journey. Normally, textbook authors like to conclude with some insightful quotation of a long-dead and usually forgotten philosopher or perhaps offer a bit of life-changing advice to carry into your future. As we have already offered our quotation, we now make a final appeal.

Never in history has there been such mixing of peoples and cultures. Nor will this mixing and blending soon slow. Driven by economic deprivation and political tyranny, people will continue to migrate to nations that hold the promise of security and a more productive life. Employment is now on a global basis—you have just as much chance of working in London as you do in Kansas City. While globalization has created a truly international economy, political states remain separate. This has produced a novel conundrum—nations are economically interdependent but separated by political and nationalistic interests. The economic ties lessen the likelihood of large-scale conflict, which leaves only dialogue to resolve the political disputes. Thus, the requirement for intercultural skills will increase during your lifetime.

With this in mind, we ask for your assistance in bringing about greater intercultural awareness, understanding, and communication competence. The requirement is clear, and the rewards are self-evident. Good luck!

SUMMARY

- Venturing into a new culture can cause anxiety and emotional distress, resulting in mental and physical fatigue.

- Culture shock is a mental state that can occur when moving from a familiar to an unfamiliar environment and finding that established patterns of behavior are ineffective.

- According to the U-curve model, cultural adaptation has four phases—honeymoon, disillusionment, recovery, and adjustment. Culture shock can occur during the disillusionment stage.

- Kim sees acculturation, or cultural adjustment, as a continuing process of stress-adaptation-growth.

- Cultural adaptation strategies include learning about the host culture and its language, avoiding ethnocentrism, and maintaining contact with your own culture.

- Obstacles to effective intercultural communication include a preference for similarities, dealing with uncertainty, the risk of withdrawal, stereotyping tendencies, problems of prejudice and racism, and issues of power.

- Prejudice is a strong feeling or attitude toward a particular social group or thing.

- Racism occurs when individuals believe that their race/ethnicity is superior to another race/ethnicity.

- Because communication is an activity that has a consequence, we must develop a communication ethic.

- The two major perspectives on ethics are relativism and universalism.

- An intercultural ethic asks you to be mindful of the power of communication, respect the worth of all individuals, seek commonalties among people and cultures, recognize the validity of differences, and take individual responsibility for your actions.

ACTIVITIES

1. Go to YouTube and search for "Examples of culture shock." You can also search for "cultural adaptation," "cultural adjustment," "reverse culture shock," or "U-curve." After viewing some of the videos, try to isolate some of the most common causes of culture shock. (Warning: "Culture shock" will bring up many nonrelated videos.)

2. Working alone or in a group, choose a country and compile a list of preparations to minimize the effects of culture shock in that specific nation.

3. To measure your implicit social attitudes about race, gender, sexual orientation, etc., go to the Harvard University–sponsored "Project Implicit" website (https://implicit.harvard.edu/implicit) and take the test(s). The tests can be taken anonymously online with results provided immediately.

4. Go to the "Shooter Task" website (http://www.csun.edu/~dma/FPST/consent.html) and read about the voluntary study to measure "implicit associations and the demographic variables." Participate if you like.

5. Working with others, discuss the components of intercultural ethics. How would you recommend that such ethics be internalized so that they are always present during intercultural exchanges?

CONCEPTS AND QUESTIONS

1. Why do so many immigrants have a difficult time adapting to a new culture? What suggestions do you have for making that process less troublesome?

2. Do you think members of a host culture have any responsibilities to make immigrants feel comfortable in the new cultural environment? Why?

3. Discuss the following statement: "Prejudice can never be eliminated because it is so deeply rooted in human nature."

4. What relationship links stereotypes, prejudice, racism, and power?

5. What are some of the merits of a relativistic approach to developing an intercultural ethic? Of a universalistic approach? What are some of the dangers?

Notes

Chapter 1

1. L. A. Samovar and R. E. Porter, *Communication Between Cultures* (Belmont, CA: Wadsworth Publishing, 1991), 3.

2. A. Cabrera and G. Unruh, *Being Global: How to Think, Act, and Lead in a Transformed World* (Boston: Harvard Business Review Press, 2012), 13–14.

3. "Import Share of Consumption," *U.S. Agricultural Trade* (U.S. Department of Agriculture, Economic Research Service, May 30, 2012), http://www.ers.usda.gov/topics/international-markets-trade/us-agricultural-trade/import-share-of-consumption.aspx (accessed February 13, 2015).

4. M. A. Hamburg, "Food Safety Modernization Act: Putting the Focus on Prevention," *Foodsafety.gov* (U.S. Department of Health & Human Services, 2015), http://www.foodsafety.gov/news/fsma.html (accessed February 13, 2015).

5. N. Eberstadt, "The Human Population Unbound," *Current History* 113, 759 (January 2014): 43–45.

6. "Global Population Growth," *Global Population Profile: 2002* (U.S. Census Bureau, 2002), 11, http://www.census.gov/ population/international/publications/index.html (accessed February 15, 2015); *World POPClock Projection* (U.S. Census Bureau, 2015), http://www.census.gov/population/popwnotes.html (accessed February 15, 2015); "World population projected to reach 9.6 billion by 2050 — UN report," *UN News Centre* (June 13, 2013), http://www.un.org/apps/news/story.asp?NewsID=45165#.VOF5fRR0y71 (accessed February 15, 2015); P. Gerland, A. E. Raftery, H.

Ševčiková, N. Li, D. Gu, T. Spoorenberg, L. Alkema, B. K. Fosdick, J. Chunn, N. Lalic, G. Bay, T. Buettner, G. K. Heilig, and J. Wilmoth, "World population stabilization unlikely this century," *Science* 346, 6206 (September 14, 2014): 234.

7. *State & County QuickFacts* (U.S. Census Bureau, February 5, 2015), http://quickfacts.census.gov/qfd/states/00000.html (accessed February 16, 2015); M. Lifsher, "Immigrant workers," *Los Angeles Times* (August 18, 2013), http://www.latimes.com/business/la-fi-capitol-business-beat-20130819,0,2787065.story (accessed February 16, 2015).

8. M. Pagel, "Does globalization mean we will become one culture?," *BBC Future* (May 23, 2013), http://www.bbc.com/future/story/20120522-one-world-order (accessed February 16, 2015).

9. S. Sengupta, "U.N. Finds Most People Now Live in Cities," *New York Times* (July 10, 2014), http://www.nytimes.com/2014/07/11/world/more-than-half-the-global-population-growth-is-urban-united-nations-report-finds.html?_r=0 (accessed February 15, 2015); *World Urbanization Prospects: The 2014 Revision* (United Nations, Department of Economic and Social Affairs, 2014), 1, http://esa.un.org/unpd/wup/Highlights/WUP2014-Highlights.pdf (accessed February 16, 2015); "Growth in Urban Population Outpaces Rest of Nation, Census Bureau Reports," *Newsroom Archive* (U.S. Census Bureau, March 2012), https://www.census.gov/newsroom/releases/archives/2010_census/cb12-50.html (accessed February 16, 2015).

10. J. P., "Mixed marriages: The mixture as before," *The Economist* (July 6, 2012),

http://www.economist.com/blogs/feastandfamine/2012/07/mixed-marriages (accessed February 17, 2015); G. Lanzieri, "Merging populations: A look at marriages with foreign-born persons in European countries," *Population and social conditions: Statistics in focus* (Eurostat, June 28, 2012), http://ec.europa.eu/eurostat/documents/3433488/5584928/KS-SF-12-029-EN.PDF/4c0917f8-9cfa-485b-a638-960c00d66da4 (accessed February 17, 2015); "International marriage: Herr and Madame, Señor and Mrs," *The Economist* (November 12, 2011), http://www.economist.com/node/21538103 (accessed February 17, 2015); T. D. Johnson and R. M. Kreider, *Mapping Interracial/Interethnic Married-Couple Households in the United States: 2010* (U.S. Census Bureau, n.d.), http://www.census.gov/hhes/socdemo/marriage/data/census/InterracialMarriages_PAA2013_FINAL.pdf (accessed February 17, 2015); "Across the aisles," *The Economist* (April 13, 2013), 36; A. Stone, "Multiracial American Population Grew Faster Than Single-Race Segment In 2010 Census," *Huffington Post* (September 27, 2012), http://www.huffingtonpost.com/2012/09/27/multiracial-americans-2010-census_n_1919070.html (accessed February 15, 2015).

11. D. Lee, "As America ages, generational gap between whites and minorities," *Los Angeles Times* (July 27, 2013), http://www.latimes.com/business/money/la-na-census-demo graphic-gap-20140626-story.html (accessed February 15, 2015); M. Muskal, "Whites to lose majority status by 2043, the census projects," *Los Angeles Times* (December 12, 2012), http://articles.latimes.com/2012/dec

/12/nation/la-na-nn-whites-to-lose
-majority-status-by-2043-the-census
-projects-20121212 (accessed February
17, 2015).

12. *Attitudes about Aging: A Global Perspective* (Pew Research Center, January 2014), 26, http://www.pewglobal
.org/files/2014/01/Pew-Research
-Center-Global-Aging-Report-FINAL
-January-30-20141.pdf (accessed Feb-
ruary 17, 2015); A. Fensom, "East
Asia's Future: Extinction?," *The
Diplomat* (August 29, 2014), http://
thediplomat.com/2014/08/east-asias
-future-extinction (accessed February
17, 2015); "Highlights," *Administration on Aging* (U.S. Department of
Health and Human Services,
Administration for Community
Living, n.d.), http://www.aoa.acl.gov
/Aging_Statistics/Profile/2013/2.aspx
(accessed January 5, 2015); C. A.
Werner, *The Older Population: 2010*
(U.S. Census Bureau: 2010 Census
Briefs, November 2011), 2–4, http://
www.census.gov/prod/cen2010/briefs
/c2010br-09.pdf (accessed February
14, 2015); *World Population Ageing
2013* (United Nations, Department of
Economic and Social Affairs, Population Division, 2013), http://www
.un.org/en/development/desa
/population/publications/pdf/ageing
/WorldPopulationAgeing2013.pdf
(accessed February 14, 2015).

13. *Why Population Aging Matters: A
Global Perspective* (National Institute
on Aging, National Institutes of
Health, Publication No. 07-6234,
March 2007), 1, http://www.nia.nih
.gov/sites/default/files/WPAM.pdf
(accessed March 6, 2015).

14. *The National Intelligence Strategy of the
United States of America* (Office of the
Director of National Intelligence,
2014), http://www.dni.gov/files/docu-
ments/2014_NIS_Publication.pdf, 5
(accessed February 18, 2015).

15. N. R. Brown, "Changing the Rules in
Global Resource Competition,"
*Testimony for the House Committee on
Foreign Affairs, Subcommittee on
Europe, Eurasia and Emerging Threats*
(July 25, 2013), http://docs.house
.gov/meetings/FA/FA14/20130725
/101216/HHRG-113-FA14-Wstate
-BrownN-20130725.pdf (accessed

February 18, 2015); S. Donnan and J.
Politi, "WTO rules against China on
'rare earths' export restrictions,"
Financial Times (March 26, 2014),
http://www.ft.com/cms/s/0/962a0ba4
-b4e6-11e3-9166-00144feabdc0
.html#axzz3S7dkBmus (accessed February 18, 2015); E. Economy and M.
Levi, *By All Means Necessary* (New
York: Oxford University Press, 2014),
5–9; "How will global energy markets
evolve to 2040?," *World Energy Outlook 2104 Factsheet* (Paris: International Energy Agency, n.d.), http://
www.worldenergyoutlook.org/media
/weowebsite/2014/141112_WEO
_FactSheets.pdf (accessed February
18, 2015); D. Jolly, "China Export
Restrictions on Metals Violate Global
Trade Law, Panel Finds," *New York
Times* (March 26, 2014), http://www
.nytimes.com/2014/03/27/business
/international/china-export-quotas
-on-rare-earths-violate-law-wto
-panel-says.html?ref=topics&_r=0
(accessed February 18, 2015).

16. B. I. Cook, T. R. Ault, and J. E.
Smerdon, "Unprecedented 21st cen-
tury drought risk in the American
Southwest and Central Plains," *Sci-
ence Advances* 1, 1 (2015):
e1400082, 1–7; S. Borenstein, "U.S.
'Megadroughts' Are Likely Later
This Century, Study Finds,"
Huffington Post (February 12, 2015),
http://www.huffingtonpost.com
/2015/02/13/us-megadroughts
-study_n_6671812.html (accessed
February 15, 2015); "Companies and
Water: Values Diluted," *The Economist* (November 8, 2014), 67; G.
Kleyn and T. Luttrell (eds.), *Water:
Our Future* (West Perth, Australia:
Future Directions, 2011), 7–8, http://
www.futuredirections.org.au/files
/WaterPublication[2].pdf (accessed
February 19, 2015); M. Mohieldin,
The Road from Thirst (Project
Syndicate) (February 11, 2014),
http://www.project-syndicate.org/
commentary/mahmoud-mohieldin
-identifies-four-areas-for-action-on
-the-water-related-challenges-that
-are-impeding-economic-development
-and-poverty-reduction (accessed
February 19, 2015); "Water World,"
Time (December 29, 2014/January 5,
2015), 58–59.

17. S. Heslot, "China's Increasing Food
Imports: The Impact on Global Markets," *Future Directions International*
(September 3, 2014), http://www
.futuredirections.org.au/publications
/food-and-water-crises/28-global-food
-and-water-crises-swa/1904-china-s
-increasing-food-imports-the-impact
-on-global-markets.html (accessed
February 15, 2015); E. Levinson,
"Global Revolutions in Agriculture:
The Challenge and Promise of 2050,"
2014 GAP Report (Washington, DC:
Global Harvest Initiative, 2014), 4,
http://www.globalharvestinitiative
.org/GAP/2014_GAP_Report.pdf
(accessed February 19, 2015); D. K.
Ray, N. D. Mueller, P. C. West, and
J. A. Foley, "Yield Trends Are Insufficient to Double Global Crop Production by 2050," *PLoS ONE* 8, 6
(June 19, 2013), http://journals.plos
.org/plosone/article?id=10.1371/jour-
nal.pone.0066428 (accessed
February 19, 2013); *Global map of
investments* (Land Matrix, 2015),
http://landmatrix.org/en/get-the-idea/
global-map-investments (accessed
February 19, 2015); "The new green
revolution: A bigger rice bowl," *The
Economist* (May 10, 2014), 21–23;
"Meat and greens," *The Economist*
(January 18, 2014), 60–61.

18. *The State of World Fisheries and
Aquaculture* (Food and Agriculture
Organization of the United Nations,
2014), http://www.fao.org/3/a-i3720e
.pdf (accessed February 14, 2015).

19. L. R. Brown, *Full Planet, Empty Place*
(New York: Norton, 2012), 17; B.
Walsh, "Ocean View," *Time*
(April 14, 2014), 42–44.

20. Brown, 2014, 14.

21. J. R. Jambeck, R. Geyer, C. Wilcox,
T. R. Siegler, M. Perryman, A.
Andrady, R. Narayan, and K. L. Law,
"Plastic waste inputs from land into
the ocean," *Science* 347, 6223 (Feb-
ruary 13, 2015): 768–70; A. B. Sielen,
"The devolution of the seas," *Foreign
Affairs* 92, 6 (2013): 124–32; "China's
underground water quality worsens:
report," *Xinhua English News.com*
(April 22, 2014), http://news.xinhua
net.com/english/china/2014-04/22/
c_126421022.htm (accessed
February 20, 2015); *Nonpoint Source*

Pollution: The Nation's Largest Water Quality Problem (U.S. Environmental Protection Agency, Pointer No. 1EPA841-F-96-004A, September 14, 2014), http://water.epa.gov/polwaste /nps/outreach/point1.cfm (accessed February 17, 2015); J. Barchfield, "Brazil Won't Clean Up Water Pollution In Guanabara Bay By 2016 Olympics, Officials Say," *The World Post* (May 18, 2014), http://www. huffingtonpost.com/2014/05/18/brazil -water-pollution-guanabara-bay-2016 -olympics_n_5347766.html (accessed February 20, 2015); T. Barboza, "Scientists say ozone from Asia contributes to the West's pollution," *Los Angeles Times* (January 31, 2015), http://www.latimes.com/science/la -me-pacific-smog-20150201-story .html#page=1 (accessed February 20, 2015); E. Wong, "China Exports Pollution to U.S., Study Finds," *New York Times* (January 20, 2014), http:// www.nytimes.com/2014/01/21/world/ asia/china-also-exports-pollution-to -western-us-study-finds.html?_r=0 (accessed February 20, 2015).

22. J. K. Boyce, "Amid climate change, what's more important: Protecting money or people?," *Los Angeles Times* (December 21, 2014), http://www .latimes.com/opinion/op-ed/la-oe -1222-boyce-climate-change -adaptation-costs-20141218-story. html (accessed February 20, 2015); "Impact of climate change 'harrowing,'" *The Japan Times* (November 4, 2013), http://www.japantimes.co.jp /life/2013/11/03/environment/impact -of-climate-change-harrowing/# .VOgQPhR0y70 (accessed February 20, 2015).

23. M. T. S. Rajan, "The implications of international copyright law for cultural diversity policies," in *Differing Diversities: Transversal Study on the Theme of Cultural Policy and Cultural Diversity*, ed. Tony Bennett (Strasbourg, France: Cultural Policy and Action Department, Council of Europe Publishing, November 2001), 142, http://www.google.com/url? sa=t&rct=j&q=&esrc=s&source= web&cd=1&ved=0CB4QFjAA &url=http%3A%2F%2Fwww.labfor culture.org%2Fde%2Fcontent% 2Fdownload%2F9708%2F120993% 2Ffile%2FEN_Diversity_Bennett .pdf&ei=UuHrVLHvHsXqoATY0o LYDg&usg=AFQjCNFOmeO- JASqVchlsYkqE_HwMJYqZC w&bvm=bv.86475890,d.cGU (accessed February 23, 2015).

24. H. Korn, "Patenting Culture: The Cultural Conflict of Intellectual Property," *The MorningSide Review* (Columbia University, 2010/2011 edition), http://morningsidereview .org/essay/patenting-culture-the -cultural-conflict-of-intellectual -property/ (accessed February 24, 2015).

25. Y. Takeo, "Japan's Parliament Ratifies Child Custody Treaty," *Wall Street Journal* (June 2, 2013), http://www .wsj.com/articles/SB1000142412788 73237343045 78540952428702518 (accessed February 24, 2015).

26. J. Bunge, "U.S. Corn Exports to China Dry Up Over GMO Concerns," *Wall Street Journal* (April 11, 2014), http://www.wsj.com/articles /SB1000142405270230387360 45 79493790405023808 (accessed February 24, 2015); D. Lynch and D. Vogel, *The Regulation of GMOs in Europe and the United States: A Case-Study of Contemporary European Regulatory Politics* (New York: Council on Foreign Relations Press, April 5, 2001), http://www.cfr.org /agricultural-policy/regulation-gmos -europe-united-states-case-study-con- temporary-european-regulatory-politics /p8688 (accessed February 24, 2015); M. C. Nisbet, "The Competition for Worldviews: Values, Information, and Public Support for Stem Cell Research," *International Journal of Public Opinion Research* 17, 1 (2005): 90, http://ijpor.oxfordjournals.org /content/17/1/90.full.pdf+html (accessed February 24, 2015); "The Validity of a Cultural Approach to Human Rights," *Human Rights Dialogue* 1, 5 (Summer 1996): "Cultural Sources of Human Rights in East Asia" (June 5, 1996), http://www .carnegiecouncil.org/publications /archive/dialogue/1_05/articles/524 .html (accessed February 24, 2015); S. Sceats and S. Breslin, *China and the International Human Rights System* (London: Chatham House, October 2012), 7, http://www.chathamhouse .org/sites/files/chathamhouse/public /Research/International%20Law /r1012_sceatsbreslin.pdf (accessed February 24, 2015).

27. K. Davenport, "History of Official Proposals on the Iranian Nuclear Issue," *Fact Sheets & Briefs* (Washington, DC: Arms Control Association, January 2014), http:// www.armscontrol.org/factsheets /Iran_Nuclear_Proposals (accessed February 25, 2015); J. Bajoria and B. Xu, "The Six Party Talks on North Korea's Nuclear Program," *Backgrounders* (Council on Foreign Relations, September 30, 2013), http://www.cfr.org/proliferation /six-party-talks-north-koreas-nuclear -program/p13593 (accessed February 25, 2015); "All of Syria's declared chemical weapons removed, official says," *CBS News* (June 23, 2014), http://www.cbsnews.com /news/all-of-syrias-declared-chemical -weapons-removed-official-says (accessed February 25, 2015); N. Notman, "Eliminating Syria's chemical weapons," *Chemistry World* (May 21, 2014), http://www.rsc.org /chemistryworld/2014/05/syrian -chemical-weapons-feature (accessed February 25, 2015).

28. "About CMF," *Combined Maritime Forces* (n.d.), http://combinedmaritime forces.com/about (accessed February 25, 2015).

29. "Peacekeeping Fact Sheet," *United Nations Peacekeeping* (United Nations, January 31, 2015), http://www.un.org /en/peacekeeping/resources/statistics /factsheet.shtml (accessed February 25, 2015); S. Schlesinger, "The dangerous, valuable work of U.N. peacekeepers," *Los Angeles Times* (September 18, 2014), http://www .latimes.com/opinion/op-ed/la-oe -schlesinger-endangered-peacekeepers -20140919-story.html (accessed February 15, 2015).

30. *Latest Trends in Religious Restrictions and Hostilities* (Pew Research Center, February 26, 2015), 4.

31. *Latest Trends*, 2015, 7.

32. J. Sacks, "Europe's Alarming New Anti-Semitism," *Wall Street Journal*

(October 2, 2014), http://www.wsj
.com/articles/europes-alarming-new
-anti-semitism-1412270003 (accessed
February 27, 2015); J. Yardley,
"Europe's Anti-Semitism Comes Out
of the Shadows," *New York Times*
(September 23, 2015), http://www
.nytimes.com/2014/09/24/world
/europe/europes-anti-semitism-comes
-out-of-shadows.html?_r=0 (accessed
February 27, 2015).

33. J. Wight, "Across Europe Nationalism
Is on the Rise," *Huffington Post Politics*
(May 27, 2014), http://www.huffing
tonpost.co.uk/john-wight/nationalism
-europe_b_5393841.html (accessed
February 27, 2015); S. Kotkin, "The
Resistible Rise of Vladimir Putin,"
Foreign Affairs 94, 2 (March/April
2015): 150; "What Hindu nationalism means," *The Economist* (May 18,
2014), http://www.economist.com
/blogs/economist-explains/2014/05
/economist-explains-8 (accessed February 27, 2015); E. Fish, "A Glimpse
Into Chinese Nationalism," *The
Diplomat* (November 7, 2014), http://
thediplomat.com/2014/11/a-glimpse
-into-chinese-nationalism (accessed
February 27, 2015); J. Anderlini,
"Patriotic education distorts China
world view," *Financial Times*
(December 23, 2012), http://www.ft
.com/cms/s/0/66430e4e-4cb0-11e2
-986e-00144feab49a.html#axzz3-
SyNZ8XmD (accessed February 27,
2015); N. Kato, "Tea Party Politics in
Japan: Japan's Rising Nationalism,"
New York Times (September 12,
2014), http://www.nytimes.com/2014
/09/13/opinion/tea-party-politics-in
-japan.html?_r=0 (accessed
February 27, 2015); J. A. Gans Jr.,
"American Exceptionalism and the
Politics of Foreign Policy," *The
Atlantic* (November 21, 2011), http://
www.theatlantic.com/international
/archive/2011/11/american
-exceptionalism-and-the-politics-of
-foreign-policy/248779 (accessed
February 27, 2015).

34. "Balfour Declaration," *Encyclopædia
Britannica* (July 15, 2014), http://
www.britannica.com/EBchecked
/topic/50162/Balfour-Declaration
(accessed February 27, 2015); F.
Jacobs, "The Elephant in the Map

Room," *New York Times* (August 7,
2012), http://opinionator.blogs
.nytimes.com/2012/08/07/the
-elephant-in-the-map-room/?_r=0
(accessed February 27, 2015); G.
Fainclough, "India–China Border
Standoff: High in the Mountains,
Thousands of Troops Go Toe-to-
Toe," *Wall Street Journal* (October 30,
2014), http://www.wsj.com/articles
/india-china-border-standoff-high-in
-the-mountains-thousands-of-troops
-go-toe-to-toe-1414704602 (accessed
February 27, 2015).

35. M. Thim, "No Strait for Aircraft
Carriers," (Center for International
Maritime Security, March 6, 2015),
http://cimsec.org/no-strait-aircraft
-carriers/15372 (accessed March 7,
2015).

36. O. Onuch, "Social networks and
social media in Ukrainian 'Euromaidan' protests," *Washington Post*
(January 2, 2014), http://www
.washingtonpost.com/blogs/monkey
-cage/wp/2014/01/02/social-networks
-and-social-media-in-ukrainian
-euromaidan-protests-2 (accessed
March 6, 2015).

37. J. M. Berger and J. Morgan, *The ISIS
Twitter Census: Defining and describing
the population of ISIS supporters on
Twitter* (Washington, DC: Brookings
Institution Press, March, 2015),
http://www.brookings.edu/~/media
/research/files/papers/2015/03/isis
-twitter-census-berger-morgan/the
-isis-twitter-census-defining-and
-describing-the-population-of-isis-sup-
porters-on-twitter.pdf (accessed March
7, 2015); S. Shane and B. Hubbard,
"ISIS Displaying a Deft Command
of Varied Media," *New York Times*
(August 30, 2014), http://www
.nytimes.com/2014/08/31/world
/middleeast/isis-displaying-a-deft
-command-of-varied-media.html?_r=0
(accessed March 6, 2015); L. Walker,
"Inside the ISIS Social Media
Campaign," *Newsweek* (March 6,
2015), http://www.newsweek.com
/inside-isis-social-media-campaign
-312062 (accessed March 6, 2015);
"Best known for scandal, Bell now
getting A's for transparency," *Los
Angeles Times* (March 14, 2013),
http://latimesblogs.latimes.com

/lanow/2013/03/best-known-for
-scandal-bell-now-getting-as-for
-transparency.html (accessed
March 7, 2015).

38. *The Global Class* (2015), http://www
.theglobalclass.org (accessed March 7,
2015).

39. J. Wildens, "Panic Virus explores dangerous trend," *San Diego Union-Tribune*
(January 24, 2011), http://www.utsan
diego.com/news/2011/jan/24/beyond
-belief (accessed March 7, 2015).

40. J. Achenbach, "The Age of Disbelief,"
National Geographic (March 2015), 45.

41. N. D. Kristof, "The Daily Me," *New
York Times* (March 19, 2009), http://
www.nytimes.com/2009/03/19
/opinion/19kristof.html?_r=0
(accessed March 7, 2015).

42. A. Smith and M. Duggan, *Online
Dating and Relationships* (Pew
Research Center, October 21, 2013),
http://www.pewinternet.org/files/old
-media//Files/Reports/2013/PIP
_Online%20Dating%202013.pdf
(accessed March 8, 2015).

43. S. Pinker, *The Blank Slate: The
Modern Denial of Human Nature*
(New York: Viking, 2002), 34.

44. J. Hooker, *Working Across Cultures*
(Stanford, CA: Stanford University
Press, 2003),60.

45. R. L. Coles, *Race and Family: A
Structural Approach* (Thousand Oaks,
CA: Sage Publications, 2006), xi.

46. *Random House Dictionary of the English
Language,* 2nd ed. Unabridged (New
York: Random House, 1987), 1336.

47. G. Ferraro and S. Andreatta, *Cultural
Anthropology: An Applied Perspective,*
8th ed. (Belmont, CA: Wadsworth
Cengage Learning, 2010), 109.

48. J. T. Wood, *Interpersonal Communi-
cation: Everyday Encounters,* 12th ed.
(Boston: Wadsworth Cengage
Learning, 2013), 29.

Chapter 2

1. C. F. Keating, "World Without
Words: Messages from Face and Body,"
in *Psychology and Culture*, ed. W. J.
Lonner and R. S. Malpass (Boston:
Allyn and Bacon, 1994), 175.

2. See R. E. Porter and L. A. Samovar, "Cultural Influences on Emotional Expression: Implications for Intercultural Communication," in *Handbook of Communication and Emotion: Research, Theory, Applications, and Contexts*, ed. P. A. Andersen and L. K. Guerrero (New York: Academic Press, 1998), 451–72.

3. J. T. Wood, *Communication Mosaics*, 7th ed. (Boston: Wadsworth Cengage Learning, 2014), 178.

4. F. E. X. Dance and C. E. Larson, *Speech Communication: Concepts and Behavior* (New York: Holt, Rinehart and Winston, 1972).

5. D. A. Infante, A. S. Racer, and D. F. Womack, *Building Communication Theory* (Prospect Heights, IL: Waveland Press, 1990), 6.

6. K. E. Andersen, *Introduction to Communication Theory and Practice* (Menlo Park, CA: Cummings, 1972), 5.

7. Andersen, 7.

8. E. T. Hall and M. R. Hall, *Understanding Cultural Differences: Germans, French, and Americans* (Yarmouth, ME: Intercultural Press, 1990), 18.

9. A. G. Smith, ed., *Communication and Culture: Readings in the Codes of Human Interaction* (New York: Holt, Rinehart and Winston, 1966), v.

10. J. T. Wood, *Interpersonal Communication: Everyday Encounters*, 7th ed. (Boston: Wadsworth Cengage Learning, 2013), 29.

11. D. Solomon and J. Theiss, *Interpersonal Communication: Putting Theory into Practice* (New York: Routledge, 2013), 11.

12. E. T. Hall, *Beyond Culture* (Garden City, NY: Anchor Doubleday, 1977), 14.

13. G. A. Rodriguez, *Bringing Up Latino Children in a Bicultural World* (New York: Fireside, 1999), 20.

14. E. T. Hall, *The Silent Language* (New York: Doubleday, 1959), 169.

15. Wood, 2014, 163.

16. T. Sowell, "Cultural Diversity: A World View," in *Intercultural Communication: A Reader*, 13th ed., ed. L. A. Samovar, R. E. Porter, and E. R.

McDaniel (Boston: Wadsworth Cengage Learning, 2012), 497.

17. L. E. Harrison and S. P. Huntington, eds., *Culture Matters: How Values Shape Human Progress* (New York: Basic Books, 2000), xv.

18. W. J. Lonner and R. S. Malpass, "When Psychology and Culture Meet: Introduction to Cross-Cultural Psychology," in *Psychology and Culture*, ed. W. J. Lonner and R. S. Malpass (Boston: Allyn and Bacon, 1994), 7.

19. H. Triandis, *Culture and Social Behavior* (New York: McGraw-Hill, 1994), 23.

20. S. P. Huntington, "The West Unique, Not Universal," *Foreign Affairs*, November/December 1996, 28.

21. H. L. Shapiro, *Aspects of Culture* (New Brunswick, NJ: Rutgers University Press, 1956), 54.

22. G. Hofstede, *Culture's Consequences: Comparing Values, Behaviors, Institutions, and Organizations Across Nations*, 2nd ed. (Thousand Oaks, CA: Sage, 2001), 10.

23. R. W. Nolan, *Communicating and Adapting Across Cultures: Living and Working in the Global Village* (Westport, CT: Bergin and Garvey, 1999), 3.

24. W. A. Haviland, H. E. L. Prins, B. McBride, and D. Walrath, *Cultural Anthropology: The Human Challenge*, 14th ed. (Belmont, CA: Wadsworth Cengage Learning, 2014), 29.

25. G. Hofstede, G. J. Hofstede, and M. Minkov, *Culture's Consequences: Intercultural Cooperation and Its Importance for Survival* (New York: McGraw-Hill, 2010), 6.

26. D. Matsumoto and H. S. Hwang, "Cultural Influences on Nonverbal Behavior," in *Nonverbal Communication: Science and Applications*, ed. D. Matsumoto, M. G. Frank, and H. S. Hwang (Los Angeles: Sage, 2013), 98.

27. G. Ferraro and S. Andreatta, *Cultural Anthropology: An Applied Perspective* (Belmont, CA: Wadsworth Cengage Learning, 2010), 29.

28. H. L. Weinberg, *Levels of Knowing and Existence* (New York: Harper and Row, 1959), 157.

29. D. G. Bates and F. Plog, *Cultural Anthropology*, 3rd ed. (New York: McGraw-Hill, 1990), 20.

30. S. Nanda and R. L. Warms, *Cultural Anthropology*, 11th ed. (Boston: Wadsworth Cengage Learning, 2014), 55.

31. E. T. Hall, *The Hidden Dimension* (New York: Doubleday, 1966).

32. E. Schuster, "Proverbs: A Path to Understanding Different Cultures," *Journal of Extension* 36, 1 (1998), http://www.joe.org/joe/1998february /tt2.php (accessed March 18, 2014).

33. S. B. Olajide, "An Assessment of Secondary School Teachers of Proverbs in Ilorin, Kwara State, Nigeria," *Journal of Educational and Social Research* 4, 3 (2013): 277.

34. J. M. Sellers, *Folk Wisdom of Mexico* (San Francisco: Chronicle Books, 1994), 7.

35. E. G. Seidensticker, foreword, in *"Even Monkeys Fall from Trees" and Other Japanese Proverbs*, comp. and trans. D. Galef (Clarendon, VT: Charles E. Tuttle, 1987), 8.

36. W. Mieder, *Encyclopedia of World Proverbs: A Treasury of Wit and Wisdom Through the Ages* (Englewood Cliffs, NJ: Prentice Hall, 1986), xi.

37. Mieder, 1986, x.

38. C. Roy, "Mexican *Dichos*: Lessons through Language," in *Intercultural Communication: A Reader*, 14th ed., ed. L. A. Samovar, R. E. Porter, E. R. McDaniel, and C. S. Roy (Boston: Cengage Learning, 2015), 224.

39. For a further listing of international proverbs, see S. Arnott, *Peculiar Proverbs: Weird Words of Wisdom from Around the World* (New York: St. Martin's Press, 2008; L. P. Canlas, *International Proverbs* (Philadelphia: Infinity Publishing, 2000); H. V. Dordry, *The Multicultural Dictionary of Proverbs: Over 20,000 Adages from More Than 120 Languages, Nationalities and Ethnic Groups* (Jefferson, NC: McFarland, 1997); G. De Lay, P. Darbo, and K. Potter, *International Dictionary of Proverbs* (New York: Hippocrene Books, 1998); J. Speake, *The Oxford Dictionary of Proverbs* (New York: Oxford University Press,

2003); and G. Titelman, *Popular Proverbs and Sayings* (New York: Gramercy Books, 1997).

40. S. Parlevliet, "Daily Chicken: The Cultural Transmission of Bourgeois Family Values in Adaptations of Literary Classics for Children," *Journal of Family History* 36 (2011): 464.

41. T. Imada and S. R. Yussen, "Reproduction of Cultural Values: A Cross-Cultural Examination of Stories People Create and Transmit," *Personality and Social Psychology Bulletin* 38 (2012): 115.

42. Rodriguez, 1999, 269.

43. M. Northrup, "Multicultural Cinderella Stories," Book Links, May 2000 (v. 9 no. 5), 1, http://www.ala.org /offices/resources/multicultural (accessed March 18, 2014).

44. P. R. Walker, *Little People: Stories from Around the World* (New York: Harcourt Brace and Company, 1997), 2.

45. Walker, 43.

46. Rodriguez, 1999, 270.

47. P'u Sung-ling, "The Taoist Priest of Lao-Shan" [folktale], in *Children and Youth in History*, item #204, http:// chnm.gmu.edu/cyh/primary-sources/ 204 (accessed March 18, 2014).

48. C. Tomlinson, "Myth of Invincibility Draws Children to Battles in Zaire," *San Diego Union-Tribune*, December 17, 1996, A21.

49. R. Erdoes and A. Ortiz, eds., *American Indian Myths and Legends* (New York: Pantheon, 1984), xv.

50. J. Campbell, *The Power of Myth* (New York: Doubleday, 1988), 6.

51. Nanda and Warms, 2014, 295.

52. "Give Us Back Our Treasures," *This Week*, April 30, 2010.

53. G. F. Will, "Understanding America through Art," *San Diego Union-Tribune*, December 25, 2008, B6.

54. Nanda and Warms, 2014, 299.

55. C. Strickland, *Art History* (New York: Sterling, 2006), 1.

56. M. K. Nydell, *Understanding Arabs: A Contemporary Guide to Arab Society*, 5th ed. (Boston: Intercultural Press, 2012) 221.

57. Ferraro and Andreatta, 2010, 381.

58. Ibid.

59. A. Hunter and J. Sexton, *Contemporary China* (New York: St. Martin's Press, 1999), 158.

60. J. Campbell, *Myths to Live By* (New York: Penguin, 1972), 106.

61. Nanda and Warms, 2014, 341.

62. D. M. Newman, *Sociology: Exploring the Architecture of Everyday Life*, 3rd ed. (Los Angeles: Sage, 2013), 73.

63. F. Williams, *The New Communications*, 2nd ed. (Belmont, CA: Wadsworth, 1989), 269.

64. "New Study Finds Children Age Zero to Six Spend As Much Time With TV, Computers and Video Games As Playing Outside," *PR Newswire* (October 28, 2003), http://www .prnewswire.com/news-releases/new -study-finds-children-age-zero-to-six -spend-as-much-time-with-tv -computers-and-video-games-as -playing-outside-72743517.html (accessed March 18, 2014). See also http://www.livescience.com/22281 -teens-video-games-health-risks.html (accessed March 18, 2014).

65. F. P. Delgado, "The Nature of Power Across Communicative and Cultural Borders" (paper presented at the annual convention of the Speech Communication Association, Miami Beach, FL, November 1993), 12.

66. See G. Gerbner, L. Gross, M. Morgan, and N. Signorielli, "Living with Television: The Dynamics of the Cultivation Process," in *Perspectives on Media Effects*, ed. J. Bryant and D. Zillman (Hillsdale, NJ: Lawrence Erlbaum Associates, 1986), 17–40; G. Gerbner, "Advancing on the Path of Righteousness (Maybe)," in *Cultivation Analysis: New Directions in Media Effects Research*, ed. N. Signorielli and M. Morgan (Newbury Park, CA: Sage, 1990); and J. D. Robinson, "Media Portrayals and Representations," in *21st Century Communication: A Reference Handbook*, ed. W. F. Eadie (Thousand Oaks, CA: Sage, 2009), 497–505.

67. D. Chandler, "Cultivation Theory," http://www.aber.ac.uk/media /Documents/short/cultiv.html (accessed March 28, 2014).

68. S. Tubbs and S. Moss, *Human Communication*, 11th ed. (New York: McGraw-Hill Higher Education, 2008), 535.

69. J. C. Hersey and A. Jordan, *Reducing Children's TV Time to Reduce the Risk of Childhood Overweight: The Children's Media Use Study* (Atlanta: Centers for Disease Control and Prevention, Nutrition and Physical Activity Communication Team), 8, http://www.rocklandsteps.org/files /TV_Time_Highligts[1].pdf (accessed March 18, 2014).

70. Newman, 2013, 71.

71. E. Yahr, "How much TV is too much TV for kids?," *Washington Post*, http:// www.washingtonpost.com/lifestyle /style/advice-on-kids-tv-watching -habits/2012/06/22/gJQAF0l3uV _story.html (accessed March 18, 2014).

72. See M. J. Gannon and R. Pillai, *Understanding Global Cultures: Metaphorical Journeys through 29 Nations, Clusters of Nations, Continents, and Diversity*, 4th ed. (Thousand Oaks, CA: Sage, 2010).

73. Gannon and Pillai, 2010, xiii.

74. E. A. Schutz and R. H. Lavenda, *Cultural Anthropology: A Perspective on the Human Condition*, 8th ed. (New York: Oxford University Press, 2012), 33

75. Nanda and Warms, 2014, 68.

76. Ibid.

77. L. Beamer and I. Varner, *Intercultural Communication in the Global Workplace*, 5th ed. (New York: McGraw-Hill Irwin, 2011), 25.

78. D. C. Barnlund, *Communicative Styles of Japanese and Americans: Images and Realities* (Belmont, CA: Wadsworth, 1989), 192.

79. G. Bailey and J. Peoples, *Essentials of Cultural Anthropology*, 3rd ed. (Boston: Wadsworth Cengage Learning, 2014), 34.

80. E. A. Hoebel and E. L. Frost, *Cultural and Social Anthropology* (New York: McGraw-Hill, 1976), 324.

81. B. J. Hall, *Among Cultures: The Challenge of Communication* (Orlando, FL: Harcourt College, 2002), 29.

82. Ferraro and Andreatta, 2010, 353.

83. Bailey and Peoples, 2014, 28.

84. Newman, 2013, 19.

85. C. M. Parkes, P. Laungani, and B. Young, eds., *Death and Bereavement Across Cultures* (New York: Routledge, 1997), 15.

86. Nolan, 1999, 3.

87. Bailey and Peoples, 2014, 40.

88. E. T. Hall, *Beyond Culture* (New York: Doubleday, 1976), 13–14.

89. Ferraro and Andreatta, 2010, 41.

90. Haviland et al., 2014, 34.

91. R. Benedict, *Patterns of Culture*, 2nd ed. (New York: Mentor, 1948), 2.

92. R. Benedict, *Patterns of Culture* (Boston: Houghton Mifflin, 1934), 21–22.

93. G. Ness, *Germany: Unraveling the Enigma* (Yarmouth, ME: Intercultural Press, 2000), 137.

94. E. W. Lynch, "Conceptual Framework: From Culture Shock to Culture Learning," in *Developing Cross-Cultural Competence*, 2nd ed., ed. E. W. Lynch and M. J. Hanson (Baltimore: Paul H. Brookes, 1998), 26.

95. B. H. Spitzberg, "A Model of Intercultural Communication Competence," in *Intercultural Communication: A Reader*, 14th ed., ed. L. A. Samovar, R. E. Porter, E. R. McDaniel, and C. S. Roy (Boston: Cengage Learning, 2015), 343.

96. Y. Y. Kim, "Intercultural Communication Competence: A Systems-Theoretic View," in *Cross-Cultural Interpersonal Communication*, ed. S. Ting-Toomey and R. Korzenny, eds. (Newbury Park, CA: Sage, 1991), 259.

97. S. P. Morreale, B. H. Spitzberg, and J. K. Barge, *Communication: Motivation, Knowledge, Skills*, 3rd ed., (New York: Peter Lang, 2013), 29.

98. Morreale et al., 2013, 30.

99. G. Chen, "Intercultural Communication Competence," in *Encyclopedia of Communication Theory*, ed. S. W. Littlejohn and K. A. Foss, eds. (Thousand Oaks, CA: Sage, 2009), 530.

100. Nydell, 2012, 89.

101. Chen, 2009, 530.

102. A. Foster, *Bargaining Across Borders: How to Negotiate Successfully Anywhere in the World* (New York: McGraw-Hill, 1992), 253.

Chapter 3

1. D. G. Bates and F. Plog, *Cultural Anthropology*, 3rd ed. (New York: McGraw-Hill, 1990), 285.

2. "The Perpetual War," *The Week*, October 22, 2010, 15.

3. S. P. Huntington, "The Clash of Civilizations," *Foreign Affairs* 72 (1993), 22.

4. Huntington, 25.

5. S. P. Huntington, *The Clash of Civilizations and the Remaking of World Order* (New York: Simon and Schuster, 1996), 128.

6. S. Kakar, *The Colors of Violence: Cultural Identities, Religion, and Conflict* (Chicago: University of Chicago Press, 1996), 189.

7. M. Guirdham, *Communicating Across Cultures* (West Lafayette, IN: Ichor Business Books, 1999), 63.

8. E. L. Lynch and M. J. Hanson, *Developing Cross-Cultural Competence: A Guide for Working with Young Children and Their Families* (Baltimore: Paul H. Brookes, 1992), 358.

9. W. A. Haviland, H. E. L. Prins, B. McBride, and D. Walrath, *Cultural Anthropology: The Human Challenge*, 14th ed. (Belmont, CA: Wadsworth Cengage Learning, 2014), 215.

10. M. K. DeGenova and F. P. Rice, "Why Examine Family Background?," in *Making Connections: Readings in Relational Communication*, 4th ed., ed. K. M. Galvin and J. P. Cooper (Los Angeles: Roxbury Press, 2006), 104.

11. M. A. Lamanna, A. Riedmann, and S. Stewart, *Marriage and Families: Making Choices in a Diverse Society*, 12th ed. (Belmont, CA: Cengage Learning, 2015), 25.

12. Lamanna et al., 24.

13. A. Swerdlow, R. Bridenthal, J. Kelly, and P. Vine, *Families in Flux* (New York: Feminist Press, 1989), 64.

14. B. Strong and T. F. Cohen, *The Marriage and Family Experience*, 12th ed. (Belmont, CA: Wadsworth Cengage Learning, 2014), 10.

15. Lamanna et al., 2015, 9.

16. S. Nanda and R. L. Warms, *Cultural Anthropology*, 13th ed. (Belmont, CA: Wadsworth Cengage Learning, 2014), 182.

17. Ibid.

18. E. A. Schultz and R. H. Lavenda, *Cultural Anthropology: A Perspective on the Human Condition*, 8th ed. (New York: Oxford University Press, 2012), 301.

19. H. C. Triandis, *Culture and Social Behavior* (New York: McGraw-Hill, 1994), 159.

20. Haviland et al., 2014, 216–17.

21. H. L. Tischler, *Introduction to Sociology*, 10th ed. (Belmont, CA: Wadsworth Cengage Learning, 2011), 269.

22. Triandis, 1994, 159.

23. D. Knox and C. Schacht, *Choices in Relationships: An Introduction to Marriage and the Family*, 11th ed. (Belmont, CA: Wadsworth Cengage Learning, 2013), 7.

24. M. W. Karraker, *Global Families*, 2nd ed. (Los Angeles: Sage, 2013), 5.

25. G. Bailey and J. Peoples, *Essentials of Cultural Anthropology*, 2nd ed. (Belmont, CA: Wadsworth Cengage Learning, 2014), 11.

26. B. S. Trask, *Globalization and Families: Accelerated Systemic Social Change* (New York: Springer, 2010), v.

27. "Migration, Remittances, Diaspora and Development," http://go.world bank.org/0IK1E5K7U0 (accessed June 6, 2015).

28. Karraker, 2013, 56.

29. Karraker, 62.

30. Karraker, 60.

31. F. Muyale-Manenji, "The effects of globalization on culture in Africa in the eyes of an African woman," http://www.oikoumene.org/en/resources/documents/wcc-programmes/public-witness-addressing-power-affirming-peace/poverty-wealth-and-ecology/neoliberal-paradigm/the-effects-of

-globalization-on-culture-in-africa-in
-the-eyes-of-an-african-woman
(accessed April 6, 2014).

32. D. M. Newman, *Sociology: Exploring
the Architecture of Everyday Life*,
3rd ed. (Los Angeles: Sage, 2013), 224.

33. A. Giddens, *Runaway World: How
Globalization Is Reshaping Our Lives*
(New York: Routledge, 2003), 4.

34. Strong and Cohen, 2014, 13.

35. D. Solomon and J. Theiss, *Interpersonal Communication: Putting Theory
into Practice* (New York: Routledge,
2013), 296–97.

36. K. J. Christiano, "Religion and the
Family in Modern American Cul-
ture," in *Family, Religion and Social
Change in Diverse Societies*, ed. S. K.
Houseknecht and J. G. Pankhurst
(New York: Oxford University Press,
2000), 43.

37. J. W. Berry, Y. H. Poortinga, M. H.
Segall, and P. R. Dasen, *Cross-
Cultural Psychology: Research and
Application* (New York: Cambridge
University Press, 1992), 22.

38. M. I. Al-Kaysi, *Morals and Manners in
Islam: A Guide to Islamic Adab*
(London: The Islamic Foundation,
1986), 36.

39. K. K. Lee, "Family and Religion in
Traditional and Contemporary
Korea," in *Religion and the Family in
East Asia*, ed. G. A. De Vos and
T. Sofue (Berkeley: University of
California Press, 1986), 185.

40. K. A. Ocampo, M. Bernal, and
G. P. Knight, "Gender, Race, and
Ethnicity: The Sequencing of Social
Constancies," in *Ethnic Identity:
The Formation and Transmission among
Hispanic and Other Minorities*, ed.
M. E. Bernal and G. P. Knight
(New York: State University of
New York Press, 1993), 106.

41. S. Trenholm and A. Jensen, *Interpersonal Communication*, 6th ed. (New
York: Oxford University Press, 2008),
259.

42. G. Pankhurst and S. K. Houseknecht,
"Introduction," in *Family, Religion and
Social Change*, ed. S. K. Houseknecht
and J. G. Pankhurst (New York:
Oxford University Press, 2000), 28.

43. B. L. Rodríguez and L. B. Olswang,
"Mexican-American and Anglo-
American Mothers' Beliefs and
Values About Child Rearing, Education, and Language," *American Journal
of Speech-Language Pathology* 12
(2003): 369.

44. J. T. Wood, *Gendered Lives: Commu-
nication, Gender, and Culture*, 10th ed.
(Belmont, CA: Wadsworth Cengage
Learning, 2013), 161.

45. Newman, 2013, 70.

46. Knox and Schacht, 2013, 47.

47. G. Bailey and J. Peoples, *Essentials
of Cultural Anthropology*, 3rd ed.
(Belmont, CA: Wadsworth Cengage
Learning, 2014), 188.

48. Bailey and Peoples, 197.

49. Tischler, 2011, 253.

50. Lamanna et al., 2015, 69.

51. Strong and Cohen, 2014, 121.

52. J. T. Wood, *Communication Mosaics:
An Introduction to the Field of Com-
munication*, 7th ed. (Boston:
Wadsworth Cengage Learning, 2014),
181; See also Newman, 2013, 102;
Wood, 2013, 21–22.

53. Wood, 2013, 169.

54. Ibid.

55. Newman, 2013, 102.

56. C. Wade and C. Tavris, "The Long
War: Gender and Culture," in *Psychology and Culture*, ed. W. J. Lonner
and R. S. Malpass (Boston: Allyn and
Bacon, 1994), 126.

57. Newman, 2013, 98.

58. M. Kim, "Transformation of Family
Ideology in Upper-Middle-Class
Families in Urban South Korea,"
*International Journal of Cultural and
Social Anthropology* 32 (1993): 70.

59. Ibid.

60. S. H. Hwang, "Family Life Education
with Asian Immigrant Families," in
*Family Life Education with Diverse
Populations*, ed. S. M. Ballard and A. C.
Taylor(Los Angeles: Sage, 2012), 192.

61. W. R. Jankowiak, *Sex, Death, and
Hierarchy in a Chinese City: An
Anthropological Account* (New York:
Columbia University Press, 1993),
166.

62. V. Hildebrand, L. A. Phenice, M. M.
Gray, and R. P. Hines, *Knowing and
Serving Diverse Families*, 3rd ed.
(Upper Saddle River, NJ: Merrill
Prentice Hall, 2008), 134.

63. T. V. Tran, "The Vietnamese
American Family," in *Ethnic Families
in America: Patterns and Variations*,
4th ed., ed. C. H. Mindel, R. W.
Habenstein, and R. Wright (Upper
Saddle River, NJ: Prentice Hall,
1998), 261.

64. L. Schneider and A. Silverman,
*Global Sociology: Introducing Five
Contemporary Societies*, 6th ed.
(Boston: McGraw-Hill Higher
Education, 2013), 18.

65. E. T. Hall and M. R. Hall, *Hidden
Differences: Doing Business with the
Japanese* (New York: Anchor Books,
1990), 47.

66. "Catechism of the Catholic Faith,"
http://www.vatican.va/archive
/ccc_css/archive/catechism/p1s2c1p1
.htm (accessed July 8, 2014).

67. P. L. Schvaneveldt and A. O.
Behnke, "Family Life Education with
Latino Immigrant Families," in
*Family Life Education with Diverse
Populations*, ed. S. M. Ballard and
A. C. Taylor (Los Angeles: Sage,
2012), 171.

68. Ibid.

69. "Understanding the Hispanic/Latino
Culture," http://www.coedu.usf.edu
/zalaquett/hoy/culture.html, (accessed
July 5, 2014).

70. Hildebrand et al., 2008, 94.

71. E. S. Kras, *Management in Two Cultures* (Yarmouth, ME: Intercultural
Press, 1995), 64.

72. Strong and Cohen, 2014, 101.

73. Karraker, 2013, 177.

74. Schneider and Silverman, 2013, 87.

75. C. E. Henderson, *Culture and Customs
of India* (Westport, CT: Greenwood
Press, 2002), 128.

76. D. Jacobson, "Indian Society and
Ways of Living," http://asiasociety
.org/countries/traditions/indian
-society-and-ways-living (accessed
July 8, 2014).

77. Henderson, 2002, 130.

78. S. Nanda and R. L. Warms, *Cultural Anthropology*, 8th ed. (Belmont, CA: Wadsworth, 2014), 172.

79. "Arranged Marriages: CNN Examines The Age-Old Practice In India," http://www.huffingtonpost.com/2012/05/31/arranged-marriage_n_1560049.html (accessed July 5, 2014).

80. Nanda and Warms, 2014, 173–74.

81. S. Wolpert, *India*, 3rd ed. (Berkeley: University of California Press, 2005), 137.

82. J. L. Esposito, *What Everyone Needs to Know About Islam*, 2nd ed., (New York: Oxford University Press, 2011), 4.

83. M. K. Nydell, *Understanding Arabs: A Contemporary Guide to Arab Society*, (Boston: Intercultural Press, 2012), xi.

84. V. Hildebrand, L. A. Phenice, M. M. Gray, and R. P. Hines, *Knowing and Serving Diverse Families*, 3rd ed. (Upper Saddle River, NJ: Merrill Prentice Hall, 2008), 134.

85. Nydell, 2012, 65.

86. Schneider and Silverman, 2013, 205.

87. Al-Kaysi, 1986, 41.

88. M. S. Sait, "Have Palestinian Children Forfeited Their Rights?," *Journal of Comparative Family Studies* 2 (2004): 214.

89. S. Irfan and M. Cowburn, "Disciplining, Chastisement and Physical Abuse: Perceptions and Attitudes of the British Pakistani Community," *Journal of Muslim Affairs* 24 (2004): 96.

90. Nydell, 2012, 69.

91. B. S. Trask, "Families in the Islamic Middle East," in *Families in Global and Multicultural Perspective*, 2nd ed., ed. B. B. Ingoldsby and S. D. Smith (Thousand Oaks, CA: Sage, 2006), 243.

92. Schneider and Silverman, 2013, 209.

93. Triandis, 1994, 172.

94. Schneider and Silverman, 2013, 79.

95. W. V. Schmidt, R. N. Conaway, S. E. Easton, and W. J. Wardrope, *Communicating Globally: Intercultural Communication and Intercultural Business* (Los Angeles: Sage, 2007), 25.

96. D. C. Thomas and K. Inkson, *Cultural Intelligence: People Skills for Global Business* (San Francisco: Berrett-Koehfer, 2004), 31.

97. Lamanna et al., 2015, 170.

98. H. C. Triandis, *Individualism and Collectivism* (San Francisco: Westview Press, 1995), 63.

99. N. Nomura, Y. Noguchi, S. Saito, and I. Tezuka, "Family Characteristics and Dynamics in Japan and the United States: A Preliminary Report from the Family Environment Scale," *International Journal of Intercultural Relations* 19 (1995): 63.

100. Newman, 2013, 68.

101. Schvaneveldt and Behnke, 2012, 169.

102. B. B. Ingoldsby, "Families in Latin America," in *Families in Global and Multicultural Perspective*, 2nd ed., ed. B. B. Ingoldsby and S. D. Smith (Thousand Oaks, CA: Sage, 2006), 281.

103. G. A. Rodriguez, *Bringing Up Latino Children in a Bicultural World* (New York: Fireside, 1999), 327.

104. Y. Sanchez, "Families of Mexican Origin," in *Families in Cultural Context: Strengths and Challenges of Diversity*, ed. M. K. DeGenova (Mountain View, CA: Mayfield, 1997), 66.

105. M. B. Zinn and A. Y. H. Pok, "Traditional and Transition in Mexican Origin Families," in *Minority Families in the United States: A Multicultural Perspective*, 3rd ed., ed. R. L. Taylor (Upper Saddle River, NJ: Prentice Hall, 2002), 84.

106. H. Carrasquillo, "Puerto Rican Families in America," in *Families in Cultural Context: Strengths and Challenges in Diversity*, ed. M.K. DeGenova (Mountain View, CA: Mayfield, 1997), 159.

107. S. W. Wilson and L. W. Ngige, "Families of Sub-Saharan Africa," in *Families in Global and Multicultural Perspective*, 2nd ed., ed. B. B. Ingoldsby and S. D. Smith (Thousand Oaks, CA: Sage, 2006), 250.

108. K. Peltzer, "Personality and Person Perception in Africa," in *Intercultural Communication: A Reader*, 11th ed., ed. L. A. Samovar, R. E. Porter, and E. R. McDaniel (Belmont, CA: Wadsworth, 2006), 135.

109. Schneider and Silverman, 2013, 148.

110. J. Esherick, *Women in the Arab World* (Philadelphia: Mason Crest Publishers, 2006), 68.

111. S. K. Farsoun, *Culture and Customs of the Palestinians* (Westport, CT: Greenwood Press, 2004), 33.

112. M. Mikulincer, A. Weller, and V. Florian, "Sense of Closeness to Parents and Family Rules: A Study of Arab and Jewish Youth in Israel," *International Journal of Psychology* 28 (2007): 323.

113. Hildebrand et al., 2008, 151.

114. Newman, 2013, 92.

115. D. Cheal, *Sociology in Family Life* (New York: Palgrave, 2002), 25.

116. C. I. Murray and N. Kimura, "Families in Japan," in *Families in Global and Multicultural Perspective*, 2nd ed., ed. B. B. Ingoldsby and S. D. Smith (Thousand Oaks, CA: Sage, 2006), 303.

117. G. Redding and G. Y. Y. Wong, "The Psychology of Chinese Organizational Behavior," in *The Psychology of the Chinese People*, ed. M. H. Bond (New York: Oxford University Press, 1987), 274.

118. H. Kissinger, *On China* (New York: Penguin, 2012), 406.

119. J. J. Ponzetti, ed., *International Encyclopedia of Marriage and Family*, 2nd ed. (New York: Gale Group, 2003), 1207.

120. G. C. Chu and Y. Ju, *The Great Wall in Ruins: Communication and Culture Change in China* (Albany: State University of New York Press, 1993), 9–10.

121. A. C. Taylor and S. M. Ballard, "Preparing Family Life Educators to Work with Diverse Populations," in *Family Life Education With Diverse Populations*, ed. S. M. Ballard and A. C. Taylor (Los Angeles: Sage, 2012), 296–97.

122. T. Cheshire, "American Indian Families: Strength and Answers from Our Past," in *Families in Global and Multicultural Perspective*, 2nd ed. (Thousand Oaks, CA: Sage, 2006), 318.

123. R. John, "Native American Families," in *Ethnic Families in America: Patterns*

and Variations, 4th ed., ed. C. H. Mindel, R. W. Habenstein, and R. Wright (Upper Saddle River, NJ: Prentice Hall, 1998), 383.

124. Haviland et al., 2014, 248.

125. Ibid.

126. Pew Research, "Social and Demographic Trends," http://www.pewsocial trends.org/2014/07/17/in-post -recession-era-young-adults-drive -continuing-rise-in-multi-generational -living (accessed July 17, 2014).

127. Schneider and Silverman, 2013, 85.

128. M. Sánchez-Ayéndez, "The Puerto Rican Family," in *Ethnic Families in America: Patterns and Variations*, 4th ed., ed. C. H. Mindel, R. W. Habenstein, and R. Wright (Upper Saddle River, NJ: Prentice Hall, 1998), 199.

129. Hildebrand et al., 2008, 97.

130. Hildebrand el al., 155.

131. A. Mir, *The American Encounter with Islam* (Broomall, PA: Mason Crest Publishers, 2004), 85.

132. D. E. Long, *Culture and Customs of Saudi Arabia* (Westport, CT: Greenwood Press, 2005), 38.

133. Nydell, 2012, 66.

134. J. Makinen, "China's 'Visit Your Parents' Law Weighs on Many in One-Child Nation," http://articles .latimes.com/2013/jul/29/world/la-fg -china-elderly-law-20130729 (accessed July 5, 2014).

135. Ibid.

136. Nanda and Warms, 2014, 180.

137. D. N. Clark, *Culture and Customs of Korea* (Westport, CT: Greenwood Press, 2000), 36.

138. H. Wenzhong and C. L. Grove, *Encountering the Chinese: A Guide for Americans*, rev. ed. (Yarmouth, ME: Intercultural Press, 1999), 7.

139. Haviland et al., 2014, 250.

140. Ibid.

141. "Native American Elderly," http://cas .umkc.edu/casww/natameers.htm (accessed June 1, 2014).

142. "Cultural Group Guides," Dimensions of Culture, http://dimensionsofculture .com/culture-fact-sheets (accessed June 1, 2014).

143. H. P. McAdoo, "African American Families," in *Ethnic Families in America: Patterns and Variations*, 4th ed., ed. C. H. Mindel, R. W. Habenstein, and R. Wright (Upper Saddle River, NJ: Prentice Hall, 1998), 362.

144. R. McCoy, "African American Elders, Cultural Traditions, and the Family Reunion," http://www.asaging.org /blog/african-american-elders-culture -traditions-and-family-reunion (accessed June 2, 2014).

145. C. Wetzstein, "1 in 10 U.S. children live with a grandparent," http:// www.washingtontimes.com/news /2011/jun/29/1-in-10-us-children -live-with-a-grandparent (accessed July 7, 2014).

146. L. Bryant and S. Lim, "Australian-Chinese Families Caring for Elderly Relatives," *Ageing & Society* 33 (2013): 140.

147. Makinen, 2014.

148. M. Izuhara, "Changing Families and Policy Responses to an Aging Japanese Society," in *The Changing Japanese Family*, ed. M. Rebick and A. Takenaka (New York: Routledge, 2006), 162–63.

149. Schneider and Silverman, 2013, 60.

150. T. J. Burke, A. Woszidlo, and C. Segrin, "Social Skills, Family Conflict, and Loneliness in Families," *Communication Reports* 25 (2012): 76.

151. R. B. Adler and R. F. Proctor, *Looking Out, Looking In*, 14th ed. (Boston: Wadsworth Cengage Learning, 2014), 285.

152. "Social Skills: Promoting Positive Behavior, Academic Success, and School Safety," http://www.nasponline .org/resources/factsheets/socials kills_fs.aspx (accessed July 12, 2014).

153. R. Park and K. King, "Cultural Diversity and Language Socialization in the Early Years," http://www.cal .org/resource-center/briefs-digests /digests (accessed July 7, 2014).

154. D. Cheal, *Sociology of Family Life* (New York: Palgrave, 2002), 12.

155. H. S. Kim "Culture and Self-Expression," http://www.apa.org /science/about/psa/2010/06/sci-brief .aspx (accessed July 18, 2014).

156. H. S. Kim and D. K Sherman, "'Express Yourself': Culture and the Effect of Self-Expression on Choice," *Journal of Personality and Social Psychology* 92 (2007): 1.

157. Park and King, 2014.

158. A. K. M. Rezanur Rahman, "Cultural Differences in Aggression: A Case Study in Bangladesh," *Journal of Life and Earth Science* 3–4 (2009): 43.

159. Ibid.

160. F. M. Moghaddam, D. M. Taylor, and S. C. Wright, *Social Psychology in Cross-Cultural Perspective* (New York: W. H. Freeman, 1993), 125.

161. A. S. Rancer, "Argumentativeness, Assertiveness, and Verbal Aggressive Theory," in *Encyclopedia of Communication Theory*, ed. S. W. Littlejohn and K. A. Foss (Thousand Oaks, CA: Sage, 2009), 45.

162. Wood, 2013, 175.

163. S. Bergmuller, "The Relationship Between Cultural Individualism-Collectivism and Student Aggression Across 62 Countries," *Aggressive Behavior* 39 (2013): 182.

164. Adler and Proctor, 2014, 362.

165. R. Cooper and N. Cooper, *Thailand: A Guide to Customs and Etiquette* (Portland, OR: Graphic Arts Center, 1982), 83.

166. Karraker, 2013, 105.

167. Taylor and Ballard, 2012, 285.

168. Ibid.

169. M. Carteret, "Culture and Family Dynamics," http://www.dimensions ofculture.com/2010/11/culture-and -family-dynamics (accessed July 5, 2014).

170. Ibid.

Chapter 4

1. G. Bailey and J. Peoples, *Essentials of Cultural Anthropology*, 3rd ed. (Belmont, CA: Wadsworth Cengage Learning, 2014), 34.

2. E. Schultz and R. H. Lavenda, *Cultural Anthropology: A Perspective on the Human Condition*, 8th ed. (New York: Oxford University Press, 2012), 174.

3. D. W. Klopf and J. C. McCroskey, *Intercultural Communication Encounters* (New York: Pearson Education, 2007), 97.

4. L. E. Harrison, *Jews, Confucians, and Protestants: Cultural Capital and the End of Multiculturalism* (New York: Rowman & Littlefield, 2013), 18–31.

5. E. A. Hoebel, *Man in the Primitive World* (New York: McGraw-Hill, 1958), 159.

6. R. H. Dana, *Multicultural Assessment Perspective for Professional Psychology* (Boston: Allyn and Bacon, 1993), 9.

7. S. A. Gunaratne, "Asian Communication Theory," in *Encyclopedia of Communication Theory*, ed. S. W. Littlejohn and K. A. Foss (Thousand Oaks, CA: Sage, 2009), 48.

8. M. P. Fisher and R. Luyster, *Living Religions* (Englewood Cliffs, NJ: Prentice Hall, 1991), 153–56.

9. P. U. Spencer, "A Native American Worldview," *Noetic Sciences Review* (Summer 1990), http://ratical.com/many_worlds/NAworldview.html (accessed June 7, 2014).

10. R. Bartels, "National Culture Business Relations: United States and Japan Contrasted," *Management International Review* 2 (1982): 5.

11. R. E. Nisbett, *The Geography of Thought* (New York: Free Press, 2003), 100.

12. I. S. Markham, *A World Religions Reader*, 2nd ed. (Malden, MA: Blackwell, 2000), 43.

13. F. Ridenour, *So What's the Difference?* (Ventura, CA: Regal Books, 2001), 192.

14. The Pew Forum on Religion and Public Life, *U.S. Religious Landscape Survey* (June 23, 2008), http://religions.pewforum.org/reports (accessed June 7, 2014).

15. E. Federman, "Atheist Mega-Churches May Help Mend Relationships with Faithful," http://www.huffingtonpost.com/eliyahu-federman/atheist-megachurches-may_b_4278761.html? (accessed June 7, 2014).

16. http://www.washingtonpost.com/blogs/worldviews/wp/2013/05/23/a-surprising-map-of-where-the-worlds-atheists-live (accessed June 7, 2014).

17. "What is Atheism?," http://atheists.org/activism/resources/what-is-atheism (accessed April 5, 2014).

18. C. Hitchens, *God Is Not Great* (New York: Hachette Book Group USA, 2007), 10.

19. D. C. Halverson, "Secularism," in *The Compact Guide to World Religions*, ed. D. C. Halverson (Minneapolis: Bethany House Publishers, 1996), 186.

20. Halverson, 191.

21. J. E. Archer, "An Atheist's World View: 15 Principles of Atheism," http://unitedstatesatheists.com/cgibin/page_display.cgi?page_nav_name=atheism101fK5 (accessed June 7, 2014).

22. K. S. Cornish, "An Atheist's Perspective on Death," http://atheistfoundation.org.au (accessed June 7, 2014).

23. R. E. Van Voorst, *RELG: World*, 2nd ed. (Stamford, CT: Cengage Learning, 2015), 338.

24. W. A. Haviland, H. E. L. Prins, B. McBride, and D. Walrath, *Cultural Anthropology: The Human Challenge*, 14th ed. (Belmont, CA: Wadsworth Cengage Learning, 2014), 299.

25. R. A. Carvalho and M. Robinson, eds., *Cultural Competence in Health Care: A Practical Guide* (San Francisco: Jossey-Bass, 1999), 102.

26. L. Schmidt, *Restless Souls: The Making of American Spirituality* (New York: HarperCollins, 2005), 12. See also "Religion vs. Spirituality—What's The Difference?," http://www.bibliotecapleyades.net/mistic/mistic_10.htm (accessed January 15, 2014), and Ridenour, 2001, 147–54.

27. K. A. Roberts, *Religion in Sociological Perspective*, 4th ed. (Belmont, CA: Wadsworth Cengage Learning, 2004), 11.

28. C. Kimball, *When Religion Becomes Evil* (New York: HarperCollins, 2002), 196.

29. T. L. Friedman, *The Lexus and the Olive Tree* (New York: Farrar, Straus and Giroux, 1999).

30. M. P. Osborne, *One World, Many Religions: The Ways of Worship* (New York: Alfred A. Knopf, 1996), vii.

31. Fisher and Luyster, 1991, 13.

32. H. Smith, *The World's Religions* (New York: HarperCollins, 1991), 9.

33. H. L. Tischler, *Introduction to Sociology*, 10th ed. (Belmont, CA: Wadsworth Cengage Learning, 2011), 302.

34. Haviland et al., 2014, 298.

35. G. W. Braswell Jr., *Understanding World Religions* (Nashville, TN: Broadman & Holman Publishers, 1994), 3.

36. G. Ferraro and S. Andreatta, *Cultural Anthropology: An Applied Perspective* (Belmont, CA: Wadsworth Cengage Learning, 2010), 364.

37. D. M. Newman, *Sociology: Exploring the Architecture of Everyday Life*, 3rd ed. (Los Angeles: Sage, 2013), 146.

38. Roberts, 2004, 397.

39. R. Schmidt, G. C. Sager, G. T. Carney, A. C. Muller, K. J. Zanca, J. J. Jackson, C. Wayne Mayhall, and J. C. Burke, *Patterns of Religion*, 3rd ed. (Boston: Wadsworth Cengage Learning, 2014), 4.

40. Y. Canfi, "Anti-Semitism on the Rise in Europe," *The Week*, September 13, 2013, 18.

41. W. E. Paden, *Religious Worlds: The Comparative Study of Religion* (Boston: Beacon Press, 1994), 170.

42. Van Voorst, 2015, 24.

43. M. Fairchild, "Christianity Today General Statistics and Facts of Christianity," http://christianity.about.com/od/denominations/p/christiantoday.htm (accessed January 24, 2014).

44. K. Barr, "Major Religions of the World Ranked by Number of Adherents," http://www.ehow.com/info_8721704_major-world-ranked-number-adherents.html#ixzz2qynsqNDp (accessed April 6, 2014).

45. Ibid.

46. D. L. Carmody and J. T. Carmody, *In the Path of the Masters: Understanding the Spirituality of Buddha, Confucius, Jesus, and Muhammad* (New York: Paragon House, 1994), preface.

47. Smith, 1991, 3.

48. Ferraro and Andreatta, 2010, 365.

49. R. E. Van Voorst, *Anthology of World Scriptures*, 8th ed. (Boston: Wadsworth Cengage Learning, 2013), xix.

50. W. Matthews, *World Religions*, 7th ed. (Belmont, CA: Wadsworth Cengage Learning, 2013), 6.

51. D. Crystal, *The Cambridge Encyclopedia of Language*, 2nd ed. (New York: Cambridge University Press, 2003), 224.

52. N. Smart, *Worldview: Crosscultural Explorations of Human Beliefs*, 3rd ed. (Upper Saddle River, NJ: Prentice Hall, 2000), 9–10.

53. J. Bowker, *World Religions: The Great Faiths Explored and Explained* (New York: DK Publishing, 2006), 8.

54. M. V. Angrosino, *The Culture of the Sacred: Exploring the Anthropology of Religion* (Prospect Heights, IL: Waveland Press, 2004), 97.

55. Paden, 1994, 96.

56. H. Smith, *The Illustrated World's Religions: A Guide to Our Wisdom Traditions* (New York: HarperCollins, 1994), 210.

57. Ibid.

58. M. D. Coogan, ed., *The Illustrated Guide to World Religions* (New York: Oxford University Press, 1998), 10.

59. J. Hendry, *Understanding Japanese Society*, 3rd ed. (New York: Routledge Curzon, 2003) 122.

60. Schmidt et al., 2014, 193.

61. R. D. Hale, "Christianity," in *The Illustrated Guide to World Religions*, ed. M. D. Coogan (New York: Oxford University Press, 1998), 54.

62. Matthews, 2013, 324.

63. Bowker, 2006, 150.

64. A. Romagosa, "Christianity and Community," http://aromagosa .easycgi.com/christianhumanism /preamble/Christianity.htm (accessed July 3, 2011).

65. Schmidt et al., 2014, 193.

66. M. B. McGuire, *Religion: The Social Context*, 5th ed. (Belmont, CA: Wadsworth, 2002), 2001.

67. K. L. Woodard, "2000 Years of Jesus," *Newsweek*, April 5, 1999, http://www

.newsweek.com/id/87939 (accessed July 13, 2011).

68. Matthews, 2013, 291.

69. Ibid.

70. Smith, 1994, 210.

71. Schmidt et al., 2014, 223.

72. M. L. Andersen and H. F. Taylor, *Sociology: The Essentials*, 6th ed. (Belmont, CA: Wadsworth Cengage Learning, 2011), 335.

73. T. C. Muck, *Those Other Religions in Your Neighborhood: Loving Your Neighbor When You Don't Know How* (Grand Rapids, MI: Zondervan, 1992), 165.

74. Smith, 191, 328.

75. R. France, "Jesus," in *Eerdmans' Handbook to the World's Religions* (Grand Rapids, MI: Eerdmans, 1982), 339.

76. Van Voorst, 2015, 283.

77. Van Voorst, 2013, 282.

78. Matthews, 2013, 325.

79. Matthews, 330.

80. W. Jackson, "The Biblical View of Death," *Christian Courier*, https:// www.christiancourier.com/articles /850-the-biblical-view-of death (accessed January 22, 2014).

81. Matthews, 2013, 330.

82. K.P. Kramer, *The Sacred Art of Dying: How World Religions Understand Death* (Mahwah, NJ: Paulist Press, 1988), 1.

83. M. Connolly, "After Death— Heaven," *Spirituality for Today* 1, 9 (April 1996), http://www.spirituality .org/is/009/page06.asp (accessed June 7, 2014).

84. C. Panati, *Sacred Origins of Profound Things* (New York: Penguin, 1996), 461.

85. "Christian Funerals: Christian Death and Burial," BBC Religions, June 23, 2009, http://www.bbc.co.uk/religion /religions/christianity/ritesrituals /funerals.shtml (accessed June 7, 2014).

86. T. Rich, "Judaism 101," http://www .jewfaq.org/populatn.htm (accessed June 7, 2014).

87. S. Prothero, *God Is Not One* (New York: HarperCollins, 2010), 245.

88. Van Voorst, 2013, 213.

89. Harrison, 2013, 55.

90. Matthews, 2013, 249.

91. S. M. Matlins and A. J. Magida, *How to Be a Perfect Stranger*, 4th ed. (Woodstock, VT: SkyLight Paths, 2006), 132.

92. D. Prager and J. Telushkin, *The Nine Questions People Ask about Judaism* (New York: Simon and Schuster, 1981), 112.

93. R. L. Torstrick, *Culture and Customs of Israel* (Westport, CT: Greenwood Press, 2004), 28.

94. C. S. Ehrlich, "Judaism," in *The Illustrated Guide to World Religions*, ed. M. D. Coogan (New York: Oxford University Press, 1998), 16.

95. "The Three Branches of Judaism," http://www.shofarbetzion.com/01 /thethreebracnesofJudaism.htm (accessed February 1, 2014).

96. "The Branches of Judaism," http:// www.icsresources.org (accessed February 1, 2014).

97. Tischler, 2011, 268.

98. Matthews, 2013, 268.

99. Osborne, 1996, 7.

100. C. Van Doren, *A History of Knowledge* (New York: Ballantine Books, 1991), 16.

101. B. A. Robinson, "Two Millennia of Jewish Persecution: Anti-Judaism: 70 to 1200 CE," Ontario Consultants on Religious Tolerance (February 7, 2010), http://www.religioustolerance .org/jud_pers1.htm (accessed June 9, 2014).

102. Prager and Telushkin, 1981, 29.

103. Matthews, 2013, 270.

104. "Anti-Semitism: 2012 Report on Global Trends in Anti-Semitism," http://www.jewishvirtuallibrary.org /jsource/anti-semitism/trendtoc.html (accessed February 3, 2014). See also "Increases in Major and Non-Major Anti-Semitic Incidents," U.S. Department of State, Contemporary Global Anti-Semitism: A Report Provided to the United States Congress (March 2008), http://www.state .gov/documents/organization/102301 .pdf (accessed June 6, 2014).

105. Van Doren, 1991, 16.

106. E. Peters, *Judaism, Christianity and Islam: The Classical Texts and Their Interpretation* (Princeton, NJ: Princeton University Press, 1990), 10.

107. L. Rosten, *Religions of America* (New York: Simon and Schuster, 1975), 143.

108. Ibid.

109. "A Portrait of Jewish Americans: October 1, 2013," Pew Research Religion and Public Life Project, http://www.pewforum.org/2013/10/01/jewish-american-beliefs-attitudes-culture-survey (accessed February 6, 2014).

110. Harrison, 2013, 49.

111. I. S. Markham and C. Lohr, *A World Religion Reader*, 3rd ed. (Malden, MA: Wiley-Blackwell, 2009), 175.

112. Smith, 1994, 189.

113. Schmidt et al., 2014, 142.

114. A. Rainey and L. Rabinowitz, "Family," in *Encyclopaedia Judaica*, vol. 6, 2nd ed., ed. M. Berenbaum and F. Skolnik (Detroit: Macmillan Reference USA, 2007), 690–95, http://go.galegroup.com/ps/i.do?id=GALE|CX2587506268&v=2.1&u=imcpl1111&it=r&p=GVRL&sw=w&asid=de7007c918975622311043113f4c6be9 (accessed July 23, 2014).

115. "What is Judaism: The Jewish People Are A Family," *Judaism 101* (n.d.), http://www.jewfaq.org/judaism.htm (accessed July 3, 2011).

116. Rosten, 1975, 575.

117. Markham and Lohr, 2009, 175.

118. Matthews, 2013, 278.

119. Matthews, 283.

120. L. Jacobs, "Jewish Attitudes Towards Death," http://www.myjewishlearning.com/life/Life_Events/Death_and_Mourning/About_Death_and_Mourning/Attitudes_Prn.shtml (accessed March 31, 2014).

121. American-Israeli Cooperative Enterprise, "Jewish Concepts: Afterlife" (2006), http://www.jewishvirtuallibrary.org/jsource/Judaism/afterlife.html (accessed June 6, 2014).

122. Prothero, 2010, 25.

123. J. L. Esposito and D. Mogahed, *Who Speaks for Islam? What a Billion Muslims Really Think* (New York: Gallup Press, 2007), ix.

124. D. Belt, "The World of Islam," *National Geographic*, January 2002, 76.

125. "The Future of the Global Muslim Population," http://www.pewforum.org/2011/01/27/the-future-of-the-global-muslim-population (accessed July 23, 2014).

126. Ibid.

127. M. Clark, "Survey: Islam is SD's Fastest Growing Religion," http://www.utsandiego.com/news/2012/jul/07/islam-san-diego-county-fastest-growing-religion (accessed July 23, 2014).

128. M. Sedgwick, *Islam and Muslims: A Guide to Diverse Experience in a Modern World* (Boston: Intercultural Press, 2006), 4.

129. K. L. Woodward, "In the Beginning, There Were the Holy Books," *Newsweek*, February 11, 2001, 52.

130. T. Reagan, *Non-Western Educational Traditions: Alternative Approaches to Educational Thought and Practice*, 2nd ed. (Mahwah, NJ: Lawrence Erlbaum Associates, 2000), 183.

131. Matthews, 2013, 131.

132. Koran, 112: 1–4.

133. Bowker, 2006, 178.

134. Van Voorst, 2015, 312.

135. Van Voorst, 2013, 302.

136. Prothero, 2010, 42.

137. J. J. Elias, *Islam* (Upper Saddle River, NJ: Prentice Hall, 1999), 21.

138. D. L. Daniel and A. A. Nahdi, *Culture and Customs of Iran* (Westport, CT: Greenwood Press, 2006), 38.

139. Van Voorst, 2013, 314.

140. C. E. Farah, *Islam*, 7th ed. (Hauppauge, NY: Barron's Educational Series, 2003), 120.

141. L. Schneider and A. Silverman, *Global Sociology: Introducing Five Contemporary Societies*, 5th ed. (New York: McGraw-Hill, 2010).

142. E. M. Caner and E. F. Caner, *Unveiling Islam* (Grand Rapids, MI: Kregel Publications, 2002), 122.

143. M. K. Nydell, *Understanding Arabs: A Guide for Modern Times*, 5th ed. (Boston: Intercultural Press, 2012), 76.

144. Matthews, 2013, 345.

145. Schneider and Silverman, 2010, 197.

146. S. K. Farsoun, *Culture and Customs of the Palestinians* (Westport, CT: Greenwood Press, 2004), 77.

147. Prothero, 2010, 34.

148. J. J. Elias, *Islam* (Upper Saddle River, NJ: Prentice Hall, 1999), 71.

149. B. Handwerk, "What Does 'Jihad' Really Mean to Muslims?," *National Geographic News*, October 24, 2003, http://news.nationalgeographic.com/news/pf/48665454.html (accessed July 23, 2014).

150. Matthews, 2013, 170.

151. Schneider and Silverman, 2010, 198.

152. K. Armstrong, *A History of God: The 4,000-Year Quest of Judaism, Christianity, and Islam* (New York: Knopf, 1994), 344.

153. K. E. Richter, E. M. Rapple, J. C. Modschiedler, and R. Peterson, *Understanding Religion in a Global Society* (Belmont, CA: Wadsworth, 2005), 366.

154. Nydell, 2012, 73.

155. M. O. Mababaya and N. Dindang, "Islam: The Complete Way of Life," http://wisdomislamic.info/texts/Islam_files/IslamComplete.htm (accessed July 23, 2014).

156. A. Esler, *The Human Venture*, 2nd ed. (Englewood Cliffs, NJ: Prentice Hall, 1992), 257–58.

157. Van Voorst, 2015, 316.

158. "Sharia," BBC Religions (March 9, 2009), http://www.bbc.co.uk/religion/religions/islam/beliefs/sharia_1.shtml (accessed July 23, 2014).

159. O. Sacirbey, "Sharia Law in the USA 101: A Guide to What It Is and Why States Want to Ban It," http://www.huffingtonpost.com/2013/07/29/sharia-law-usa-states-ban_n_3660813.html? (accessed July 23, 2014).

160. L. Taraki, "The Role of Women," in *Understanding The Contemporary Middle East*, 2nd ed., ed. D. J. Gerner and

J. Schwedler (Boulder, CO: Lynne Rienner Publishers, 2004), 335.

161. S. Magin, "Illiteracy in the Arab Region: A Meta Study," http://www.gial.edu/images/gialens/vol4-2/Magin-Arab-Illiteracy.pdf (accessed July 23, 2014).

162. J. Esherick, *Women in the Modern Arab World* (Philadelphia: Mason Crest Publishers, 2005), 53.

163. Esposito and Mogahed, 2007, 107.

164. Van Voorst, 2013, 323.

165. Matthews, 2013, 365.

166. Van Voorst, 2015, 315.

167. Matthews, 2013, 368.

168. V. Narayanan, "Hinduism," in *The Illustrated Guide to World Religions*, ed. M. D. Coogan (New York: Oxford University Press, 1998), 126.

169. Van Voorst, 2015, 64.

170. Markham and Lohr, 2009, 32.

171. C. Shattuck, *Hinduism* (Upper Saddle River, NJ: Prentice Hall, 1999), 17.

172. Matthews, 2013, 73.

173. D. M. Knipe, "Veda," in *The Perennial Dictionary of World Religions*, ed. K. Crim (New York: HarperCollins, 1989), 785.

174. Schmidt et al., 2014, 341.

175. S. R. Stroud, "Hindu Communication Theory," in *Encyclopedia of Communication Theory*, ed. S. W. Littlejohn and K. A. Foss (Thousand Oaks, CA: Sage, 2009), 476.

176. B. Usha, *A Ramakrishna-Vedanta Wordbook* (Hollywood, CA: Vedanta Press, 1971), 79–80.

177. T. A. Robinson and H. P. Rodrigues, *World Religions: A Guide to the Essentials* (Peabody, MA: Hendrickson Publishers, 2006), 165.

178. V. Narayanan, *Understanding Hinduism* (London: Duncan Baird Publishers, 2006), 23.

179. D. J. Boorstin, *The Creators* (New York: Random House, 1992), 4–5.

180. Matthews, 2013, 97.

181. D. Jurney, ed., *Gems of Guidance: Selections from the Scriptures of the World* (Kidlington, UK: George Ronald, Publisher, 1992), 48.

182. R. Kumer and A. K. Sethi, *Doing Business in India* (New York: Palgrave Macmillan, 2005), 57.

183. Van Voorst, 2015, 69.

184. S. Prabhavanda, *The Spiritual Heritage of India*, 2nd ed. (Hollywood, CA: Vedanta Press, 1969), 335.

185. "Heart of Hinduism: Four Main Paths," http://hinduism.iskcon.org/practice (accessed February 20, 2014).

186. Ibid. See also Matthews, 2013, 81–82.

187. http://www.hinduwebsite.com/hinduwaymain1.asp (accessed June 6, 2014).

188. C. E. Henderson, *Culture and Customs of India* (Westport, CT: Greenwood Press, 2002), 32.

189. Van Voorst, 2015, 189.

190. A. Dhand, "The Dharma of Ethics, the Ethics of Dharma: Quizzing the Ideals of Hinduism," *Journal of Religious Ethics* 30 (2002): 347–72.

191. "Karma (Hinduism)," http://berkleycenter.georgetown.edu/resources/essays/karma-hinduism (accessed June 6, 2014) (n.p.).

192. Prothero, 2010, 146.

193. Matthews, 2013, 80.

194. See Van Voorst, 2013, 37.

195. Van Voorst, 2015, 79.

196. S. Nikhilananda, "Ethics," http://www.hinduism.co.za/ethics.htm (accessed June 8, 2014) (n.p.).

197. Van Voorst, 2013, 97.

198. Narayanan, 2004, 90.

199. Jarayam V, "Hinduism: Life and Death," http://www.hinduwebsite.com/hinduism/h_death.asp (accessed April 2, 2014).

200. "Pew Research: Religion and Public Life: Buddhist," http://pewforum.org/2012/12/18/global-religious-landscape-buddhist (accessed April 2, 2014).

201. J. Coleman, "The Face of Western Buddhism," *Buddhadharma: The Practitioner's Quarterly*, Fall 2011, 49.

202. A. Powell, *Living Buddhism* (Berkeley: University of California Press, 1989), 10.

203. N. Thera, *An Outline of Buddhism* (Singapore: Palelai Buddhist Temple Press, n.d.), 19.

204. Schmidt et al., 2014, 257.

205. H. Smith and P. Novak, *Buddhism: A Concise Introduction* (New York: HarperCollins, 2003), 4.

206. P. Garfinkel, "Buddha Rising," *National Geographic*, December 2005, 96.

207. D. N. Clark, *Culture and Customs of Korea* (Westport, CT: Greenwood Press, 2000), 31.

208. R. H. Robinson, W. L. Johnson, and T. Bhikku, *Buddhist Religions: A Historical Introduction*, 5th ed. (Belmont, CA: Wadsworth, 2005), 7.

209. W. Dissanayake, "Buddhist Communication Theory," in *Encyclopedia of Communication Theory*, ed. S. W. Littlejohn and K. A. Foss (Thousand Oaks, CA: Sage, 2009), 84.

210. M. Wood, *India* (New York: Basic Books, 2007), 65.

211. Smith and Novak, 2003, 3–4.

212. Markham and Lohr, 2009, 78.

213. B. Bodhi, *The Buddha and His Dhamma* (Sri Lanka: Buddhist Publication Society, 1999), 15.

214. B. Bodhi, *Nourishing the Roots and Other Essays on Buddhist Ethics* (Sri Lanka: Buddhist Publication Society, 1978), 7.

215. Van Voorst, 2015, 124.

216. Bodhi, 1999, 25.

217. "The Four Noble Truths," BBC: Religion (November 17, 2009), http://www.bbc.co.uk/religion/religions/buddhism/beliefs/fournobletruths_1.shtml (accessed April 6, 2014).

218. Van Voorst, 2015, 123.

219. Van Voorst, 2013, 81.

220. For a more detailed description of the Eightfold Path see Bodhi, 1999, 32; B. H. Gunaratana, *Eight Mindful Steps to Happiness* (Boston: Wisdom Publications, 2001); Matthews, 2013, 117; A. Newberg, *Why We Believe What We Believe* (New York: Free Press, 2006), 172; Schmidt et al. 2014, 273–74; and Van Voorst, 2015, 125.

221. Dissanayake, 2009, 85.

222. R. Brabant-Smith, "Two Kinds of Language," *The Middle Way: Journal of the Buddhist Society* 68 (1993): 123.

223. T. Thien-An, *Zen Philosophy, Zen Practice* (Emeryville, CA: Dharma, 1975), 17.

224. T. Nhat Hanh, "The Practice of Looking Deeply Using Three Dharma Seals: Impermanence, No Self and Nirvana," http://shambhalasun.com/index.php?option=content&task=view&id=1647 (accessed February 28, 2014).

225. Ibid.

226. K. N. Jayatilleke, *The Message of the Buddha* (Sri Lanka: Buddhist Publication Society, 2000), 141.

227. P. Novak, 1994, *The World's Wisdom: Sacred Texts of the World's Religions* (New York: HarperCollins, 1994), 67.

228. R. Bogoda, *A Simple Guide to Life* (Sri Lanka: Buddhist Publication Society, 1994), 43.

229. K. Thera, "Buddhist Ethics," http://www.budsas.org/ebud/whatbudbeliev/main.htm (accessed March 1, 2014).

230. Van Voorst, 2015, 126.

231. Van Voorst, 127.

232. Schmidt et al., 2014, 379.

233. Markham and Lohr, 2009, 94.

234. P. Hawter, "Death and Dying in the Tibetan Buddhist Tradition," http://buddhanet.net/deathtib.htm (accessed June 7, 2014).

235. A. Ottama, *The Message in the Teachings of Kamma, Rebirth, Samsara* (Sri Lanka: Buddhist Publication Society, 1998), 43.

236. T. Tu, "What to Think About at Death" *Tricycle: The Buddhist Review* 86 (Winter 2012): 53.

237. C. Lamb, "Buddhist Rites of Passage," *Inquiring Mind* 27 (Spring 2011): 8–9.

238. J. Yin, "Confucian Communication Theory," in *Encyclopedia of Communication Theory*, ed. S. W. Littlejohn and K. A. Foss (Thousand Oaks, CA: Sage, 2009), 170.

239. L. E. Harrison, "Promoting Progressive Cultural Change," in *Culture Matters: How Values Shape Human Progress*, ed. L. E. Harrison and S. P. Huntington (New York: Basic Books, 2000), 296.

240. Prothero, 2010, 105.

241. Matthews, 2013, 189.

242. J. Oldstone-Moore, "Chinese Traditions," in *The Illustrated Guide to World Religions*, ed. M. D. Coogan (New York: Oxford University Press, 1998), 205.

243. I. P. McGreal, *Great Thinkers of the Eastern World* (New York: HarperCollins, 1995), 3.

244. Harrison, 2013, 83.

245. T. I. S. Leung, "Confucianism," in *The Compact Guide to World Religions*, ed. D. C. Halverson (Minneapolis: Bethany Publishers, 1996), 75.

246. S. Dragga, "Ethical Intercultural Technical Communication: Looking Through the Lens of Confucian Ethics," in *Intercultural Communication: A Reader*, 11th ed., ed. L. A. Samovar, R. E. Porter, and E. R. McDaniel (Belmont, CA: Wadsworth, 2006), 421.

247. Matthews, 2013, 190.

248. Bowker, 2006, 101.

249. Smith, 1994, 110.

250. Matthews, 2013, 191.

251. Schmidt et al., 2014, 495.

252. Smith, 1994, 111.

253. M. J. Gannon and R. Pillai, *Understanding Global Cultures*, 4th ed. (Thousand Oaks, CA: Sage, 2010), 438.

254. Smith, 1994, 111.

255. Yin, 2009, 171.

256. C. Chiu and Y. Hong, *Social Psychology of Culture* (New York: Psychology Press, 2006), 178.

257. Schmidt et al., 2014, 501.

258. G. Gao and S. Ting-Toomey, *Communicating Effectively with the Chinese* (Thousand Oaks, CA: Sage, 1998), 75.

259. J. O. Yum, "Confucianism and Interpersonal Relationships and Communication Patterns in East Asia," in *Intercultural Communication: A Reader*, 9th ed., ed. L. A. Samovar and R. E. Porter (Belmont, CA: Wadsworth, 2000), 70.

260. D. Wong, "Chinese Ethics," *The Stanford Encyclopedia of Philosophy* (Spring 2013 Edition), ed. Edward N. Zalta, http://plato.stanford.edu/archives/spr2013/entries/ethics-chinese (accessed June 9, 2014).

261. Van Voorst, 2013, 151.

262. Matthews, 2013, 200.

263. Ibid.

264. Ibid.

265. Prothero, 2010, 106.

266. Schmidt et al., 2014, 500.

267. Prothero, 2010, 334–35.

268. Bowker, 2006, 208.

269. Schmidt et al., 2014, 16.

270. Prothero, 2010, 335.

271. T. Blair, "Religious Differences, Not Ideology, Will Fuel This Century's Epic Battles," http://www.theguardian.com/politics/2014/jan/25/extremist-religion-wars-tony-blair (accessed March 29, 2014).

272. J. Beversluis, *A Source Book for Earth's Community of Religions* (New York: Global Education Associates, 1995), 138.

273. T. L. Friedman, "A War We Can't Win with Guns Only," *San Diego Union-Tribune*, November 28, 2001, B-8.

274. Ibid.

Chapter 5

1. P. N. Stearns, "Why Study History?," *American Historical Association* (1998), http://www.historians.org/about-aha-and-membership/aha-history-and-archives/archives/why-study-history (accessed January 5, 2015).

2. W. Huber, "The Judeo-Christian Tradition," in *The Cultural Values of Europe*, ed. H. Joas and K. Weigandt, trans. Alex Skinner (Liverpool: Liverpool University Press, 2009), 43.

3. E. O. Reischauer and J. K. Fairbank, *East Asia: The Great Tradition* (Boston: Houghton Mifflin, 1960), 43.

4. T. Bender, *A Nation Among Nations: America's Place in World History* (New York: Hill and Wang, 2006), 3–4.

5. M. MacMillan, *Dangerous Games: The Uses and Abuses of History* (New York: Modern Library, 2010), 88–89.

6. B. Lewis, *The Shaping of the Modern Middle East* (New York: Oxford University Press, 1994), 11; B. Lewis, *The Middle East: A Brief History of the Last*

2,000 Years (New York: Scribner, 1995), 67.

7. B. Kerblay, *Modern Soviet Society* (New York: Pantheon, 1983), 271.

8. MacMillan, 2010, 19.

9. J. H. McElroy, *American Beliefs: What Keeps a Big Country and Diverse People United* (Chicago: Ivan R. Dee, 1999), 51, 220. (Comment: We recognize that Spain had established a colony in what is now Florida prior to 1607. However, we contend that the English settlers had a greater impact on U.S. national character.)

10. C. S. Fischer, *Made in America* (Chicago: University of Chicago Press, 2010), 12.

11. A. Chua, *Day of Empire* (New York: Doubleday, 2007), 234–39.

12. "United States," *The World Factbook* (Central Intelligence Agency, June 20, 2014), https://www.cia.gov /library/publications/the-world -factbook/geos/us.html (accessed January 9, 2015); data contained in the "Country Statistics" tables in this chapter were obtained from the *CIA World Factbook* (https://www.cia .gov/library/publications/the-world -factbook) unless otherwise noted.

13. "DP-05 ACS Demographic and Housing Estimates: 2009–2013 American Community Survey 5-Year Estimates," *American Fact Finder* (U.S. Census Bureau, n.d.), http:// factfinder.census.gov/faces/table services/jsf/pages/productview.xhtml? src=CF (accessed January 9, 2013).

14. C. Ryan, *Language Use in the United States: 2011* (U.S. Census Bureau: American Community Survey Reports, 2013 August), http://www .census.gov/prod/2013pubs/acs-22.pdf (accessed January 9, 2015).

15. F. Newport, *In U.S., 77% Identify as Christian* (Gallup, 2012), http://www .gallup.com/poll/159548/identify -christian.aspx (accessed February 15, 2015).

16. C. Van Doren, *A History of Knowledge* (New York: Ballantine Books, 1991), 224; A. M. Schlesinger Jr., *The Cycles of American History* (Boston: Houghton Mifflin), 89.

17. G. Althen, *American Ways*, 2nd ed. (Yarmouth, ME: Intercultural Press, 2003), 120.

18. J. H. McElroy, *Finding Freedom: America's Distinctive Cultural Formation* (Carbondale: Southern Illinois University Press, 1987), 65.

19. S. D. Cohen, *An Ocean Apart* (Westport, CT: Praeger, 1998), 141.

20. E. C. Stewart and M. J. Bennett, *American Cultural Patterns*, rev. ed. (Yarmouth, ME: Intercultural Press, 1991), 136.

21. Fischer, 2010, 10.

22. McElroy, 1987, 143.

23. C. Fox, "The 15 Most Amazing Places Uncle Sam Could Send You," *Huffington Post* (April 29, 2014), http://www.huffingtonpost.com/2014 /04/29/best-military-bases-around -the-world_n_5216682.html (accessed January 10, 2015).

24. Bender, 2006, 187–88.

25. R. Griswold del Castillo, *The Treaty of Guadalupe Hidalgo: A Legacy of Conflict* (Norman: University of Oklahoma Press, 1990), 4.

26. Stewart and Bennett, 1991, 119–23.

27. F. Fukuyama, "America in Decay: The Sources of Political Dysfunction," *Foreign Affairs* 93, 5 (September/ October 2014): 26.

28. J. Kohan, "A Mind of Their Own," *Time*, December 7, 1992, 66.

29. A. C. Kuchins, "Why Russia is so Russian," *Current History*, 108, 720 (2009): 318–24.

30. R. V. Daniels, *Russia: The Roots of Confrontation* (Cambridge, MA: Harvard University Press, 1985), 55.

31. A. Esler, *The Human Venture*, 3rd ed. (Upper Saddle River, NJ: Prentice Hall, 1996), 668.

32. "Russia," *CIA World Factbook* (June 20, 2014), https://www.cia.gov /library/publications/the-world -factbook/geos/rs.html (accessed January 14, 2015).

33. Kuchins, 2009, 320.

34. J. Minahan, *One Europe, Many Nations: A Historical Dictionary of European National Groups* (Westport,

CT: Greenwood Publishing Group, 2000), 567.

35. "The Uses and Abuses of History," *The Economist*, May 7, 2005, 43

36. M. Bergelson, "Russian Cultural Values and Workplace Communication Patterns," in *Intercultural Communication: A Reader*, 13th ed., ed. L. A. Samovar, R. E. Porter, and E. R. McDaniel (Boston: Wadsworth Cengage, 2012), 191.

37. N. Ryan, "Byzantine Influence on Russia Through the Ages," *Culture & Memory*, Special Issue of *Modern Greek Studies* (Australia and New Zealand, 2006), 279, http://open journals.library.usyd.edu.au/index .php/MGST/article/viewFile/6760 /7405 (accessed January 15, 2015).

38. P. Kolsto, "Nation-Building in Russia: A Value Oriented Strategy," in *Nation Building and Common Values in Russia*, ed. P. Kolsto and H. Blakkisrud (Lanham, MD: Rowman & Littlefield, 2004), 2.

39. Kuchins, 2009, 323.

40. J. J. Mearsheimer, "Why the Ukraine Crisis is the West's Fault," *Foreign Affairs*, September/October, 2014, 82–83.

41. V. Fursova and G. Simons, "Social Problems of Modern Russian Higher Education: The Example of Corruption," *International Education Studies* 7, 10 (2014): 25.

42. K. Rapoza, "Russia's Three Biggest Problems," *Forbes* (January 24, 2013), http://www.forbes.com/sites/kenrapoza /2013/01/24/russias-three-biggest -problems (accessed January 15, 2015).

43. T. Mazumdar, "Vodka blamed for high death rates in Russia," *BBC News* (January 31, 2014), http://www .bbc.com/news/health-25961063 (accessed January 15, 2015); M. Mirovalev, "Russia Drug Abuse Top Problem, According to Poll," *The World Post* (September 11, 2012), http://www.huffingtonpost .com/2012/07/12/russia-drug-abuse_n _1667786.html (accessed January 15, 2015).

44. P. Herlihy, "Russia's 'family values' experiment," *Los Angeles Times* (June 19, 2013), http://www.latimes

.com/news/opinion/commentary/la-oe-herlihy-russia-anti-gay-20130619,0,3118119.story (accessed January 1, 2015).

45. Andrew Wilson, "The High Stakes of the Ukraine Crisis," *Current History* 113, 765 (2014): 273–75.

46. D. Treisman, *The Return: Russia's Journey from Gorbachev to Medvedev* (New York: Free Press, 2011), 344.

47. M. Bird, "China Just Overtook the US as the World's Largest Economy," *Business Insider* (October 8, 2014), http://www.businessinsider.com/china-overtakes-us-as-worlds-largest-economy-2014-10 (accessed January 18, 2015).

48. O. A. Westad, *Restless Empire* (New York: Basic Books, 2012), 2.

49. I. Morris, *Why the West Rules—For Now* (New York: Farrar, Straus and Giroux, 2010), 123.

50. C. O. Hucker, *China's Imperial Past* (Stanford, CA: Stanford University Press, 1975), 26.

51. Hucker, 1975, 2.

52. Morris, 2010, 285.

53. J. K. Fairbank, E. O. Reischauer, and A. M. Craig, *East Asia: Tradition and Transformation*, (Boston: Houghton Mifflin, 1973), 20.

54. "China," *The World Factbook* (Central Intelligence Agency, June 22, 2014), https://www.cia.gov/library/publications/the-world-factbook/geos/ch.html (accessed January 19, 2015).

55. X. Zuo, "China's policy towards minority languages in a globalising age," *Transnational Curriculum Inquiry* 4, 1 (2007): 84, http://ojs.library.ubc.ca/index.php/tci/article/viewFile/42/74 (accessed February 3, 2015).

56. Westad, 2012, 336.

57. "World Development Indicators: Urbanization," *World Bank* (December 2014), http://wdi.worldbank.org/table/3.12 (accessed January 21, 2014).

58. D. Shambaugh, "New China Requires a New US Strategy," *Current History* 109, 728 (2010): 219–26; see also Z. Wang, *Never Forget National Humiliation* (New York: Columbia University Press, 2012).

59. J. Makinen, "Artists finding inspiration in China's bad air," *Los Angeles Times* (May 7, 2014), http://www.latimes.com/world/great-reads/la-fg-c1-china-art-pollution-20140507-story.html#page=1 (accessed January 22, 2015); T. Marslen, "Are China's Plans to Tackle Water Pollution Sufficient?," *Future Directions International* (March 19, 2014), http://www.futuredirections.org.au/publications/food-and-water-crises/28-global-food-and-water-crises-swa/1586-are-china-s-plans-to-tackle-water-pollution-sufficient.html (accessed January 2, 2015).

60. Y. Xie and X. Zhou, "Income inequality in today's China," *Proceedings of the National Academy of Sciences of the United States of America* 111, 19 (2014): 6928, http://www.pnas.org/content/111/19/6928.full.pdf+html?sid=e07a8e89-7f28-46f4-b86d-f3da31d5ad5e (accessed January 22, 2014).

61. "3-5 Basic statistics on national population census in 1953, 1964, 1982, 1990, 2000 and 2010," *China Statistical Yearbook 2011* (Beijing: National Bureau of Statistics of China, n.d.), http://www.stats.gov.cn/tjsj/ndsj/2011/indexeh.htm (accessed January 22, 2015).

62. "China's urbanization level to reach 60 pct by 2020," *Xinhua* (March 16, 2014), http://news.xinhuanet.com/english/china/2014-03/16/c_133190605.htm (accessed January 2, 2015); D. K. Gardner, "China's planned urban growth bodes ill for environment," *Los Angeles Times* (April 21, 2014), http://www.latimes.com/opinion/commentary/la-oe-gardner-china-pollution-20140422,0,3971313.story#axzz2zekP096N (accessed January 22, 2015).

63. W. Feng and M. Hvistendahl, "China's Population Destiny: The Looming Crisis," *Current History*, 728, 244 (2010): 250.

64. "Official vows China will correct gender imbalance," *Xinhua–English News* (May 24, 2012), http://news.xinhuanet.com/english/china/2012-05/24/c_131608451.htm (accessed December 22, 2015); A. Jacobs, "For

Many Chinese Men, No Deed Means No Dates," *New York Times* (April 14, 2011), http://www.nytimes.com/2011/04/15/world/asia/15bachelors.html (accessed June 6, 2015).

65. G. Mu, "A two-child policy for all," *China Daily USA* (August 11, 2014), http://usa.chinadaily.com.cn/opinion/2014-08/11/content_18283036.htm (accessed January 22, 2015); "Paying for the grey," *The Economist*, April 5, 2014, 37; "One-child proclivity," *The Economist*, July 19, 2014, 40.

66. I. Johnson, "Educated Chinese move abroad in record numbers," *International Herald Tribune* (November 2, 2012), 1; D. Shambaugh, "The Illusion of Chinese Power," *The National Interest* (June 25, 2014), http://nationalinterest.org/feature/the-illusion-chinese-power-10739 (accessed January 22, 2015).

67. R. Gifford, *China Road: A Journey into the Future of a Rising Power* (New York: Random House, 2007), 278.

68. "Japan," *The World Factbook* (Central Intelligence Agency, June 22, 2014), https://www.cia.gov/library/publications/the-world-factbook/geos/ja.html (accessed January 23, 2015).

69. J. W. Dower, *Embracing Defeat: Japan in the Wake of World War II*, (New York: Norton, 1999), 29.

70. E. O. Reischauer and M. B. Jansen, *The Japanese Today: Change and Continuity* (Cambridge, MA: Harvard University Press, 1995), 32.

71. J. Soble, "Japan stands by immigration controls despite shrinking population," *Financial Times* (June 2, 2014), http://www.ft.com/cms/s/0/32788ff0-ea00-11e3-99ed-00144feabdc0.html#axzz3Pf3sMl4v (accessed January 23, 2015).

72. C. Burgess, "Japan's 'no immigration principle' looking as solid as ever," *Japan Times* (June 18, 2014), http://www.japantimes.co.jp/community/2014/06/18/voices/japans-immigration-principle-looking-solid-ever/#.VMJ0RBR0y70 (accessed January 23, 2015); C. Matthews, "Can immigration save a struggling, disappearing Japan?," *Fortune* (November 20,

2014), http://fortune.com/2014/11/20/japan-immigration-economy (accessed January 23, 2015).

73. M. B. Jansen, *The Making of Modern Japan* (Cambridge, MA: Belknap Press, 2000), 97; A. Gordon, *A Modern History of Japan* (New York: Oxford University Press, 2003), 16.

74. B. L. De Mente, *Behind the Japanese Bow* (Chicago: Passport Books), 1–2, 12.

75. J. Kingston, *Contemporary Japan: History, Politics, and Social Change Since the 1980s* (Chichester: Wiley, 2011), 17.

76. T. S. Lebra, *Japanese Patterns of Behavior* (Honolulu: University of Hawaii Press, 1976), various.

77. Jansen, 2000, 111.

78. Reischauer and Jansen, 1995, 15–16.

79. Jansen, 2000, 111.

80. M. Hoffman, "Nothing is clear about court ruling on illegitimate kids," *Japan Times* (September 28, 2013), http://www.japantimes.co.jp/news/2013/09/28/national/media-national/nothing-is-clear-about-court-ruling-on-illegitimate-kids/#.VMKtfxR0y70 (accessed January 22, 2015).

81. Kingston, 2011, 129.

82. "Chapter 2. Population," *Statistical Handbook of Japan 2014* (Tokyo: Ministry of Internal Affairs and Communications: Statistics Japan, n.d.), http://www.stat.go.jp/english/data/handbook/c0117.htm#c02 (accessed January 23, 2015); A. Harney, "Japan's Silver Democracy The Costs of Letting the Elderly Rule Politics," *Foreign Affairs* (July 18, 2013), http://www.foreignaffairs.com/articles/139589/alexandra-harney/japans-silver-democracy (accessed January 23, 2015); "Number of newborn babies in Japan fell to record low in 2014," *Japan Times* (January 1, 2015), http://www.japantimes.co.jp/news/2015/01/01/national/number-newborn-babies-japan-fell-record-low-2014/#.VKYQzxR0y70 (accessed January 1, 2015).

83. Kingston, 2011, 19–20.

84. J. S. Black and A. J. Morrison, *Sunset in the Land of the Rising Sun* (New York: Palgrave Macmillan, 2010), various; see also "Sunset in the Land of the Rising Sun" (YouTube), https://www.youtube.com/watch?v=P5giYFnRK24.

85. Y. Sugimoto, *An Introduction to Japanese Society*, 3rd ed. (New York: Cambridge University Press, 2010), 190.

86. For a more comprehensive discussion, see S. Kawano, G. S. Roberts, and S. O. Long, eds., *Capturing Contemporary Japan: Differentiation and Uncertainty* (Honolulu: University of Hawaii Press, 2014).

87. S. Wolpert, *India*, 3rd ed. (Berkeley: University of California Press, 2005), 2.

88. "India's outsourcing business: On the turn," *The Economist* (January 19, 2013), http://www.economist.com/news/special-report/21569571-india-no-longer-automatic-choice-it-services-and-back-office-work-turn (accessed January 24, 2015); 76; H. Timmons, "Outsourcing to India Draws Western Lawyers," *New York Times* (August 4, 2010), http://www.nytimes.com/2010/08/05/business/global/05legal.html (accessed January 24, 2015).

89. *The Rise of Asian Americans* (Washington, DC: Pew Research Center, April 4, 2013), 7, 44, http://www.pewsocialtrends.org/files/2013/04/Asian-Americans-new-full-report-04-2013.pdf (accessed January 26, 2015); M. Kripalani, "Indian Americans Come Out," *Los Angeles Times* (January 21, 2007), http://www.latimes.com/news/printedition/asection/la-oe-kripalani20jan20,0,1385820.story (accessed January 24, 2015).

90. N. Grihault, *Culture Smart! India* (London: Kuperard, 2007), various; C. E. Henderson, *Culture and Customs of India* (Westport, CT: Greenwood Press, 2002), various; "India," *CIA World Factbook* (Central Intelligence Agency, June 22, 2014), https://www.cia.gov/library/publications/the-world-factbook/geos/in.html (accessed January 26, 2015).

91. "India," 2014.

92. Grihault, 2007, 24; Henderson, 2002, 13; D. R. SarDesai, *India: The Definitive History* (Boulder, CO: Westview Press, 2008), 18; Wolpert, 2005, 25–27.

93. Henderson, 2002, 13–15; Wolpert, 2005, 29–38.

94. Wolpert, 2005, 40–41.

95. Henderson, 2002, 15.

96. Wolpert, 2005, 42.

97. D. Brown, *A New Introduction to Islam* (Malden, MA: Blackwell, 2004), 192; Henderson, 2002, 26.

98. Henderson, 2002, 17.

99. Grihault, 2007, 29.

100. Wolpert, 2005, 51.

101. Ibid.

102. Grihault, 2007, 28; Henderson, 2002, 21; Wolpert, 69.

103. "GDP Ranking," *The World Bank* (December 16, 2014), http://data.worldbank.org/data-catalog/GDP-ranking-table (accessed January 25, 2015).

104. K. Mahr, "The New Face of India," *Time*, June 2, 2014, 20; L. R. Brown, "India's dangerous 'food bubble,'" *Los Angeles Times* (November 29, 2013), http://www.latimes.com/opinion/commentary/la-oe-brown-india-food-bubble-famine-20131129,0,4895563.story#axzz2m490YgsR (accessed January 29, 2014); "India elections a reminder of the ties that bind us," *Sydney Morning Herald* (April 6, 2014), http://www.smh.com.au/comment/smh-editorial/india-elections-a-reminder-of-the-ties-that-bind-us-20140405-zqr5y.html (accessed January 25, 2015); SarDesai, 2008, 10.

105. R. Bansal, "India's Remix Generation," *Current History* 106, 699 (2007): 168.

106. I. Bagchi, "The Struggle for Women's Empowerment in India," *Current History* 113, 716 (April 2014): 145.

107. Ibid., 148.

108. Rural Urban Distribution of Population," *Census of India 2011* (Registrar General & Census Commissioner, India: Ministry of Home Affairs, July 11, 2011), http://censusindia.gov.in/2011-prov-results/paper2/data_files

/india/Rural_Urban_2011.pdf (accessed January 25, 2015); B. Sivakumar, "Literacy rate jumps 10% in a decade in India," *The Times of India* (November 23, 2014), http://timesofindia.indiatimes.com/india/Literacy-rate-jumps-10-in-a-decade-in-India/articleshow/45244626.cms (accessed January 25, 2015); "India tops in adult illiteracy: U.N. report," *The Hindu* (January 14, 2014), http://www.thehindu.com/features/education/issues/india-tops-in-adult-illiteracy-un-report/article5629981.ece (accessed January 25, 2015).

109. "Poverty and Equity," *World Bank* (2012), http://povertydata.worldbank.org/poverty/country/IND (accessed January 25, 2015); K. K. Kundu, "Young, Jobless and Indian," *Wall Street Journal* (November 23, 2012), http://blogs.wsj.com/indiarealtime/2012/11/23/young-jobless-and-indian/?mg=blogs-wsj&url=http%253A%252F%252Fblogs.wsj.com%252Findiarealtime%252F2012%252F11%252F23%252Fyoung-jobless-and-indian (accessed February 15, 2015).

110. "Remaking India: Yes, prime minister," *The Economist* (October 18, 2014), http://www.economist.com/news/asia/21625857-more-moderniser-market-reformer-narendra-modi-relies-his-bureaucrats-yes-prime-minister (accessed January 25, 2015); B. Xu and E. Albert, "Governance in India: Infrastructure," Council on Foreign Affairs (October 1, 2014), http://www.cfr.org/india/governance-india-infrastructure/p32638 (accessed January 25, 2015); "A Village in a Million," *The Economist*, December 18, 2010, 63.

111. Mahr, 2014, 21; S. Ganguly, "India Held Back," *Current History* 107, 712 (November 2008): 370.

112. A. R., "The Economist explains: Why caste still matters in India," *The Economist* (February, 14, 2014), http://www.economist.com/blogs/economist-explains/2014/02/economist-explains-9 (accessed February 15, 2015); S. Bengali and M. N. Parth, "Indian rights groups cite discrimination in deadly rape case," *Los Angeles Times* (April 4, 2014), http://www.latimes.com/world/asia/la-fg-india-rights-groups-rape-20140603-story.html (accessed February 15, 2015).

113. L. Sankaran, "Caste is not past," *New York Times*, (June 15, 2013), http://www.nytimes.com/2013/06/16/opinion/sunday/caste-is-not-past.html?_r=0 (accessed January 25, 2015).

114. Personal correspondence between A. P. Ramasay and Edwin R. McDaniel, March 18, 2014, Taipei, Taiwan.

115. "Ambient (outdoor) air pollution in cities database 2014," *Public health, environmental and social determinants of health (PHE)* (World Health Organization, 2014), http://www.who.int/phe/health_topics/outdoorair/databases/cities/en (accessed February 15, 2015); G. Harris, "Cities in India Among the Most Polluted, W.H.O. Says, *New York Times* (May 8, 2014), http://www.nytimes.com/2014/05/09/world/asia/cities-in-india-among-the-most-polluted-who-says.html (accessed January 26, 2015).

116. *San Ysidro Land Port of Entry* (U.S. General Services Administration, September 15, 2014), http://www.gsa.gov/portal/content/104872 (accessed February 15, 2015).

117. *U.S. Relations With Mexico* (U.S. Department of State: Bureau of Western Hemisphere Affairs Fact Sheet, September 10, 2014), http://www.state.gov/r/pa/ei/bgn/35749.htm (accessed January 26, 2015).

118. A. Gonzalez-Barrera and M. H. Lopez, *A Demographic Portrait of Mexican-Origin Hispanics in the United States* (Pew Research Center, Pew Hispanic Center, May 1, 2013), http://www.pewhispanic.org/files/2013/05/2013-04_Demographic-Portrait-of-Mexicans-in-the-US.pdf (accessed January 26, 2015).

119. L. Schneider and A. Silverman, *Global Sociology: Introducing Five Contemporary Societies*, 5th ed. (Boston: McGraw-Hill, 2010), 72.

120. "Mexico," *CIA World Factbook* (Central Intelligence Agency, June 20, 2014), https://www.cia.gov/library/publications/the-world-factbook/geos/mx.html (accessed February 13, 2015).

121. L. V. Foster, *A Brief History of Mexico* (New York: Facts on File, 1997), 2; J. D. Cockcroft, *Mexico's Hope: An Encounter with Politics and History* (New York: Monthly Review Press, 1998), 13; Schneider and Silverman, 2010, 60.

122. R. Kaplan, "What is the origin of zero? How did we indicate nothingness before zero?" *Scientific American* (January 16, 2007), http://www.scientificamerican.com/article/what-is-the-origin-of-zer (accessed January 27, 2015).

123. "The Conquest of Mexico: On the trail of Hernán Cortés," *The Economist*, December 20, 2014, 53–55; Schneider and Silverman, 2010, 72–73.

124. Cockcroft, 1998, 19.

125. "The Conquest of Mexico," 2014, 53.

126. Foster, 1997, 65–66.

127. Ibid., 96.

128. F. Merrell, *The Mexicans: A Sense of Culture* (Boulder, CO: Westview Press, 2003), 53–56.

129. Schneider and Silverman, 2010, 74.

130. Foster, 1997, 111.

131. C. J. Johns, *The Origins of Violence in Mexican Society* (Westport, CT: Praeger, 1995), 202.

132. M. V. Meed, *The Mexican War 1846–1848* (Oxford: Osprey Publishing, 2002), 7.

133. E. Krauze, "Border Battle: The Ugly Legacy of the Mexican-American War," *Foreign Affairs*, November/December, 2013, 155.

134. "The Treaty of Guadalupe Hidalgo," *Hispanic Reading Room* (Library of Congress, February 14, 2011), http://www.loc.gov/rr/hispanic/ghtreaty (accessed January 28, 2015).

135. Griswold del Castillo, 1990, xii.

136. J. Samora and P. V. Simon, *A History of Mexican-American People* (London: University of Notre Dame Press, 1977), 98.

137. Krauze, 2013, 155.

138. A. Esler, *The Human Venture*, 3rd ed. (Upper Saddle River, NJ: Prentice Hall, 1996), 613.

139. Schneider and Silverman, 2010, 75.

140. "Poverty headcount ratio at national poverty lines (% of population)," *Mexico: Data* (World Bank, 2015), http://data.worldbank.org/country /mexico (accessed January 28, 2015); P. R. Mallén, "Poverty Increases In Mexico To 45 Percent Of Population: 53 Million Mexicans Under Poverty Line," *International Business Times* (July 30, 2013), http://www .ibtimes.com/poverty-increases -mexico-45-percent-population-53 -million-mexicans-under-poverty-line -1364753 (accessed January 28, 2015).

141. D. Cohn, A. Gonzalez-Barrera, and D. Cuddington, *Remittances to Latin America Recover—but Not to Mexico* (Pew Research Center, Hispanic Trends, November 15, 2013), http:// www.pewhispanic.org/2013/11/15 /remittances-to-latin-america -recover-but-not-to-mexico (accessed February 12, 2015).

142. N. Miroff and W. Booth, "Mexico's drug war is at a stalemate as Calderon's presidency ends," *Washington Post* (November 27, 2012), http://www .washingtonpost.com/world/the _americas/calderon-finishes-his-six -year-drug-war-at-stalemate/2012/11 /26/82c90a94-31eb-11e2-92f0 -496af208bf23_story.html (accessed January 28, 2015); I. Grillo, "Mexico's Drug War Leads to Kidnappings, Vigilante Violence," *Time* (January 17, 2014), http://world.time .com/2014/01/17/mexico-drug-war -kidnapping (accessed January 28, 2015); D. Estevez, "Mexico's Astonishing Costs of Fighting Drug Cartels Have Not Reduced Violence," *Forbes* (June 19, 2014), http://www.forbes. com/sites/doliaestevez/2014/06/19 /mexicos-astonishing-spending-on -fighting-drug-cartels-has-not-reduced -violence (accessed January 28, 2015); I. Grillo, "Mexico's Deadly Narco -Politics," *New York Times* (October 9, 2014), http://www.nytimes.com/2014 /10/10/opinion/mexicos-deadly-narco -politics.html (accessed January 28, 2015); Editorial Board, "Law and Order in Mexico," *New York Times* (November 11, 2014), http://www. nytimes.com/2014/11/12/opinion /murder-in-mexico.html?_r=0 (accessed January 28, 2014).

143. A. Taylor, "Mexico's Vigilantes," *The Atlantic* (May 13, 2014), http://www .theatlantic.com/photo/2014/05 /mexicos-vigilantes/100734 (accessed January 28, 2015); F. E. Gonzalez, "Mexico's Drug Wars Get Brutal," *Current History* 108, 715 (2009): 74–75; Schneider and Silverman, 2010, 775–76; "The Catholic Church's position in Mexico," *BBC News* (March 12, 2013), http://www .bbc.com/news/world-latin-america -21745882 (accessed January 28, 2015).

144. D. Agren, "Model for megacities? Mexico City cleans up its air," *Christian Science Monitor* (April 22, 2013), http://www.csmonitor.com/World /Americas/2013/0422/Model-for -megacities-Mexico-City-cleans-up -its-air (accessed 27 January, 2015); "Mexico," *CIA World Factbook* (June 20, 2015), https://www.cia.gov /library/publications/the-world -factbook/geos/mx.html (accessed January 27, 2015).

145. D. Desilver, "World's Muslim population more widespread than you might think," *Fact Tank* (Pew Research Center, June 7, 2013), http://www.pewresearch.org/fact -tank/2013/06/07/worlds-muslim -population-more-widespread-than -you-might-think (accessed January 28, 2015).

146. "Muslims," *The Global Religious Landscape* (Pew Research Center, Religion & Public Life, December 18, 2012), http://www.pewforum.org /2012/12/18/global-religious -landscape-muslim (accessed January 29, 2015).

147. *The Future of the Global Muslim Population: Projections for 2010–2030* (Pew Research Center, Forum on Religion & Public Life, January 2011), 13–15, 141, http://www .pewforum.org/files/2011/01/Future GlobalMuslimPopulation-WebPDF -Feb10.pdf (accessed January 29, 2015).

148. "Muslims," 2012.

149. I. R. Manners and B. M. Parmenter, "The Middle East: A Geographic Preface," in *Understanding the Contemporary Middle East*, 2nd ed., ed. D. J. Gernerand and J. Schwedler (Boulder, CO: Lynne Rienner Publishers, 2004), 5–32; A. Goldschmidt Jr., "The Historical Context," in *Understanding the Contemporary Middle East*, 2nd ed., ed. D. J. Gerner and J. Schwedler (Boulder, CO: Lynne Rienner Publishers, 2004), 33–78.

150. A. L. W. Admec, *Historical Dictionary of Islam*, 2nd ed. (Lanham, MD: Scarecrow Press, 2001), 146.

151. Goldschmidt, 2004, 39.

152. Ibid.

153. F. M. Donner, "Muhammad and the Caliphate," in *The Oxford History of Islam*, ed. J. L. Esposito (New York: Oxford University Press, 1999), 11.

154. P. Lunde, *Islam* (New York: DK Publishing, 2002), 8.

155. Donner, 1999, 11.

156. Ibid., 13.

157. Lunde, 2002, 52, 61.

158. "Muslims," 2012.

159. *Mapping the Global Muslim Population: A Report on the Size and Distribution of the World's Muslim Population* (Pew Research Center, Forum on Religion & Public Life, October, 2009), 9, http://www.pewforum.org/files/2009 /10/Muslimpopulation.pdf (accessed January 27, 2015).

160. J. L. Esposito, *What Everyone Needs to Know About Islam*, 2nd ed. (New York: Oxford University Press, 2011), 50; for a comprehensive discussion of the Sunni–Shia schism, see *The Sunni-Shia Divide*, a Council on Foreign Relations InfoGuide presentation at http://www.cfr.org /sunnishia.

161. Lunde, 2002, 54–56.

162. J. I. Smith, "Islam and Christendom," in *The Oxford History of Islam*, ed. J. L. Esposito (New York: Oxford University Press, 1999), 312, 337.

163. E. Rogers and E. M. Steinfatt, *Intercultural Communication* (Prospect Heights, IL: Waveland Press, 1999), 9.

164. Smith, 1999, 339.

165. B. Lewis, *The Crisis of Islam* (New York: Random House, 2004), 59.

166. S. V. R. Nasr, "European Colonialism and the Emergence of Modern Muslim States," in *The Oxford History of Islam*, ed. J. L. Esposito (New York: Oxford University Press, 1999), 552.

167. Lewis, 2004, xix.

168. D. Brown, *A New Introduction to Islam* (Malden, MA: Blackwell, 2004), 18–19.

169. Lewis, 1994, 27.

170. Esposito, 2011, 223; E. E. Curtis IV, *Encyclopedia of Muslim-American History* (New York: Facts on File, 2010), 20.

171. B. Lewis, "The Revolt of Islam," *The New Yorker*, November 19, 2001, 52.

172. "Tethered by history," *The Economist*, July 5, 2014, 20–22; "A climate of change," *The Economist*, July 13, 2013, 1–16; "Waking from Its Sleep: A Special Report on the Arab World," *The Economist*, July 25, 2009, 1–16.

173. *Rethinking Economic Growth: Towards Productive and Inclusive Arab Societies* (United Nations International Labour Organization, 2012), 52, http://www.ilo.org/wcmsp5/groups/public/—arabstates/—ro-beirut/documents/publication/wcms_208346.pdf (accessed February 13, 2015).

174. Esposito, 2011, 47.

175. "The abolition of the Caliphate," *The Economist* (March 8, 1924), http://www.economist.com/node/11829711 (accessed January 31, 2015).

176. Esposito, 2011, 47; A. M. Shahrur, "A Call for Reformation," in "Voices within Islam: Four Perspectives on Tolerance and Diversity," B. Baktiari and A. R. Norton, *Current History* 104, 658 (2005): 39–43.

177. Esposito, 2011, 47–48.

178. J. L. Esposito, *The Future of Islam* (New York: Oxford University Press, 2010), 195–96.

179. R. Eslan, "Bill Maher Isn't the Only One Who Misunderstands Religion," *New York Times* (October 8, 2014), http://www.huffingtonpost.com/2015/01/27/nicholas-kristof-bill-maher_n_6550400.html?cps=gravity_2677_1542977224934004197 (accessed January 31, 2015).

Chapter 6

1. S. Hawking and L. Mlodinow, *The Grand Design* (New York: Bantam Books, 2010), 46.

2. W. B. Gudykunst, *Bridging Differences: Effective Intergroup Communication*, 4th ed. (Thousand Oaks, CA: Sage, 2004), 105.

3. P. T. Moran, P. R. Harris, and S. V. Moran, *Managing Cultural Differences: Leadership Skills and Strategies for Working in a Global World*, 8th ed. (New York: Elsevier, 2011), 464–65.

4. N. J. Adler with A. Gunderson, *International Dimensions of Organizational Behavior*, 5th ed. (Mason, OH: Thomson South-Western, 2008), 73.

5. Ibid., 79–80.

6. C.-Y. Chiu and Y.-Y. Hong, *Social Psychology of Culture* (New York: Psychology Press, 2006), 83.

7. J. Cromby, "Beyond belief," *Journal of Health Psychology* 17, 7, (2012): 943–57, DOI: 10.1177/1359105312448866.

8. "The Debate Over Universal Values," *The Economist*, October 2, 2010, 43.

9. Charlemagne, "Help them to help themselves," *The Economist*, June 26, 2010, 56.

10. M. K. Nydell, *Understanding Arabs: A Contemporary Guide to Arab Society*, 5th ed. (Boston: Intercultural Press, 2012), 18.

11. J. M. Charon and L.G. Vigilant, *The Meaning of Sociology*, 8th ed. (Upper Saddle River, NJ: Pearson Prentice Hall, 2009), 87.

12. E. Y. Kim, *The Yin and Yang of American Culture: A Paradox* (Yarmouth, ME: Intercultural Press, 2001), xv.

13. "Robert Kohls," *Washington Post* (September 2, 2006), http://www.washingtonpost.com/wp-dyn/content/article/2006/09/01/AR2006090101637.html (accessed May 1, 2014).

14. Table adapted from L. Robert Kohls, *The Values Americans Live By* (1986), http://www.claremontmckenna.edu/pages/faculty/alee/extra/American_values.html (accessed May 1, 2014).

15. G. Althen and J. Bennett, *American Ways*, 3rd ed. (Yarmouth, ME: Intercultural Press, 2011), 15.

16. A. R. Lanier, *Living in the USA*, 6th ed., rev. J. C. Davis (Boston: Intercultural Press, 2005), 22–23.

17. Lanier, 2005, 82–83.

18. M. J. Gannon and R. Pillai, *Understanding Global Cultures*, 4th ed. (Thousand Oaks, CA: Sage, 2010), 263.

19. *Declaration of Independence*, http://www.archives.gov/exhibits/charters/declaration_transcript.html (accessed May 2, 2014).

20. *Constitution of the United States*, Section 9, http://www.archives.gov/exhibits/charters/constitution_transcript.html (accessed May 2, 2014).

21. M. J. Hanson, "Families with Anglo-European Roots," in *Developing Cross-Cultural Competence: A Guide for Working with Children and Their Families*, 2nd ed., ed. E. W. Lynch and M. J. Hanson (Baltimore: Paul H. Brookes, 1998), 104–5.

22. M. K. Datesman, J. Crandall, and E. N. Kearny, *American Ways: An Introduction to American Culture*, 3rd ed. (White Plains, NY: Pearson, 2005), 29.

23. E. C. Stewart and M. J. Bennett, *American Cultural Patterns: A Cross-Cultural Perspective* (Yarmouth, ME: Intercultural Press, 1991), 133.

24. C. S. Fischer, *Made in America* (Chicago: University of Chicago Press, 2010), 12.

25. Gannon and Pillai, 2010, 255.

26. Adler and Gunderson, 2008, 33.

27. Lanier, 2005, 17–18; Althen and Bennett, 2011, 23–26.

28. Althen and Bennett, 2011, 23.

29. T. Bender, *A Nation Among Nations: America's Place in World History* (New York: Hill and Wang, 2006), 187.

30. "The Tyranny of Choice: You choose," *The Economist*, December 18, 2010, 123. http://www.economist.com/node/17723028 (accessed May 3, 2014).

31. R. J. House, "Illustrative Examples of GLOBE Findings," in *Culture,*

Leadership, and Organizations: The GLOBE Study of 62 Societies, ed. R. J. House, P. J. Hanges, M. Javidan, P. W. Dorfman, and V. Gupta, eds. (Thousand Oaks, CA: Sage, 2004), 3–8; F. Trompenaars and C. Hampden-Turner, *Riding the Waves of Culture*, 3rd ed. (New York: McGraw-Hill, 2012).

32. F. R. Kluckhohn and F. L. Strodtbeck, *Variations in Value Orientations* (New York: Row and Peterson), 1960.

33. P.-J. Fu, "Human Nature and Human Education: On Human Nature as Tending Toward Goodness," in *Chinese Foundations for Moral Education and Character Development*, ed. T. V. Doan, V. Shen, and G. McLean (Washington, DC: Council for Research in Values and Philosophy, 1991), 20.

34. N. C. Jain and E. D. Kussman, "Dominant Cultural Patterns of Hindus in India," in *Intercultural Communication: A Reader*, 9th ed., ed. L. A. Samovar and R. E. Porter, eds. (Belmont, CA: Wadsworth, 2000), 89.

35. O. A. Westad. *Restless Empire: China and the World Since 1750* (New York: Basic Books, 2012), 2.

36. E. T. Hall and M. R. Hall, *Understanding Cultural Differences* (Yarmouth, ME: Intercultural Press, 1990), 87.

37. J. Luckmann, *Transcultural Communication in Nursing* (Albany, NY: Delmar Publishers, 1999), 31.

38. N. J. Adler and M. Jelinek, "Is 'Organization Culture' Culture Bound?," in *Culture, Communication and Conflict: Readings in Intercultural Relations*, 2nd ed., ed. G. R. Weaver, ed. (Boston: Pearson, 2000), 130.

39. Kim, 2001, 115.

40. E. T. Hall, *Beyond Culture* (Garden City, NY: Doubleday, 1976), 91.

41. Ibid., 85.

42. Hall and Hall, 1990, 6.

43. Hall, 1976, 91.

44. Hall and Hall, 1990, 6.

45. D. A. Foster, *Bargaining Across Borders* (New York: McGraw-Hill, 1992), 280.

46. Gudykunst, 2001, 32.

47. H.-C. Chang, "Communication in the Analects of Confucius," in *The Global Intercultural Communication Reader*, ed. M. K. Asante, Y. Miike, and J. Yin (New York: Routledge, 2008), 97.

48. Hall and Hall, 1990, 7.

49. Althen, 2011, 25.

50. G. Hofstede, *Culture's Consequences: International Differences in Work-Related Values*, 2nd ed. (Beverly Hills, CA: Sage, 2001); see also G. Hofstede, G.J. Hofstede, and M. Minkov, *Cultures and Organizations: Software of the Mind*, 3rd ed. (New York: McGraw-Hill, 2010).

51. P. B. Smith, M. H. Bond, and Ç. Kağitçibaşi, *Understanding Social Psychology Across Cultures* (Thousand Oaks, CA: Sage, 2006), 34.

52. P. A. Andersen, M. L. Hecht, G. D. Hoobler, and M. Smallwood, "Nonverbal Communication Across Cultures," in *Cross-Cultural and Intercultural Communication*, ed. W. B. Gudykunst (Thousand Oaks, CA: Sage, 2003), 77.

53. H. C. Triandis, *Individualism and Collectivism* (Boulder, CO: Westview Press, 1995); see also H. C. Triandis, "Cross-Cultural Studies of Individualism and Collectivism," in *Cross-Cultural Perspectives*, ed. J. J. Berman (Lincoln: University of Nebraska Press, 1990), 41–133.

54. D. Brooks, "Harmony and the Dream," *New York Times* (August 11, 2008), http://www.nytimes.com/2008/08/12/opinion/12brooks.html (accessed May 4, 2014).

55. Hofstede et al., 2010, 90.

56. C. Triandis, "Cross-Cultural Studies of Individualism and Collectivism," in *Cross-Cultural Perspectives*, ed. J. J. Berman (Lincoln: University of Nebraska Press, 1990), 52.

57. D. Etounga-Manguelle, "Does Africa Need a Cultural Adjustment Program?," in *Culture Matters: How Values Shape Human Progress*, ed. L. Harrison and S. P. Huntington (New York: Basic Books, 2000), 71.

58. T. Y.-J. Shim, M.-S. Kim, and J. N. Martin, *Changing Korea: Understanding Culture and Communication* (New York: Peter Lang, 2008), 27.

59. K. Belson and N. Onishi, "In Deference to Crisis, a New Obsession Sweeps Japan: Self- Restraint," *New York Times* (March 27, 2011), http://www.nytimes.com/2011/03/28/world/asia/28tokyo.html?ref=world (accessed May 4, 2014); "S. Korean psyche hit hard by sunk ferry," *Japan Times* May 20, 2014, 1–4.

60. Hofstede et al., 2010, 191.

61. E. Warnock. "Japanese Students Not Hot on Study Aboard," *Wall Street Journal: Japan* (April 12, 2012), http://blogs.wsj.com/japanrealtime/2012/04/12/japanese-students-not-hot-on-study-abroad, accessed May 5, 2014).

62. "Young People Not Interested in Overseas Work," *Japan Times* (May 28, 2014). http://www.japantimes.co.jp/news/2014/05/28/business/young-people-interested-overseas-work/#.U4udpBROW70 (accessed June 1, 2014).

63. Hofstede et al., 2010, 205.

64. Ibid., 55.

65. Ibid., 61.

66. W. B. Gudykunst, *Bridging Differences: Effective Intergroup Communication* (Thousand Oaks, CA: Sage, 2001), 62.

67. C. Calloway-Thomas, P. J. Cooper, and C. Blake, *Intercultural Communication: Roots and Routes* (Boston: Allyn and Bacon, 1999), 196.

68. J. Jang and J.-M. Park, "Children's corpses reveal desperate attempts to escape Korean ferry," *Reuters* (April 23, 2014) http://uk.reuters.com/article/2014/04/23/uk-korea-ship-idUKBREA3M03H20140423 (accessed May 6, 2014).

69. Adler and Gunderson, 2008, 57–58.

70. Hofstede et al., 2010, 140.

71. Adler and Gunderson, 2008, 57.

72. *Women in Elective Office, 2014: Fact Sheet* (Center for American Women and Politics, Eagleton Institute of Politics, Rutgers, the State University of New Jersey, 2014), http://www.cawp.rutgers.edu/fast_facts/levels_of_office/documents/elective.pdf (accessed May 5, 2014).

73. Hofstede et al., 2010, 140.

74. "Country overview," in *Global Database of Quotas for Women* (Quota Project, 2011 and 2013), http://www.quotaproject.org/country.cfm?SortOrder=Percentage (accessed May 5, 2014).

75. R. Hausmann, L. D. Tyson, Y. Bekhouche, and S. Zahidi, *The Global Gender Gap Index 2013* (Geneva, Switzerland: World Economic Forum, 2013), http://www3.weforum.org/docs/WEF_GenderGap_Report_2013.pdf (accessed May 5, 2014).

76. Chinese Culture Connection, "Chinese Values and the Search for Culture-Free Dimensions of Culture," *Journal of Cross-Cultural Psychology* 18 (1987): 143–64; see also G. Hofstede and M. H. Bond, "Confucius and Economic Growth: New Trends in Culture's Consequence," *Organizational Dynamics* 16 (1988): 4–21.

77. Hofstede, 2001, 351, 354.

78. Ibid., 351, 355.

79. M. Minkov and G. Hofstede, "Hofstede's Fifth Dimension: New Evidence from the World Values Survey," *Journal of Cross-Cultural Psychology*, December 15, 2010, 2, DOI: 10.1177/0022022110388567; For information on the World Values Survey, see http://www.worldvaluessurvey.org/wvs.jsp.

80. Ibid., 9.

81. Hofstede et al., 2010, 239, 254.

82. Minkov and Hofstede, 2010, 9.

83. Hofstede et al., 2010, 251.

84. M. Minkov, *Cultural Differences in a Globalized World* (United Kingdom: Emerald, 2011).

85. Ibid., 128; see also M. Minkov, "Monumentalism versus Flexumility," SIETAR Europa Congress (2007), http://www.sietareuropa.org/congress2007/files/congress2007_paper_Michael_Minkov.doc

86. Ibid., 195.

87. J. F. Embree, "Thailand—A Loosely Structured Social System," *American Anthropologist* 52, 2 (1950): 159–80; P. J. Pelto, "The Differences Between 'Tight' and 'Loose' Societies," *Transaction* 5, 5 (1968): 37–40; M. J. Gelfand et al., "Differences Between Tight and Loose Cultures: A 33-Nation Study," *Science* 332 (May 27, 2011): 1100–4; M. J. Gelfand, "Culture's Constraints: International Differences in the Strength of Social Norms," *Current Directions in Psychological Science*, 21, 16 (2012): 420–24.

88. H. C. Hu, "The Chinese Concepts of 'Face,'" *American Anthropologist*, 46, 1 (1044): 45–64.

89. K. Domenici and S. W. Littlejohn, *Facework: Bridging Theory and Practice* (Thousand Oaks, CA: Sage, 2006), 10.

90. S. Ting-Toomey, "The Matrix of Face: An Updated Face-Negotiation Theory," in *Theorizing About Intercultural Communication*, ed. W. B. Gudykunst (Thousand Oaks, CA: Sage, 2005), 73.

91. R. M. March, *Reading the Japanese Mind* (Tokyo: Kodansha, 1996), 28.

92. G. Gao and S. Ting-Toomey, *Communicating Effectively with the Chinese* (Thousand Oaks, CA: Sage, 1998), 54.

93. Smith et al., 2006, 159.

94. J. Oetzel, S. Ting-Toomey, M. I. Chew-Sanchez, R. Harris, R. Wilcox, and S. Stumpf, "Face and Facework in Conflicts With Parents and Siblings: A Cross-Cultural Comparison of Germans, Japanese, Mexicans, and U.S. Americans," *Journal of Family Communication* 3, 2 (2003): 67–93.

95. M. S. Kim, *Non-Western Perspectives on Human Communication* (Thousand Oaks, CA: Sage, 2002), 65.

96. S. Ting-Toomey and A. Kurogi, "Facework Competence in Intercultural Conflict: An Updated Face-Negotiation Theory," *International Journal of Intercultural Relations* 22 (1998): 202.

Chapter 7

1. K. Tracy and J. S. Robles, *Everyday Talk: Building and Reflecting Identities* (New York: Guilford Press, 2013), 21.

2. S. Ting-Toomey, "Identity Negotiation Theory: Crossing Cultural Boundaries," in *Theorizing About Intercultural Communication*, ed. W. B. Gudykunst (Thousand Oaks, CA: Sage, 2005), 212.

3. M. Fong, "Identity and the Speech Community," in *Communicating Ethnic and Cultural Identity*, ed. M. Fong and R. Chuang (Lanham, MD: Rowman & Littlefield, 2004), 6.

4. Ibid.

5. S. Ting-Toomey and L. C. Chung, *Understanding Intercultural Communication* (Los Angeles: Roxbury, 2005), 93.

6. I. E. Klyukanov, *Principles of Intercultural Communication* (Boston: Pearson Education, 2005), 12.

7. F. Dervin, "Cultural identity, representation, and Othering," in *The Routledge Handbook of Language and Intercultural Communication*, ed. J. Jackson (New York: Routledge, 2012), 183.

8. J. C. Turner, *Rediscovering the Social Group: A Self-Categorization Theory* (Oxford: Basil Blackwell, 1987), 45.

9. B. J. Hall, *Among Cultures: The Challenge of Communication*, 2nd ed. (Belmont, CA: Thomson-Wadsworth, 2005), 108–9.

10. W. B. Gudykunst, *Bridging Differences: Effective Intergroup Communication*, 4th ed. (Thousand Oaks, CA: Sage, 2004), 77.

11. J. S. Phinney, "A Three-Stage Model of Ethnic Identity Development in Adolescence," in *Ethnic Identity: Formation and Transmission Among Hispanics and Other Minorities*, ed. M. E. Bernal and G. P. Knight (Albany: State University of New York Press, 1993), 62.

12. K. R. Humes, N. A. Jones, and R. R. Ramirez, *Overview of Race and Hispanic Origin: 2010* (Washington, DC: U.S. Census Bureau), http://www.census.gov/prod/cen2010/briefs/c2010br-02.pdf (accessed December 29, 2014), 4, 9–10.

13. A. Brittingham and G. P. de la Cruz, *Ancestry: 2000*, Census 2000 Brief (Washington, DC: Census 2000 Brief, U.S. Census Bureau), http://www.census.gov/prod/2004pubs/c2kbr-35.pdf (accessed December 29, 2014) 3, 9.

14. M. L. Hecht, R. L. Jackson II, and S. A. Ribeau, *African American Communication: Exploring Identity and Culture*, 2nd ed. (Mahwah, NJ: Lawrence Erlbaum Associates, 2003), 62.

15. M. MacMillan, *Dangerous Games: The Uses and Abuses of History* (New York: Modern Library, 2010), 54–58.

16. W. A. Haviland, H. E. L. Prins, B. McBride, and D. Walrath, *Cultural Anthropology: The Human Challenge*, 14th ed. (Belmont, CA: Wadsworth Cengage Learning, 2014), 96.

17. P. B. Smith, M. H. Bond, and Ç. Kağitçibaşi, *Understanding Social Psychology Across Cultures: Living and Working in a Changing World* (Thousand Oaks, CA: Sage, 2006), 224.

18. "Explore the Form" *United States Census 2010*, http://www.census.gov /2010census/about/interactive-form .php (accessed December 29, 2014).

19. C. P. Kottak and K. A. Kozaitis, *On Being Different: Diversity and Multiculturalism in the North American Mainstream*, 2nd ed. (New York: McGraw-Hill, 2003), 92.

20. Ting-Toomey, 2005, 213.

21. R. Felder, "Manly Manicures End in Color," *New York Times* (June 12, 2013), http://www.nytimes.com/2013 /06/13/fashion/manly-manicures-end -in-color.html (accessed December 29, 2013).

22. P. Cohen, "Professor is a Label That Leans to the Left," *New York Times* (January 18, 2010), http://www .nytimes.com/2010/01/18/arts /18liberal.html (accessed December 28, 2014).

23. L. Gross, "More Men Join Nursing Field as Stigma Starts to Fade," *USA Today* (July 10, 2013), http://www .usatoday.com/story/news/nation /2013/07/10/men-join-nursing-field -as-stigma-fades/2504803 (accessed June 16, 2015).

24. W. L. Williams, "The 'two-spirit' people of indigenous North Americans," *The Guardian* (October 11, 2010), http://www.theguardian.com /music/2010/oct/11/two-spirit-people -north-america (accessed June 16, 2015).

25. H. Beech, "Where the 'Ladyboys' Are," *Time World* (July 7, 2008), http://www.time.com/time/world /article/0,8599,1820633,00.html (accessed November 29, 2014).

26. "A question of sex," *The Economist* (October 17, 2010), http://www .economist.com/node/14646491 (accessed November 29, 2014).

27. K. Steinmetz, "America's Transition," *Time* (June 9, 2014), 38–40.

28. M. J. Collier, "Researching Cultural Identity: Reconciling Interpretive and Postcolonial Perspectives," in *Communication and Identity Across Cultures*, ed. D. V. Tanno and A. Gonzalez (Thousand Oaks, CA: Sage, 1998), 38.

29. V. Chen, "(De)hyphenated Identity: The Double Voice of the Woman Warrior" in *Our Voices*, 4th ed., A. González, M. Houston, and V. Chen, eds. (Los Angeles: Roxbury, 2004), 20.

30. T. R. Reid, *The United States of Europe* (New York: Penguin Press, 2004), 200.

31. K. Willsher, "'My absolute priority is housing,' says Paris' first female mayor," *Los Angeles Times* (July 27, 2014), http://www.latimes.com/world /europe/la-fg-france-paris-hidalgo-q-a -20140727-story.html (accessed December 28, 2014).

32. G. W. Allport, *The Nature of Prejudice* (Reading, MA: Addison-Wesley, 1954), 116.

33. P. J. Spiro, "The evolving acceptance of dual citizenship," *Los Angeles Times* (October 29, 2014), http://www .latimes.com/opinion/op-ed/la-oe -spiro-dual-citizenship-advantages -20141030-story.html (accessed June 16, 2015). For a more comprehensive discussion, see Peter J. Spiro, *Beyond Citizenship: American Identity After Globalization* (New York: Oxford University Press, 2008).

34. R. Dixon, "Rwanda makes great progress 20 years after genocide," *Los Angeles Times* (April 7, 2014), http:// www.latimes.com/world/africa/la-fg -rwanda-genocide -20140407,0,326593.story#axz z2yEQDH9xT (accessed June 16, 2015); J. Tepperman, "Progress,

Rwandan style," *Los Angeles Times* (April 6, 2014), http://www.latimes .com/opinion/commentary/la-oe -tepperman-rwanda -20140406,0,7721887.story#axz z2y9UokcZI (accessed June 16, 2015).

35. K. Maurer, "Afghan commandos' esprit de corps transcends tribe," *Seattle Times* (September 12, 2009), http://seattletimes.nwsource.com /html/nationworld/2009854105 _apasafghancommandos.html (accessed December 17, 2014).

36. C. J. Williams, "In Lviv, Ukraine, the nation's east-west divide is on display," *Los Angeles Times* (May 25, 2014), http://www.latimes.com/world /europe/la-fg-ukraine-identity -20140525-story.html (accessed December 17, 2014).

37. S. E. Cross, E. E. Hardin, and B. Gercek-Swing, "The What, How, Why, and Where of Self-Construal," *Personality and Social Psychology Review* 15, 2 (2011: 142–79. DOI: 10.1177/1088868310373752; see also S. Adams, "Information Behavior and the Formation and Maintenance of Peer Cultures in Massive Multiplayer Online Role-Playing Games: A Case Study of City of Heroes," *Proceedings of DiGRA 2005 Conference: Changing Views – Worlds in Play*, Digital Games Research Conference 2005, June 16–20, 2005, Vancouver, British Columbia, Canada, http://www.digra.org /wp-content/uploads/digital-library /06278.15067.pdf (accessed December 19, 2014).

38. S. Cross, "Self-Construal," *Oxford Bibliographies* (2011), http://www. oxfordbibliographies.com/view /document/obo-9780199828340 /obo-9780199828340-0051.xml (accessed December 19, 2014).

39. Cross et al., 2011, 144.

40. J. Suler, "Identity Management in Cyberspace," *Journal of Applied Psychoanalytic Studies*, 4, 4 (2002): 455.

41. Ibid., 457.

42. "Growing opportunities for games, comics and animation in Hong Kong," Hong Kong Trade Development Council (HKTDC) (2014), http://www.hktdc.com/info/webcast /v/en/en/1X04C7E1/Growing

-Opportunities-For-Games-Comics
-And-Animation-In-Hong-Kong.htm
(accessed June 16, 2015).

43. M. Cieply and B. Barnes, "Large
Crowds Spend Little at Comic-Con,"
New York Times (July 27, 2014),
http://www.nytimes.com/2014/07/28
/business/media/large-crowds-spend
-little-at-comic-con.html?_r=0
(accessed December 20, 2014).

44. C. Shalev and JTA, "Study: Orthodox community boosts New York
City's Jewish population," *Haaretz*
(June 12, 2012), http://www.haaretz.
com/jewish-world/jewish-world-news
/study-orthodox-community-boosts
-new-york-city-s-jewish-population
-1.436007 (accessed June 16, 2015);
S. Otterman, "Jewish Population Is
Up in the New York Region," *New
York Times* (January 17, 2013), http://
www.nytimes.com/2013/01/18/nyre
gion/reversing-past-trend-new-yorks
-jewish-population-rises.html?_r=0
(accessed December 28, 2014).

45. "Hijab couture," *The Economist*,
April 26, 2014, 58.

46. F. F. Zakaria, "Why they still hate us,
13 years later," *Washington Post*
(September 4, 2014), http://www.
washingtonpost.com/opinions/fareed
-zakaria-why-they-still-hate-us-13-
years-later/2014/09/04/64f3f4fa-3466
-11e4-9e92-0899b306bbea_story.
html (accessed December 21, 2014).

47. Ting-Toomey, 2005, 211.

48. W. Meissner, "China's Search for
Cultural and National Identity from
the Nineteenth Century to the
Present," *China Perspectives* 68
(November–December 2006): 41,
http://chinaperspectives.revues.org
/3103 (accessed June 16, 2015).

49. Ting-Toomey, 2005, 212.

50. Phinney, 1993, 61–79, 66.

51. J. N. Martin, R. L. Krizek, T. K.
Nakayama, and L. Bradford, "Exploring Whiteness: A Study of Self Labels
for White Americans, *Communication
Quarterly* 44 (1996): 125.

52. Phinney, 1993, 69.

53. D. V. Tanno, "Names, Narratives,
and the Evolution of Ethnic Identity,"
in *Our Voices*, 4th ed., ed. A.

González, M. Houston, and V. Chen
(Los Angeles: Roxbury, 2004), 39.

54. Phinney, 1993, 76.

55. J. N. Martin and T. K. Nakayama,
*Intercultural Communication in Con-
texts*, 6th ed. (New York: McGraw-
Hill, 2012), 179–85.

56. Ibid.

57. Ibid.

58. "Background," *'Hafu'/Half Japanese*
(2010), http://www.hafujapanese.org
/index.html (accessed June 16, 2015).

59. *The Hapa Project* (n.d.), http://www
.thehapaproject.com (accessed
June 16, 2015).

60. Hall, 2005, 117.

61. G. A. Yep, "My Three Cultures: Navi-
gating the Multicultural Identity
Landscape," in *Readings in Intercultural
Communication*, ed. J. N. Martin,
T. K. Nakayama, and L. A. Flores
(Boston: McGraw-Hill, 2002), 63.

62. A. D. Buckley and M. C. Kenney,
*Negotiating Identity: Rhetoric,
Metaphor, and Social Drama in
Northern Ireland* (Washington, DC:
Smithsonian Institution Press, 1995).

63. J. A. Drzewiecka and N. Draznin,
"A Polish Jewish American Story:
Collective Memories and Intergroup
Relations," in *Intercultural Communi-
cation: A Reader*, 11th ed., ed. L. A.
Samovar, R. E. Porter, and E. R.
McDaniel (Belmont, CA: Thomson-
Wadsworth, 2005), 73.

64. H. C. Triandis, *Individualism and
Collectivism* (Boulder, CO: Westview
Press, 1995), 71; see also Martin and
Nakayama, 2008, 91.

65. M. Y. Ishikida, *Japanese Education in
the 21st Century* (New York: iUni-
verse, 2005), 59.

66. H. W. Gardiner and C. Kosmitzki,
Lives Across Cultures, 4th ed. (Boston:
Allyn and Bacon, 2008), 71.

67. D. H. Palfrey, "La Quinceañera: a
celebration of budding womanhood,"
(1997), http://www.mexconnect.com
/articles/3192-la-quincea%C3%
B1eraa-celebration-of-budding
-womanhood (accessed June 16,
2015).

68. Gardiner and Kosmitzki, 2008, 73.

69. G. David and K. K. Ayouby, "Being
Arab and Becoming Americanized:
Forms of Mediated Assimilation in
Metropolitan Detroit," in *Muslim
Minorities in the West*, ed. Y. Y.
Haddad and J. I. Smith (Walnut Creek,
CA: Altamira Press, 2002), 131.

70. Ibid.

71. Ibid.

72. A. Giddens, *Runaway World: How
Globalization is Reshaping our Lives*
(New York: Routledge, 1999), 13.

73. A. Naz, W. Khan, M. Hussain, and
U. Daraz, "The Crises of Identity:
Globalization and Its Impacts on
Socio-Cultural and Psychological
Identity among Pakhtuns of Khyber
Pakhtunkhwa Pakistan," *International
Journal of Academic Research in
Business and Social Sciences* 1, 1
(April 2011): 2, http://www.hrmars.
com/admin/pics/8.pdf (accessed
December 24, 2014).

74. S. Erlanger, "French Mosque's
Symbolism Varies With Beholder,"
New York Times (December 27,
2009), http://www.nytimes.com/2009
/12/28/world/europe/28marseille
.html?pagewanted=all (accessed
December 28, 2014).

75. P. Simon, *French National Identity and
Integration: Who Belongs to the
National Community?* (Washington,
DC: Transatlantic Council on
Migration, 2012), 2, http://www
.migrationpolicy.org/research/TCM
-french-national-identity (accessed
December 28, 2014).

76. R. Chuang, "Theoretical Perspective:
Fluidity and Complexity of Cultural
and Ethnic Identity," in *Communicating Ethnic and Cultural Identity*, ed.
M. Fong and R. Chuang (Lanham,
MD: Rowman & Littlefield, 2004),
65.

77. J. N. Martin, T. K. Nakayama, and L.
A. Flores, "Identity and Intercultural
Communication" in *Readings in
Intercultural Communication*, ed.
J. N. Martin, T. K. Nakayama, and
L. A. Flores (Boston: McGraw-Hill,
2002), 33.

78. J. Hitt, "The Newest Indians," *New
York Times Magazine*, August 21,
2005, http://www.nytimes.com/2005

/08/21/magazine/21NATIVE.html? pagewanted=print&_r=0 (accessed June 16, 2015).

79. J. Kotkin and T. Tseng, "Happy to Mix It All Up," *Washington Post*, June 8, 2003, B-1.

80. Hitt, 2005.

81. C. Onwumechili, P. O. Nwosu, R. L. Jackson II, and J. James-Hughes, "In the Deep Valley with Mountains to Climb: Exploring Identity and Multiple Reacculturation," *International Journal of Intercultural Relations* 27 (2003): 42; C. Onwumechili, P. O. Nwosu, and R. L. Jackson II, "Straddling Cultural Borders: Exploring Identity in Multiple Reacculturation," in *Intercultural Communication: A Reader*, 14th ed., ed. L. A. Samovar, R. E. Porter, E. R. McDaniel, and C. S. Roy (Boston: Cengage Learning, 2015), 92–104.

82. Hitt, 2005.

83. Hecht et al., 61.

84. T. T. Imahori and W. R. Cupach, "Identity Management Theory: Face Work in Intercultural Relations," in *Theorizing About Intercultural Communication*, ed. W. B. Gudykunst (Thousand Oaks, CA: Sage, 2005), 197.

85. M. J. Collier, "Cultural Identity and Intercultural Communication," in *Intercultural Communication: A Reader*, 14th ed., ed. L. A. Samovar, R. E. Porter, E. R. McDaniel, and C. S. Roy (Boston: Cengage Learning, 2015), 59.

Chapter 8

1. E. A. Schultz and R. H. Lavenda, *Cultural Anthropology: A Perspective on the Human Condition*, 8th ed. (New York: Oxford University Press, 2012), 90.

2. D. M. Newman, *Sociology: Exploring the Architecture of Everyday Life*, 3rd ed. (Los Angeles: Sage, 2013), 29–30.

3. C. Ryan, "Language Use in the United States: 2011," http://www .census.gov/prod/2013pubs/acs-22.pdf (accessed December 8, 2014).

4. G. P. Ferraro, *The Cultural Dimension of International Business*, 5th ed.

(Upper Saddle River, NJ: Pearson Prentice Hall, 2006), 47.

5. D. Crystal, *The Cambridge Encyclopedia of Language*, 2nd ed. (New York: Cambridge University Press, 2003), 10.

6. Ibid., 42.

7. Z. Hua, *Exploring Intercultural Communication: Language in Action* (New York: Routledge, 2014), 203.

8. Crystal, 2003, 21.

9. D. Solomon and J. Theiss, *Interpersonal Communication: Putting Theory into Practice* (New York: Routledge, 2013), 131.

10. R. West and L. H. Turner, *Understanding Interpersonal Communication: Making Choices in Changing Times*, 2nd ed. (Boston: Wadsworth Cengage Learning, 2009), 121.

11. G. Bailey and J. Peoples, *Essentials of Cultural Anthropology*, 3rd ed. (Belmont, CA: Wadsworth Cengage Learning, 2014), 55.

12. G. Deutscher, *Through the Language Glass: Why the World Looks Different in Other Languages* (New York: Henry Holt and Company, 2010), 130.

13. D. G. Mandelbaum, ed., *Selected Writings of Edward Sapir* (Berkeley: University of California Press, 1949), 162.

14. S. Nanda and R. L. Warms, *Cultural Anthropology*, 11th ed. (Belmont, CA: Wadsworth Cengage Learning, 2014), 90.

15. E. M. Rogers and T. M. Steinfatt, *Intercultural Communication* (Prospect Heights, IL: Waveland Press, 1998), 25.

16. Hua, 2014, 175.

17. N. Bonvillain, *Language, Culture, and Communication: The Meaning of Messages*, 4th ed. (Upper Saddle River, NJ: Prentice Hall, 2003), 46.

18. Z. Salzmann, *Language, Culture, and Society: An Introduction to Linguistic Anthropology*, 4th ed. (Boulder, CO: Westview Press, 2007), 58.

19. "American Indians: Gambling on Nation-building," *The Economist*, April 7, 2012, 35.

20. B. F. Shearer, "Context: The Land, the People, the Past, the Present," in

Culture and Customs of the United States, vol. 1, ed. B. F. Shearer (Westport, CT: Greenwood Press, 2008), 31.

21. A. C. Cargile, "Language Matters," in *Intercultural Communication: A Reader*, 14th ed., ed. L. A. Samovar, R. E. Porter, E. R. McDaniel, C. S. Roy (Boston: Cengage Learning, 2015), 251.

22. T. Novinger, *Intercultural Communication: A Practical Guide* (Austin: University of Texas Press, 2001), 49.

23. W. V. Schmidt, R. N. Conaway, S. E. Easton, and W. J. Wardrope, *Communicating Globally: Intercultural Communication and International Business* (Los Angeles: Sage, 2007), 87.

24. D. Crystal, *How Language Works: How Babies Babble, Words Change Meanings, and Languages Live or Die* (New York: Overlook Press, 2006), 290.

25. http://www.english.wisc.edu/rfyoung /336/dialects.pdf (accessed July 17, 2014).

26. Schmidt et al., 2007, 87.

27. Crystal, 2003, 314.

28. Ibid., 53.

29. D. Crystal, *Words, Words, Words* (New York: Oxford University Press, 2006), 113.

30. Ferraro, 2006, 29.

31. C. Ryan, 2011, 2.

32. E. Y. Kim, *The Yin and Yang of American Culture: A Paradox* (Yarmouth, ME: Intercultural Press, 2001), 31.

33. J. C. Condon, *Good Neighbors: Communicating with the Mexicans* (Yarmouth, ME: Intercultural Press, 1985), 50.

34. A. Riding, *Distant Neighbors: A Portrait of Mexico* (New York: Knopf, 1985), 8.

35. N. Crouch, *Mexicans and Americans: Cracking the Cultural Code* (Yarmouth, ME: Nicholas Brealey Publishing, 2004), 56.

36. T. Novinger, *Communicating with Brazilians: When "Yes" Means "No"* (Austin: University of Texas Press, 2003), 154.

37. Ibid., 156.

38. Ibid., 157.

39. J. Yin, "Confucian Communication Theory," in *Encyclopedia of Communication*, ed. S. W. Littlejohn and K. A. Foss (Thousand Oaks, CA: Sage, 2009), 172.

40. Y. Miike, "An Asiacentric Reflection on Eurocentric Bias in Communication Theory," *Communication Monographs* 74, 2 (June 2007): 274.

41. H. Wenzhong and C. Grove, *Encountering the Chinese*, 3rd ed. (Boston: Intercultural Press, 2010), xxv–xxvii.

42. G. Gao and S. Ting-Toomey, *Communicating Effectively with the Chinese* (Thousand Oaks, CA: Sage, 1998), 17.

43. Wenzhong and Grove, 2010, 4.

44. C. Lee, *Cowboys and Dragons* (Chicago: Dearborn Trade Publishing, 2003), 81.

45. Gao and Ting-Toomey, 1998, 60–81.

46. Wenzhong and Grove, 2010, 39–42.

47. T. Y. Shim, M-S. Kim, and J. N. Martin, *Changing Korea: Understanding Culture and Communication* (New York: Peter Lang, 2008), 57.

48. Ibid., 65.

49. D. W. Klopf and J. C. McCroskey, *Intercultural Communication Encounters* (Boston: Pearson Education, 2007), 189.

50. J. Hendry, *Understanding Japanese Society* 3rd ed. (New York: Routledge, 2003), 52.

51. D. C. Barnlund, *Communicative Styles of Japanese and Americans* (Belmont, CA: Wadsworth Publishing Company, 1989), 42.

52. R. Patai, *The Arab Mind*, rev. ed. (New York: Hatherleigh Press, 2002), 45–46; "A God-given way to communicate," *The Economist*, April 24, 2010, 47.

53. M. K. Nydell, *Understanding Arabs*, 5th ed. (Boston: Intercultural Press, 2013), 89.

54. *Public Relations Review* 21, 3 (1995): 245–46.

55. Ibid., 249.

56. Nydell, 2013, 99.

57. E. Feghali, "Arab Cultural Communication Patterns," *International Journal of Intercultural Relations* 21, 3 (1997): 361.

58. E. T. Hall and M. R. Hall, *Understanding Cultural Differences* (Yarmouth, ME: Intercultural Press, 1990), 49.

59. G. Ness, *Germany: Unraveling the Enigma* (Yarmouth, ME: Intercultural Press, 2000), 63.

60. Hall and Hall, 1990, 49.

61. Ness, 2000, 79.

62. T. Morrison and W. A. Conaway, *Kiss, Bow or Shake Hands: Sales and Marketing* (New York: McGraw-Hill, 2012), 83.

63. C. Kellogg, "Before Translation, It Was Nothing but Babel," *Los Angeles Times*, October 16, 2011, E12.

64. J. Sharples, "With half the world's population speaking English, it's a great time to be a teacher," http://www.telegraph.co.uk/education/expat education/4195890/With-half-the -worlds-population-speaking-English -its-a-great-time-to-be-a-teacher.html (accessed June 17, 2015).

65. "Translation and the European Union," http://ec.europa.eu/dgs/trans lation/translating/index_en.htm (accessed June 18, 2015).

66. *2010 Language Need and Interpreter Use California Superior Courts*, (The Institute of Social Research: California State University, Sacramento, May 2010), http://www.courts.ca.gov /documents/language-interpreterneed -10.pdf (accessed June 17, 2015).

67. C. Knoll, "After federal probe, state examines need for civil court interpreters," *Los Angeles Times*, http:// www.latimes.com/local/countygo vernment/la-me-language-access -courts-20141105-story.html#page=1 (accessed December 5, 2014).

68. T. Kumeh, "Patient-interpreter Bill Aims to Overcome Language Barriers," *Los Angeles Times*, http://www .latimes.com/news/local/la-me -interpreters-20130819,0,56108.story (accessed August 13, 2014).

69. J. E. Rudd and D. R. Lawson, *Communicating in Global Business Negotiations: A Geocentric Approach* (Los Angeles: Sage, 2007), 87.

70. "Skype to Feature Real-time Translation," *This Week*, June 13, 2014, 16.

71. http://www.extremetech.com /extreme/12208-microsoft-unveils -universal-translator-that-converts -your-voice-into-another-language (accessed August 15, 2014).

72. D. Crystal, *How Language Works*, 2006, 484.

73. B. B. Lai, "Three Worlds: Inheritance and Experience," in *Translating Lives: Living with Two Languages and Cultures*, ed. M. Besemeres and A. Wierzbicka (Queensland, Australia: University of Queensland, 2007), 27.

74. J. Wong, "East Meets West, or Does It Really?," in *Translating Lives: Living with Two Languages and Cultures*, ed. M. Besemeres and A. Wierzbicka (Queensland, Australia: University of Queensland, 2007), 22.

75. Personal conversation with Bert Adams, Metris Company, Nagoya, Japan, July 2008.

76. Crystal, 2003, 362.

77. "Special Eurobarometer 386: Europeans and Their Languages," (June 2012) European Commission, http://ec.europa.eu/public_opinion /archives/ebs/ebs_386_en.pdf (accessed August 24, 2015).

78. T. Fukada, "Takaki Stresses Value of Foreign Languages," *Japan Times*, October 13, 2011, 3.

79. "Benefits of Mindfulness," http:// www.helpguide.org/harvard/mindful ness.htm (accessed September 10, 2014).

80. W. G. Gudykunst, *Bridging Differences*, 4th ed. (Thousand Oaks, CA: Sage, 2004), 32.

81. D. Morales, "Battling language's law of diminishing returns," *Japan Times*, October 20, 2011, 13.

82. Ferraro, 2006, 72.

83. Crystal, 2003, 8.

84. L. H. Chaney and J. S. Martin, *Intercultural Business Communication*, 4th ed. (Upper Saddle River, NJ: Pearson Prentice Hall, 2007), 102.

85. Ibid., 103.

86. Ferraro, 2006, 72.

87. Schmidt et al., 2007, 195.

Chapter 9

1. J. Silverman and P. Kinnersley, "Doctors' Non-verbal Behaviour in Consultations: Look at the Patient Before You Look at the Computer," *British Journal of General Practice* 60 (2010): 76.

2. D. C. Barnlund, *Interpersonal Communication: Survey and Studies* (Boston: Houghton Mifflin, 1968), 536–37.

3. E. Goffman, *The Presentation of Self in Everyday Life* (New York: Doubleday, 1957), 2.

4. L. Knapp, J. A. Hall, and T. G. Horgan, *Nonverbal Communication in Human Interaction*, 8th ed. (Boston: Wadsworth Cengage Learning, 2014), 8.

5. S. P. Morreale, B. H. Spitzberg, and J. K. Barge, *Human Communication: Motivation, Knowledge, and Skills*, 2nd ed. (Belmont, CA: Thomson Wadsworth, 2007), 113.

6. A. Tucker, "The Body of Work," Smithsonian, October 2010, 56. For a further examination of nonverbal communication and identity, see J. T. Wood, *Communication Mosaics*, 6th ed. (Boston: Wadsworth Cengage Learning, 2011), 103.

7. V. P. Richmond, J. C. McCroskey, and M. L. Hickson III, *Nonverbal Behavior in Interpersonal Relations*, 7th ed. (New York: Allyn & Bacon, 2012), 11.

8. L. Beamer and I. Varner, *Intercultural Communication in the Global Workplace* (New York: McGraw-Hill, 2001), 160.

9. D. Matsumoto, M. G. Frank, and H. S. Hwang, *Nonverbal Communication: Science and Application* (Los Angeles: Sage, 2013) 113–14.

10. P. C. Rosenblatt, "Grief in Small-Scale Societies," in *Death and Bereavement Across Cultures*, ed. C. M. Parks, P. Laungani, and B. Young (New York: Routledge, 1997), 36.

11. E. T. Hall, *The Silent Language* (New York: Fawcett, 1959), xii–xiii.

12. *The Week*, February 1, 2013, 16.

13. Knapp et al., 2014, 154–55.

14. Richmond et al., 2012, 25.

15. Ibid., 33–34.

16. Y. Richmond and P. Gestrin, *Into Africa: Intercultural Insights* (Yarmouth, ME: Intercultural Press, 1998), 45.

17. H. Wenzhong, C. N. Grove, and Z. Enping, *Encountering the Chinese*, 3rd ed. (Yarmouth, ME: Intercultural Press, 2010), 120.

18. *The Week*, July 16, 2010, 6.

19. M. S. Remland, *Nonverbal Communication in Everyday Life* (New York: Houghton Mifflin, 2000), 113–14.

20. S. Dolnick, "Ethnic Differences Emerge in Plastic Surgery," *New York Times* (February 18, 2011), http://www.nytimes.com/2011/02/19nyregion/19plastic.html?pagewanted=all (accessed January 9, 2014).

21. L. A. Vazquez, E. Garcia-Vazquez, S. A. Bauman, and A. S. Sierra, "Skin Color, Acculturation, and Community Interest among Mexican-American Students: A Research Note," *Hispanic Journal of Behavioral Sciences* 19 (1997): 337.

22. E. Folb, "Who's Got the Room at the Top? Issues of Dominance and Non-dominance in Intracultural Communication," in *Intercultural Communication: A Reader*, 14th ed., ed. L. A. Samovar, R. E. Porter, E. R. McDaniel, and C. S. Roy (Boston: Wadsworth Cengage Learning, 2014), 154–61.

23. G. E. Codina and F. F. Montalvo, "Chicano Phenotype and Depression," *Hispanic Journal of Behavioral Sciences* 16 (1994): 296–306.

24. S. Watson and P. F. Dejong, "Ethical Responses to Public Allegations of Skin Tone Manipulation in Print Advertising: Consumer Indifference or Consumer Concern," *Journal of Promotion Management* 17 (2011): 397.

25. D. Levin, "Beach Essentials in China: Flip-Flops, a Towel and a Ski Mask," *New York Times* (August 3, 2012), http://nytimes.com/imagepages/2012/08/04/world/asia/MASKS.html (accessed June 22, 2015).

26. R. Ross, *Clothing: A Global History* (Malden, MA: Polity Press, 2008), 3.

27. M. Hamilton, "Teen Who Murdered Baby in Dad's Arms Gets 90 Years to Life," *Los Angeles Times*, (June 21, 2013), http://articles.latimes.com/2013/jun/21/local/la-me-gangmember-sentenced-20130622 (accessed January 9, 2014).

28. S. B. Kaiser, "Women's Appearance and Clothing within Organizations," in *The Nonverbal Communication Reader*, 3rd ed., ed. L. K. Guerrero and M. L. Hecht (Lake Grove, IL: Waveland Press, 2008), 74–81.

29. S. M. Torrawa, "Every Robe He Dons Becomes Him," *Parabola*, Fall 1994, 21.

30. Torrawa, 1994, 25.

31. "Women and Veils: Running for Cover," *The Economist* (May 13, 2010), http://www.economist.com/node/16113091 (accessed June 22, 2015).

32. M. Cohen, "France Uncovered," review of *Why the French Don't Like Headscarves*, by J. Bowen, *New York Times* (April 1, 2007), http://www.nytimes.com/2007/04/01/books/review/Cohen.t.html (accessed January 8, 2014).

33. "Helping to Free Muslim Women," *The Week*, April 16, 2010, 15.

34. W. V. Ruch, *International Handbook of Corporate Communication* (Jefferson, NC: McFarland, 1989), 242.

35. E. T. Hall and M. R. Hall, *Understanding Cultural Differences: Germans, French and Americans* (Yarmouth, ME: Intercultural Press, 1990), 53.

36. T. Gochenour, *Considering Pilipinos* (Yarmouth, ME: Intercultural Press, 1990).

37. E. McDaniel, "Nonverbal Communication: A Reflection of Cultural Themes," in *Intercultural Communication: A Reader*, 14th ed., ed. L. A. Samovar, R. E. Porter, E. R. McDaniel, and C. S. Roy (Boston: Wadsworth Cengage Learning, 2014), 246.

38. Y. Yamada, O. Takahashi, S. Ohde, G. Deshpande, and T. Fukui, "Patients' Preferences for Doctors'

Attire in Japan," *Internal Medicine* 49 (2010): 1521.

39. G. E. Adamo, "Nigerian Dress as a Symbolic Language," *Semiotica* 184 (2011): 8.

40. T. J. Whande, "Look! My body is talking to you," *Sunday Standard*, Online ed., (July 22, 2007), http://www.sundaystandard.info/article.php?NewsID=1796&GroupID=2 (accessed June 22, 2015).

41. S. Stevenson, "How to be Invisible," *Newsweek*, April 19, 2010, 12.

42. Richmond et al., 2012, 51.

43. S. Loygren, "Fear Is Spread by Body Language, Study Says," *National Geographic News* (November 16, 2004), http://news.nationalgeographic.com/news/2004/11/1116_041116_fear_posture.html (accessed March 27, 2014).

44. "Row Over the Bow," *Newsweek*, November 30, 2009, 15.

45. S. Ishii, "Characteristics of Japanese Nonverbal Communication Behavior," *Communication* 2 (1973): 163–80.

46. G. Ness, *Germany: Unraveling an Enigma* (Yarmouth, ME: Intercultural Press, 2000), 93.

47. Remland, 2000, 229.

48. R. Cooper and N. Cooper, *Culture Shock: Thailand* (Portland, OR: Graphic Arts Center, 1994), 22–23.

49. M. L. Hecht, M. J. Collier, and S. A. Ribeau, *African American Communication: Ethnic Identity and Cultural Interpretation* (Newbury Park, CA: Sage, 1993), 102.

50. D. Glanton, "Obama's Ways Cool to Some, New to Others," *Chicago Tribune*, January 25, 2009.

51. D. Archer, "Unspoken Diversity: Cultural Differences in Gestures," *Qualitative Sociology* 20 (1997): 81.

52. R. G. Harper, A. N. Wiens, and J. D. Matarazzo, *Nonverbal Communication: The State of the Art* (New York: Wiley, 1978), 164.

53. P. Ekman and W. V. Friesen, "Hand Movements," in *The Nonverbal Communication Reader*, 3rd ed., ed. L. K. Guerrero and M. L. Hecht (Long Grove, IL: Waveland Press, 2008), 105.

54. D. Matsumoto and H. S. Hwang, "Body and Gestures," in *Nonverbal Communication: Science and Applications*, ed. D. Matsumoto, M. G. Frank, and H. S. Hwang (Los Angeles: Sage, 2013), 79.

55. Hamiru-aqui, *70 Japanese Gestures: No Language Communication* (Tokyo: IBC Publishing, 2004), 49.

56. Ibid., 99.

57. *Handbook for Teaching Korean-American Students* (Sacramento: California Department of Education, 1992), 95.

58. M. K. Nydell, *Understanding Arabs: A Contemporary Guide to Arab Society*, 5th ed. (Boston: Intercultural Press, 2012), 28.

59. T. Novinger, *Communicating with Brazilians* (Austin: University of Texas Press, 2003), 173.

60. Nydell, 2012, 27.

61. M. Kim, "A Comparative Analysis of Nonverbal Expression as Portrayed by Korean and American Print-Media Advertising," *Howard Journal of Communications* 3 (1992): 321.

62. Ruch, 1989, 191.

63. Richmond et al., 2012, 73.

64. Ibid., 74–75.

65. P. Ekman, "Face Muscles Talk Every Language," *Psychology Today*, September 1975, 35–39. See also P. Ekman, W. Friesen, and P. Ellsworth, *Emotion in the Human Face: Guidelines for Research and an Integration of the Findings* (New York: Pergamon Press, 1972).

66. P. A. Andersen, "The Basis of Cultural Differences in Nonverbal Communication," in *Intercultural Communication: A Reader*, 13th ed., ed. L. A. Samovar, R. E. Porter, and E. R. McDaniel (Boston: Wadsworth Cengage Learning, 2011), 294.

67. R. E. Porter and L. A. Samovar, "Cultural Influences on Emotional Expression: Implications for Intercultural Communication," in *Handbook of Communication and Emotion: Research, Theory Applications, and Contexts*, ed. P. A. Andersen and

L. K. Guerrero (San Diego: Academic Press, 1998), 454.

68. Richmond et al., 2012, 77.

69. A. Mehrabian, *Nonverbal Communication* (New Brunswick, CT: Aldine Transaction, 2007), 144.

70. M. Maynard, "An Apology from Toyota's Leader," *New York Times* (February 24, 2010), http.nytimes.com/2010/02/25/business/global/25toyota.html?pagewanted=print (accessed May 30, 2011).

71. M. Sharifabad and S. Vali, "A Comparative Study of Native and Non-Native Body Language: The Case of Americans' Kinesics vs. Persian Speakers," *Journal of Intercultural Communication*, 26 (July 2011): 6.

72. R. E. Kruat and R. E. Johnson, "Social and Emotional Messages of Smiling," in *The Nonverbal Communication Reader: Classic and Contemporary Readings*, 2nd ed., ed. L. K. Guerrero, J. A. De Vito, and H. L. Hecht (Prospect Heights, IL: Waveland Press, 1999), 140.

73. K. Nishiyama, *Doing Business in Japan: Successful Strategies for Intercultural Communication* (Honolulu: University of Hawaii Press, 2000), 22.

74. N. Dresser, *Multicultural Manners*, rev. ed. (New York: Wiley, 2005), 21.

75. G. Nees, *Germany: Unraveling an Enigma* (Yarmouth, ME: Intercultural Press, 2000), 93.

76. "The Evil Eye: A Stare of Envy," *Psychology Today*, December 1977, 154.

77. Nydell, 2012, 95.

78. M. E. Zuniga, "Families with Latino Roots," in *Developing Cross-Cultural Competence*, 2nd ed., ed. E. W. Lynch and M. J. Hanson (Baltimore: Paul H. Brookes, 1998), 231.

79. W. G. Grumet, "Eye Contact: The Core of Interpersonal Relatedness," in *The Nonverbal Reader*, 3rd ed., ed. L. K. Guerrero and M. L. Hecht (Long Grove, IL: Waveland Press, 2008), 125–26.

80. H. Triandis, *Culture and Social Behavior* (New York: McGraw-Hill, 1994), 198.

81. Richmond et al., 2012, 101.

82. Dresser, 2005, 22.

83. Richmond and Gestrin, 1998, 88.

84. F. Meleis and M. Meleis, "Egyptian Americans," in *Transcultural Health Care: A Culturally Competent Approach*, ed. L. D. Purnell and B. J. Paulanka (Philadelphia: F. A. Davis, 1998), 221.

85. E. Feghali, "Arab Cultural Communication Patterns," *International Journal of Intercultural Relations* 21 (1997): 346.

86. T. Morrison and W. A. Conaway, *Kiss, Bow, or Shake: Sales and Marketing* (New York: McGraw-Hill, 2012), 164.

87. For a discussion of homosexual nonverbal communication, see W. F. Eadie, "In Plain Sight: Gay and Lesbian Communication and Culture," in *Intercultural Communication: A Reader*, 14th ed., ed. L. A. Samovar, R. E. Porter, E. R. McDaniel, and C. S. Roy (Boston: Wadsworth Cengage, 2014), 190–203.

88. L. D. Purnell, "Mexican-Americans," in *Transcultural Health Care: A Culturally Competent Approach*, ed. L. D. Purnell and B. J. Paulanka (Philadelphia: F. A. Davis, 1998), 400.

89. "Eye contact," *Handspeak.com* (n.d.) http://www.handspeak.com/byte/e/index.php?byte=eyecontact (accessed March 27, 2014).

90. J. D. Salinger, *The Catcher in the Rye* (New York: Grosset and Dunlap, 1945), 103.

91. R. M. Bereko, L. B. Rosenfeld, and L. A. Samovar, *Connecting: A Culture-Sensitive Approach to Interpersonal Communication Competency*, 1st Canadian ed. (Toronto: Harcourt-Brace Canada, 1998).

92. P. A. Andersen, *Nonverbal Communication: Forms and Functions* (Mountain View, CA: Mayfield, 1999) 78.

93. Feghali, 2006, 364.

94. Morrison and Conaway, 2014, 38.

95. J. Condon, *Good Neighbors: Communicating with the Mexicans* (Yarmouth, ME: Intercultural Press, 1985), 60.

96. M. Hickson, D. W. Stacks, and N. Moore, *Nonverbal Communication: Studies and Applications* (Los Angeles: Roxbury Publishing Company, 2004), 69.

97. Richmond et al., 2012, 186.

98. E. McDaniel and P. A. Andersen, "International Patterns of Interpersonal Tactile Communication," *Journal of Nonverbal Communication Behavior* 22 (Spring 1998): 70.

99. D. Rowland, *Japanese Business Etiquette* (New York: Warner, 1985), 53.

100. Dresser, 2005, 15.

101. Richmond, McCroskey, and Hickson, 2012, 187. See also Knapp, Hall, and Horgan, 2012, 249–50.

102. S. Kershaw, "Hellos Give Way to Hugs for Current Crop of Teens," *San Diego Union-Tribune*, (May 28, 2009), A-1.

103. K. E. Y. Low, *Scents and Scent-Sibilities: Smell and Everyday Life Experiences* (Newcastle, UK: Cambridge Scholars Publishing, 2009), 3, http://www.cambridgescholars.com/download/sample/60348 (accessed March 26, 2014).

104. Richmond et al., 2012, 167.

105. Knapp et al., 2014, 179.

106. http://www.david-howes.com/senses/Consert-Odor.htm (accessed July 6, 2013).

107. C. Classen, "Foundations for an Anthropology of the Senses," *International Social Science Journal*, September 1997, 401–11.

108. E. B. Furlow, "The Smell of Love," in *The Nonverbal Communication Reader: Classic and Contemporary Readings*, 3rd ed., ed. L. K. Guerrero and M. L. Hechet (Long Grove, IL: Waveland Press, 2008), 87.

109. Gochenour, 1990, 61.

110. Richmond et al., 2012, 210.

111. M. I. Al-Kaysi, *Morals and Manners in Islam: A Guide to Islamic Adab* (London: The Islamic Press, 1986), 84.

112. E. T. Hall, *The Hidden Dimension* (New York: Doubleday, 1966), 149.

113. Richmond et al., 2012, 105.

114. Knapp et al., 2014, 337–56.

115. Nydell, 2012, 93

116. Ruch, 1989, 191.

117. Hecht et al., 1993, 113.

118. Andersen, 2008, 125–26.

119. Al-Kaysi, 1996, 55.

120. E. W. Lynch, "From Culture Shock to Cultural Learning," in *Developing Cross-Cultural Competence*, 2nd ed., ed. E. W. Lynch and M. J. Hanson (Baltimore: Paul H. Brookes Publishing, 1998), 26.

121. L. Skow and L. Samovar, "Cultural Patterns of the Maasai," in *Intercultural Communication: A Reader*, 14th ed., ed. L. A. Samovar, R. E. Porter, E. R. McDaniel, and C. S. Roy (Boston: Cengage Learning, 2014), 241.

122. E. T. Hall and M. R. Hall, *Hidden Differences: Doing Business with the Japanese* (New York: Anchor Books, 1990), 113.

123. E. R. McDaniel, "Japanese Nonverbal Communication: A Review and Critique of Literature," paper presented at the annual convention of the Speech Communication Association, Miami Beach, FL, November 1993, 18.

124. E. T. Hall, *The Hidden Dimension* (New York: Anchor Books, 1966), 1.

125. Hall and Hall, 1990, 12–13.

126. Hall, 1959.

127. Triandis, 1994, 201. See also Matsumoto and Hwang, 2013, 85.

128. Morrison and Conaway, 2012, 27.

129. Ruch, 1989, 239.

130. Dresser, 2005, 130.

131. M. S. Remland, T. S. Jones, and H. Brinkman, "Interpersonal Distance, Body Orientation, and Touch: Effects of Culture, Gender and Age," *Journal of Social Psychology* 135 (1995): 282.

132. K. S. Young and H. P. Travis, *Communicating Nonverbally: A Practical Guide to Presenting Yourself More Effectively* (Long Grove, IL: Waveland Press, 2008), 58. See also Andersen, 2008, 120; Moore et al., 2010, 84–85; and Knapp et al., 2014, 137.

133. L. A. Siple, "Cultural Patterns of Deaf People," *International Journal of Intercultural Relations* 18 (1994): 345–67.

134. Knapp et al., 2014, 142.

135. "Seating Arrangement," *China Highlights* (n.d.), http://www.chinahighlights.com/travelguide/chinese-food/seating-arrangement.htm (accessed June 2, 2011).

136. L. K. Matocha "Chinese-Americans," in *Transcultural Health Care: A Culturally Competent Approach*, ed. L. D. Parnell and B. J. Paulanka (Philadelphia: F. A. Davis, 1998) 167.

137. McDaniel, 2006, 270.

138. N. N. Singh, J. D. McKay, and A. N. Singh, "Culture and Mental Health: Nonverbal Communication," *Journal of Child and Family Studies* 7 (1998): 408.

139. http://www.governingwithcode.org/journal_articles/pdf/how_architecture_regulates.pdf (accessed September 20, 2013).

140. Nishiyama, 2000, 26.

141. Hall and Hall, 1990, 91.

142. J. H. Flaskerud, "Western Notions of Time and Stress," *Issues in Mental Health Nursing,* 34 (2012): 560.

143. A. Gonzales and P. G. Zimbardo, "Time Perspective," in *The Nonverbal Communication Reader*, 3rd ed., ed. L. K. Guerrero and M. L. Hecht (Long Grove, IL: Waveland Press, 2008), 245.

144. K. L. Egland, M. A. Stelzner, P. A. Andersen, and B. H. Spitzberg, "Perceived Understanding, Nonverbal Communication and Relational Satisfaction," in *Intrapersonal Communication Process*, ed. J. L. Aitken and L. Shedletsky (Annandale, VA: Speech Communication Association, 1997), 386–95. See also Guerrero and Floyd, 2006, 112.

145. N. Moore, M. Hickson, and D. W. Stacks, *Nonverbal Communication: Studies and Applications*, 5th ed. (New York: Oxford University Press, 2010), 291.

146. Flaskerud, 2013, 558.

147. N. Crouch, *Mexicans and Americans: Cracking the Cultural Code* (Yarmouth, ME: Nicholas Brealey Publishers, 2004), 34.

148. M. Argyle, "Inter-cultural Communication," in *Cultures in Contact: Studies in Cross-Cultural Interaction*, ed. S. Bochner (New York: Pergamon Press, 1982), 68.

149. Nishiyama, 2000, 28.

150. Nydell, 2012, 49.

151. Richmond and Gestrin, 1998, 108.

152. E. Y. Kim, *The Yin and Yang of American Culture: A Paradox* (Yarmouth, ME: Intercultural Press, 2001), 115.

153. Crouch, 2005, 39.

154. G. Asselin and R. Maston, *Au Contraire! Figuring Out the French* (Yarmouth, ME: Intercultural Press, 2001), 233.

155. R. Brislin, *Understanding Culture's Influence on Behavior* (Fort Worth: Harcourt Brace Jovanovich, 1993), 211.

156. Ruch, 1989, 278.

157. P. Abu Gharbieh, "Arab-American," in *Transcultural Health Care: A Culturally Competent Approach*, ed. L. D. Purnell and B. J. Paulanka (Philadelphia: F. A. Harris, 1998), 140.

158. E. T. Hall, *The Dance of Life: Other Dimensions of Time* (New York: Anchor Press/Doubleday, 1983), 42.

159. P. B. Smith and M. H. Bond, *Social Psychology Across Cultures: Analysis and Perspective*, 2nd ed. (Boston: Allyn and Bacon, 1994), 149.

160. Hall and Hall, 1990, 16.

161. Andersen, 2008, 80.

162. Hall, 1959, 19.

163. Smith and Bond, 1994, 147.

164. Dresser, 2005, 26.

165. Richmond and Gestrin, 1998, 109.

166. Feghali, 1997, 367.

167. Hall and Hall, 1990, 18.

168. A. Jaworski, "The Power of Silence in Communication," in *The Nonverbal Communication Reader*, 3rd ed., ed. L. K. Guerrero and M. L. Hecht (Long Grove, IL: Waveland Press, 2008), 179. See also Knapp et al., 2014, 135.

169. T. J. Bruneau, "How Americans Use Silence and Silences to Communicate," *China Media Research* 4 (2008): 77–85.

170. D. Crystal, *The Cambridge Encyclopedia of Language*, 2nd ed. (New York: Cambridge University Press, 1997), 174.

171. A. Braithwaite, "Cultural Uses and Interpretations of Time," in *The Nonverbal Communication Reader: Classic and Contemporary Reading*, 2nd ed., ed. L. K. Guerrero, J. A. De Vito, and H. L. Hecht (Prospect Heights, IL: Waveland Press, 1999), 164.

172. Bruneau, 2008, 83.

173. R. D. Lewis, *When Cultures Collide: Managing Successfully Across Cultures* (London: Nicholas Brealey, 1999), 13.

174. A. J. V. Chandrakanthan, "The Silence of Buddha and His Contemplation of the Truth," *Spirituality Today* 40, 2 (Summer 1988): 145, http://www.spiritualitytoday.org/spir2day/884025chandrak.html (accessed May 30, 2011).

175. D. C. Barnlund, *Communicative Styles of Japanese and Americans: Images and Realities* (Belmont, CA: Wadsworth, 1989), 142.

176. S. Chan, "Families with Asian Roots," in *Developing Cross-Cultural Competence*, 2nd ed., ed. E. W. Lynch and M. J. Hanson (Baltimore: Paul H. Brookes, 1998), 321–22.

177. R. L. De Mente, *Japan Unmasked: The Character and Culture of the Japanese* (Tokyo: Tuttle Publishing, 2005), 179.

178. A. Kerr, *Dogs and Demons: Tales from the Dark Side of Japan* (New York: Hill and Wang, 2001), 105.

179. I. Nakane, "Silence and Politeness in Intercultural Communication in University Seminars," *Journal of Pragmatics* 11 (2006): 1811–35.

180. N. Jain and A. Matukumalli, "The Functions of Silence in India: Implications for Intercultural Communication Research," paper presented at the Second International East Meets West Conference in Cross-Cultural Communication, Comparative Philosophy, and Comparative Religion, Long Beach, CA (1993), 7.

181. Smith and Bond, 1999, 141.

182. G. A. Plank, "What Silence Means for Educators of American Indian

Children," *Journal of American Indian Education* 34 (1994): 1–19.

183. For a detailed analysis of methods to improve nonverbal communication competency, see S. P. Morreale, B. H. Spitzberg, and J. K. Barge, *Communication: Motivation, Knowledge, Skills*, 3rd ed. (New York: Peter Lang, 2013), 95–102.

Chapter 10

1. J. T. Wood, *Interpersonal Communication: Everyday Encounters*, 8th ed. (Boston: Wadsworth Cengage Learning, 2015), 110.

2. S. P. Morreale, B. H. Spitzberg, and J. K. Barge, *Human Communication: Motivation, Knowledge, and Skills*, 2nd ed. (Belmont, CA: Thomson Wadsworth, 2007), 168–69.

3. M. K. Nydell, *Understanding Arabs: A Guide for Westerners*, 5th ed. (Boston: Intercultural Press, 2012), 55; "First lady forgoes headscarf in Saudi Arabia," *PBS News Hour* (January 27, 2015), http:// www.pbs.org/newshour/rundown /first-lady-forgoes-headscarf-saudi -arabia (accessed March 14, 2015).

4. T. Morrison and W. A. Conway, *Kiss, Bow, or Shake Hands: Europe: How to do Business in 25 European Countries* (Avon, MA: Adams Media, an F+W Publications Company, 2007), 294.

5. "Holiday shopping abroad has become easier with online payment services," *Los Angeles Times* (December 23, 2014), http://www.latimes.com/busi ness/la-fi-holiday-shopping-abroad -20141223-story.html (accessed March 12, 2015).

6. D. C. Thomas and K. Inkson, *Cultural Intelligence: Living and Working Globally*, 2nd ed. (San Francisco: Berrett-Koehler, 2009), 7–11; D. C. Thomas, *Cross-Cultural Management: Essential Concepts*, 2nd ed. (Los Angeles: Sage, 2008), 1–18.

7. D. C. Davis, "Global Managers: Developing a Mindset for Global Competitiveness," in *Readings and Cases in International Management: A Cross-Cultural Perspective*, ed. D. C. Davis (Thousand Oaks, CA: Sage, 2003), 4.

8. J. S. Martin and L. H. Chaney, *Global Business Etiquette: A Guide to International Communication and Customs*, 2nd ed. (Westport, CT: Praeger, 2012), 74.

9. *Foreign Corrupt Practices Act* (U.S. Department of Justice, n.d.), http:// www.justice.gov/criminal/fraud/fcpa (accessed March 17, 2015); *Travel, Entertainment, Gift, and Car Expenses: Publication 463* (Internal Revenue Service, February 4, 2015), http:// www.irs.gov/pub/irs-pdf/p463.pdf (accessed March 17, 2015).

10. R. T. Moran, P. R. Harris, and S. V. Moran, *Managing Cultural Differences*, 8th ed. (Boston: Elsevier, 2011), 282.

11. "Labor Force Characteristics of Foreign-Born Workers Summary," *Economic News Release* (U.S. Department of Labor, Bureau of Labor Statistics, May 22, 2014), http://www.bls.gov /news.release/forbrn.nr0.htm (accessed March 18, 2015); L. Wides-Munoz and P. Wiseman, "Backlash stirs in U S against foreign worker visas," *Yahoo News* (July 6, 2014), http://news.yahoo.com/back lash-stirs-us-against-foreign-worker -visas-135208422–finance.html (accessed March 18, 2015).

12. *Evolution of Work and the Worker* (London: The Economist Intelligence Unit, February 2014), 39, http:// whitepaper-admin.eiu.com/future hrtrends/wp-content/uploads/sites/2 /2014/06/6-14-EIU-Report-Web.pdf (accessed March 19, 2015).

13. T. L. Coyner and S-H Jang, *Mastering Business in Korea: A Practical Guide* (Seoul: Seoul Selection, 2007), 38–39; Y. Sugimoto, *An Introduction to Japanese Society*, 3rd ed. (New York: Cambridge University Press), 24; A. Yeung, K. Xin, W. Pfoertsch, and S. Liu, *The Globalization of Chinese Companies* (Singapore: Wiley, 2011), 104.

14. L. Burkitt, "The Chinese Dream vs. the American Dream," *Wall Street Journal: China Realtime* (May 9, 2014), http://blogs.wsj.com/chinareal time/2014/05/08/the-chinese-dream -vs-the-american-dream-in-4-charts (accessed March 11, 2015).

15. N. J. Adler, *International Dimensions of Organizational Behavior*, 5th ed. (Mason, OH: Thompson South-Western, 2008), 184.

16. M. I. Bright, "Can Japanese mentoring enhance understanding of Western mentoring," *Employee Relations* 27, 4/5 (2005): 325, 334.

17. *Working Conditions Laws Report: A Global Review* (Geneva, Switzerland: International Labour Organization, 2013), 20–29.

18. J. Makinen, "Bar's Buddha poster lands 3 in Myanmar prison for insulting religion," *Los Angeles Times* (March 17, 2015), http://www.latimes.com/world /asia/la-fg-myan mar-bar-buddha -prison-20150317-story.html (accessed March 18, 2015).

19. H. Wenzhong, C. N. Gove, and Z. Enping, *Encountering the Chinese*, 3rd ed. (Boston: Intercultural Press, 2010), 79; M. G. Martinsons and R. M. Davison, "Strategic decision making and support systems: Comparing American, Japanese and Chinese management," *Decision Support Systems* 43 (2007): 293–98, http:// www.is.cityu.edu.hk/staff/isrobert /is6600/dss431.pdf (accessed March 21, 2015).

20. W. Yuan, "Conflict management among American and Chinese employees in multinational organizations in China," *Cross Cultural Management: An International Journal* 17, 3 (2010): 299–311, DOI: 10.1108/13527601011068388.

21. M. H. Bond, *Beyond the Chinese Face: Insights from Psychology* (Hong Kong: Oxford University, 1991), 65–66; Z. Ma, "Chinese Conflict Management Styles and Negotiation Behaviours: An Empirical Test," *International Journal of Cross Cultural Management* 7, 7 (2007): 113–14. DOI: 10.1177 /1470595807075177; Yuan, 2010, 302, 307.

22. M. Guirdham, *Communication Across Cultures at Work*, 3rd ed. (New York: Palgrave Macmillan, 2011), 314–16; Moran et al., 2011, 75.

23. Information used to construct the table and discussion of Chinese and U.S. negotiations was taken from

multiple sources, including the following: A. Akgunes and R. Culpepper, "Negotiations Between Chinese and Americans: Examining the Cultural Context and Salient Factors," *Journal of International Management Studies* 7 (2012), 191–200; J. L. Graham and M. N. Lam, "The Chinese Negotiation," *Harvard Business Review*, October 2003, 2–11; P. Ghauri and T. Fang, "Negotiating with the Chinese," in *Readings and Cases in International Management: A Cross-Cultural Perspective*, ed. D. C. Davis, (Thousand Oaks, CA: Sage, 2003), 163–75; X. Lin and J. Guan, "Negotiating Across the Pacific," in *Readings and Cases in International Management: A Cross-Cultural Perspective*, ed. D. C. Davis (Thousand Oaks, CA: Sage, 2003), 230–37; Z. Ma, "Negotiating into China: The impact of individual perception on Chinese negotiation styles," *International Journal of Emerging Markets* 1, 1 (2006): 64–83, DOI: 10.1108/17468800610645013; R. Prasad and Y. Cao, "Improving Negotiation Outcomes Between American and Chinese Partners: A Framework for Practice," *Journal of Applied Business Research* 28, 1 (2012): 1–8; J. K. Sebenius and C. Qian, "Cultural notes on Chinese negotiating behavior," *Harvard Business School: Working Paper 09-076* (2008), 1–10, http://www.hbs.edu/faculty/Publication%20Files/09-076.pdf (accessed March 27, 2015); Y-J. Song and C. L. Hale, "The Business Negotiation Styles of the Chinese and the Japanese, and South Koreans: Similarities and Differences Found in East Asian Cultural Groups," in *The Same and Different: Acknowledging the Diversity Within and Between Cultural Groups*, International and Intercultural Communication Annual, vol. XXIX, ed. M. P. Orbe, B. J. Allen, and L. A. Flores (Washington, DC: National Communication Association, 2006), 267–92; C. A. Warden and J. F. Clyde, "Chinese Negotiators' Subjective Variations in Intercultural Negotiations," *Journal of Business Ethics* 88 (2009): 529–37, DOI: 10.1007/s10551-009-0300-0; Yeung et al., 2011; W. Yuan, 2010, 299–311.

24. J. S. Black and A. J. Morrison, *Sunset in the Land of the Rising Sun: Why Japanese Multinational Corporations Will Struggle in the Global Future* (New York: INSEAD Business Press, Palgrave Macmillan, 2010), various; "Galapagos effect: How can Japan capture global value from Japan's technologies and new business models?," *Eurotechnology Japan KK* (2013), http://www.eurotechnology.com/insights/galapagos (accessed April 6, 2015); Y. Gao, *China as the workshop of the world* (New York: Routledge, 2012), various; "Global 500," *CNN Money* (n.d.), http://money.cnn.com/magazines/fortune/global500/2012/full_list (accessed March 30, 2015); J. Makinen, "A subculture of entrepreneurship hatches in Japan," *Los Angeles Times* (March 29, 2015), http://www.latimes.com/world/asia/la-fg-japan-entrepreneurs-20150329-story.html#page=1 (accessed June 28, 2015); W. Pesek, "Japan Inc. Needs to Get Off Galapagos," Bloomberg-View (December 5, 2013), http://www.bloombergview.com/articles/2013-12-04/japan-inc-needs-to-get-off-galapagos (accessed March 30, 2015).

25. *The Condition of Education 2014* (U.S. Department of Education, May 2014), 52, http://nces.ed.gov/pubs2014/2014083.pdf (accessed April 3, 2015); "Selected Social Characteristics in the United States: 2009–2013 American Community Survey 5-Year Estimates," *U.S. Census Bureau, 2009–2013 5-Year American Community Survey* (U.S. Census Bureau, American Fact Finder, n.d.), http://factfinder.census.gov/faces/tableservices/jsf/pages/productview.xhtml?pid=ACS_13_5YR_DP02&src=pt (accessed April 4, 2015); O. Kagan, "Schools should help the children of immigrants become truly bilingual," *Los Angeles Times* (December 21, 2014), http://www.latimes.com/opinion/op-ed/la-oe-1222-kagan-heritage-languages-20141222-story.html (accessed April 4, 2015); C. Malveaux, "Crawford players ace Football 101," *San Diego Union-Tribune* (September 12, 2013), http://www.utsandiego.com/news/2013/sep/12/crawford-players-ace-football-101 (accessed June 27, 2015).

26. *The Condition of Education 2014*, 2014, 48.

27. L. Foderaro, "More Foreign-Born Scholars Lead U.S. Universities," *New York Times* (March 9, 2011), http://www.nytimes.com/2011/03/10/education/10presidents.html?_r=0 (accessed April 6, 2015); A. Paulson, "Record 900,000 international students in US: the top countries they hail from," *Christian Science Monitor* (November 17, 2014), http://www.csmonitor.com/USA/Education/2014/1117/Record-900-000-international-students-in-US-the-top-countries-they-hail-from (accessed April 6, 2014).

28. "Top 25 Places of Origin of International Students, 2012/13–2013/14," in *Open Doors Report on International Educational Exchange* (Institute of International Education, 2014), http://www.iie.org/Research-and-Publications/Open-Doors/Data/International-Students/Leading-Places-of-Origin/2012-14 (accessed March 6, 2015).

29. J. Tobin and A. Hayashi, "[Japan, China, USA] The Preschool in Three Cultures Studies," *ECEC around the World* (Child Research Net, December 9, 2011), http://www.childresearch.net/projects/ecec/2011_05.html (accessed April 4, 2015); E. Rauhala, "China's Big Test," *Time*, April 13, 2015, 41; "Teaching and Teaching Strategies (US and China)," *Comparing U.S. and Chinese Public School Systems* (University of Michigan, n.d.), http://sitemaker.umich.edu/vanschaack.356/reference_list (accessed April 17, 2015); J. B. Starr, *Understanding China*, 3rd ed. (New York: Hill and Wang), 262–70; K. Chen, "Cultural Perspectives on Student Behaviors: A Study of American and Chinese Students," *US-China Education Review* 2, 1 (January 2005): 27.

30. J. M. McHugh, "Cultural attitudes toward education in the US," *Lincoln Times-News* (September, 13, 2013), http://www.lincolntimesnews.com/2013/09/13/cultural-attitudes

-toward-education-in-the-us (accessed April 11, 2015).

31. M. Nisen and V. Giang, "These 19 Insanely Successful College Dropouts Prove You Don't Need A Degree," *Business Insider* (September 3, 2013), http://www.businessinsider.com/most -successful-college-dropts-2013-9 (accessed April 11, 2015).

32. A. Ripley, *The smartest kids in the world* (New York: Simon and Schuster, 2013), 109.

33. J. Fairbank, E. O. Reischauer, and A. M. Craig, *East Asia: Tradition and Transformation* (Boston: Houghton Mifflin, 1973), 188–91; Rauhala, 2015, 38–41; Ripley, 2013, 54–55; S. Tiezzi, "The Gaokao Exam: A Tough Test for China," *The Diplomat* (June 7, 2014), http://thediplomat .com/2014/06/the-gaokao-exam-a -tough-test-for-china (accessed April 10, 2015); "9.42m to sit for college entrance exam," *Xinhua* (June 6, 2015), http://www.china daily.com.cn/china/2015-06/06/con tent_20926958.htm (accessed June 27, 2015); Banyan, "Test-taking in South Korea: Point me at the SKY, *Economist* (November 8, 2013), http://www.economist.com/blogs/ban yan/2013/11/test-taking-south-korea (accessed June 27, 2015).

34. F. Shyong, "For Asian Americans, a changing landscape on college admissions," *Los Angeles Times* (February 21, 2015), http://www .latimes.com/local/california/la-me -adv-asian-race-tutoring-20150222 -story.html (accessed April 11, 2015); E. Knowlton, "24 Photos of China's Insanely Stressful College Entrance Exam Process," *Business Insider* (June 12, 2014), http://www.busines sinsider.com/24-stunning-photos-of -chinas-college-entrance-exams -2014-6 (accessed April 11, 2015); B. Larmer, "Inside a Chinese Test -Prep Factory," *New York Times Magazine* (December 31, 2014), http://www.nytimes.com/2015/01/04 /magazine/inside-a-chinese-test-prep -factory.html?_r=0 (accessed April 11, 2015); M. Mason, "Affirmative action non-action still causing waves in Sacramento," *Los Angeles Times* (March 30, 2014), http://www

.latimes.com/local/la-me-affirmative -action-20140331,0,2270777.story #axzz2xZOVt2P2 (accessed April 4, 2015); L. Gordon, "UC enrolling more new students from other states and nations," *Los Angeles Times* (July 22, 2014), http://www.latimes .com/local/lanow/la-me-ln-uc-nonresi dent-20140722-story.html (accessed June 28, 2015).

35. "College or bust," *The Economist* (Special Report: America's Hispanics, March 14, 2015), 13; C. Walford, "The chattering classes: The British primary school where pupils speak 31 different languages," *Daily Mail* (June 7, 2012), http://www.dailymail.co.uk /news/article-2155938/The-primary -school-pupils-speak-31-different -languages–class-just-single-British -pupil.html (accessed April 12, 2015).

36. S. A. Reyes and T. L. Vallone, "Toward an Expanded Understanding of Two-Way Bilingual Immersion Educa- tion: Constructing Identity through a Critical, Additive Bilingual/Bicultural Pedagogy," *Multicultural Perspectives* 9, 3 (July 2007): 5–9, http://www.diversi tylearningk12.com/articles/Reyes _Vallone_Two-Way_Bilingual _Education.pdf (accessed April 12, 2015).

37. K. N. Robins, R. B. Lindsey, D. B. Lindsey, and R. D. Terrell, *Culturally Proficient Instruction: A Guide for People Who Teach* (Thousand Oaks, CA: Corwin Press, 2002), 4.

38. R. E. Nisbett, *The Geography of Thought* (New York: Simon and Schuster, 2003), 82; E. Redden, "Chinese Students in the Classroom," *Inside Higher Ed* (April 9, 2014), https://www.insidehighered.com /news/2014/04/09/new-research -examines-how-chinese-students -respond-challenges-classroom (accessed April 13, 2015).

39. C. O. Airhihenbuwa, *Healing Our Differences: The Crisis of Global Health and Politics of Identity* (Lanham, MD: Rowman & Littlefield, 2007), 192; E. Hanson, "Oral Traditions," *Indigenous Foundations* (University of British Columbia, First Nations Studies Programs, n.d.), http://indigenous foundations.arts.ubc.ca/home/culture /oral-traditions.html (accessed April

13, 2015); R. Wollmering, *Cross- Cultural Dialogue* (World Wise Schools, Peace Corps, n.d.), http:// www.peacecorps.gov/wws/stories /cross-cultural-dialogue (accessed April 6, 2015); E. O. Reischauer and J. K. Fairbank, *East Asia: The Great Tradition* (Boston: Houghton Mifflin, 1960), 43; A. C. Madrigal, "Oral Culture, Literate Culture, Twitter Culture, *The Atlantic* (May 31, 2011), http://www.theatlantic.com/technol ogy/archive/2011/05/oral-culture -literate-culture-twitter-culture /239697 (accessed April 15, 2015).

40. L. Fish, *Building Blocks: The First Steps of Creating a Multicultural Classroom*, (Critical Multicultural Pavilion, Research Room, n.d.) http://www .edchange.org/multicultural/papers /buildingblocks.html (accessed April 4, 2015).

41. Adapted from a variety of sources, including J. G. Thompson, "Cultur ally Responsive Teaching," *Middle Web* (August 24, 2013), http://www .middleweb.com/9471/culturally -responsive-classrooms (accessed June 28, 2015).

42. D. M. Gollnick and P. C. Chinn, *Multicultural Education in a Pluralistic Society*, 9th ed. (New York: Pearson, 2013), 24.

43. L. D. Purnell, *Transcultural Health Care: A Culturally Competent Approach* (Philadelphia: F. A. Davis, 2013), 3.

44. "Countries," *Medecines sans Frontieres /Doctors Without Borders* (n.d.), http:// www.doctorswithoutborders.org/our -work/countries (accessed April 23, 2015).

45. K. McCabe, "Foreign-Born Health Care Workers in the United States," Migration Policy Institute, June 27, 2012, http://www.migrationpolicy. org/article/foreign-born-health-care -workers-united-states (accessed April 22, 2015).

46. *2013 State Physician Workforce Data Book* (Center for Workforce Studies, American Association of Medical Colleges, November 2013), https:// www.aamc.org/download/362168 /data/2013statephysicianworkforceda tabook.pdf (accessed April 22, 2015); H. Siddique, "Figures show extent of

NHS reliance on Foreign Nationals," *The Guardian* (January 26, 2014), http://www.theguardian.com/society /2014/jan/26/nhs-foreign-nationals -immigration-health-service (accessed April 22, 2015).

47. Purnell, 2013, 3.

48. J. Campinha-Bacote, "People of African American Heritage," in *Transcultural Health Care: A Culturally Competent Approach*, ed. L. D. Purnell (Philadelphia: F. A. Davis, 2013), 107; K. W. Huttlinger, "People of Appalachian Heritage," in *Transcultural Health Care: A Culturally Competent Approach*, L. D. Purnell (Philadelphia, PA: F. A. Davis, 2013), 151; K. B. Wright, L. Sparks, and H. D. O'Hair, *Health Communication in the 21st Century*, 2nd ed. (Malden, MA: Wiley, 2012), 124.

49. M. M. Andrews, "The Influence of Cultural and Health Belief Systems on Health Care Practices," in *Transcultural Concepts in Nursing Care*, 5th ed., ed. M. M. Andrews and J. S. Boyle (Philadelphia: Lippincott Williams & Wilkins, 2008), 67.

50. J. M. Colin and G. Paperwalla, "People of Haitian Heritage," in *Transcultural Health Care: A Culturally Competent Approach*, ed. L. D. Purnell (Philadelphia: F. A. Davis, 2013), 284; G.-A. Galanti, *Caring for Patients from Different Cultures* (Philadelphia: University of Pennsylvania Press, 2015), 236.

51. Galanti, 2015, 92, 299–300.

52. "Holistic health care," *Mosby's Medical Dictionary*, 9th ed. (St. Louis, MO: Elsevier, 2013), 849–80.

53. S. Ceasar, "Navajo Nation confronts HIV and AIDS," *Los Angeles Times* (January 4, 2012), http://articles .latimes.com/2012/jan/05/nation/la -na-navajo-hiv-20120105 (accessed April 21, 2015).

54. Galanti, 2015, 242; See also A. du Pré, *Communicating About Health*, 4th ed. (New York: Oxford University Press, 2014), 175, and H-M. Tsai, "People of Chinese Heritage," in *Transcultural Health Care: A Culturally Competent Approach*, ed. L. D. Purnell (Philadelphia: F. A. Davis, 2013), 191–92.

55. "TCM training course held on PLA Navy's 'Peace Ark' hospital ship," *China Military Online* (July 10, 2014), http://eng.chinamil.com.cn/news -channels/china-military-news/2014 -07/10/content_6043102.htm (accessed April 21, 2015); K. Mizokami, "Peace Ark: Onboard China's Hospital Ship," *USNI News* (July 23, 2014), http://news.usni.org/2014/07/ 23/peace-ark-onboard-chinas-hospi tal-ship (accessed April 25, 2015).

56. C. O'Neil, "Traditional Healing," *The Navajo: Yesterday and Today* (PBS, 2003), http://www.pbs.org/wgbh/mys tery/american/navajoland/yestertoday .html (accessed April 25, 2015); R. Zoucha and C. A. Zamarripa, "People of Mexican Heritage," in *Transcultural Health Care: A Culturally Competent Approach*, ed. L. D. Purnell (Philadelphia: F. A. Davis, 2013), 385–86.

57. Andrews, 2008, 69; du Pré, 2014, 167; Galanti, 2015, 27; L. D. Purnell, "People of European American Heritage," in *Transcultural Health Care: A Culturally Competent Approach*, ed. L. D. Purnell (Philadelphia: F. A. Davis, 2013), 226.

58. du Pré, 2014, 173.

59. G. Jucket, "Caring for Latino Patients," *American Family Physician* 87, 1 (January 1, 2013): 48–54; G. Jucket, "Cross-Cultural Medicine," *American Family Physician* 72, 11 (December 1, 2005): 2268; Galanti, 2015, 100; A. D. Kulwicki and S. Ballout, "People of Arab Heritage," in *Transcultural Health Care: A Culturally Competent Approach*, ed. L. D. Purnell (Philadelphia: F. A. Davis, 2013), 173.

60. J. N. Giger, *Transcultural Nursing: Assessment and Intervention*, 6th ed. (St. Louis, MO: Elsevier Mosby, 2013), 220.

61. Galanti, 2015, 100; Giger, 2013, 348.

62. C. Ryan, *Language Use in the United States: 2011* (U.S. Census Bureau: American Community Survey Reports, August, 2013), 9, https:// www.census.gov/prod/2013pubs/acs -22.pdf (accessed April 27, 2015).

63. E. Brown, "Number of Latino doctors isn't keeping pace with population, study says," *Los Angeles Times* (February 19, 2015), http://www.latimes .com/local/california/la-me-latino -doctors-20150220-story.html (accessed April 21, 2015).

64. Galanti, 2015, 35–36.

65. du Pré, 2014, 167.

66. A. Shahzad, "Cultural Taboos Fuel Breast Cancer Toll in Pakistan," *San Diego Union Tribune* (January 21, 2014), A8, http://www.utsandiego .com/news/2014/jan/21/tp-cultural -taboos-fuel-breast-cancer-toll-in (accessed April 29, 2015).

67. Galanti, 2015, 128; S. O. Long, *Final Days: Japanese Culture and Choice at the End of Life* (Honolulu: University of Hawaii Press, 2005), 130–31; C. C. Munoz, "People of Filipino Heritage," in *Transcultural Health Care: A Culturally Competent Approach*, ed. L. D. Purnell (Philadelphia: F. A. Davis, 2013), 245.

68. B. Stulberg, "No one wants to talk about death, but you need to anyway," *Los Angeles Times* (December 30, 2013), http://www.latimes.com /opinion/commentary/la-oe-stulberg -advance-healthcare-planning -20131230,0,5263335.story#axzz2p 0jZpc83 (accessed April 21, 2015); Ceasar, 2012; Zoucha and Zamarripa, 2013, 384.

69. R. L. Wiseman, "Intercultural Communication Competence," in *Handbook of International and Intercultural Communication*, 2nd. ed., ed. W. B. Gudykunst and B. Moody (Thousand Oaks, CA: Sage, 2002), 207–24.

70. L. D. Purnell, "Transcultural diversity and Health Care," in *Transcultural Health Care: A Culturally Competent Approach*, ed. L. D. Purnell (Philadelphia: F. A. Davis, 2013), 4; N. K-F. Tsang and J. Ap, "Tourists' Perceptions of Relational Quality," *Journal of Travel Research* 45 (2007): 355–366, DOI: 10.1177/0047287506295911.

71. *ABB* (2015), http://www.abb.com (accessed May 1, 2015); "Global 500 2014," *Fortune* (n.d.), http://fortune .com/global500/abb-259.

72. A. Yeung, K. Xin, W. Pfoertsch, and S. Liu, *The Globalization of Chinese companies* (Singapore: Wiley, 2011), 107.

Chapter 11

1. C. Ward, S. Bochner, and A. Furnham, *The Psychology of Culture Shock*, 2nd ed. (New York: Routledge, 2001), 9.

2. Ibid., 270.

3. S. Lysgaard, "Adjustment in a foreign society: Norwegian Fulbright Grantees Visiting the United States," *International Social Science Bulletin* 7 (1955): 45–51.

4. J. T. Gullahorn and J. E. Gullahorn, "An Extension of the U-Curve Hypothesis," *Journal of Social Science* 17 (1963): 33–47.

5. J. W. Berry, "Stress Perspectives on Acculturation," in *The Cambridge Handbook of Acculturation Psychology*, ed. D. L. Sam and J. W. Berry (New York: Cambridge University Press), 50; Ward et al., 2006, 231.

6. Y. Y. Kim, *Becoming Intercultural: An Integrative Theory of Communication and Cross-Cultural Adaptation* (Thousand Oaks, CA: Sage, 2001), 54–61.

7. Y. Y. Kim, "Adapting to a New Culture: An Integrative Communication Theory," in *Theorizing About Intercultural Communication*, ed. W. B. Gudykunst (Thousand Oaks, CA: Sage, 2005), 384.

8. Ward et al., 2001, 271.

9. A-M. Masgoret and C. Ward, "Cultural Learning Approach to Acculturation," in *The Cambridge Handbook of Acculturation Psychology*, ed. D. L. Sam and J. W. Berry (New York: Cambridge University Press), 50; Ward et al., 2006, 63.

10. C. Gouttefarde, "Host National Culture Shock: What Management Can Do," *European Business Review* 92, 4 (1992): 1.

11. E. C. Stewart and M. J. Bennett, *American Cultural Patterns* (Yarmouth, ME: Intercultural Press, 1991), x.

12. "The future of mobility," *The Economist*, May 28, 2011, 87.

13. W. B. Gudykunst, "An Anxiety/ Uncertainty Management (AUM) Theory of Effective Communication," in *Theorizing About Intercultural Communication*, ed. W. B. Gudykunst

(Thousand Oaks, CA: Sage, 2005), 286.

14. Ibid., 289–90.

15. W. Kremer and C. Hammond, "Hikikomori: Why are so many Japanese men refusing to leave their rooms?," *BBC News Magazine* (July 4, 2013), http://www.bbc.com/news/magazine-23182523 (accessed August 16, 2014).

16. D. L. Hamilton and T. K. Trolier, "Stereotypes and stereotyping: An overview of the cognitive approach," in *Prejudice, Discrimination, and Racism: Theory and Research*, ed. J. F. Dovidio and S. L. Gaertner (San Diego, CA: Academic Press, 1986), 142.

17. D. J. Schneider, *The Psychology of Stereotypes* (New York: Guilford Press, 2004), 341.

18. J. T. Wood, *Gendered Lives: Communication, Gender and Culture*, 6th ed. (Belmont, CA: Wadsworth/Thomson Learning, 2005), 234.

19. N. J. Adler, *International Dimensions of Organizational Behavior*, 5th ed. (Eagan, MN: Thomson/South Western, 2008), 79. See also P. B. Smith, M. H. Bond, and C. Kagitcibasi, *Understanding Social Psychology Across Cultures* (Thousand Oaks, CA: Sage, 2006).

20. M. Guirdham. *Communicating Across Cultures* (West Lafayette, IN: Purdue University Press, 1999), 163.

21. D. S. Meshel and R. P McGlynn, "Intergenerational Contact, Attitudes, and Stereotypes of Adolescents and Older People," *Educational Gerontology* 30 (2004): 461.

22. Ibid., 262.

23. S. Ting-Toomey and L. C. Chung, *Understanding Intercultural Communication*, 2nd ed. (New York: Oxford University Press, 2011), 167.

24. Ibid., 168.

25. D. C. Thomas, *Cross-Cultural Management*, 2nd ed. (Thousand Oaks, CA: Sage, 2008).

26. G. W. Allport, *The Nature of Prejudice* (New York: Addison-Wesley, 1979), 9.

27. E. M. Rogers and T. M. Steinfatt, *Intercultural Communication*,

(Prospects Heights, IL: Waveland Press, 1999), 55.

28. J. B. Ruscher, *Prejudiced Communication: A Social Psychological Perspective* (New York: Guilford Press, 2001), 6.

29. R. Brislin, *Understanding Culture's Influence on Behavior*, 2nd ed. (New York: Harcourt, 2000), 209.

30. For a detailed account of the functions of prejudice, see Brislin, 2000, 208–13; D. Katz, "The Functional Approach to the Study of Attitudes," *Public Opinion Quarterly* 24 (1960): 164–204; and B. J. Hall, *Among Cultures*, 2nd ed. (Belmont, CA: Thomson-Wadsworth, 2005), 108–9.

31. W. G. Stephan and C. W. Stephan, "An Integrated Threat Theory of Prejudice," in *Reducing Prejudice and Discrimination*, ed. S. Oskamp (Mahwah, NJ: Lawrence Erlbaum Associates, 2000), 25.

32. Allport, 1979, 14.

33. Ibid., 49.

34. S. Oskamp, "Multiple Paths to Reducing Prejudice and Discrimination," in *Reducing Prejudice and Discrimination*, ed. S. Oskamp (Mahwah, NJ: Lawrence Erlbaum Associates, 2000), 7.

35. Oskamp, 2000, 9.

36. Stephan and Stephan, 2000, 40.

37. Ibid.

38. "The Immigration Act of 1924 (The Johnson-Reed Act)," U.S. Department of State, Office of the Historian (n.d.), http://history.state.gov/milestones/1921-1936/immigration-act (accessed September 18, 2014).

39. E. Vora and J. A. Vora, "Undoing Racism in America: Help from a Black Church," *Journal of Black Studies* 32 (2002): 389.

40. S. Netter, "Racism in Obama's America One Year Later," *ABC World News* (January 27, 2010), http://abcnews.go.com/WN/Obama/racism-obamas-america-year/story?id=9638178 (accessed August 31, 2014).

41. S. J. Gold, "From Jim Crow to Racial Hegemony: Evaluating Explanations of Racial Hierarchy," *Ethnic and Racial Studies* 27 (2004): 953.

42. B. Leone, *Racism: Opposing Viewpoints* (Minneapolis: Greenhaven Press, 1978), 1.

43. S. Nanda and R. L. Warms, *Cultural Anthropology*, 11th ed. (Belmont, CA: Wadsworth, 2014), 15.

44. L. Blum, *I'm not a Racist, But …* (Ithaca, NY: Cornell University Press, 2002), 9.

45. "Voting Rights Timeline," *The Annenberg Classroom* (n.d.), http://www.annenbergclassroom.org/Files/Documents/Timelines/Voting Rights.pdf (accessed August 31, 2014).

46. Constitution of the United States, Fourteenth Amendment, U.S. Senate (n.d.). http://www.senate.gov/civics/constitution_item/constitution.htm#amdt_14_(1868) (accessed September 1, 2014).

47. M. Angelou, *Won't Take Nothing for My Journey Now* (New York: Random House, 1993).

48. B. Russell, *Power: A New Social Analysis* (NewYork: Routledge Classics, 2004), 4.

49. S. R. Clegg and M. Haugaard, "Introduction: Why Power is the Central Concept of the Social Sciences," in *The SAGE Handbook of Power*, ed. M. Haugaard and S. R. Clegg (Thousand Oaks, CA: Sage, 2009), 1.

50. R. Swedberg, *The Max Weber Dictionary: Key Words and Central Concepts* (Stanford, CA: Stanford University Press, 2005), 205.

51. R. A. Barraclough and R. A. Stewart, "Power and Control: Social Science Perspectives," in *Power in the Classroom*, ed. V. P. Richmond and J. McCroskey (Hillsdale, NJ: Prentice Hall, 1991), 1–4.

52. M. G. Harper, "Ethical Multiculturalism: An Evolutionary Concept Analysis," *Advances in Nursing Science* 29, 2 (2006): 6.

53. D. B. Wong, *Natural Moralities: A Defense of Pluralistic Relativism* (New York: Oxford University Press, 2006), xxi.

54. C. J. Robertson and W. F. Crittenden, "Mapping Moral Philosophies: Strategic Implications for Multinational Firms," *Strategic Management Journal* 24, 4 (April 2003): 386.

55. M. C. E. Van Der Bly, "Globalization and the Rise of One Heterogeneous World Culture: A Microperspective of a Global Village," *International Journal of Comparative Sociology* 48, 2–3 (2007): 234–56, DOI: 10.1177/0020715207075401.

56. K. J. P. Quintelier, D. De Smet, and D. M. T. Fessler, "The Moral Universalism-Relativism Debate," *Revue Philosophique* 27 (2013): 211–62, http://www.revue-klesis.org/pdf/Klesis-philosophie-experimentale-8-Katinka-J.P.-Quintelier-Delphine-De-Smet-Daniel-M.T.-Fessler-The-moral-universalism-relativism-debate.pdf (accessed September 3, 2014).

57. Ibid., 252.

58. *Universal Declaration of Human Rights*, United Nations, Office of the High Commissioner for Human Rights (1948), http://www.ohchr.org/EN/UDHR/Pages/Language.aspx?LangID=eng (accessed June 29, 2015).

59. M. K. DeGenova, *Families in Cultural Context: Strength and Challenges in Diversity* (Mountain View, CA: Mayfield, 1997), 6.

60. S. Huntington, *The Conflict of Civilizations and the Remaking of World Order* (New York: Simon and Schuster, 1996), 320.

61. D. C. Barnlund, *Communication Styles of Japanese and Americans* (Belmont, CA: Wadsworth, 1989), 92–93.

62. R. Evanoff, "A Communicative Approach to Intercultural Dialogue on Ethics," in *Intercultural Communication: A Reader*, 14th ed., ed. L. A. Samovar, R. E. Porter, E. R. McDaniel, and C. S. Roy (Boston: Cengage Learning, 2015), 418–19.

63. G. Bateson, *Mind and Nature: A Necessary Unity* (New York: Bantam, 1980), 8.

Index